OPENNESS AND IDEALISM

SOVIET POSTERS
1985–1991

OPENNESS AND IDEALISM

SOVIET POSTERS 1985–1991

MARTHA H. AND J. SPEED
CARROLL COLLECTION

SKIRA

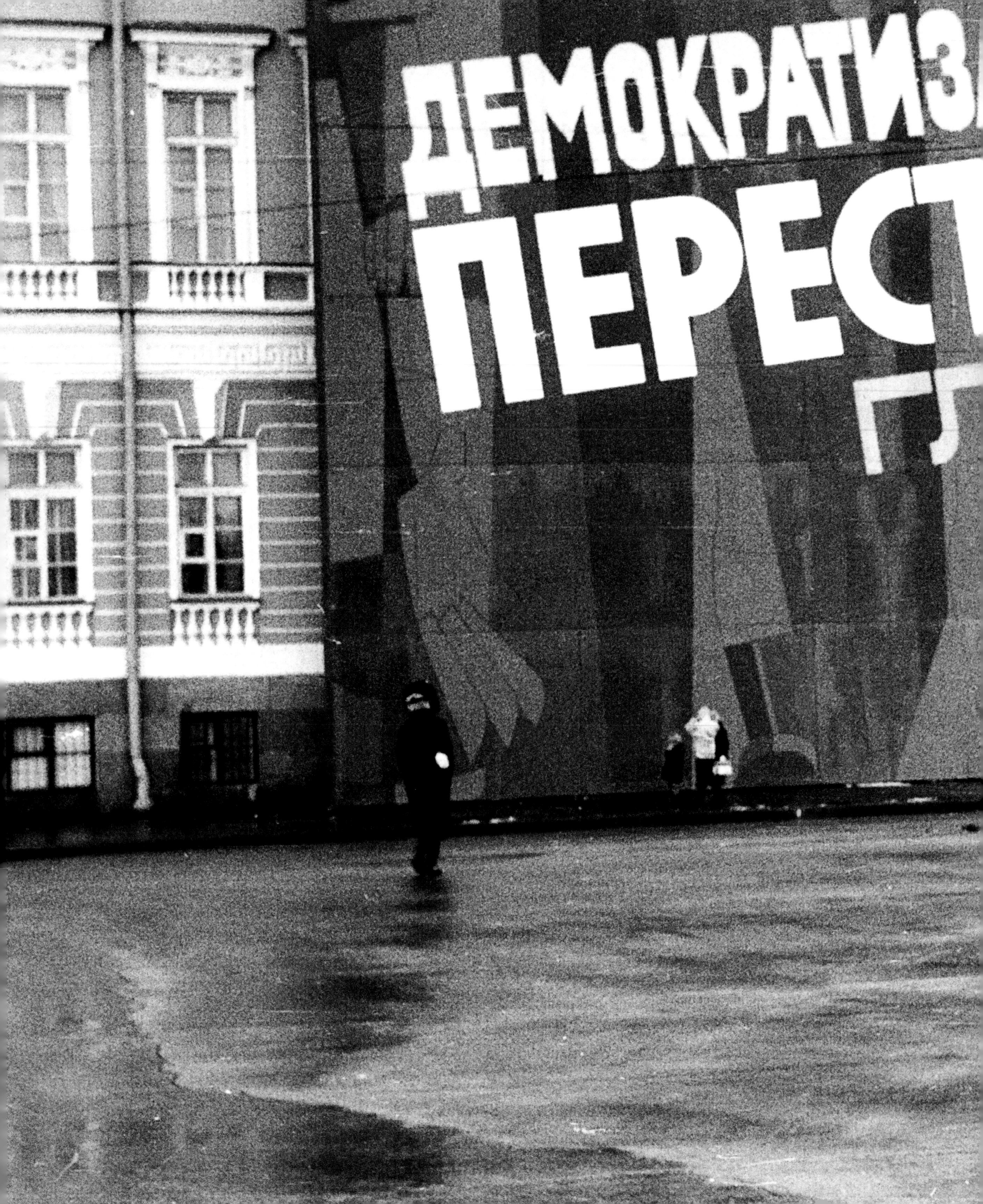
ДЕМОКРАТИЗ
ПЕРЕСТ

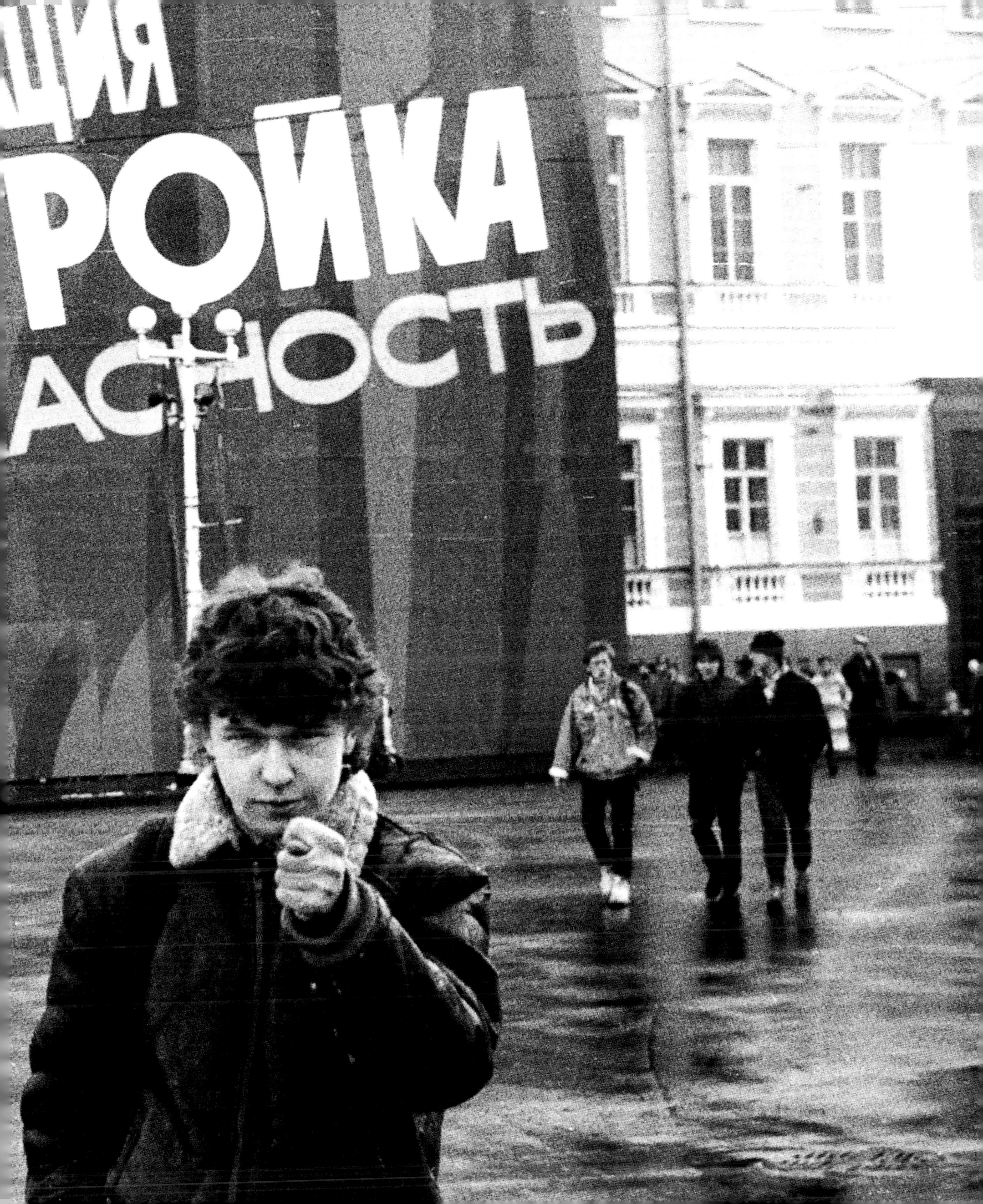
ЦИЯ
РОЙКА
АСНОСТЬ

To Martha H. Carroll [1936–2014], whose vision and sustained passion for the arts is manifested in this unique collection of glasnost and perestroika posters. She understood not only the beauty of their powerful graphic aesthetic, but also their documentary heritage, as records of the sociopolitical upheavals and ideological ambitions of glasnost during this momentous period in Russian history. Here, the poster will be presented as a means of living glasnost in the moment, with all its uncertainties, with all its possibilities.

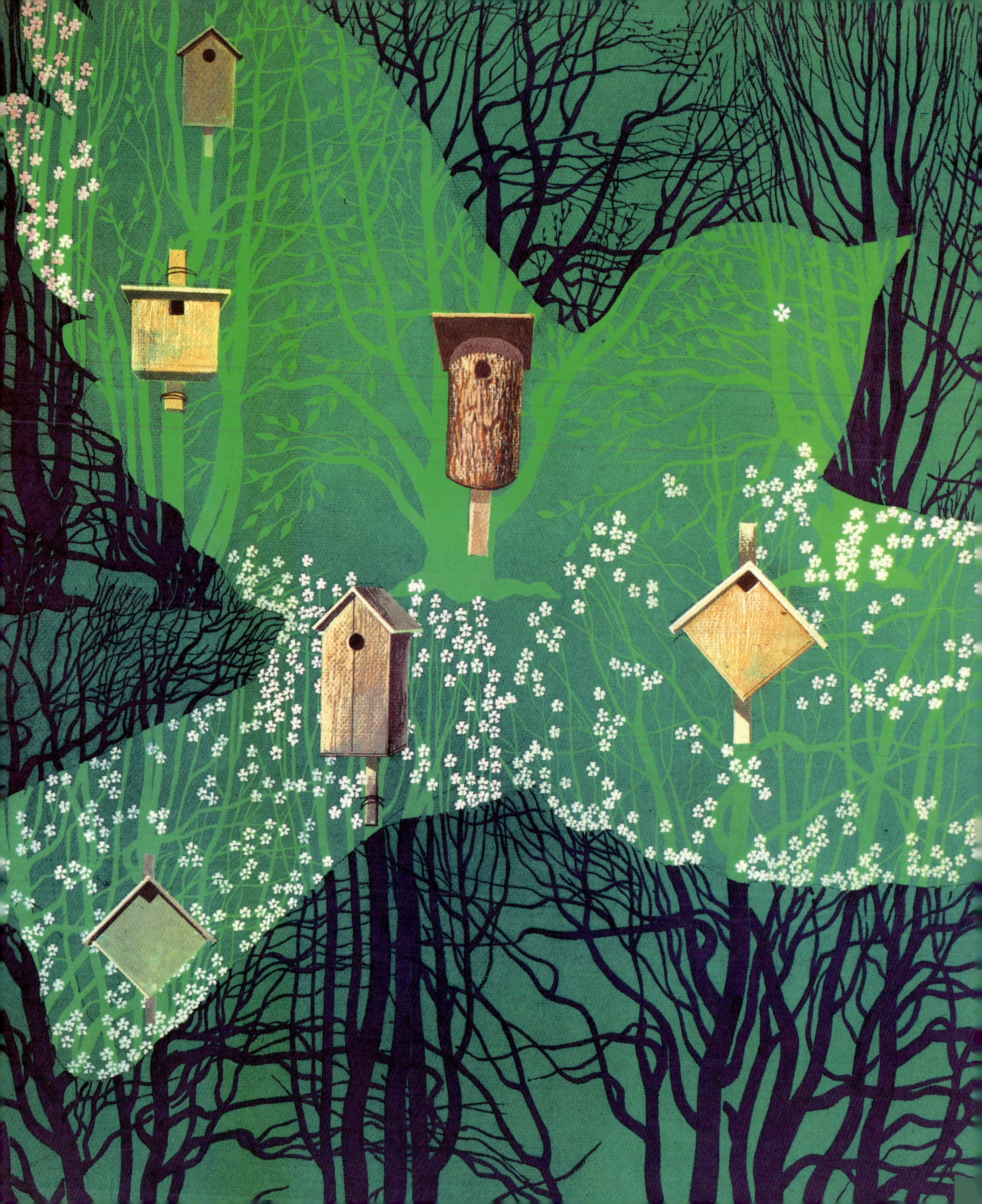

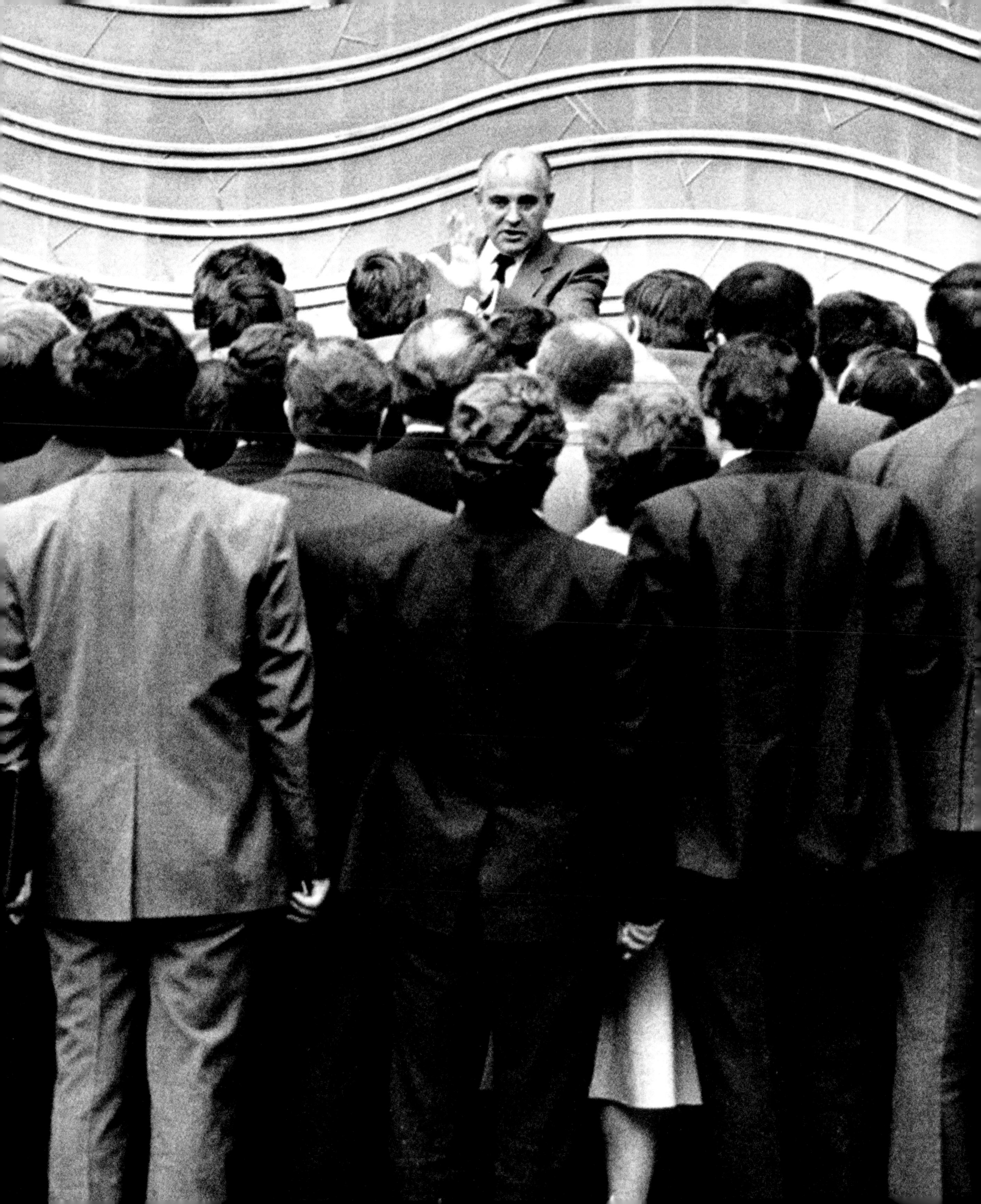

INTRODUCTION

J. SPEED CARROLL

I have been an enthusiastic collector of posters since May 1968. The chance acquisition at that time of political posters from China and the French students' rebellion then unfolding opened my eyes to the unique role of poster art. No medium is better suited to quickly communicate the thoughts and attitudes prevailing in contemporary society, especially those undergoing transformational change. In this as in so many other ways, Martha became an immediate and enthusiastic cosponsor of my newfound enthusiasm.

One day, near where we lived in New York, Martha saw a young Russian man sitting on the sidewalk with a few posters for sale. They turned out to be from the "glasnost" and "perestroika" period of the Soviet Union (roughly 1985–1991) but varied widely in theme and by artist. The man turned out to be the former manager of a Russian rock group, a free spirit who, after the band performed a few times in the US, had stayed behind just because he liked it here. He hoped to support himself for a while by selling glasnost posters, easily available to him, since his band was once again touring the smaller cities of the Soviet Union.

Martha bought several of the posters and inquired whether more were to be had. The young fellow replied yes, absolutely, because while on tour his friends in the band could buy more for what amounted to pennies and then ship them to him in New York. While the shops in Moscow and Leningrad (now St. Petersburg) quickly sold out of these items, they were easy to obtain in the provinces. Martha vigorously encouraged the young entrepreneur to do just that, and, thereafter, each time he received a new shipment, he brought them to our apartment posthaste. In effect, she got the pick of the litter every time. This continued until the young man either returned to Russia or his musician colleagues ran out of material.

Since Martha gave me these posters in large batches as birthday or Christmas presents, I'm not at all sure when she acquired them. The entire process did, I believe, take place while Mikhail Gorbachev was still in office. She was, amazingly, able to purchase around 500 posters and build a collection around these two historic initiatives: glasnost and perestroika.

The artistic quality of these images varies greatly. As many posters as we have, books from this period show that some outstanding examples are missing from our collection. Whatever the total volume of material produced may have been, it was certainly vast. The remarkable fact is that all the artists produced these posters while on the government payroll. Even more stunning, they seem to have been almost totally free of any political restraint. They could freely criticize and make fun of the government, its agencies, and its policies. As far as I know, this case of a government subsidizing the production of attacks on itself is without precedent anywhere in the world.

Why is such a significant body of work so little known, either within Russia or outside its borders? There are at least two reasons. First, Gorbachev's bold initiative came too late to save the Soviet Union, which collapsed in 1991 into its constituent elements. Second, the package of negative messages formed by the entirety of glasnost/perestroika doctrine was hardly designed for use otherwise than internally.

During a visit to St. Petersburg in 2013, Martha and I befriended two young women who worked at the State Hermitage Museum. They volunteered to check their sources to see whether there were other major collections of the glasnost posters. At the time, they could not find any, although of course scholarship and research techniques may have made considerable strides since then.

What should we learn from this remarkable moment? Certainly, the Soviet Union of that period offered no shortage of available targets, organized as it was around state agencies, national campaigns, and regional concerns. The sheer number of problems and abuses brought to the fore by these posters is absolutely staggering. Moreover, there is relatively little overlap in the subjects these artists chose to address. The lack of central guidance seems to have encouraged individual artists to seek out a multitude of styles which certainly develop many rich lines of inquiry into this fascinating but little-known period.

These chance elements enabled Martha to assemble a superlative, sharply focused poster collection. The happenstance collaboration between Martha and an unknown rock group manager has yielded a massive documentary resource that will richly reward further inquiry. Since Martha's loss I have been delighted to produce the next generation and I am very happy to introduce this combined resource to the public in these pages.

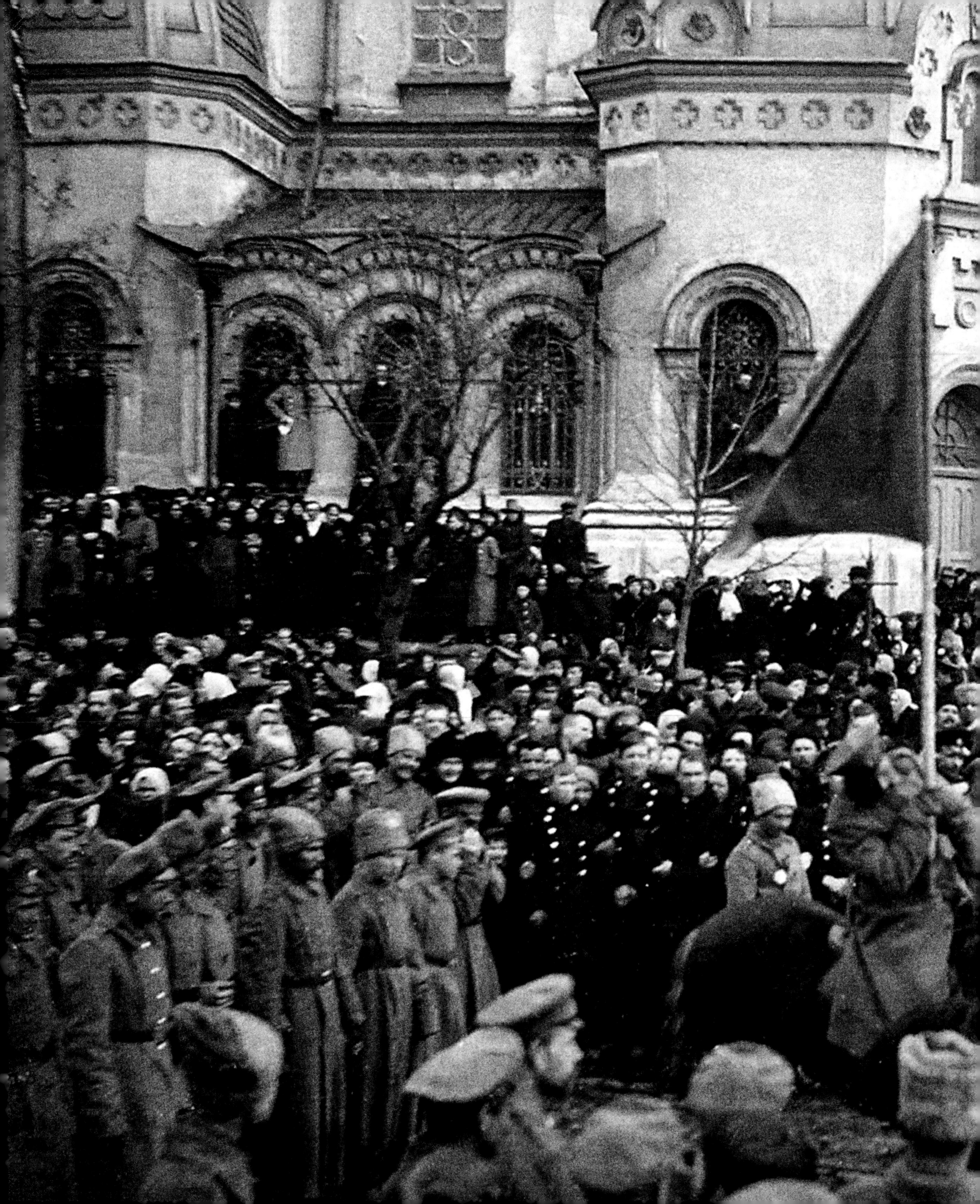

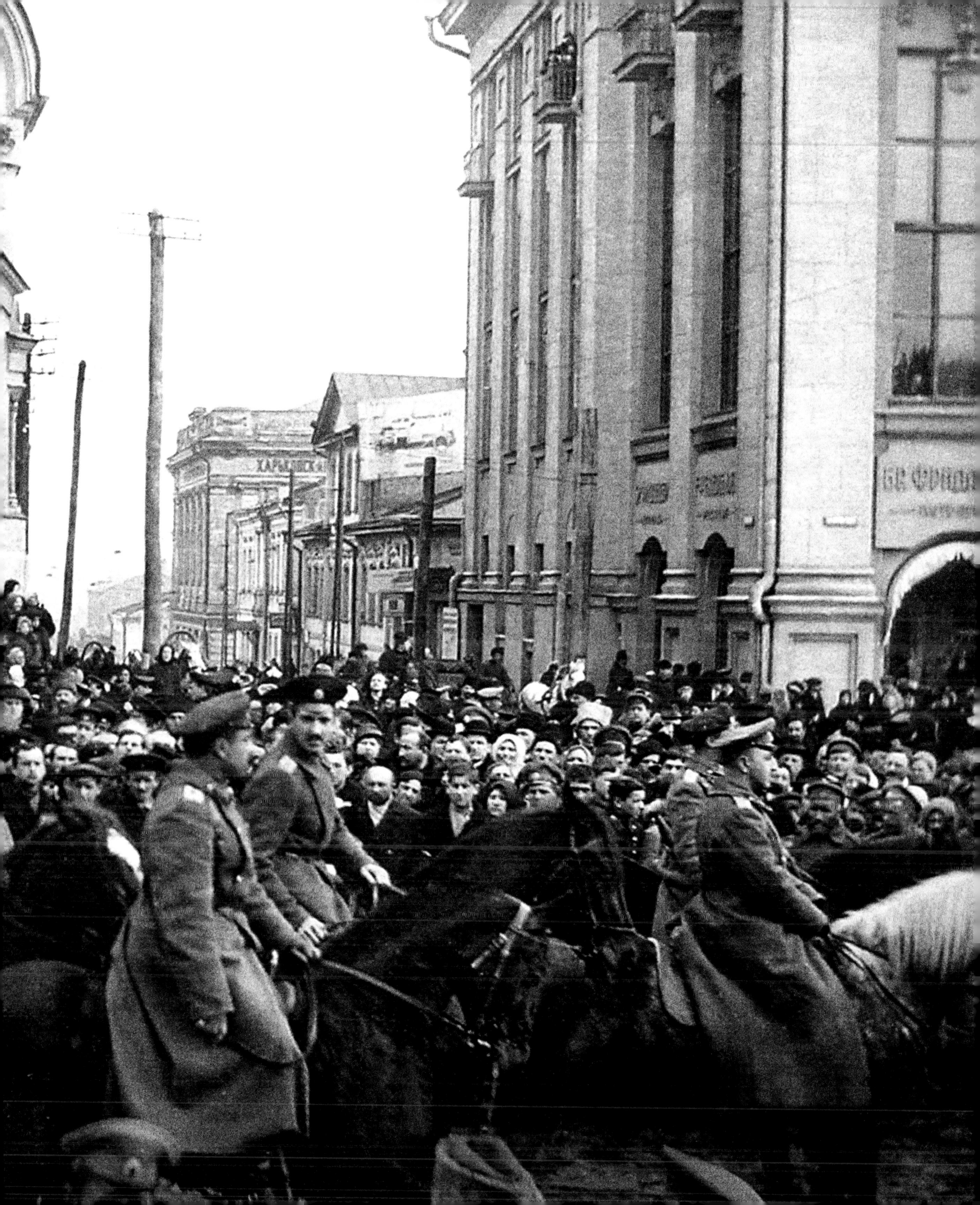

PAST

LENIN AND STALIN

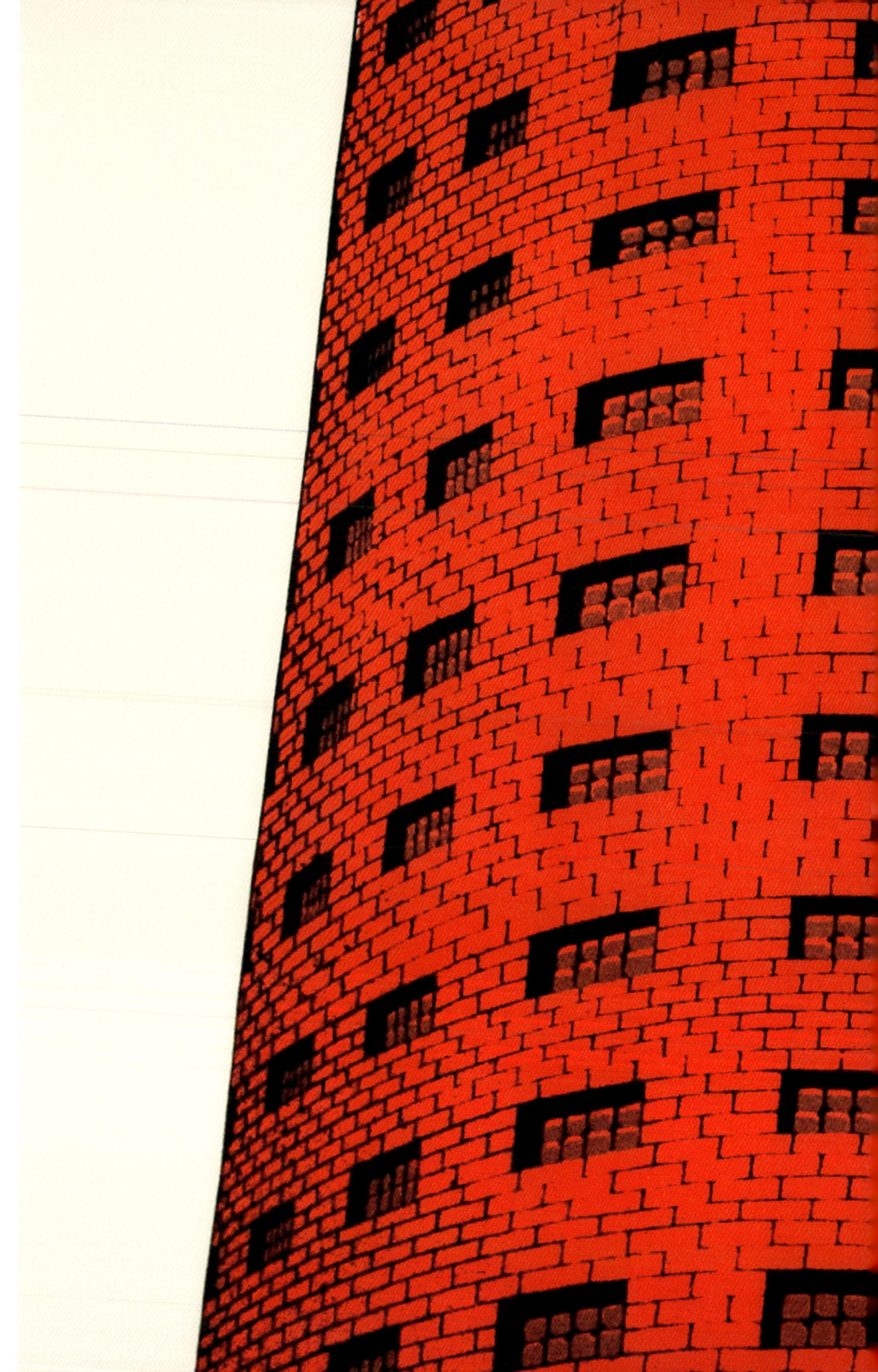

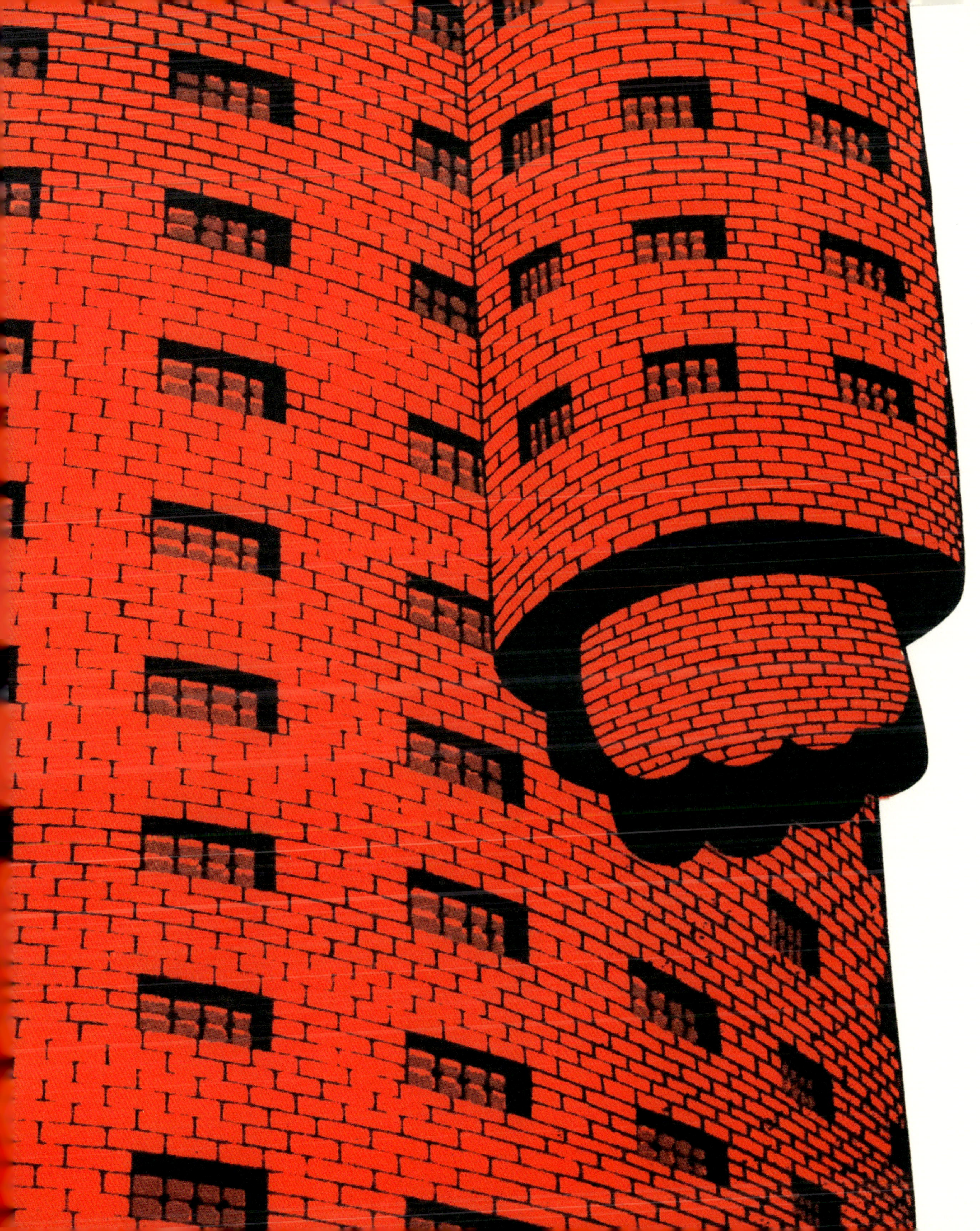

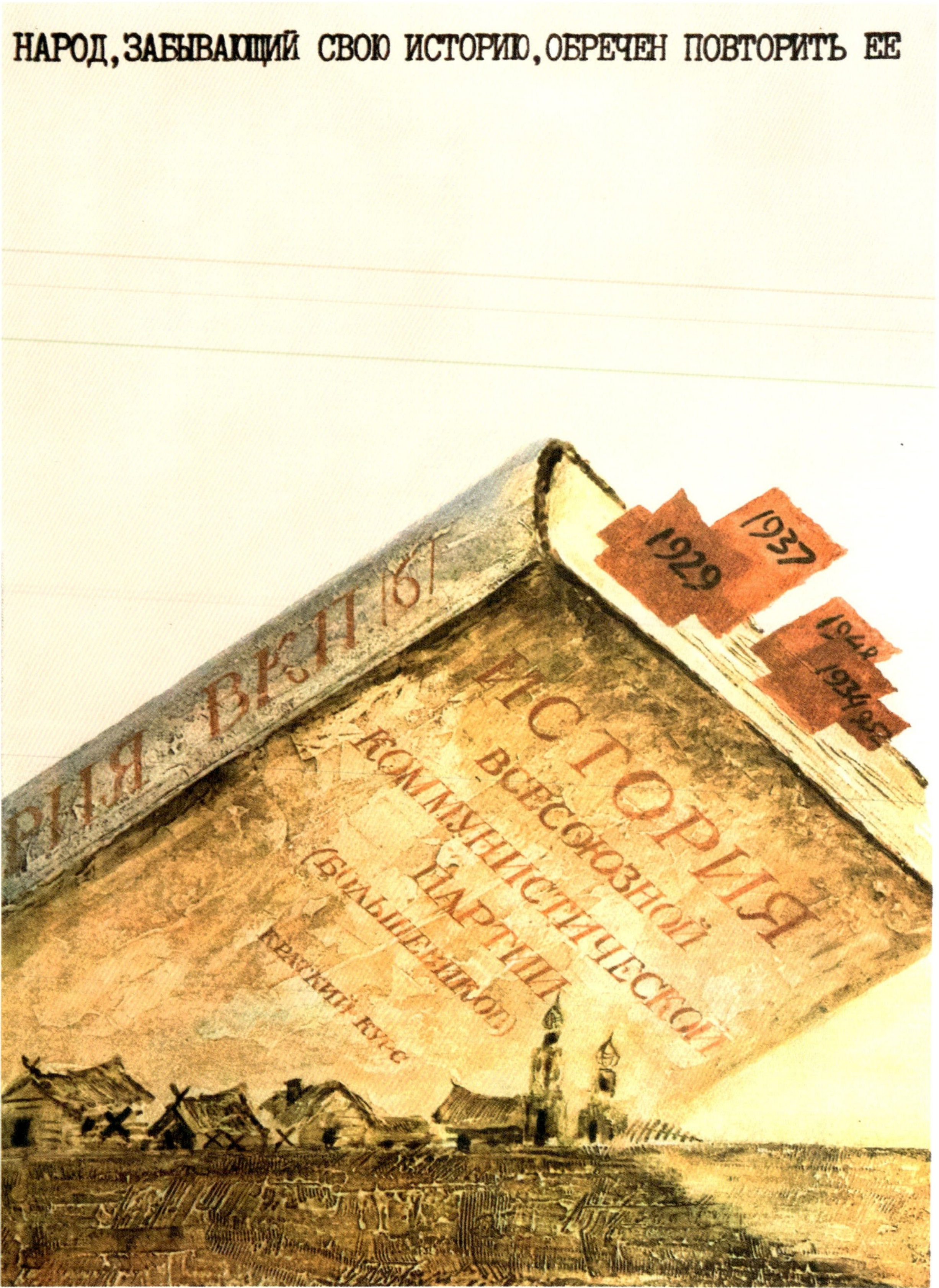
НАРОД, ЗАБЫВАЮЩИЙ СВОЮ ИСТОРИЮ, ОБРЕЧЕН ПОВТОРИТЬ ЕЕ
ВКП(б)
1929
1937
ИСТОРИЯ
ВСЕСОЮЗНОЙ
КОММУНИСТИЧЕСКОЙ
ПАРТИИ

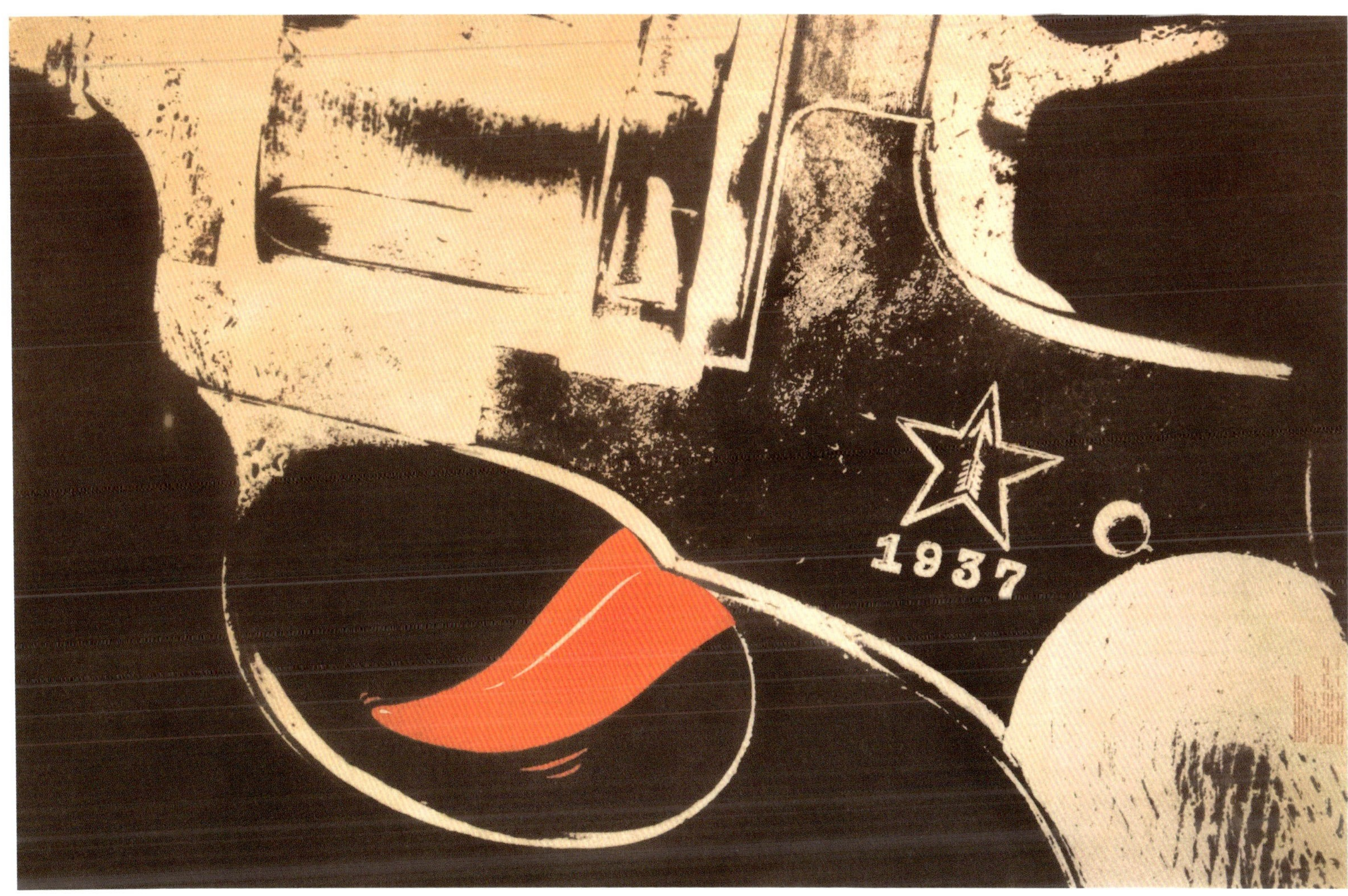

◄ Л. Ковалева (L. Kovaleva) | 1988

A NATION THAT FORGETS ITS HISTORY IS DOOMED TO REPEAT IT

The book depicted in this poster was written by Joseph Stalin in 1938 and titled *History of the All-Soviet Communist Party (Bolsheviks): A Brief Course*. It was later published in English as *History of the Communist Party of the Soviet Union (Bolsheviks): A Short Course*. The red bookmarks signal momentous dates in Stalin's career: 1929 (collectivization); 1934 (17th "Congress of Victors," in which Stalin vanquished his rivals, thus winning absolute power); 1937 (the first year of Stalin's purges); 1948 (Stalin's participation in the creation of the state of Israel); and 1952 (the first time since 1912 that the Soviet Union, then the Russian Empire, competed in the summer Olympics.)

▲ Р. Н. Найден (R. N. Nayden), А. П. Новожилов (A. P. Novozhilov) | 1990

The pistol is inscribed with 1937, the peak of Stalin's Terror, during which hundreds of thousands of people were imprisoned and executed. The gun's trigger has been replaced by a tongue in reference to the informants who facilitated these crimes in aims of retaining or elevating their statuses within the system.

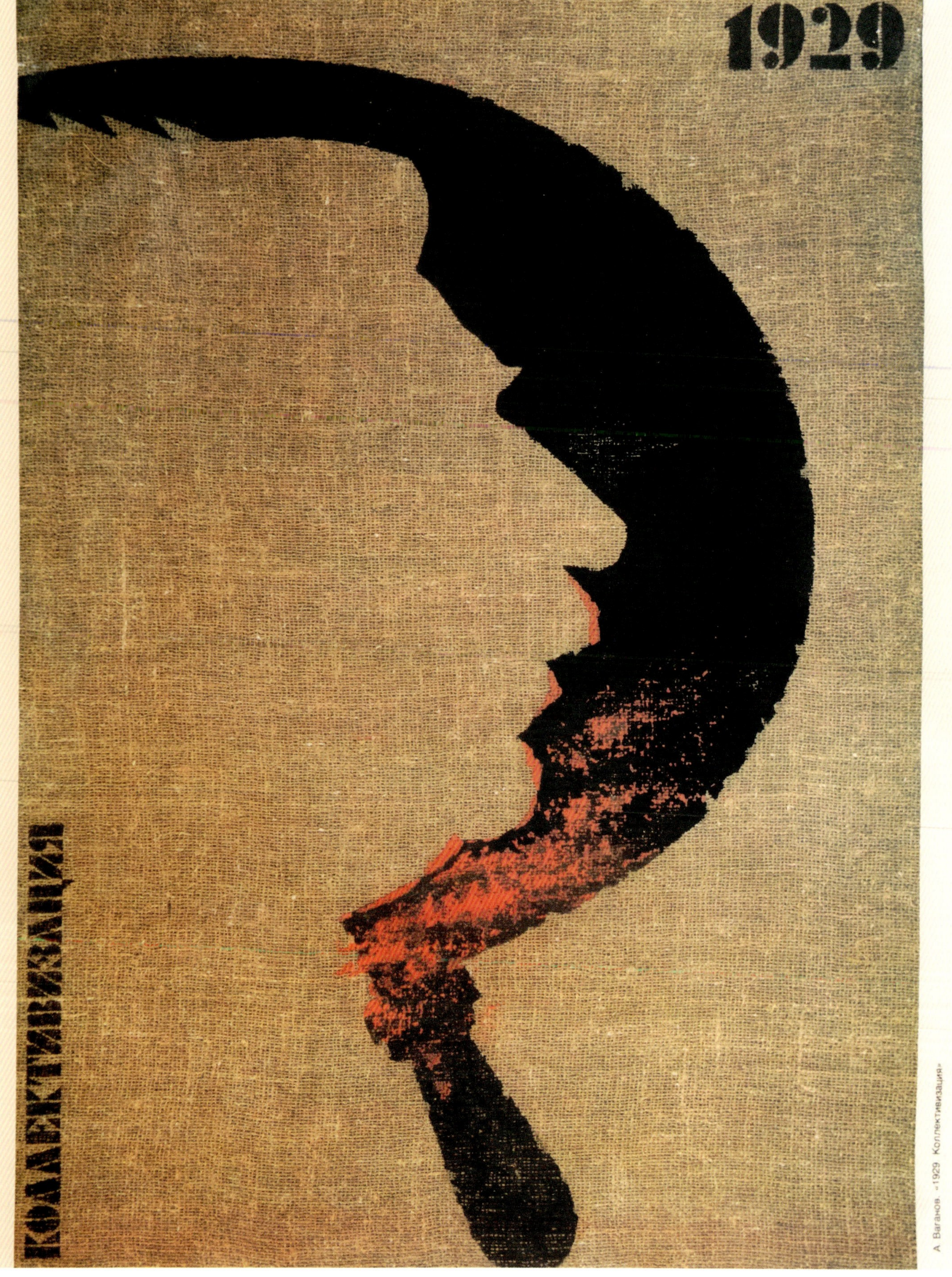
1929
Коллективизация
А Ваганов. «1929 Коллективизация»

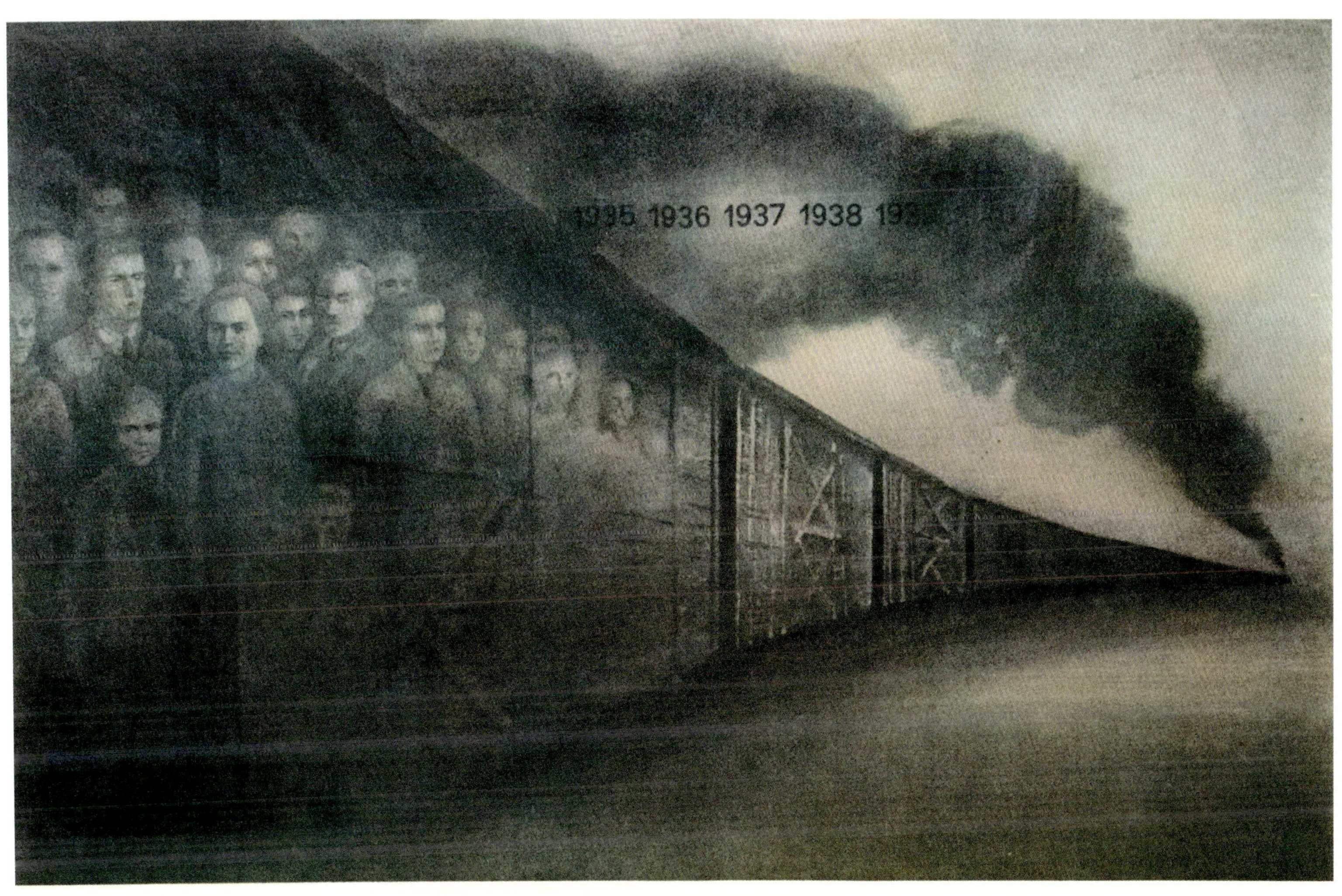

А Лозенко «1935... 1940»

◂ **А. Баранов (A. Baranov) | 1988**

1929
COLLECTIVIZATION
The sickle's inner edge traces the profile of Stalin. The date marks the commencement of his program to collectivize farm production. The blood on the sickle represents the millions who died as a result, many of starvation.

▴ **А. Лозенко (A. Lozenko) | 1988**

A freight train in a somber landscape stretches out into the distance bearing a tightly packed crowd. A sequence of years is framed in the engine's black smoke: 1935, 1936, 1937, 1938, with 1937—the height of Stalin's Great Terror—emerging with particular clarity. This poster commemorates those killed and imprisoned during the years that Stalin consolidated his total control of the USSR.

А. Кондуров (A. Kondurov) | 1988 ➤

A question mark appears at the top of a torn-open red envelope. This symbol supplants the digit in the millions place in order to ask: HOW MANY MILLIONS OF DESTINIES? The envelope's flaps are demarcated by barbed wire, and bear two stamps: a black one that appears to seal the envelope closed, and another, part of a white postmark that seems integral to opening it. In the center, the black stamp represents the 17th Congress of the Communist Party of the Soviet Union held in 1934. The same Congress carried two other names, one, "The Congress of Victors"; the other, more revealing in this context, "The Congress of the Condemned." The latter is named as such because, shortly after its adjournment, a very large number of those elected at the Congress were either executed or sent to the gulag, thereby not only consolidating Stalin's power, but also beginning the darkest period of the Soviet Union. The 20th Congress in 1956, on the other hand, was the moment when Khrushchev secretly denounced Stalin and his brutally repressive regime. This Congress and this action, signified here by the white stamp, are considered to mark the end of the gulag.

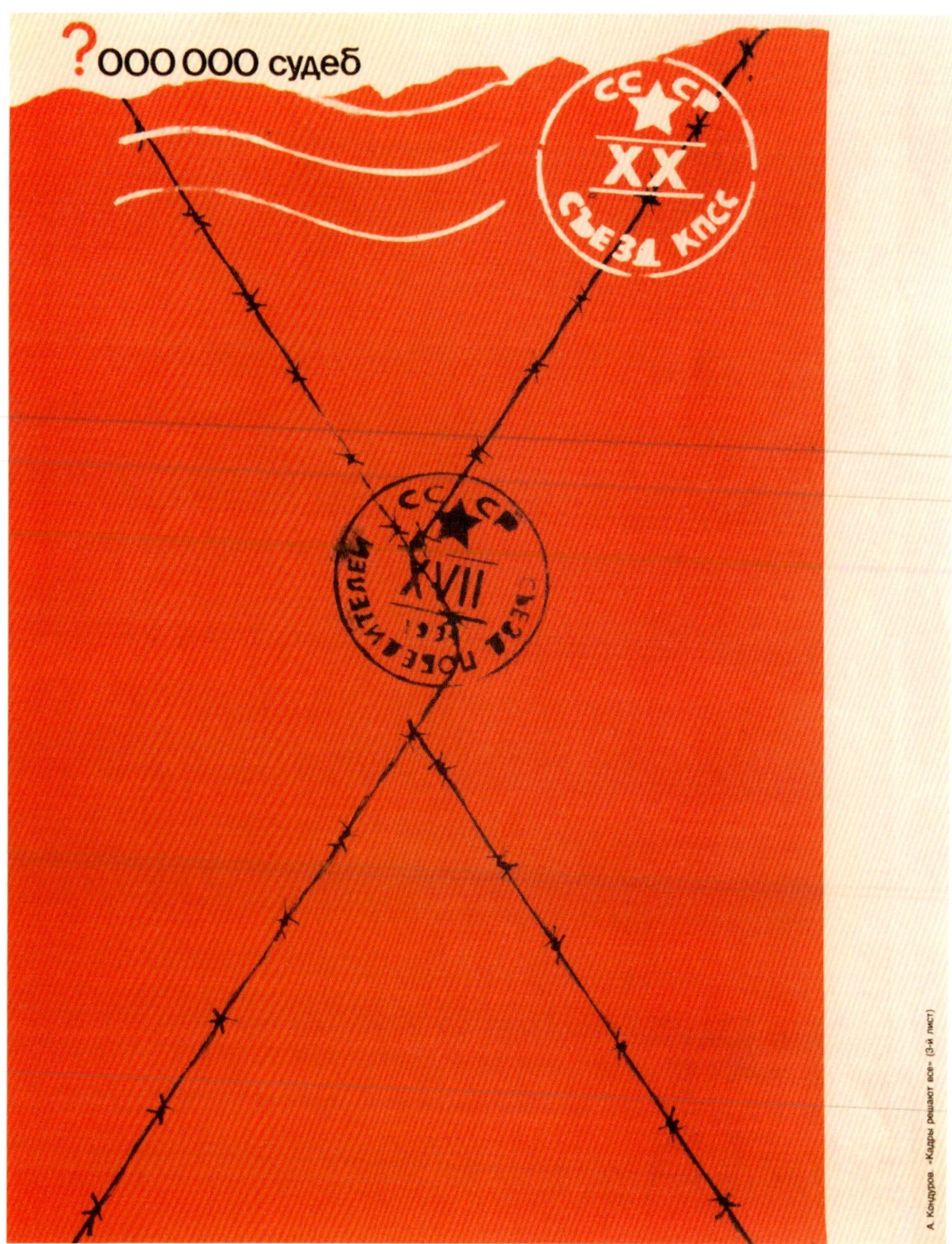

А. Кондуров (A. Kondurov) | 1988 ➤

WE WON'T LET THIS HAPPEN AGAIN!
This iconic image of Stalin in a Napoleonic stance blatantly reveals a flawed attempt to reflect his invulnerability by portraying himself as an indomitable, towering dictator.

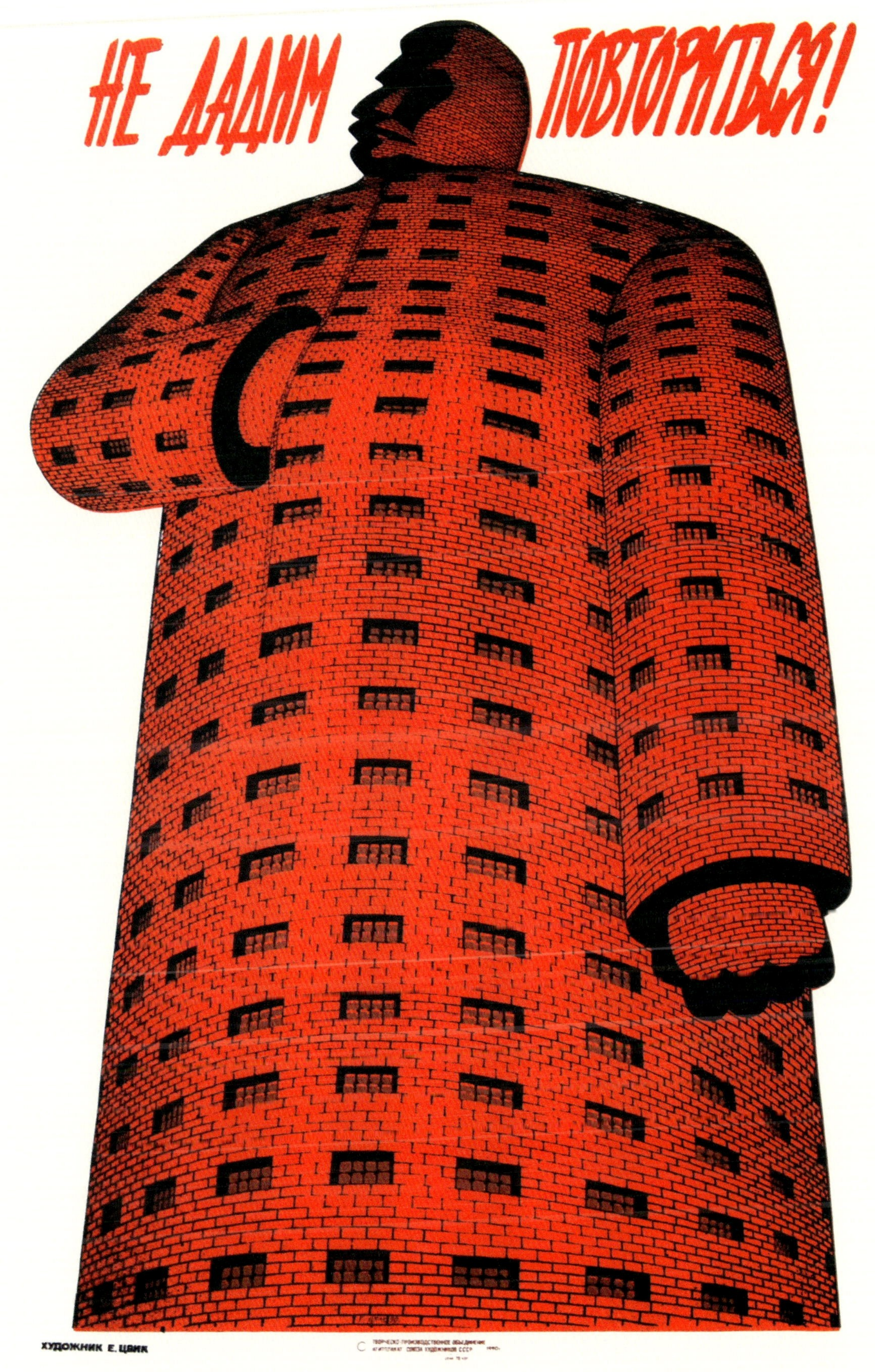
НЕ ДАДИМ ПОВТОРИТЬСЯ!
ХУДОЖНИК Е. ЦВИК

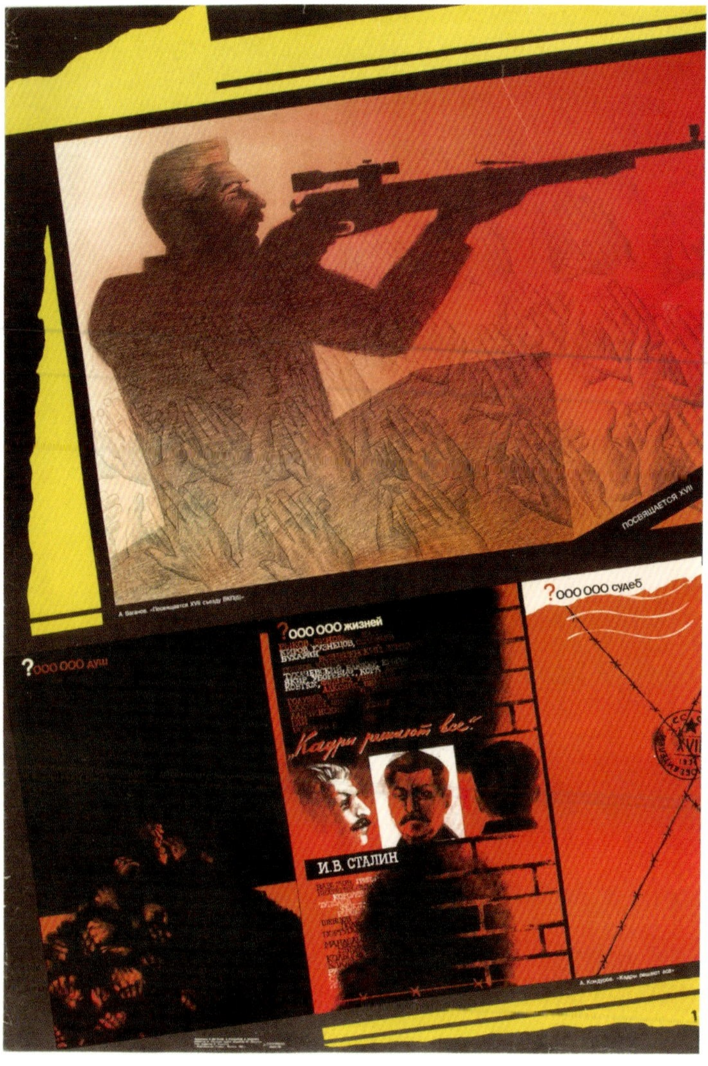

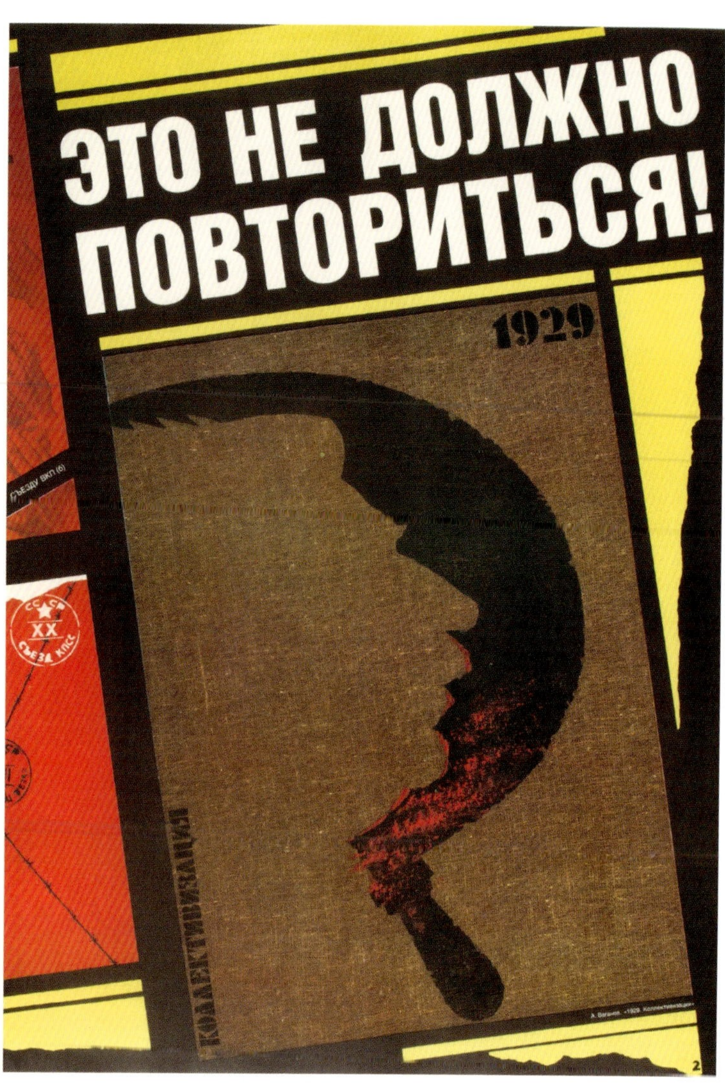

А. Ваганов (A. Vaganov), А. Кондуров (A. Kondurov), А. Лозенко (A. Lozenko) | 1988

Panel 1 of a triptych with reproductions of smaller posters that address the millions of people killed during Stalin's Great Terror. Panel 1 includes the words DEDICATED TO 17TH [continued on second panel] CONGRESS OF THE CPSU.

Panel 2 includes a poster showing Stalin's profile in a sickle, reading COLLECTIVIZATION, vertically in lower left corner, 1929, and across the top, THIS CANNOT HAPPEN AGAIN!

Panel 3 includes two other posters reading REQUIEM and 1937, and, below, IT IS THE FAULT OF STALIN AS WELL AS THOSE CLOSEST TO HIM, BEFORE THE PARTY AND BEFORE THE PEOPLE, FOR ALLOWING MASSIVE PERSECUTIONS TO TAKE PLACE. THE LAWLESSNESS WAS ENORMOUS AND UNFORGIVABLE. *PRAVDA*, APRIL 5, 1988.

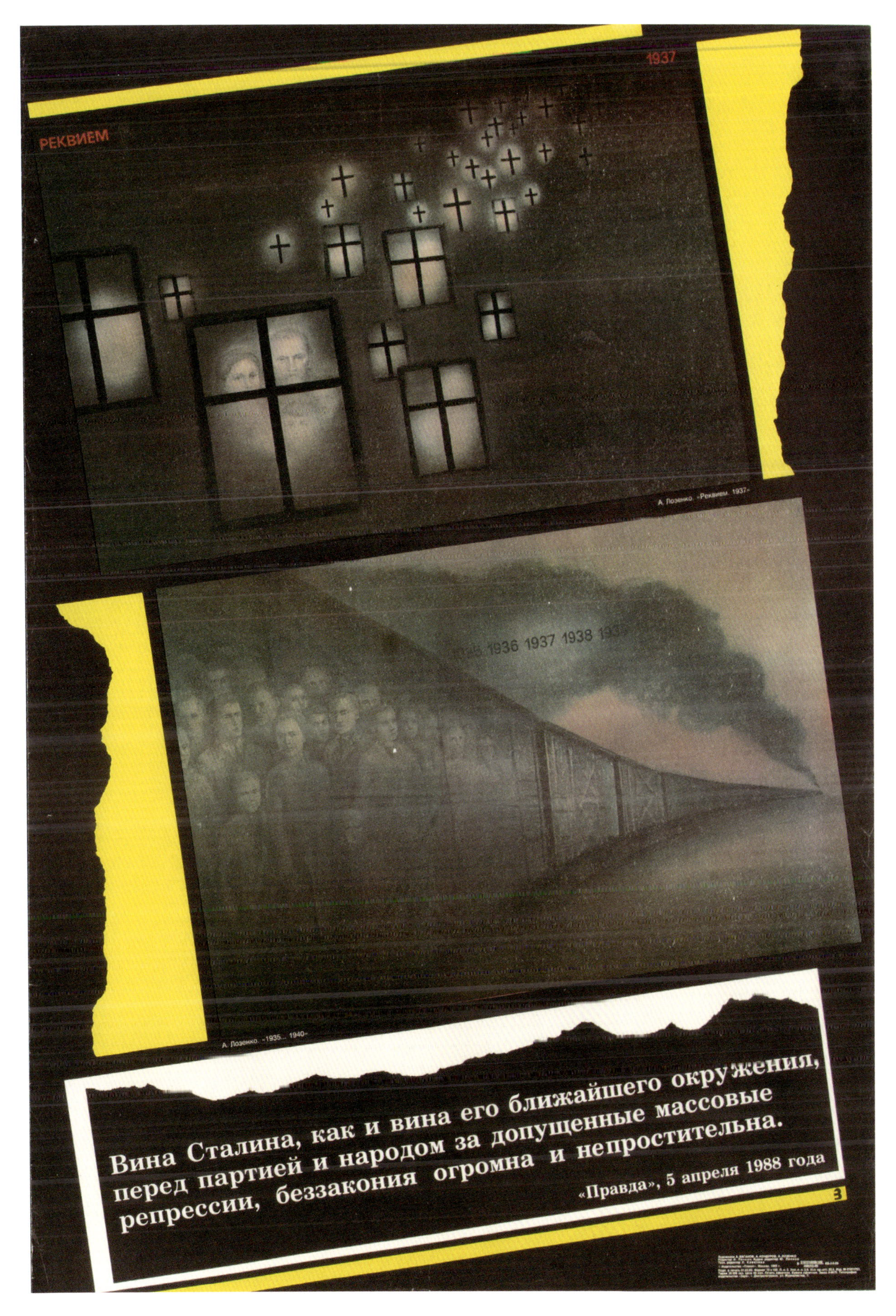
1937
РЕКВИЕМ
А. Лозенко. «Реквием. 1937»
1936 1937 1938
А. Лозенко. «1935... 1940»
Вина Сталина, как и вина его ближайшего окружения, перед партией и народом за допущенные массовые репрессии, беззакония огромна и непростительна.
«Правда», 5 апреля 1988 года
3

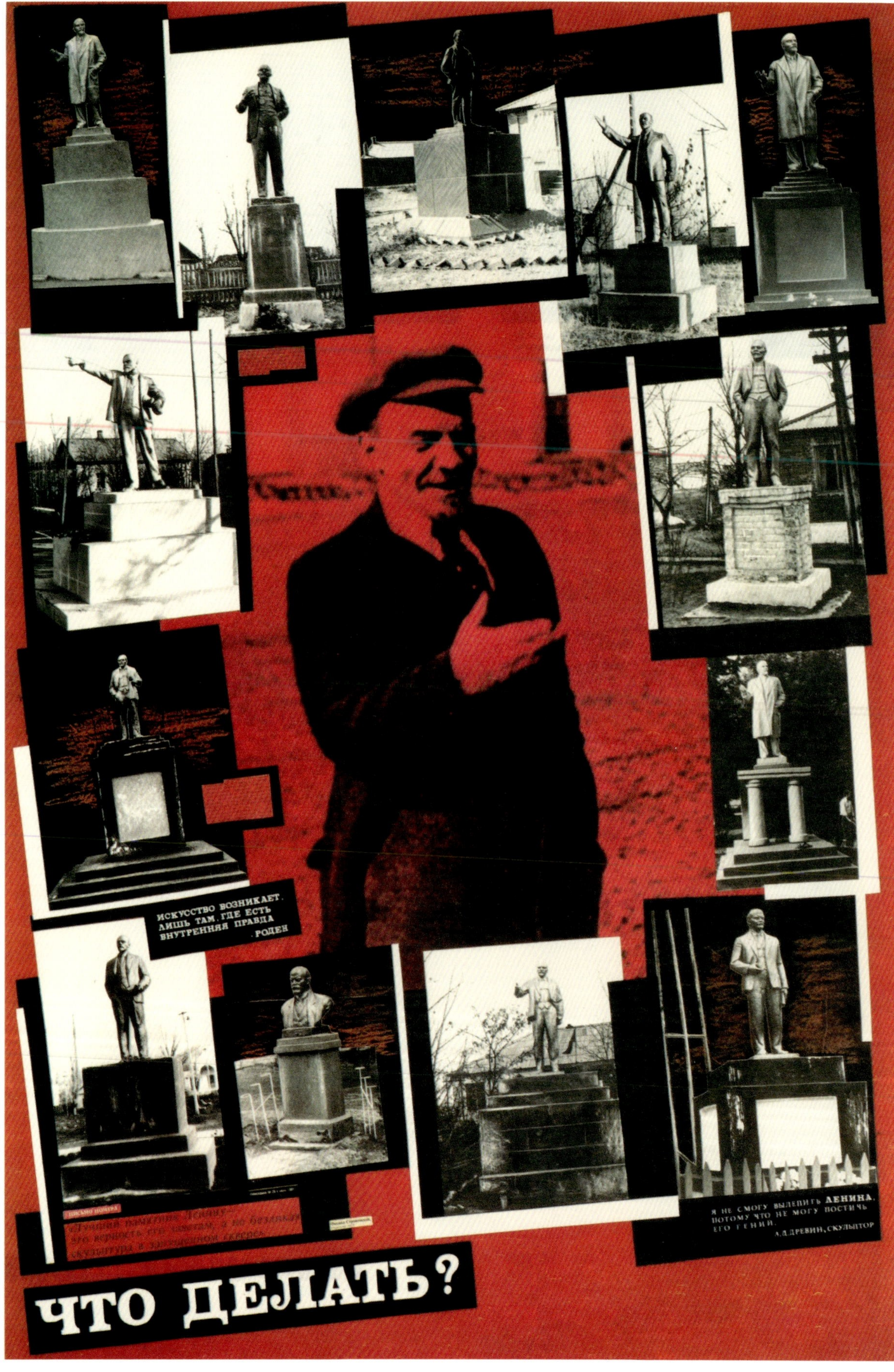
ИСКУССТВО ВОЗНИКАЕТ.
ЛИШЬ ТАМ, ГДЕ ЕСТЬ
ВНУТРЕННЯЯ ПРАВДА
. РОДЕН
Я НЕ СМОГУ ВЫЛЕПИТЬ ЛЕНИНА,
ПОТОМУ ЧТО НЕ МОГУ ПОСТИЧЬ
ЕГО ГЕНИЙ.
А.Д.ДРЕВИН, СКУЛЬПТОР
ЧТО ДЕЛАТЬ?

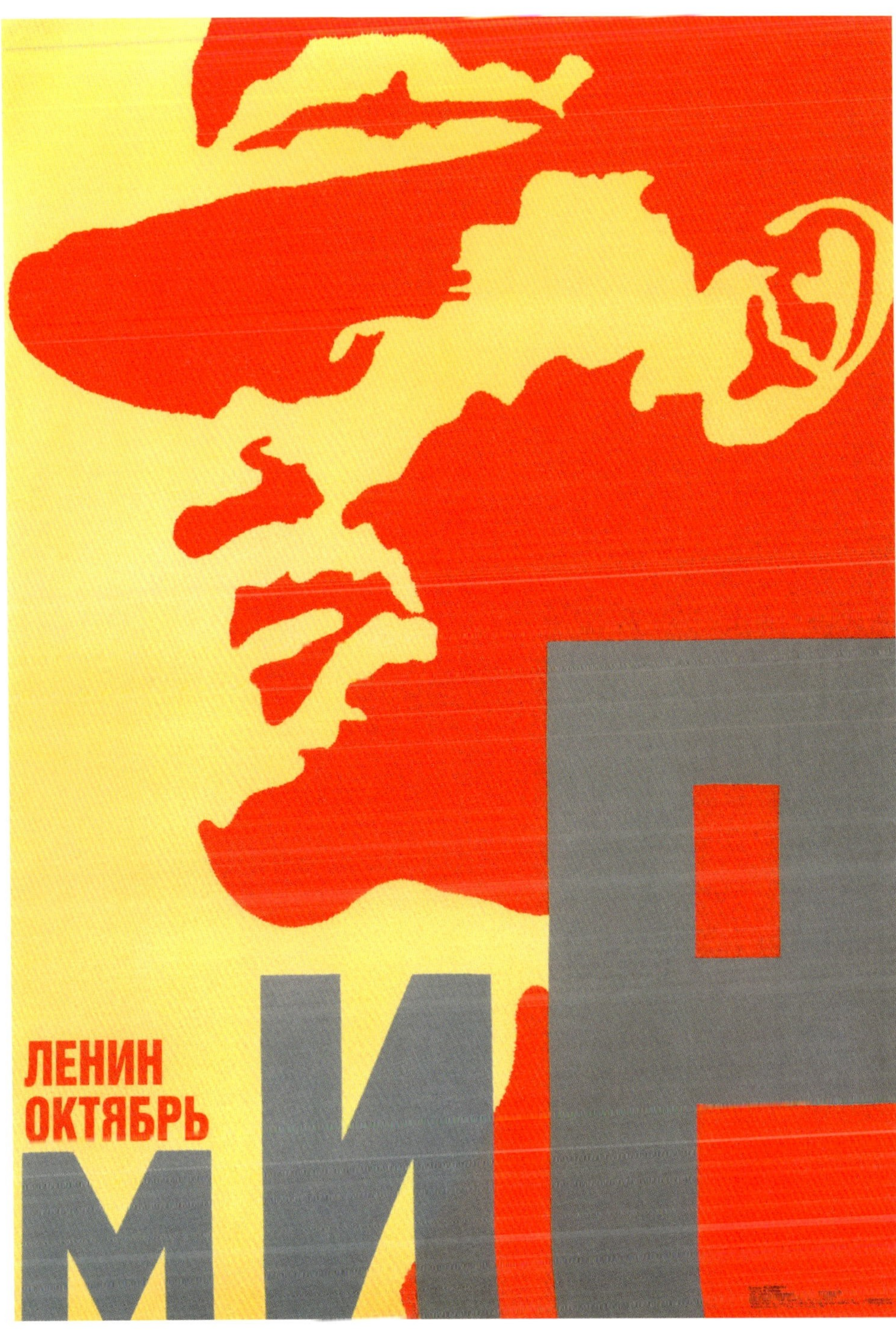

◂ В. Черенов (V. Cherenov), А. Решетов (A. Reshetov), В. Козлов (V. Kozlov) | n.d.

WHAT IS TO BE DONE?
A photo of Lenin is surrounded by photos of statues of Lenin, with the statues here acting as a metaphor for the late Soviet debate on whether to return to Lenin's ideas or abandon communist ideology altogether. At left, there is a quote, ART ONLY ARISES FROM WHERE THERE IS AN INNER TRUTH –RODIN. At right, another quote, THE BEST MONUMENT TO LENIN IS FAITHFULNESS TO HIS VISION, NOT FACELESS SCULPTURES OR NEGLECTED SQUARES –A. L. DREVIN, SCULPTOR.

▴ Ю. Палка (Y. Palka) | 1987

LENIN
OCTOBER
PEACE

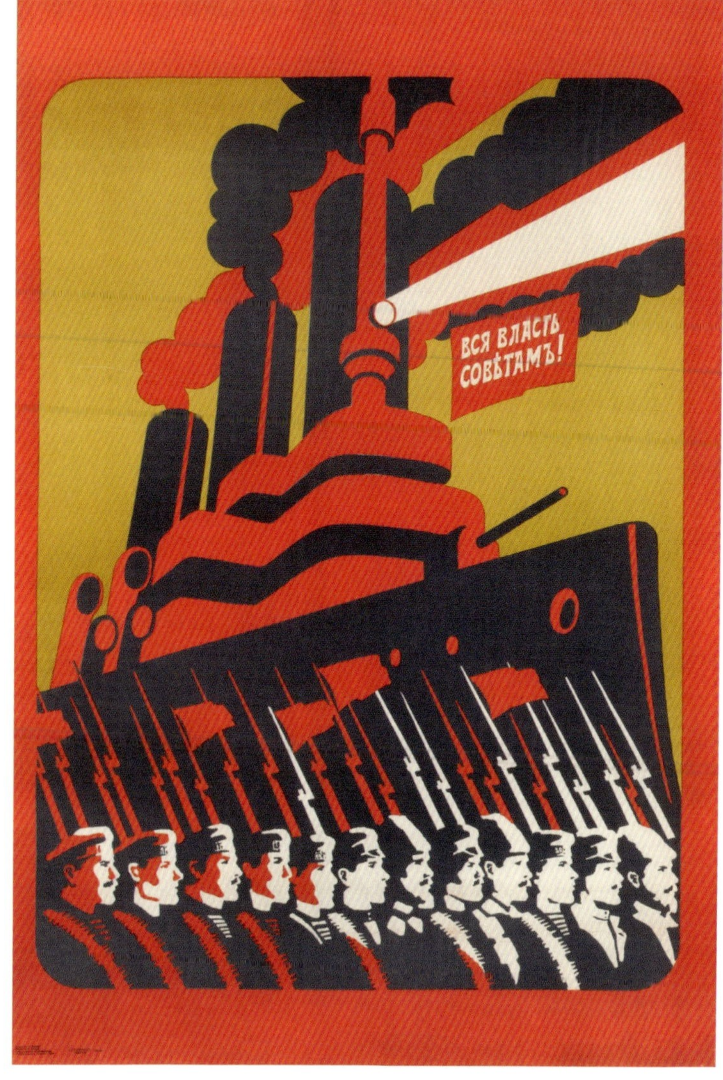

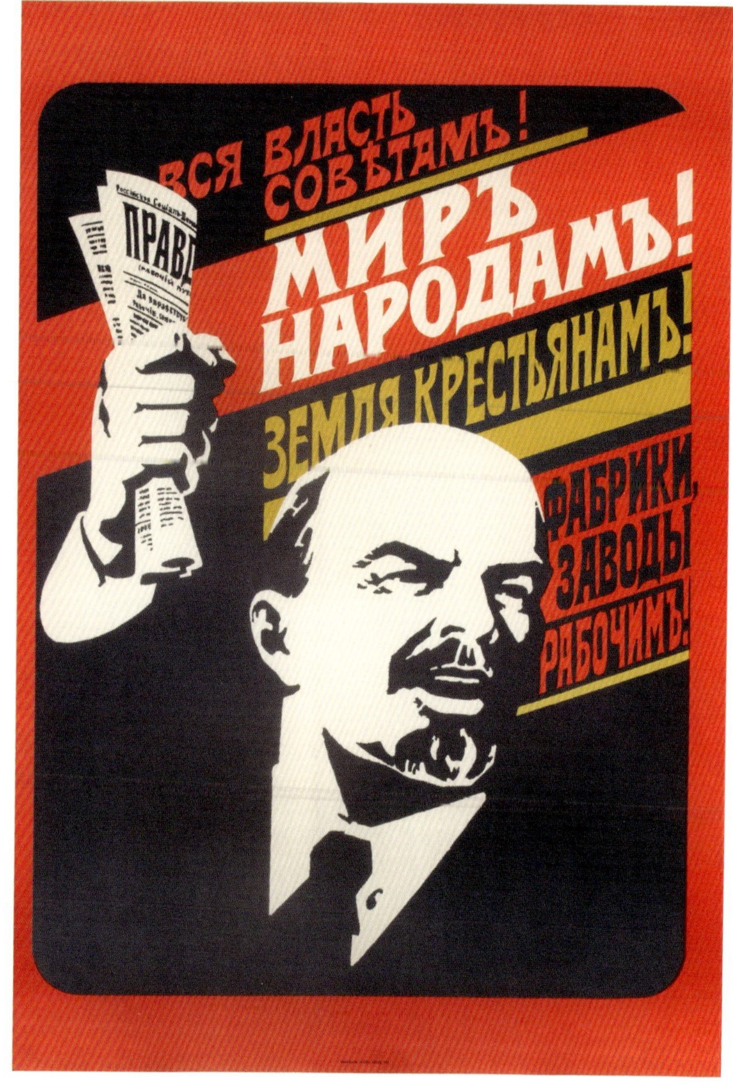

Н. Бабин (N. Babin) | 1988

Three panels of a triptych. Panel 1 diplays a battleship flanked by marching soldiers with bayonets. ALL POWER TO THE SOVIETS! was the slogan of the October Revolution. Depicted here is the ship *Aurora*, from which the first shot was fired at the onset of the revolution. This event marked the beginning of the military coup d'état.

Panel 2 features Lenin brandishing an issue of *Pravda*, which was founded in 1912 and was the official newspaper of the Communist Party of the Soviet Union. He is surrounded by early Soviet slogans: ALL POWER TO THE SOVIETS! PEACE TO THE PEOPLE OF ALL NATIONS! LAND TO THE PEASANTS! FACTORIES AND PLANTS TO THE WORKERS! All of these slogans were re-embraced during perestroika in order to legitimize the movement and galvanize the public's support.

Panel 3 includes a factory with workers and the following text: LONG LIVE THE REVOLUTION OF THE WORKERS, SOLDIERS AND PEASANTS! PEACE! BREAD! LAND!

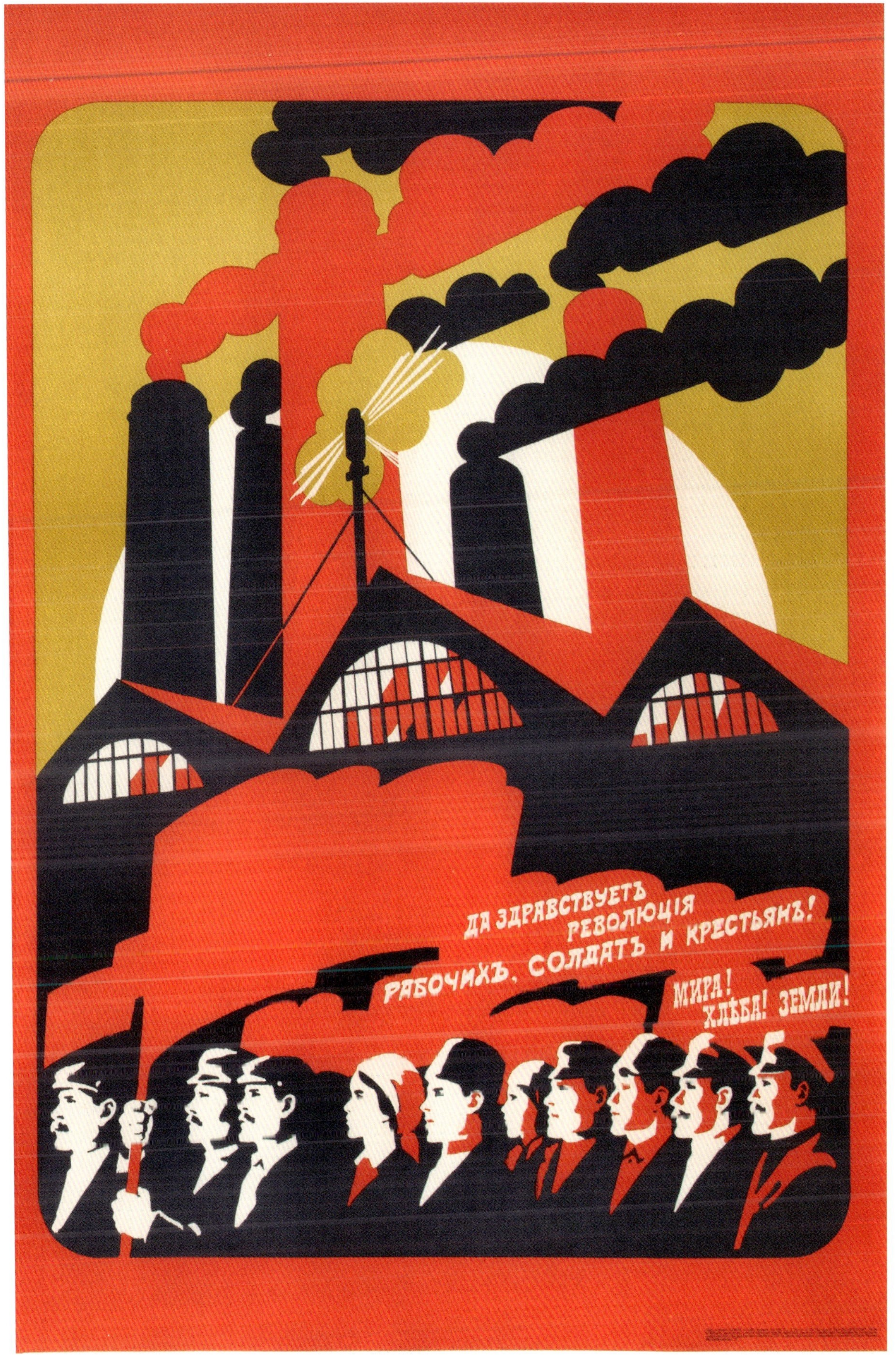
ДА ЗДРАВСТВУЕТЪ
РЕВОЛЮЦІЯ
РАБОЧИХЪ, СОЛДАТЪ И КРЕСТЬЯНЪ!
МИРА!
ХЛѢБА! ЗЕМЛИ!

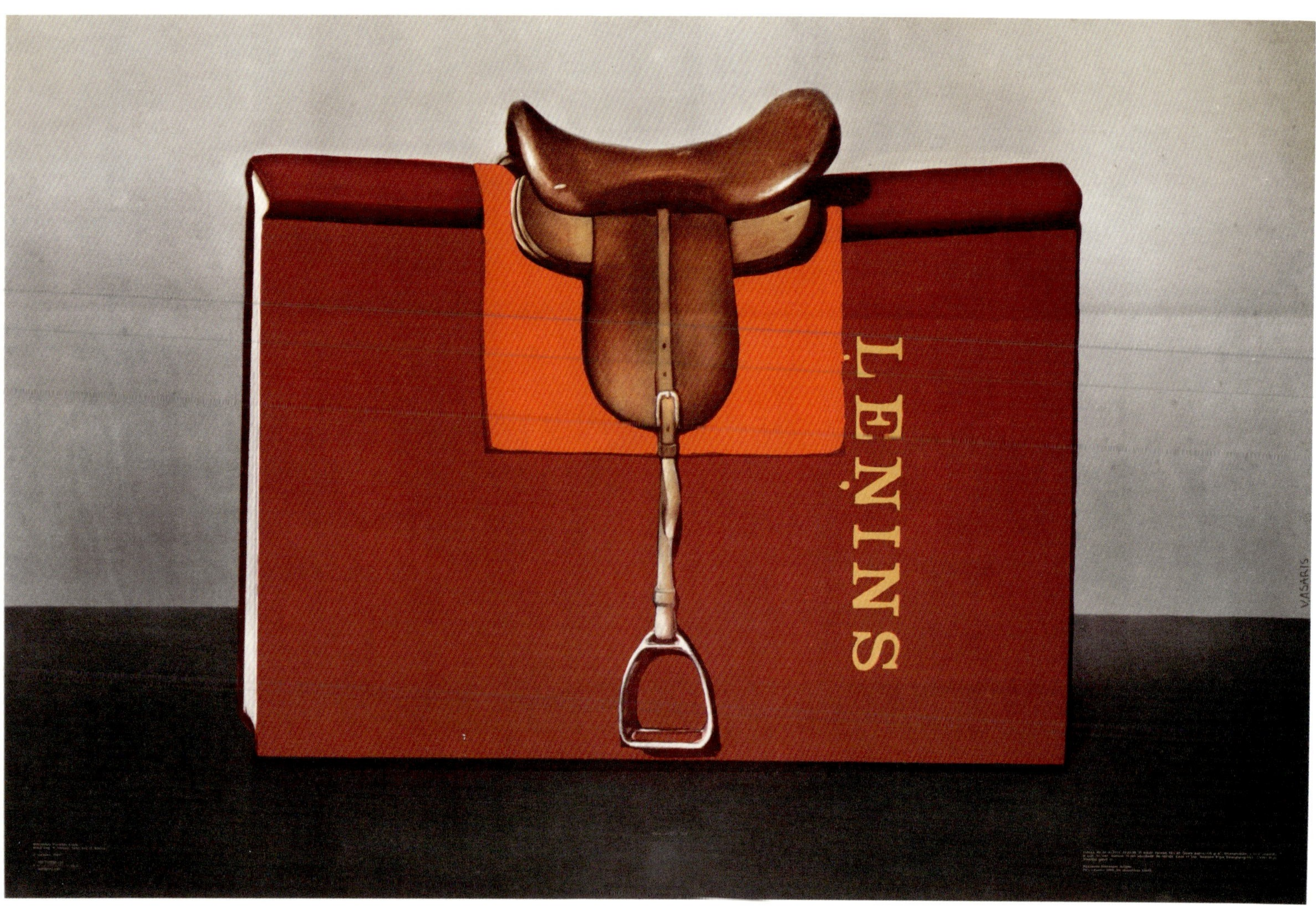

▲ Ю. Палка (Y. Palka) | 1987

A red, presumably communist, saddle blanket and saddle are mounted on a book of Lenin's theories. This composition is a reference to Lenin's New Economic Policy, which instituted a mixed economy and produced significant growth (later to disappear under Stalin). Notably, Gorbachev wanted to go back to much of the same economic policy as Lenin.

А. Кравченко (A. Kravchenko) | n.d. ➤

A TIME TO SCATTER STONES

This phrase referencing Ecclesiastes 3:5 is used to refer to old Soviet monuments. The stones scattered over a continuum of small hills are seemingly metaphors for the statues of statesmen. The message conveyed here is to encourage the removal of these monuments, symbolic of the old regime—such as those of Lenin and Stalin—for the sake of progress.

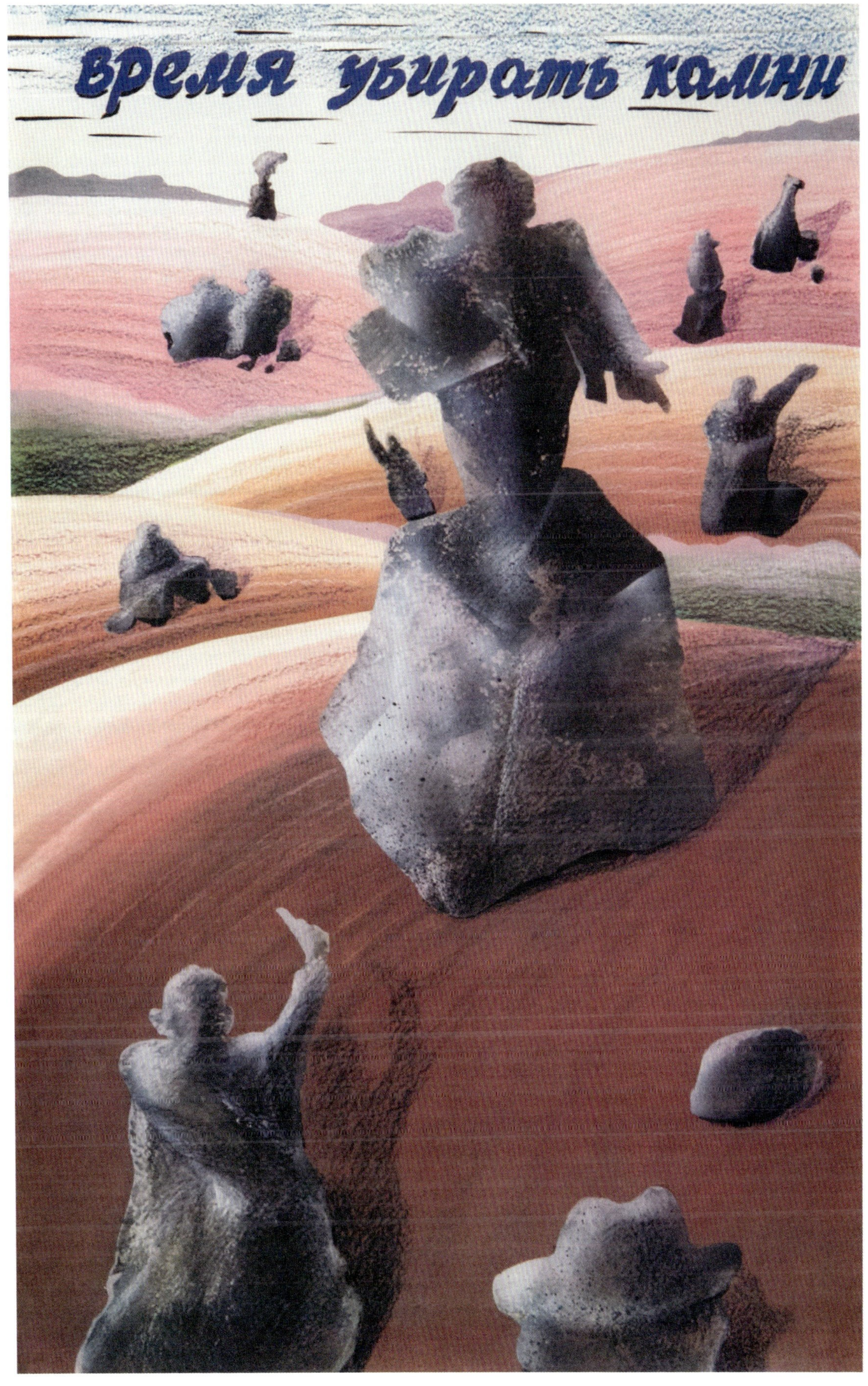
Время убирать камни

HISTORY

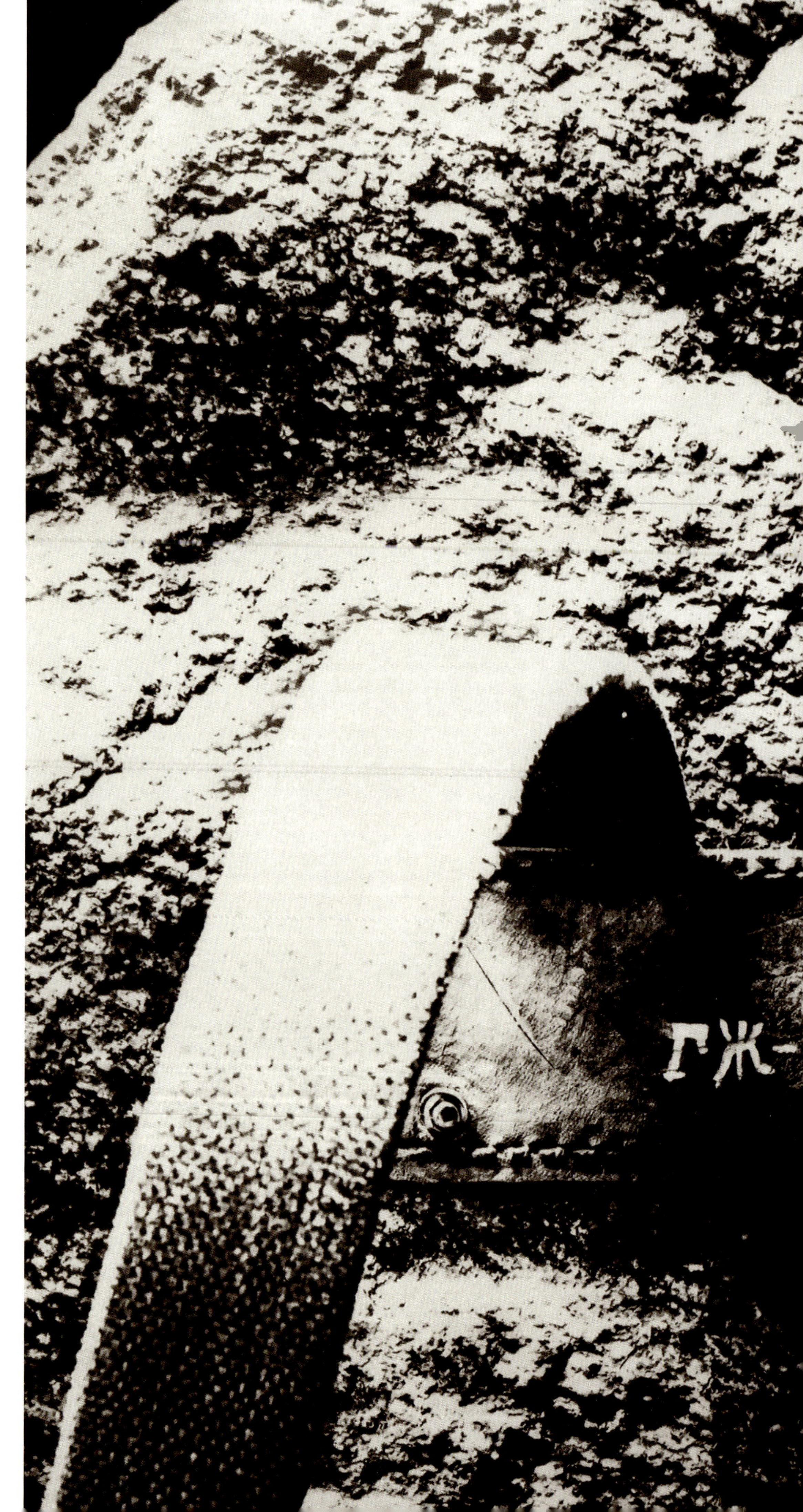

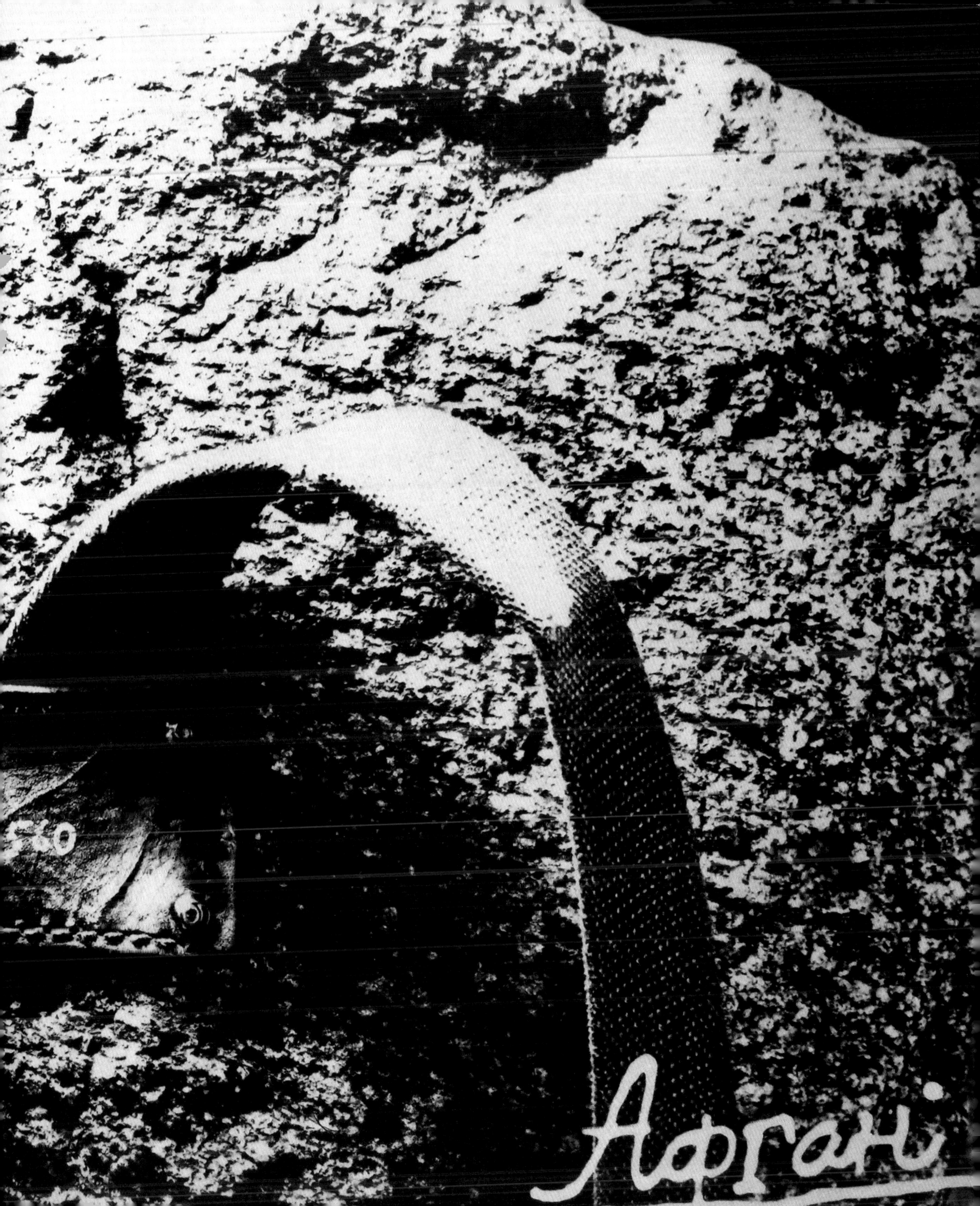

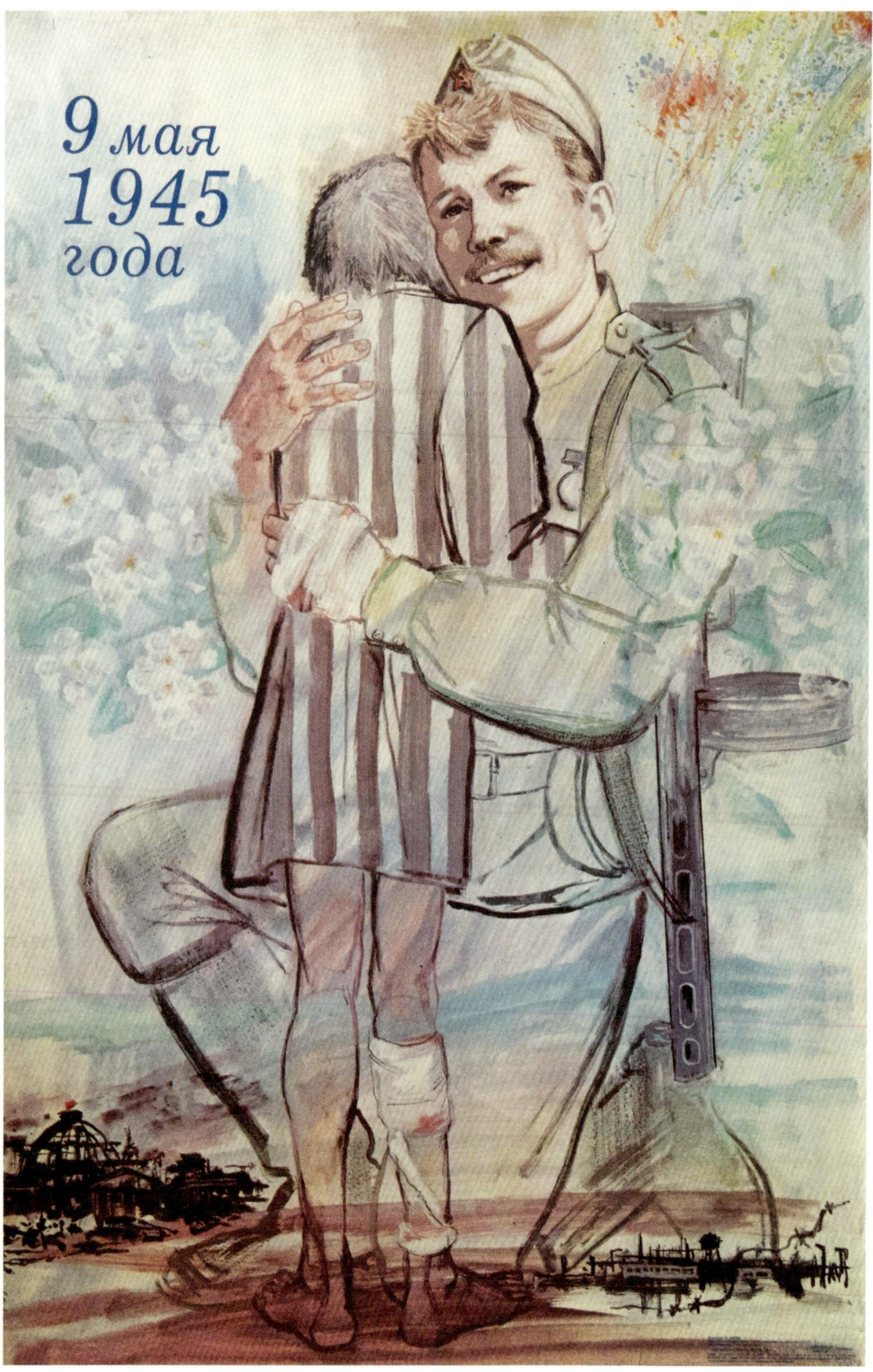

Ю. Царев (Y. Tsarev) | 1989

MAY 9, 1945, is a direct reference to "Victory Day," celebrated in Russia on that date and initially by the fifteen republics of the USSR. Victory Day marks the end of World War II and the victory of the Allied Forces in 1945.

А. Ваганов (A. Vaganov) | 1989

GLORY! GLORY! GLORY!
A soldier walks through shouts of "glory" and fireworks, but looks forlorn.

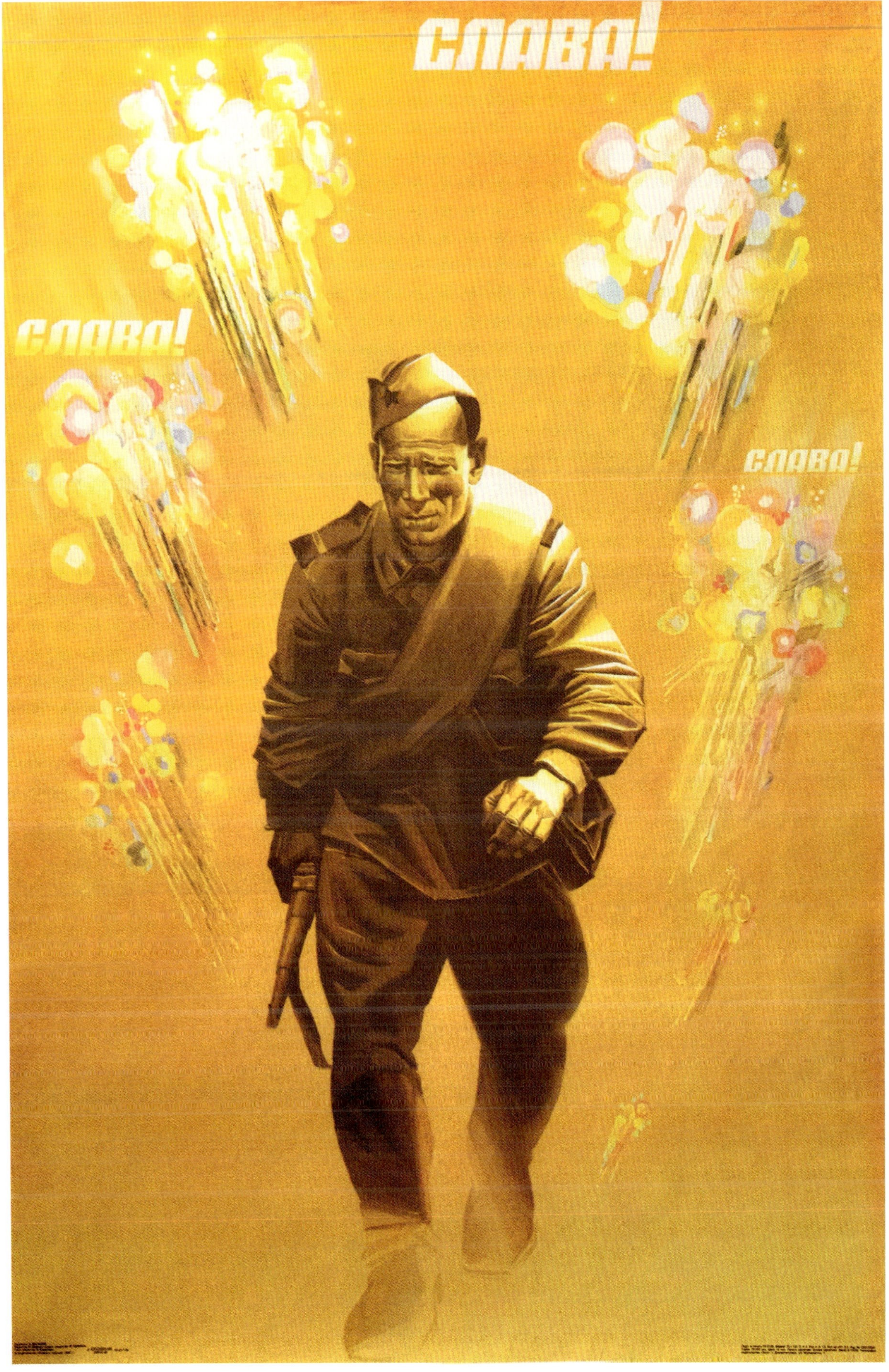
СЛАВА!
СЛАВА!
СЛАВА!

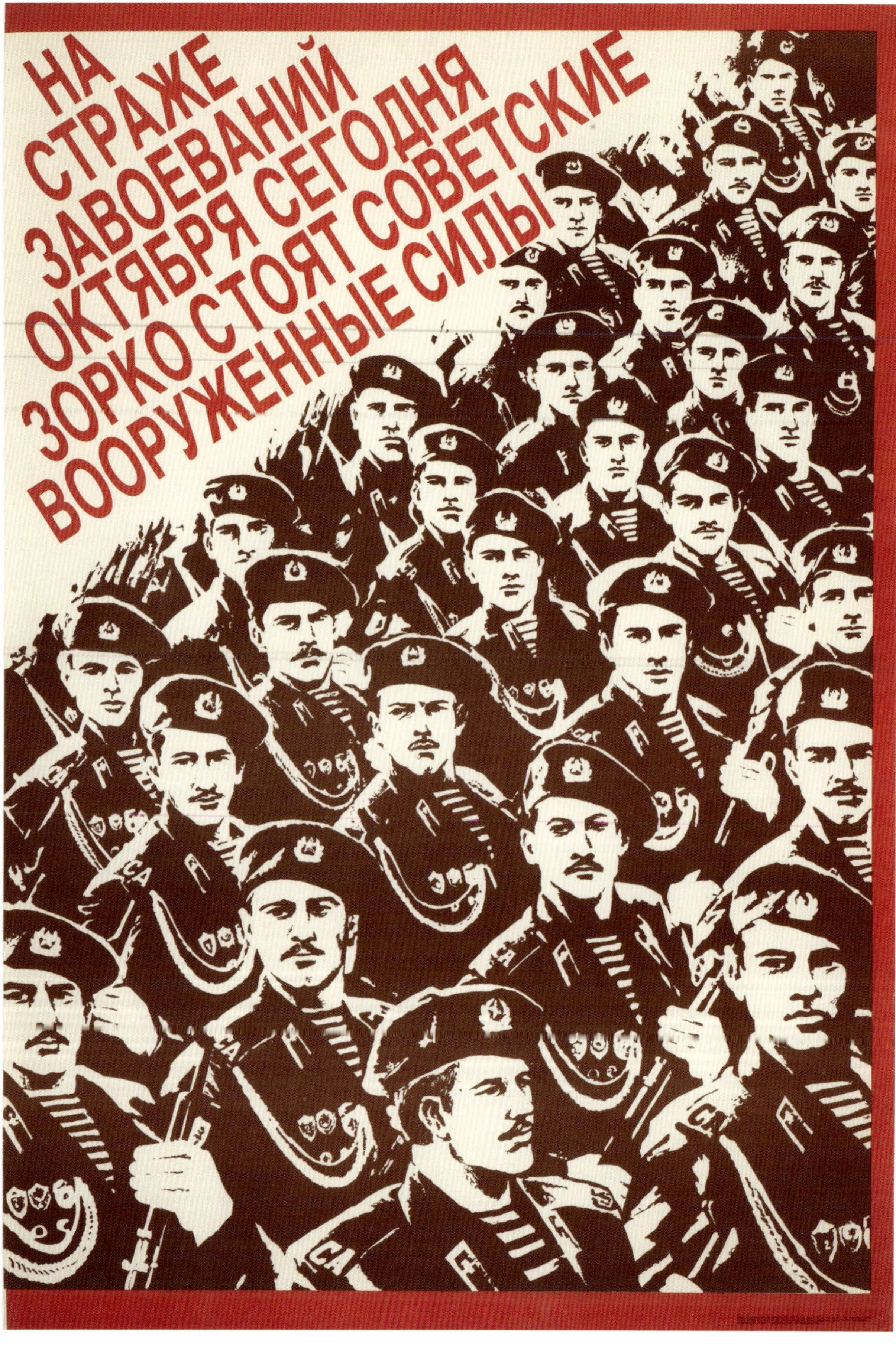
НА
СТРАЖЕ
ЗАВОЕВАНИЙ
ОКТЯБРЯ СЕГОДНЯ
ЗОРКО СТОЯТ СОВЕТСКИЕ
ВООРУЖЕННЫЕ СИЛЫ

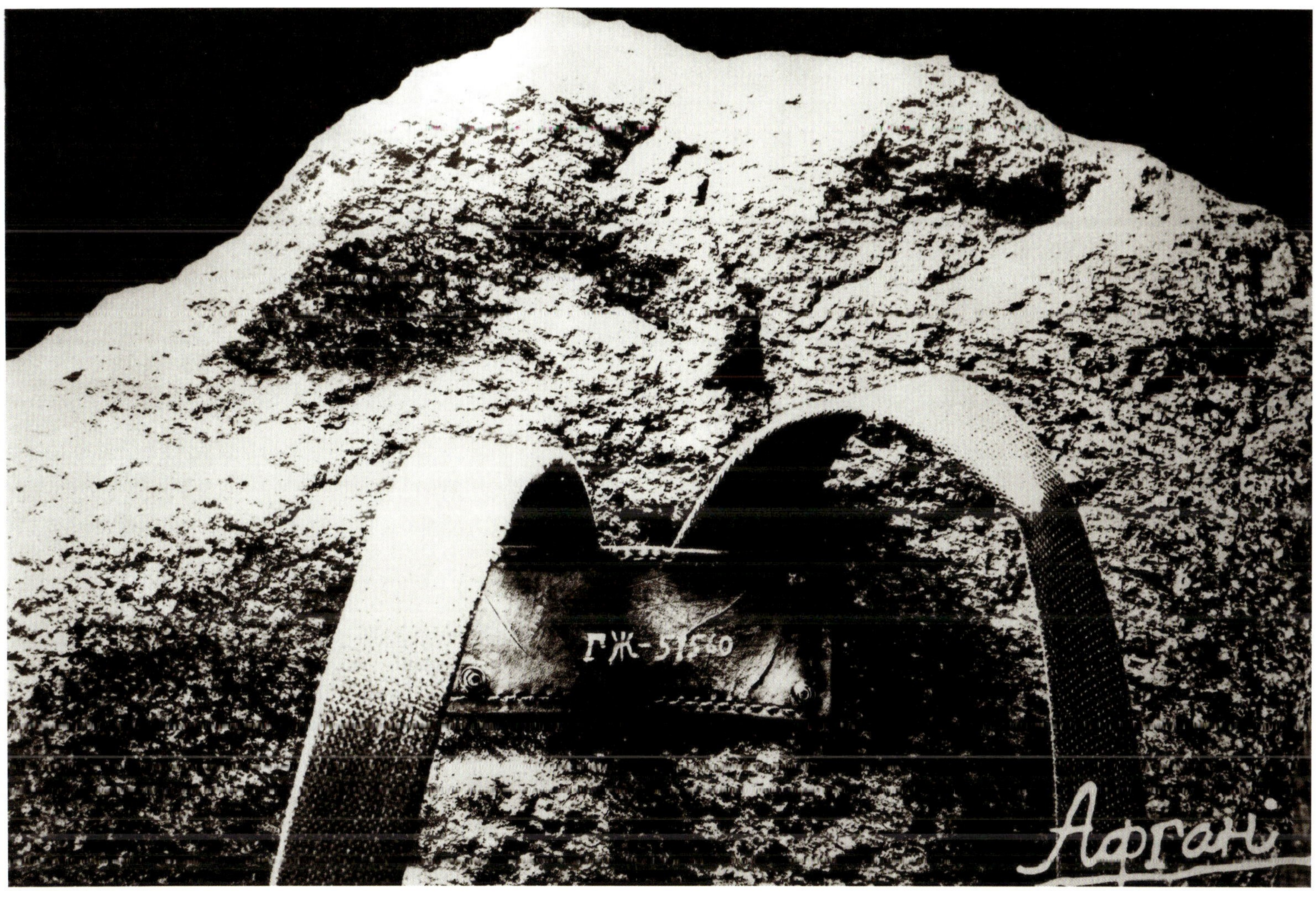

◀ **Artist unknown | 1988**

TODAY'S SOVIET ARMED FORCES STAND GUARD OVER THE CONQUESTS OF THE OCTOBER REVOLUTION

▲ **Artist unknown | 1989**

The straps of a military backpack bearing a soldier's serial number are attached to a heavy stone. The poster is signed AFGHAN—soldier slang for "Afghanistan," analagous to "Nam" for "Vietnam" in the US.

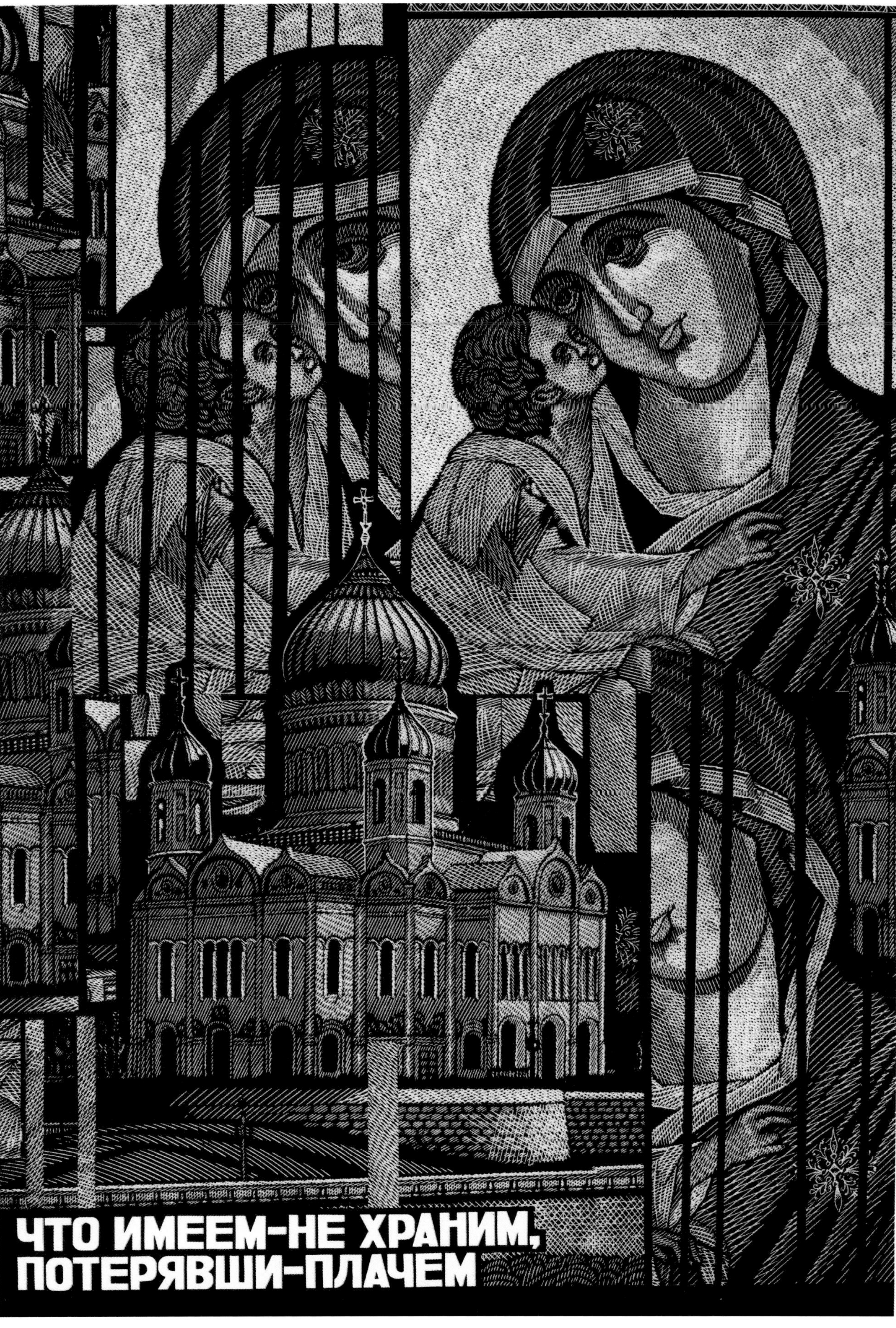
ЧТО ИМЕЕМ-НЕ ХРАНИМ,
ПОТЕРЯВШИ-ПЛАЧЕМ

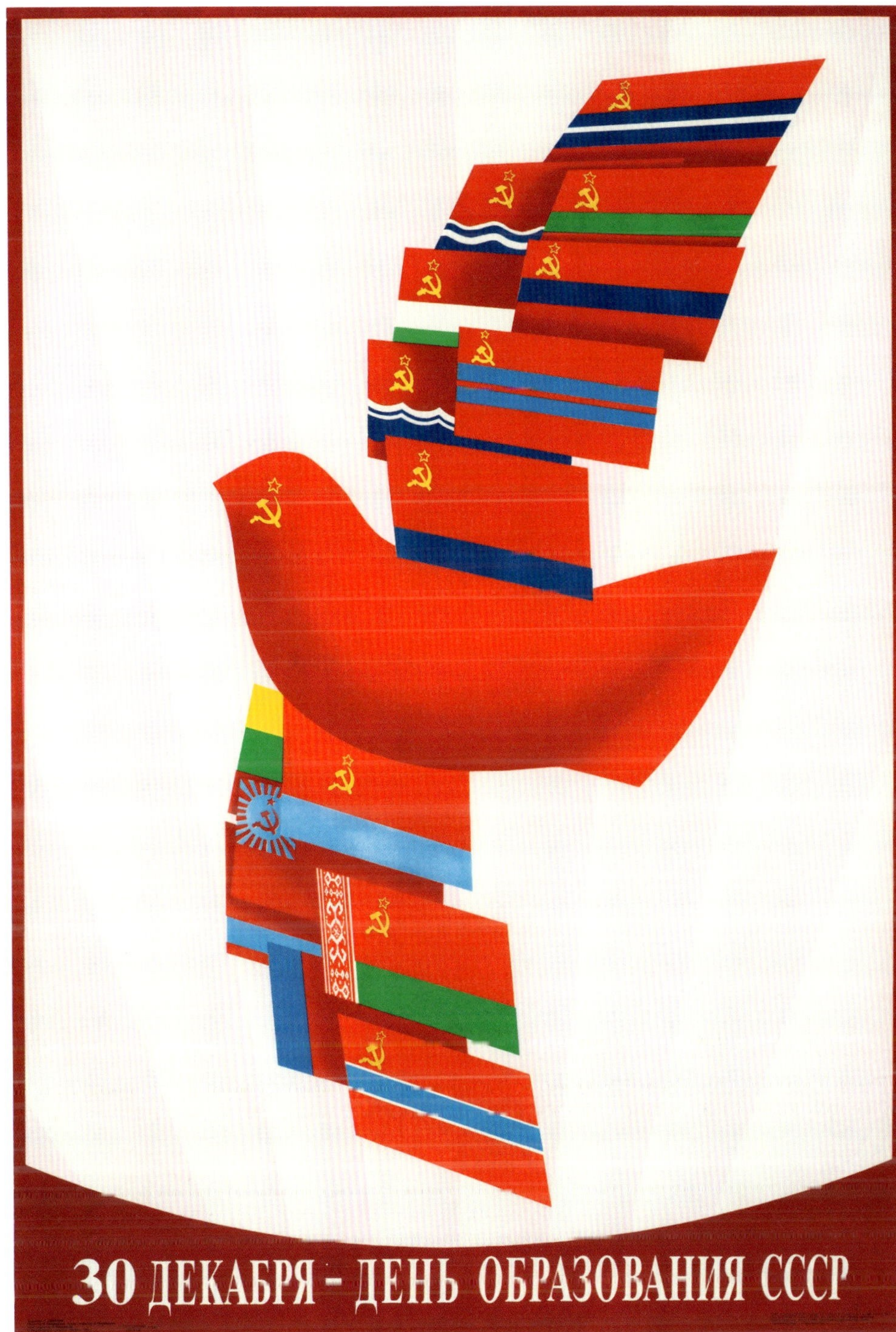

◂ М. Ахунов (M. Akhunov) | 1990

WE DON'T TAKE CARE OF WHAT WE HAVE AND ONCE IT'S LOST, WE WEEP

This poster evokes the idea of preserving the country's cultural heritage and artifacts.

С. Смирнов (S. Smirnov) | 1989 ▸

DECEMBER 30 IS THE DAY OF THE FORMATION OF THE USSR

The body of the dove represents the entirety of the USSR (commonly referred to as the Soviet Union); its wings, the flags of each of the initial fifteen constituent republics when the USSR (Union of Soviet Socialist Republics) was formed in 1922.

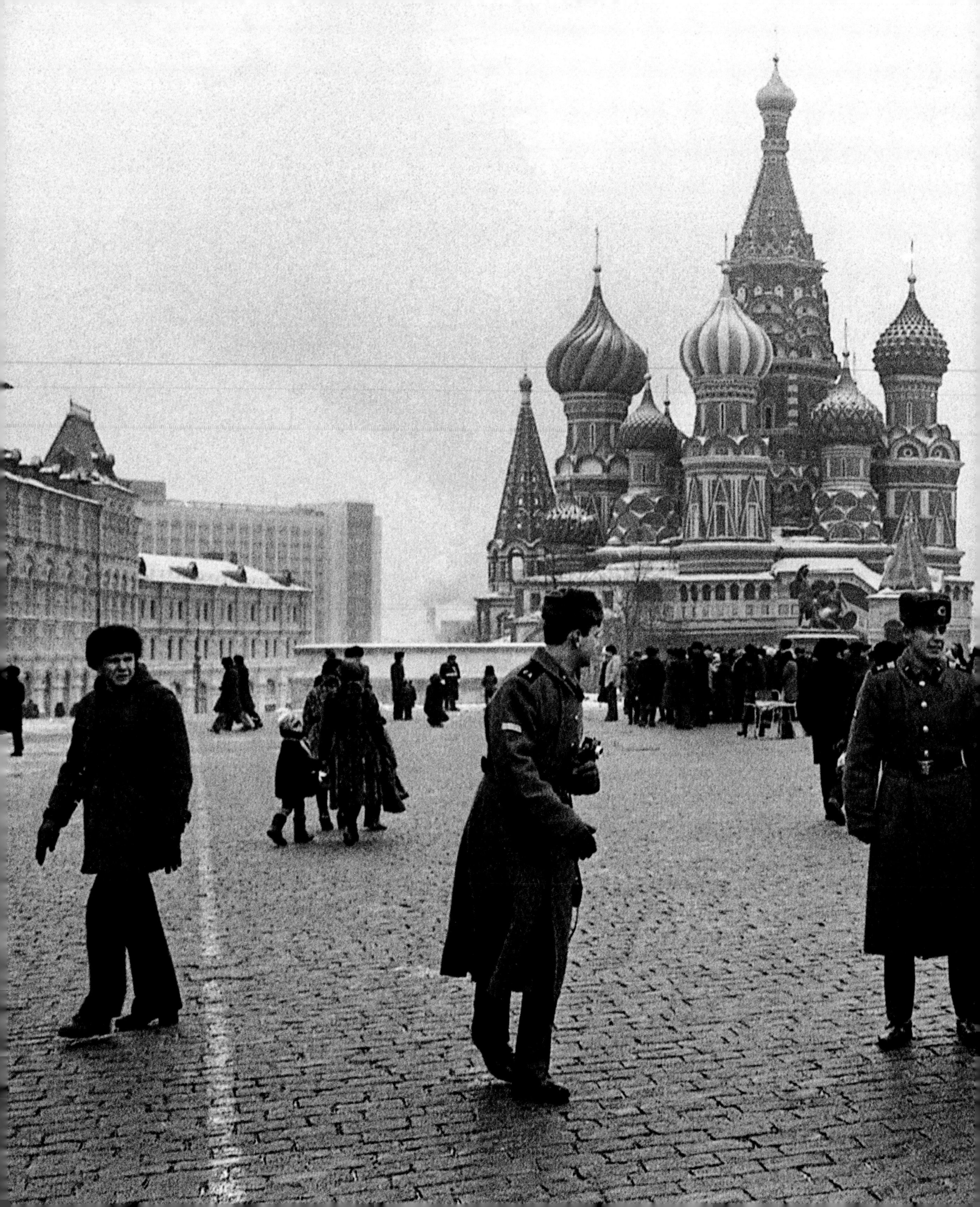

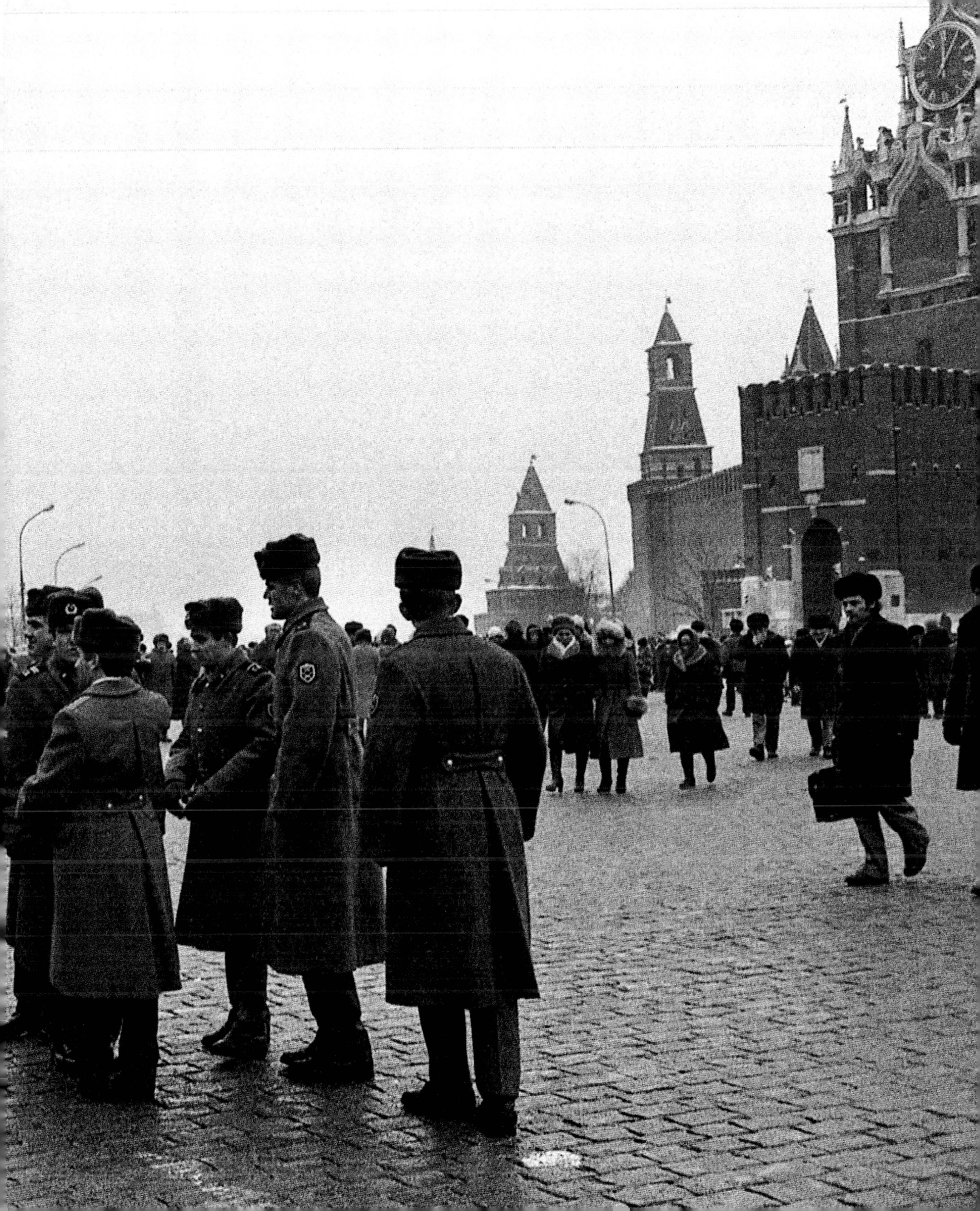

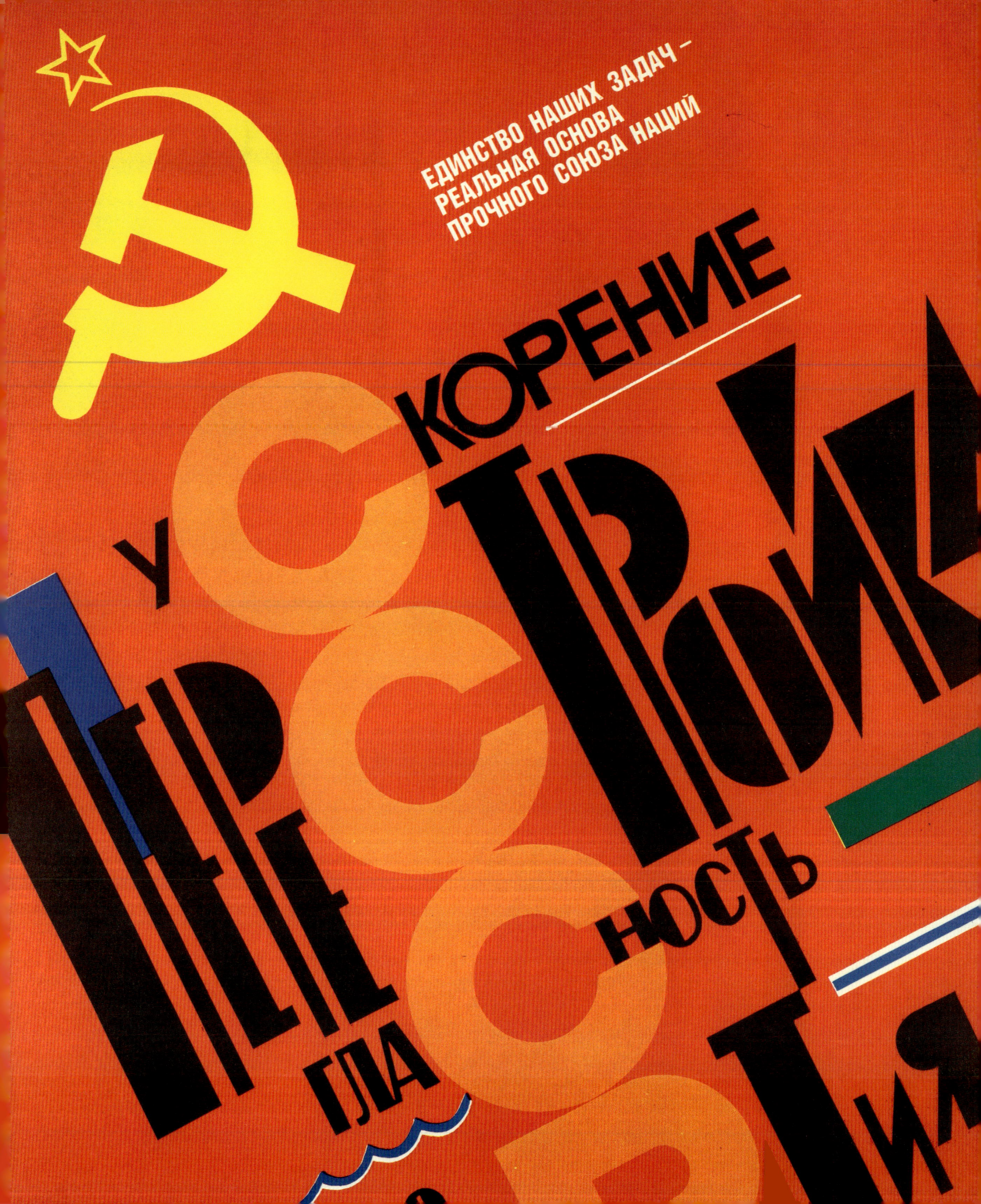
ЕДИНСТВО НАШИХ ЗАДАЧ –
РЕАЛЬНАЯ ОСНОВА
ПРОЧНОГО СОЮЗА НАЦИЙ
УСКОРЕНИЕ
ГЛАСНОСТЬ

GLASNOST IN THE STREETS

ANDY WILLIMOTT

"There is no democratization, nor can there be, without glasnost . . . [The USSR] depends on glasnost to become a trouble-free functioning system. You need glasnost in the center, but just as much, maybe even more at the base, where humans live and work."

—Mikhail Gorbachev, February 25, 1986

Glasnost—from the Russian root *golos* (voice)—might be bluntly translated as "free voice." Entering the global vocabulary in the mid-1980s, glasnost is now widely understood to mean "openness" or "transparency." Part of Mikhail Gorbachev's attempt to overhaul the Soviet system, glasnost and perestroika (restructuring) were seen as the twin prongs of a reform agenda aimed at rejuvenating the struggle for socialism in the Soviet Union. After the deadening malaise and economic stagnation of the Brezhnev era, the promise of a Red Dawn seemed remoter than ever. Gorbachev wanted to kick-start the planned economy and reawaken a citizenry of socialism. He believed true reform was dependent on this twin-pronged approach: perestroika would entail overcoming the vested bureaucratic interests and personal power bases that prevented innovation, while glasnost would unleash the plurality of thought necessary to reignite the population's engagement with socialism, and provide the system with a source of change. In other words, Gorbachev intended, with the help of glasnost, to initiate a critical public discussion of the Soviet state and economy in order to facilitate, stimulate, and increase demand for reform.

Many Western commentators, somewhat narrow-mindedly, viewed glasnost and perestroika as a straightforward attempt to replicate the successes of liberal democracies. They wanted to argue that the West had triumphed and should be declared the ideological victor of the Cold War. The us-versus-them mentality of the period obscured much of the picture.[1] In fact, as recent research has shown, Soviet economic reform under Gorbachev was modeled, in large part, on the runaway success of the "Asian Tigers"—South Korea, Taiwan, Hong Kong, and Singapore—as well as Japan and China. During the 1970s and 1980s, these Asian economies became celebrated for their ability to turn poverty into wealth through sound policy and rational reorganization. Soviet economists and scholars, it should not be forgotten, were also keen to draw lessons from the various experiments that had been permitted in the centrally planned economies of their Eastern European neighbors from the 1960s.[2] Soviet experts and policymakers had a fuller, more dynamic picture of the global economy and economic structures than many in the West have assumed. Here, then, was some of the plurality of thought that glasnost promised to unleash.

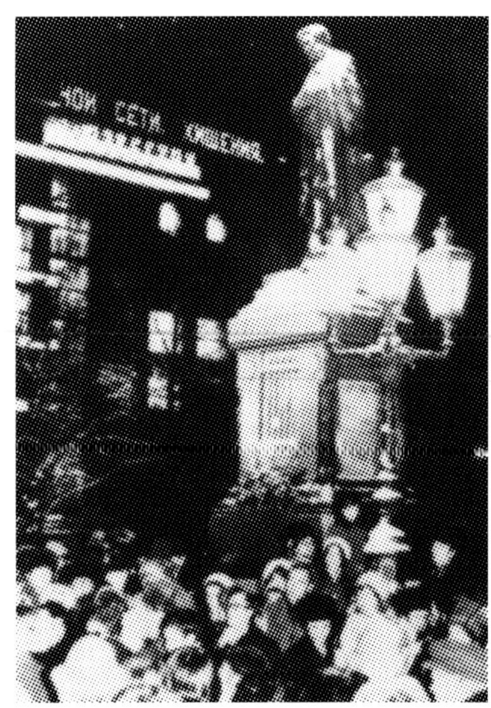

Fig. 1 Protest in Pushkin Square, Moscow, December 5, 1965.

Fig. 2 Soviet leader Mikhail Gorbachev standing in the center at the 27th Congress of the Soviet Communist Party, 1986.

Fig. 3 View of Yuri Gagarin Monument devoted to the achievements of the Soviet people in space exploration and built for the 1980 Olympics. Behind the monument the Moscow television tower (the tallest reinforced concrete structure in the world) can be seen.

Likewise, glasnost was no mere Western import. The word "glasnost" first gained significant modern currency during the reign of the "Czar Liberator," Aleksandr II (who ruled 1855–1881), whose own reform package included the introduction of court hearings to the public. As the Russian human rights activist Lyudmila Alexeyeva subsequently commented, the term appeared in the dictionaries and law books of modern Russia as an "ordinary, hardworking, nondescript word that was used to refer to . . . any process of justice or government being conducted in the open."[3] But by the mid-1960s, glasnost acquired added meaning and a newfound topical importance. At the 20th Party Congress of 1956, Nikita Khrushchev repudiated Stalin's purges, which initiated a series of reactions that gave rise to protests against closed trials. This was a rejection of the arbitrary and unaccountable brutality that countless Soviet citizens had started to associate with Stalin after 1956. Indeed, on December 5, 1965, in response to the closed trial of two Soviet writers, a crowd assembled in Moscow's Pushkin Square to demand "glasnost" in the form of public admittance, press access, and observers (fig. 1). Protests against closed trials continued in the wake of the Pushkin Square rally. Committed dissidents continued to draw attention to the regime's arbitrary actions.

Gorbachev, at fifty-four years old the youngest Soviet leader since Stalin, led a generation shaped by the 20th Party Congress. This generation passionately believed in socialism, the Communist Party, and the planned economy; people were enthusiastic about Khrushchev's reforms, which they saw as a return to Leninist principles; they lamented the curtailment of these reforms under Brezhnev; and they were queasy about the crushing of the 1968 Prague Spring.[4] By the same token, Gorbachev and his advisers were aware of the historical and contemporary significance of adopting the word "glasnost" as they vied to cement a lasting place for public discussion within the Soviet system.

The Brezhnev generation of officials—the class of 1937—survived the purges and found themselves in senior positions. They felt instinctively that innovation was dangerous.[5] In the 1930s, they had seen those who advocated anything akin to a "free voice" suffer brutal repression during the years of Stalin's Great Terror. And balking at Khrushchev's permissive reforms—fearing that this gruff, unorthodox character from provincial Ukraine had opened a Pandora's box that would implicate them all—they engineered his ouster in 1964, and Brezhnev ascended to power. But Ilya Ehrenburg's short novel *The Thaw* (1955) had already spoken of the terror, and given name to the liberalized Khrushchev era. Aleksandr Solzhenitsyn's serialized novel, *One Day in the Life of Ivan Denisovich* (1962), had earlier opened up discussion of the horrors of the gulag. An alternative to such brutality had been glimpsed, and a semblance of "free voice" permitted. Dissidents were emboldened to form reading groups, collate information on Stalin's victims, and question assumptions. Young enthusiasts and aspiring Communist Youth League members formed grassroots initiatives modeled on a romantic view of collective revolutionary action that drove events in 1917 and through the 1920s.[6] Even as Brezhnev's farcical tenure set in—with pretended amnesia traded for stability and a quiet life—the promise of an alternative continued to hang in the air.

Gorbachev, touched by the prospect of this alternative and repelled by Brezhnev's increasingly geriatric old guard, was appointed to the Central Committee in 1978, hoping to harness the energies of the post-Stalin, post-'56 generation. His decision, upon ascending to the office of General Secretary in 1985, to

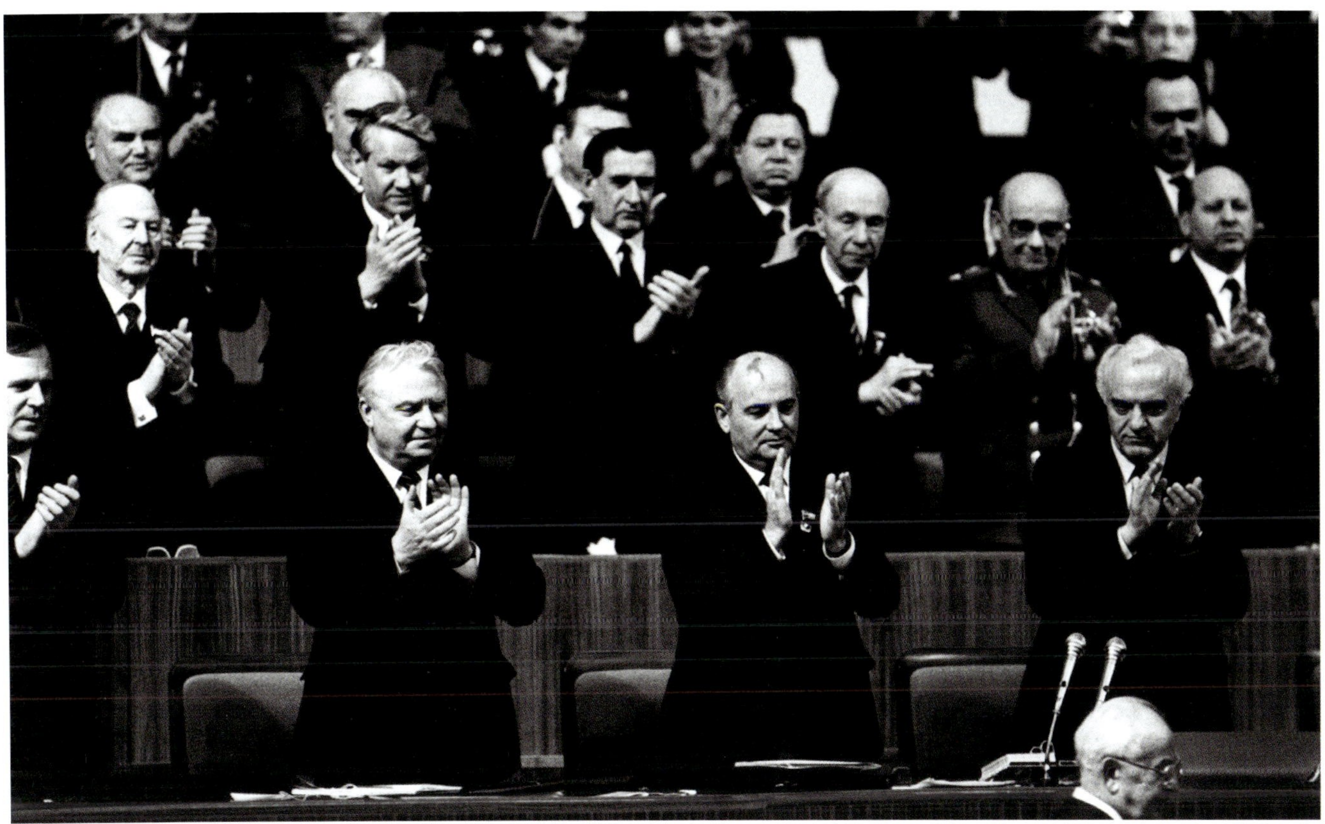

introduce glasnost was profoundly idealistic, even naive, a product of Gorbachev's lofty revolutionary aspirations (fig. 2). Stoked by Khrushchev's reforms, he, like many of his generation, sought a return to the purity of Leninism. The post-'56 generation, much like their counterparts in the West, proved idealistic, and even the dissidents among them—often lauded in the West as supporters of an anti-Soviet vision of "freedom"—often remained committed to the communist path. They abhorred their government's disregard for ordinary citizens, but, aside from a few out-and-out religious dissenters, they did not object to the goals of Marxism Leninism. They were proud of the Soviet Union's achievements, such as Sputnik and cosmonauts Yuri Gagarin and Valentina Tereshkova (fig. 3).[7] Those who joined the Pushkin Square rally in 1965 did not seek the end of the Soviet Union; they wanted it to live up to its promises. They wanted the state to adhere to the 1936 Constitution that promised freedom of assembly and the right to an open trial.

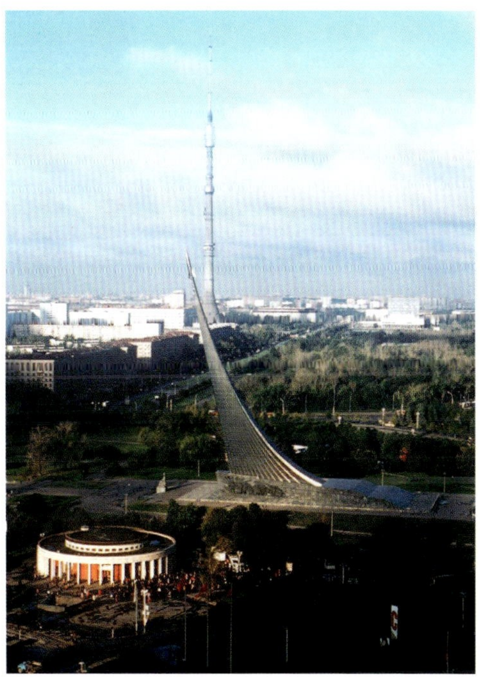

Glasnost came from within. It was the product of Soviet experience and aspiration—something not always fully appreciated in the West. While the West has celebrated "Gorby" and honored him with awards, in Russia he has been widely derided for causing the collapse of the Soviet Union, the loss of its superpower status, and the economic catastrophe that followed. The tragedy of the man—he is the Hamlet of the Soviet drama—has overshadowed a fuller assessment of glasnost's origins and significance. The experiment all begins to make more sense once we acknowledge that glasnost drew upon an existing language to recapitulate longstanding revolutionary conceptions.

In posters such as Vladimir Zhukov's stunning "1985" (fig. 4), the image of Lenin was revitalized. Zhukov shows Lenin behind a filthy glass pane, largely obscured except for where a freshly wiped portion reveals the unfaltering eyes of the great leader, which bore deep into the viewer. Lenin's stare, penetrating the dirt and detritus of a stagnant, wayward Soviet Union, suggests he expects more from the next generation. We await a legendary Lenin scolding: "What the hell have you done?!" Similarly, in a dynamic print by N. Babin, Lenin and his slogans (1988, pp. 28–29)—"All Power to the Soviets!" "Peace to the People of all Nations!" "Factories and Plants to the Workers!"—are reenergized. Here the use of tonal contrast breaks with traditional Soviet poster norms, borrowing from the style of contemporary cartooning to create a vibrancy that highlights Lenin's renewed relevance in the here and now of glasnost.

Just as crucially—and this is abundantly reflected in the posters of the era—glasnost built upon a longstanding Soviet vision of "public life," or *obshchestvennost'*. This Russian word, which, unlike glasnost, has not made its way into the global vocabulary, is hard to translate. Signifying a professional association, public identity, or imagined civic community engaged in constructing a socialist vision of society, *obshchestvennost'* has most often been rendered as "civic-mindedness." In the wake of October 1917, the Bolsheviks adopted it as a means of encouraging participation in the revolutionary project. As editor of *Pravda* between 1917 and 1929, Nikolai Bukharin thought he might cultivate *obshchestvennost'* through an amateur letter-writing section in the paper—a space where ordinary people could raise local grievances, press

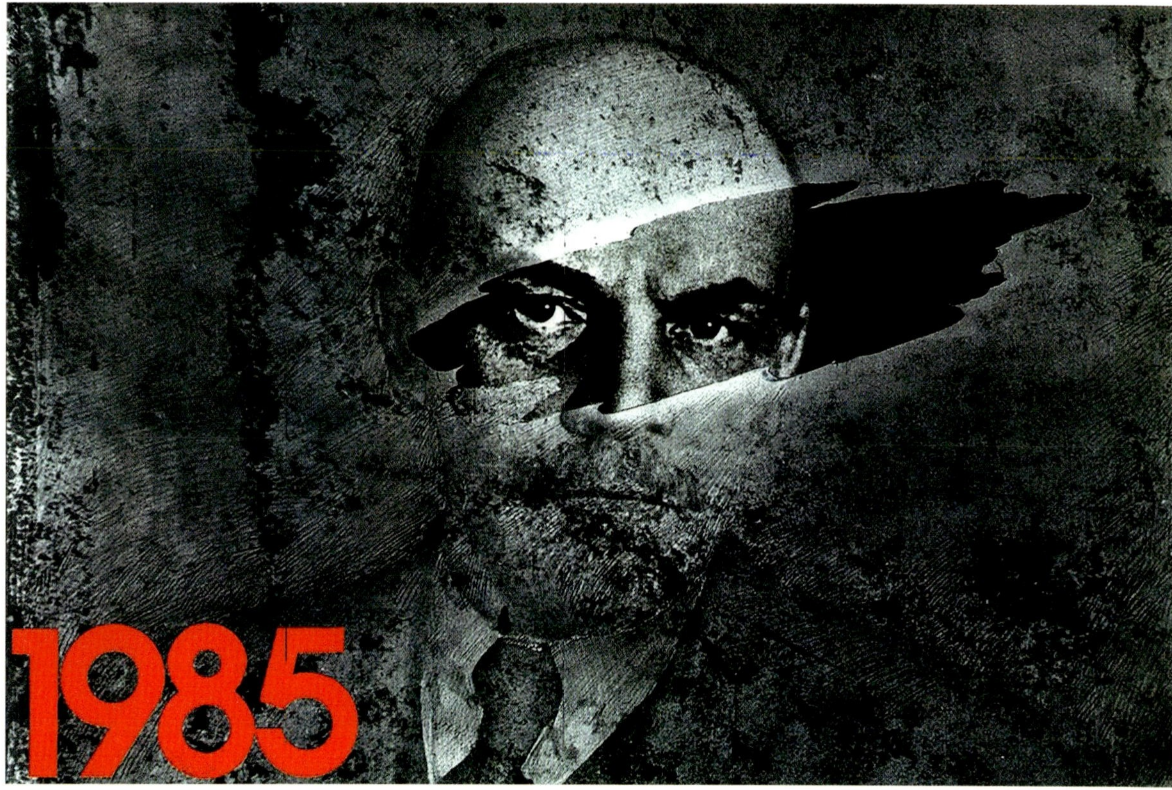

Fig. 4 Vladimir Zhukov. "1985," 1988.

for improvements in line with revolutionary goals, and develop an authentic proletarian public forum.[8] Throughout the 1920s, activists also engaged in a form of semi-independent *obshchestvennost'* by leading local cultural campaigns against illiteracy, religion, and drunkenness, as well as by forming "political clubs" and "discussion circles." Such activities formed an important part of the state-building project, and activists were encouraged to make up for shortcomings in the revolutionary mission.[9] Civic action like this was permissible as long as it did not overstep the limit by calling into question the dictatorship of the proletariat or the wisdom of a party-state system. The boundaries of acceptability would periodically shift—narrowing significantly under Stalin, widening under Khrushchev, and narrowing again under Brezhnev. "For many," as one leading historian observes, "participation in it may have become an empty ritual, like voting in a single-candidate election." But for others, Soviet *obshchestvennost'* may have "preserved certain forms and values developed earlier."[10] After 1956, a series of "writers' communities" (*pisatel'skaia obshchestvennost'*) were formed, and they acted as the opinion leaders of the Thaw—a period of lessened cultural censorship and repression.[11] The Communist Youth League activists who carried out grassroots initiatives during the Thaw also demonstrated a reemergent *obshchestvennost'*.

To the degree that civil participation remained part the Soviet dream, the glasnost poster continued to draw attention to shortcomings in Soviet public life, calling on citizens to be part of the solution. G. Belozerov's emblematic blank-page "Pravda" (1988, p. 148) points to the lack of authentic news in the Soviet Union's leading press organ—a red pencil, once the tool of the censor, hangs by a string from the newspaper's masthead, inviting the viewer to fill in the blank page below. In the same vein, countless other posters rallied citizens to unite against bureaucracy, corruption, nepotism, alcoholism, and all manner of social ills associated with the stagnation of Lenin's vision.

Whether emergent or residual, public revolutionary participation remained part of the Soviet mission. Soviet voices calling for glasnost in the 1960s, activists looking to become public-opinion leaders, dissidents calling the government to account—none were anathema to the Soviet revolutionary experience. And so, in 1985, calls for a "free voice" become integral to Soviet life once more. Herein lies the purpose of this volume. Not enough attention has been paid to glasnost as an idealistic venture founded on revolutionary visions and revolutionary heritage. What has been largely overlooked is the feel, color, and energy of glasnost—the lived experience of the reform agenda. Focus has tended to fall not on the day-by-day tone of reform, but rather on the political machinations and personalities that drove it. The glasnost poster provides us with a tangible emblem of the era—the revolutionary ambition driving it, the ideas it unleashed, the creativity of those pushing for it. This Collection of posters gives us a better sense of how reform manifested itself on the street, "at the base, where humans live and work."

We can see glasnost come to life in the Soviet poster—posters created by freed minds and approved for public display, to be pinned up in shop windows. Other posters, less palatable to the authorities, were nonetheless exhibited in pop-up galleries and viewed by thousands. By focusing on the visual product of glasnost in this way, we can rekindle some of the experience of reform on its own terms—provisional, optimistic, filled with possibility.

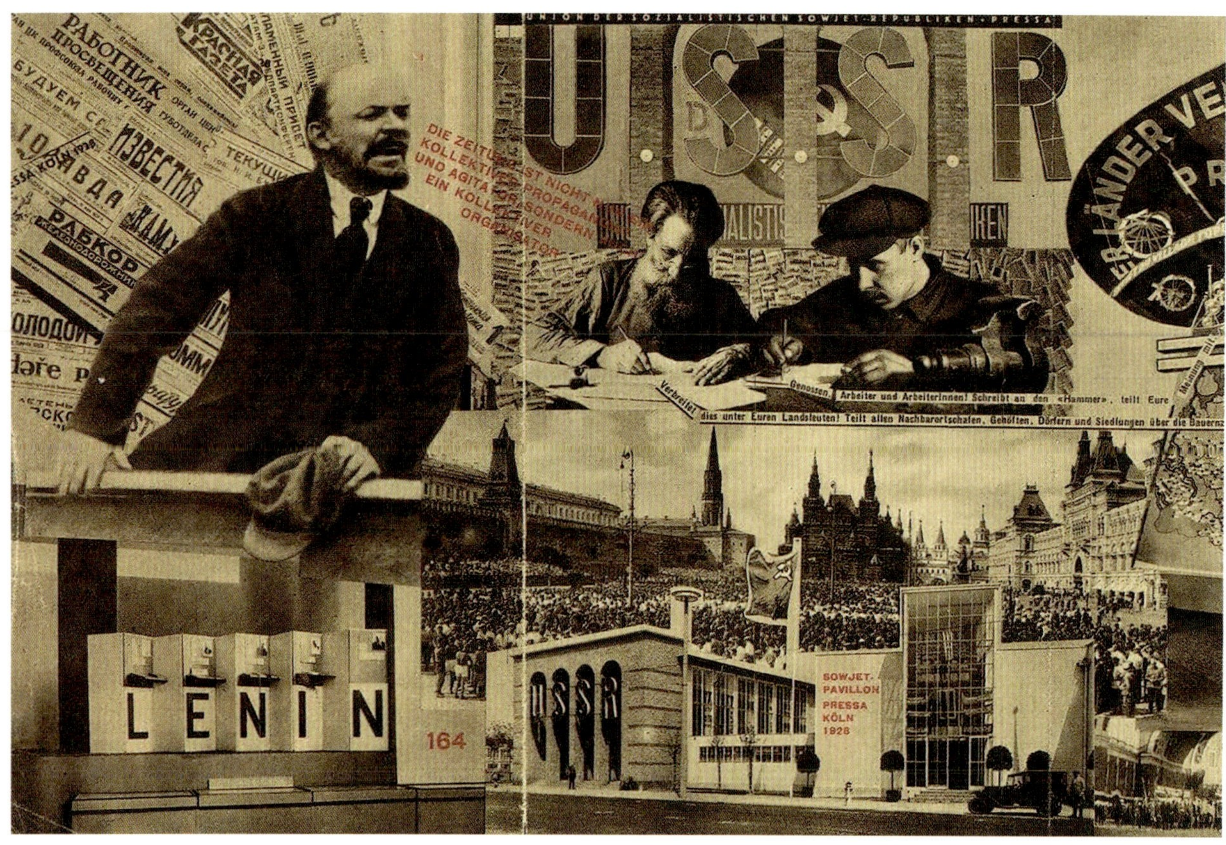

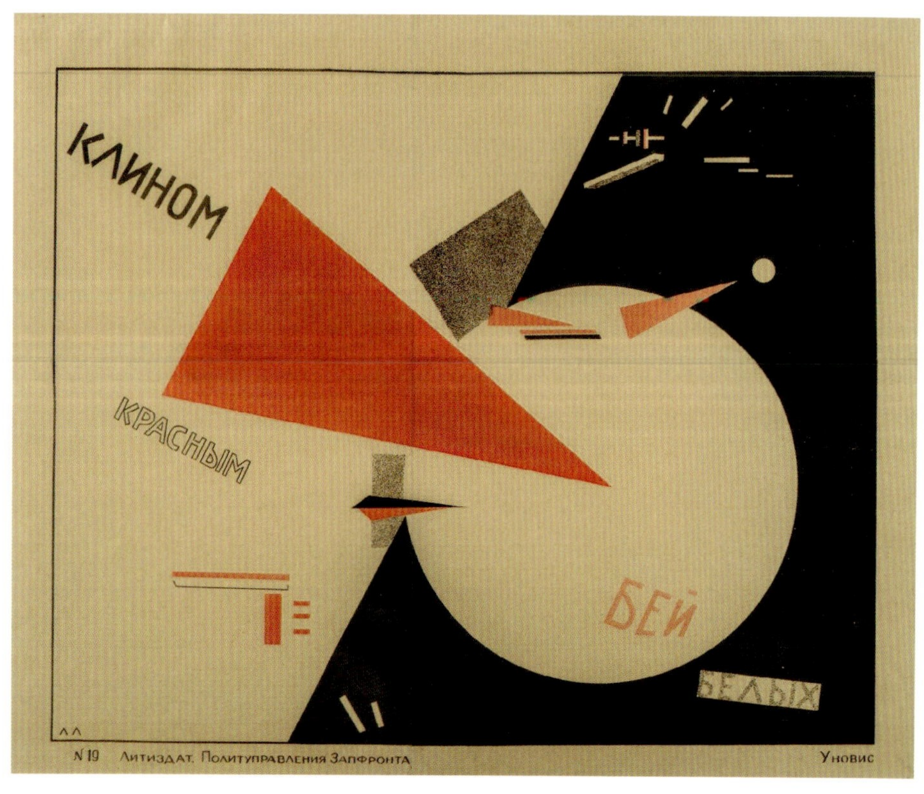

Fig. 5 El Lissitzky and Sergei Senkin. *The Task of the Press is the Education of the Masses* (detail), 1928. Photogravure photomontage from the *Union of Soviet Socialist Republics: Catalogue of the Soviet Pavilion at the International Press Exhibition*, Cologne. Collection of Tate Archive, London.

Fig. 6 El Lissitzky. *Beat the Whites with the Red Wedge*, 1920 (printed 1966). Color lithograph, 10 × 24 ½ in. (51 × 62 cm). Collection of the Museum of Fine Arts, Boston.

GLASNOST THROUGH THE POSTER

Change came, as it had at various points in the Russian/Soviet past, slowly then all at once. The actuality of glasnost was nowhere more visually apparent than in the contrast between political posters, old and new. The tired, familiar, disingenuous messages of the Brezhnev era—promoting workplace productivity, lauding heroic feats, celebrating unreal images of Soviet society—gave way to more dynamic and daring variations. Starting in 1985–86, the formulaic templates of Soviet poster design were one by one cast aside.

At first the stylistic and artistic quality did not alter radically; rather, new rallying messages appeared against the old backdrop of red banners. Soviet insignia and memorabilia still cluttered the studios and minds of Soviet poster designers, in part because the scope and possibility of glasnost were not yet fully apparent to them. What they knew for certain was that the old graphic templates were all but guaranteed to be accepted by Party authorities and Soviet publication organs, so the designers made use of them.

In February 1986, at the 27th Party Congress, Gorbachev signaled his intent to relax Soviet censorship. Glasnost and perestroika were put center stage. Encountering resistance from within the Soviet bureaucratic machine, and facing criticism following the initial cover-up of the April 1986 Chernobyl disaster, Gorbachev decided to accelerate his "new course." By 1986–87, when change was official Soviet policy, Soviet poster designers felt confident enough to experiment. Thereafter the political poster paradigm was transformed.

Confidence bred creativity. The new posters demonstrated an unprecedented variety of styles and forms. And, just as in 1917, ordinary citizens had to be prepared to master a remarkable range of new expressive idioms.[12] Traditional symbols were recast in dynamic ways—none more so than the hammer and sickle. Avant-garde influences from the 1920s, including photomontage (fig. 5) and Constructivist composition (fig. 6), were rekindled and repurposed. Pop art influences emerged in highly stylized, often ironic depictions. M. Mkrtchyan's "School" (1988, p. 132), for instance, presents a comb that is shown to function as a mold, making all Soviet children alike. The message is clear: the Soviet system had for too long stifled the individual, a much-needed component for a healthy and creative society. The colorful and playful style of Soviet cartoon proved a popular means of polemical depiction, as seen, for example, in V. Zavyalov's "Reconstruction Project / Proposal / New Technologies" (undated, p. 125), which depicts a Soviet bureaucrat with a meat grinder for a head. No matter what new progressive concepts are fed into his mind, the same old bureaucratic mantra comes out: "Tread softly, go far . . . ." In addition to the animated style, vivid color and computer graphics brought an aggressively contemporary quality to many posters. This trend can be seen in the stylized fonts used in L. Tarasova's "Glasnost / Brave Assessments / A Culture of Discussion" (1988, p. 146) and Romanenko and V. Cheremkhin's "Implement, Deepen, Protect—Perestroika" (1990, pp. 114–115), as well as in the lurid hues of G. Tkachenko's "But the 'emperor' . . . has no clothes!" (1989, p. 75). In numerous ways, poster designers were inspired to surprise and engage viewers, drawing them and their experience into the frame. This was glasnost not just on display, but also in action.

The glasnost poster addressed a number of themes and past taboos head-on. Most predominant among these was the suppressive nature of the Soviet system. Whereas previously Soviet propaganda suggested that a citizen's duty was to serve the greater good of the Party, now the political poster placed the individual at a critical distance from power. Most significantly, the crimes of Stalin and Stalinism were broached once more—just as they had been under Khrushchev in 1956.

L. Kovaleva's "A nation that forgets its history is doomed to repeat it" (1988, p. 18) offers one of the most striking reflections on Stalinism, showing Stalin's infamous treatise the *Short Course* (1935) looming over a traditional Russian village, threatening to crush it with the weight of falsified Party history.[13] Key dates are identified with red bookmarks—1929, 1934, 1937. The egregious manipulation of facts within this text is highlighted by two more bookmarks, 1948 and 1952, years not even covered in the book. The *Short Course* was the central text of Stalin's ideological canon. It has been referred to as the "master narrative—a hegemonic statement on history, philosophy, and ideology that scripted Soviet society for the better part of a generation."[14] Over 40 million copies of the book circulated in over a dozen languages. It governed all references to the Soviet historical experience and was cited in school textbooks and academic scholarship decade after decade. Khrushchev's failure to completely repudiate the text meant that the *Short Course* effectively continued to stymie Party and ideological reform through to the 1980s.

Kovaleva's poster followed hot on the heels of Gorbachev's 1988 rallying call for a more diligent critical reappraisal of Stalinism—part of Gorbachev's continued struggle with the Party's old guard.[15] Gorbachev's official endorsement opened the way to a broader reconceptualization of Stalin's crimes. In 1989, former Colonel General D. A. Volkogonov wrote that the *Short Course* had taught Soviet society to assume a submissive relationship to political authority. He noted that it had also trained citizens to believe that all Soviet shortcomings were the result of "sabotage" and "wrecking," rather than the failings of a party-state system shaped by Stalinist ideology.[16] The *Short Course* was a ubiquitous feature of Soviet life, and a powerful symbol of past crimes. There was no greater obstacle to reform than the "lessons" of the *Short Course*.

A. Baranov's "1929—Collectivization" (1988, p. 20) uses the inner edge of a Soviet sickle to trace the profile of Stalin. The year marks the start of Stalin's disastrous, breakneck agricultural policy. The lower end of the sickle is splattered with blood—a reminder of the millions who died as a result of this policy, many through starvation. R. N. Nayden and A. P. Novozhilov's "1937" (1990, p. 19) invokes another infamous year, the height of the Great Terror, with the depiction of a gun. The trigger takes the form of a red tongue—red because it belongs to someone who shows himself to be a true communist of the Stalinist sort, denouncing comrades, condemning them to death through a bullet to the head or exile to the gulag. The crimes of the past and the complicity of a submissive society were being put in the spotlight. Glasnost elevated the previously unmentionable to a topic of hot debate. Such debate was seen as a catharsis essential to the advance of Soviet socialism. For glasnost to succeed, the past had to be tackled honestly.

S. Minenok's "They Did Everything For Us" (1989, p. 65) presents an aged veteran of the Great Patriotic War struggling with a heavy bag of potatoes while a young skater whizzes by—an image of the moral decay of Soviet society in the wake of the Brezhnev era's economic and political stagnation. Other posters focus on the gap between promise and reality in the supply of food and consumer goods. B. Semenov's "You're swindling your own father!" (1990, p. 85) presents the realities of Soviet social consequence:

the father is shocked that his son puts a finger on the scales while serving him in a shop, though it was he who raised his son to cheat. The ugly, unwritten norms of Soviet life are here laid bare. As well as decrying the falsifications of past regimes, glasnost continued to challenge Soviet citizens to shed bad habits and improve themselves. Soviet *obshchestvennost'* was still an imperative, but so too was an ideological belief in the perfectibility of mankind. In 1922, Alexandra Kollontai wrote advice literature for revolutionary youths, declaring that by rejecting "bourgeois morality" and submitting oneself to a new "rational . . . collective regime," a "person can be taught to think like a communist."[17] In 1924, Leon Trotsky proclaimed that under full communism the "average human type will rise to the heights of an Aristotle, a Goethe, or a Marx. And above this ridge new peaks will rise."[18] Now, in the glasnost era, Soviet citizens were being asked to struggle against the insufficient norms and mores that had become entrenched under the hypocrisy of past regimes. It was time to look ahead once more to the possibilities of the future. Prometheus was not yet unbound.

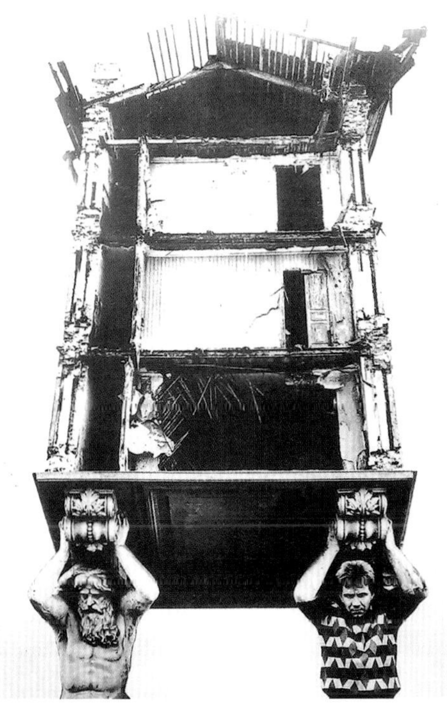

Fig. 7 Alexander Vasilchenko. "Concern means work!," 1988.

The call for Soviet *obshchestvennost'* and civic action were further evident in posters such as Alexander Vasilchenko's "Concern means work!" (1988, fig. 7) and "Let's revive our abundant beauty" (1990). Both address the need for volunteers and Soviet pride in the fight to save and restore historic buildings and monuments. The former even depicts an ordinary Soviet citizen standing in for a missing classical pillar—the citizen shown as integral to the restoration effort and equal to any celebrated figures from antiquity. Here the fight to save the material culture of the Soviet Union was shown to be glorious—a Promethean tale of civilization in progress.

Glasnost also expounded a new concern for the environment. P. Davidyuk's "Green it" (1986, p. 204), an early example, depicts the tender shoots of a young tree tied to a brick chimney, the branches's bright yellow stems and fresh green leaves bringing life to a feature typical of the Soviet Union's heavily industrialized landscape. The environmental damage caused by large-scale industrial and agricultural projects, as well as the wastefulness and inefficiencies of the Soviet economy, became a primary concern during glasnost. Davidyuk draws attention to this plight, while also invoking the spirit of Soviet *obshchestvennost'*, urging citizens to help bring nature and greenery back into their cities. Chernobyl heightened public awareness of the dangers to health posed by various forms of pollution. Environmental activism and concern gathered momentum during glasnost, peaking in the late 1980s. In advance of the March 1989 elections to the Congress of People's Deputies, many candidates even campaigned on environmental issues and complaints. The destructive swagger and disdain of early twentieth-century Soviet modernity—with its hydroelectric dams changing the course of rivers, its huge consumption of fossil fuels, and its drive to "conquer" nature—were being called to account. What's more, environmental concerns merged with ethnic and national tensions within the republics of the USSR. Environmentalist campaigners in Lithuania, Latvia, Estonia, Ukraine, and Armenia accused Moscow of ecological colonialism. Kazakhstan raised grievances over the hundreds of nuclear weapons tests that had been conducted in the country's eastern regions over the preceding decades.[19]

Glasnost and the posters celebrating it challenged bureaucracy, past crimes, corruption, entrenched power bases and nepotism, social degradation, and environmental negligence. Soviet citizens were exhorted to rekindle revolutionary goals and rise to the challenge of forging a bright non-capitalist future that would stand as a beacon for all of humanity, with the eventual goal of nuclear arms reduction, and, ultimately, world peace.

GLASNOST UNFURLED

Until 1991, the ideological orientation, concerns, and language of the period's political posters were overseen by the CPSU Central Committee's Department of Ideology. The Central Committee maintained control and regulatory oversight, as it had always done, since it remained the ultimate purchaser of all political posters and propaganda material. In practice this meant that the state publishing houses that printed these images remained subordinate to the Central Committee. In 1984–85, the Department of Ideology set the initial parameters of the glasnost poster through assigned briefs and "annual thematic plans." At first these briefs revolved around the promotion of perestroika and glasnost, as well as the accompanying anti-corruption and anti-bureaucratic campaigns. But the Central Committee was less draconian than it had been in past decades, and by 1987 it was largely unwilling to interfere on matters of style and design, preferring to delegate responsibility. The editors of the publishing houses had greater license than before when commissioning designs. Poster designers were free to offer their own sketches in open competition. Fees for accepted designs also increased. The result was an unprecedented array of posters and proposals from which the publishing houses and Party authorities could choose.[20]

Preference was given to those designs that served the political and ideological goals of glasnost, but artists no longer faced recrimination for exercising their full creativity or pushing the boundaries of acceptability. As glasnost progressed, with ever more inventive designs and sentiments finding an outlet, the political poster became more and more of a collaborative enterprise.

As Speed Carroll astutely observed in considering the posters of this period, "Few artists have earned state salaries by holding their paymasters to ridicule." O. Kacher's "Off You Go Son" (1989, p. 111) is a prime case in point, critiquing the pervasive nepotism of the Party elite and the nomenclature system. A young boy, set for a red-carpet life, sports the same oversized suit as his father and, despite a presumed lack of achievement, already has his Order of the Red Star medals pinned prominently on his breast. With a sharp wit and evident feeling, the artist calls out the inequities and blatant hypocrisy of the Soviet system. Speed and Martha Carroll, attuned to poster art and ephemera, were struck by the wider stylistic shift of Soviet propaganda during glasnost. Having lived in the fifth arrondissement of Paris during the student rebellion of May 1968, Speed was well aware of poster art's unique ability to capture and communicate contemporary attitudes and grievances. He became a serious collector of posters and ephemera. Martha, sharing in Speed's passions, acquired the present collection of posters during the glasnost period. The enduring import and value of these visual artifacts were immediately apparent to Speed and Martha. They discerned a crucial historical moment vividly documented through the supposedly temporary medium of the political poster.

Designs that won in open competition were published in large poster format, some in large runs, others in relatively small quantities. The public encountered these new, sometimes startling images in the streets, on state buildings, and plastered on official billboards. They saw them replicated on the pages of the print media. In some cases, winning designs were assembled in "posters of posters" presentations, as seen in K. Romanenko and V. Cheremkhin's triptych "Implement, Deepen, Protect—Perestroika" showcasing anti-bureaucratic messages in support of economic perestroika, especially as it pertained to agricultural productivity.

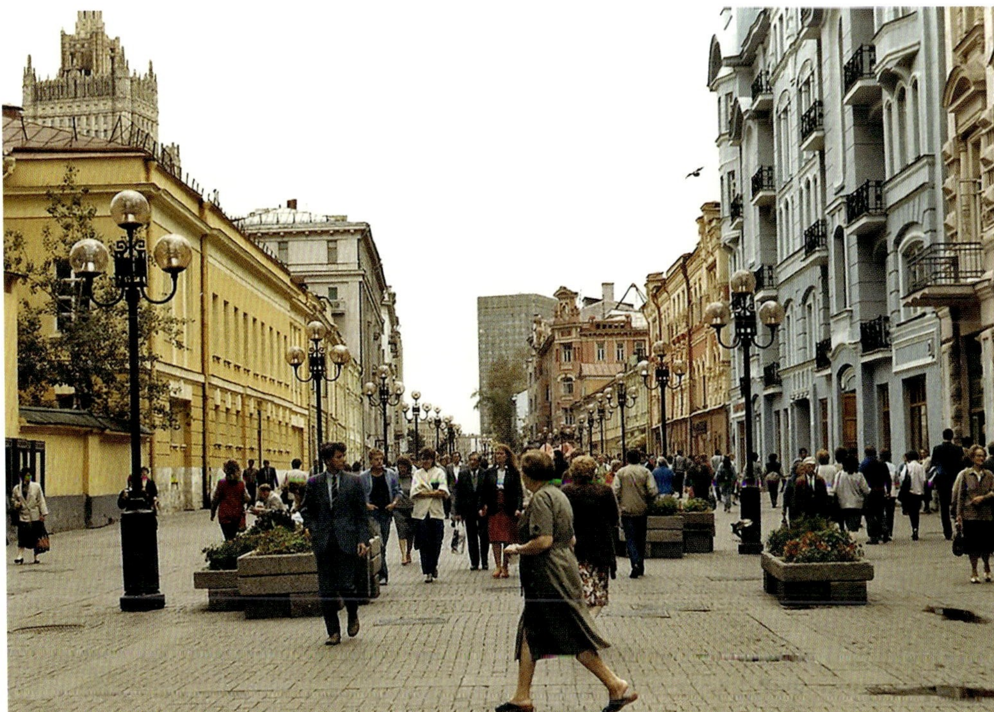

Fig. 8 The Arbat district of Moscow, 1988.

Of course, there were many posters that did not meet Party approval or did not gain commission for whatever reason. Indeed, it has been estimated that only about one-third of posters on historical themes were published in large format.[21] Some were published in journals and art magazines only; others were exhibited at poster exhibitions, but did not attain mass circulation; still others remained unpublished. Those posters whose history and printing dates are now hard to verify may fall into this "less widely distributed" category. But it is worth noting that large-print, large-run editions were not the only way that the Soviet public encountered the glasnost poster. A number of expositions provided lively and sometimes provocative venues in which the public came face to face with the messages of the new "open voice." In 1989, for instance, the Union of Artists of Ukraine and the Regional Committee of the Communist Youth League organized an "All-Union Showcase of the Political Poster" in Odessa. Rather than exhibit in a traditional space, the organizers displayed posters in shop windows along Odessa's central Deribasovskaya Street, enabling ordinary residents and visitors alike to encounter glasnost outdoors. The exhibition lasted two weeks. From the trees that lined this famous thoroughfare, paper and pencils were hung. A microphone was provided. The public was being invited to comment and express their opinions.[22] For all intents and purposes, Deribasovskaya became a street-wide pop-up gallery. Again, this was not just a visual representation of glasnost, it was glasnost in action. The success of the event prompted the organizers to repeat it the following year.

On Moscow's famous Arbat Street, a prime tourist site, the *Poster—Perestroika* (1988) exhibition, organized jointly by the Poster Publishing house of the Russian Soviet Federative Socialist Republic (RSFSR) and the USSR Union of Artists, attracted huge crowds twenty-four hours a day during its run (fig. 8). Indeed, the organizers were forced to extend the show to meet the demand. This event, which included a large range of posters, was arranged around a primary exhibition hall, but images and discussion spilled onto the street, too. That same year, the Communist Youth League organized an All-Union poster competition and an accompanying exhibition titled *Perestroika and We*. Marking the seventieth anniversary of the Youth League, the theme was young people and their relation to reform.[23] Around 500–600 entries were submitted. In a demonstration of glasnost, visitors were encouraged to provide critical feedback on the event. Some took the opportunity to criticize the organizers for the cramped display, suggesting that the contents of the exhibition should have been in the street. As one person commented, "the bureaucrat will never go to this exhibition." Such material should be "branded and nailed" where it can thrive.[24]

The glasnost poster, like all Soviet propaganda before it, was created to serve the policy interests of leading authorities. But increasingly, as artists and designers began to feel more emboldened, internalizing the message of glasnost, many also came to view the poster as reflecting the critical moods and evolving experience of contemporary society. The Soviet poster, far more dynamic in this new incarnation, initiated new means of expression. As often happens with official policies, in practice it took unexpected directions. In 1988, the Moscow-based Street Poster Group formed with the express aim of "exhibiting" unauthorized images in the streets, plastering posters to walls and shop windows at will. Founded by A. Agaev, V. Mokhov, and Yu. Gerepanov, artists who became well known for their satirical creations, this group pushed things to an extreme. Their public works sometimes provoked violent reactions. Their displays were often forcibly removed, and their actions dismissed as juvenile. They managed to rile both anti-reform loyalists, who saw the group as the nadir of glasnost, and pro-reform figures, who feared their penchant for disruption would go too far. Here the political poster had all but freed itself from any obligation to serve the interests of the authorities. New needs and wants found expression. In August 1991, on the eve of the attempted coup d'état designed to oust Gorbachev, the Union of Artists had arranged a political poster exhibition on Kuznetsk Bridge, in central Moscow. Once the coup, which amounted to a hardliner attempt to halt reform, was quashed in early September, some of the most politically active artists in the show took their works across to the White House, the main government residence of the RSFSR, and put together an improvised open-air exhibition.[25] By this point, visual commentaries were becoming embroiled in new master narratives.

In the end, glasnost could not be restricted to officially prescribed topics of concern or templates of expression. Once they were declared necessary, debate and criticism abounded. What finally finished the Soviet Union was the division stoked by unfettered criticism and amplified discontent, as well as the new politics to which these expressions gave rise. Ethnic and inter-republic tensions, for example, fed an ever-mounting disquiet in the run-up to the 1990s, as depicted in M. J. Dimiters's "Dialogues?" (1989, p. 148). Printed in Riga, Latvia, this poster reflects a cynical view of center-periphery relations and the prospect of a new politics under glasnost. It speaks to the long-brewing discontent of the Baltic states, the dominance of Moscow, and an underlying Russian chauvinism. The poster renders the word "Dialogues" in English, indicating that in the Soviet context open and honest debate is a distinctly foreign concept. With power residing exclusively in the Party and Moscow, how can such dialogue possibly take place? As Dimiters suggests in his poster's imagery, we may as well imagine a discussion between the chicken and the axe—an interaction more befitting Latvia's historic relationship with Russia.

The forces released through glasnost ultimately proved unwieldy. The fracture lines exposed were too many and too deep. Gorbachev's naiveté has drawn much critical comment—deservedly—but if we view glasnost as an attempt to rekindle revolutionary *obshchestvennost'*, then it must also be noted that the transgressions committed over the preceding thirty or forty years really provided the force that splintered the Soviet project. In its very structure, then, as well as in its failings, glasnost was a Soviet experience.

Despite their divisions, in the 1991 referendum on whether the republics should remain unified, the vast majority of Soviet people voted in favor of preserving the USSR. The revolutionary project that Gorbachev so dearly wished to revitalize, and the sense of purpose that the Soviet Union provided its citizenry, had not lost its meaning. Amid all the contradiction and confusion of the period, the explosion of idealism, the debates and criticisms, a consensus on union was still firmly expressed—perhaps a suitably idealistic epitaph to glasnost itself. As many of the posters of this time make plain, glasnost represented a short-lived yet resounding explosion of Soviet idealism. For many, this was a time when a sense of revolutionary mission returned to the surface of Soviet life. Glasnost promoted political advance through democratization and debate, economic advance through worker-sponsored reforms challenging bureaucratic inertia, and social advance through morally laden depictions of human relations in the workplace, at home, and in society at large. Glasnost, responsible for a seismic shift in the politics of a continent, was born, above all, from a sense of Soviet possibility.

1. cf. Francis Fukuyama, *The End of History and the Last Man* (New York, NY: Free Press, 1992).

2. Chris Miller, *The Struggle to Save the Soviet Economy: Mikhail Gorbachev and the Collapse of the USSR* (Chapel Hill: University of North Carolina Press, 2016), esp. 11–16.

3. Lyudmila Alexeyeva and Paul Goldberg, *The Thaw Generation: Coming of Age in the Post-Stalin Era* (Pittsburgh, PA: University of Pittsburgh Press, 1990), 108–109.

4. Stephen Kotkin, *Armageddon Averted: The Soviet Collapse 1970–2000* (Oxford: Oxford University Press, 2003), esp. 2–3.

5. Miller, *The Struggle to Save the Soviet Economy*, 18.

6. Andy Willimott, *Living the Revolution: Urban Communes & Soviet Socialism, 1917–1932* (Oxford: Oxford University Press, 2017), 168–169.

7. cf. Oliver Bullough, *That Last Man in Russia and the Struggle to Save a Dying Nation* (London: Penguin Books, 2014), 76.

8. Zenji Asaoka, "Nikolai Bukharin and the *Rabsel'kor* Movement: *Sovetskaia Obshchestvennost'* under the 'Dictatorship of the Proletariat,'" in *Obshchestvennost' and Civic Agency in Late Imperial and Soviet Russia: Interface between State and Society*, ed. Yasuhiro Matsui (London: Palgrave Macmillan, 2015), 82–108.

9. Willimott, "Revolutionary Participation, Youthful Civic-Mindedness," in *The Fate of the Bolshevik Revolution: Illiberal Liberation*, eds. Lara Douds, James Harris, and Peter Whitewood (London: Bloomsbury, 2020), chap. 14.

10. Michael David-Fox, "Review: Obshchestvennye organizatsii Rossii v 1920-e gody," *Kritika: Explorations in Russian and Eurasian History* 3, no. 1 (2002): 180.

11. Karl Loewenstein, "Obshchestvennost' as Key to Understanding Soviet Writers of the 1950s: *Moskovskii Literator*, October 1956–March 1957," *Journal of Contemporary History* 33 (2009): 473–492.

12. cf. Ekaterina Betekhina, "Style in Lower-Class Writing in 1917," in *Voices of Revolution, 1917*, ed. Mark D. Steinberg (New Haven, CT: Yale University Press, 2001), 338. Also see: Mark D. Steinberg, *The Russian Revolution, 1905–1921* (Oxford: Oxford University Press, 2017), chap. 1.

13. Full title: *History of the Communist Party of the Soviet Union (Bolsheviks): Short Course*, ed. CPSU.

14. David Brandenburger and Mikhail Zelenov, eds., *Stalin's Master Narrative: A Critical Edition of the History of the Communist Party of the Soviet Union (Bolsheviks)* (New Haven, CT: Yale University Press, 2019), 37.

15. Ibid., 37–38.

16. Ibid., 38–39; D. A. Volkogonov, *Triumf i tragediia—Politicheskii portret I. V. Stalina*, 2 vols., 2 pts. (Moscow: Izd-vo APN, 1989), 2/2: 148.

17. A. M. Kollontai, "Pis'ma k trudiasheisia molodezhi. Kakim dolzhen byt' kommunist?," *Molodaia gvardiia*, no. 1–2, April–May (1922): 1–10.

18. Leon Trotsky, *Literature and Revolution*, ed. William Keach, trans. Rose Strunsky (1924; Chicago, IL: Haymarket Books, 2005), 207.

19. Charles E. Ziegler, "Russian and Post-Soviet Studies" Environment," in *International Encyclopaedia of the Social and Behavioral Sciences*, ed. James D. Wright, 2nd ed. (Amsterdam: Elsevier, 2015), 831–851.

20. Nina Baburnia and Karl Nashik, *Real'nost' utopii: Istusstvo russkogo plakata XX veka*, Rossiisko-Germanskie kult'urnye vstrechi, (2003): 307–308.

21. Ibid., 323.

22. Ibid., 309–312.

23. While many of these posters did not acquire mass circulation, some were reproduced shortly after in published album collections. A. Egorov, ed., *The Posters of Glasnost and Perestroika* (London: Penguin Books, 1989); Н. Бабрина, ed., Россия XX век. История страны в плакате (Moscow: Panorama, 1993).

24. Nashik and Baburina, *Real'nost' utopii*, 312–313; *Perestroika and We*, exh. cat. Moscow, 1989, 114.

25. Ibid., 313

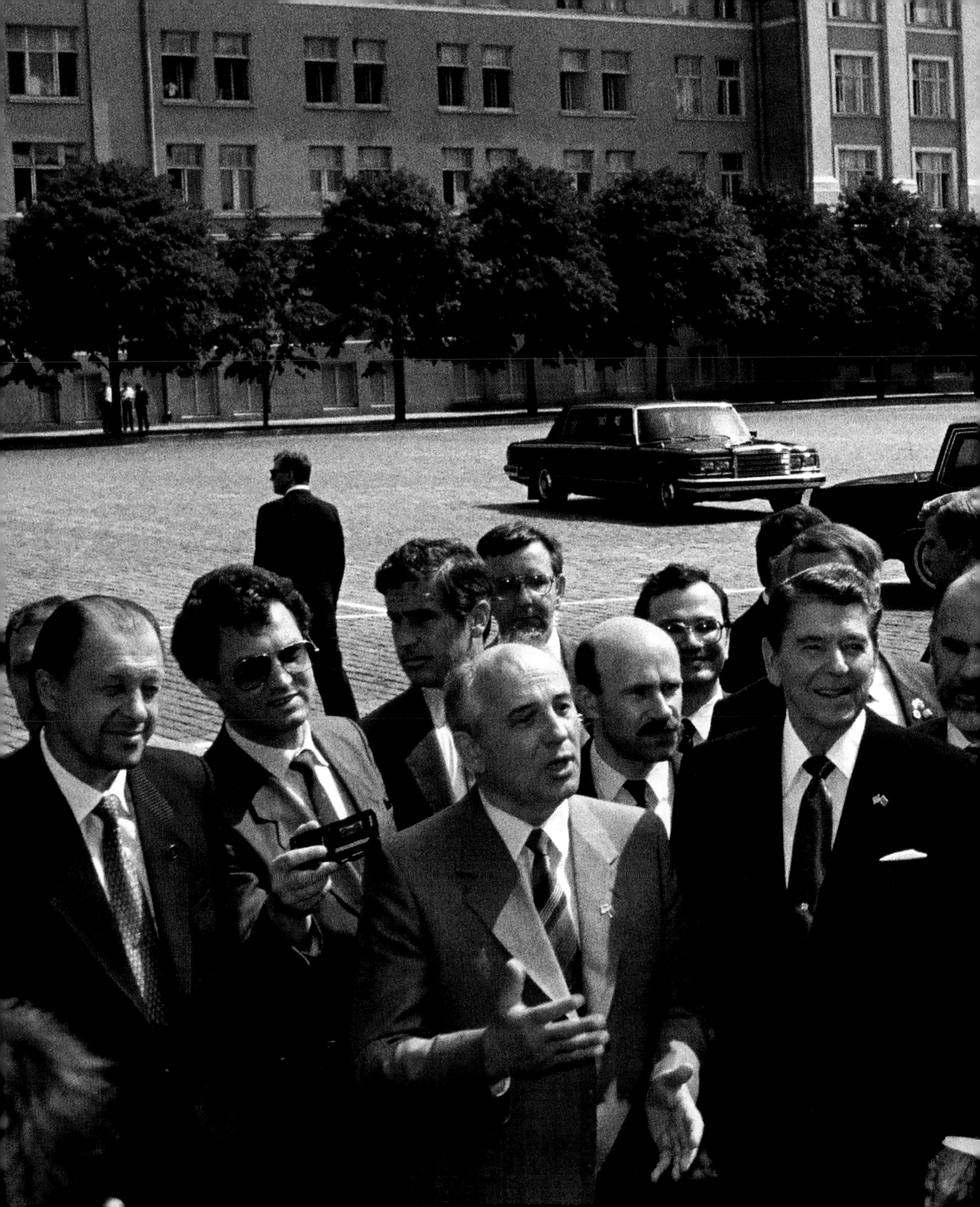

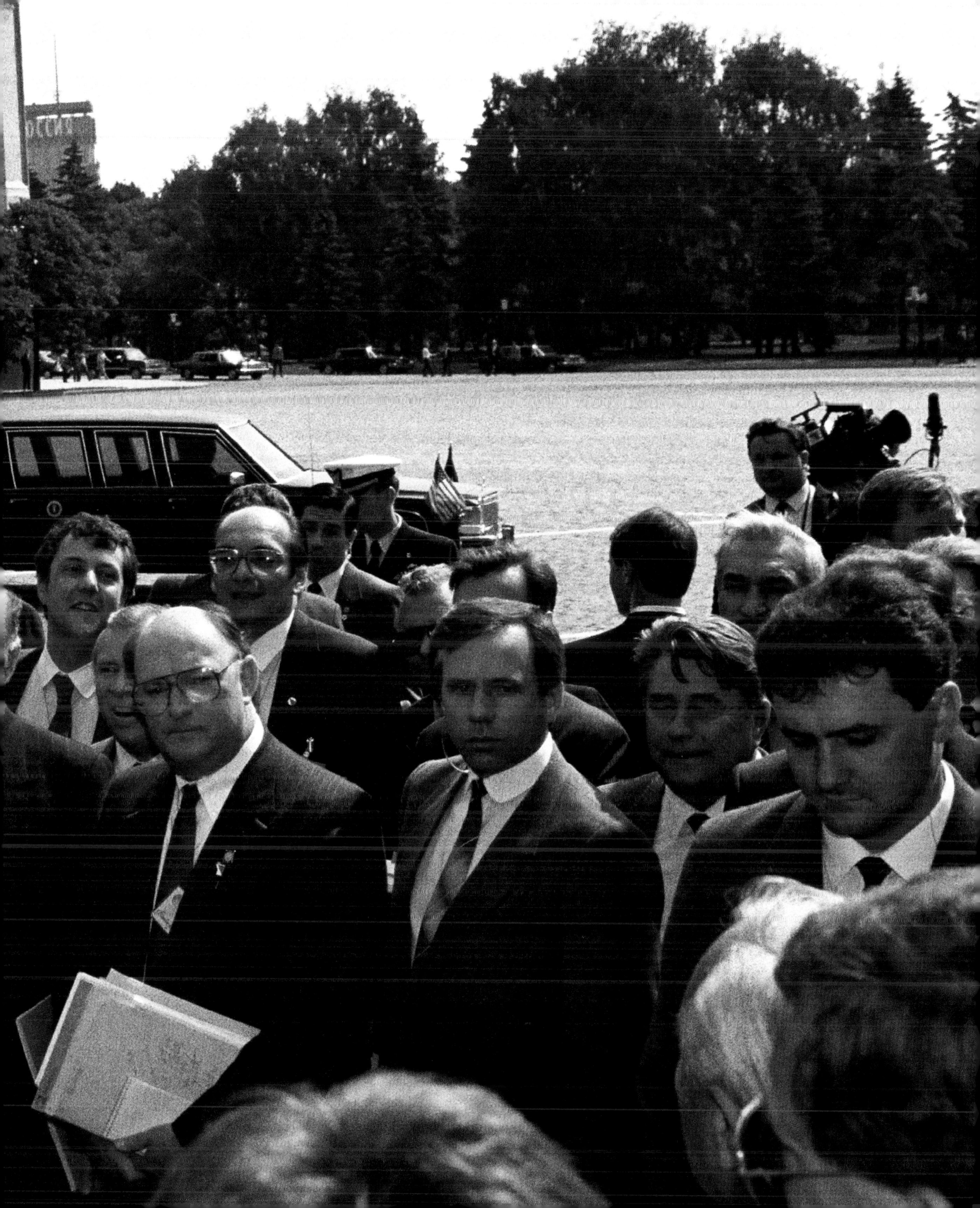

PRESENT

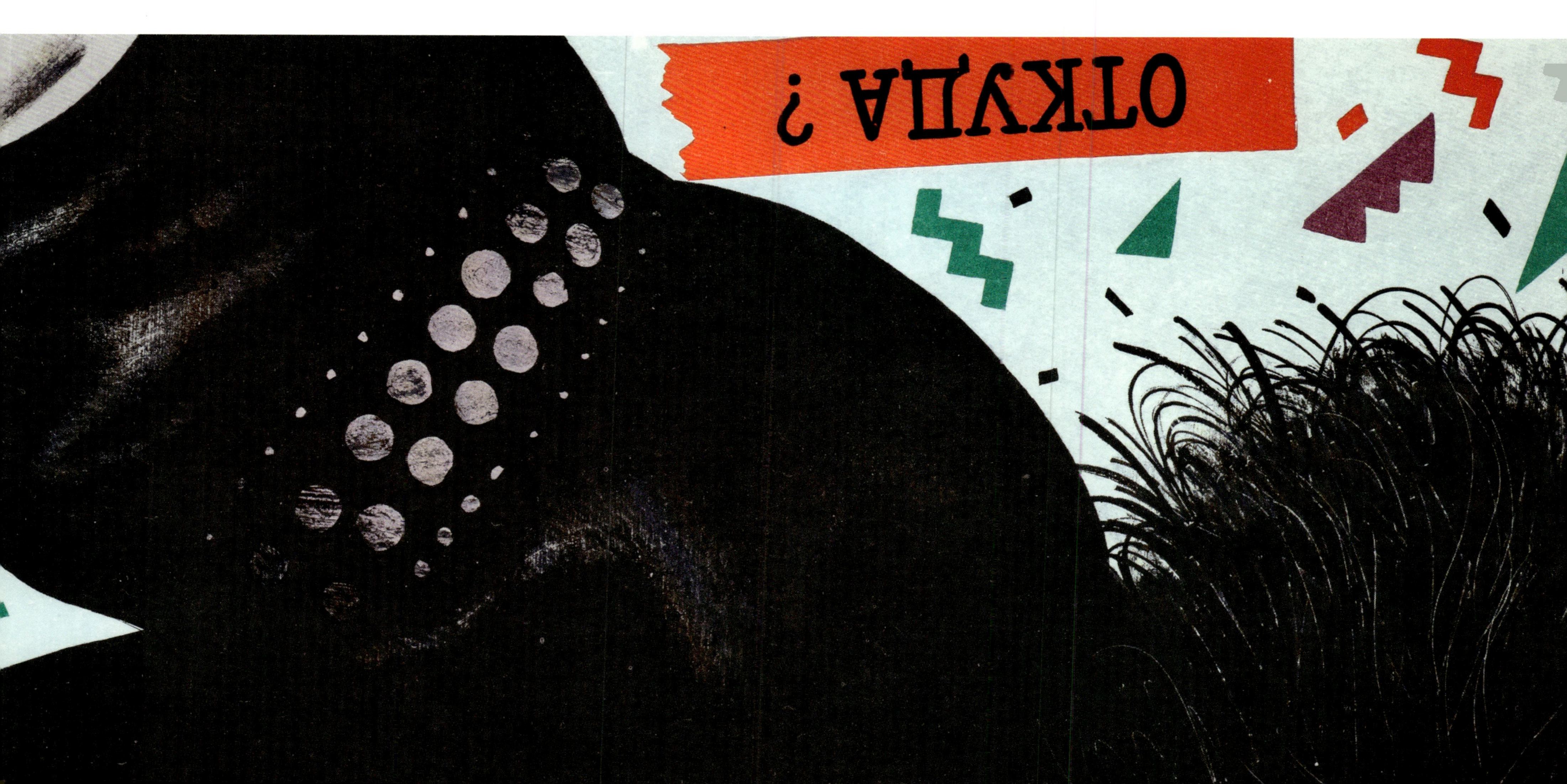
ОТКУДА ?

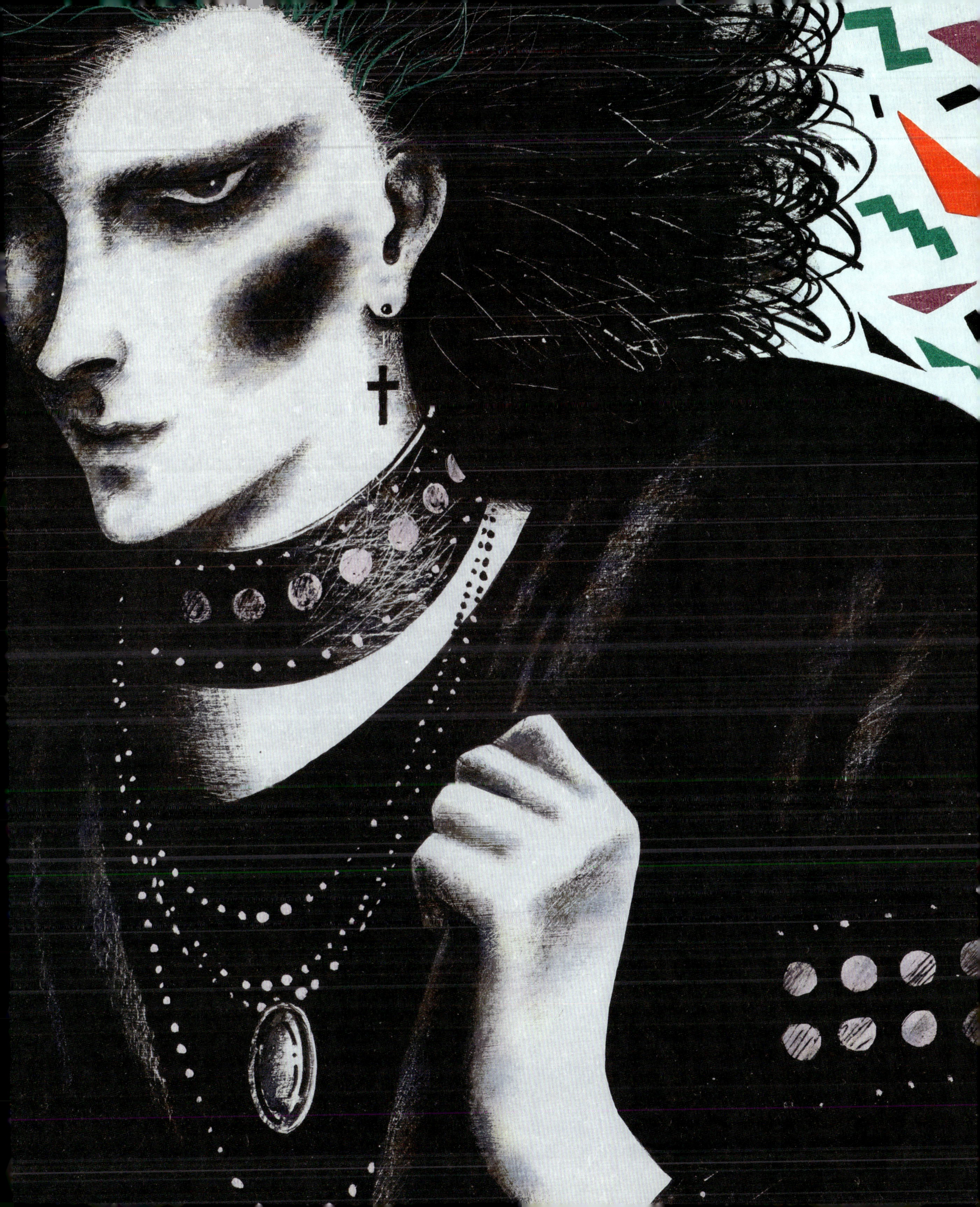

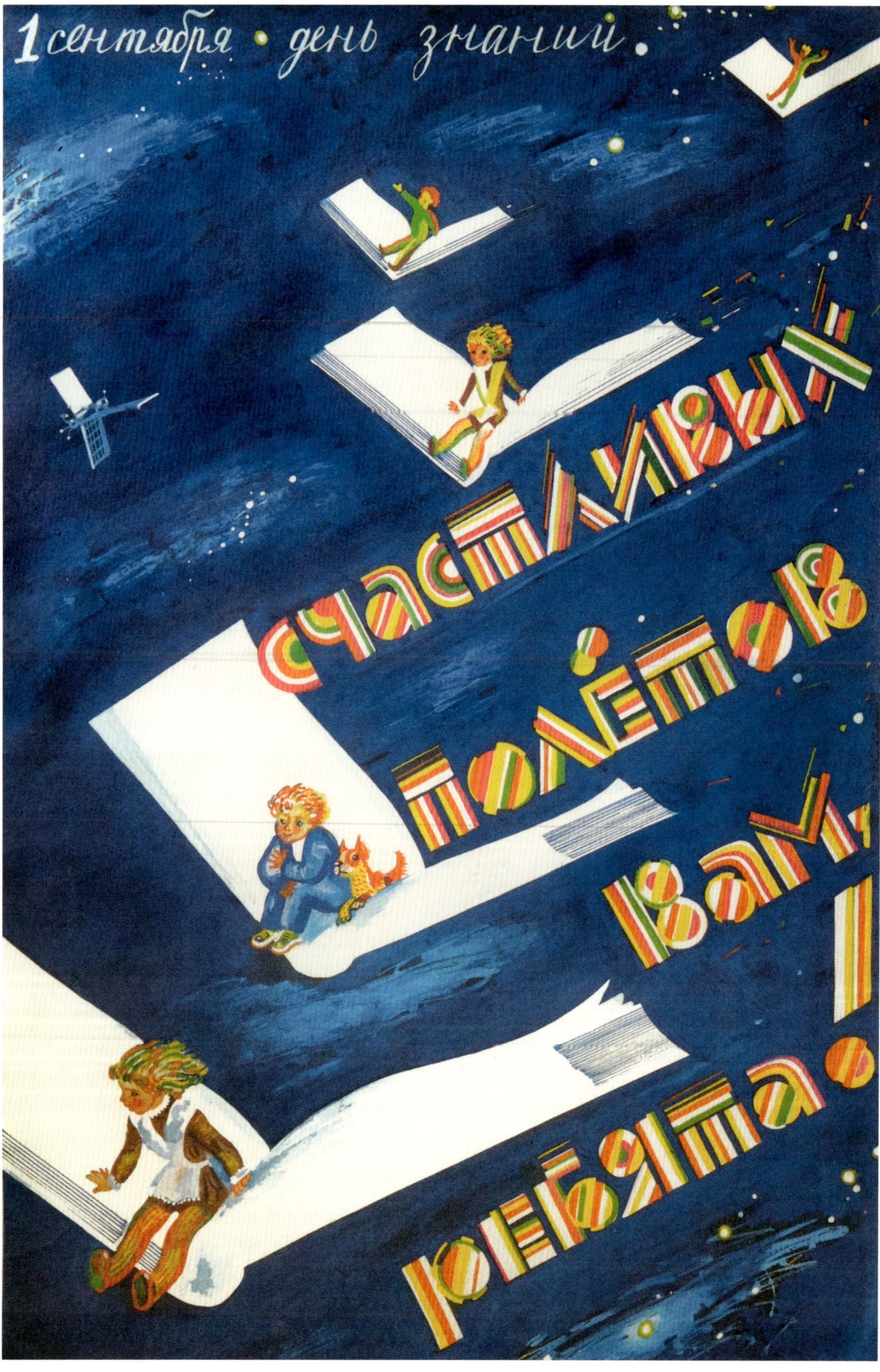
1 сентября • день знаний
счастливых
полётов
вам,
ребята!

◂ Л. Непомнящий (L. Nepomnyashchiy) | 1990

SEPTEMBER 1ST
KNOWLEDGE DAY
HAPPY FLIGHTS TO YOU, CHILDREN!

This date is traditionally the first day of the Russian school year. School children fly through space on open books whose shapes echo the space satellite pictured in the distance at left. The message conveyed in this poster is that only serious education will enable the advance of science and technology.

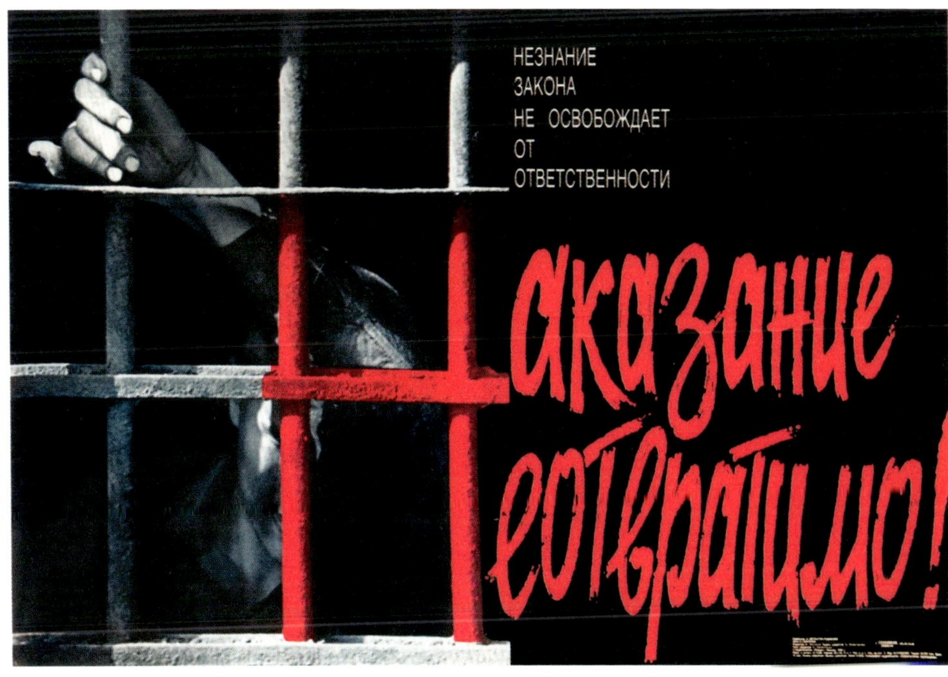

▴ И. Петрыгин-Родионов (I. Petrygin-Rodionov) | 1990

IGNORANCE OF THE LAW IS NO EXCUSE
PUNISHMENT IS INEVITABLE!

◂ А. Кондуров (A. Kondurov) | 1988

CHILDREN'S FOUNDATION NAMED AFTER THE V. I. LENIN ACCT. # 707

The government's bank account number, featured in red, is included in this poster so that people could contribute to the orphanage. The view of a child inside the orphanage through a rain-streaked window gives the impression he is crying. He has written MAMA! on the window; we read it in reverse above his head.

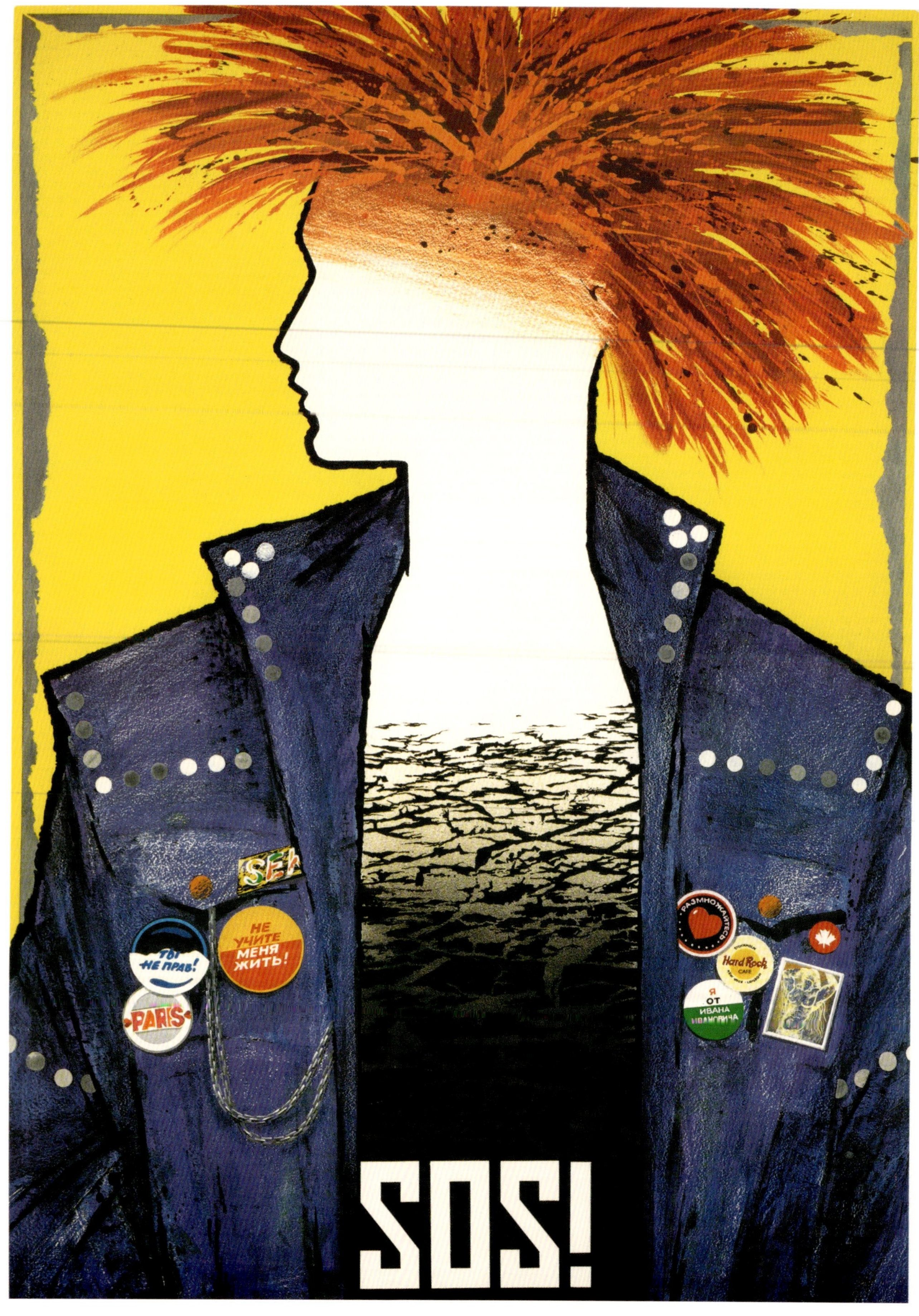
ТЫ НЕ ПРАВ!
PARIS
НЕ УЧИТЕ МЕНЯ ЖИТЬ!
РАЗМНОЖАЙТЕСЬ
Hard Rock CAFE
Я ОТ ИВАНА
SOS!

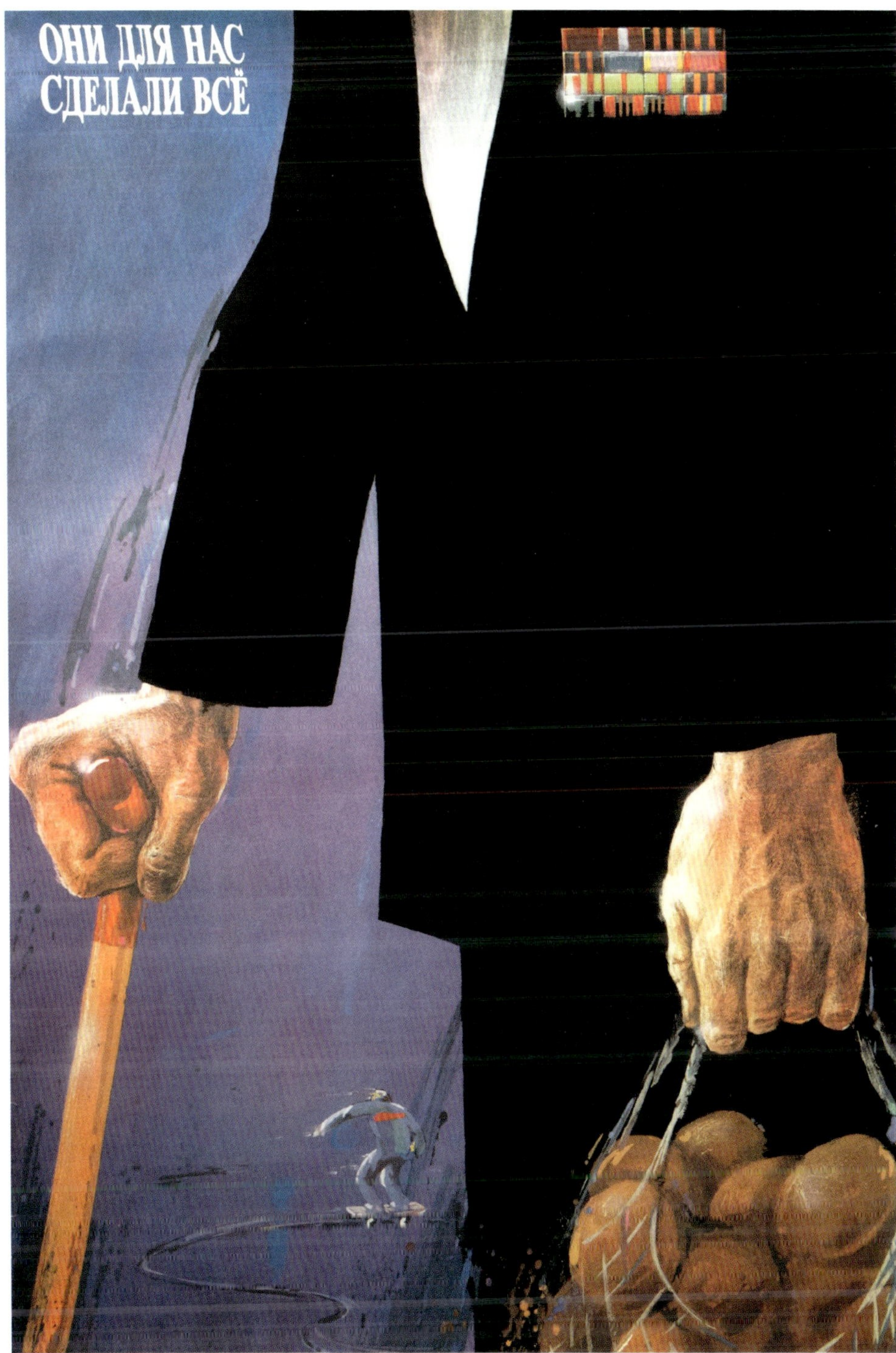

◂ Н. Журавлева (N. Zhuravleva) | 1990

SOS!
A youth sports an array of contradictory messages, fashionable at the time, because he doesn't know or care about sociopolitical problems or the morality behind them. He is presented as a mindless conformist, seeking to be fashionably shocking—thus his exploding hair. His conformism and ignorance are conveyed by his facelessness; the aridity he represents, by the cracked and polluted landscape on his chest. His buttons are incoherently mixed-up and some feature the latest "in" catchphrase—YOU'RE WRONG!—originating from Gorbachev's famous retort to the conservative Igor Ligachev. Other similar quips on the youth's buttons include: DON'T TEACH ME HOW TO LIVE / PROCREATE / IVAN IVANOVICH SENT ME. The last of these was used if you wanted to buy something under the counter, the Russian equivalent to "John Doe sent me." The "SOS!" sends a signal of distress to this young man, and to others of his generation who need help and direction.

▴ С. Миненок (S. Minenok) | 1989

THEY DID EVERYTHING FOR US
An old veteran of World War II, who must use a cane, is carrying a heavy bag of potatoes, while a young skateboarder ignores him as he whizzes by. This poster broaches the lack of social consciousness and empathy on the part of youth. Moreover, this image suggests a collective sense of loss and a renewed search for a national purpose following the Brezhnev years.

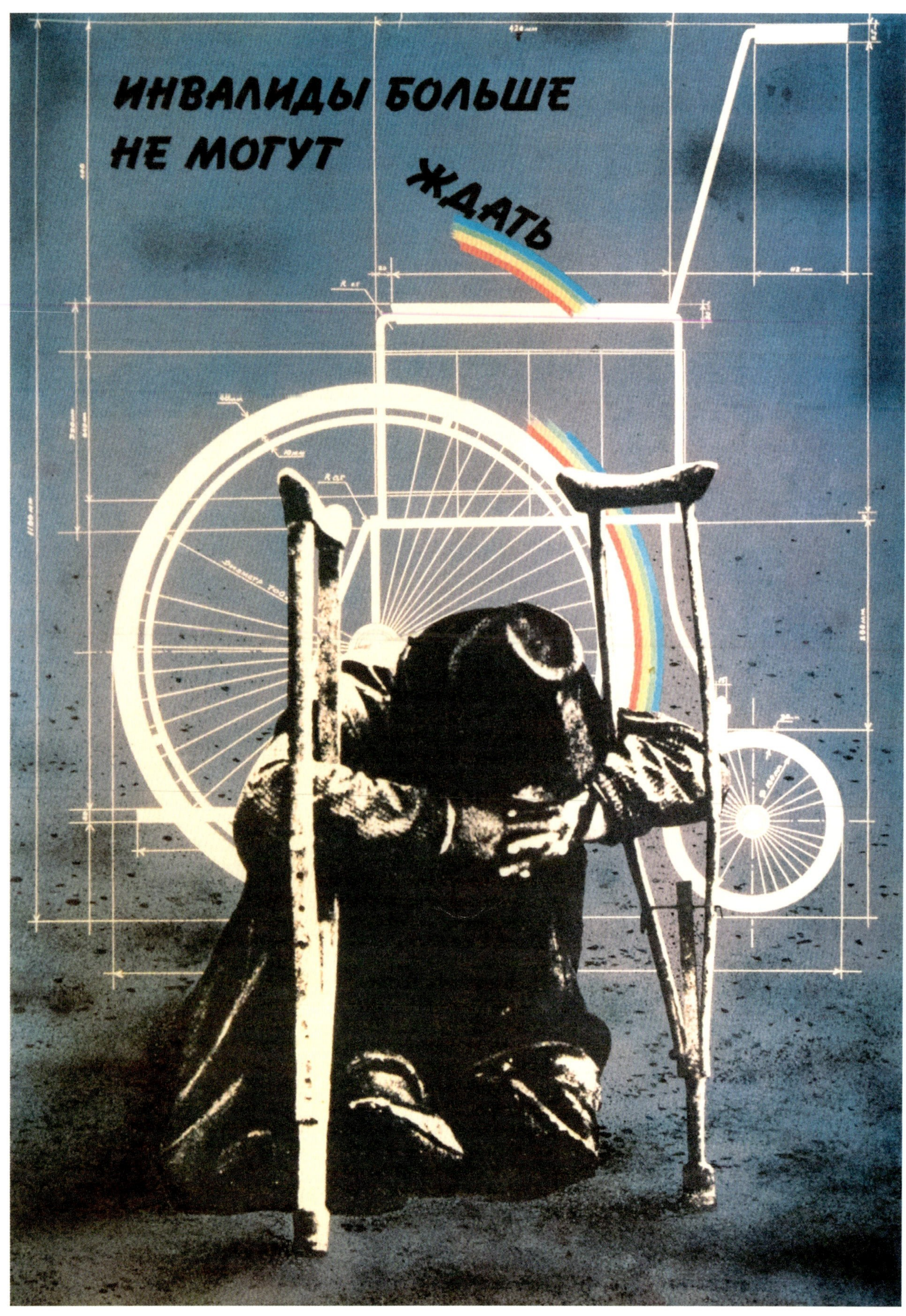
ИНВАЛИДЫ БОЛЬШЕ
НЕ МОГУТ
ЖДАТЬ

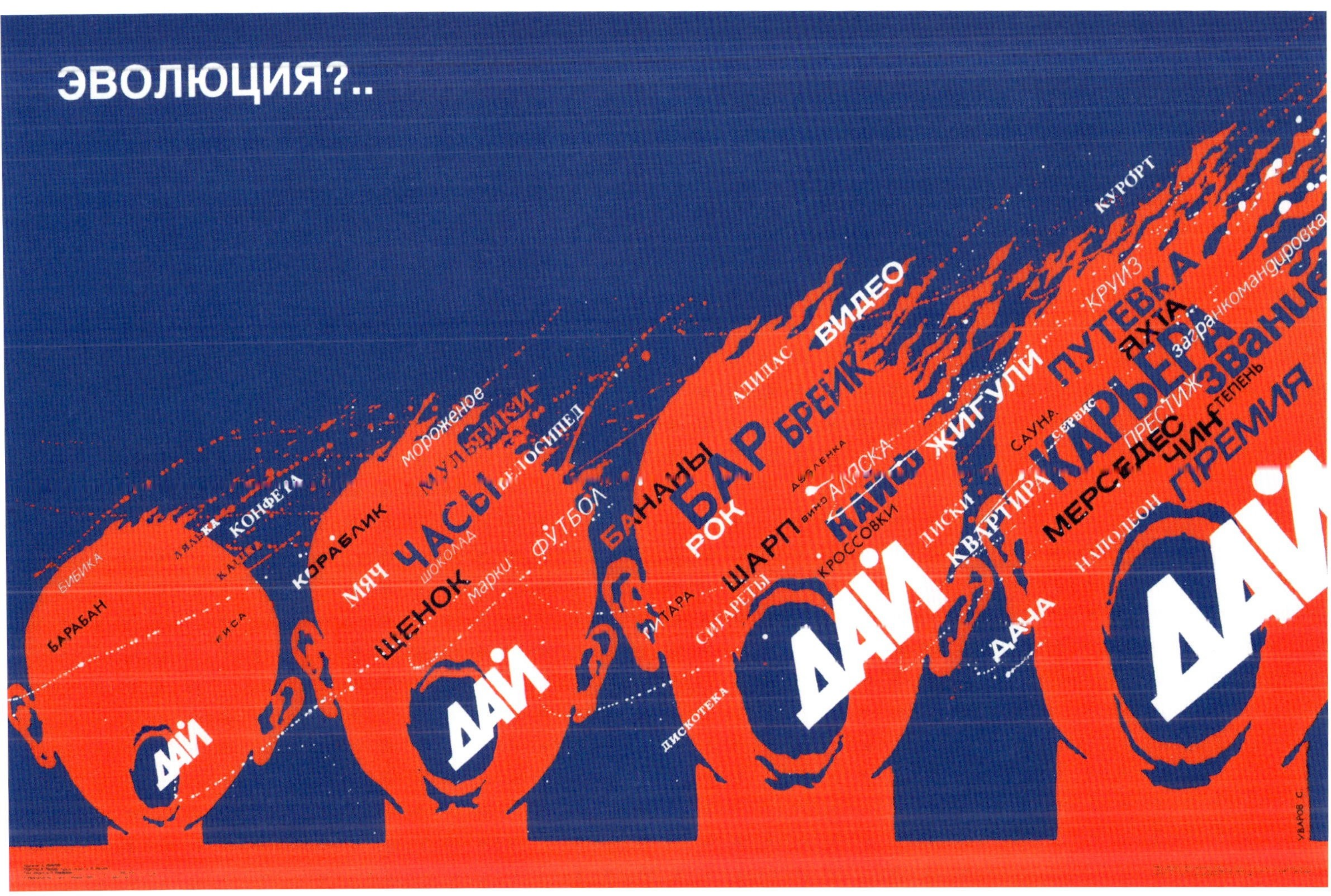

◄ О. Качер (O. Kacher) | ca. 1988

THE DISABLED CAN'T WAIT ANY LONGER
The depiction of an injured man with crutches presents the very picture of despair. The blueprint of a coveted wheelchair is shown behind him. Under the word WAIT, a broken rainbow indicates that this dream, too, is broken—his hope of receiving the necessary support from the government is futile. The Soviet Union is not providing for veterans returning from Afghanistan: the industrial system has failed even to produce sufficient wheelchairs for their needs.

▲ С. Уваров (S. Uvarov) | 1989

Text at top left: EVOLUTION? This question serves as a satirical critique of the growing demand for material possessions and personal ambition during the perestroika/glasnost era. The four heads represent different stages of life as the word GIMME spews from each mouth. Swirling around each of the heads are objects that they respectively desire as well as goals, moods, or aspirations at that moment in time. The words spewing from the toddler's mouth: KITTY / DRUM / BEEP-BEEP / CANDY; the words from the older child's mouth: SHIP / BALL / ICE CREAM / CARTOONS / WATCH / BIKE / CHOCOLATE / PUPPY / STAMP; from the teenager's mouth: BANANAS / ADIDAS / VIDEO / BAR / BREAK-DANCING / GUITAR / ROCK / PARKA /CIGARETTES / HIGH / DISCOTHEQUE / RECORDS /SNEAKERS / ALASKA. The words attributed to the adult implicatively shed light on a new and more sophisticated mindset during this period in Russian history: ZHIGULI [car] / CRUISE / RESORT / SAUNA / VACATION / YACHT / APARTMENT / CAREER / BUSINESS TRIP ABROAD / MERCEDES / PRESTIGE / VOCATION / POSITION / DEGREE / DACHA / NAPOLEON [cake] / AWARD.

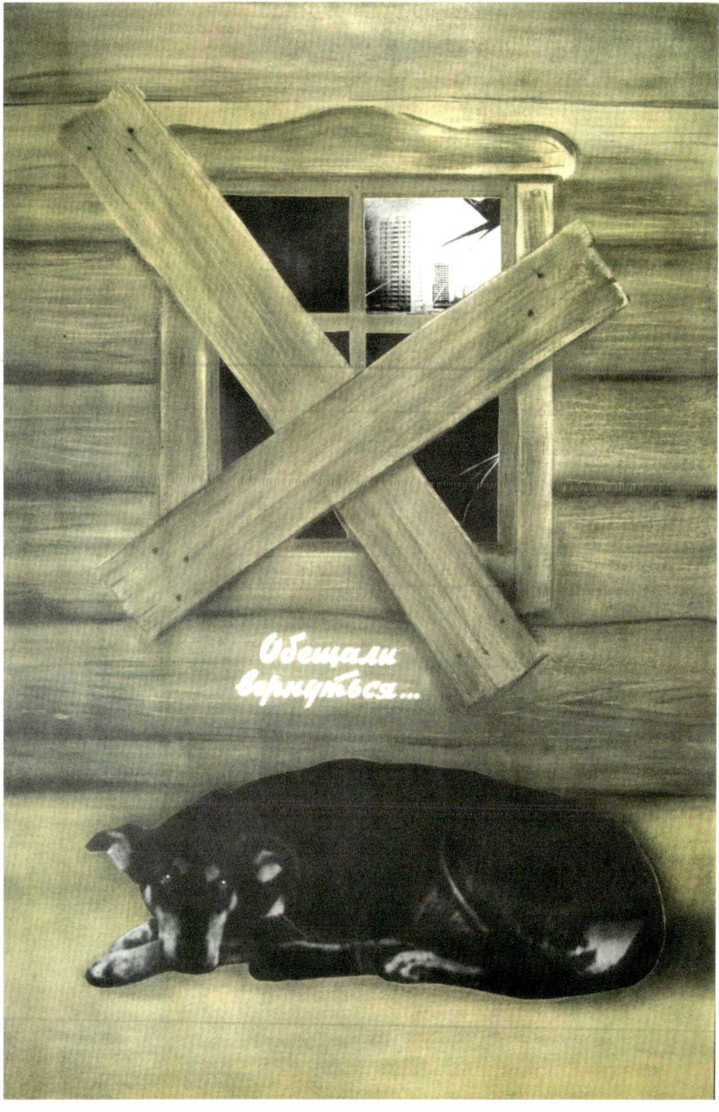

▲ С. Дьячков (S. Dyachkov) | 1987

YOU PROMISED YOU WOULD RETURN . . .
The window of this house is boarded up and the dog looks forlorn. In earlier days, each household in a Russian village would typically have a big guard dog, but people have abandoned agriculture and the village for the big city. This poster seems to indicate that this way of life has become obsolete.

▼ В. Ермаков (V. Yermakov), Ю. Жаров (Y. Zharov) | 1989

Text at top left: ALMOST 5000 CHILDREN ARE KILLED ON THE ROAD EVERY YEAR
Text at center: PREVENT ANOTHER TRAGEDY!

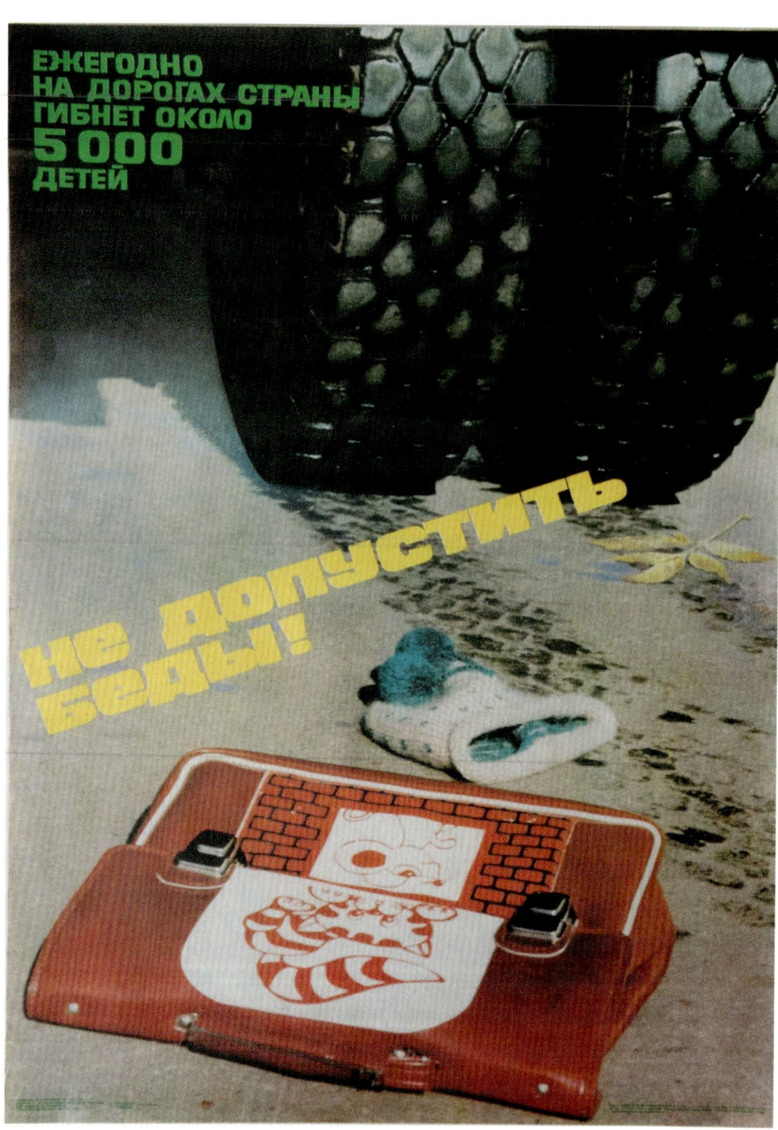

М. Рождествин (M. Rozhdestin) | 1990 ➤

Clockwise from top: WHO ARE WE? / ARE WE GOING ANYWHERE? / TO WHERE / FROM WHERE?

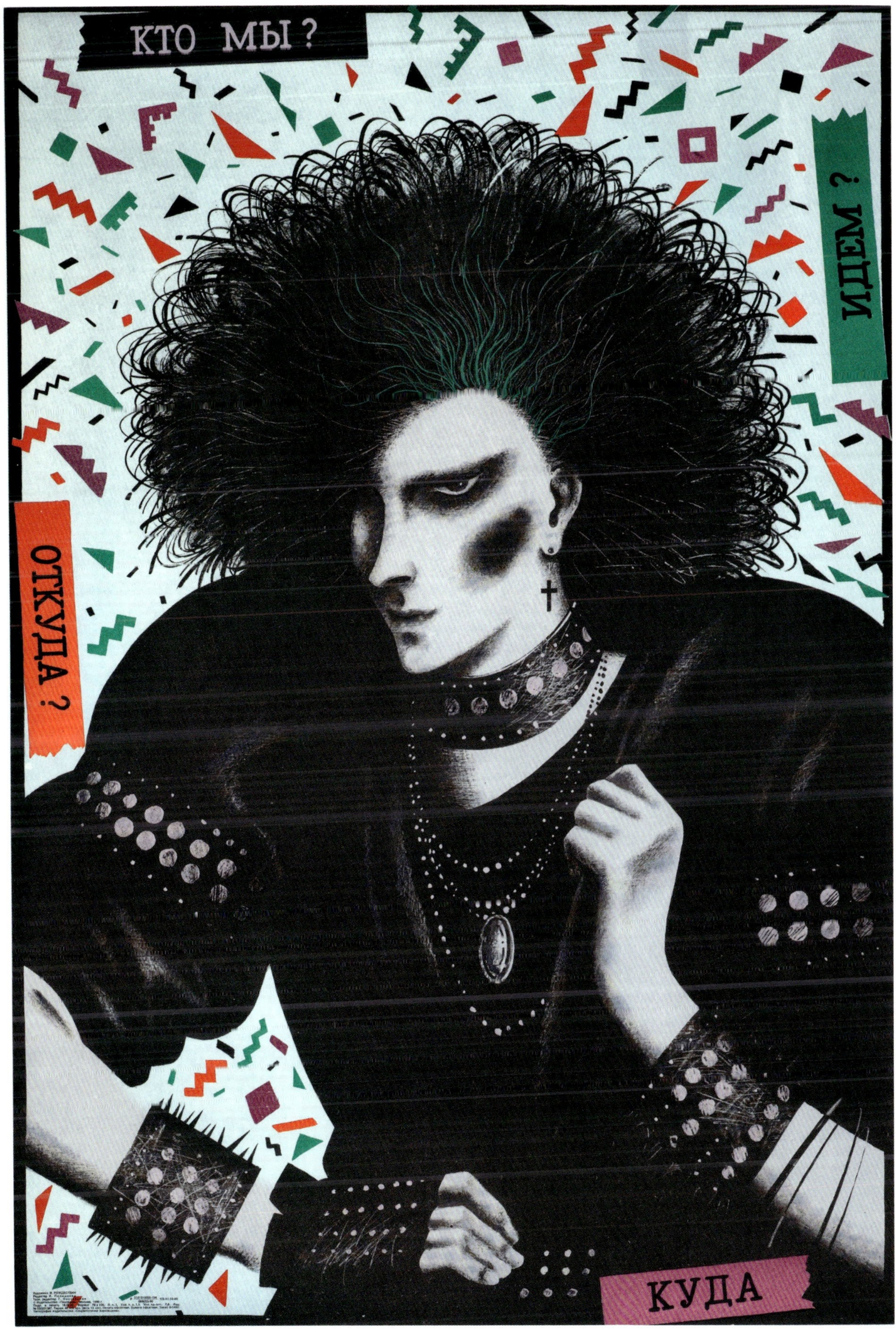
КТО МЫ?
ОТКУДА?
ИДЕМ?
КУДА

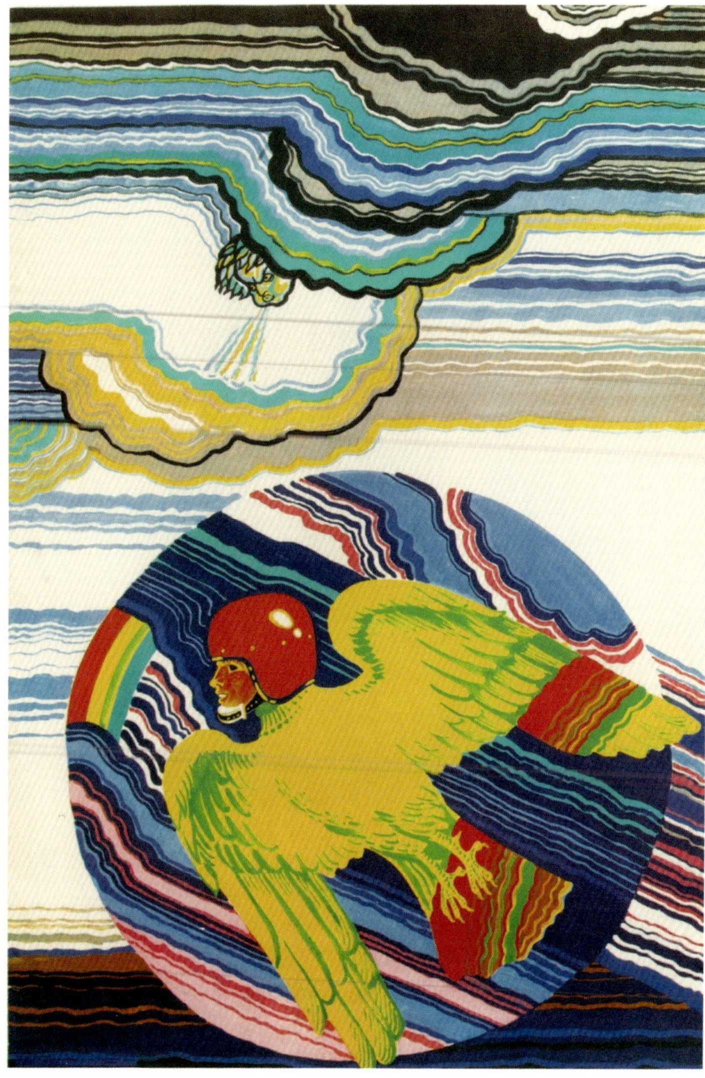

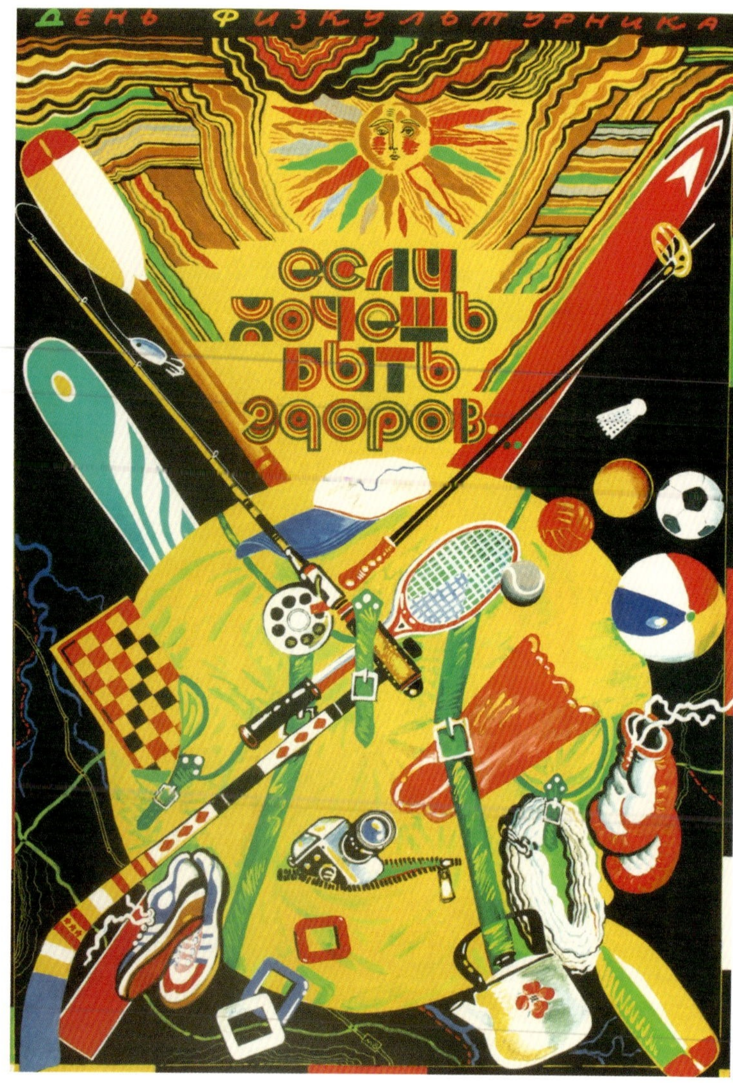

Л. Непомнящий (L. Nepomnyashchiy) | 1990

Three panels of a tryptich on the theme of sports and recreation. Text on center panel, at top, reads: PHYSICAL CULTURE DAY; text at center: IF YOU WANT TO BE HEALTHY.

During the perestroika and glasnost periods, Soviet officials were capitalizing on a period of harmonious relations with the United States to make a permanent commitment to sports expansion on the international level. They viewed sports as a means of fostering good will with the United States, and destroying myths and stereotypes.

The Soviet sports establishment—an arm of the government—kept the lion's share of all the money generated by its athletes in endorsements, appearance fees, prize money, and salaries. A 1989 article in the *New York Times* reported that the Soviets made over $100 million between 1985 and 1988 in such revenues.

According to the article, the president of a US-based marketing firm had even been "approached by a Soviet official who was interested in putting McDonald's patches on the uniforms of Soviet hockey teams." There had also been a major rebirth of tennis in the Soviet Union in the 1980s as the sport returned to the Olympics.

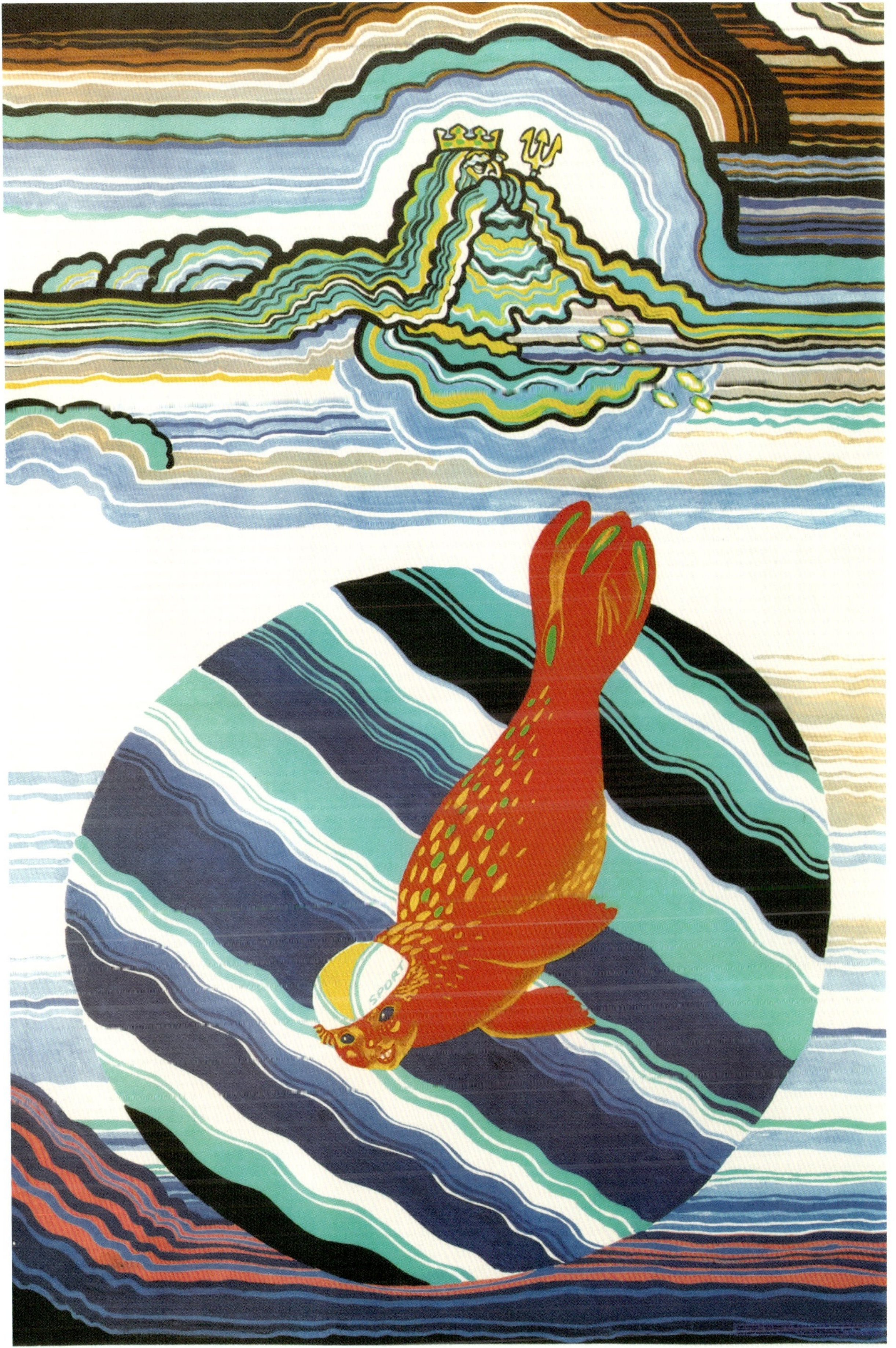
SPORT

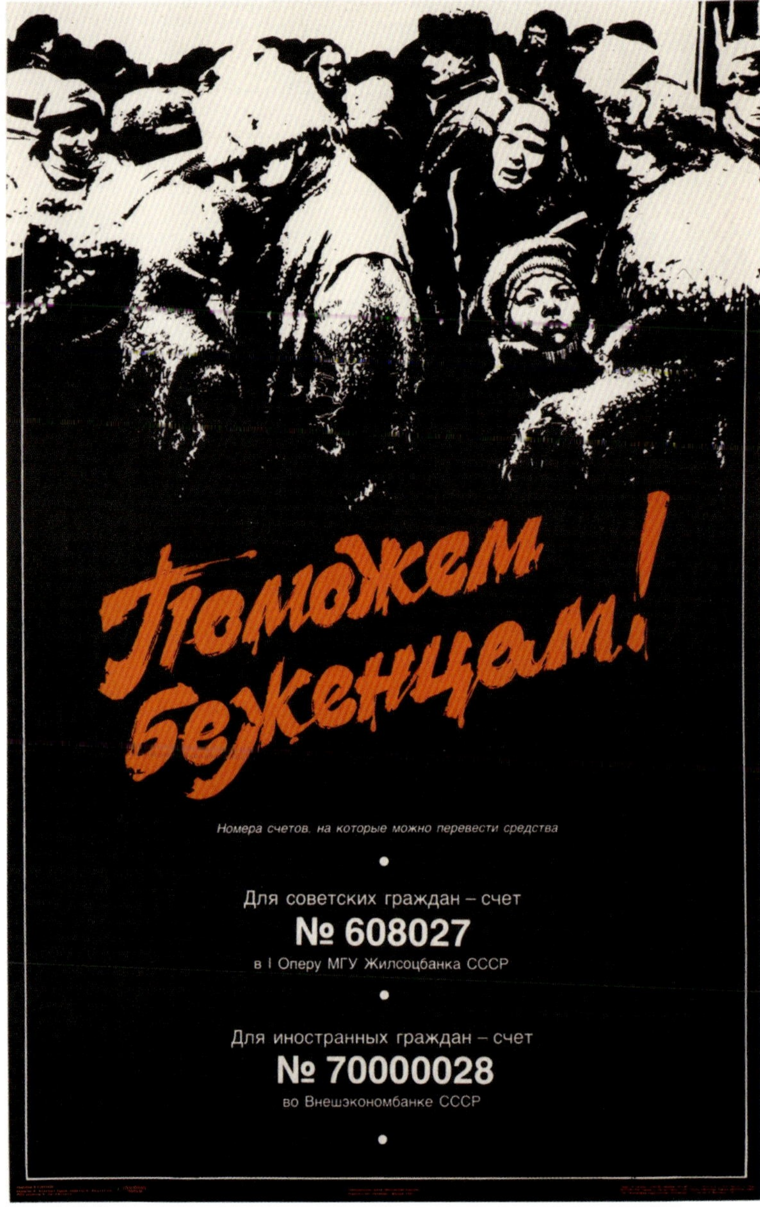

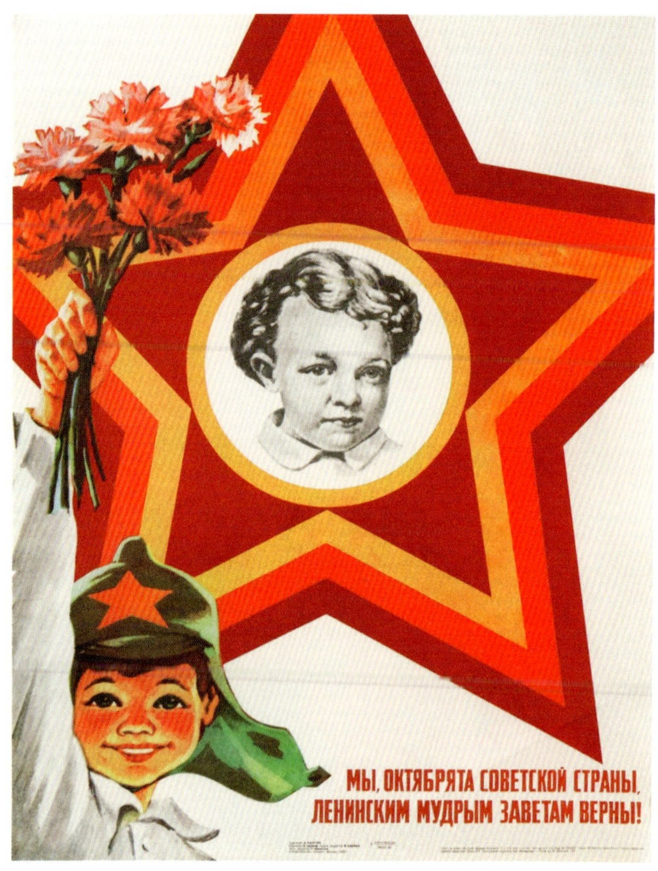

▲ В. Горохов (V. Gorokhov) | 1990

WE WILL HELP THE REFUGEES!
Text at center: FOR SOVIET CITIZENS, ACCOUNT NO. 608027, TO THE OPERATION DEPARTMENT #1 OF THE MGU ZHILSOTSBANK OF THE USSR. FOR FOREIGNERS, ACCOUNT NO. 70000028 OF THE VNESHEKONOMBANK OF THE USSR.

А. Качугин (A. Kachugin) | 1988 ▲

WE ARE THE LITTLE OCTOBRISTS OF THE SOVIET UNION, FAITHFUL TO LENIN'S WISE COMMANDMENTS!
A baby picture of Lenin appears in the center of a red star. This motif was featured on a badge worn by children of the Little Octobrists, a Communist youth organization.

И. Вахитов (I. Vakhitov) | 1990 ►

SAY HELLO TO CARDIN
This late perestroika poster was created in response to the highly publicized announcement that renowned French designer Pierre Cardin would be having the first fashion show from Paris in the Soviet Union. The image of a female construction worker in a revealing outfit cinched with a rope is clearly targeted at a Russian audience. Cardin's love of the Soviet Union led him to use Russian motifs in his collections, and to receive commissions to dress Russian ballerinas and first ladies, including Raisa Gorbacheva, Gorbachev's wife. His iconic "Cosmos" collection of dresses was inspired by Russian cosmonaut Yuri Gagarin's flight into space.

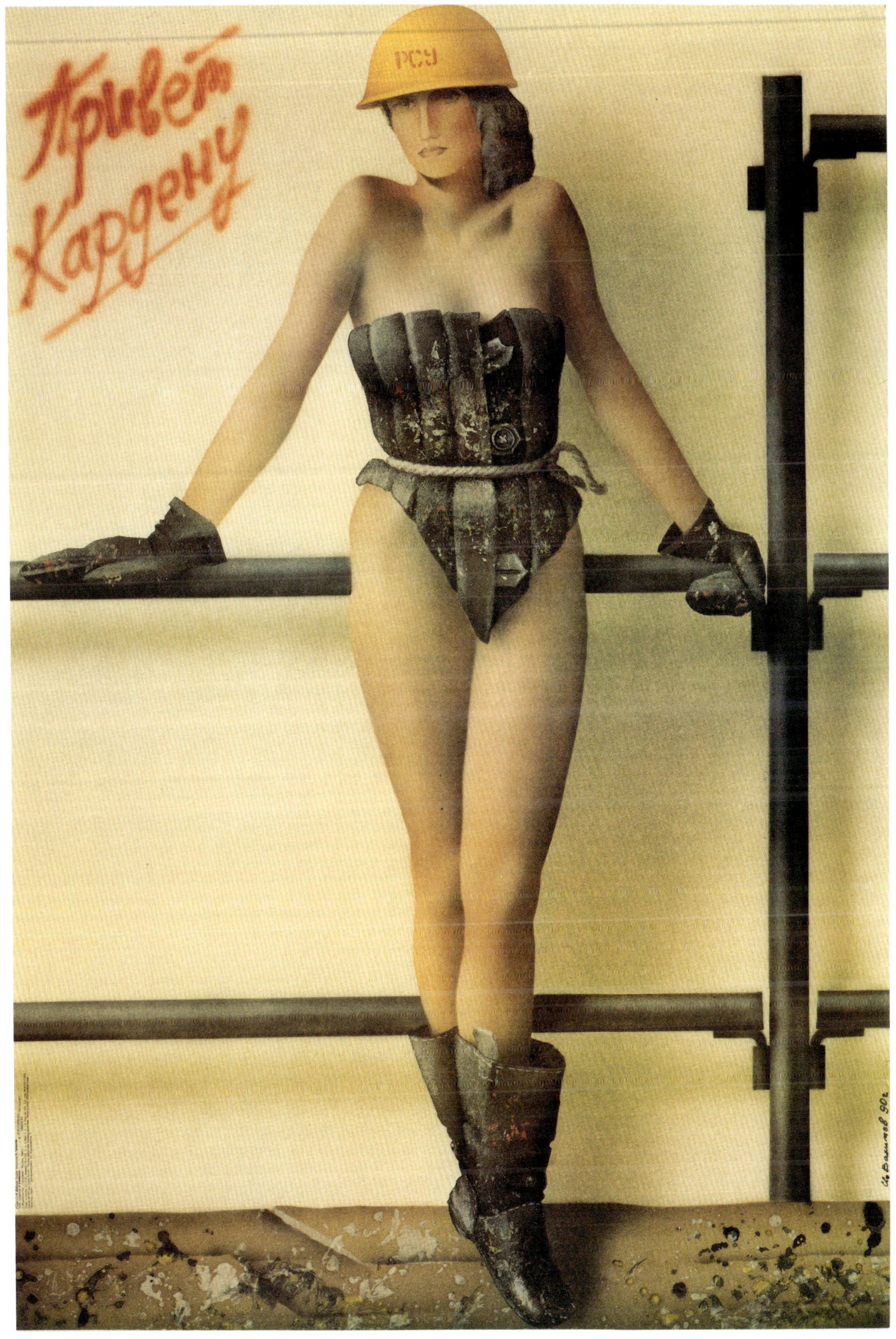
Привет
Кардену
РСУ

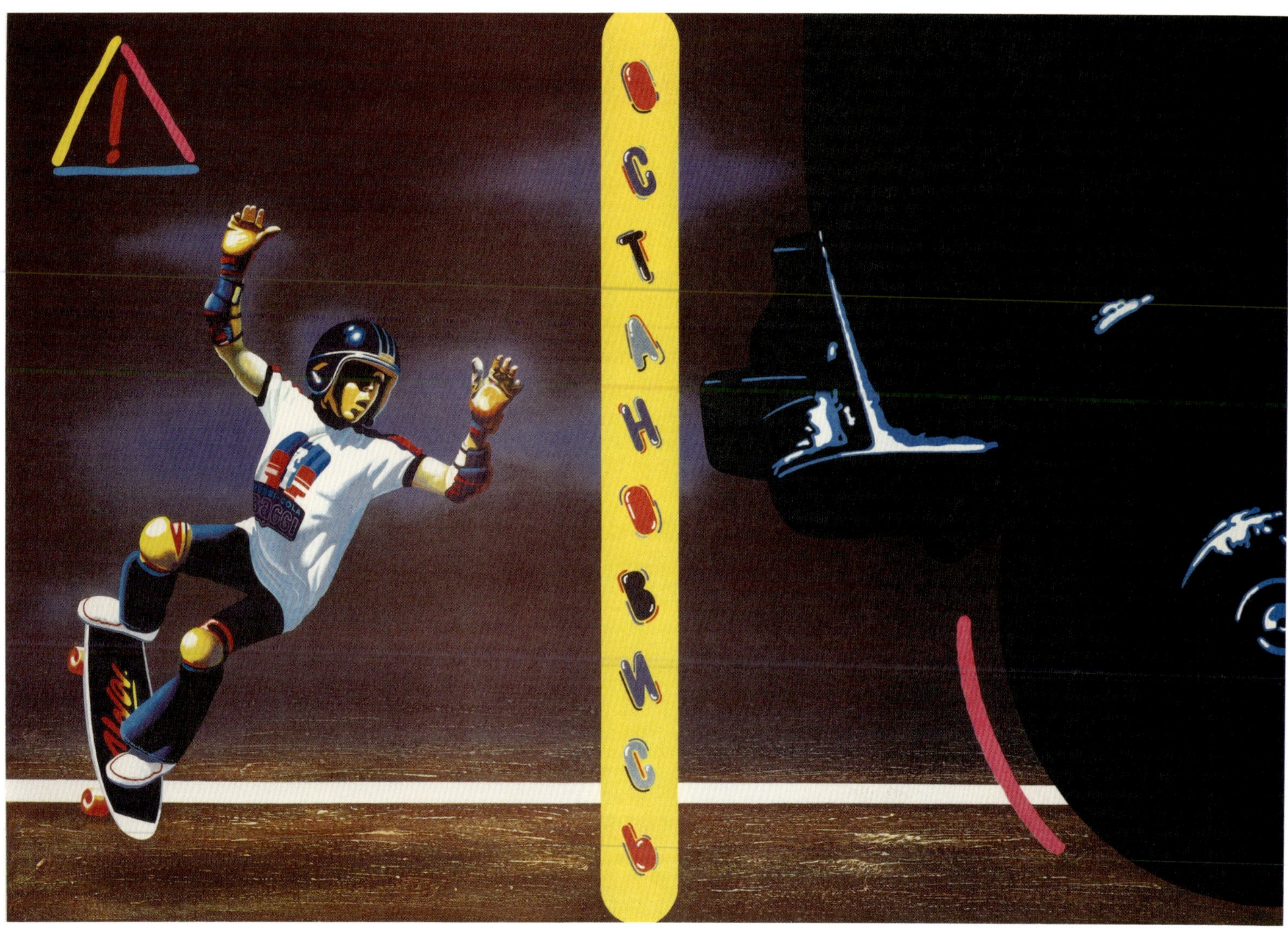

▲ С. Сухарев (S. Sukharev) | 1990

STOP
This poster was issued for a campaign to stop skateboarding in the street.

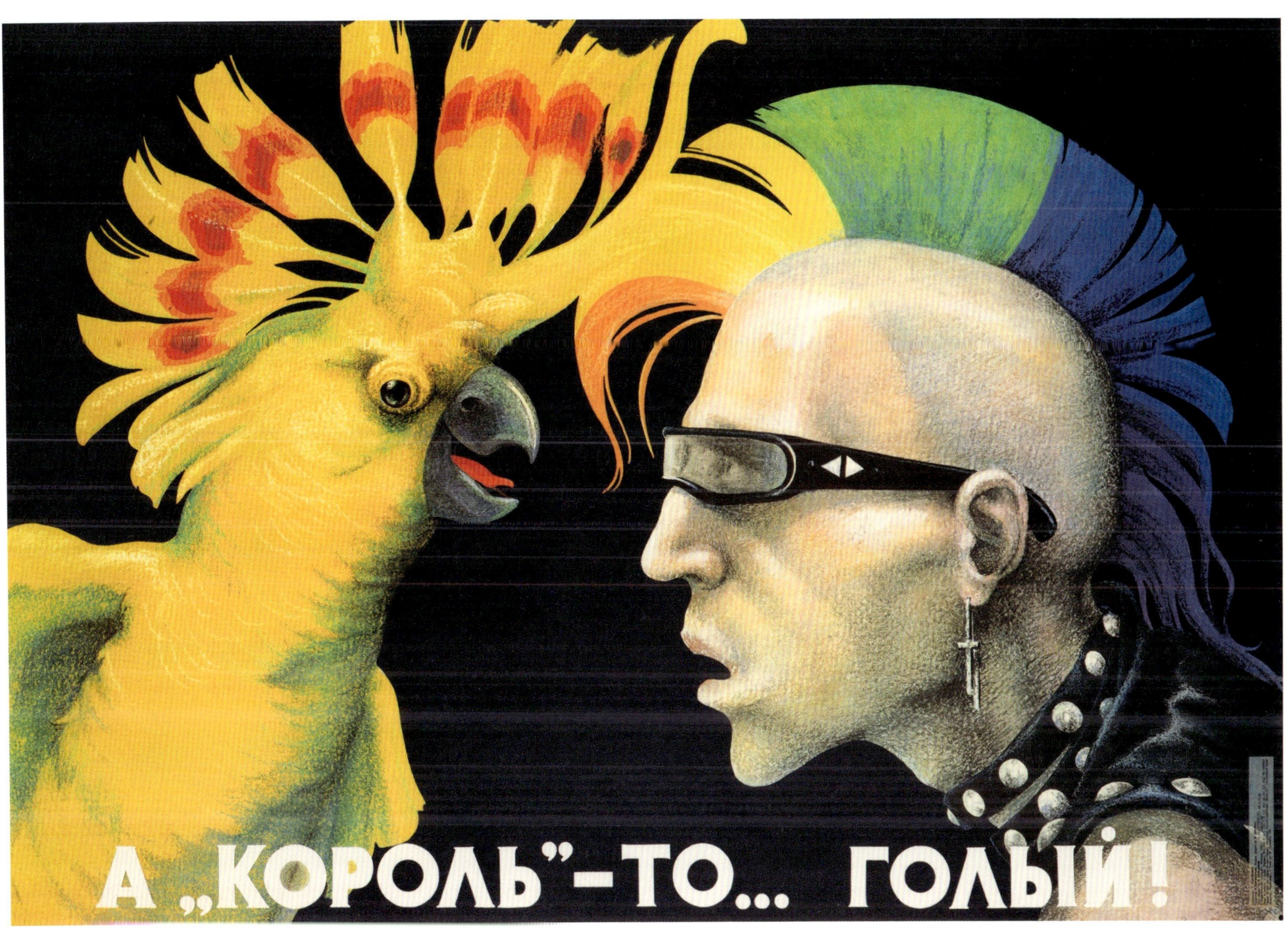

▲ Г. Ткаченко (G. Tkachenko) | 1989

BUT THE "EMPEROR" . . . HAS NO CLOTHES!
While this young punk seeks to stand out and project a notion of individualism to challenge the conformity of Soviet society, according to this poster, he is only emptily parroting his rebellious gesture from others and lacks the ability to effect true change.

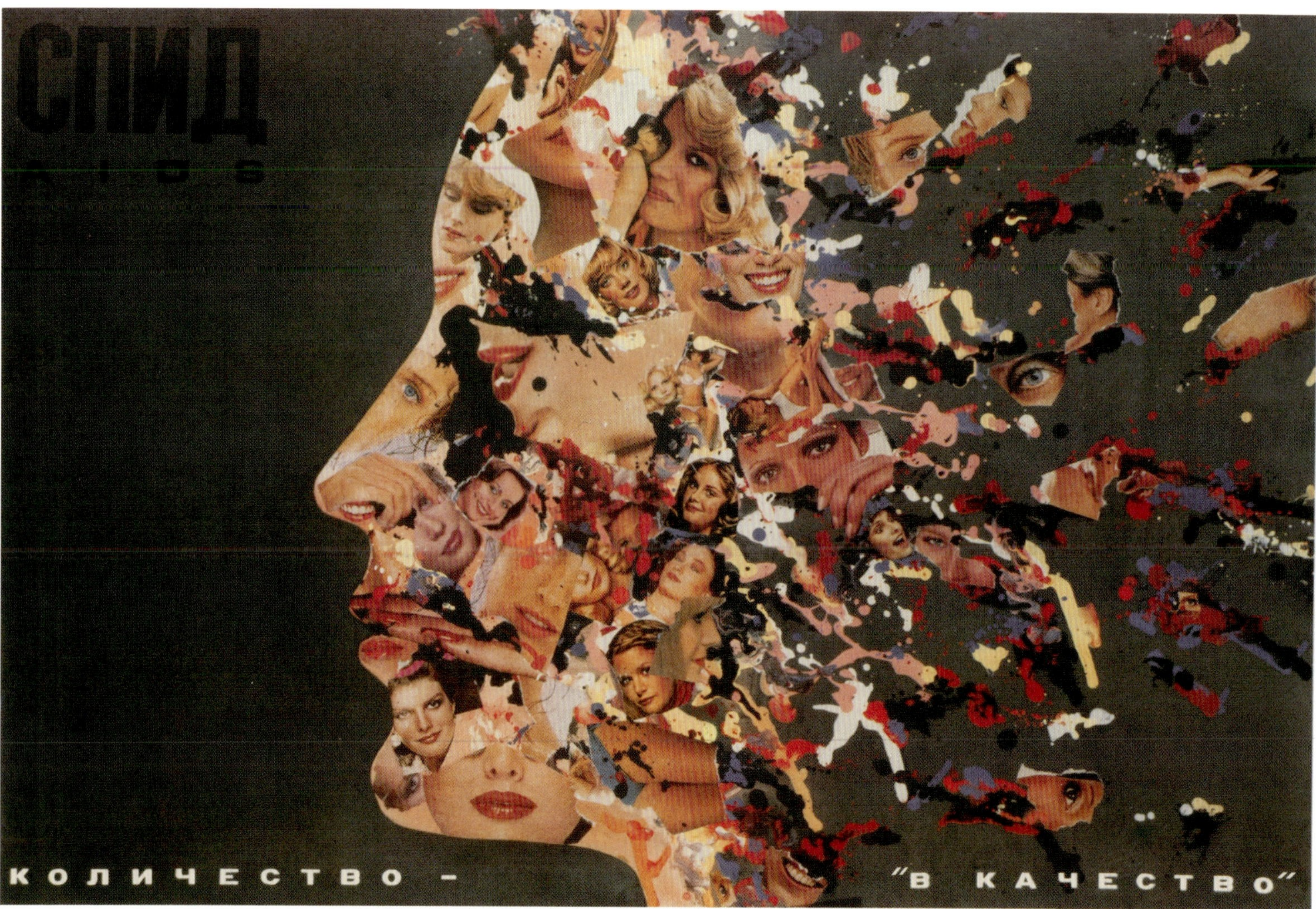

▲ Ю. Боксер (Y. Boxer) | 1989

AIDS (spelled out in both Russian and English) TURNS QUANTITY INTO "A QUALITY" In other words, the quantity of sexual partners could turn into the personal quality of having AIDS.

В. Валсамаки (V. Valsamaki), Н. Червоткин (N. Chervotkin), Г. Шлыков (G. Shlykov) | 1989 ➤

REMEMBER: AIDS IS CONTRACTED THROUGH CASUAL SEXUAL ENCOUNTERS. FAITH? HOPE? LOVE? Faith, Hope, and Love are all common Russian women's names.

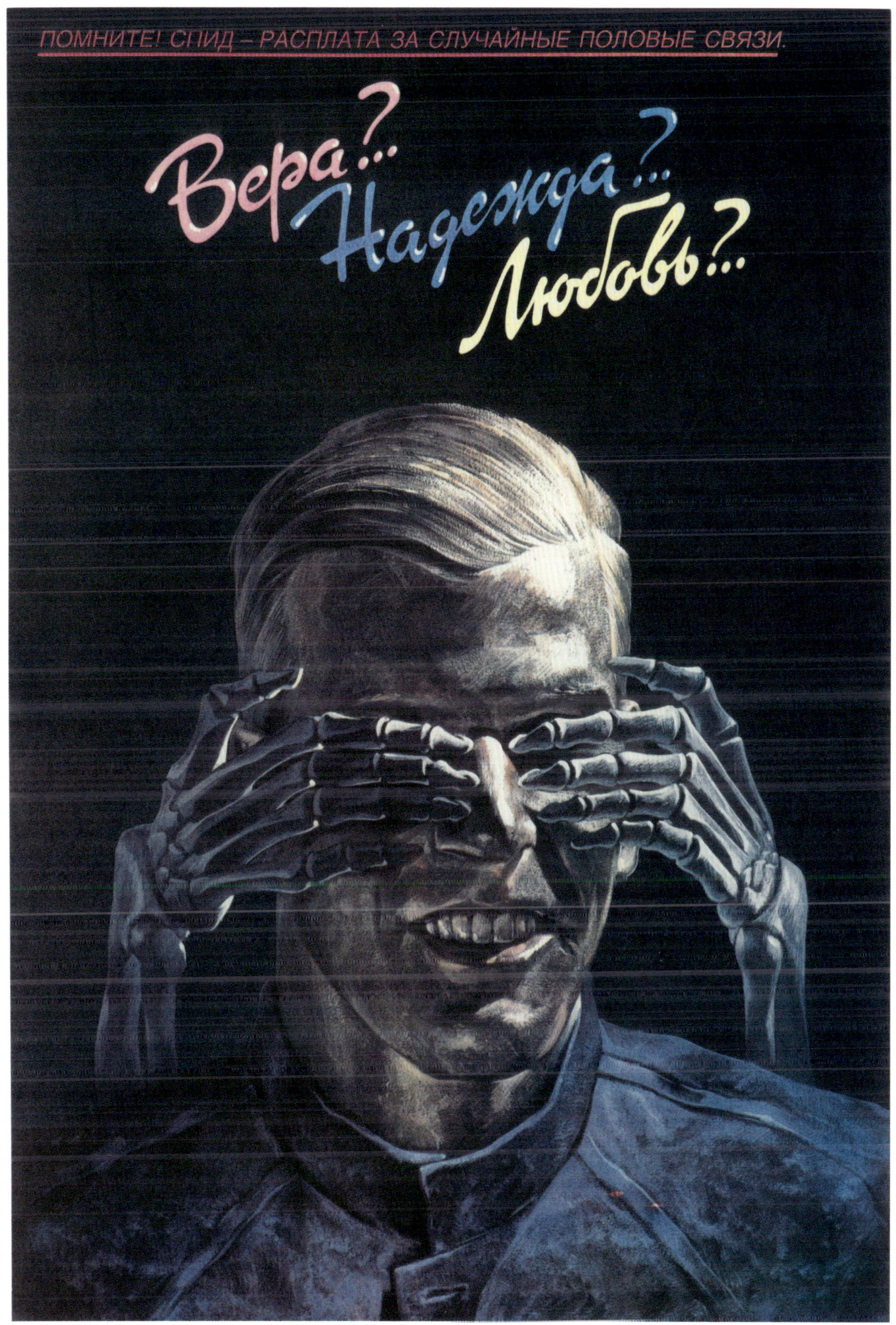
ПОМНИТЕ! СПИД – РАСПЛАТА ЗА СЛУЧАЙНЫЕ ПОЛОВЫЕ СВЯЗИ.
Вера?.. Надежда?.. Любовь?..

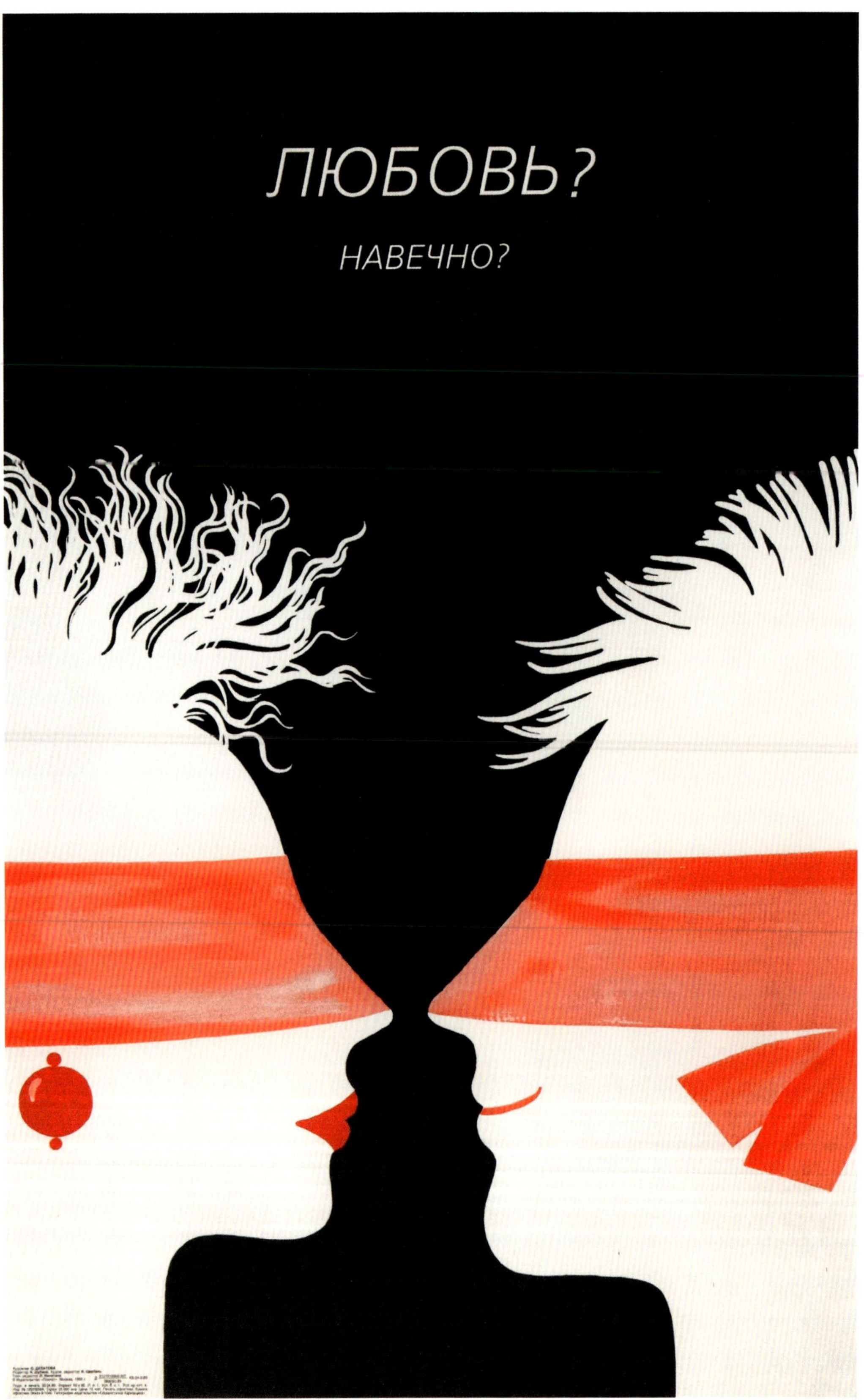

▲ О. Дулатова (O. Dulatova) | 1989

LOVE? FOREVER?

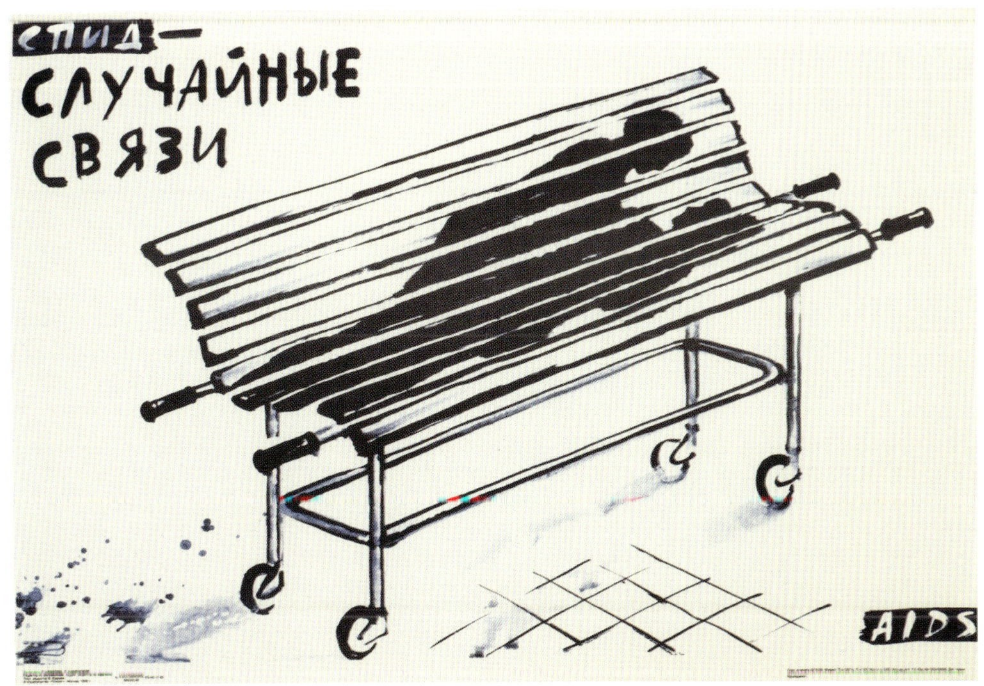

◂ Г. Немков (G. Nemkov) | 1989

AIDS COMES FROM CASUAL ENCOUNTERS

▾ О. Дулатова (O. Dulatova) | 1990

AIDS NEVER SLEEPS!
A harpy, harking back to Greek and Roman mythology, is shown with wings made up of syringes.

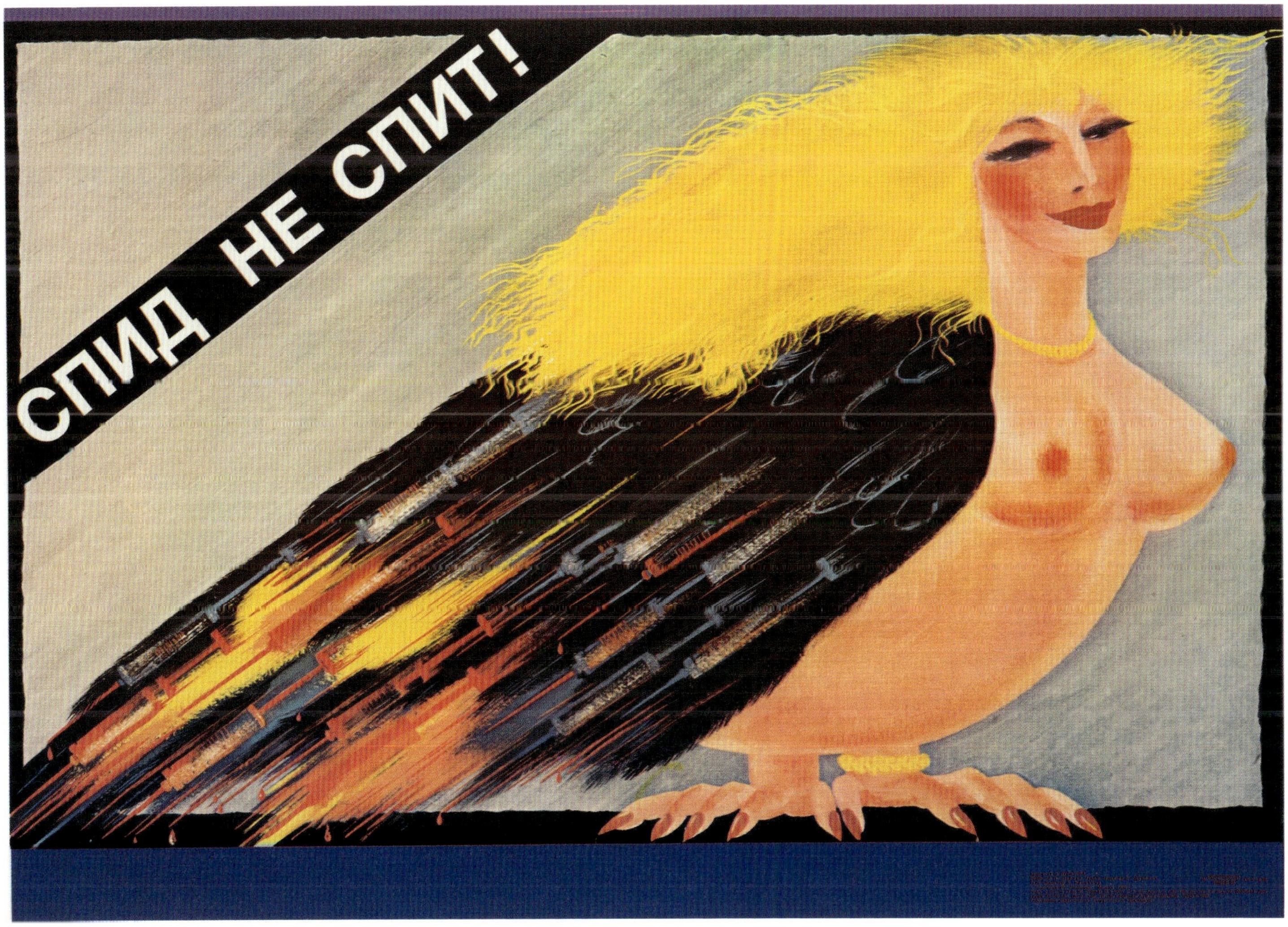

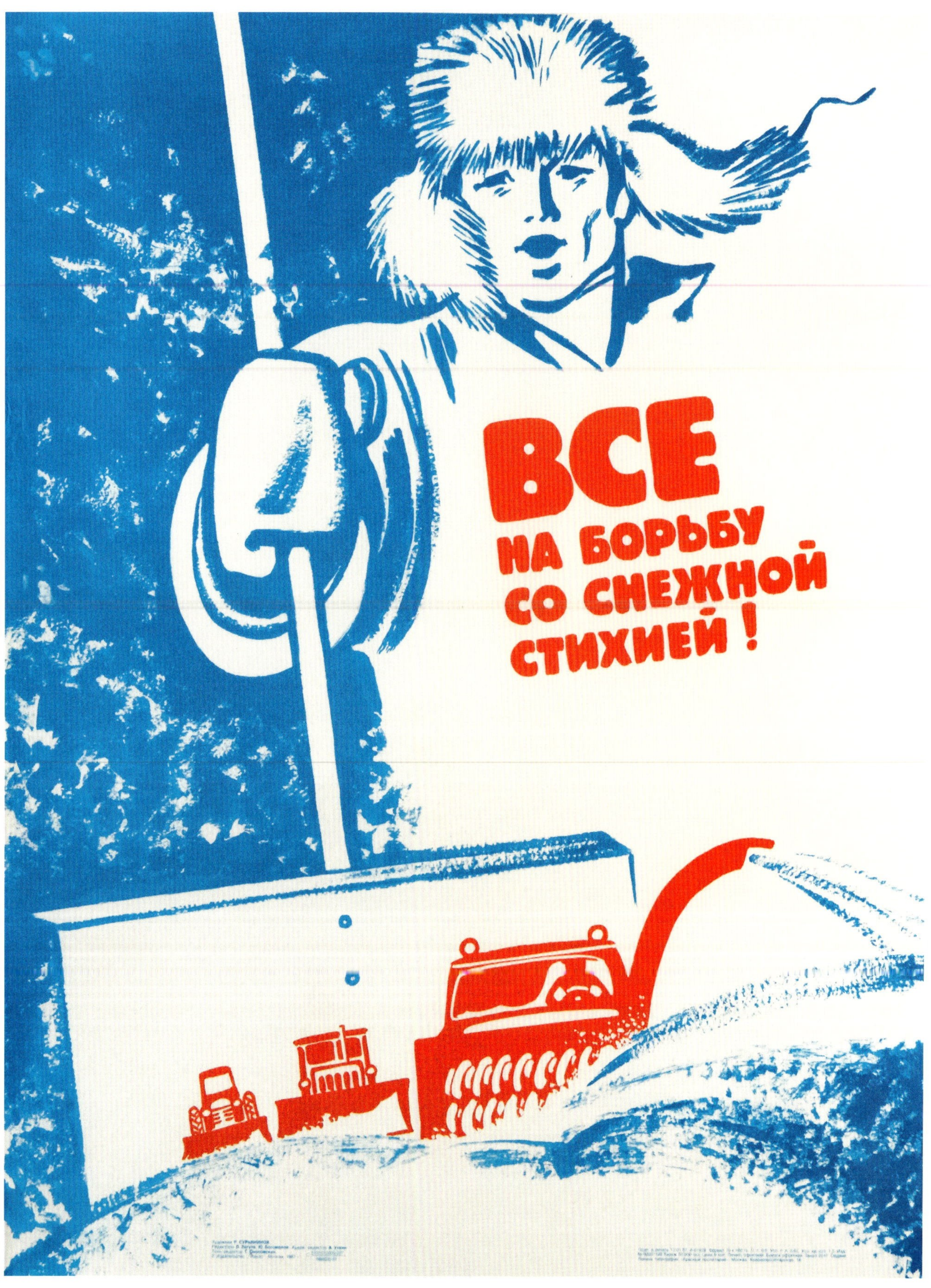
ВСЕ
НА БОРЬБУ
СО СНЕЖНОЙ
СТИХИЕЙ !

◂ Р. Сурьянинов (R. Suryaninov) | 1987

EVERYONE COME FIGHT THE WAR ON SNOW!

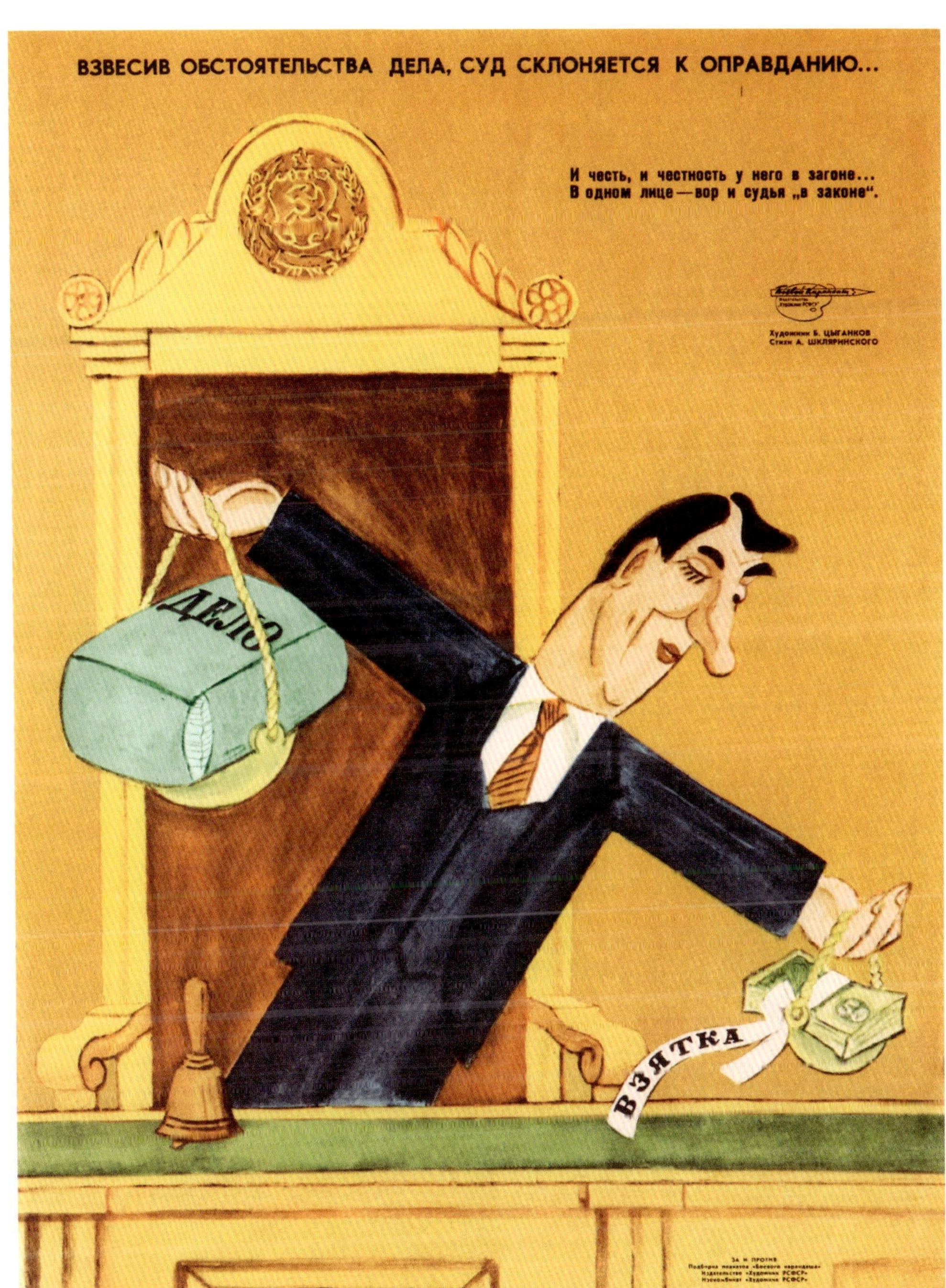

Б. Цыганков (B. Tsygankov) | n.d. ▸

Text along top: WEIGHING THE CIRCUMSTANCES OF THE CASE, THE COURT RULES NOT GUILTY . . . A judge, as the symbol of justice, balances CASE in one hand and BRIBE in the other. Despite weighing much less, the sheaf of bills clearly counts more than the case does. Text at upper right: HONOR AND HONESTY ARE TRAPPED . . . THERE IS THE SAME FACE FOR THE THIEF AND THE JUDGE "IN JUSTICE."

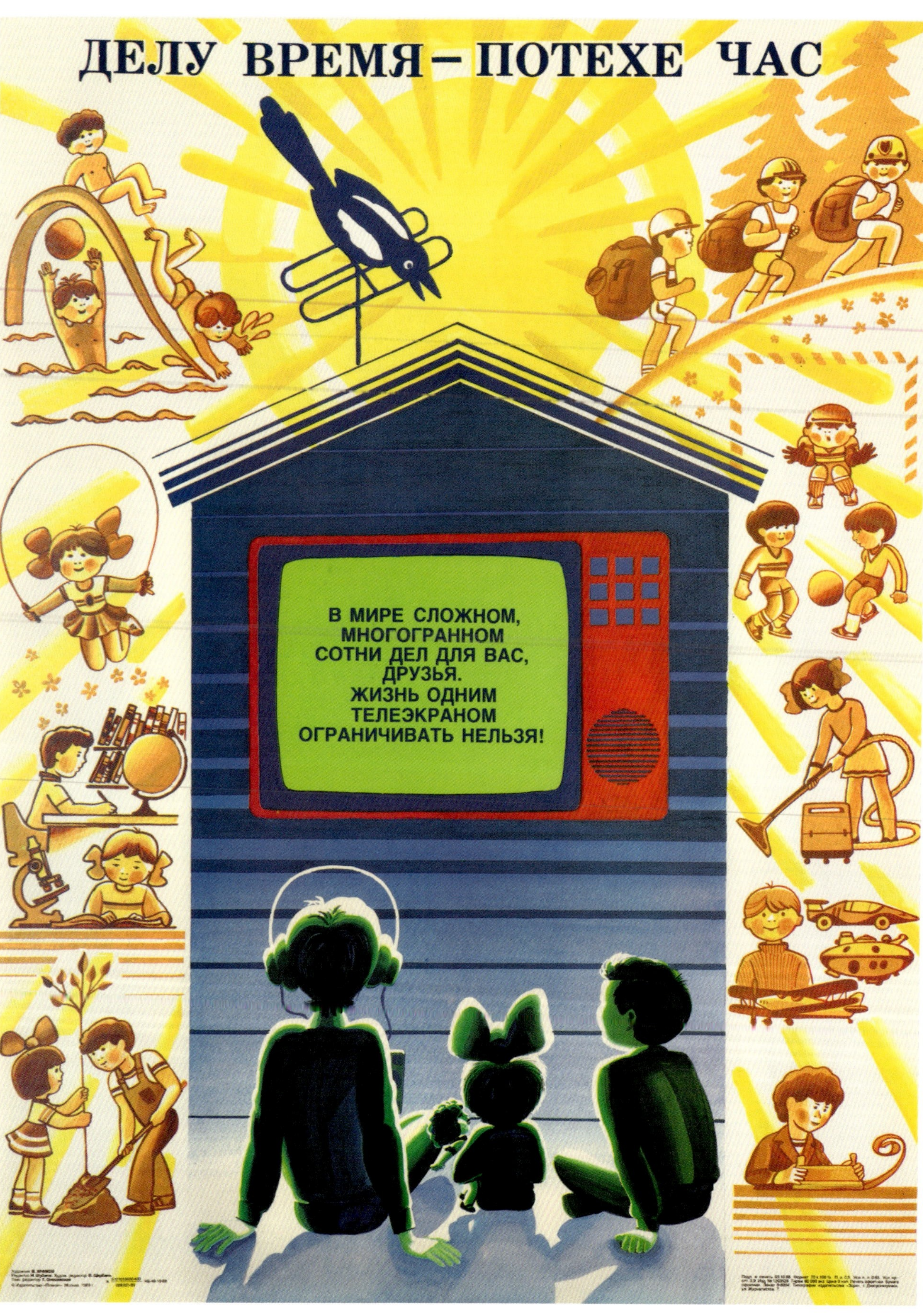
ДЕЛУ ВРЕМЯ – ПОТЕХЕ ЧАС
В МИРЕ СЛОЖНОМ,
МНОГОГРАННОМ
СОТНИ ДЕЛ ДЛЯ ВАС,
ДРУЗЬЯ.
ЖИЗНЬ ОДНИМ
ТЕЛЕЭКРАНОМ
ОГРАНИЧИВАТЬ НЕЛЬЗЯ!

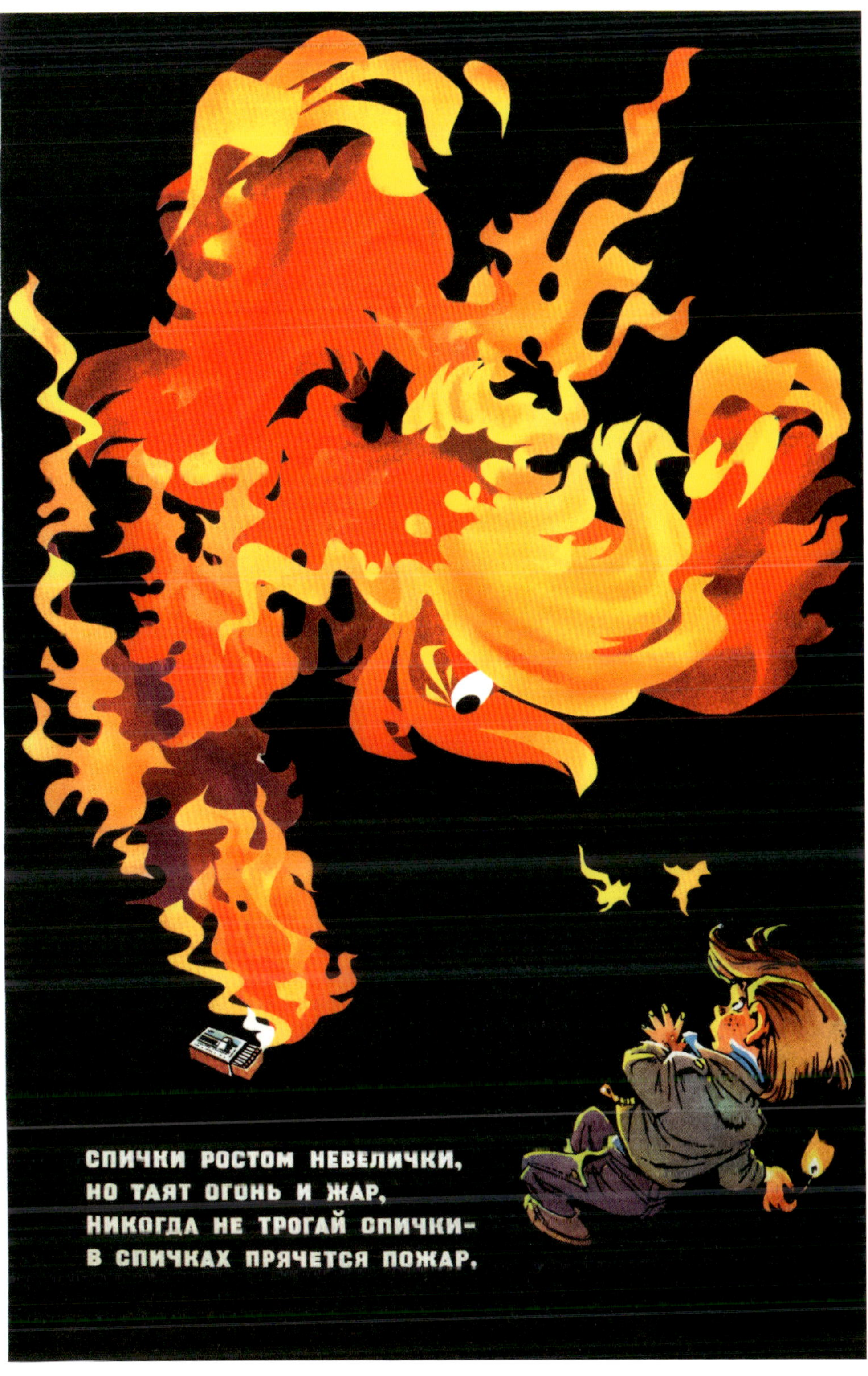

◀ В. Храмов (V. Khramov) | 1989

Text along top:
HAVE YOUR FUN WHEN WORK IS DONE
Text on the television screen: IN THIS COMPLEX, BUSY WORLD, THERE'S SO MUCH FOR YOU TO DO. DON'T JUST SPEND ALL OF YOUR TIME SITTING, STARING AT THE TUBE!

▲ Мигунов (E. Migunov) | 1989

ALTHOUGH MATCHES ARE QUITE SLIGHT,
IN THEIR HEARTS THEY HIDE A HEAT,
TOUCHING MATCHES WILL BACKFIRE,
FOR INSIDE THEY HIDE A FIRE.

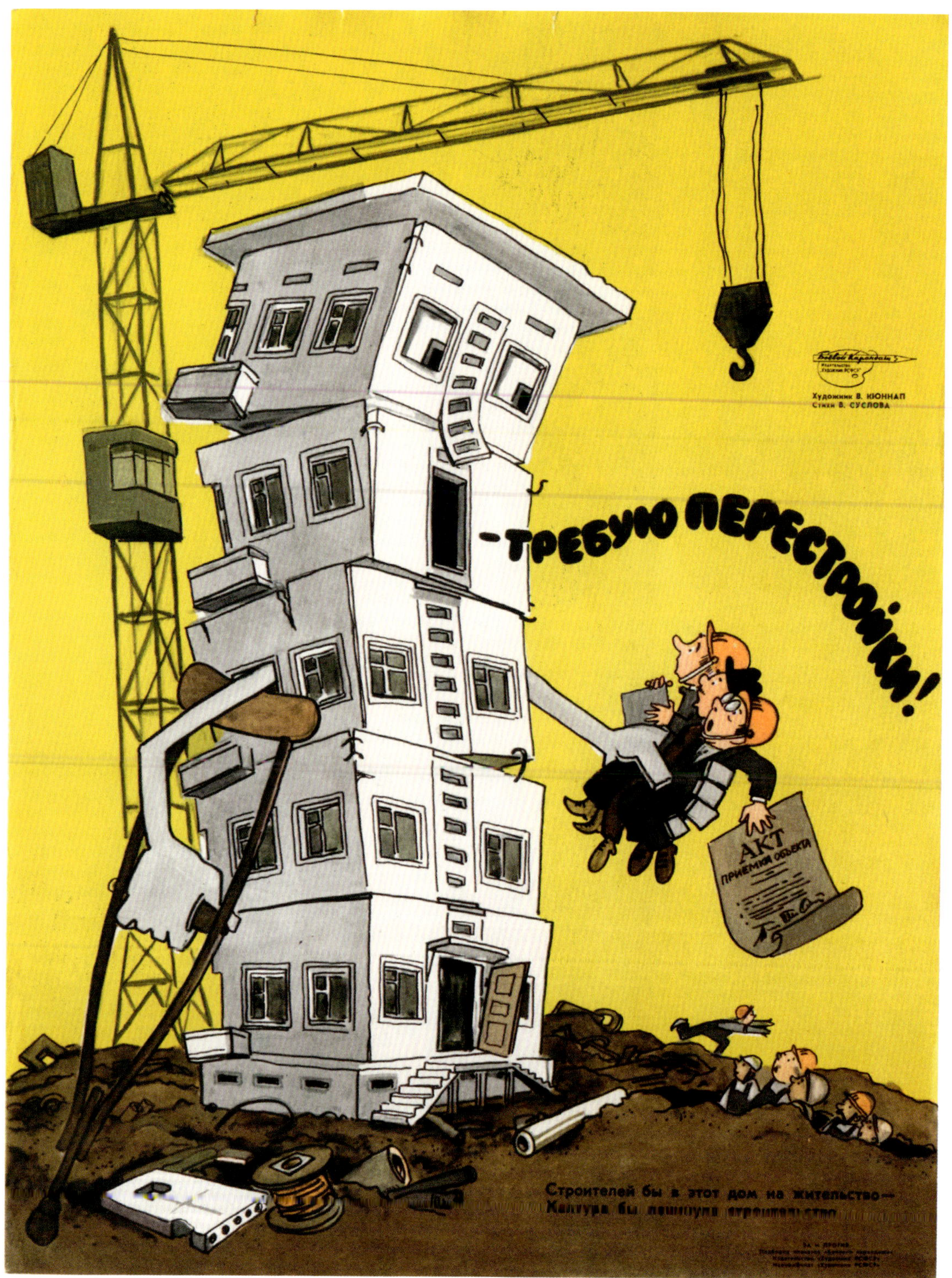

▲ В. Кюннап (V. Kunnap) | n.d.

The builders hold their construction contract, but the rickety, teetering building protests: I DEMAND PERESTROIKA! Text at bottom right: WE NEED TO MAKE THE CONTRACTORS LIVE IN THIS BUILDING, SO THAT MAYBE WE COULD GET RID OF HACKWORK.

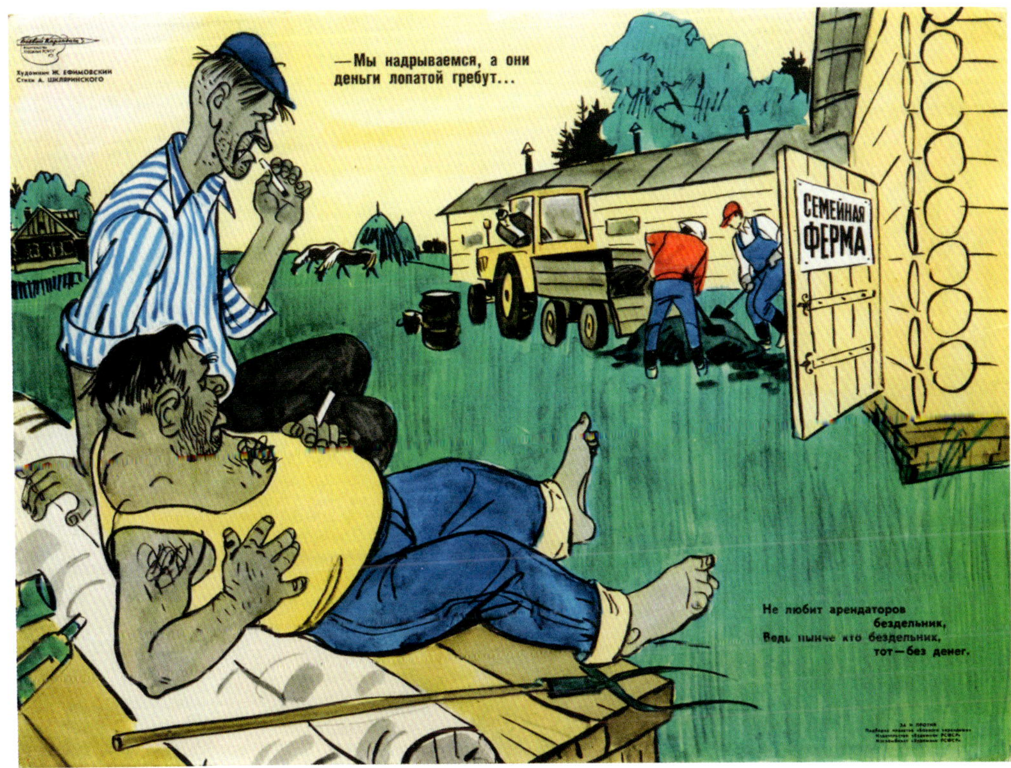

Ж. Ефимовский (J. Efimovsky) | n.d.

WE'RE BREAKING OUR BACKS HERE WHILE THOSE GUYS JUST SHOVEL IN THE CASH . . . Two idlers enviously observe a family who has received a lease for working private land for themselves. The sign on the barn door reads: FAMILY FARM. Text at bottom right: THE IDLERS DON'T SEEM TO LIKE THE RENTERS THAT THEY MEET BECAUSE TODAY, IF YOU DON'T WORK, THEN YOU CAN'T EAT

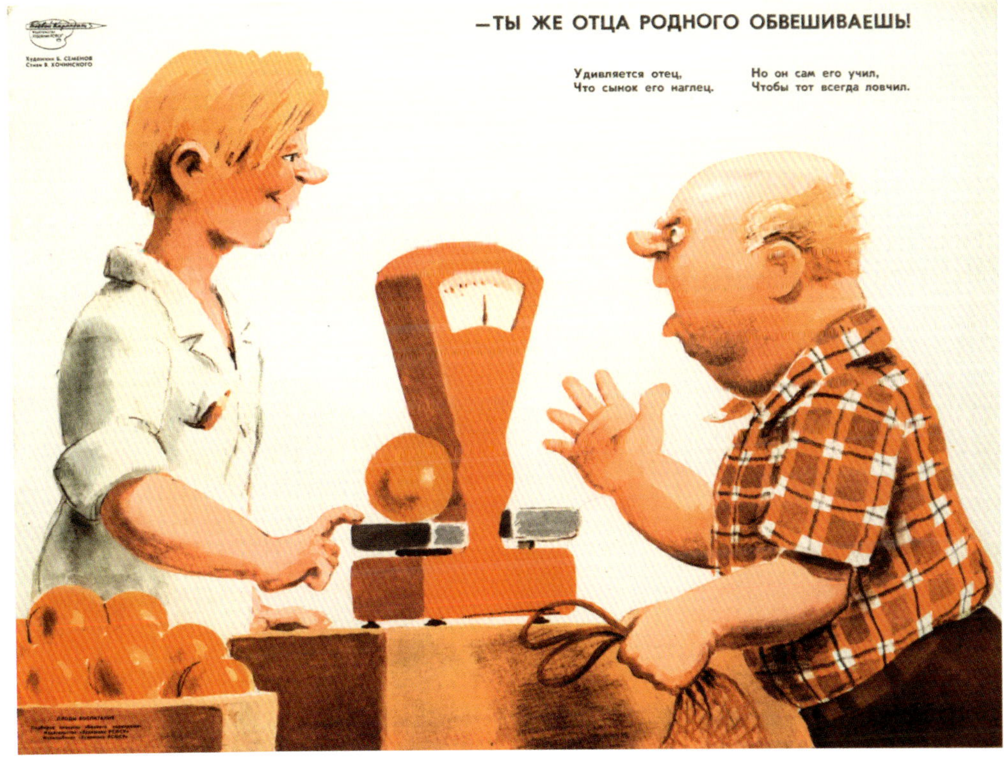

Б. Семенов (B. Semenov) | 1990

YOU'RE SWINDLING YOUR OWN FATHER!
A sales person weighs an orange, but presses his finger on the scale.
NOW THE FATHER IS SURPRISED
THAT HIS SON IS A BAD GUY
BUT HE WAS THE ONE WHO TAUGHT HIM
HOW TO CHEAT AND HOW TO LIE.

M. Мазрухо (M. Mazruho) | n.d ➤

Text across torn document:
PROPERTY SETTLEMENT
Text across the top:
DON'T MAKE YOUR CHILD'S LIFE INTO HELL /
AS THOUGH YOUR DIVORCE WERE HIS FAULT

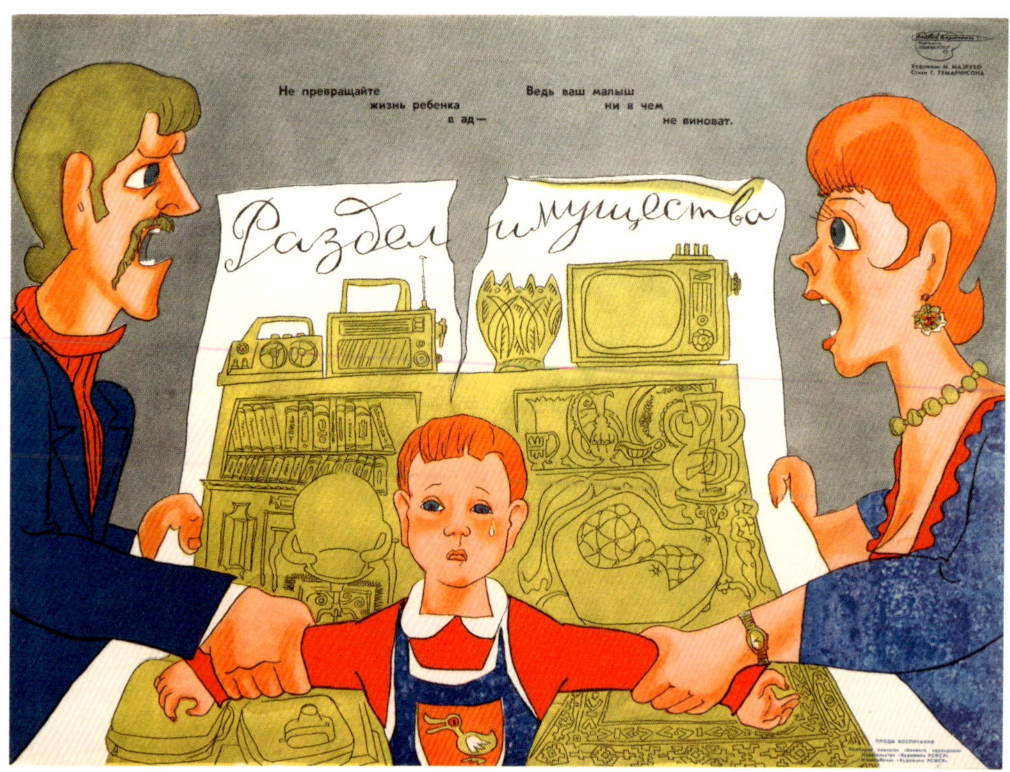

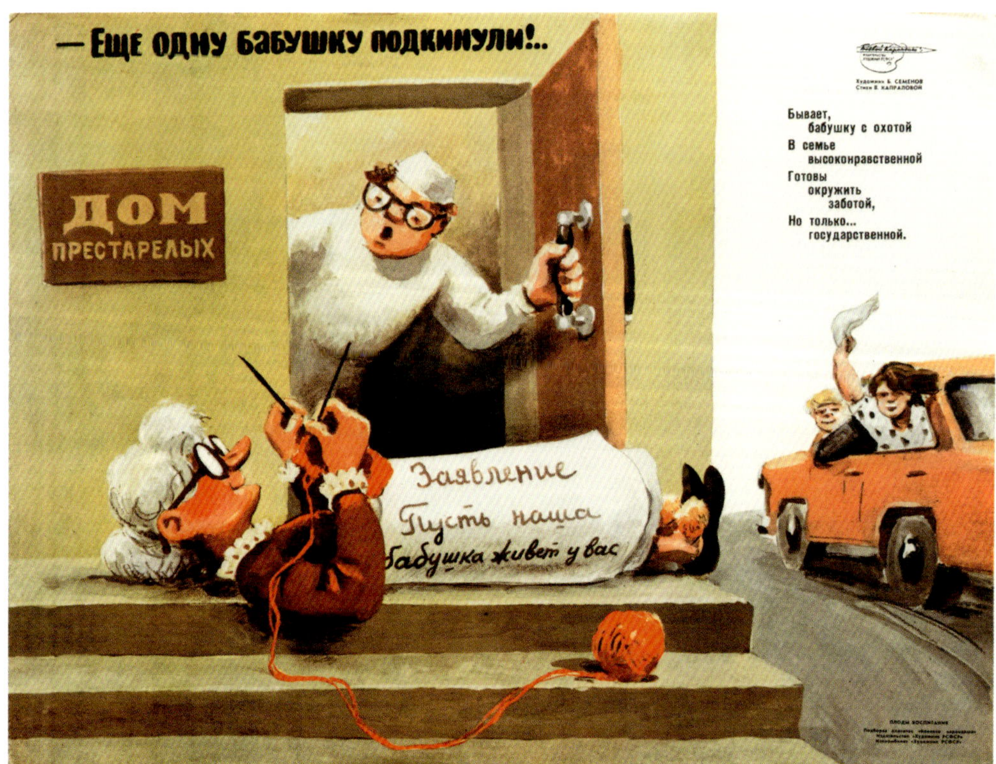

◂ Б. Семенов (B. Semenov) | n.d.

Text along top: SOMEONE DROPPED OFF ANOTHER GRANNY! Text on sign: OLD FOLKS' HOME. Scripted on her paper garment: PLEASE LET OUR GRANDMOTHER LIVE WITH YOU
Text at right: GOOD FAMILIES CAN BE PREPARED
TO TREAT THE ELDERLY WITH CARE
PROVIDE THEM WITH THE LOVE AND TIME
THAT THEY CAN GET ON THE STATE'S DIME

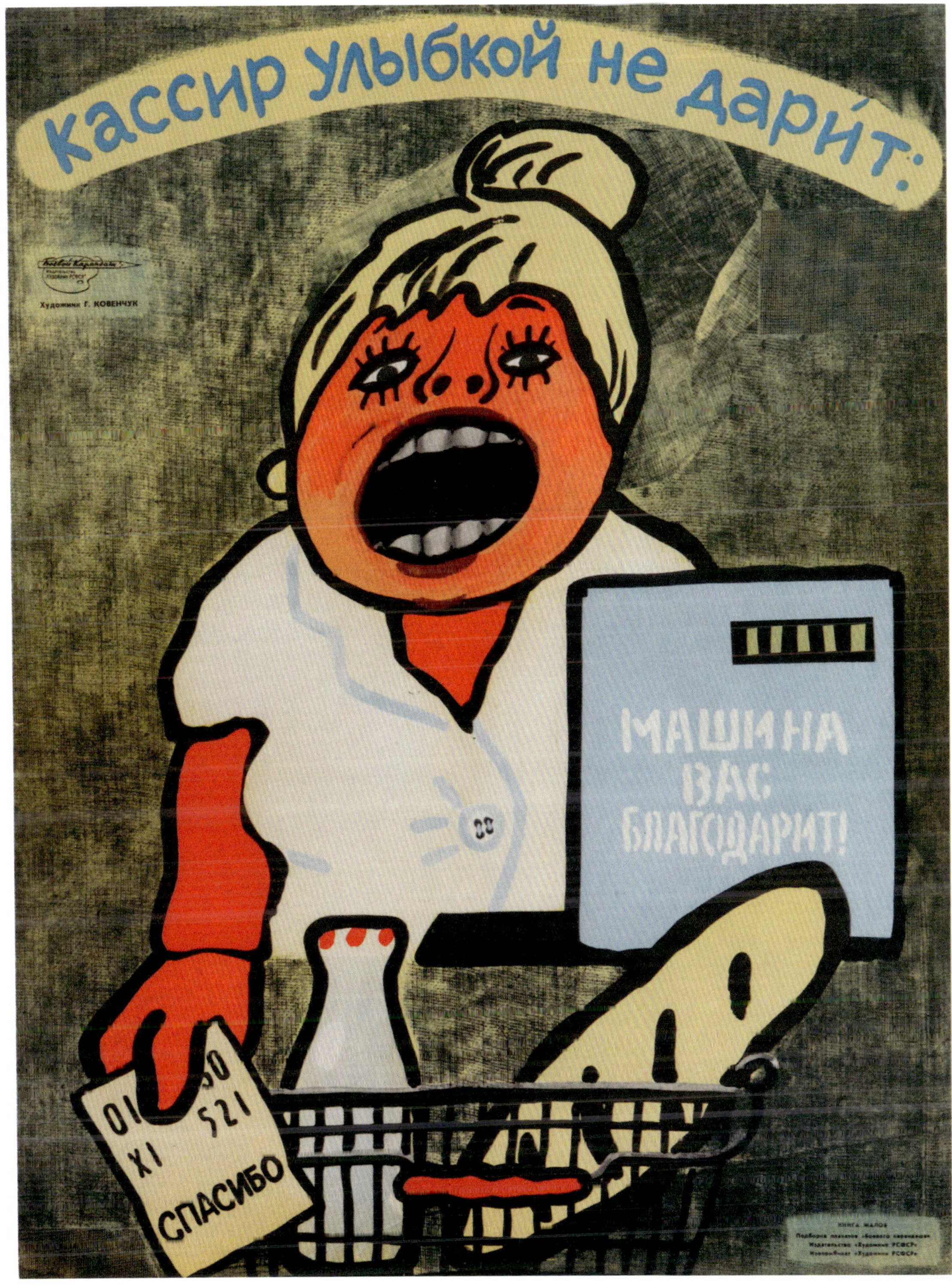

Г. Ковенчук (G. Covenchuk) | n.d. ▲

Text combined above cashier and on cash register:
WHEN THE CASHIER IS IN A BAD MOOD: THE MACHINE GIVES YOU GRATITUDE!
Text on receipt: THANK YOU

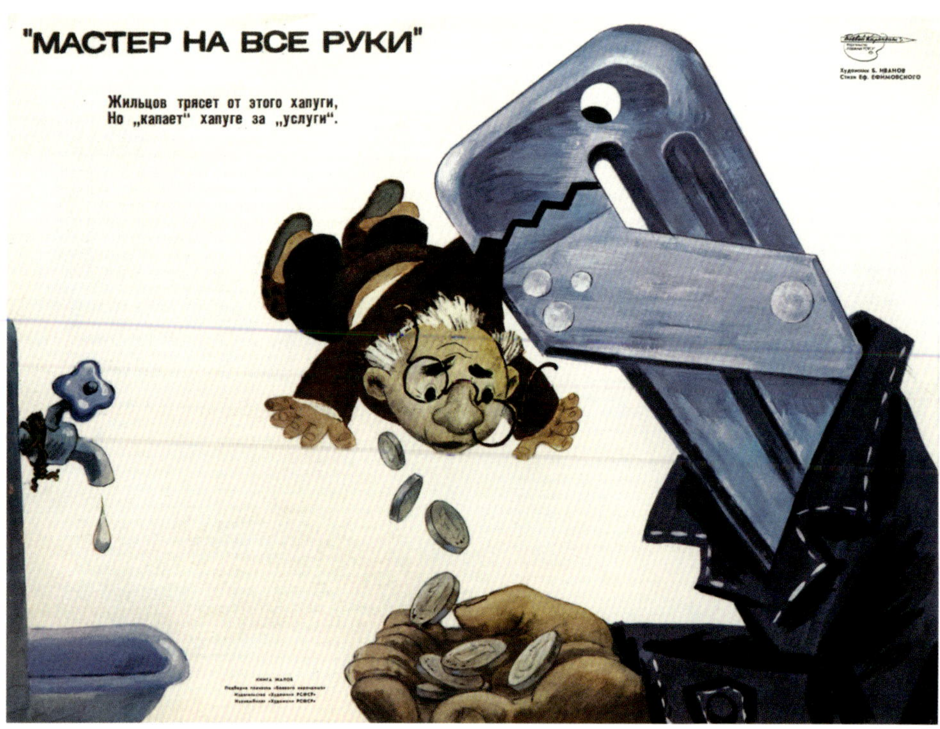

◂ Б. Иванов (B. Ivanov) | n.d.

Text at top left: "JACK OF ALL TRADES"
THIS "SUPER" MAKES THE RESIDENTS ALL SHAKE IN FEAR
SHAKING THEM DOWN INSTEAD OF DOING THEIR REPAIRS

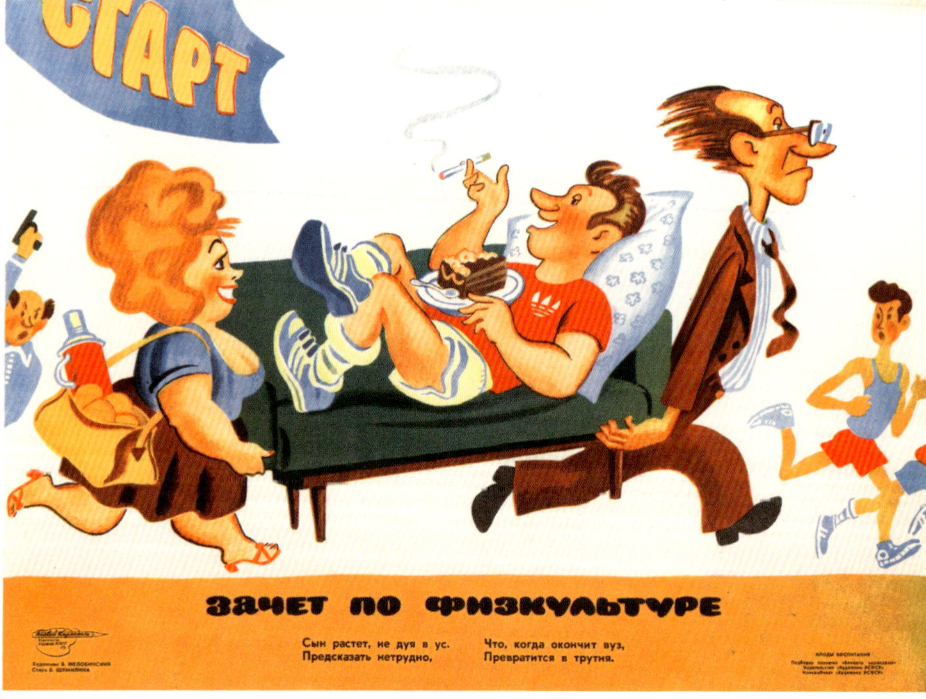

◂ В. Желобинский (V. Zhelobinsky) | n.d.

PHYSICAL FITNESS TEST
THE GROWING BOY DOESN'T DO MUCH
IT'S NOT HARD TO SEE
WHEN THEY GIVE HIM HIS DEGREE
HE'LL BECOME A MOOCH
Text on banner at top left: START

В. Кюннап (V. Kunnap) | n.d. ▸

Text along top: SCHOOL MANUFACTURING APPRENTICESHIP WORKSHOP
Text at bottom: THE ROBOT WON'T ALLOW THE STUDENT IN THE FACTORY. HIS GRADES ARE SIMPLY TOO UNSATISFACTORY.
"IF YOUR SCHOOL PROGRAM IS TOO MUCH, IT IS A SIGN YOU PROBABLY WON'T MANAGE HERE WITH MINE."

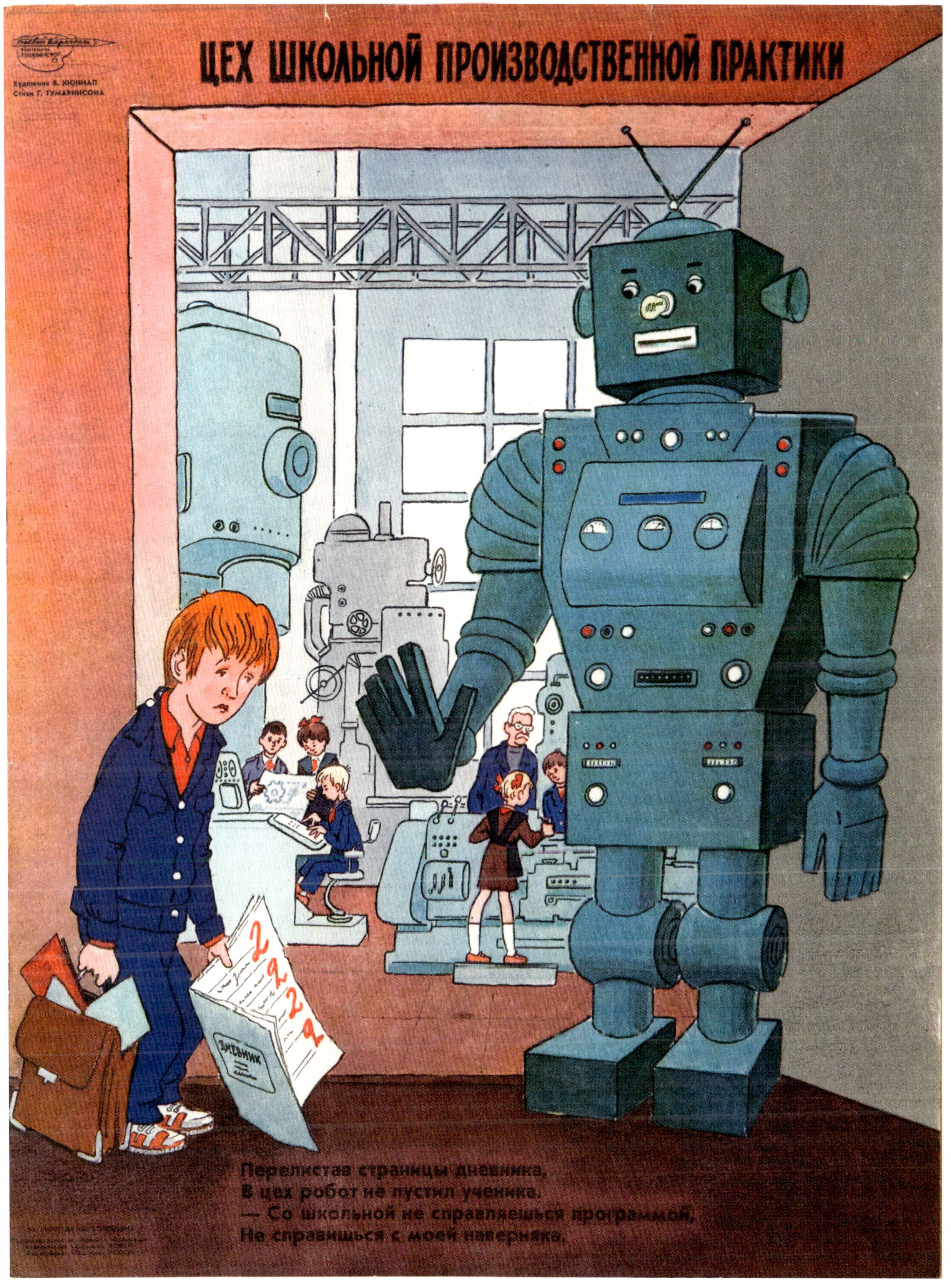
ЦЕХ ШКОЛЬНОЙ ПРОИЗВОДСТВЕННОЙ ПРАКТИКИ
Художник В. КЮННАП
Стихи Г. ТУМАРИНСОНА
ДНЕВНИК
Перелистав страницы дневника,
В цех робот не пустил ученика.
— Со школьной не справляешься программой,
Не справишься с моей наверняка.

SUBSTANCE ABUSE

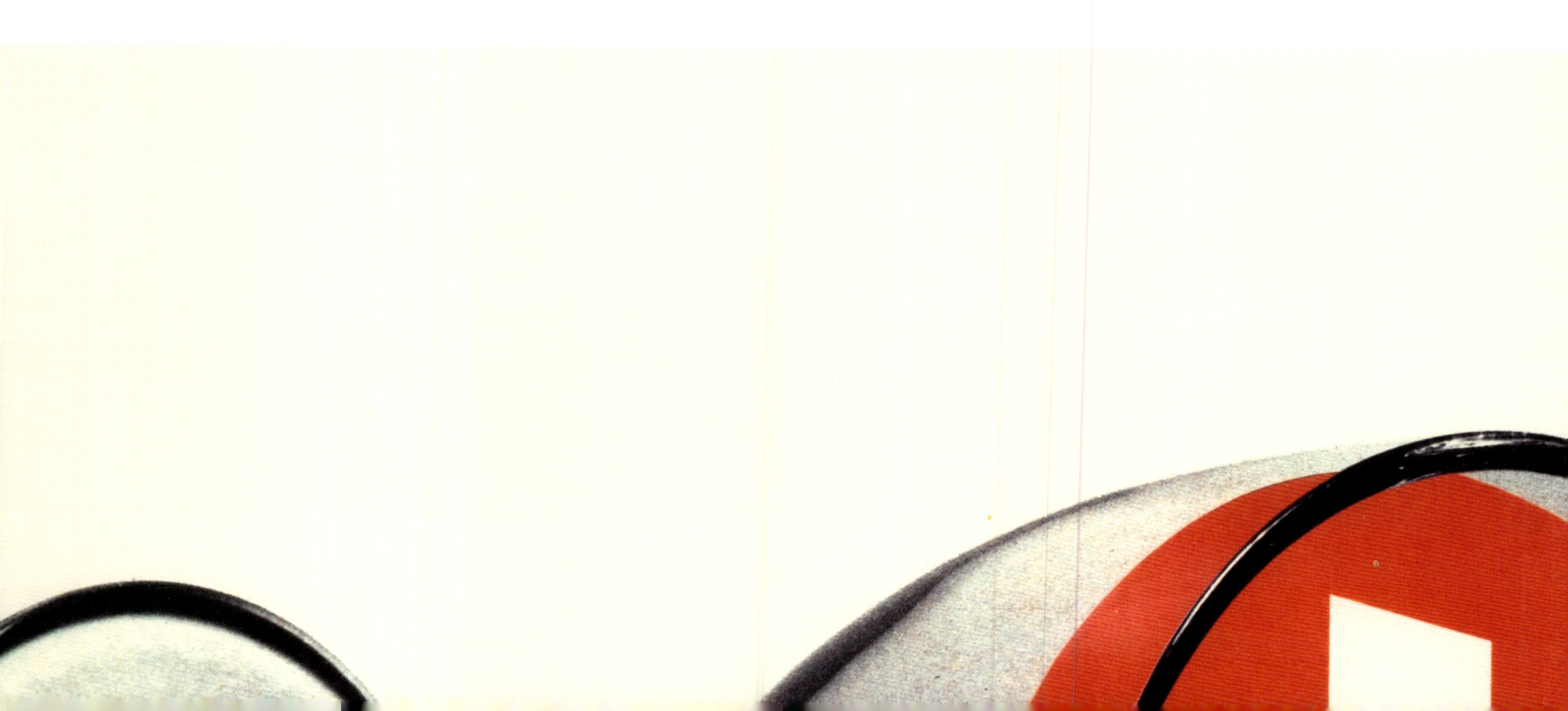

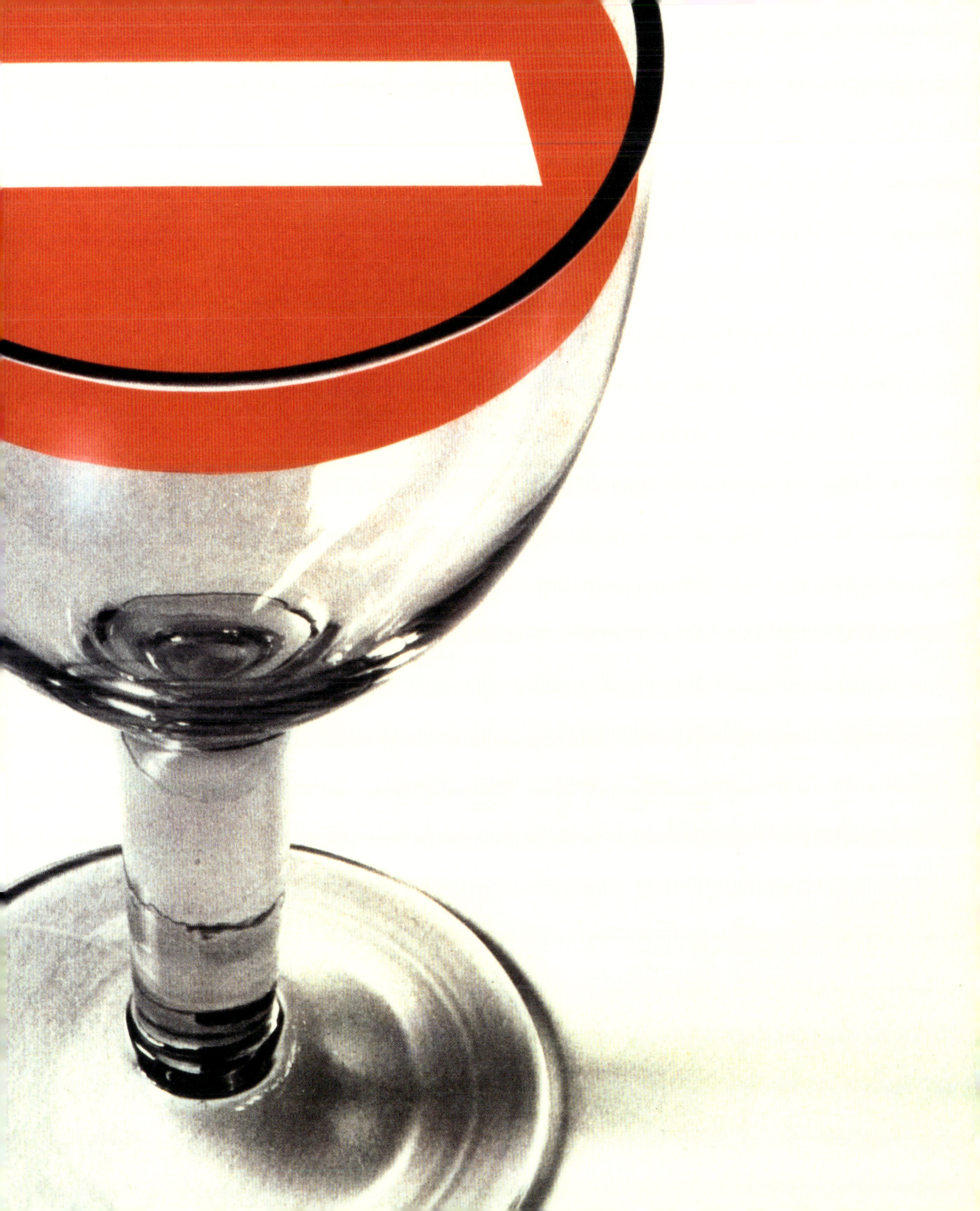

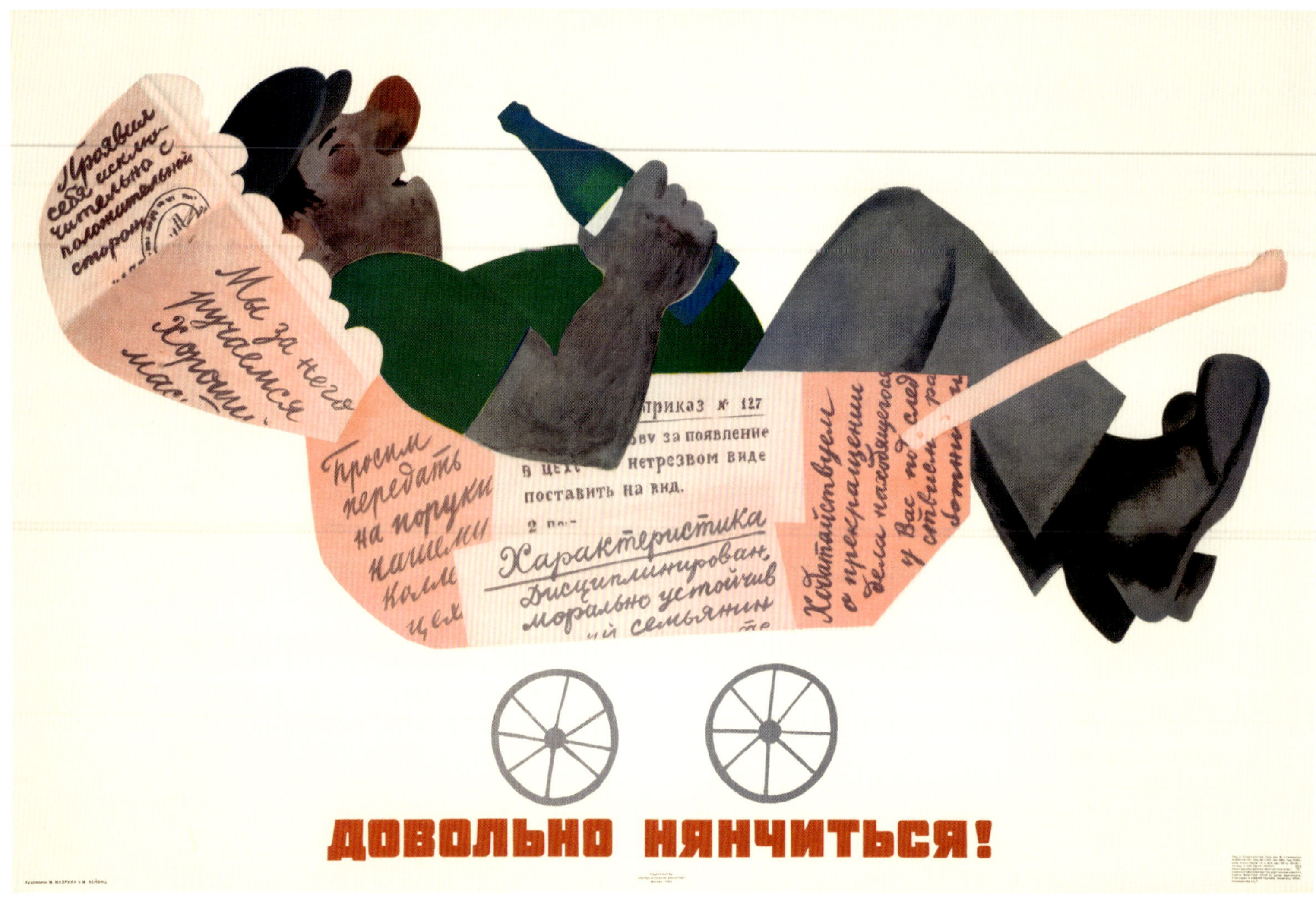

▲ М. Мазруха (M. Mazruha) | 1973

STOP THE CODDLING!
Someone has covered this baby carriage in fragments from reference letters sardonically describing this job candidate as "disciplined," "morally stable," and that "he displays exceptionally good conduct."

Л. Помянский (L. Pomiansky) | 1988 ▶

WINE TURNS MEN BOVINE AND BESTIAL . . .
—F. M. DOSTOEVSKY

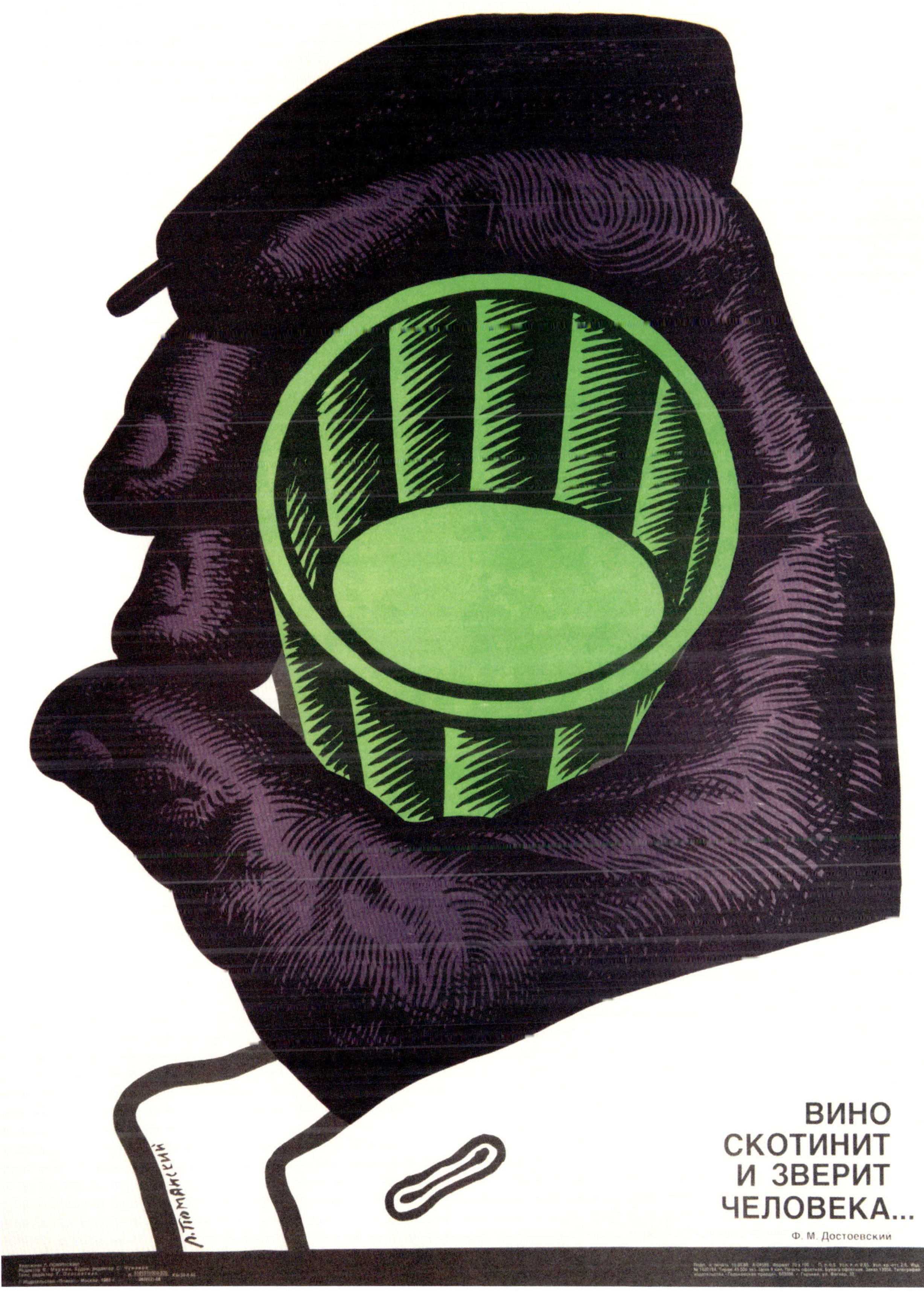
ВИНО
СКОТИНИТ
И ЗВЕРИТ
ЧЕЛОВЕКА...
Ф. М. Достоевский
Л. ТОМАНСКИЙ

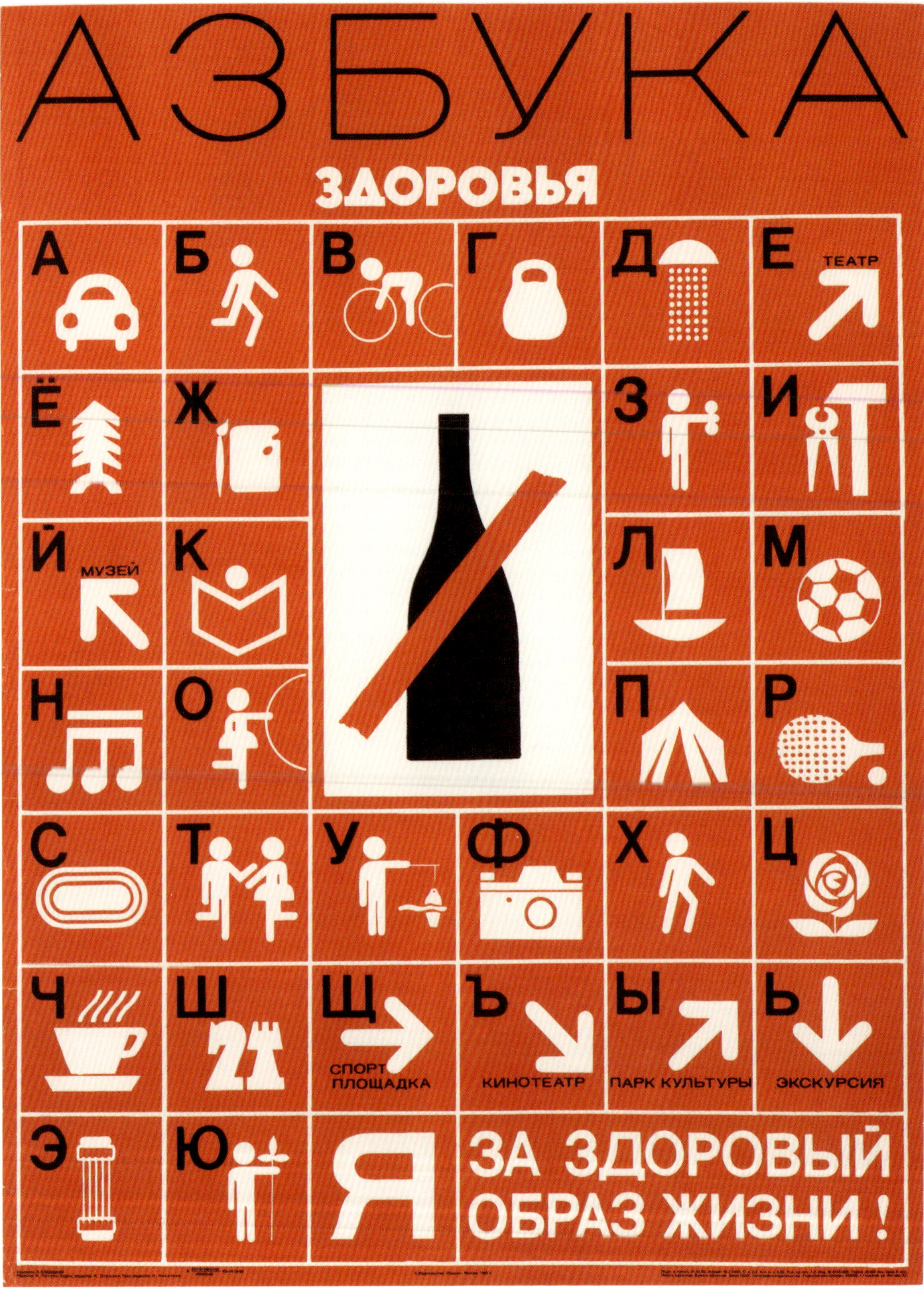

Л. Клевицкий (L. Klevitsky) | 1989

Text along top: THE ABCS OF HEALTH; text at bottom: FOR A HEALTHY LIFESTYLE! The letters in the Cyrillic alphabet that do not come at the beginning of the names of healthy activities feature arrows directing viewers to go to outdoor recreation areas, movie theaters, parks of culture, and on guided tours.

Н. Свиридов (N. Sviridov) | 1988

ABSENTEEISM IS LABOR DESERTION
The label on the bottle reads: WINE

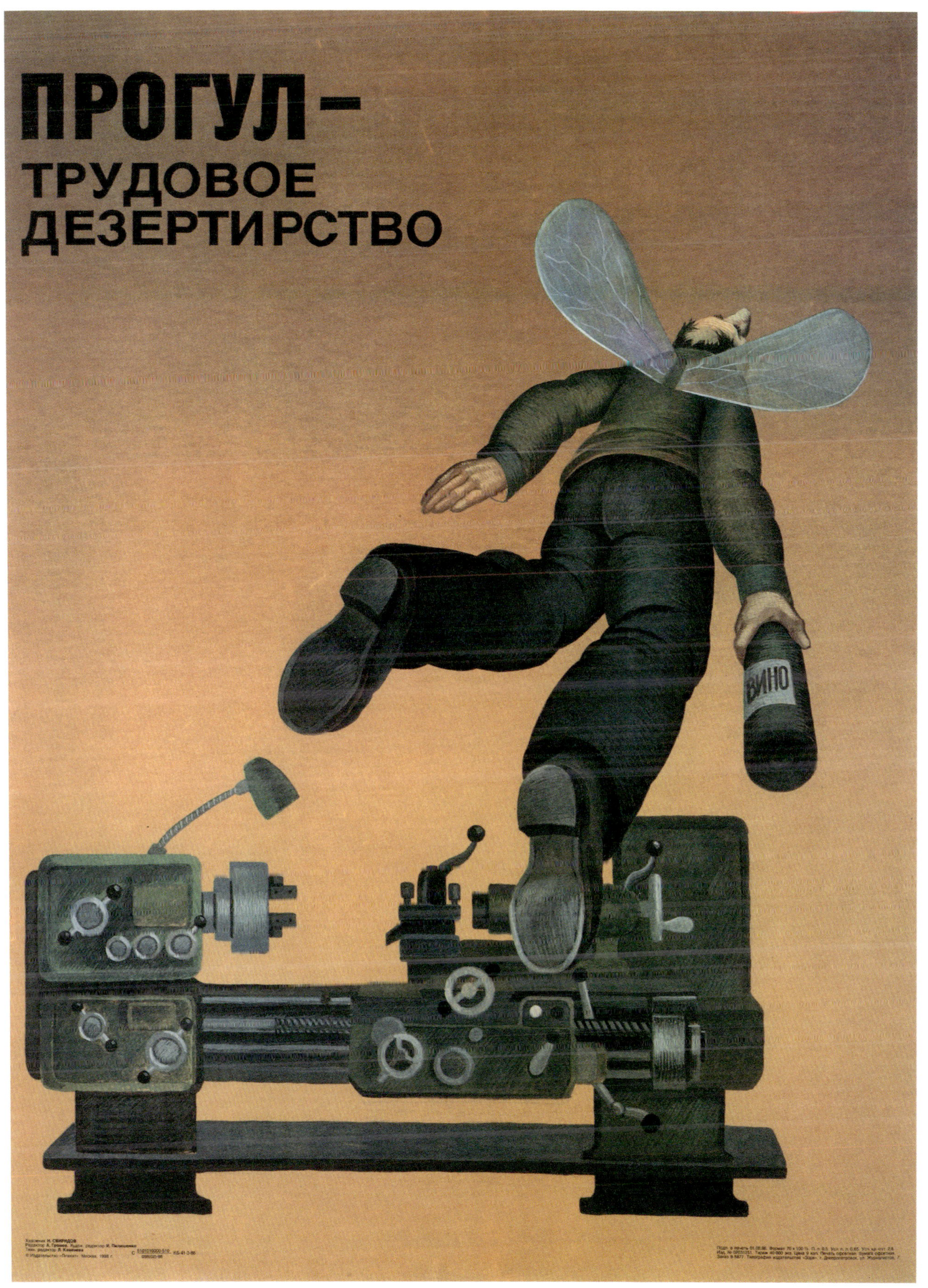
ПРОГУЛ –
ТРУДОВОЕ
ДЕЗЕРТИРСТВО
ВИНО

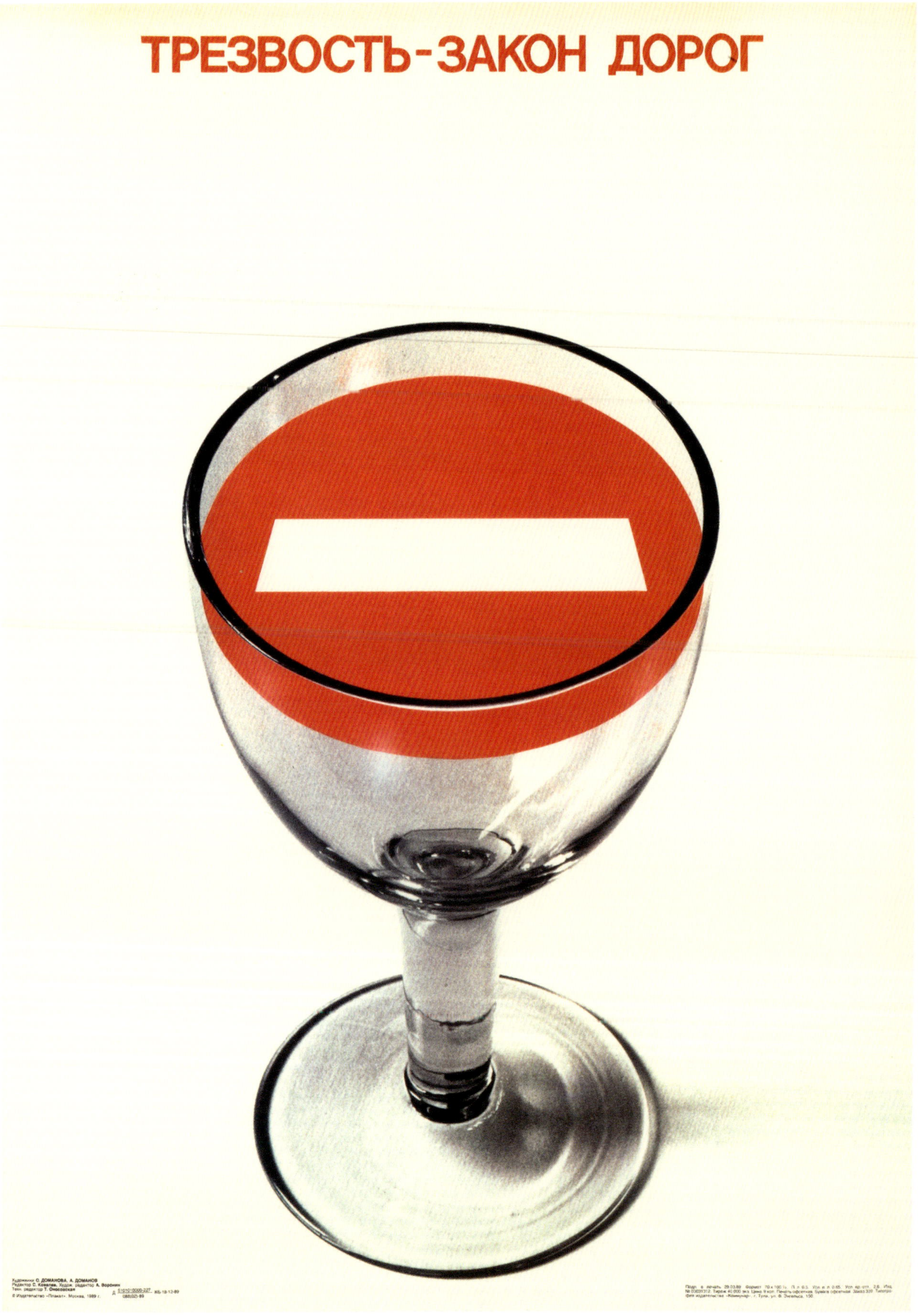
ТРЕЗВОСТЬ-ЗАКОН ДОРОГ

◂ О. Доманова (O. Domanova), А. Доманов (A. Domanov) | 1989

SOBRIETY IS THE LAW OF THE ROAD

▾ Artist unknown | n.d.

Text on right half of poster at top: AGAINST DRUNKENNESS – AS A TEAM. Below, the headers on the three blank boxes to be filled out, from top to bottom, read: PEOPLE WHO IMPAIR YOUR WORK / LOSSES INCURRED BY YOUR COLLECTIVE / PUNITIVE MEASURES (i.e., what would you recommend as punishment?) Top left: DRUNKENNESS IS VOLUNTARY MADNESS —SENECA

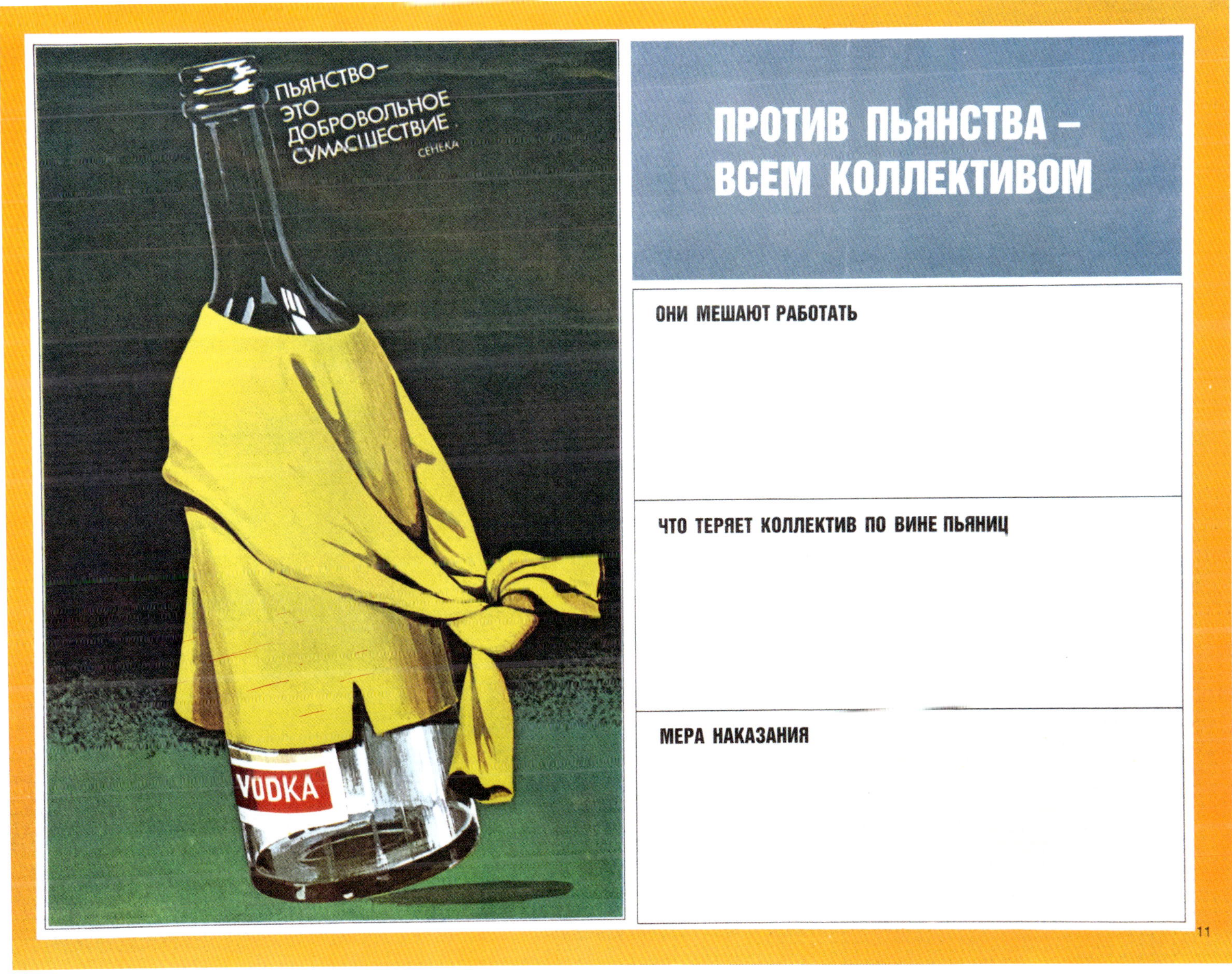

SUBSTANCE ABUSE

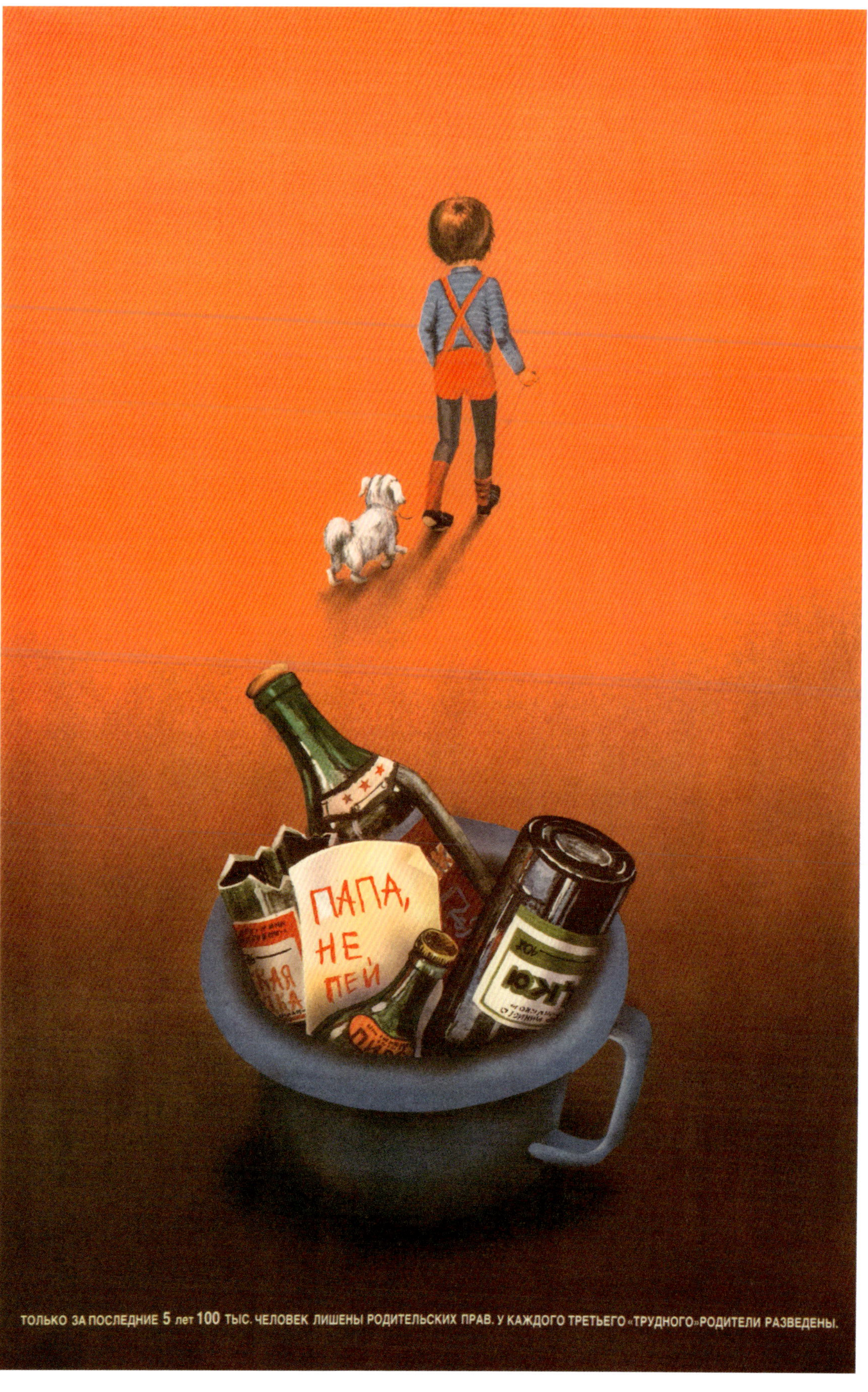

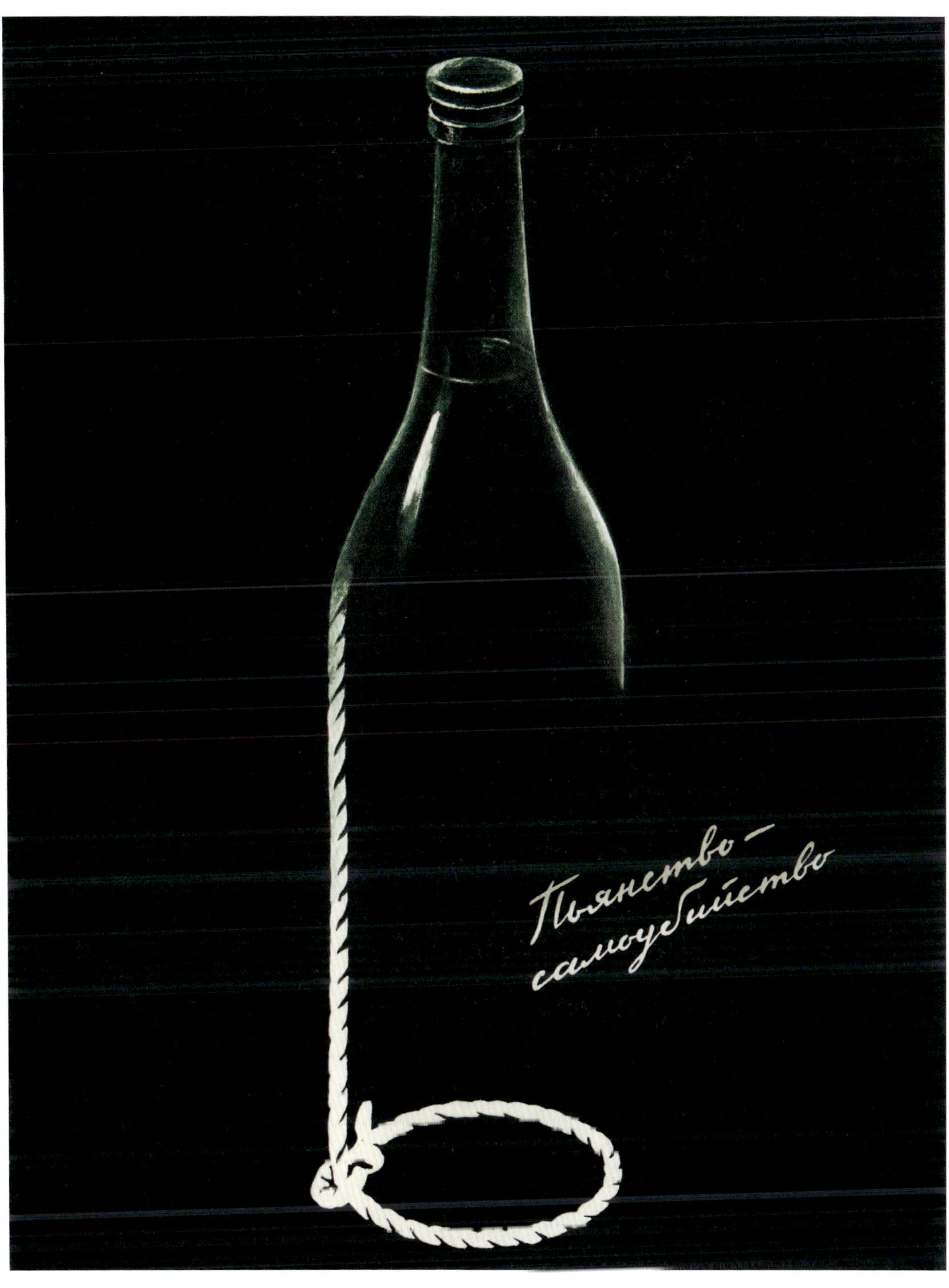

◂ Н. Жээренчиев (N. Zheerenchiev), Т. Искакова (T. Iskakova) | 1989

Text on handwritten note inside mug: DADDY, DON'T DRINK
Text at the bottom: IN JUST THE PAST FIVE YEARS, 100,000 INDIVIDUALS HAVE HAD THEIR PARENTAL RIGHTS TERMINATED. ONE IN EVERY THIRD "PROBLEM" CHILD HAS DIVORCED PARENTS.

▴ А. Лозенко (A. Lozenko) | 1988

ALCOHOLISM IS SUICIDE

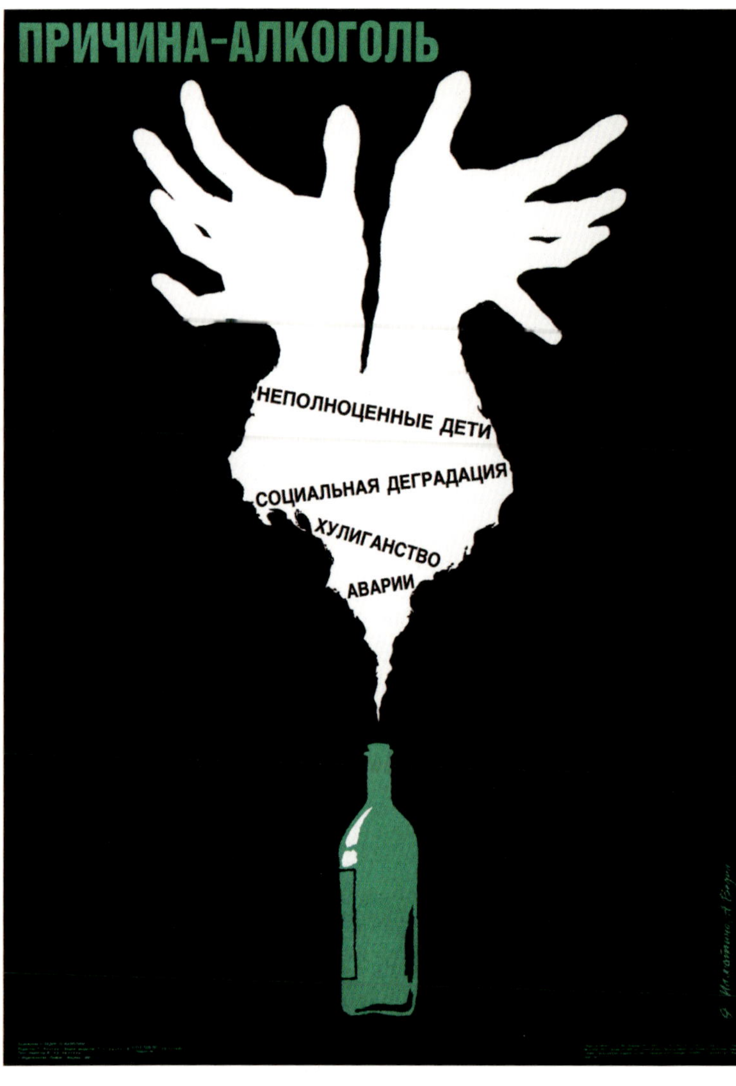

◄ А. Ведин (A. Vedin), О. Малютина (O. Malyutina) | 1990

THE REASON IS ALCOHOL
Text inside pair of white silhouetted hands: CHILDREN WITH BIRTH DEFECTS / SOCIAL DEGRADATION / HOOLIGANISM / TRAFFIC ACCIDENTS

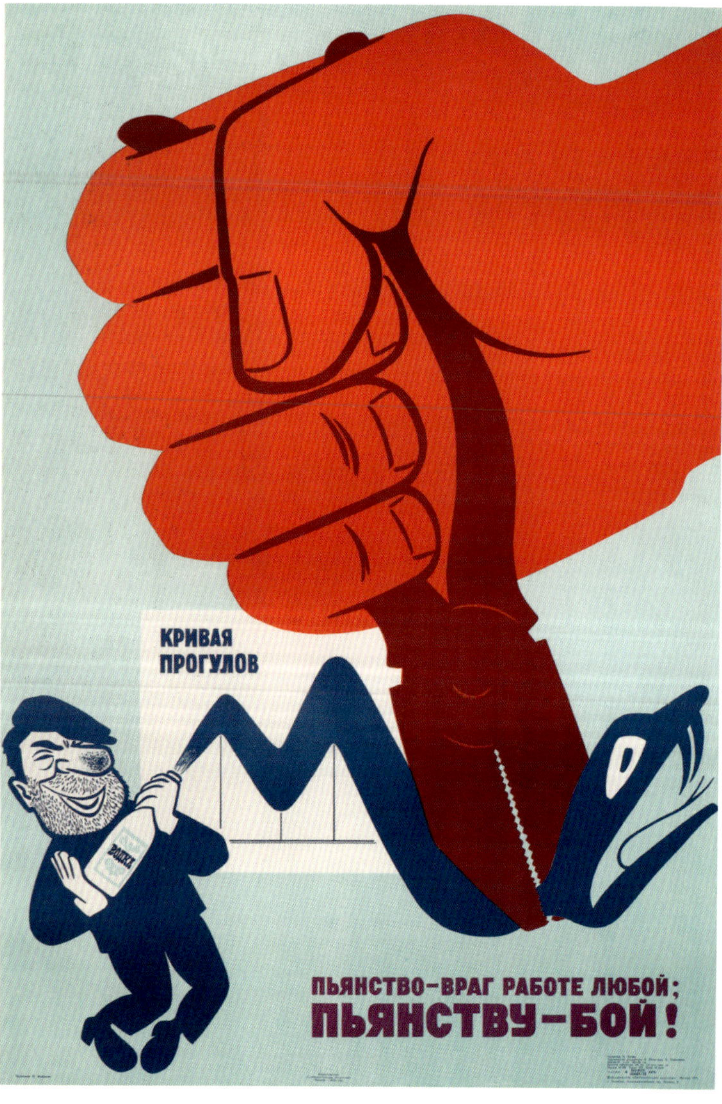

И. Фридман (I. Friedman) | 1973 ►

DRUNKENNESS: THE ENEMY OF WORKING. DOWN WITH DRINKING!
A drunkard holds a bottle of vodka. A serpent emerges from it, and the undulations of its body create a graph labeled THE TRUANCY CURVE. Meanwhile, the red fist of communism cuts off the serpent's head with a pair of pliers.

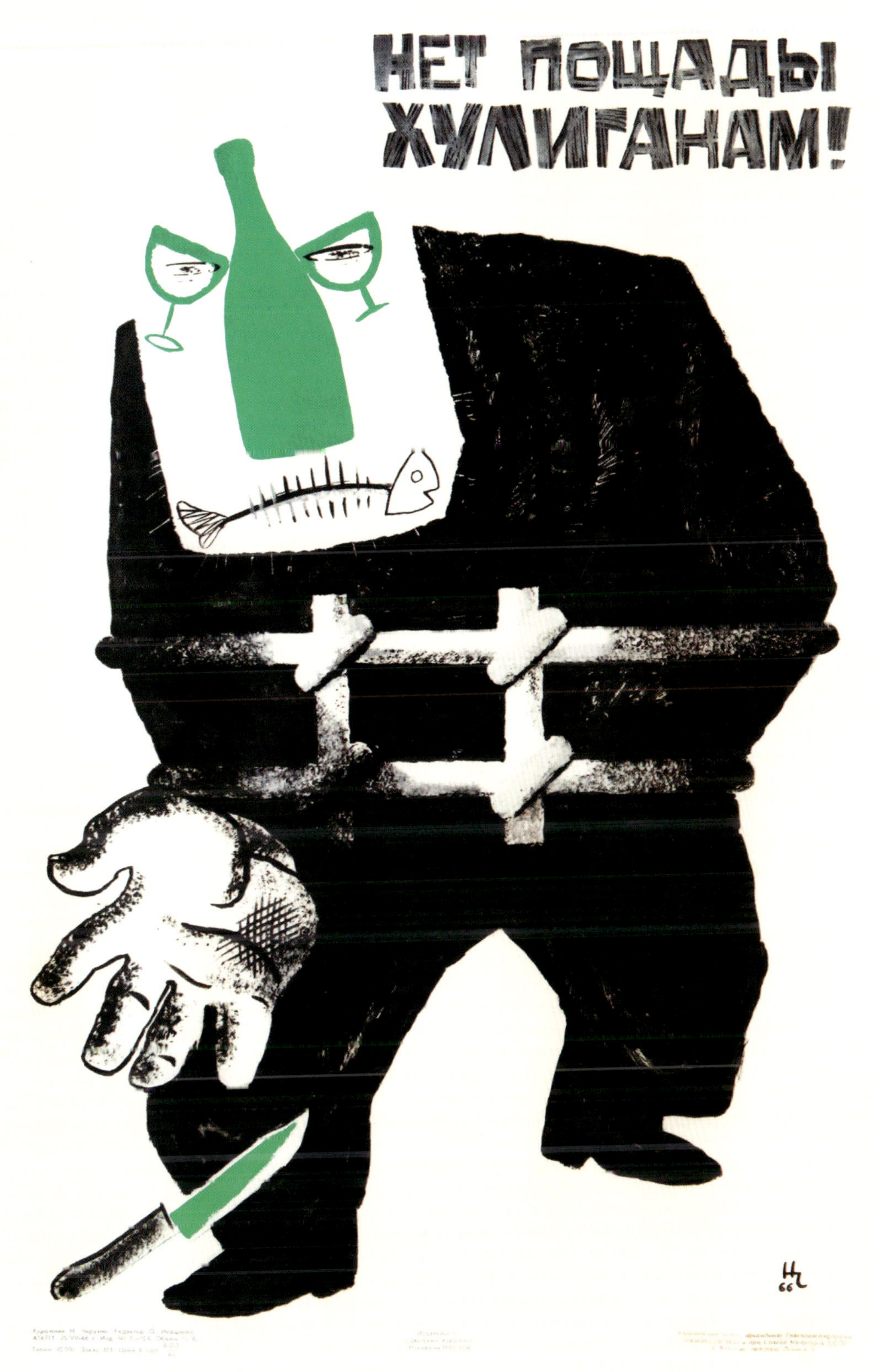

Н. Чарухин (N. Charukhin) | 1966 ➤

NO MERCY FOR HOOLIGANS!
The drunkard's angry mouth is rendered as the skeleton of a fish, the typical food consumed with alcohol. Moreover, his body appears to be held back by prison bars.

SUBSTANCE ABUSE

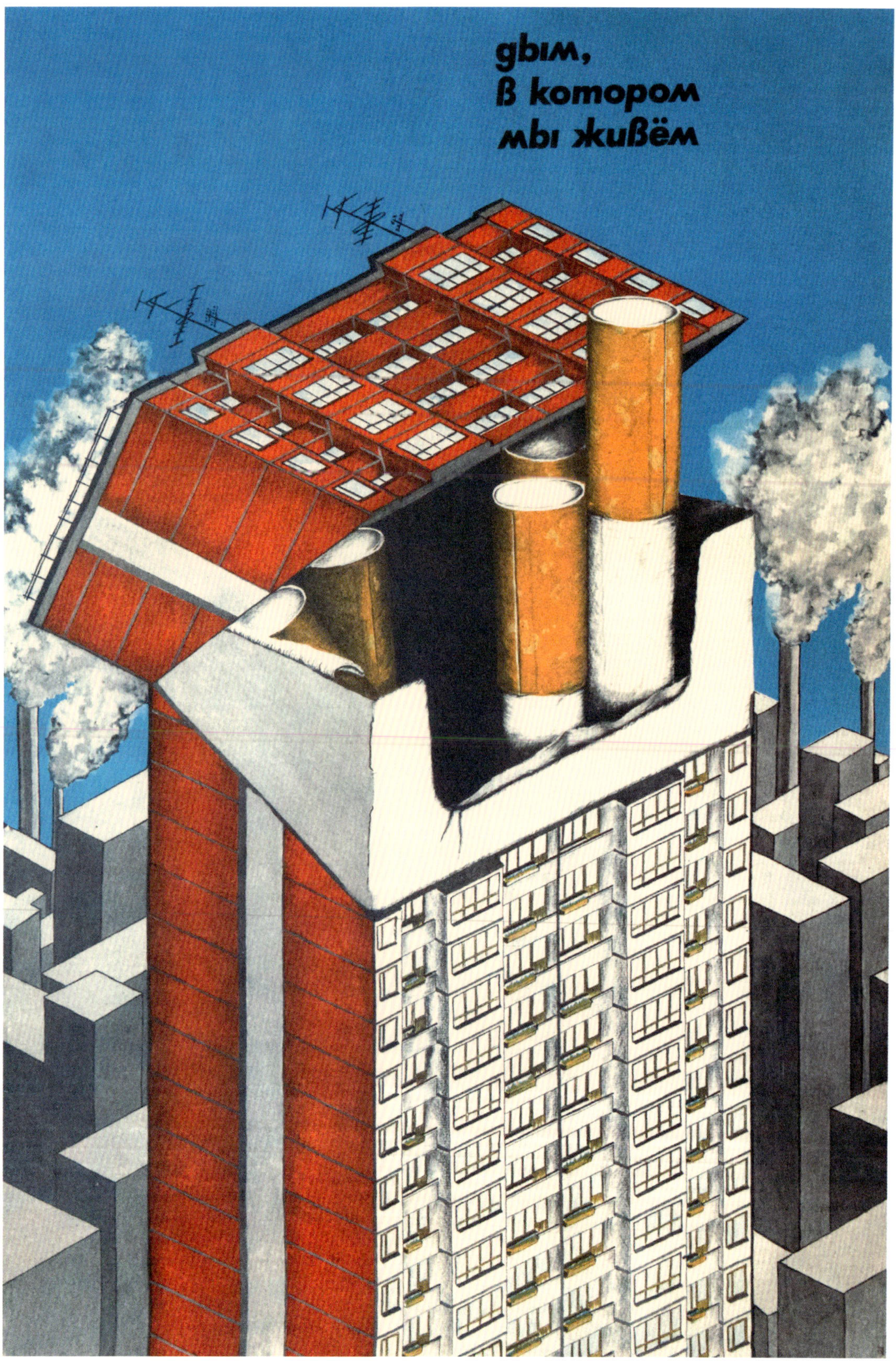

Artist unknown | 1988

THE SMOKE WE LIVE IN

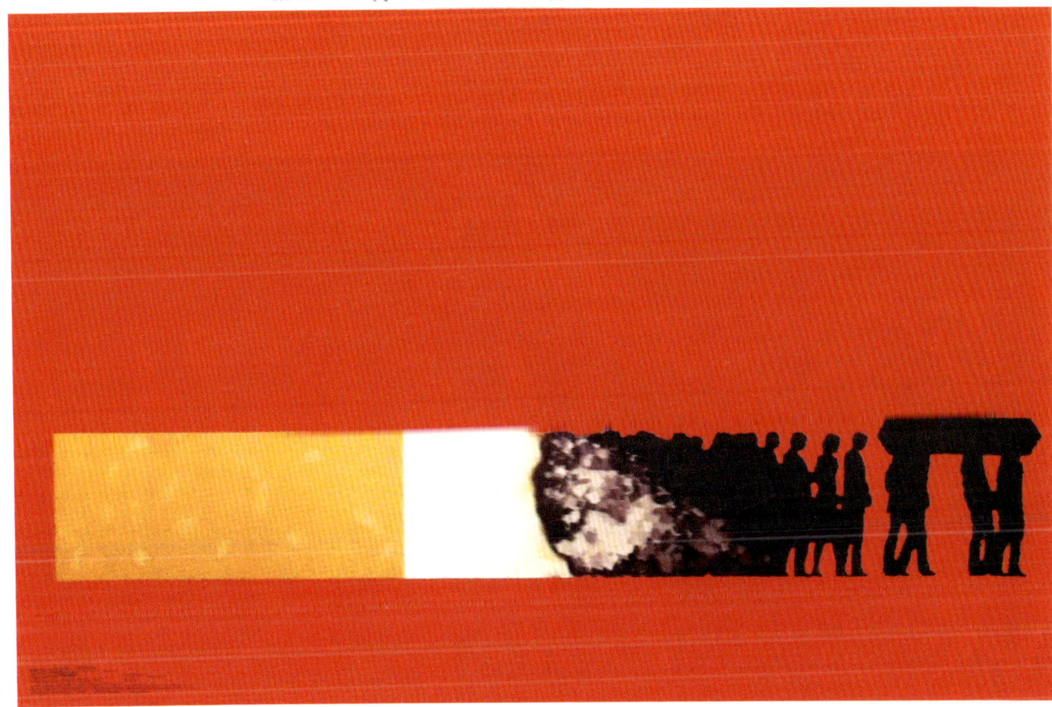

◂ В. Волков (V. Volkov), А. Марченко (A. Marchenko) | 1988

THE MINISTRY OF HEALTH WARNED YOU . . .
The people carrying the coffin are morphing into cigarette ash.

Artist unknown | n.d. ▸

On the left half of the poster is a picture of an hourglass, but the top of the hourglass is a coin purse. Inside the bottom of the hourglass is a pile of lit cigarettes with smoke filtering up to the top. In the top half of the hourglass, the text reads: THE MORE YOU SMOKE ON COMPANY TIME, THE MORE THE PROFITS WILL DECLINE! Beneath the hourglass, the text reads: VALUE EVERY MINUTE OF WORK! On the right half of the poster, at the top, the text reads: HOLD THE VIOLATORS OF LABOR DISCIPLINE AND SOCIAL ORDER ACCOUNTABLE! Beneath are three boxes to be filled out: 1) WHO VIOLATED AND WHEN 2) DAMAGE TO THE COMPANY 3) VIOLATOR PUNISHED

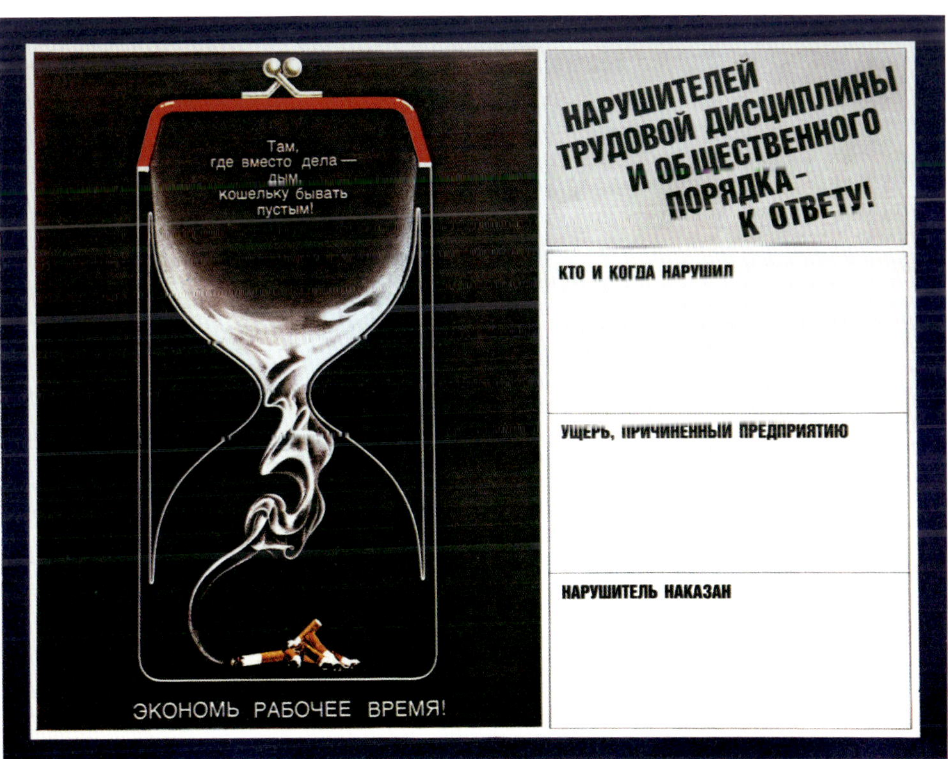

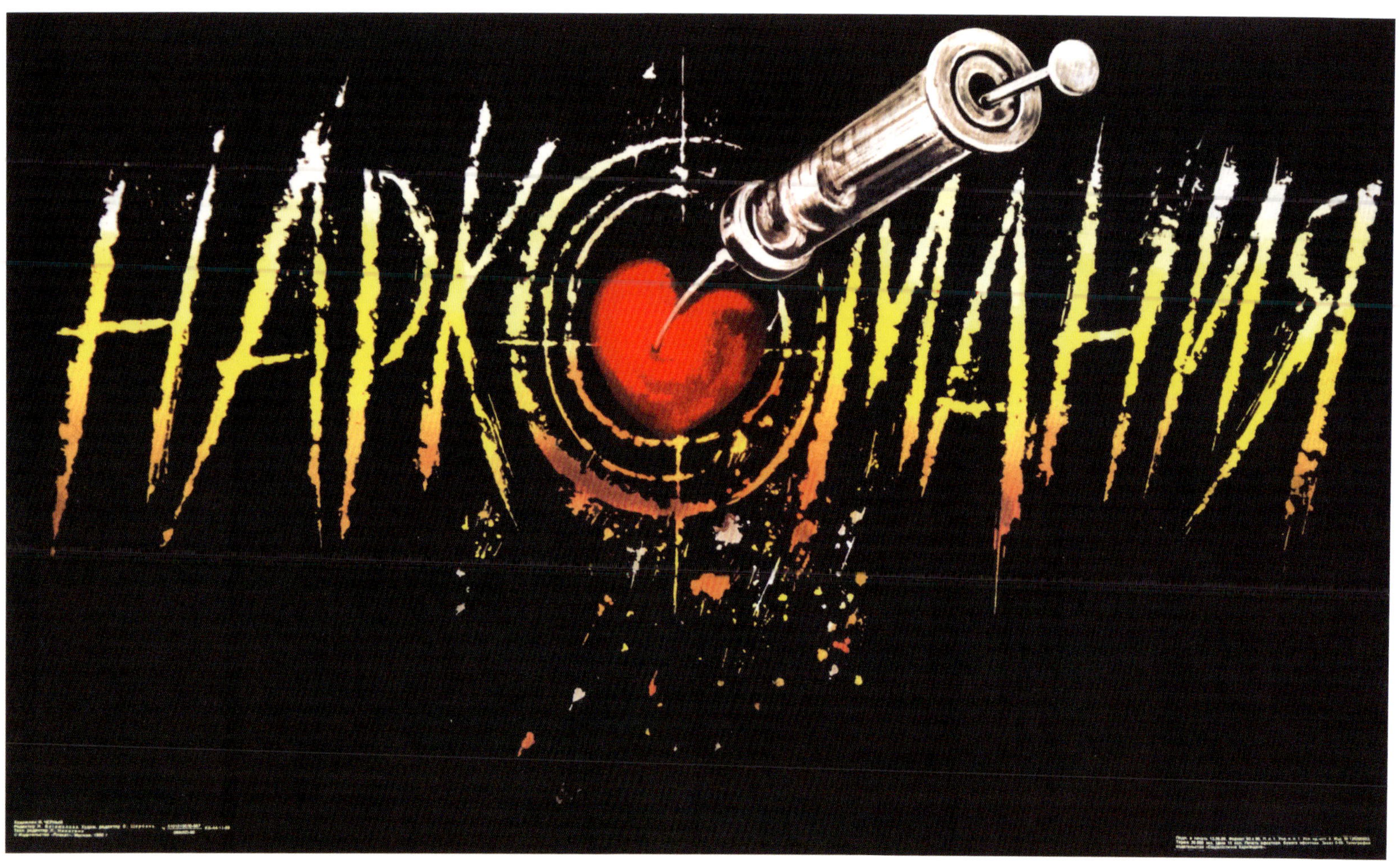

▲ И. Черный (I. Chernyy) | 1990

NARCOMANIA

С. Булкин (S. Bulkin), Е. Михеева (E. Mikheeva) | 1988 ➤

DRUG ADDICTION IS SUICIDE!

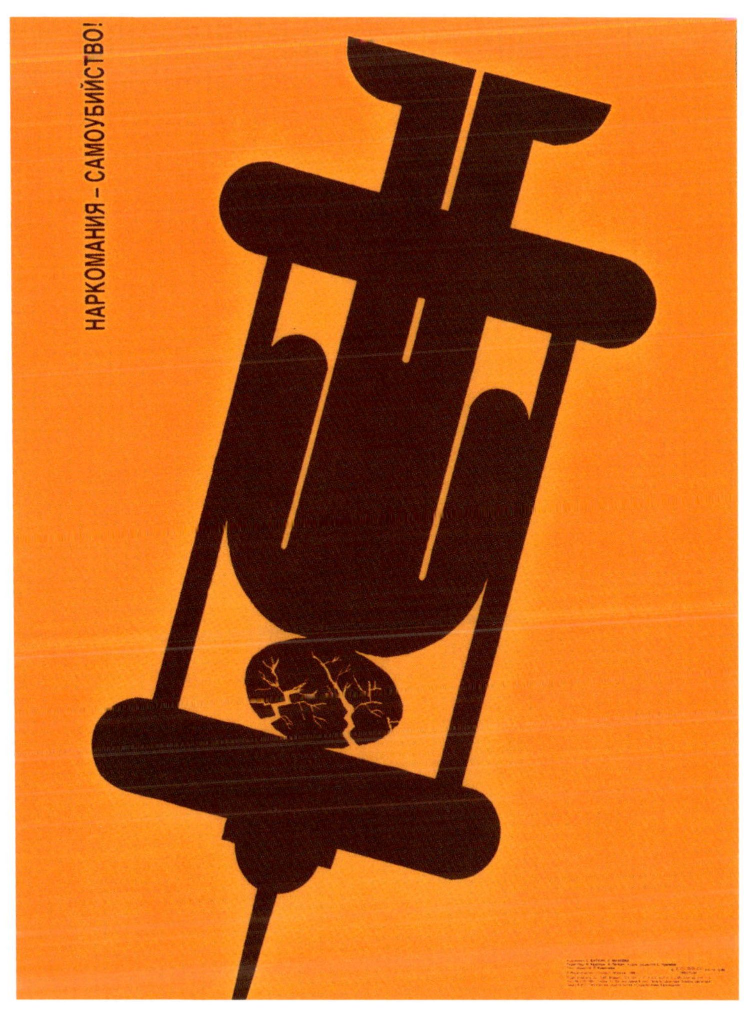

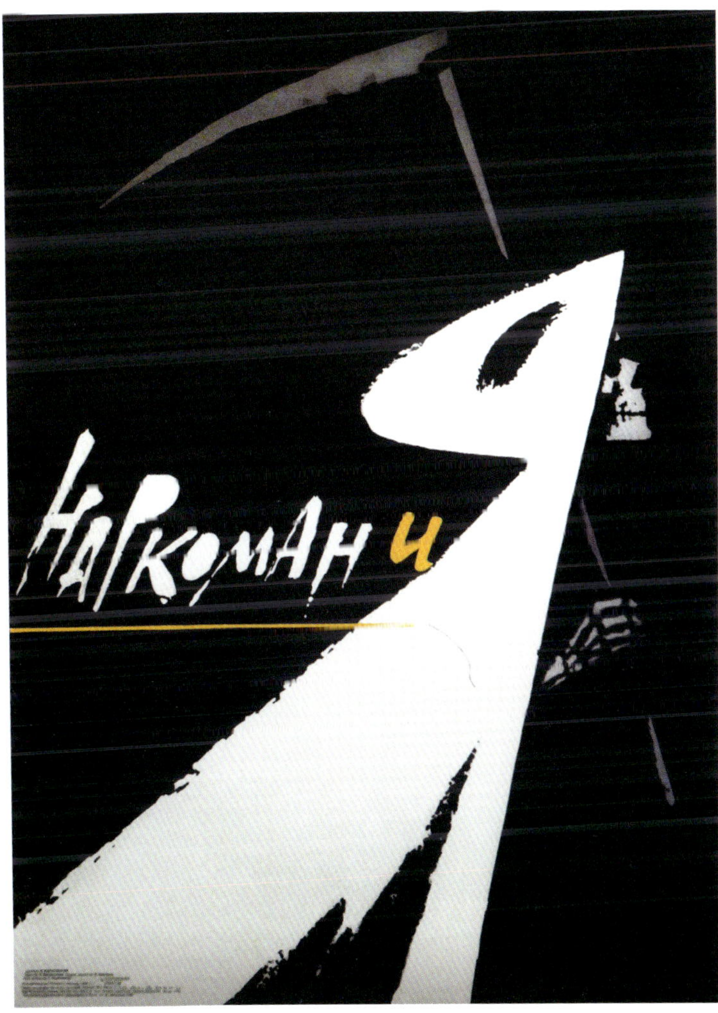

➤ И. Марковский (I. Markovsky) | 1988

NARCOMANIA

The yellow letter in "mania" means "and" in Russian. The final letter, which forms the hooded cape of Death, also means "I" in the sense of a person. The message implies both "drug addiction" as well as "Death and I together," suggesting that "Death" is speaking of himself. This is an example of visually expressed wordplay and rhyme in Russian.

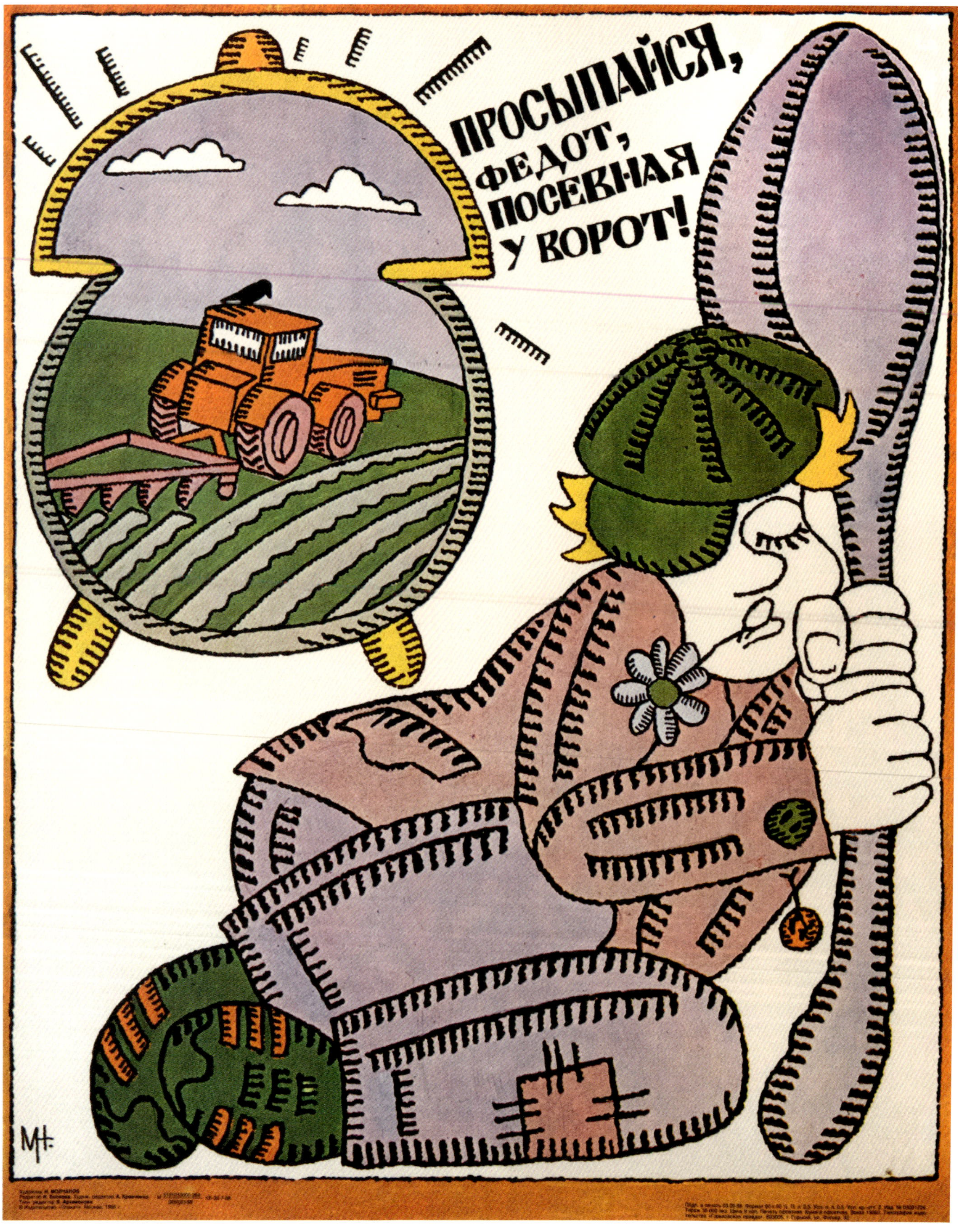
ПРОСЫПАЙСЯ,
ФЕДОТ,
ПОСЕВНАЯ
У ВОРОТ!

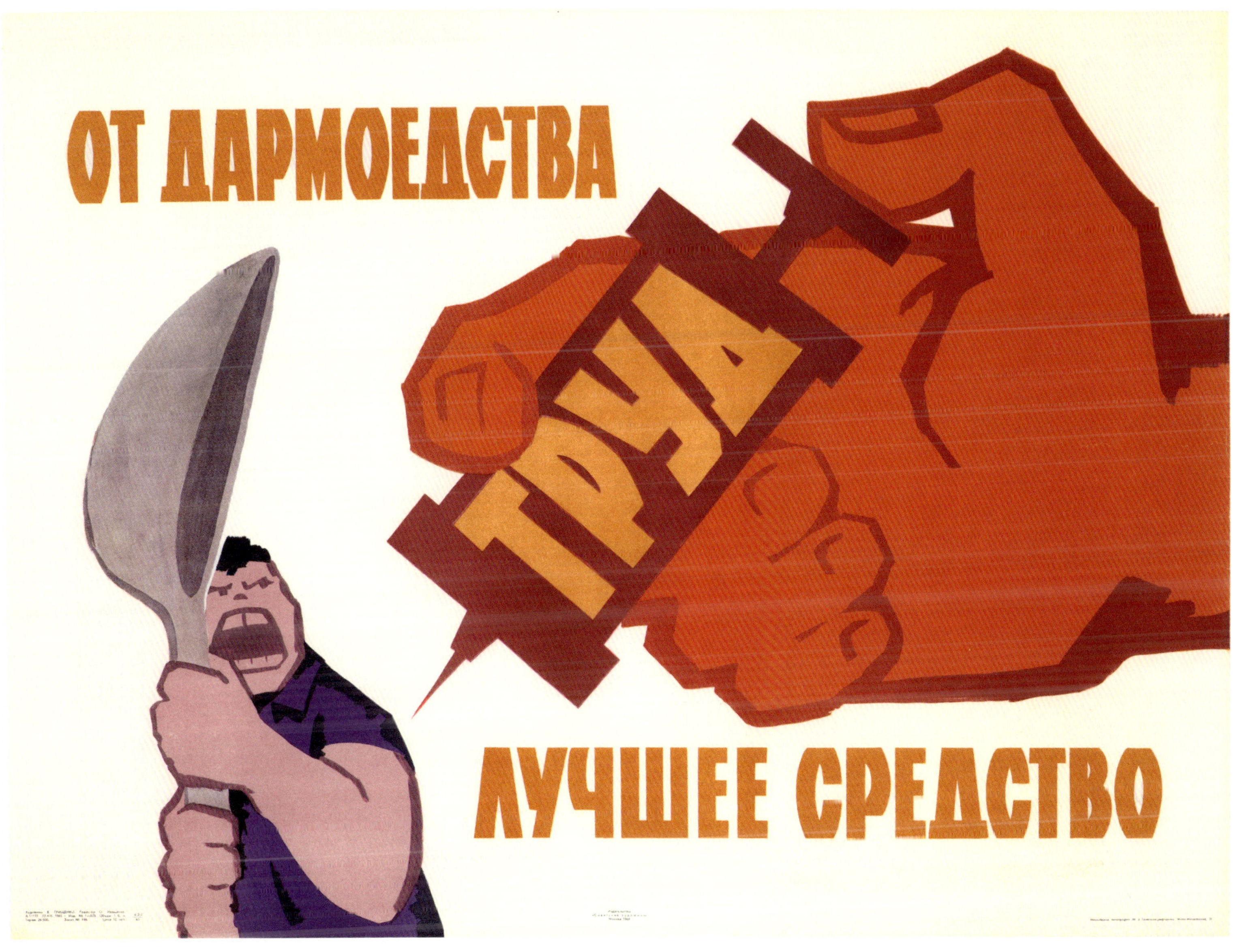

◀ Н. Молчанов (N. Molchanov) | 1988

WAKE UP FEDOT, THE TRACTOR IS WAITING AT THE GATE!
An impoverished heroin addict is too far gone to wake up at the sound of his alarm.

▲ В. Грищенко (V. Grishchenko) | 1965

THE BEST MEDICINE FOR FREELOADERS
Text on syringe: LABOR

BUREAUCRACY

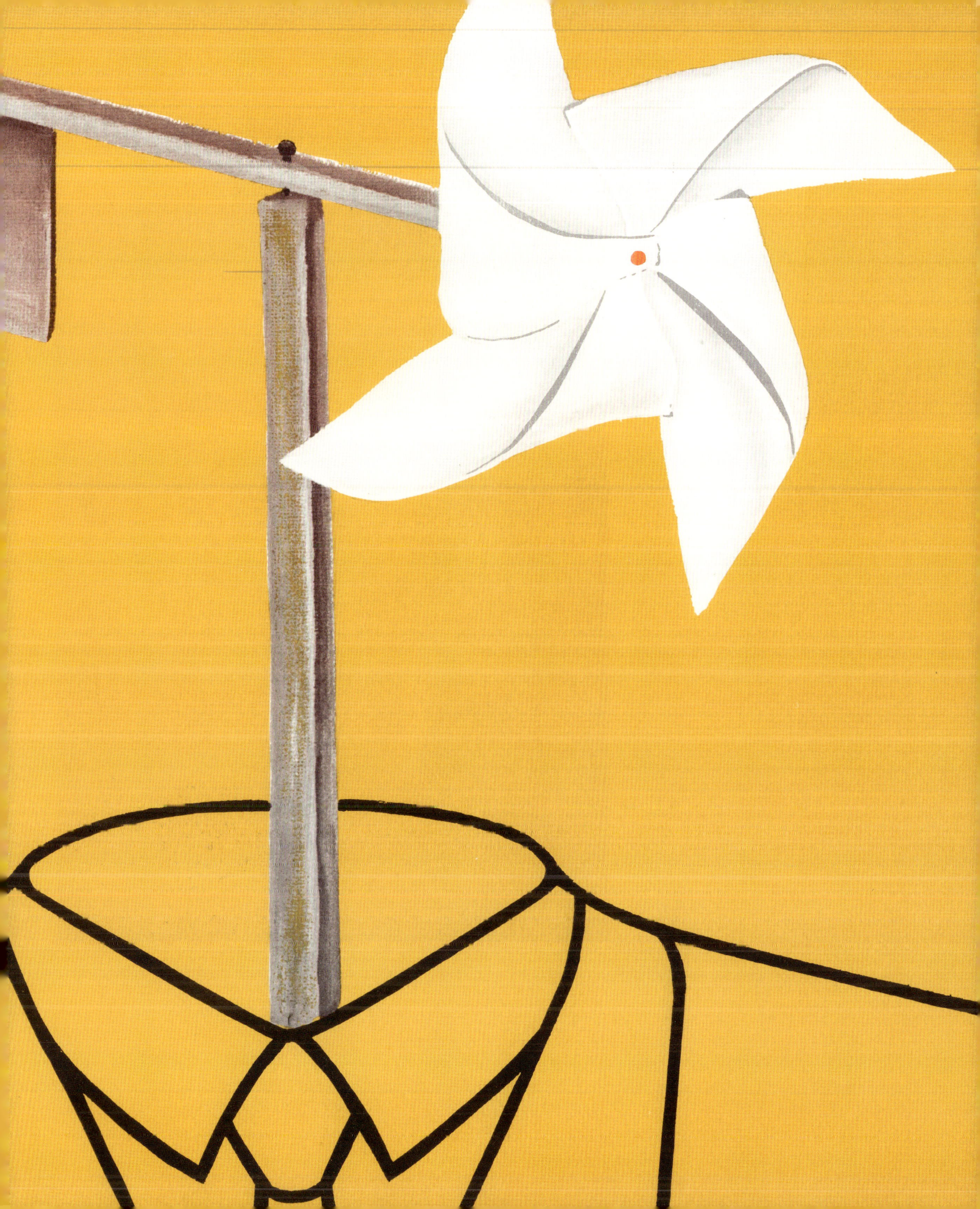

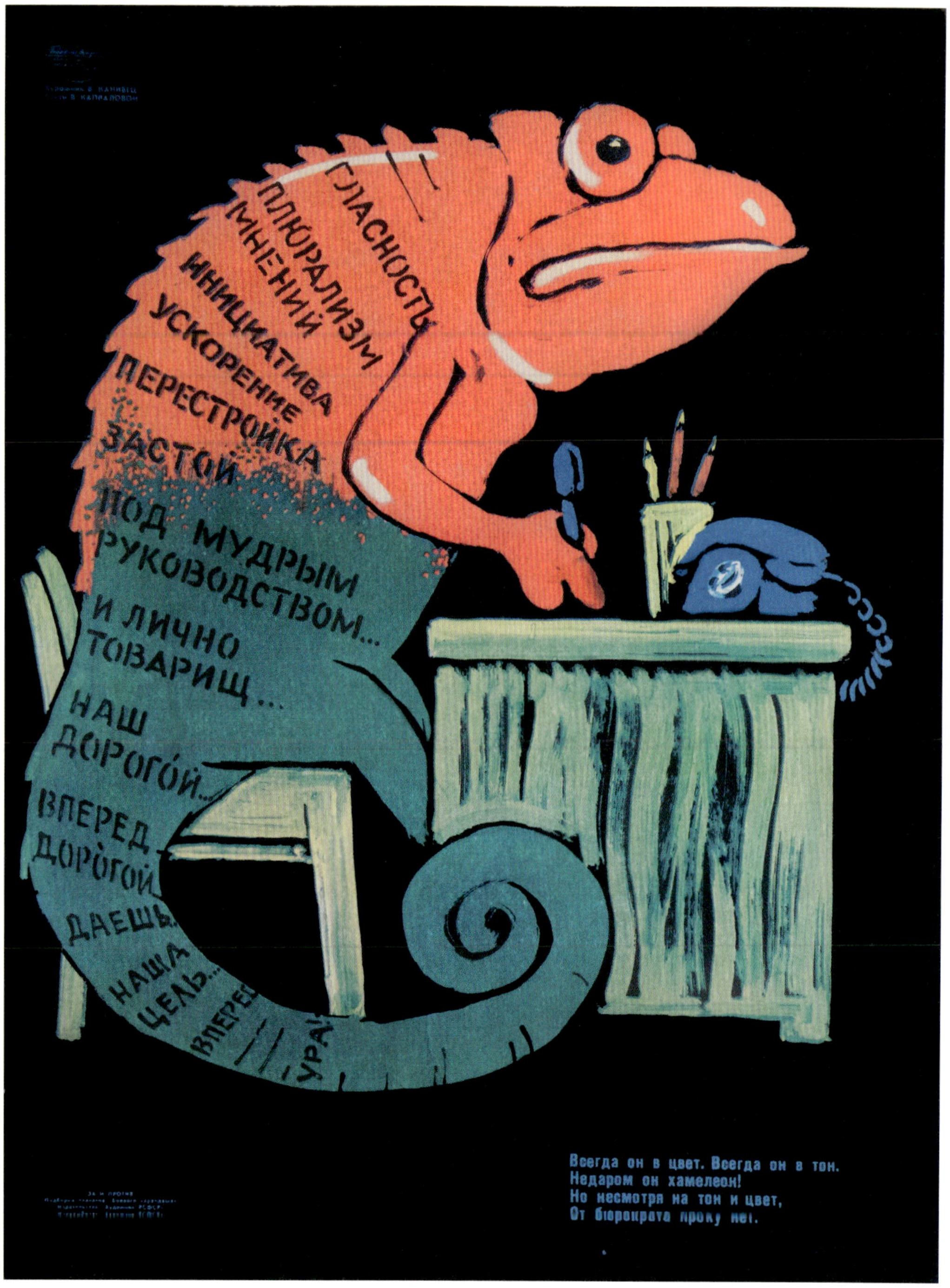

BUREAUCRACY

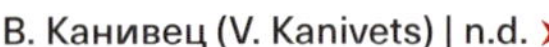

В. Канивец (V. Kanivets) | n.d.

A bureaucrat is depicted as a chameleon. The top of his body is red, demonstrating his loyalty to the Communist Party and its slogans of the day, written on his skin: GLASNOST / PLURALISM OF PERSPECTIVES / INITIATIVE / ACCELERATION / PERESTROIKA. However, these intentions come to a halt at the line where he changes color, labeled STAGNATION. Beneath this line, under the desk, the lizard hides his prehensile tail, turned green, embellished with the platitudes he uses with those he seeks to flatter: UNDER THE WISE SUPERVISION... / PERSONAL COMRADE... / OUR DEAR... / YOU SHOW US THE WAY FORWARD... / OUR COMMON GOAL... / FORWARD... / HURRAH! Conceivably, his lower half is turning green with envy of the superiors he addresses.
Text at lower-right corner:
ALWAYS THE RIGHT COLOR.
ALWAYS THE RIGHT TONE.
THAT'S WHY HE'S A CHAMELEON.
BUT NO MATTER HIS COLOR,
NO MATTER HIS RUSE
THE BUREAUCRAT IS OF NO USE.

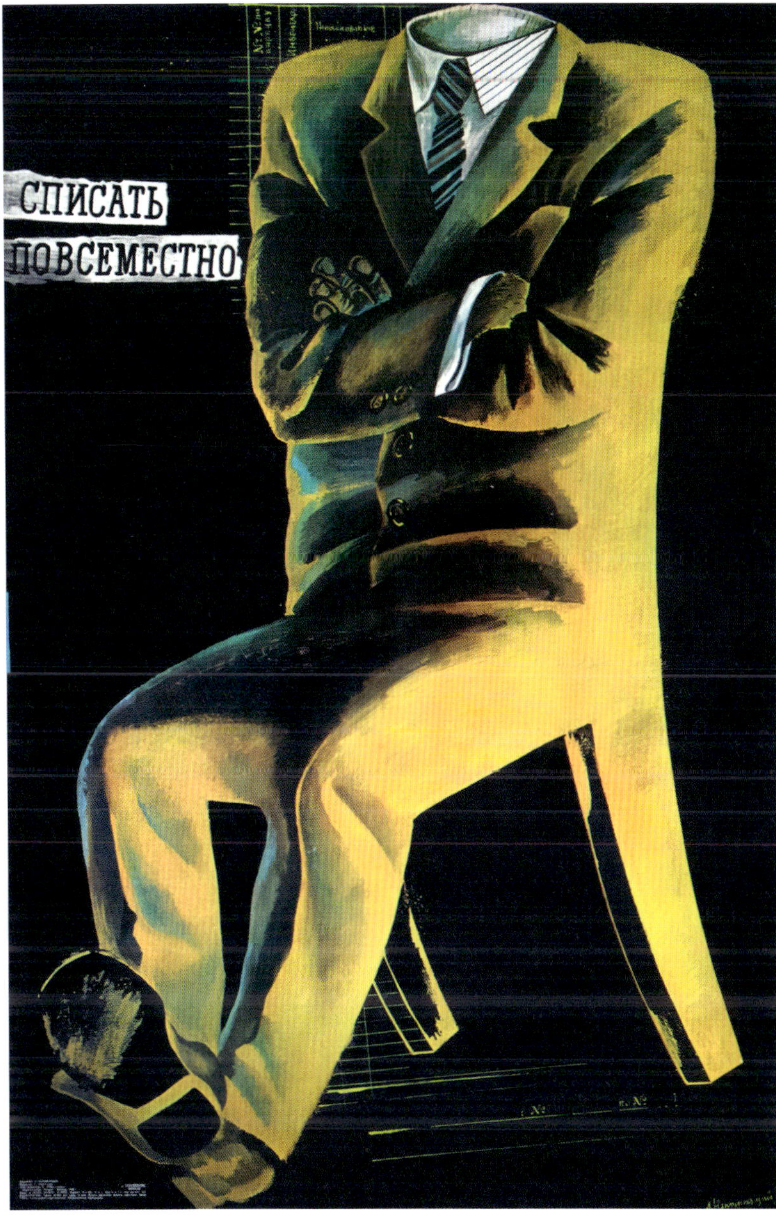

Л. Непомнящий (L. Nepomnyashchiy) | 1988

TOTAL WRITE-OFF
A headless bureaucrat has not moved for so long he has melded with his chair. Behind him, a blank ledger sheet indicates that he is now worthless.

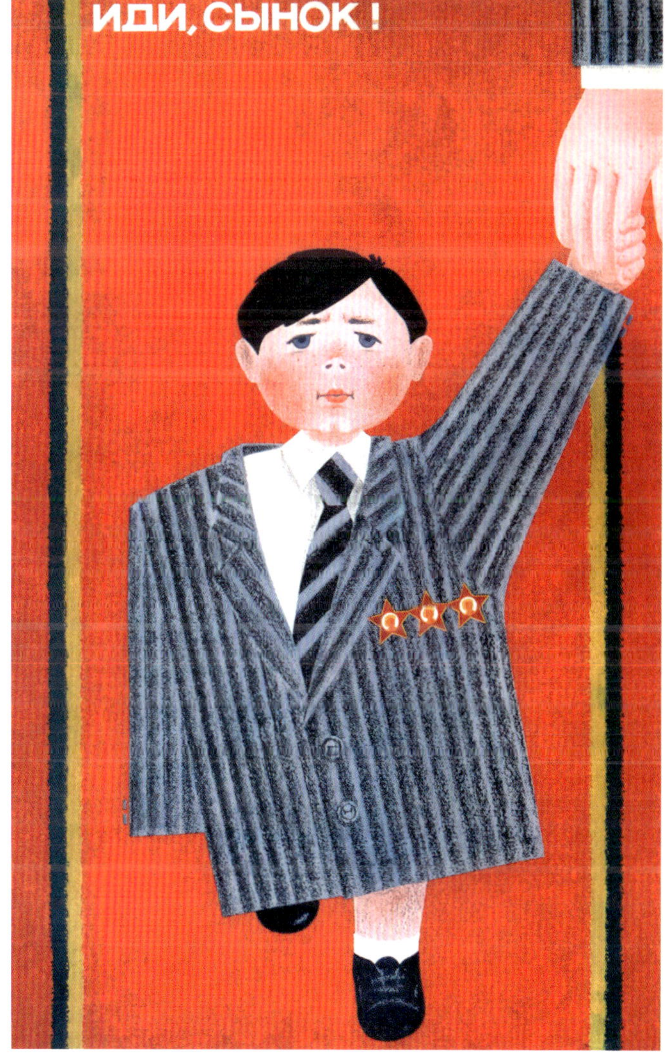

О. Качер (O. Kacher) | 1989

OFF YOU GO, SON!
This anti-nepotism poster tacitly refers to General Secretary Leonid Brezhnev, who ruled the Soviet Union from 1964 to 1982, and was known for abusing his power by awarding himself unearned medals. One of the most blatant examples of such abuse was when Brezhnev bestowed World War II medals on his son-in-law, who was only five years old when the fighting began.

BUREAUCRACY

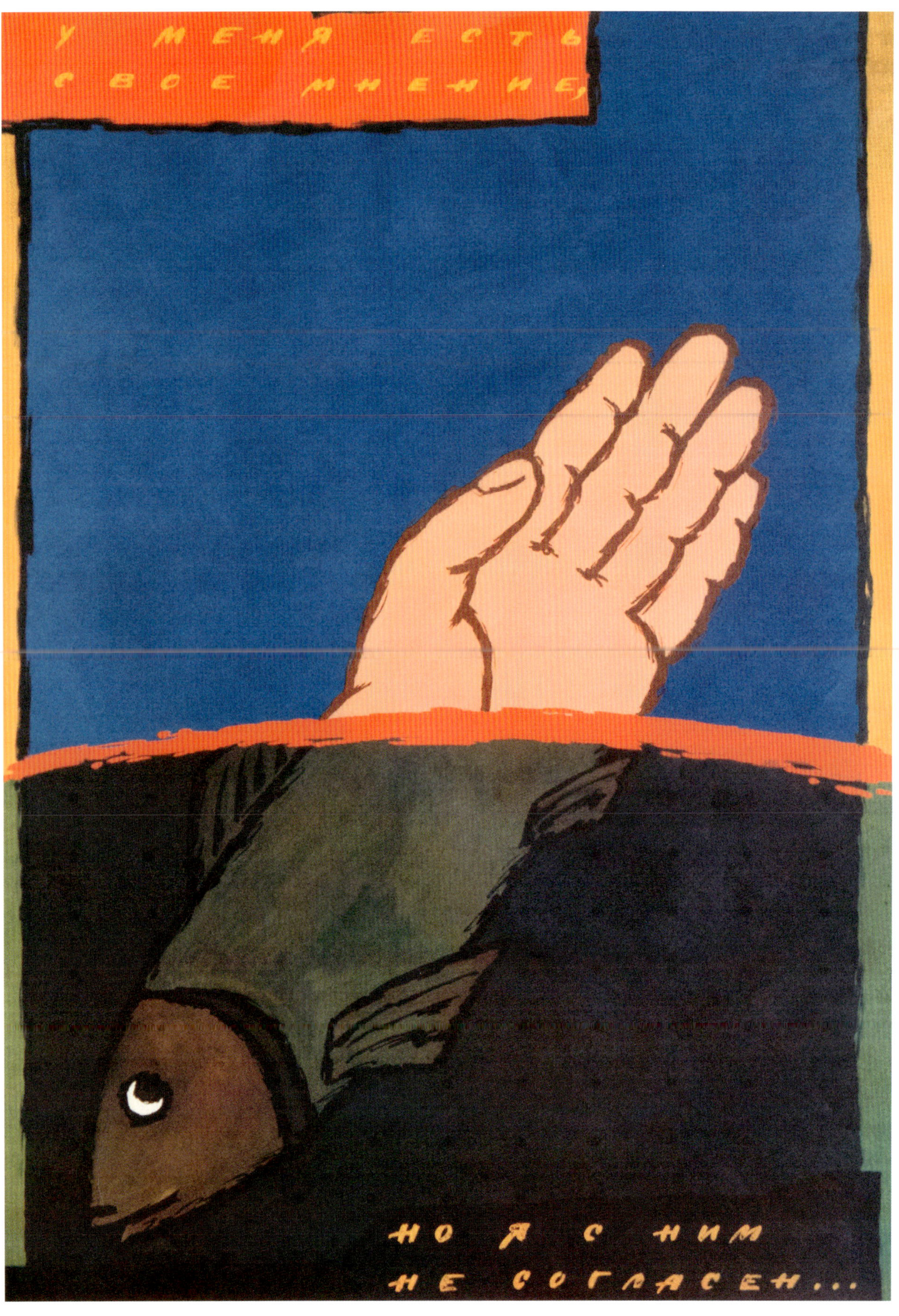

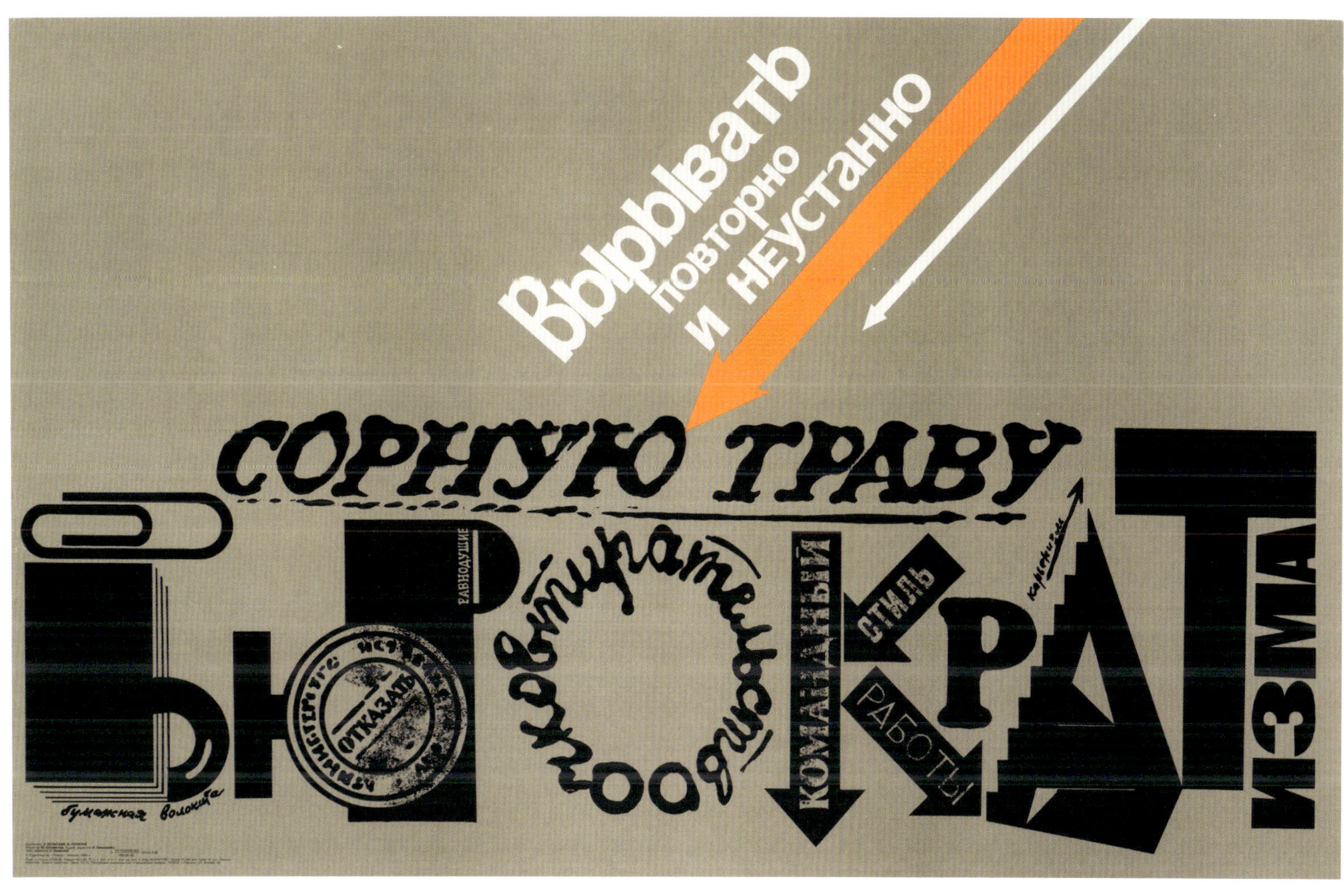

◄ Ю. Леонов (Y. Leonov) | 1988

I HAVE MY OWN OPINION, BUT I DON'T AGREE WITH IT . . .

A hand raised in the Soviet gesture signifying public support of official policy is also covertly pictured as a fish diving into the murky depths of secret personal dissent.

▲ Л. Бельский (L. Belsky), В. Потапов (V. Potapov) | 1989

ROOT OUT THE WEEDS OF BUREAUCRATISM EVERY TIME, TIRELESSLY

The words interspersed through the letters spelling out "bureaucratism" include: PAPER TRAILS OF RED TAPE / REFUSED / INDIFFERENCE / CHEATING / TOP-DOWN MANAGEMENT / CAREERISM

К. Романенко (K. Romanenko), В. Черемхин (V. Cheremkhin) | 1990

Three panels of a triptych. Red text running contiguously across the center of all three panels reads: PERESTROIKA! Text along top: IMPLEMENT, DEEPEN, PROTECT. Proclamation on yellow label at bottom left: AFFIRM, DEEPEN, PROTECT PERESTROIKA! THE WONDERFUL IDEAS OF PERESTROIKA CANNOT FAIL TO TRIUMPH. SO THAT NO ONE MAY EVER DARE TO TRAMPLE OR DESTROY THE WORKING MAN'S RENEWED FEELING THAT HE IS THE MASTER OF HIS LAND.

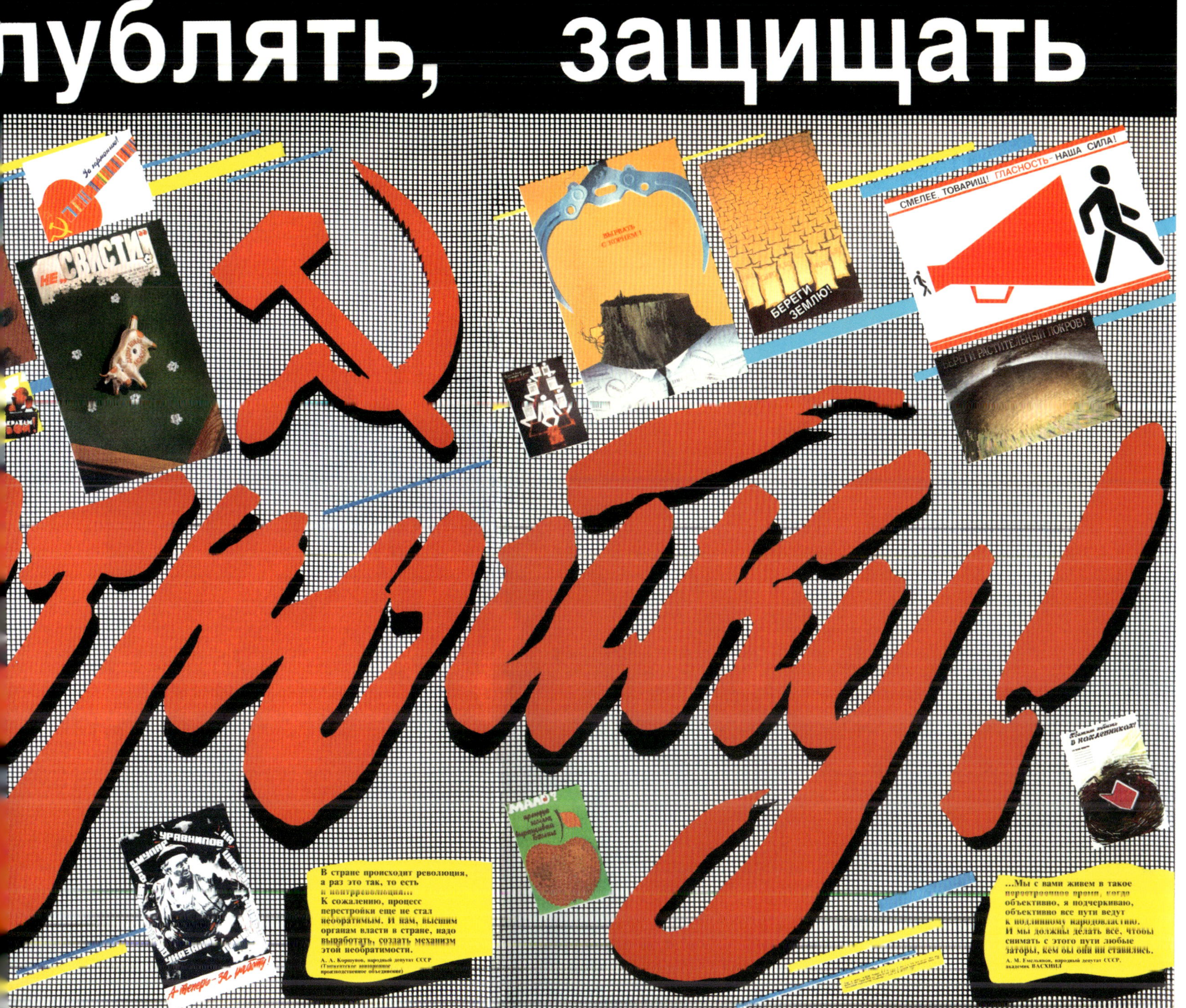

Proclamation on yellow label at bottom center:
THERE IS A REVOLUTION HAPPENING IN OUR COUNTRY, WHICH MEANS THAT THERE'S ALSO A COUNTERREVOLUTION. UNFORTUNATELY, THE PROCESS OF PERESTROIKA HAS YET TO BECOME IRREVERSIBLE. AND WE, THE TOP AUTHORITIES IN OUR COUNTRY, NEED TO CREATE A MECHANISM FOR ITS IRREVERSIBILITY.

Proclamation on yellow label at bottom right:
WE ARE CURRENTLY LIVING IN A TIME OF RECONSTRUCTION WHEN OBJECTIVELY—I EMPHASIZE, OBJECTIVELY—ALL ROADS LEAD TO TRUE POPULAR SOVEREIGNTY. WE MUST DO EVERYTHING IN OUR POWER TO REMOVE ALL ROADBLOCKS IN THIS PATH NO MATTER WHO HAS PLACED THEM THERE.

BUREAUCRACY

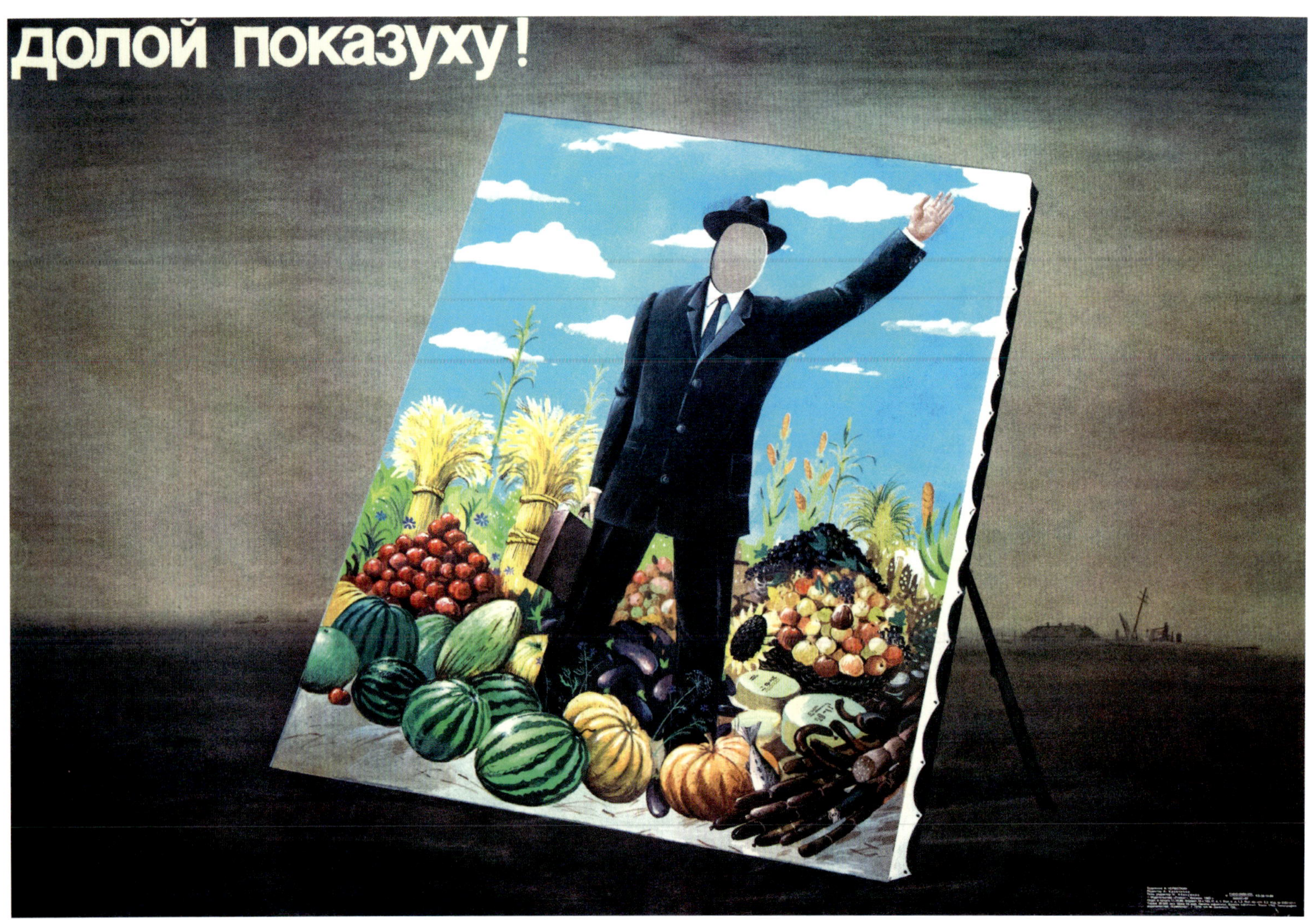

▲ И. Червоткин (I. Chervotkin) | 1989

DOWN WITH SHAM VENEERS!

A placard depicting a bureaucrat standing amid a bountiful harvest stands in a wasteland, ready for an official to insert his face where the bureaucrat's has been cut out. The Potemkin Village of Catherine the Great's Russia is still standing in the Soviet Union, where propagandistic images of successful production are used to cover up abject failures. The term translated here as "sham veneers," *pokazukha*, meaning something that's done just for show, was commonly used to characterize the efforts of government officials during the period.

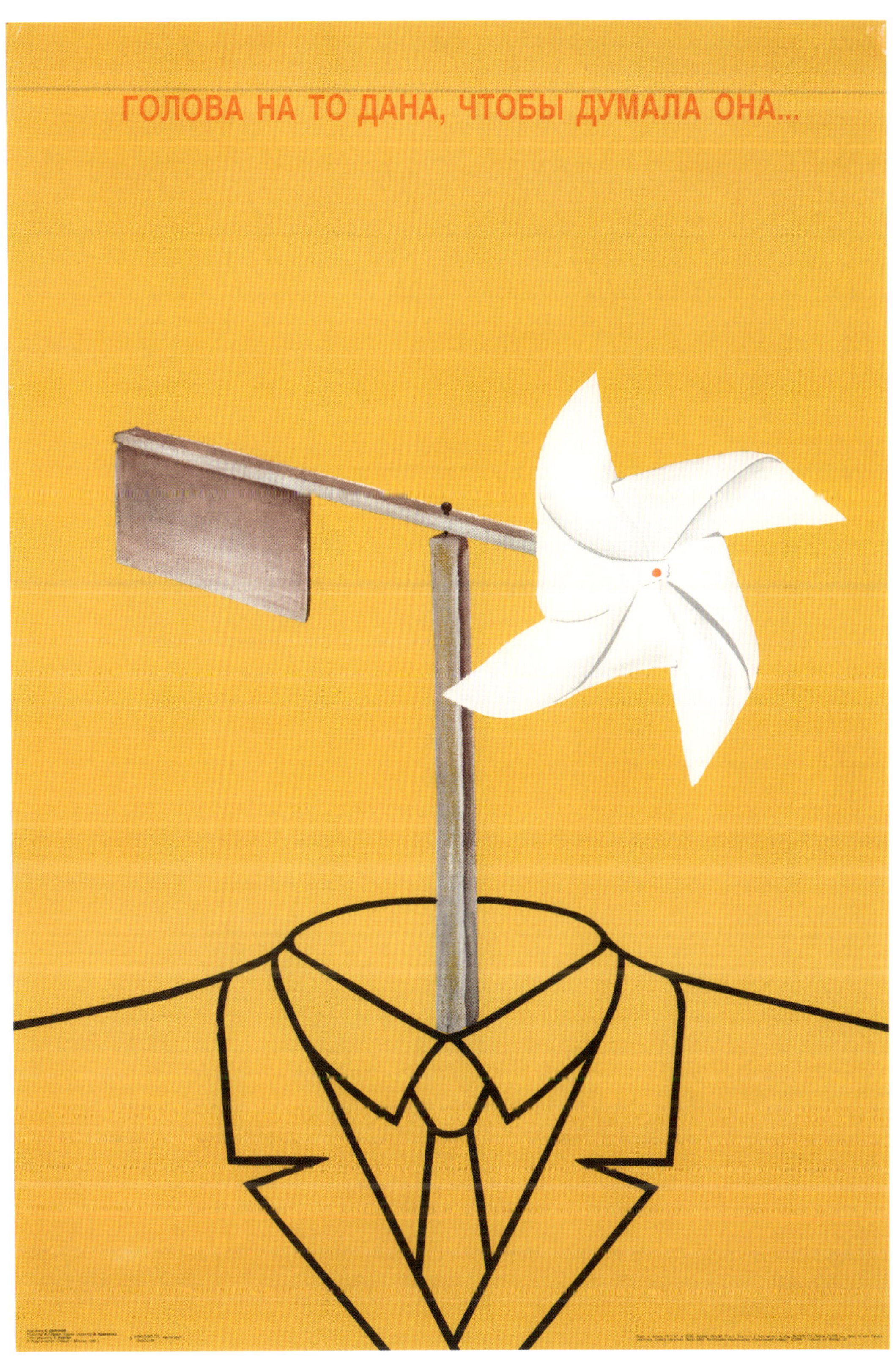

С. Дьячков (S. Dyachkov) | 1988 ➤

GOT A BRAIN, SO USE IT THEN . . .

A pinwheel has been inserted in place of a bureaucrat's head; it moves in whichever direction the wind blows.

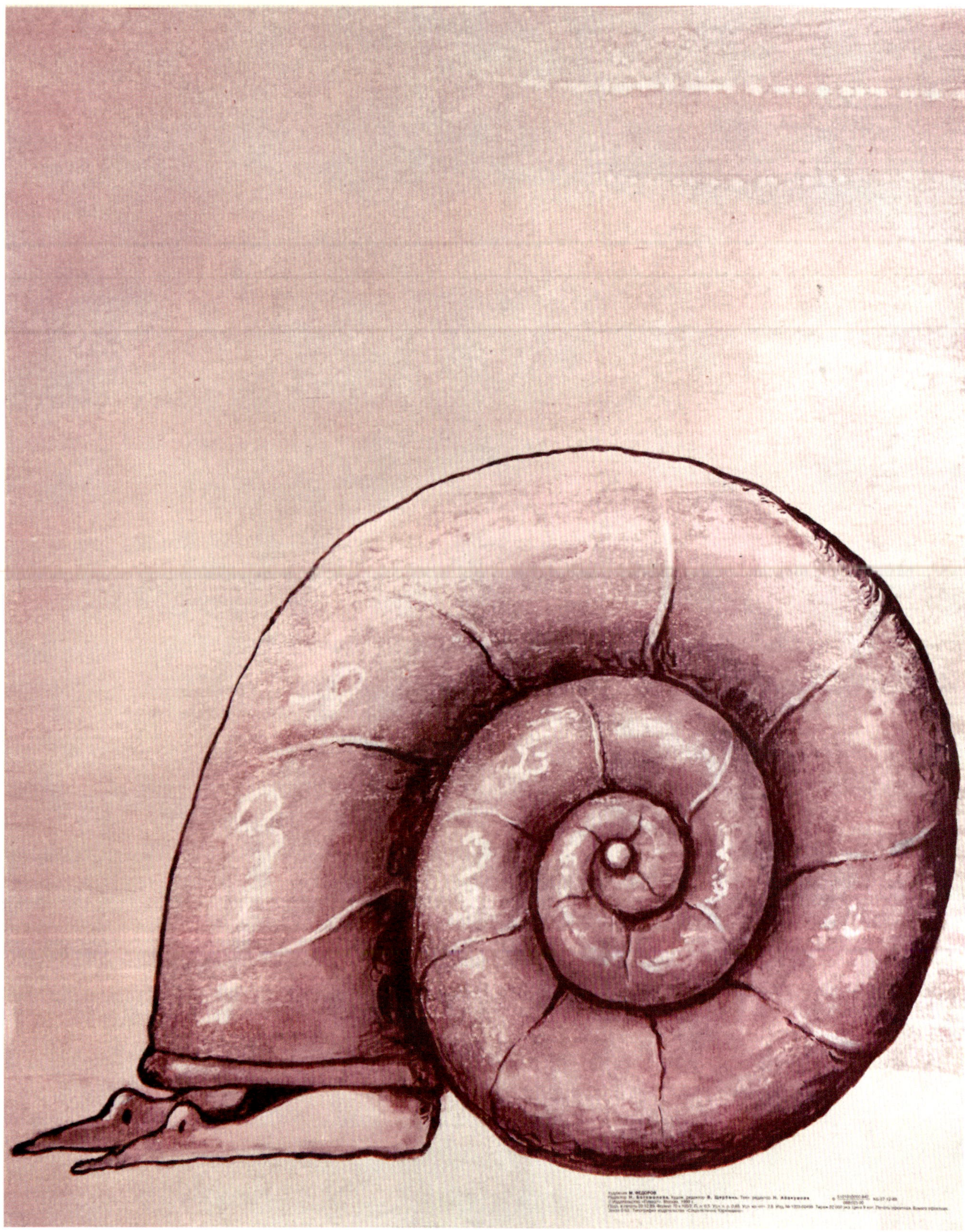
НЕ ТВОЯ ЛИ ЭТО ПОЗИЦИЯ?

◂ М. Федоров (M. Fedorov) | 1990

ISN'T THIS YOUR POSITION?
This image of a snail is a metaphor for an ignorant bureaucrat who doesn't want to acknowledge the truth of a situation and hides, attempting to conceal his incompetence by deliberately moving very slowly.

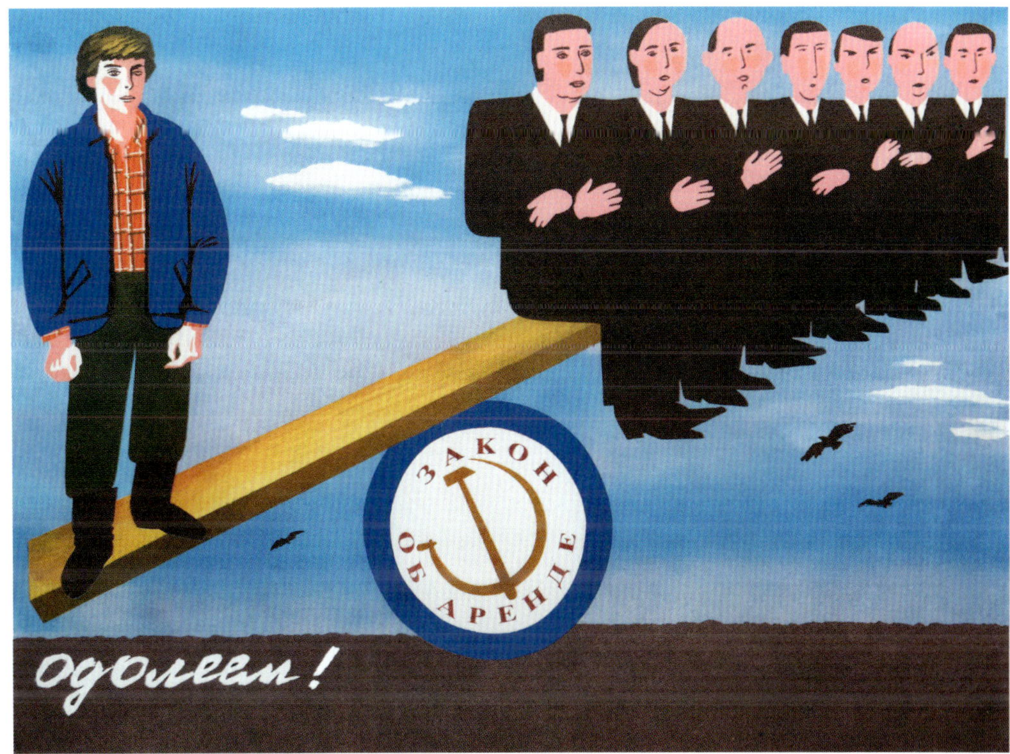

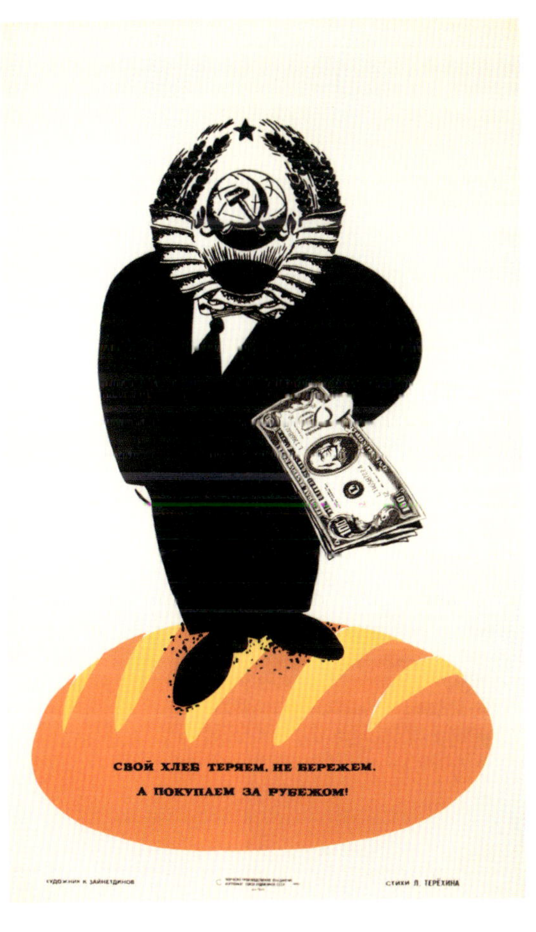

◂ К. Зайнетдинов (K. Zaynetdinov) | 1990

WE WASTE OUR OWN BREAD. WE DON'T CONSERVE IT, AND INSTEAD WE BUY IT FROM ABROAD!
A bureaucrat whose head has morphed into the seal of the Soviet Union, encircled by sheaves of wheat, holds out a fistful of dollars while standing on a loaf of bread.

▴ О. Зайкова (O. Zaykova) | 1989

WE WILL OVERCOME THE LAW ON LEASING LAND!
A peasant counterweighs a group of bureaucrats who prevent him from leasing land in order to farm more productively.

BUREAUCRACY

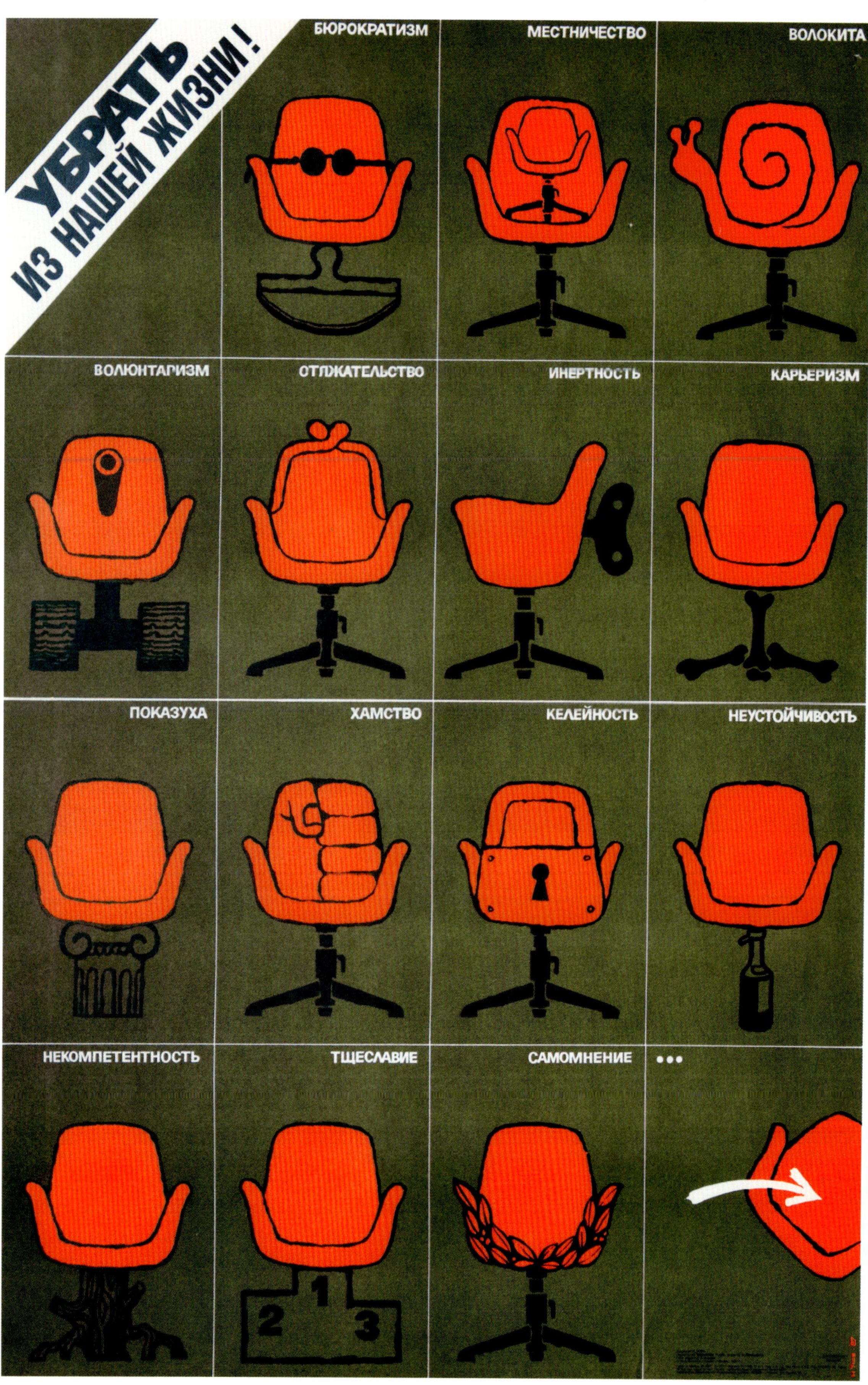

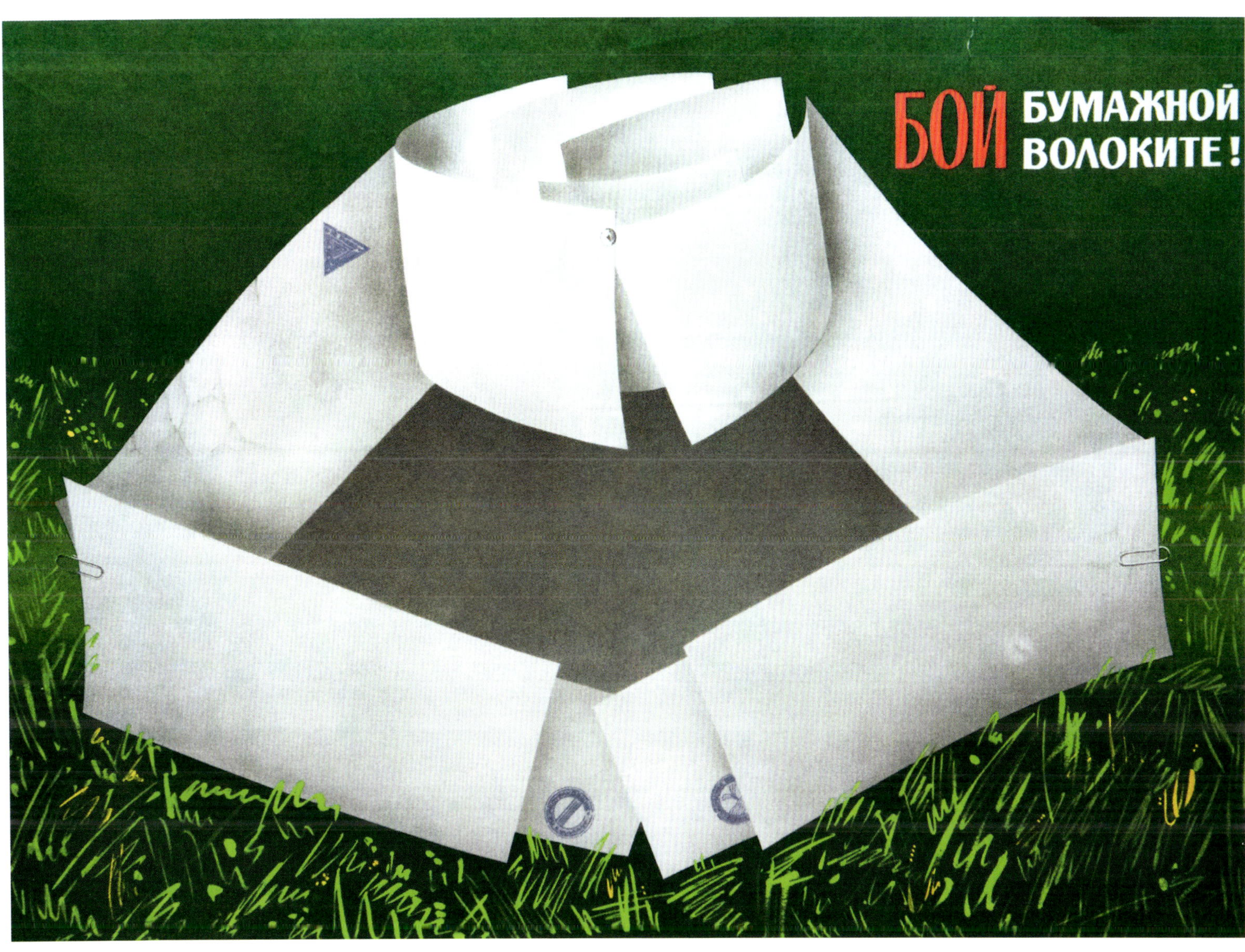

Н. Усов (N. Usov) | 1988

GET RID OF THEM!
Each desk chair is drawn and labeled to visually represent bureaucratic negatives, from left to right, top to bottom: BUREAUCRATISM / PROVINCIAL NEPOTISM / RED TAPE / ARBITRARY AUTHORITY / MONEY GRUBBING / STAGNANCY / CAREERISM / SHAM PAGEANTRY / RUDENESS / CLANNISHNESS / INSTABILITY / INCOMPETENCE / VANITY / EGO

Г. Кирке (G. Kirke) | 1988

FIGHT PAPERWORK DELAYS!

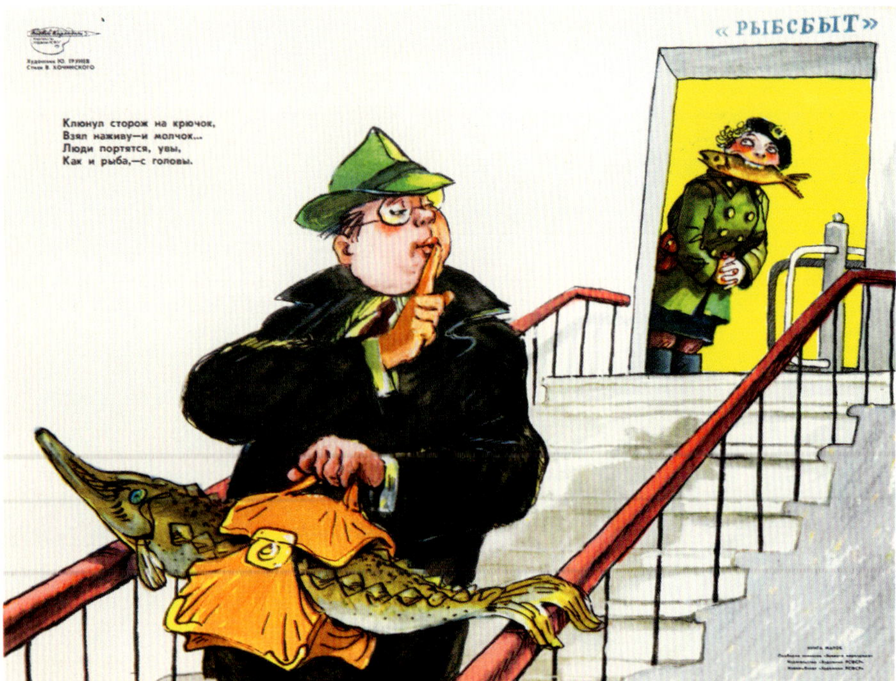

◂ Ю. Трунев (Yu. Trunev) | n.d.

THE WATCHMAN TOOK THE BAIT
AND BIT HIS LIP, IT IS TOO BAD
THAT PEOPLE ARE SO MUCH LIKE FISH
THEY ALSO SPOIL FROM THE HEAD.

A watchman, who is smuggling a sturgeon in his briefcase out of a FISHERY, looks on as a bureaucrat smuggles one out in her mouth.

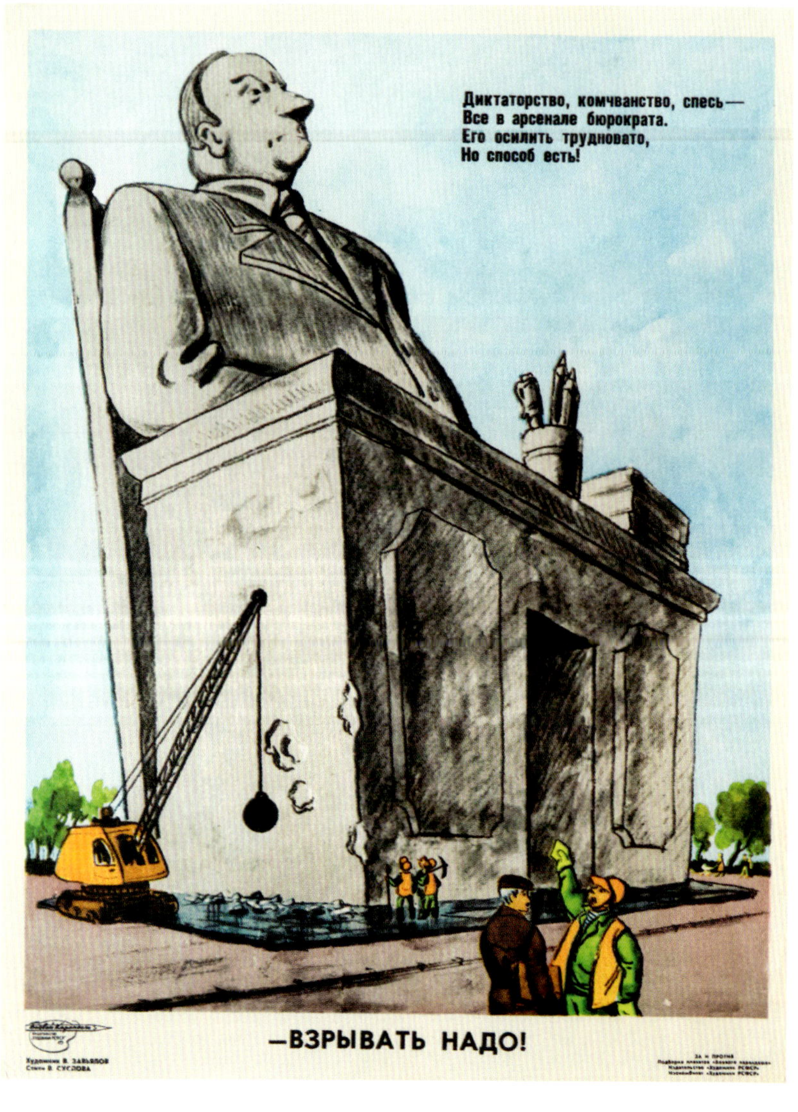

В. Завьялов (V. Zavyalov) | n.d. ▸

Text at bottom: DEMOLISH THEIR BASTION!
Text at top: DICTATORSHIP, HIGH-HANDEDNESS, ARROGANCE—THESE ARE THE WEAPONS BUREAUCRATS HAVE READILY AT HAND. IT'S ALMOST IMPOSSIBLE TO DEFEAT THEM, YET WE HAVE A WAY!

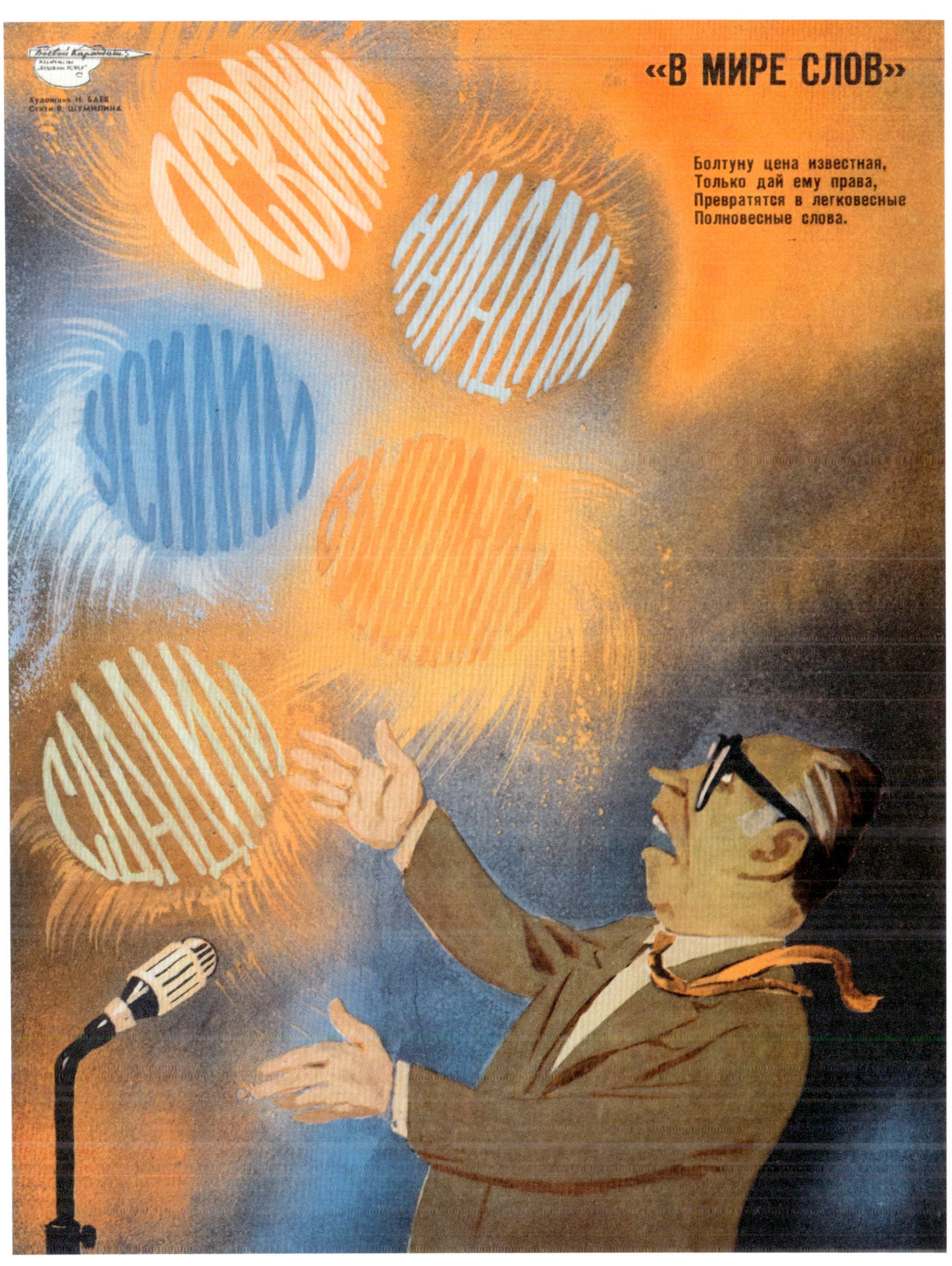

Н. Баев (N. Baev) | n.d. ➤

IN THE WORLD OF WORDS
EVERYONE KNOWS WHAT A WINDBAG IS WORTH
AS SOON AS YOU GIVE HIM THE RIGHT
HE'LL TURN EVEN THE HEAVIEST WORDS
FEATHER-LIGHT.

Text in bubbles:
MASTER / FIX / EFFORTS / FULFILL / SUBMIT

BUREAUCRACY

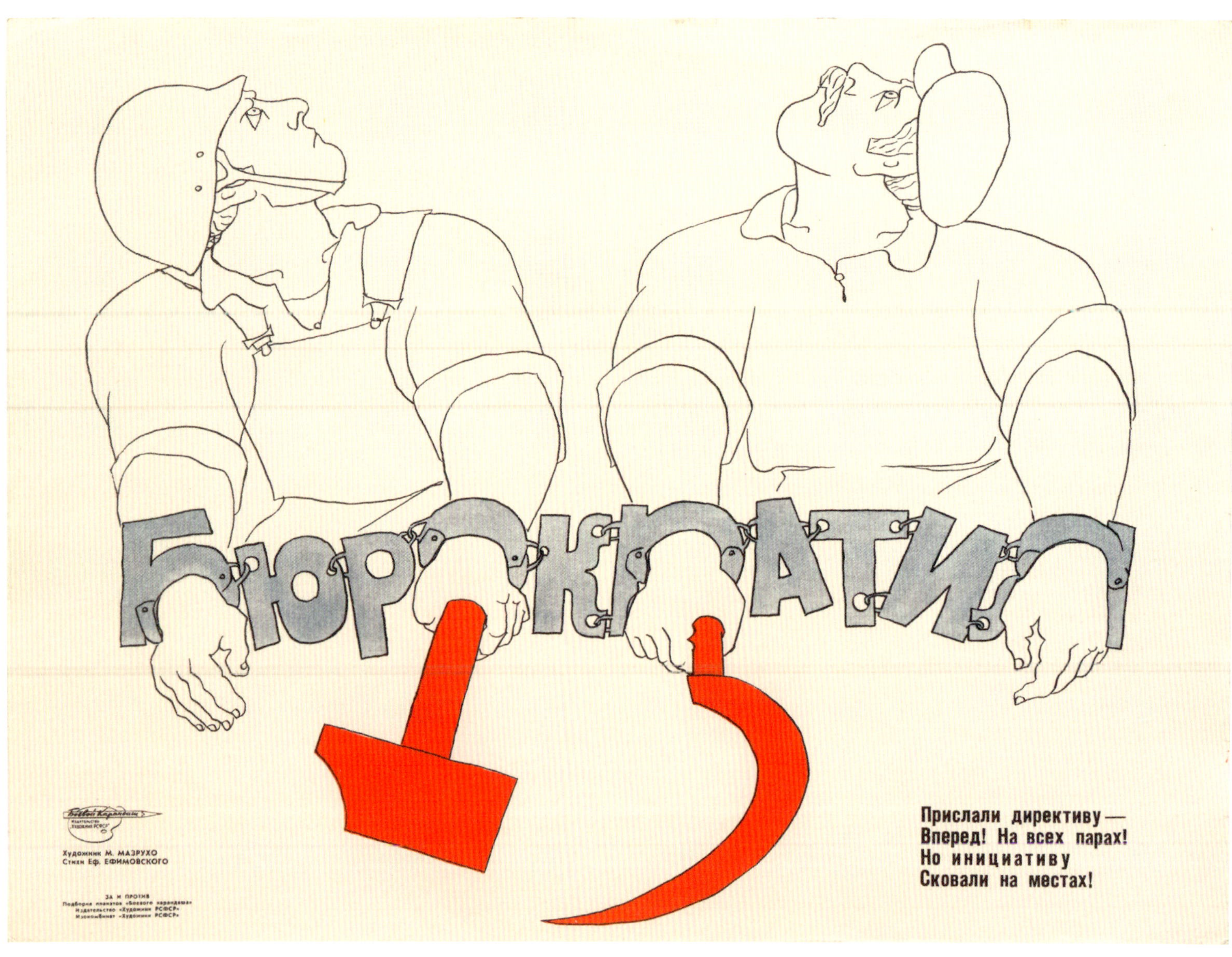

▲ **М. Мазрухо (M. Mazruho) | n.d.**

Two men, a worker and a peasant, have their wrists bound by handcuffs that spell out the word BUREAUCRACY, so that they cannot use the emblematic Soviet tools—the hammer and sickle—to do any work.
Text below: THEY SENT OUT A DIRECTIVE
TO MOVE FULL SPEED AHEAD
BUT PARALYZED INITIATIVE
IN FETTERS MADE OF LEAD!

В. Завьялов (V. Zavyalov) | n.d. ➤

Texts written on dossiers and papers inserted into a meat grinder in lieu of a bureaucrat's head: RECONSTRUCTION PROJECT / PROPOSAL / NEW TECHNOLOGIES. These concepts are all thrown into a supposedly "new" kitchen appliance and ground up together to reproduce the standard old bureaucratic rules. Spewing out from the grinder plate: TREAD SOFTLY, GO FAR . . .
Text at bottom: WE PEEKED IN THE
BUREAUCRAT'S RECIPE BOOK.
WHAT IS HE COOKING? TAKE A GOOD LOOK.

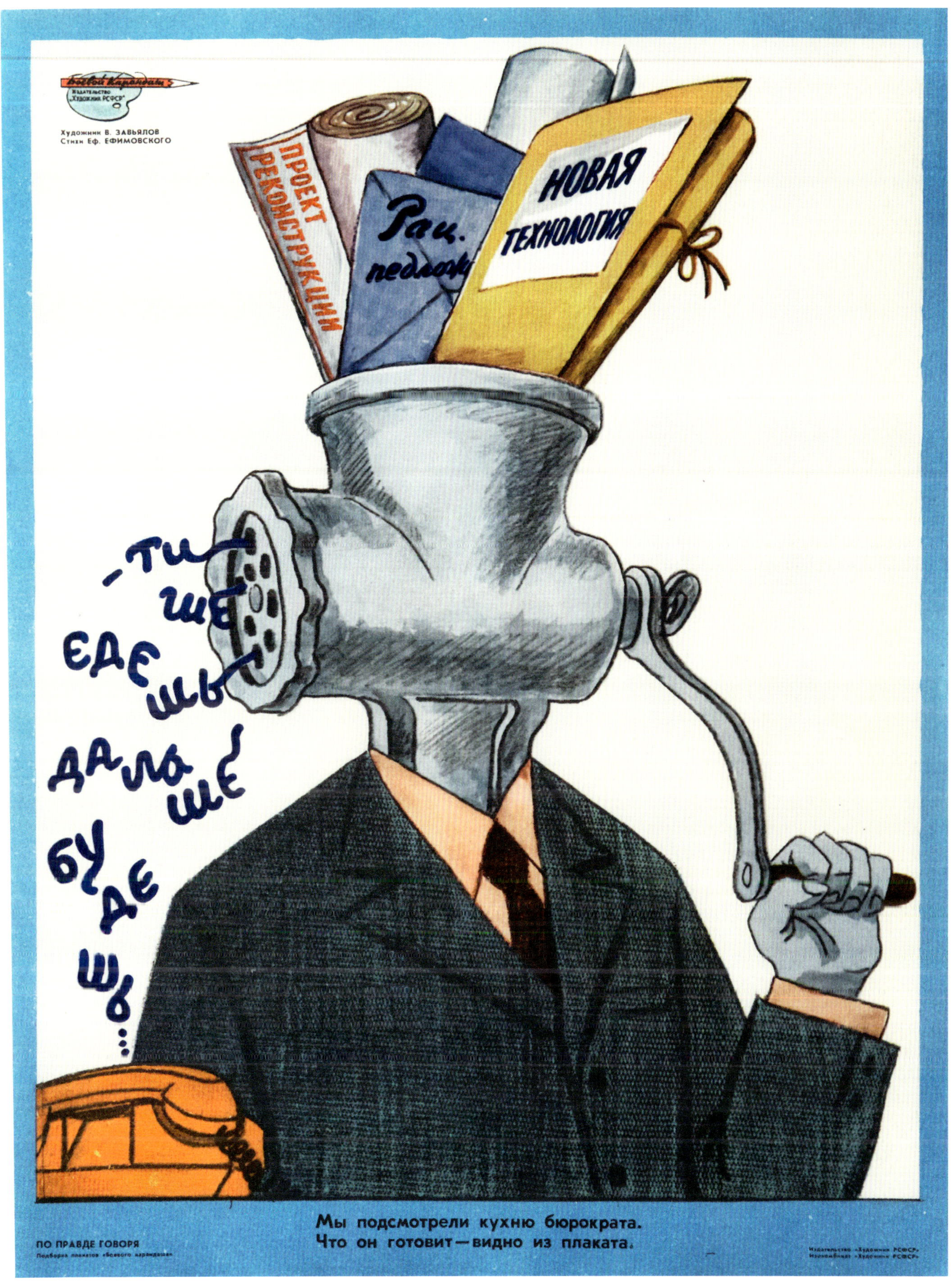
Издательство „Художник РСФСР"
Художник В. ЗАВЬЯЛОВ
Стихи Еф. ЕФИМОВСКОГО
ПРОЕКТ РЕКОНСТРУКЦИИ
Рац. предлож
НОВАЯ ТЕХНОЛОГИЯ
-ТИ-ШЕ ЕДЕШЬ ДАЛЬШЕ БУДЕШЬ...
Мы подсмотрели кухню бюрократа.
Что он готовит — видно из плаката.
ПО ПРАВДЕ ГОВОРЯ

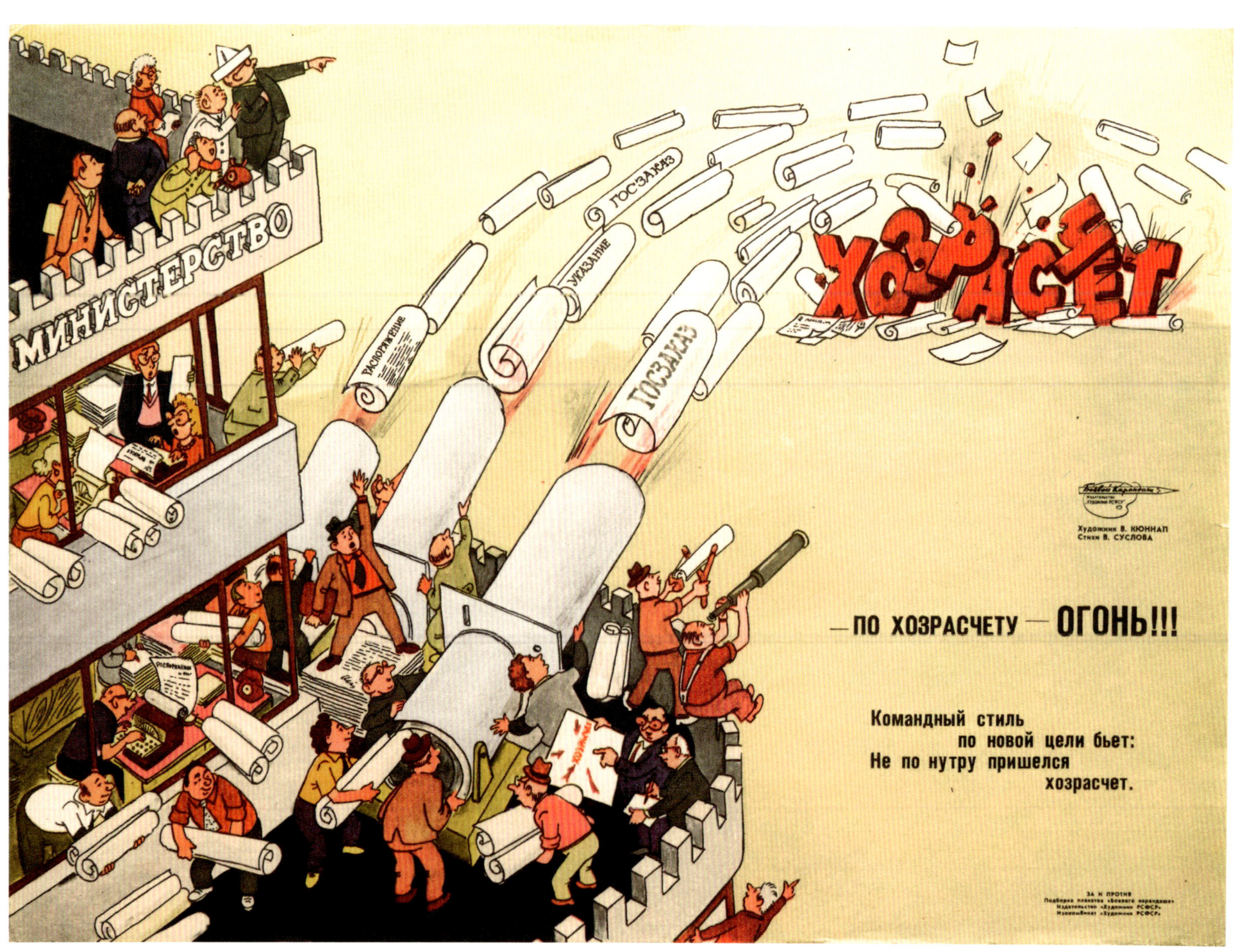

▲ В. Кюннап (V. Kunnap) | n.d.

A fortified castle labeled MINISTRY, with the minister at the top level wearing a paper hat and with a hand in his jacket in imitation of Napoleon. "The troops" are firing paper canons with paper shells, marked DECREE / DIRECTIVE / GOVERNMENT ORDER, at the words FOR-PROFIT MODEL. It appears that not many of the projectiles have been able to hit their mark.
Text at lower right: FIRE ON THE FOR-PROFIT MODEL!!! THE COMMAND HAS A NEW TARGET TO SHELL LOOKS LIKE PROFIT AND LOSS AREN'T SITTING WELL.

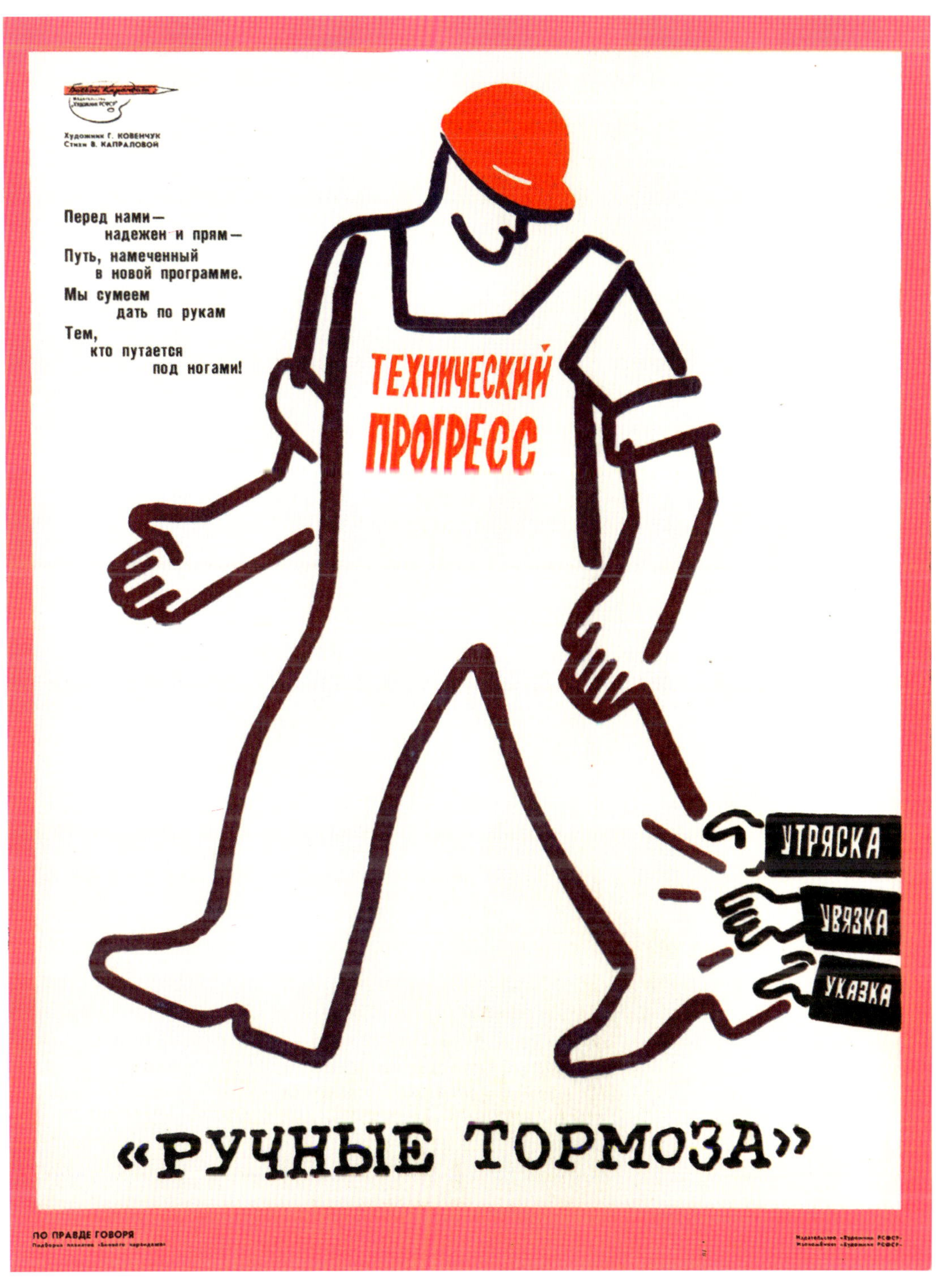

Г. Ковенчук (G. Covenchuk) | n.d.

This worker of TECHNICAL PROGRESS (printed on his overalls) is held back by HANDBRAKES (text along bottom). Three sleeved arms with the words: SHAKEDOWNS / TAKEDOWNS / HOLDUPS grab the worker's pants. Text at top left: RELIABLE AND STRAIGHT: THE ROAD AHEAD—THE PATH SET OUT IN OUR NEW PROGRAM. AS WE ADVANCE WE WILL BE SURE TO OVERCOME ALL THOSE WHO TRY TO STOP US UNDERFOOT!

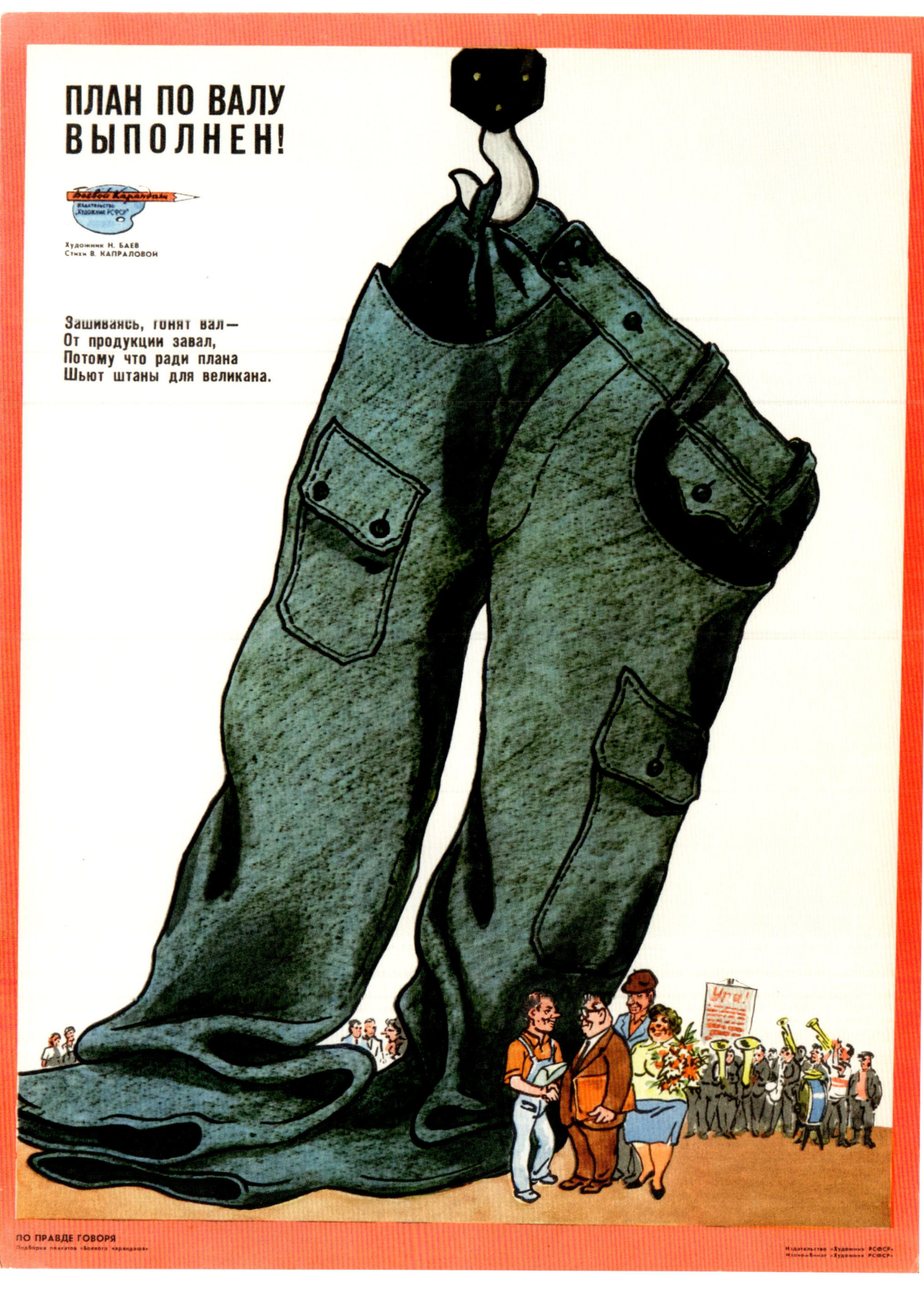
ПЛАН ПО ВАЛУ
ВЫПОЛНЕН!
Боевой Карандаш
Художник Н. БАЕВ
Стихи В. КАПРАЛОВОЙ
Зашиваясь, гонят вал—
От продукции завал,
Потому что ради плана
Шьют штаны для великана.
Ура!
ПО ПРАВДЕ ГОВОРЯ
Подборка плакатов «Боевого карандаша»
Издательство «Художник РСФСР»

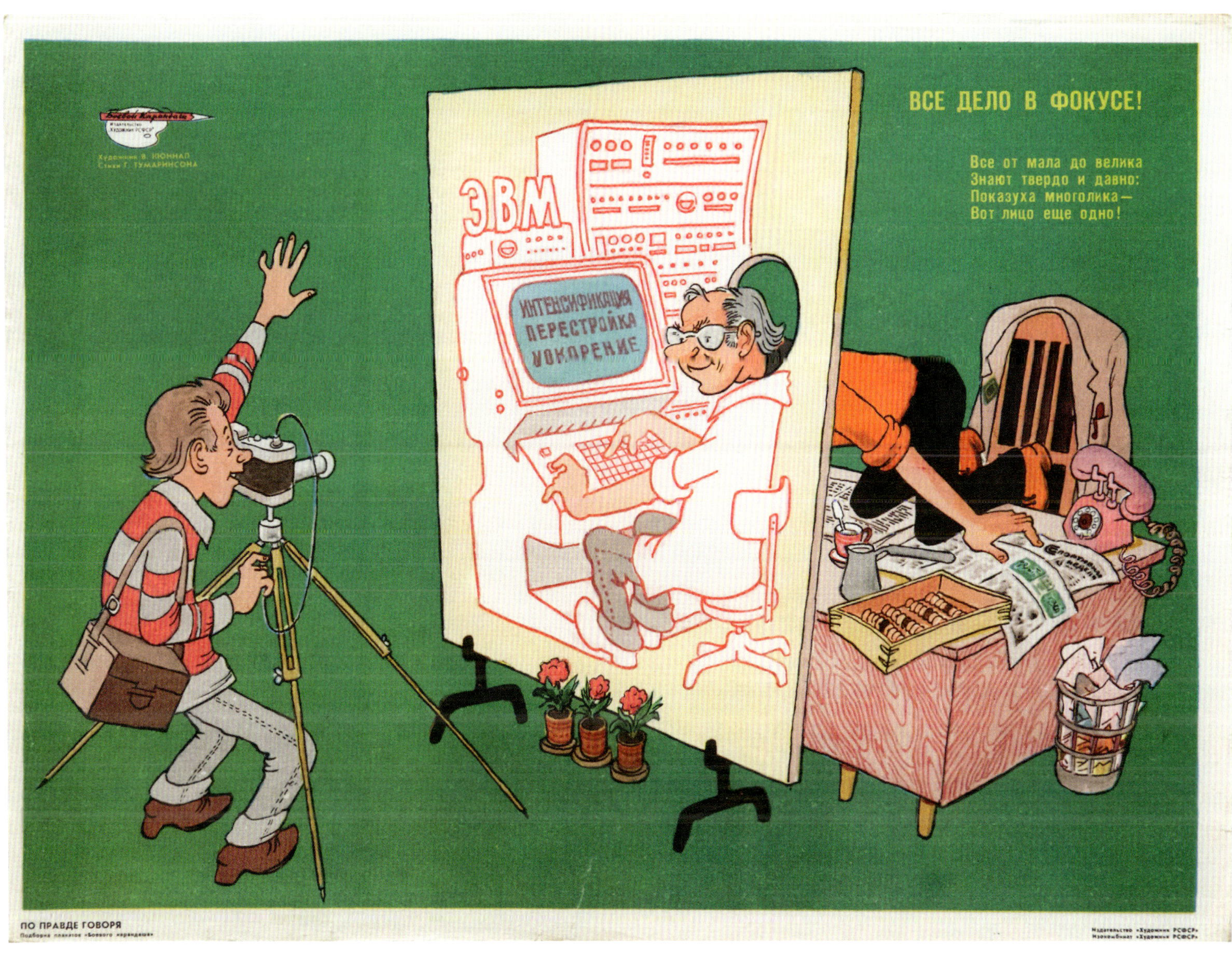

◀ **Н. Баев (N. Baev) | n.d.**

QUOTA FOR SURPLUS PRODUCTION: EXCEEDED!

THEY'RE PUSHING THEIR PRODUCTION TO THE LIMIT AND BLASTING THROUGH THE ROOF OF EVERY QUOTA BECAUSE THEY FOUND A WAY TO MAKE THE ENDS MEET: JUST MAKE A PAIR OF PANTS FIT FOR A GIANT. A band plays and someone carries a sign that reads HURRAH! A bureaucrat shakes hands with a worker while a woman waits to present him with a bouquet of flowers in recognition of his achievement.

▲ **В. Кюннап (V. Kunnap) | n.d.**

Text on upper right corner:
THE WHOLE THING IS IN FOCUS!

EVERYBODY YOUNG AND OLD
KNOWS HOW THESE THINGS GO
HERE IS JUST ANOTHER WAY
OF PUTTING ON A SHOW.

On the false front: IBM / INTENSIFICATION / PERESTROIKA / ACCELERATION

PERESTROIKA

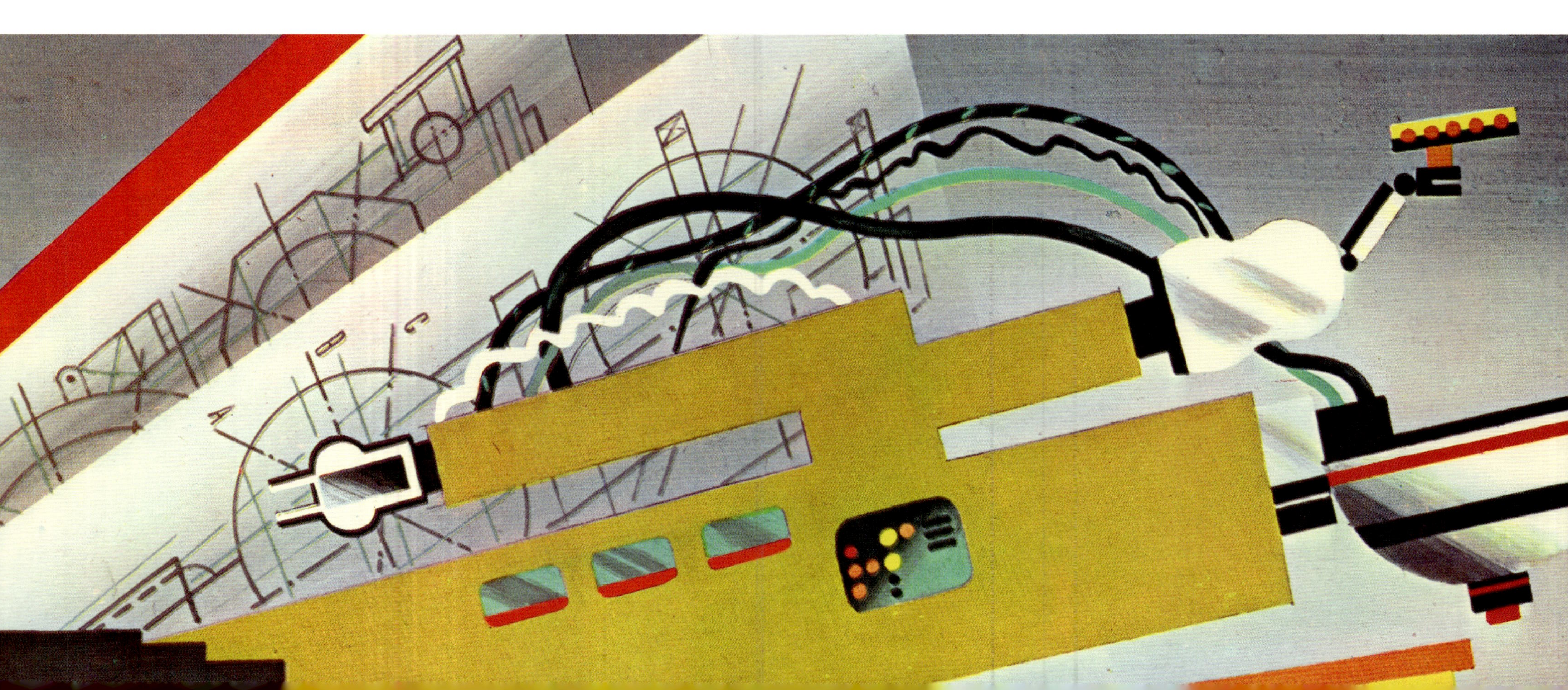

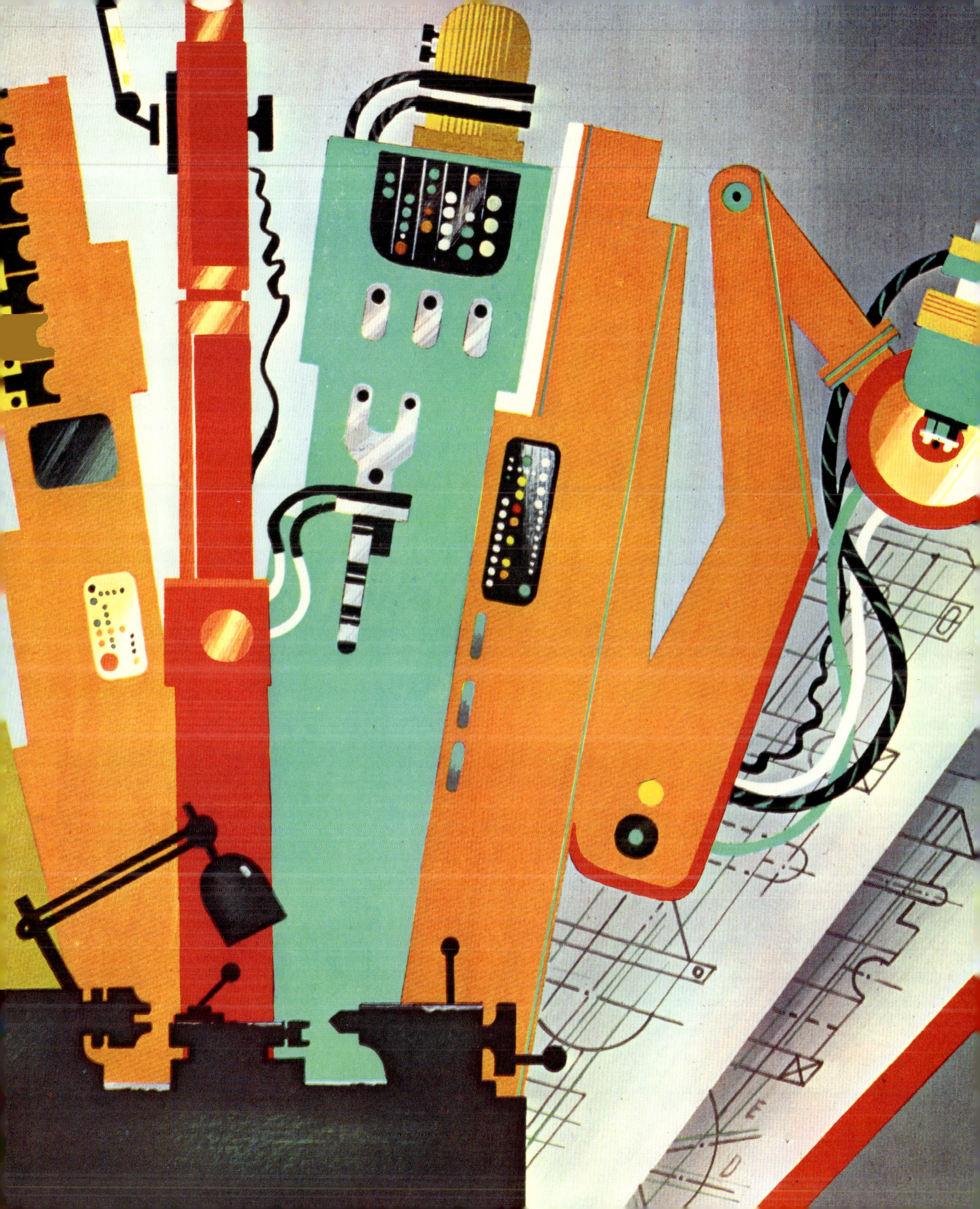

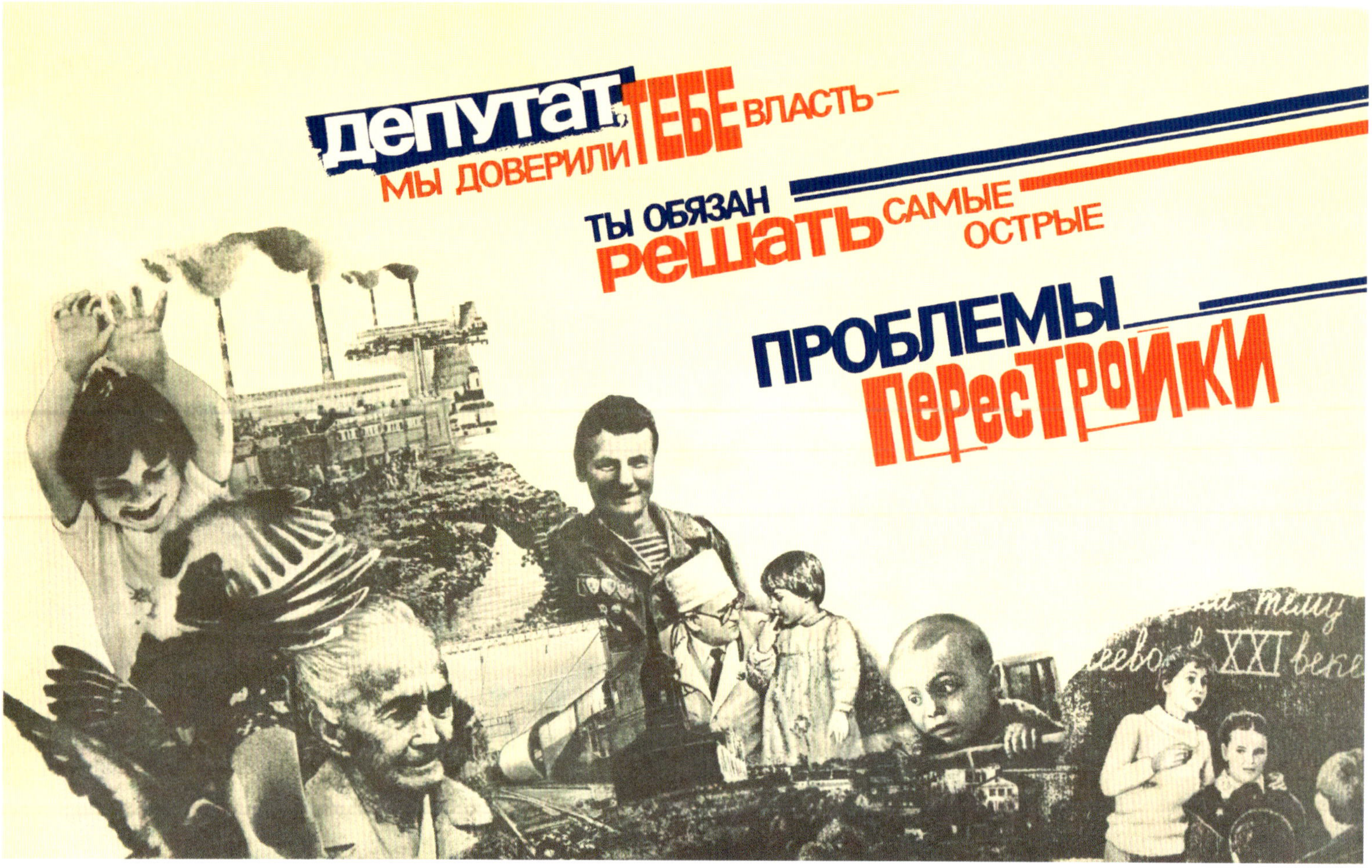

▲ **Н. Верди (N. Verdi), В. Коваленко (V. Kovalenko) | 1989**

DEPUTY [referring to the People's Deputies of the Soviet Union]: WE HAVE ENTRUSTED YOU WITH POWER—YOU MUST SOLVE THE MOST ACUTE PROBLEMS OF PERESTROIKA.

М. Мкртчьян (M. Mkrtchyan) | 1988 ►

Text on comb: SCHOOL. Text at bottom: EVERY STUDENT IS AN INDIVIDUAL! Here, the repeated anonymous silhouettes of students between the comb's teeth evoke the Russian saying: "everyone's hair is cut with the same comb." As such, the poster invokes criticism of anti-individual, pro-conformity education in the Soviet school system.

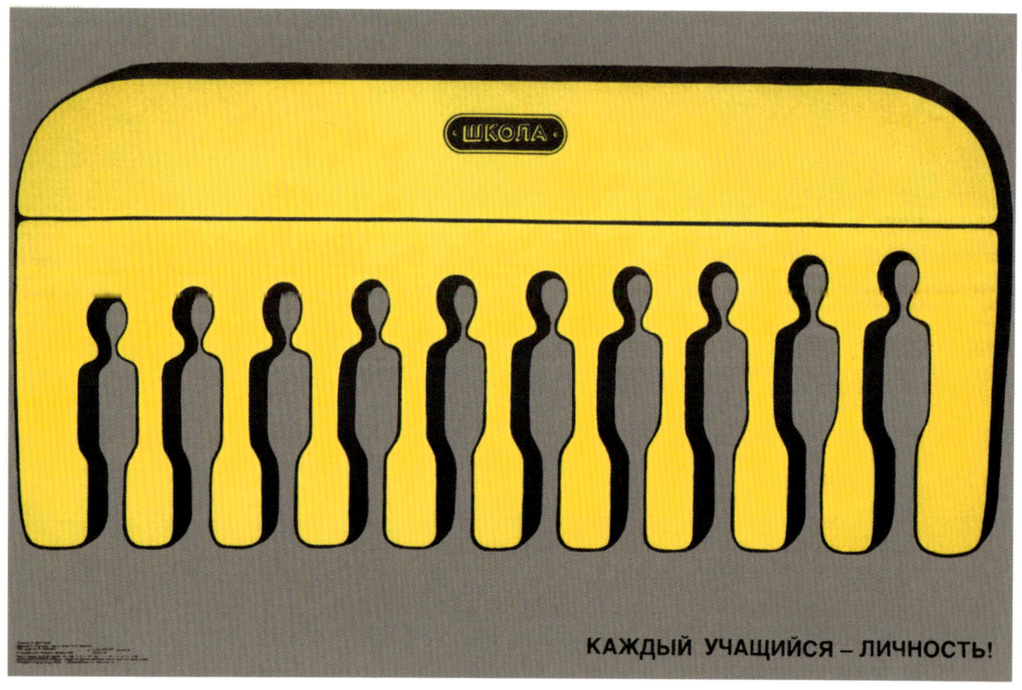

С. Сухарев (S. Sukharev) | 1990 ➤

Text at top: NO MORE EXPERIMENTS . . . LET THE PEASANTS HAVE THE LAND! A naked peasant, reduced to insignificance, supposedly outpaced by scientific agriculture, is isolated on the stage of a microscope. He sticks out his tongue, in the only small gesture of rebellion left to him. The slogan harks back to the very early years of the Soviet Revolution when peasants could farm privately. Perestroika reforms sought to reestablish a mixed economy, similar to what existed in the time of Lenin's New Economic Policy (NEP), in hopes of reinvigorating and maximizing productivity.

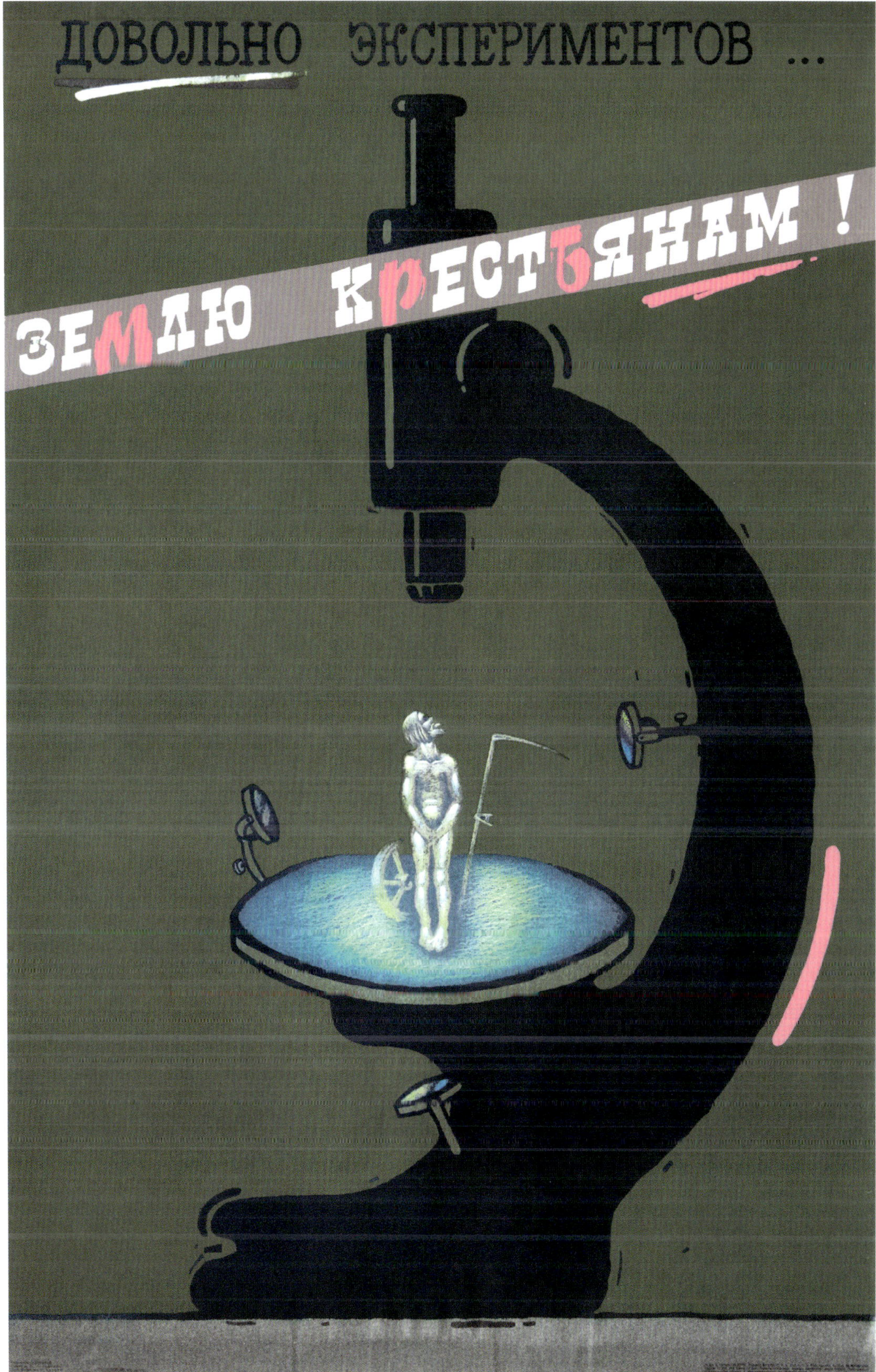

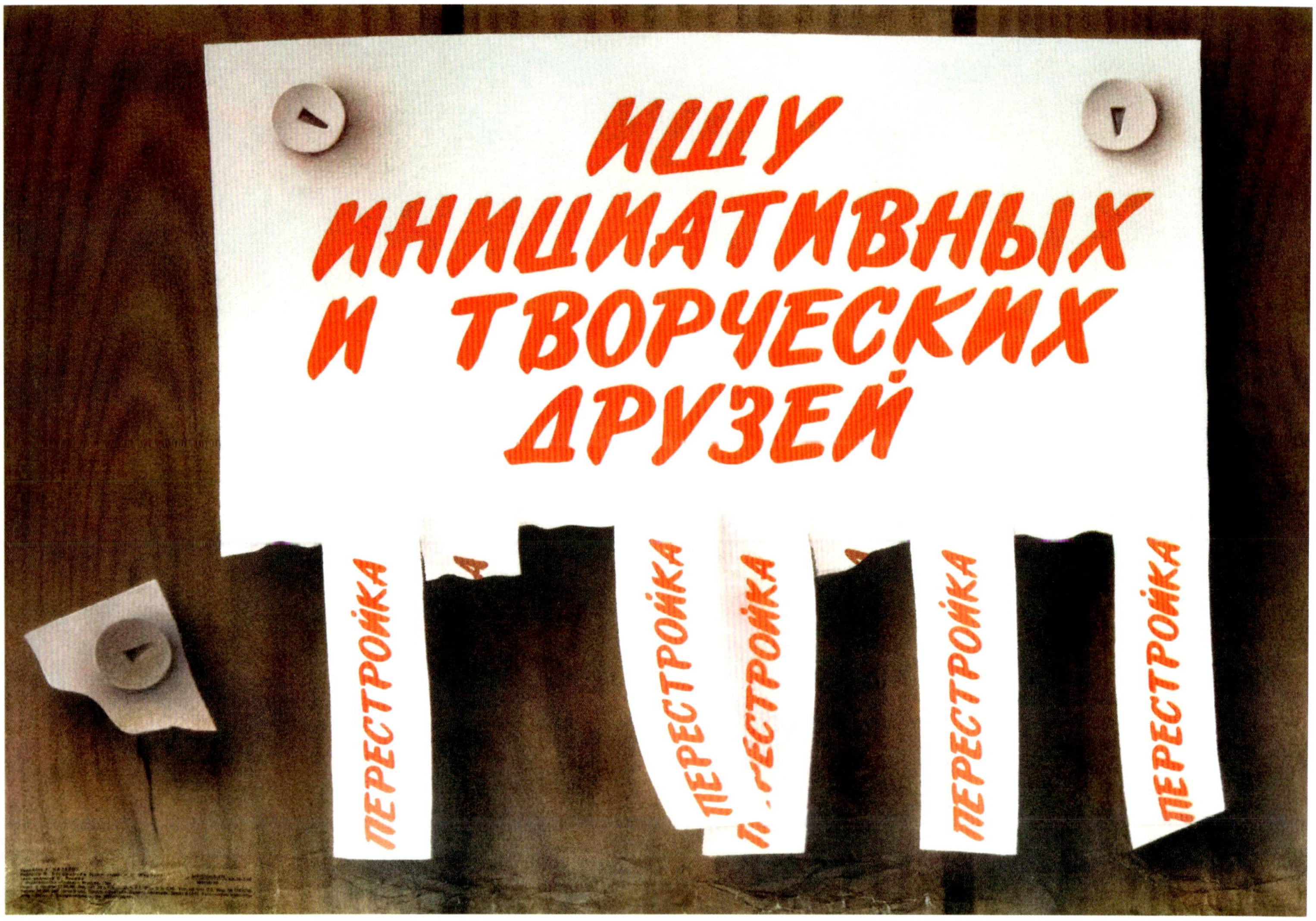

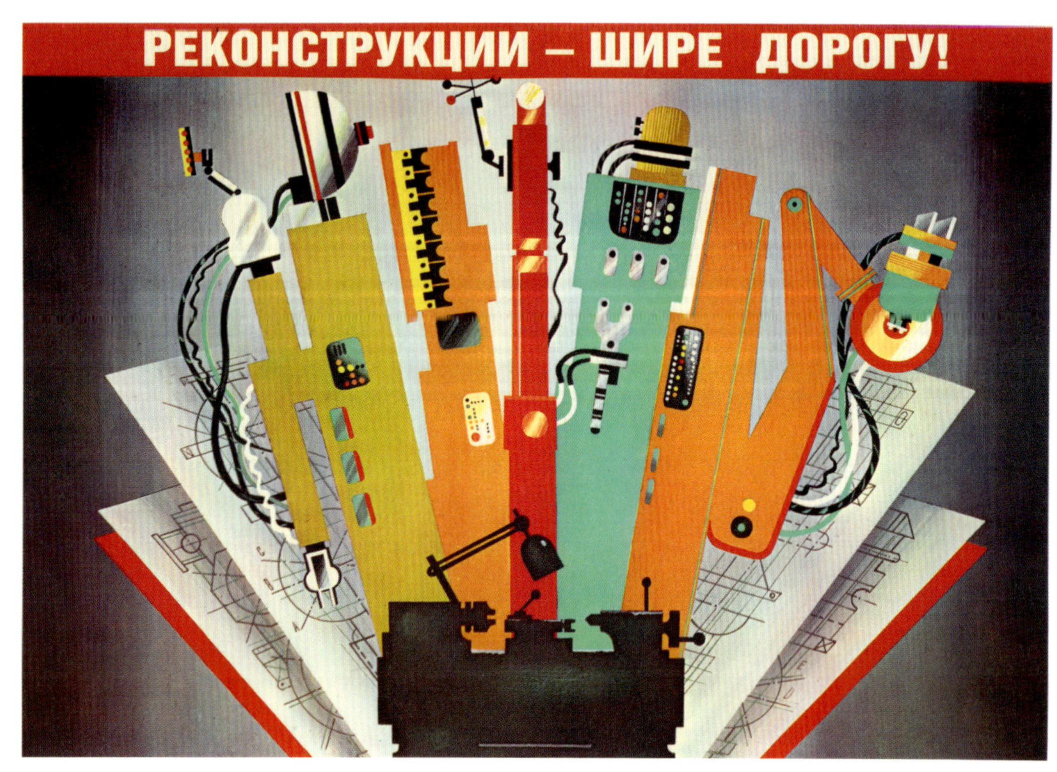

▲ Г. Назаров (G. Nazarov) | 1988

SEEKING ENTREPRENEURIAL AND CREATIVE FRIENDS
A sign on a bulletin board. Instead of a phone number, the contact information is listed on each tab of paper simply as PERESTROIKA.

Е. Родионова (E. Rodionova) | 1988 ▶

Text along top: MAKE MORE ROOM FOR RECONSTRUCTION!
Behind a realistic-looking large black lathe, a colorful burst of fantasy plans and machines imagines what the lathe could produce if those using the tool did so creatively. Again, this poster is attempting to exhort the population to apply a broadly entrepreneurial spirit to reform.

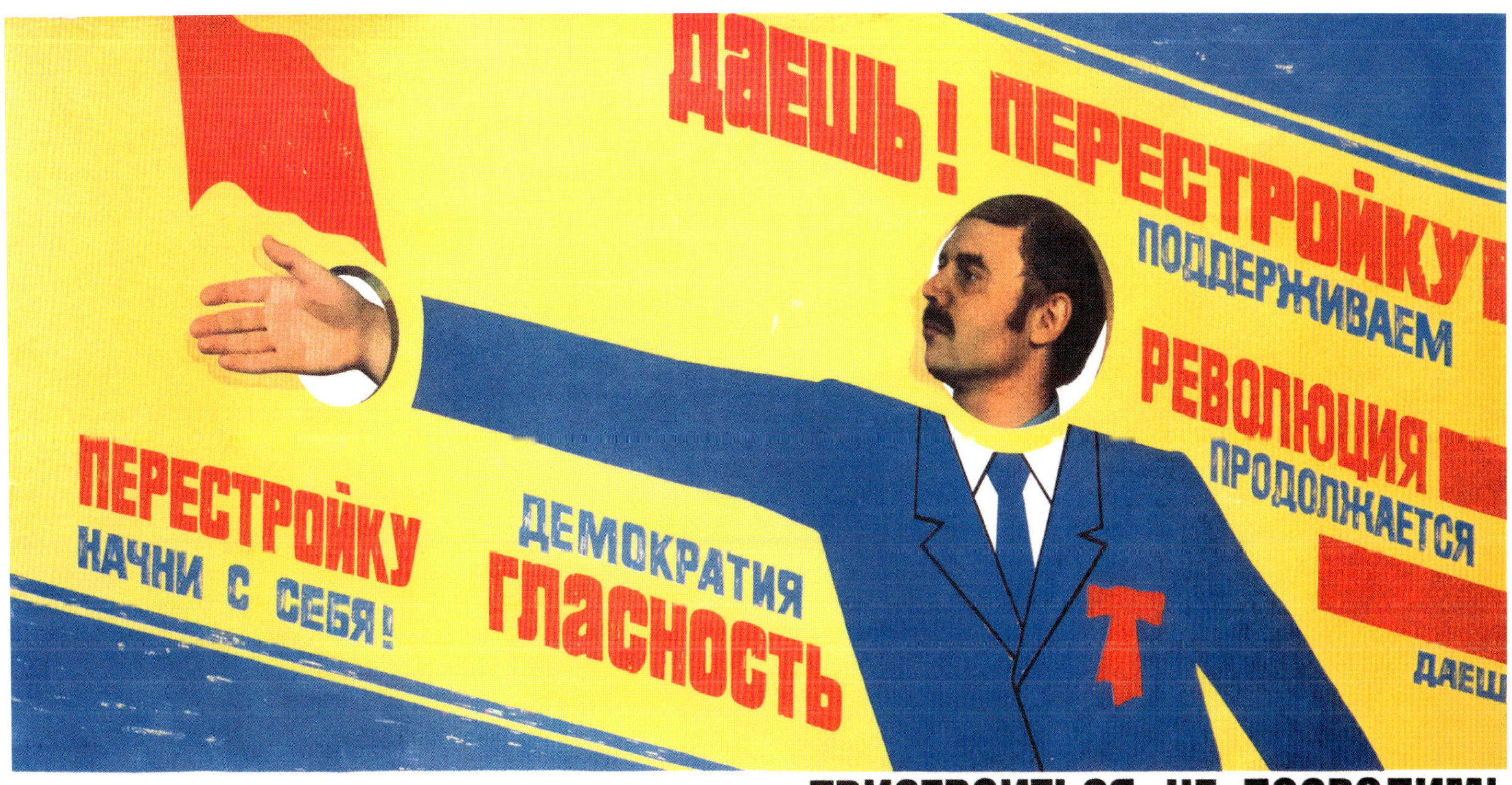

▲ Б. Янин (B. Yanin) | 1989

WE SUPPORT PERESTROIKA!
THE REVOLUTION CONTINUES
PERESTROIKA BEGINS WITH YOU
DEMOCRACY
GLASNOST

A man's hand and face poke through a billboard. A very long arm is extended in a commanding gesture strongly identified with Lenin; the red ribbon on the jacket was worn in Lenin's time to show support. The image is a typical symbol of a "Potemkin" or *pokazukha* performance—a false front used to photograph someone in order to hide the real situation.
Black text on white at bottom:
WE WON'T ALLOW THEM TO JUST PLAY ALONG!

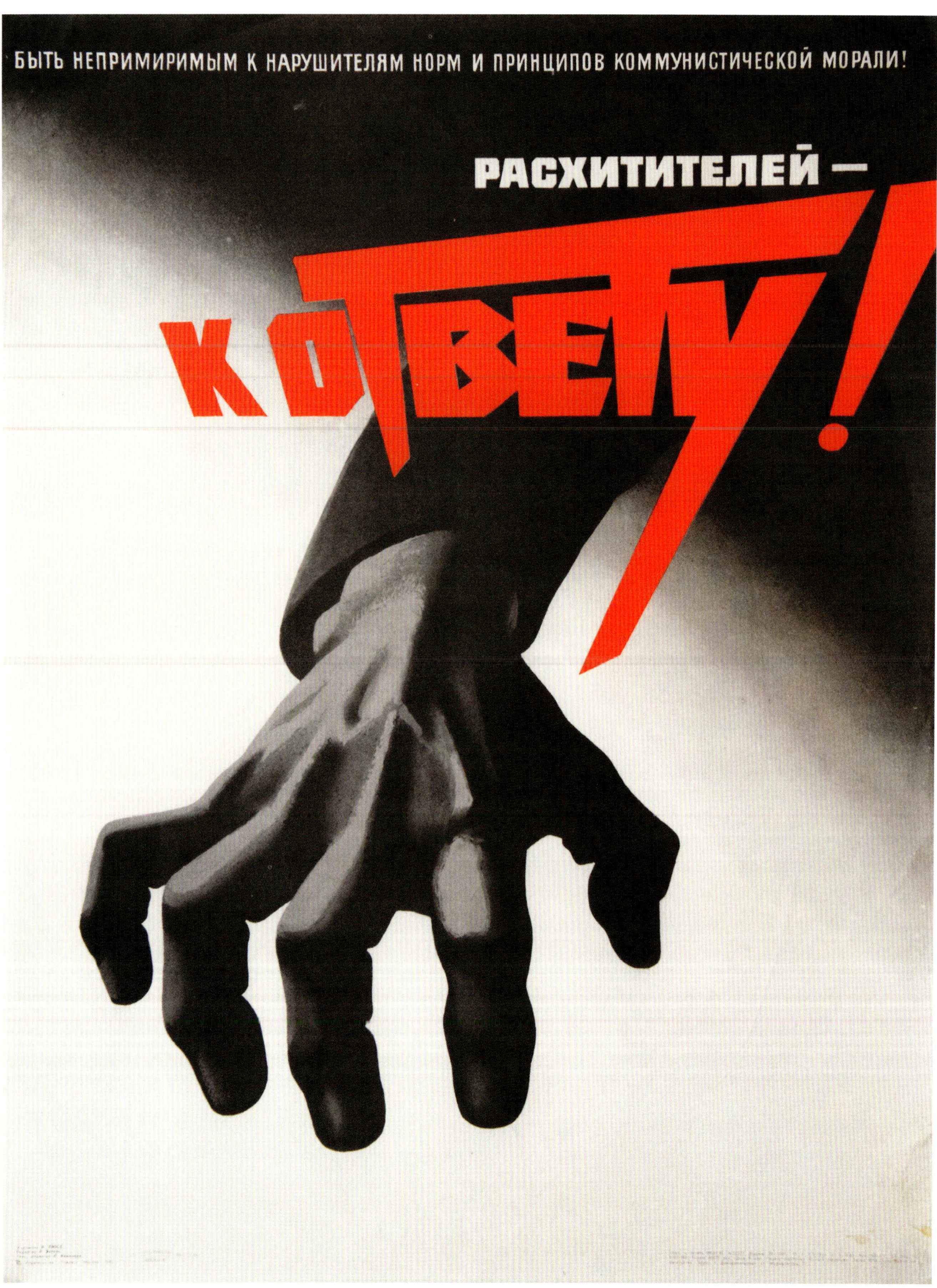
БЫТЬ НЕПРИМИРИМЫМ К НАРУШИТЕЛЯМ НОРМ И ПРИНЦИПОВ КОММУНИСТИЧЕСКОЙ МОРАЛИ!
РАСХИТИТЕЛЕЙ —
К ОТВЕТУ!

◀ К. Пюсс (K. Pyuss) | 1985

Text at top: DON'T TOLERATE THOSE WHO VIOLATE THE NORMS AND PRINCIPLES OF COMMUNIST MORALITY!
Text below:
HOLD THE PLUNDERERS RESPONSIBLE!

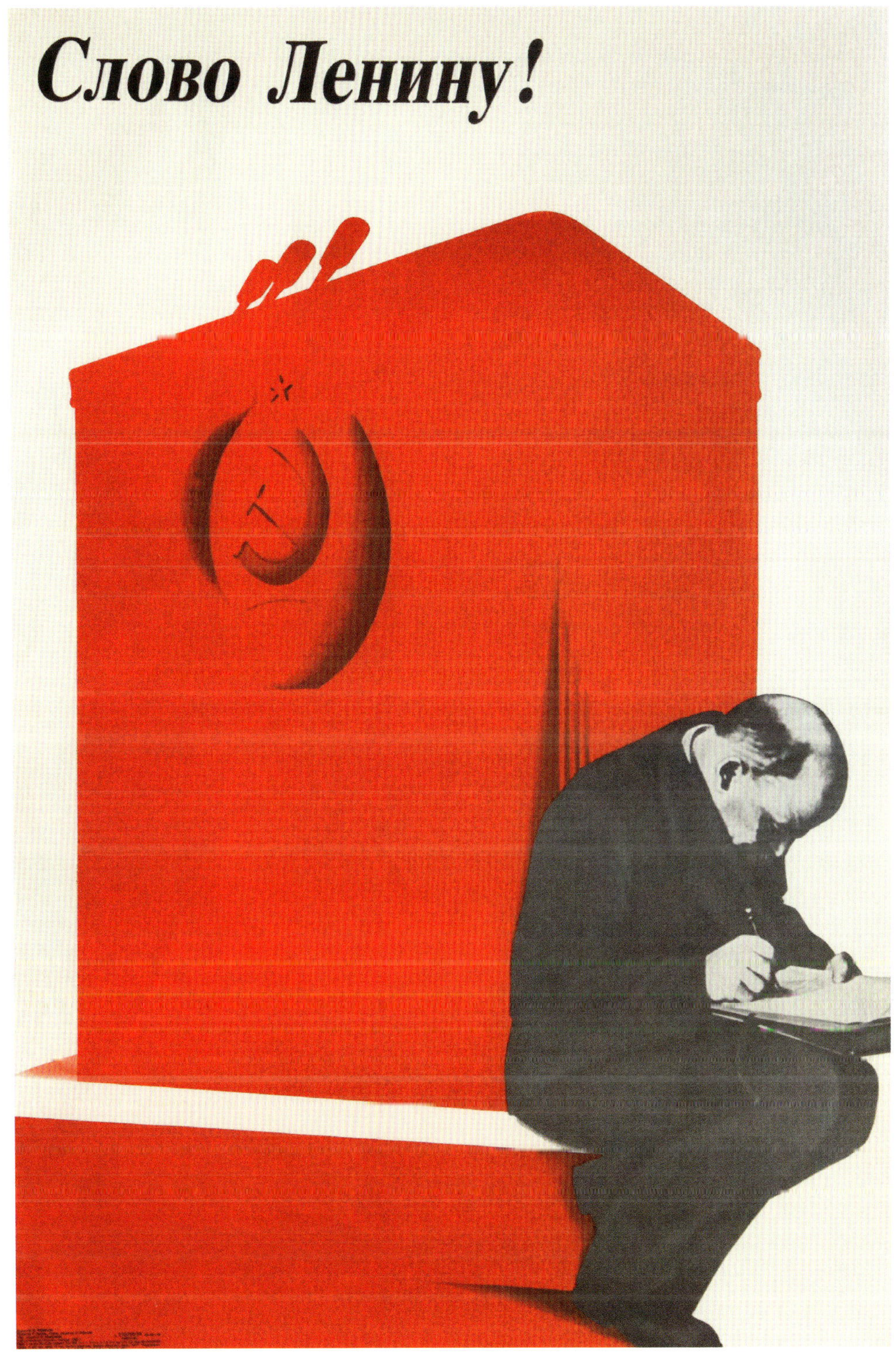

В. Чумаков (V. Chumakov) | 1990 ▶

LET LENIN TAKE THE FLOOR!
Lenin is sitting with the speaker's podium behind him. The message here is that his ideas are valid, and therefore the USSR should once again embrace his sociopolitical concepts.

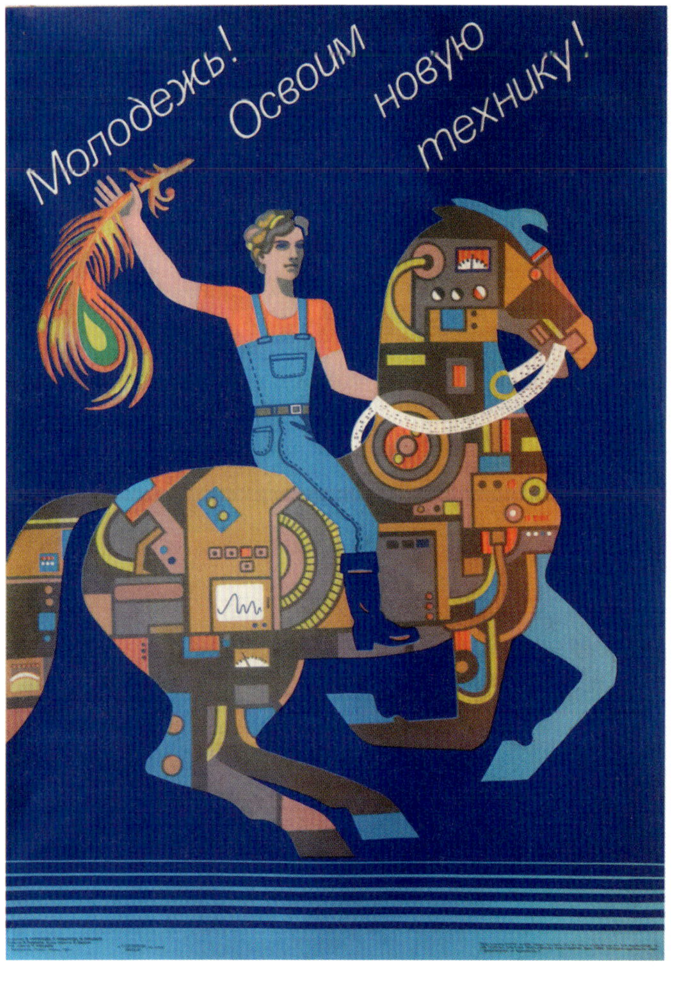

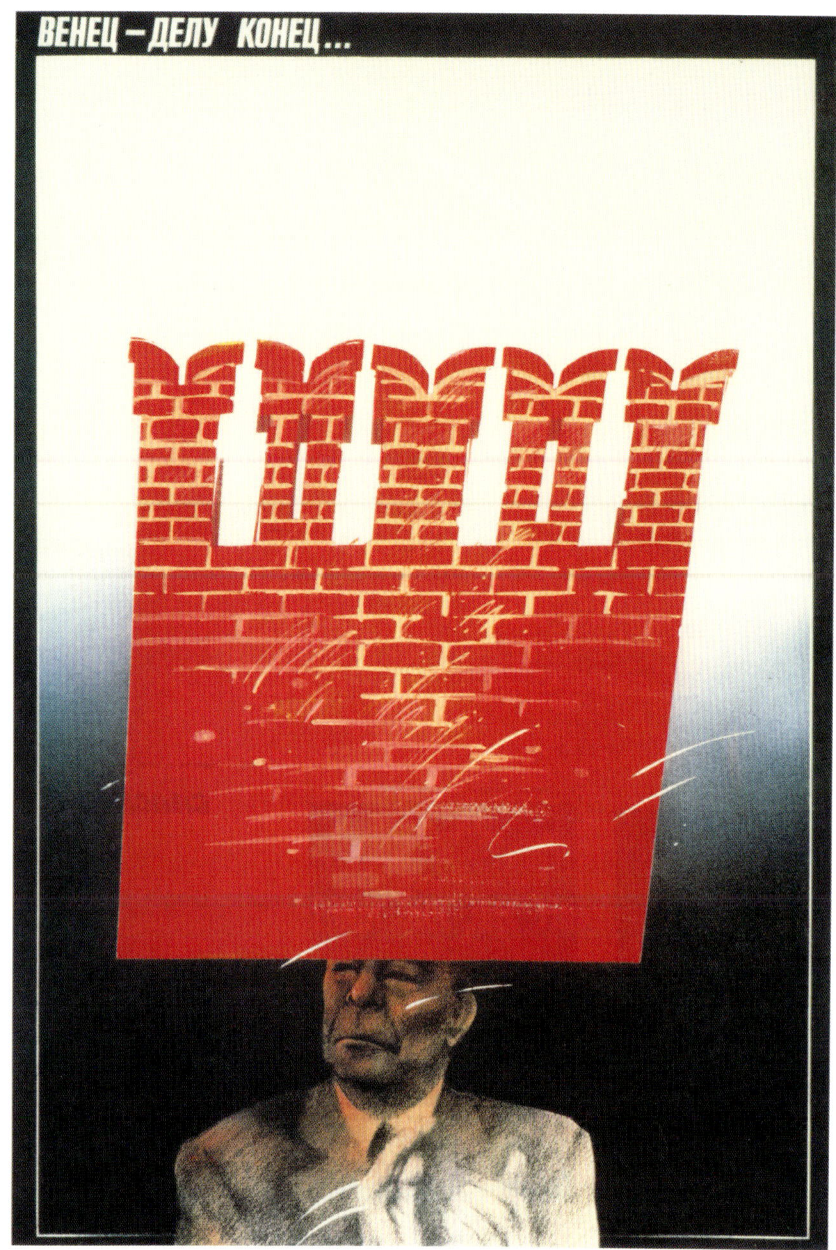

▲ С. Мосиенко (S. Mosiyenko) | 1988

THE CROWN ENDS ALL . . .
The figure of Brezhnev is crowned with a section of the Kremlin's red brick wall. But it is a medieval-type defensive wall with battlements. Indeed, the Russian word "kremlin" means a fortress. "The crown ends all," it says here, but the old Russian proverb is: "The End Crowns All." The suggestion is that for Brezhnev, the only strategy in politics was to be a Tsar, or dictator. To a lesser degree than Stalin, Brezhnev was an example of what not to do.

▲ В. Каракашев (V. Karakashev), Л. Левшунова (L. Levshunova), М. Лукьянов (M. Lukyanov) | 1987

YOUNG PEOPLE!
WE WILL MASTER NEW TECHNOLOGY!
A young worker is pictured riding an electronic horse.

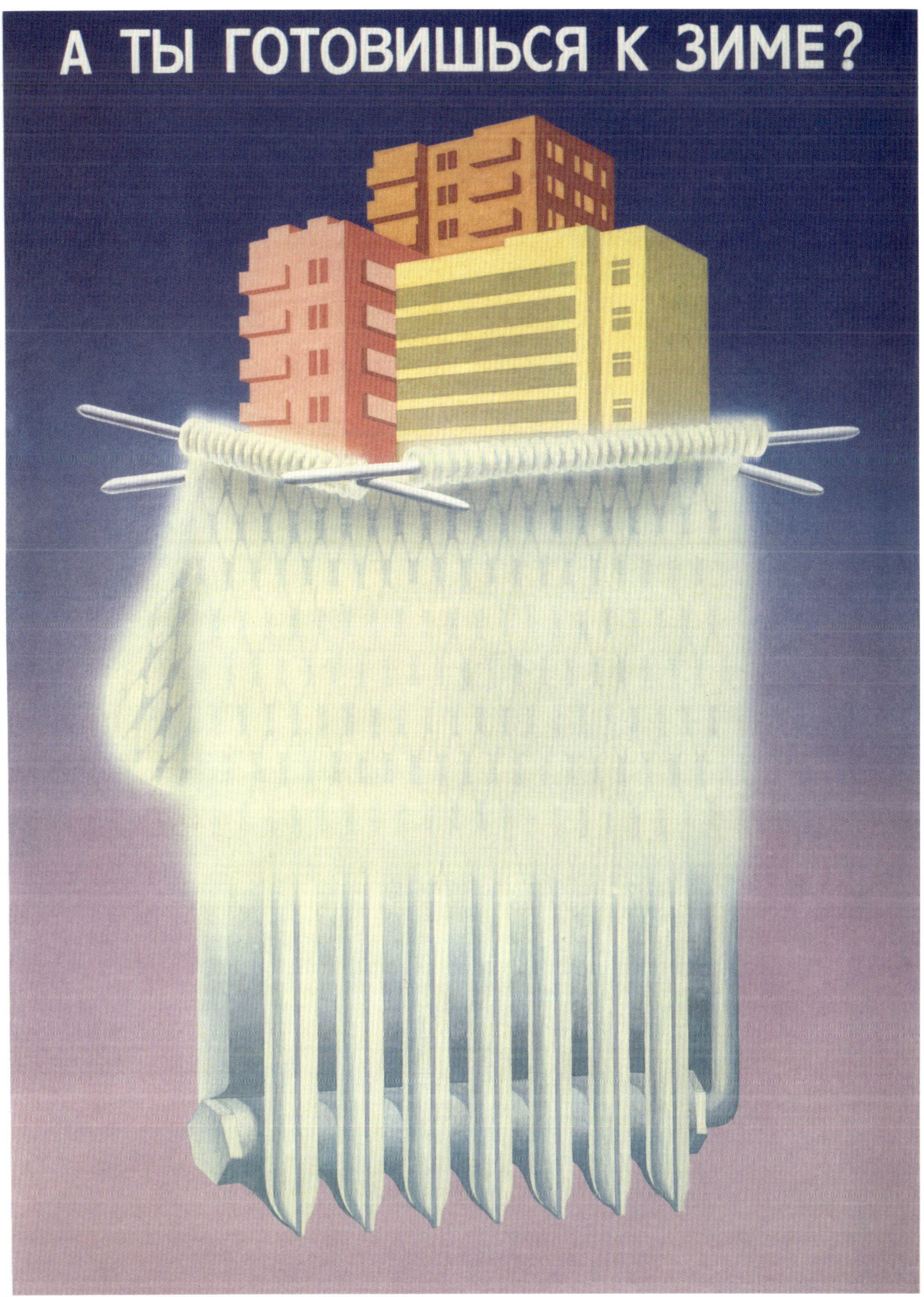

А. Стрелов (A. Strelov) | 1987

ARE YOU GETTING READY FOR WINTER?

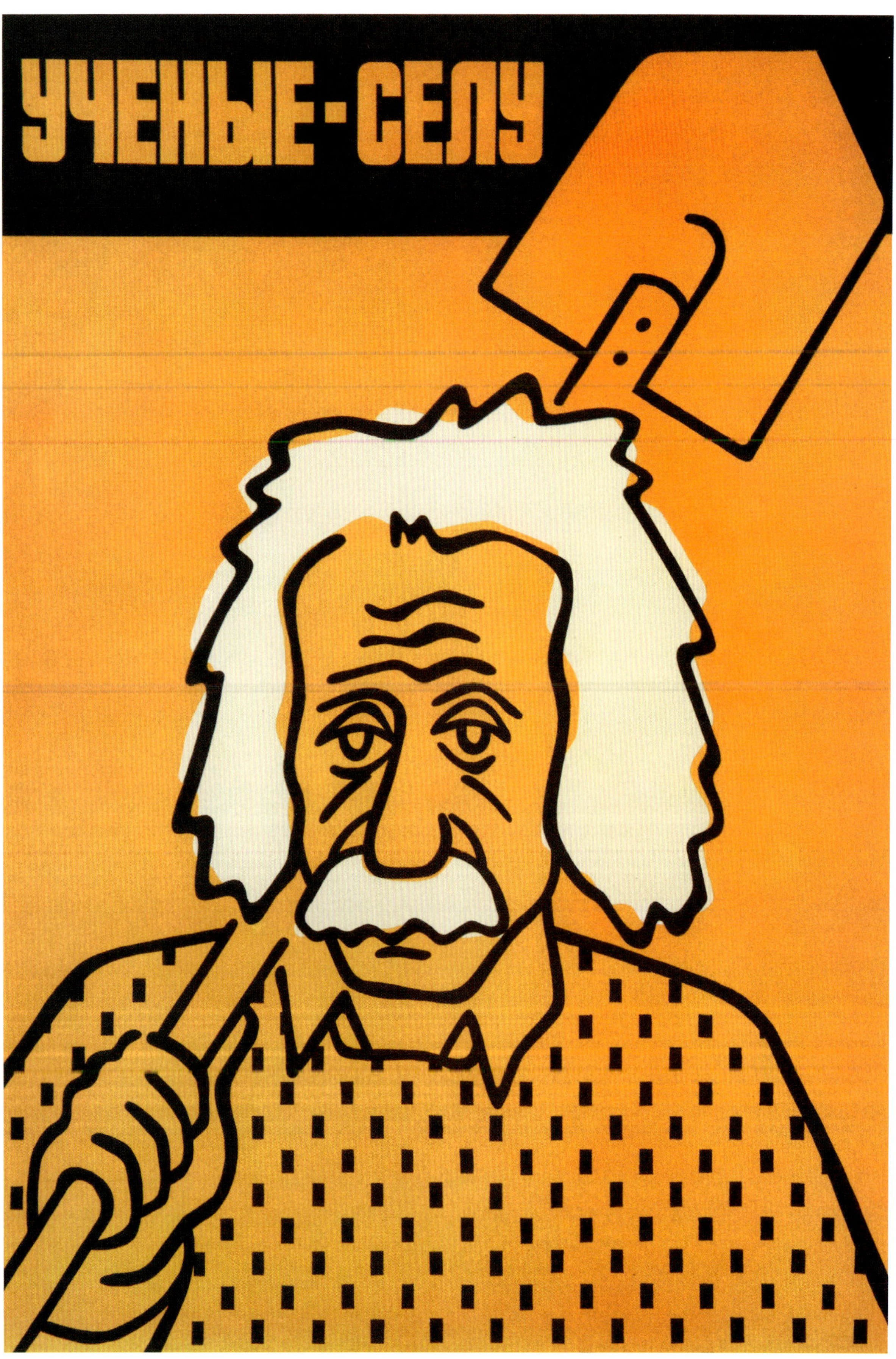
УЧЕНЫЕ - СЕЛУ

◂ М. Паршиков (M. Parshikov) | n.d.

SEND SCIENTISTS TO THE VILLAGES

М. Абрамов (M. Abramov), А. Андреев (A. Andreev) | 1990 ▸

THEY OUGHT TO BE SOWERS AND PLOWERS, NOT STANDING AROUND SELLING FLOWERS. The text displayed on the man's t-shirt reads: PERESTROIKA IS MY MOTHER. His carnations cost three rubles each

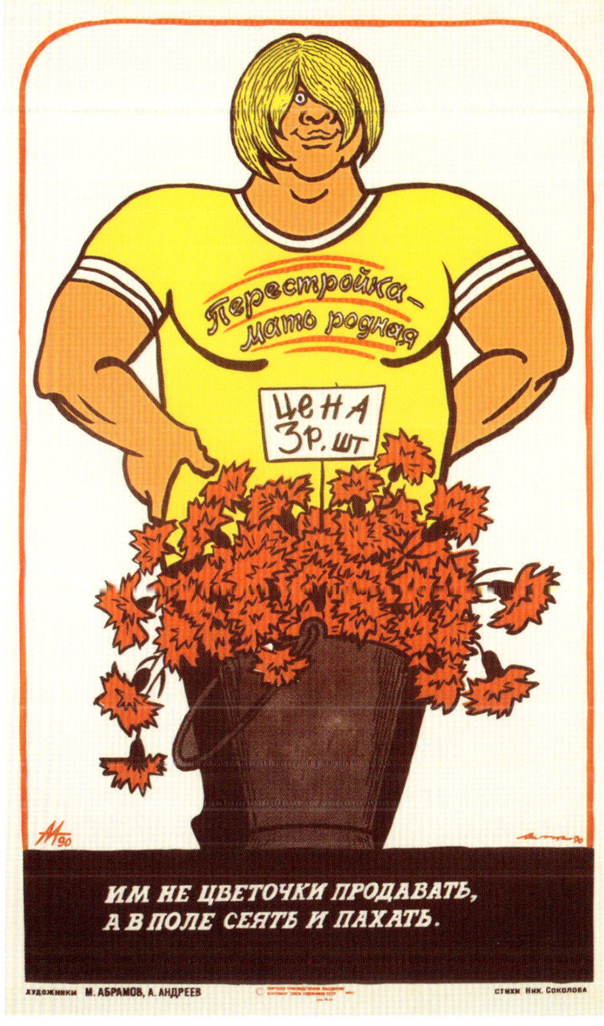

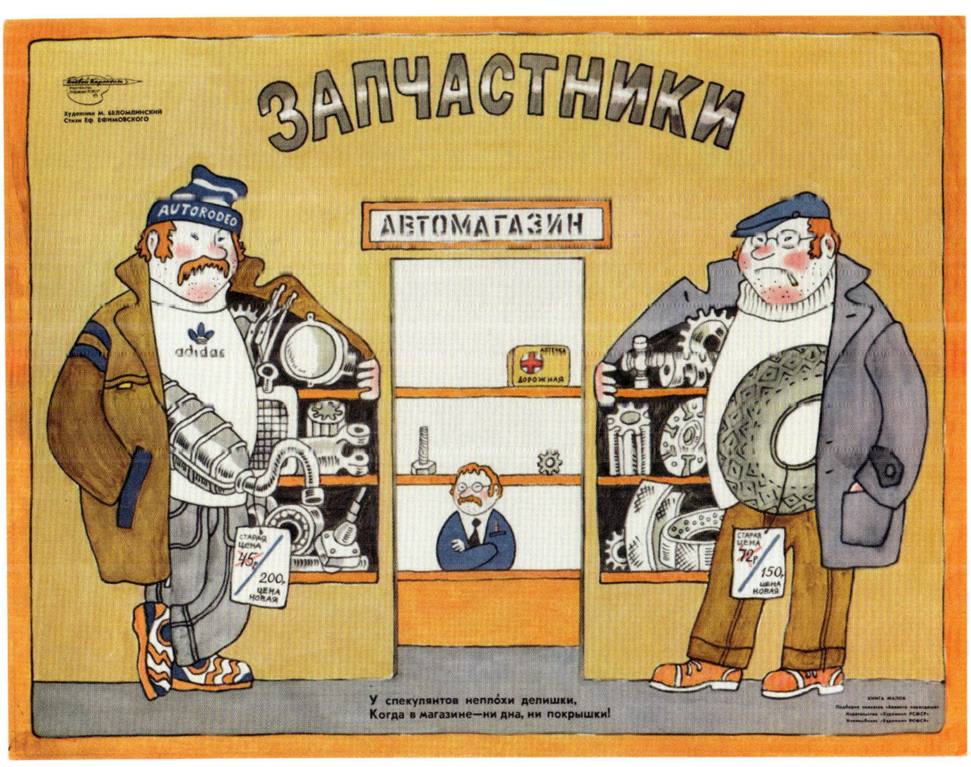

◂ М. Беломлинский (M. Belomlinsky) | n.d.

Text along top: REPAIR SHOP AUTO PARTS
Labels hanging from the muffler and spare tire inside the repairmen's coats:
OLD PRICE/NEW PRICE
THE BLACK MARKET MEN DO PRETTY WELL WHEN THE STORES DON'T HAVE ANY SPARE PARTS TO SELL!
The auto parts store is empty because the car mechanics have bought all the parts and radically marked them up. If someone wants their car repaired, they have no choice but to pay this exorbitant price.

Б. Цыганков (B. Tsygankov) | n.d.

A bureaucrat is opening a huge can of food stamped PROPERTY OF THE PEOPLE. His can opener has assumed the form of the hammer and sickle of the Soviet Union. Text at bottom:
PEOPLE'S PATRIMONY
HOW MANY YEARS DID HE ABUSE HIS POWER TO STUFF HIS OWN FACE AT THE PEOPLE'S COST!

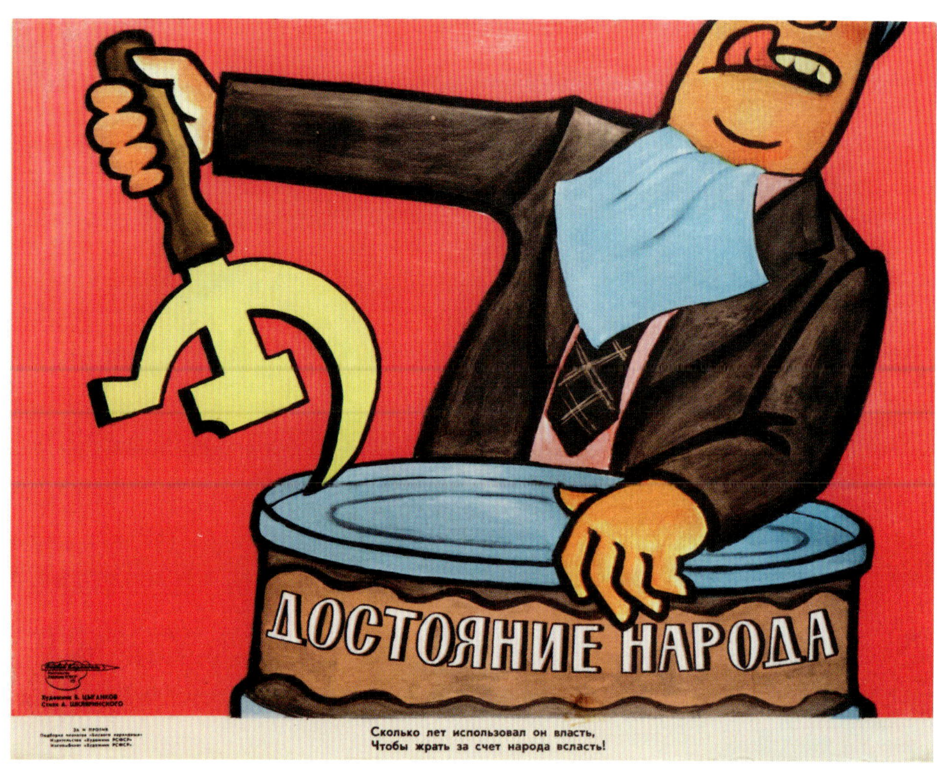

М. Беломлинский (M. Belomlinsky) | n.d.

THREE "HEROES"
Three men are depicted selling cigarettes, fruit, and soft drinks on their tables in the street. In the background, cranes denote an active construction site. On the fence surrounding them are signs offering work for any number of jobs: engineers, carpenters, helpers, blacksmiths, stokers, roofers, etc. The three strong men are references to characters in Russian folk-tales. LOOK AT THESE STRONG GUYS WHO COULD DO ANYTHING. THEY SHOULD BE WORKING ON MACHINES. THEY SHOULD BE CONSTRUCTING THE MIRACULOUS TOWNS OF FOLKTALES, BUT THEY CHOSE SOMETHING QUITE DIFFERENT—THE BLACK MARKET.

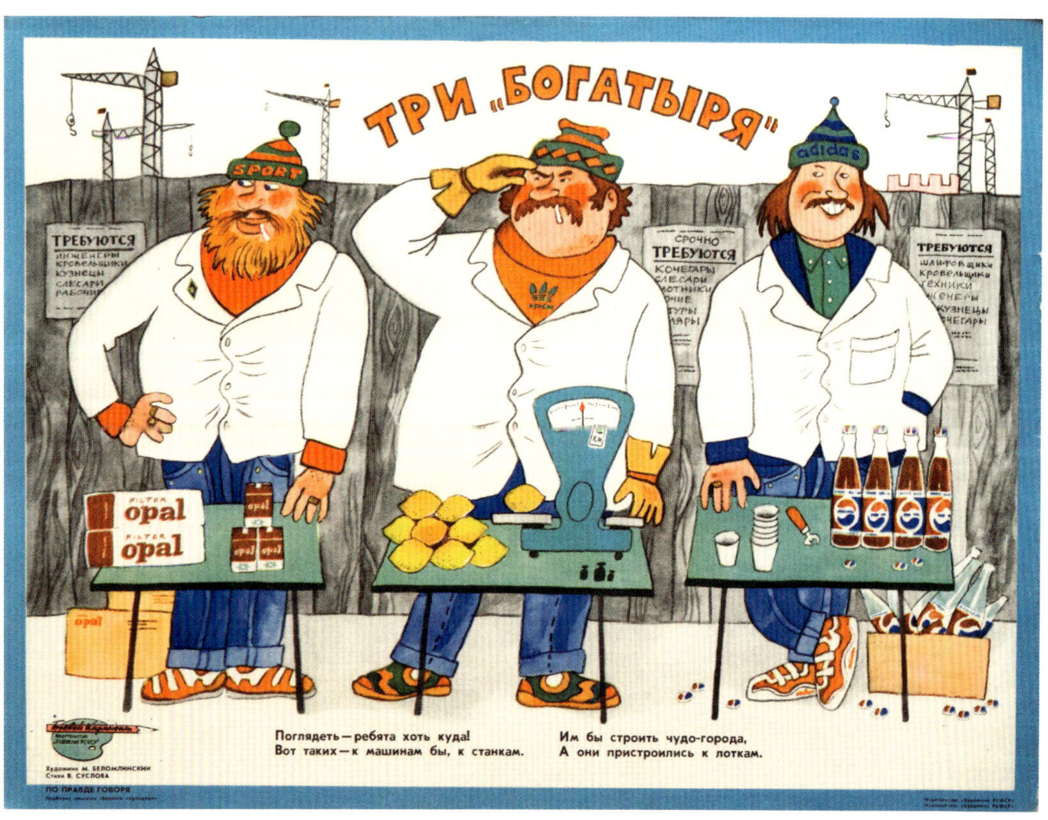

Б. Семенов (B. Semenov) | n.d. ➤

Sign behind the bureaucrat's desk reads: WORK A NEW WAY! Text at bottom: A WORTHY MOTTO WILL RING HOLLOW IF IT ISN'T FOLLOWED.

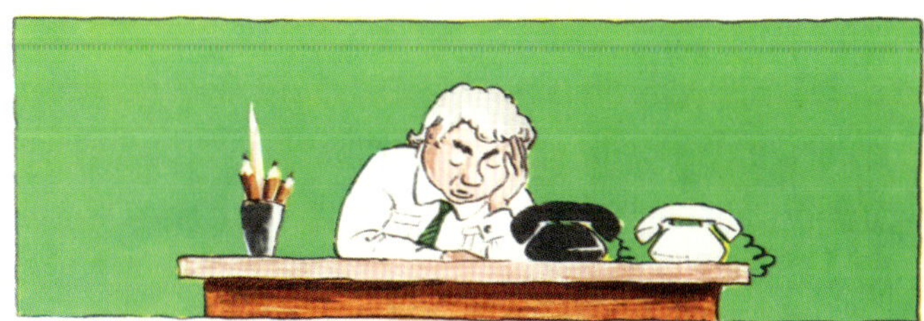

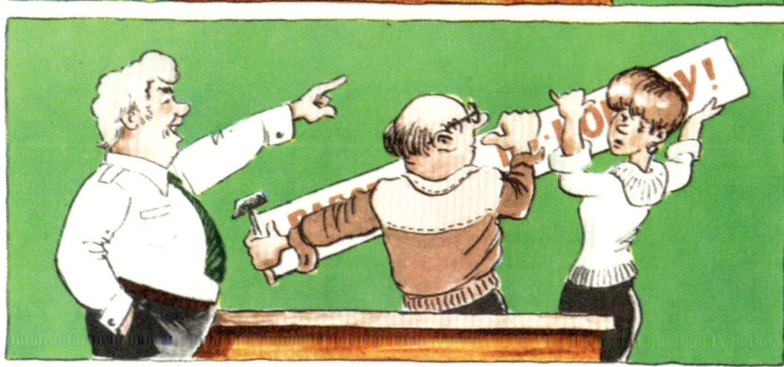

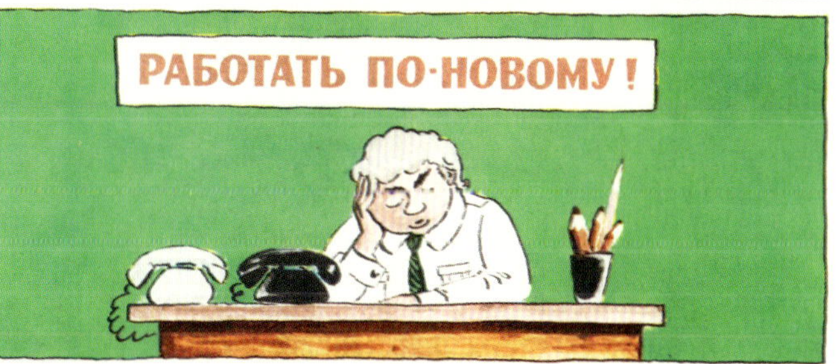

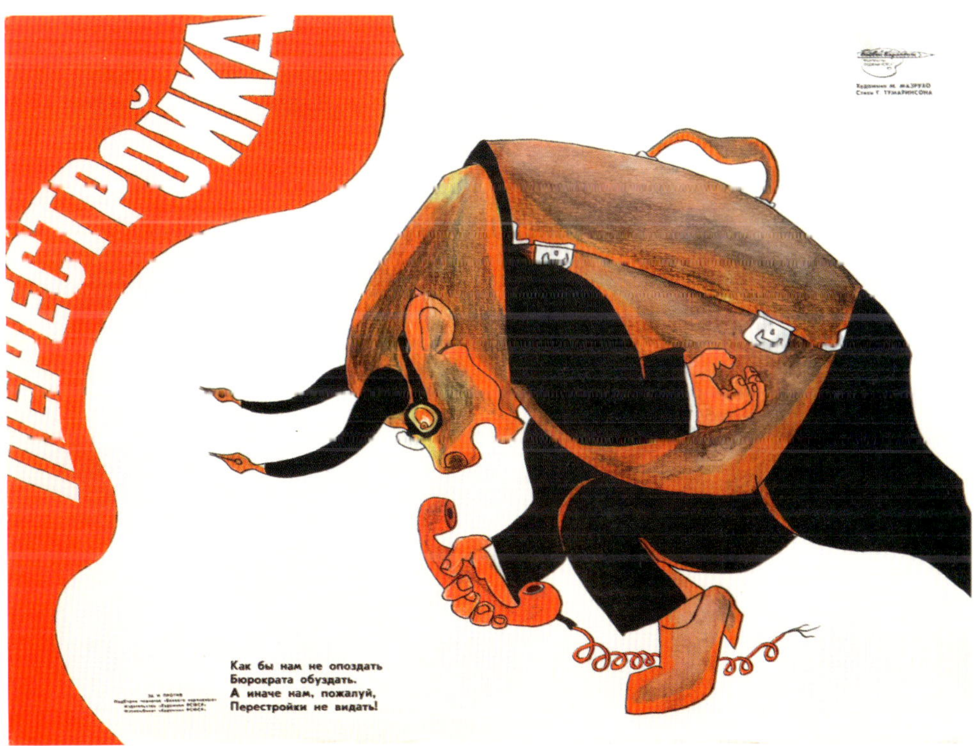

➤ М. Мазрухо (M. Mazruho) | n.d.

A bureaucrat is portrayed in the image of a bull wearing a suit, encased in a briefcase with horns that are pens. He is charging at a flag labeled PERESTROIKA. He is also wearing glasses and holding a disconnected telephone receiver. Poem at lower left:

WE MUST RUSH WITH ALL OUR MIGHT
TO REIN IN BUREAUCRACY
OTHERWISE, PERESTROIKA
MAY BE SOMETHING WE NEVER SEE!

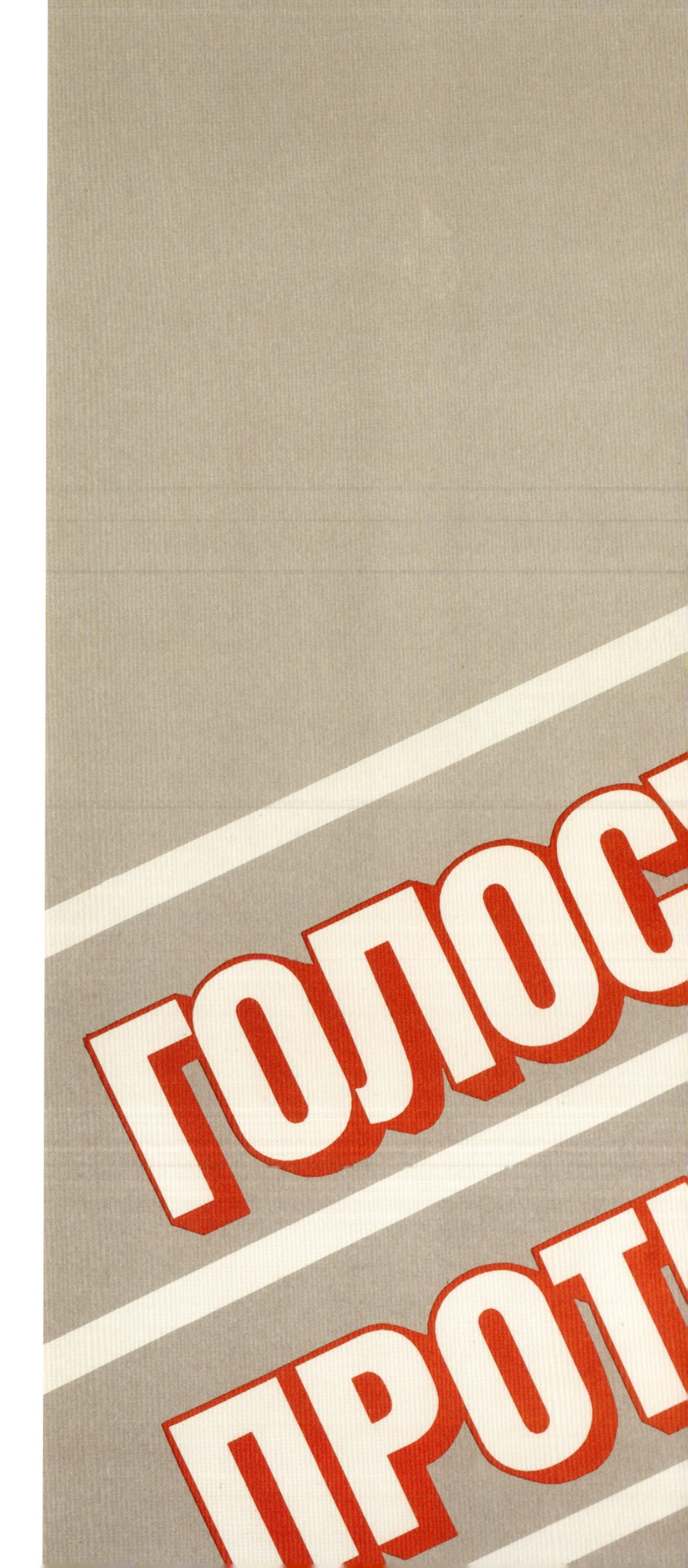

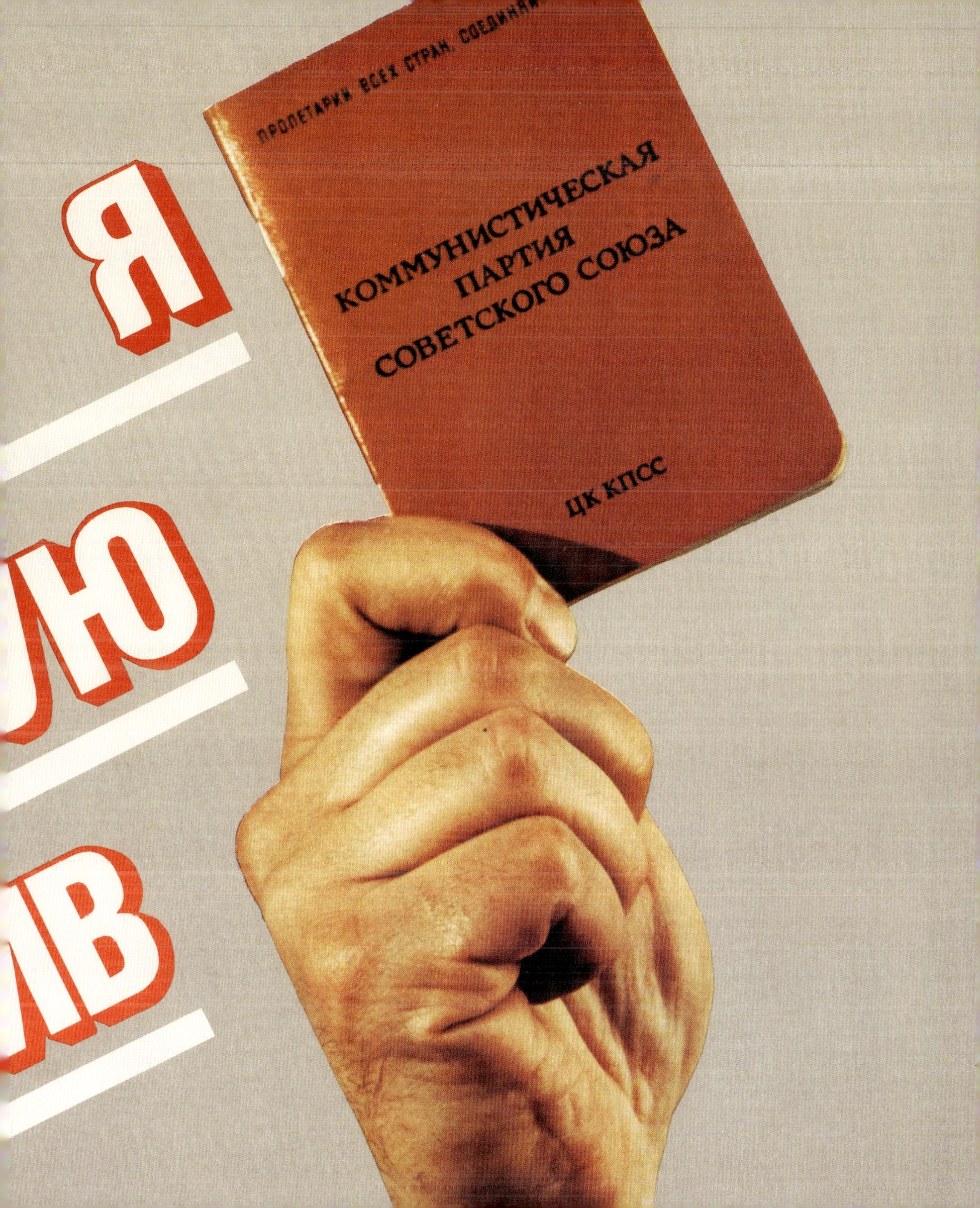
Я
ПРОЛЕТАРИИ ВСЕХ СТРАН,
КОММУНИСТИЧЕСКАЯ
ПАРТИЯ
СОВЕТСКОГО СОЮЗА
ЦК КПСС

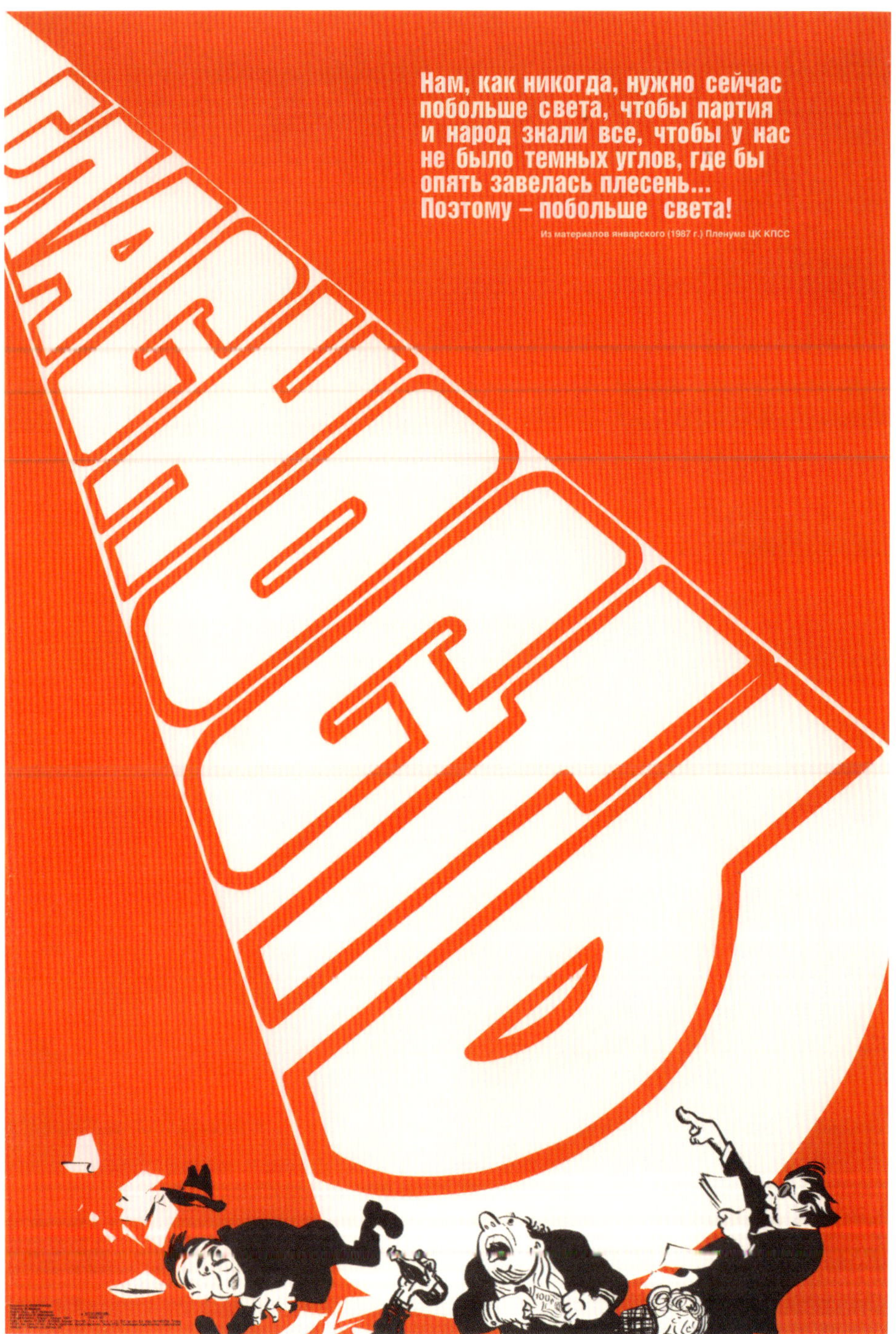

◂ Б. Решетников (B. Reshetnikov) | 1987

Diagonal text: GLASNOST
Text at top right: NOW, MORE THAN EVER BEFORE, WE NEED MORE LIGHT, SO THAT THE PARTY AND THE PEOPLE MAY SEE EVERYTHING CLEARLY, SO WE NO LONGER HAVE ANY DARK CORNERS WHERE MOLD CAN GROW. . . AND SO: LET THERE BE MORE LIGHT! FROM THE MATERIALS OF THE JANUARY 1987 PLENUM OF THE CENTRAL COMMITTEE OF THE CPSU [Communist Party of the Soviet Union]. This excerpt is from an address given by Gorbachev in which he outlined his proposals for political reform. At this time, perestroika was increasingly geared towards political reform, and focused on intra-party democracy.

Л. Тарасова (L. Tarasova) | 1988 ▸

GLASNOST, BRAVE ASSESSMENTS, A CULTURE OF DISCUSSION: THESE ARE THE MOST IMPORTANT ELEMENTS OF A PARTY CAUCUS'S WORK
Text in red square at upper right: INCREASE THE MILITANCY OF PARTY ORGANIZERS

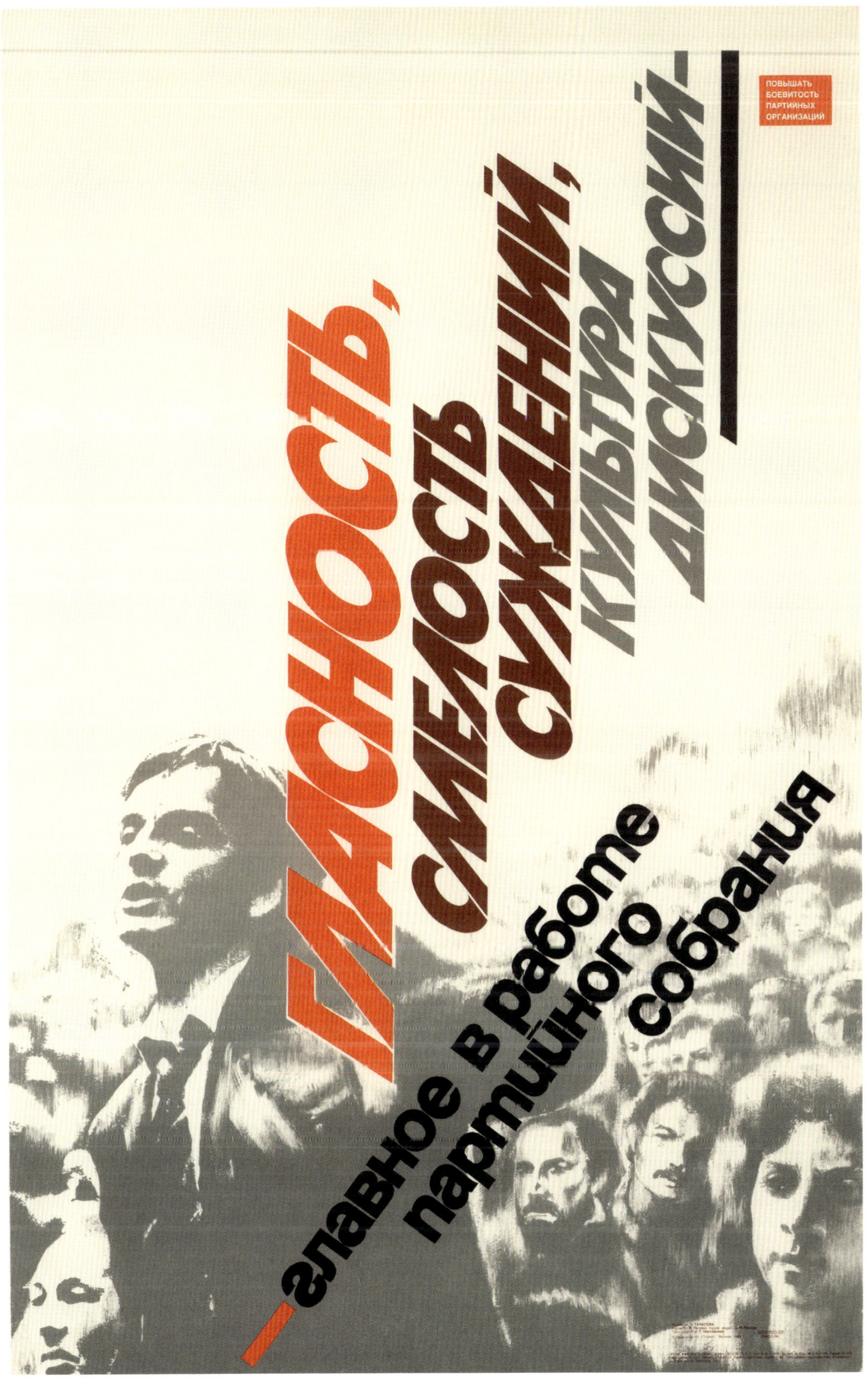
ПОВЫШАТЬ БОЕВИТОСТЬ ПАРТИЙНЫХ ОРГАНИЗАЦИЙ
ГЛАСНОСТЬ,
СМЕЛОСТЬ СУЖДЕНИЙ,
КУЛЬТУРА ДИСКУССИЙ—
—главное в работе партийного собрания

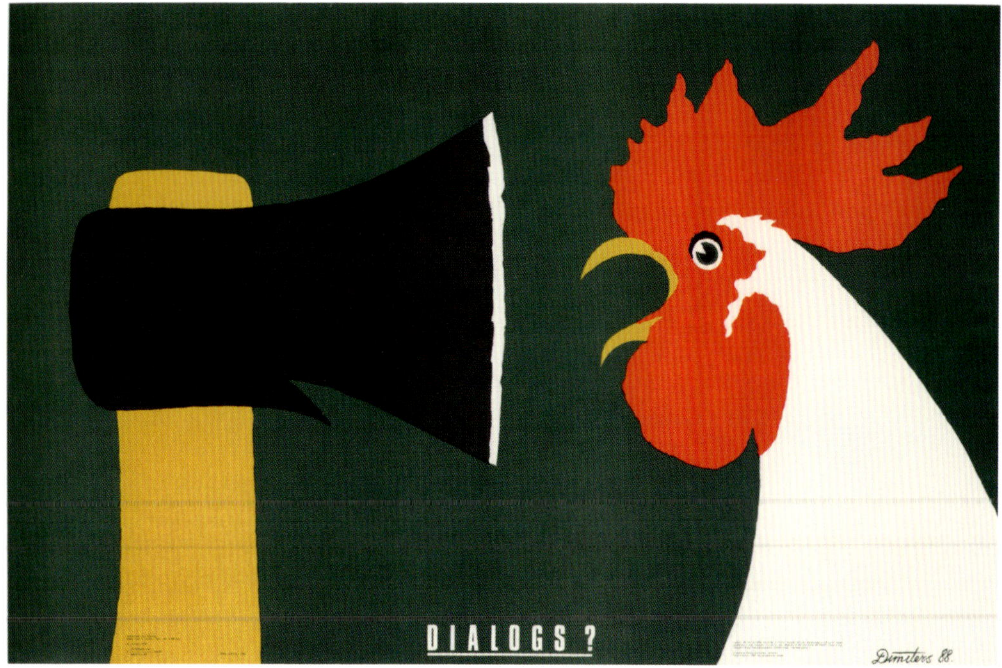

▲ Ю. Димитерс (M. J. Dimiters) | 1989

DIALOGUES?
The word exists in Russian, but only as a poorly assimilated import from the West, explaining why it is written here in Roman characters—a clear indication that in the Soviet context open and honest debate was a distinctly foreign concept. The rooster is similar to those depictions of the bird in folk art. As such, it becomes a symbol of common folk and farming. In contrast, here, the hatchet, a symbol of aggression, suggests the sleeves and cuffs of the standard jacket worn by a Russian bureaucrat. The inequality of power between these two parties evoked by this poster questions the possibility of a true dialogue between the people and government, despite glasnost's call for criticizing the state.

Г. Белозеров (G. Belozerov) | 1988 ➤

The front page of PRAVDA [Truth], the official newspaper of the Communist Party of the Soviet Union, is blank. A red pencil, normally a symbol of censorship, hangs from the masthead. However, here the text on the pencil reads GLASNOST. The implication offered here is that, through the policies of glasnost, people may fill in the page that was once filled with propaganda now with truth.

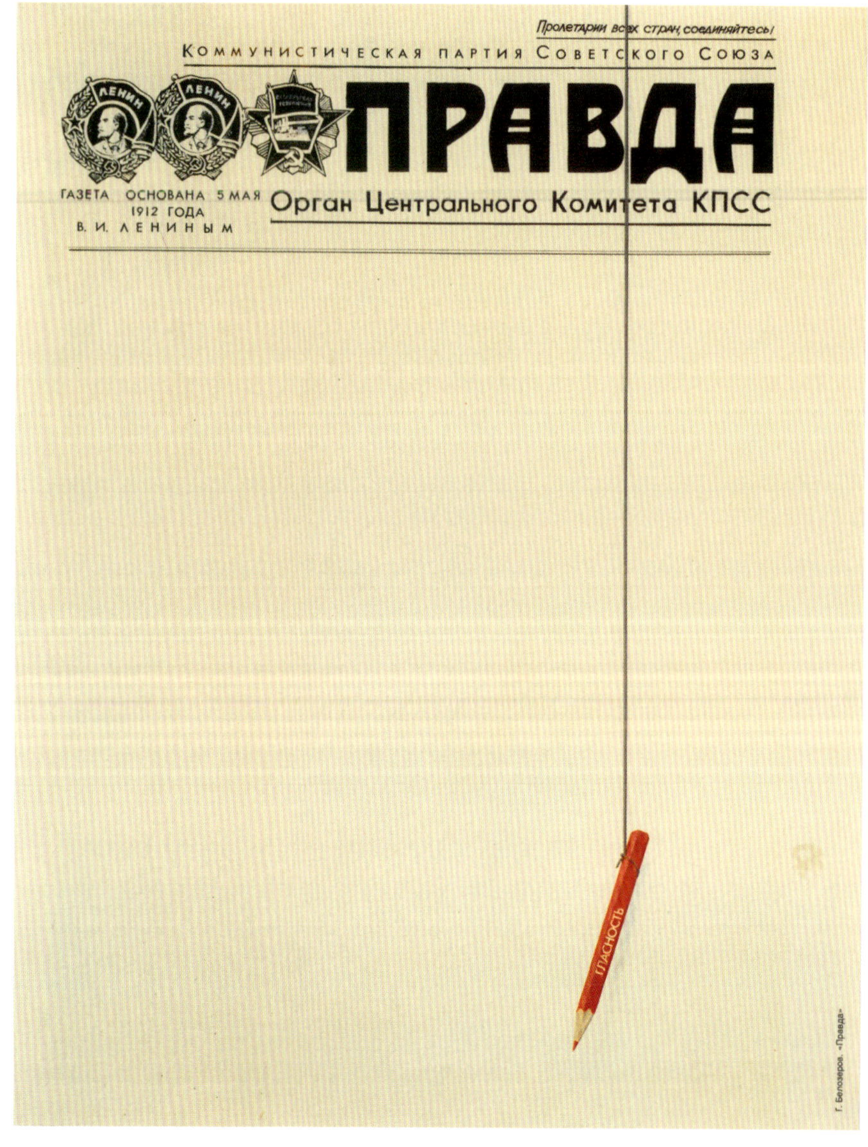

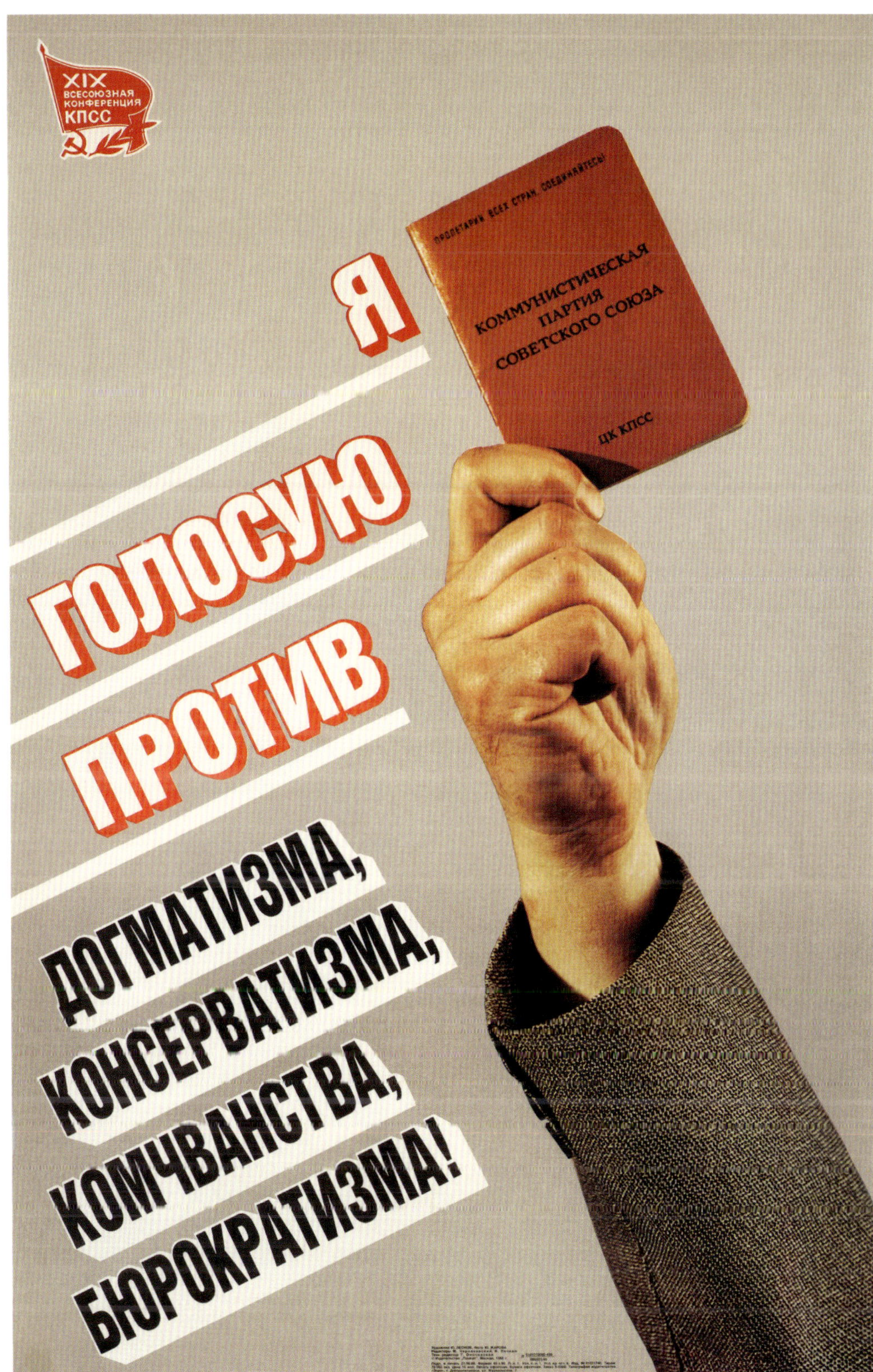

Ю. Леонов (Y. Leonov) | 1988 ➤

Text in small banner at top left: XIXTH ALL-UNION CONFERENCE OF THE CPSU
A hand holds up a Party membership booklet entitled COMMUNIST PARTY OF THE SOVIET UNION. Text at left: I VOTE AGAINST DOGMATISM, CONSERVATISM, COMMUNIST CONCEIT, BUREAUCRATISM! In 1988, at a historic Congress of the Communist Party, Gorbachev pushed for discussion of democratizing and revitalizing both the Party and society generally. Though the conference was revolutionary—the first in a series of glasnost conferences— ironically, the style of the poster remains old-fashioned.

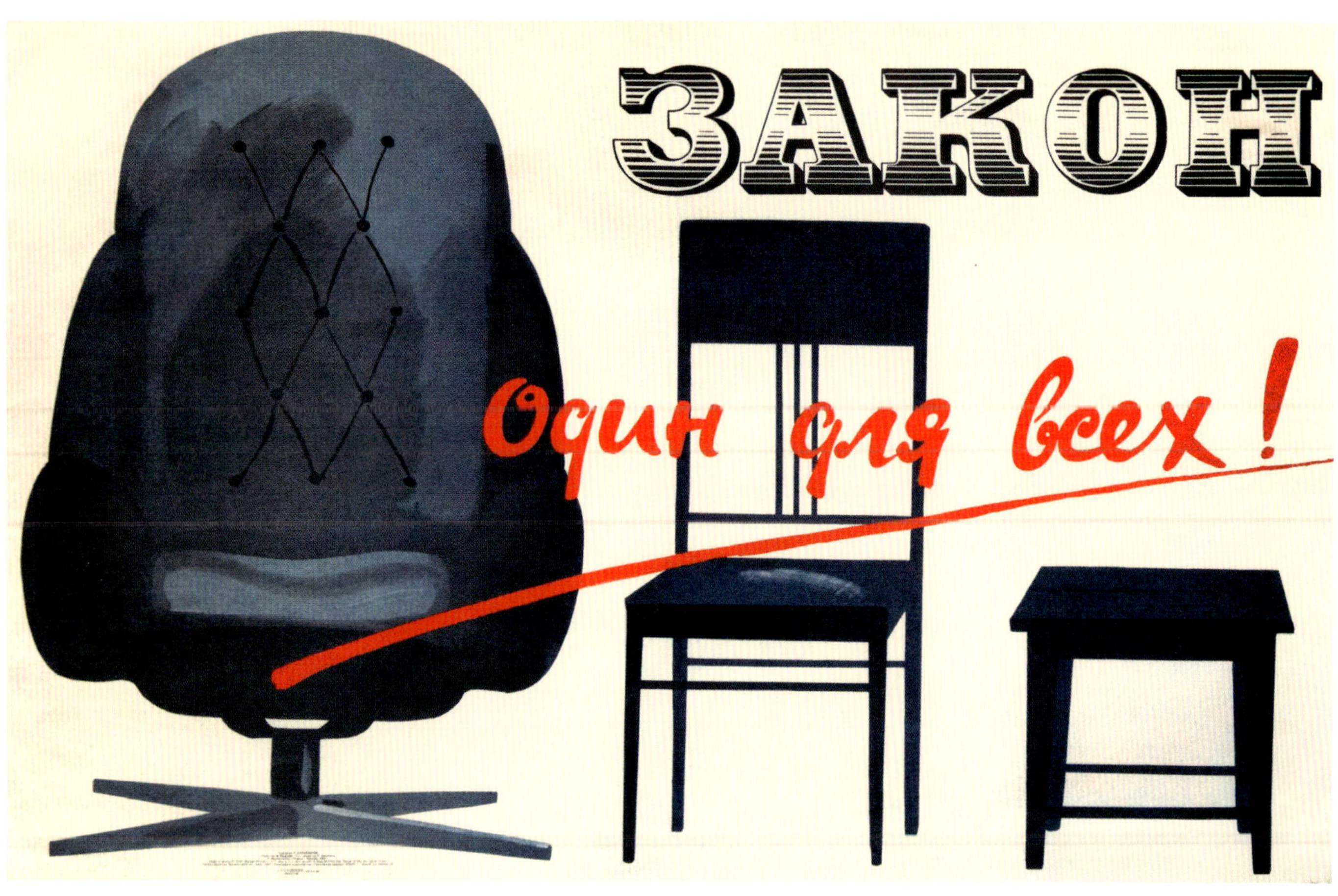

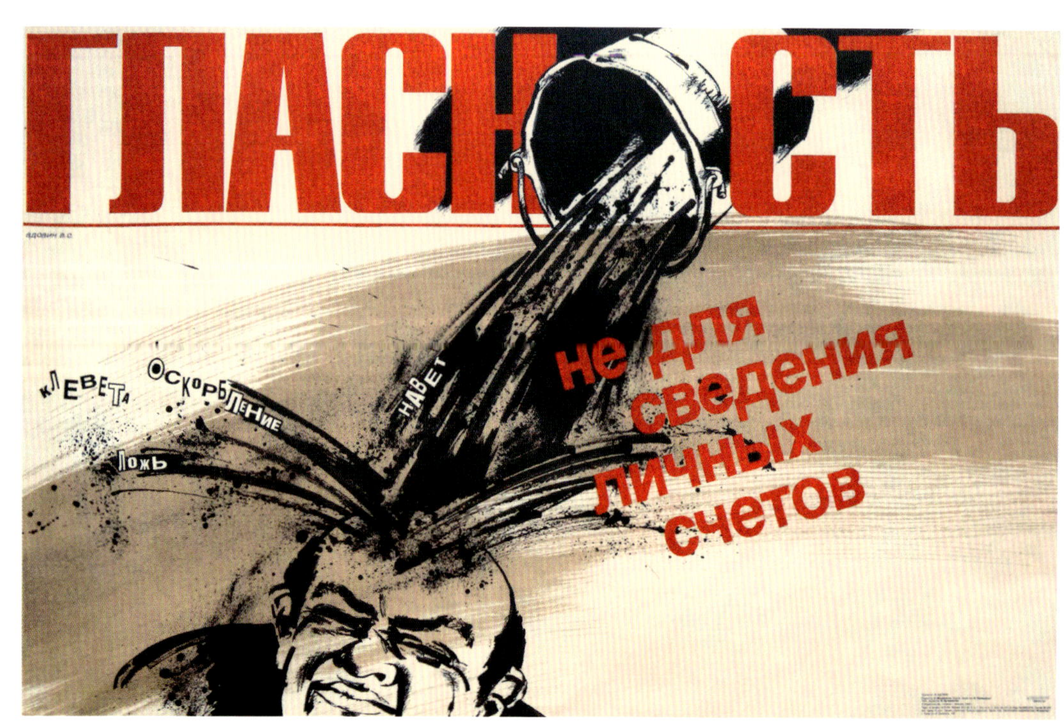

▲ Р. Сурьянинов (R. Suryaninov) | 1988

THE LAW:
THE SAME FOR EVERYONE!

В. Вдовин (V. Vdovin) | 1989 ➤

GLASNOST IS NOT FOR SETTLING PERSONAL ACCOUNTS! A bucket of filth is dumped on a bureaucrat's head. The mouth of the bucket forms the "o" in "glasnost." The words in the slop, from left to right: LIES / SLANDER / INSULTS / MUDSLINGING.

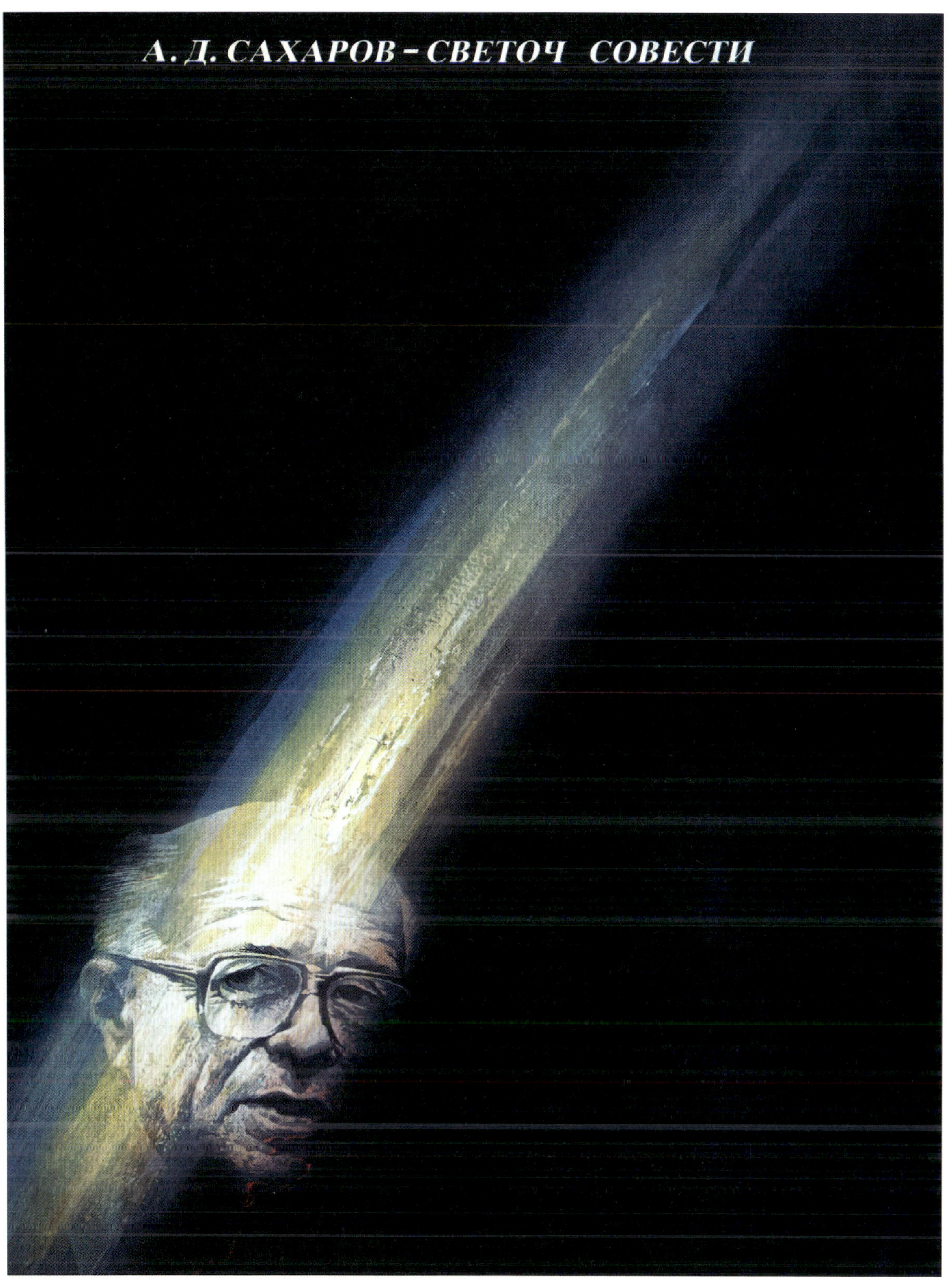

А. Ваганов (A. Vaganov) | 1990

A. D. SAKAROV—A BASTION OF CONSCIENCE
This famous physicist and dissident who campaigned for human rights was awarded the Nobel Peace Prize in 1975, and became a worldwide hero.

▼ Л. Заболотский (L. Zabolotsky) | 1990

Text at top: IT'S ALL GOOD A stylized face wears cracked rose-colored glasses through which the individual sees the following, counterclockwise: GREED / SPECULATION / CRIMINAL RACKETS / UNEARNED INCOME / MAFIA / INDIFFERENCE / VIOLENCE / CRIME / USING POSITIONS AT WORK FOR PERSONAL GAIN / IGNORANCE / RUDENESS. Text at bottom: LOVERS OF THIS COLOR [rose-colored]—WE ARE TAKING YOU TO TASK!

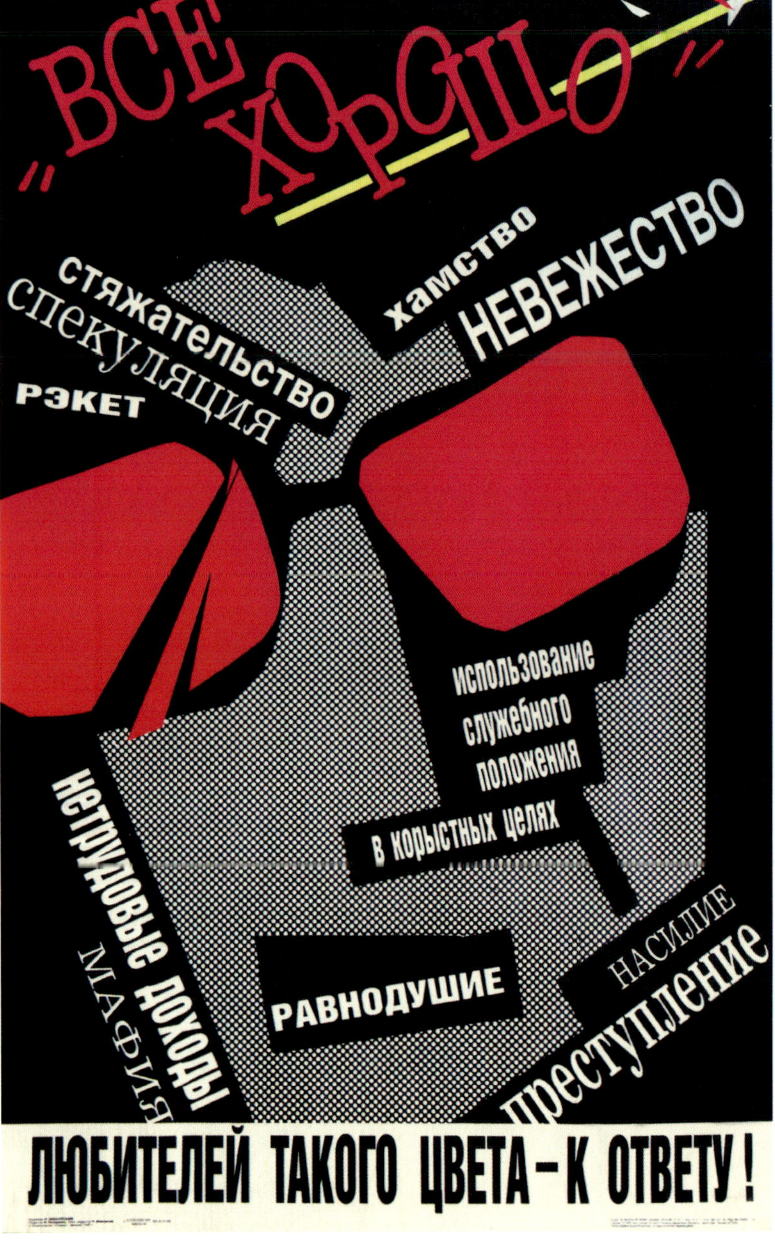

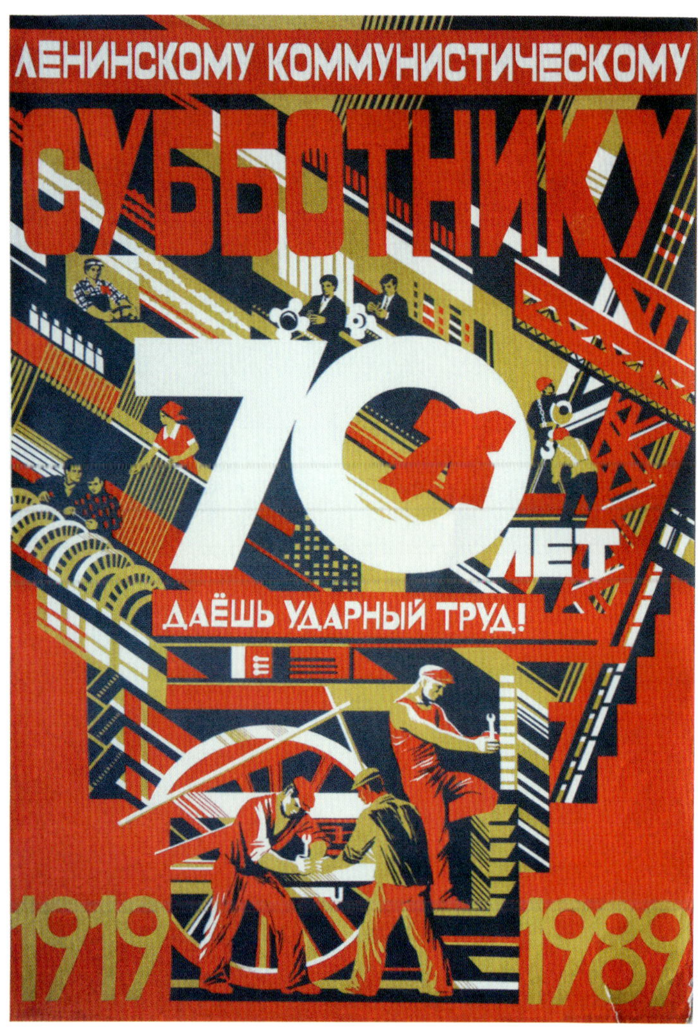

▲ С. Мосиенко (S. Mosiyenko) | 1988

LENIN'S COMMUNIST SUBBOTNIK TURNS 70 YOU'VE BEEN CONTRIBUTING YOUR SHOCK WORK FOR 70 YEARS!

А. Васильева (A. Vasilyeva), А. Сягина (A. Syagina) | n.d. ▶

STATEMENT OF THE SECRETARY GENERAL OF THE CENTRAL COMMITTEE OF THE CPSU —M. S. GORBACHEV
Red text across the front: I VOTE YES!
Headline and inscription on the front page of PRAVDA displaying affirming signatures. *Pravda* was formerly the official newspaper of the Communist Party of the Soviet Union.

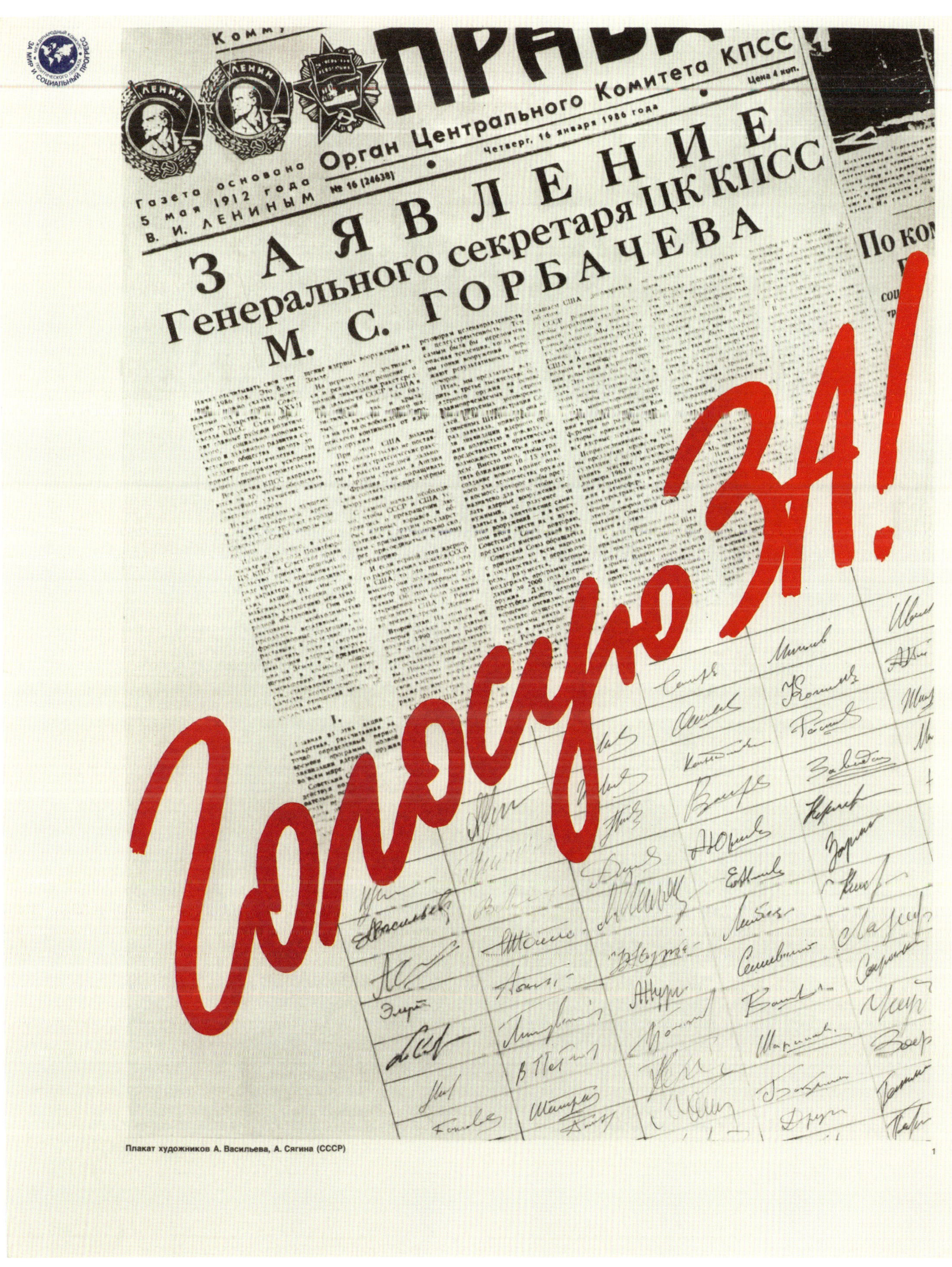

Плакат художников А. Васильева, А. Сягина (СССР)

1

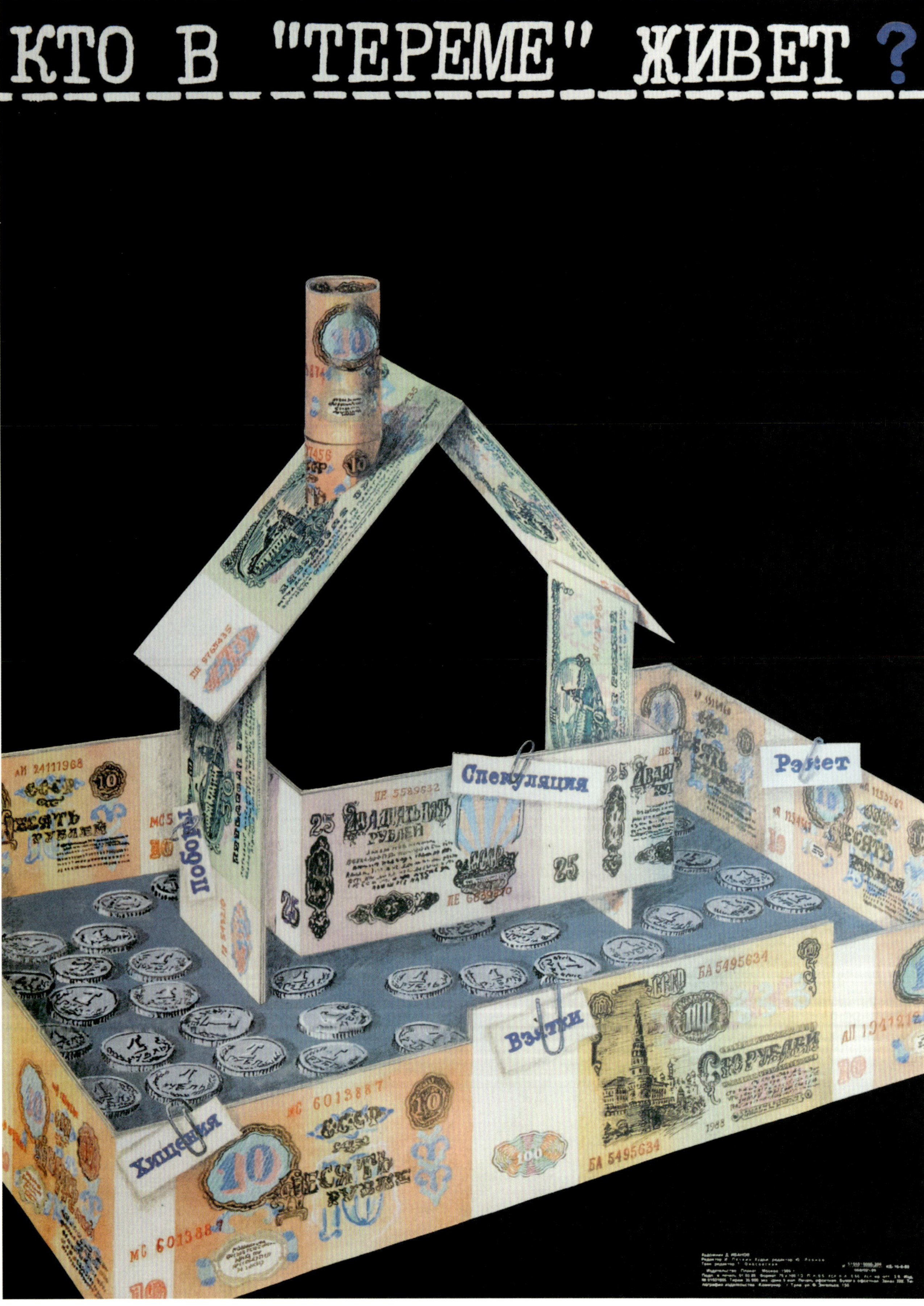
КТО В "ТЕРЕМЕ" ЖИВЕТ?
Спекуляция
Рэкет
Поборы
Взятки
Хищения

◀ Д. Иванов (D. Ivanov) | 1989

WHO LIVES IN THIS "LITTLE HUT"?
Paper labels are clipped to a country house and yard built out of rubles and kopeks. Counterclockwise, they read: EXTORTION / STEALING / BRIBERY / CRIMINAL RACKETS / SPECULATION.

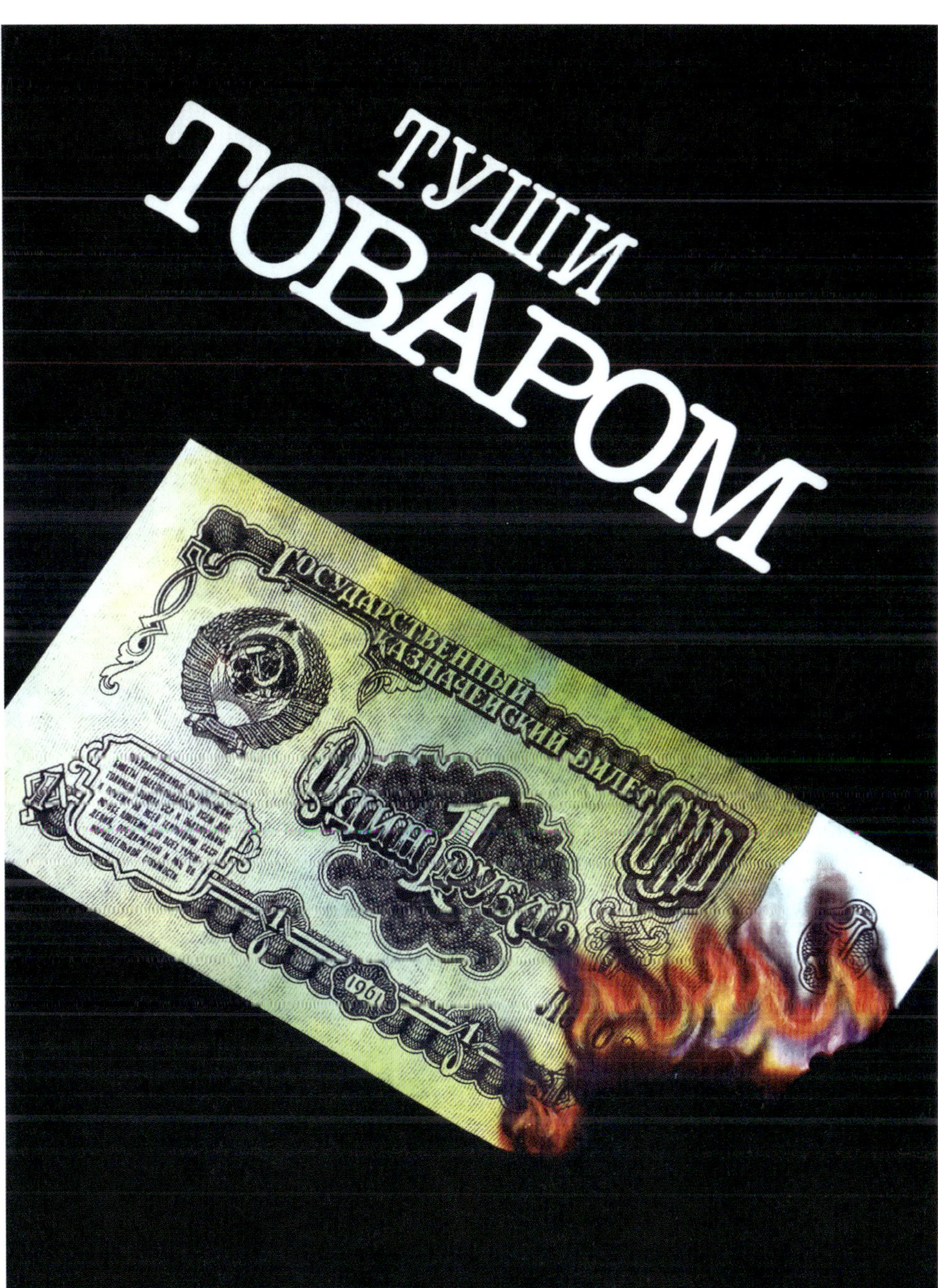

Л. Заволока (L. Zavoloka) | 1990 ▶

PUT OUT THE FIRE WITH COMMODITIES
The economic situation in the Soviet Union was becoming dire during this time period. The source of its most sacred commodity, wheat, had to be imported. Consumer goods were not to be had. The idea here is that if agriculture were to be reformed and quality consumer goods manufactured in the home country, the trade deficit could disappear and the ruble regain its value.

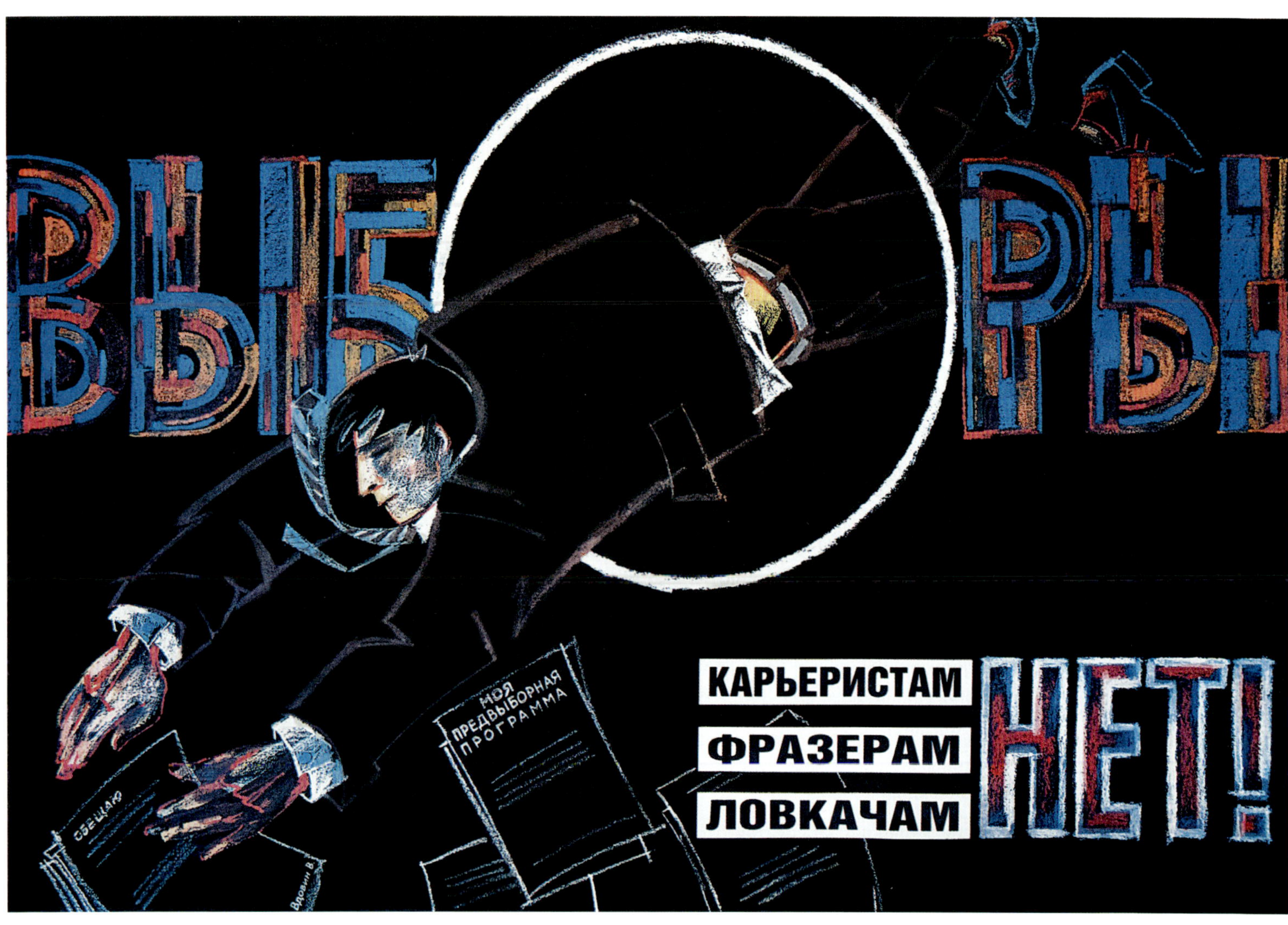

▲ В. Вдовин (V. Vdovin) | 1989

ELECTIONS
A candidate jumps through the "o" in the word "elections" toward documents reading I PROMISE and MY CAMPAIGN. Text at right: NO CAREERISTS! / NO BLOWHARDS! / NO CHARLATANS!

В. Мулгачев (V. Mulgachev), А. Панков (A. Pankov) | 1990 ➤

A set of faceless dummies in different costumes and uniforms stand in for Stalin, Khrushchev, and Brezhnev. Stalin: LIFE IS BETTER, LIFE IS MORE JOYFUL. Khrushchev: THIS GENERATION WILL LIVE TO SEE COMMUNISM. Brezhnev: THE ECONOMY SHOULD BE ECONOMICAL. Text at bottom: TOSS OLD SLOGANS IN THE TRASH!

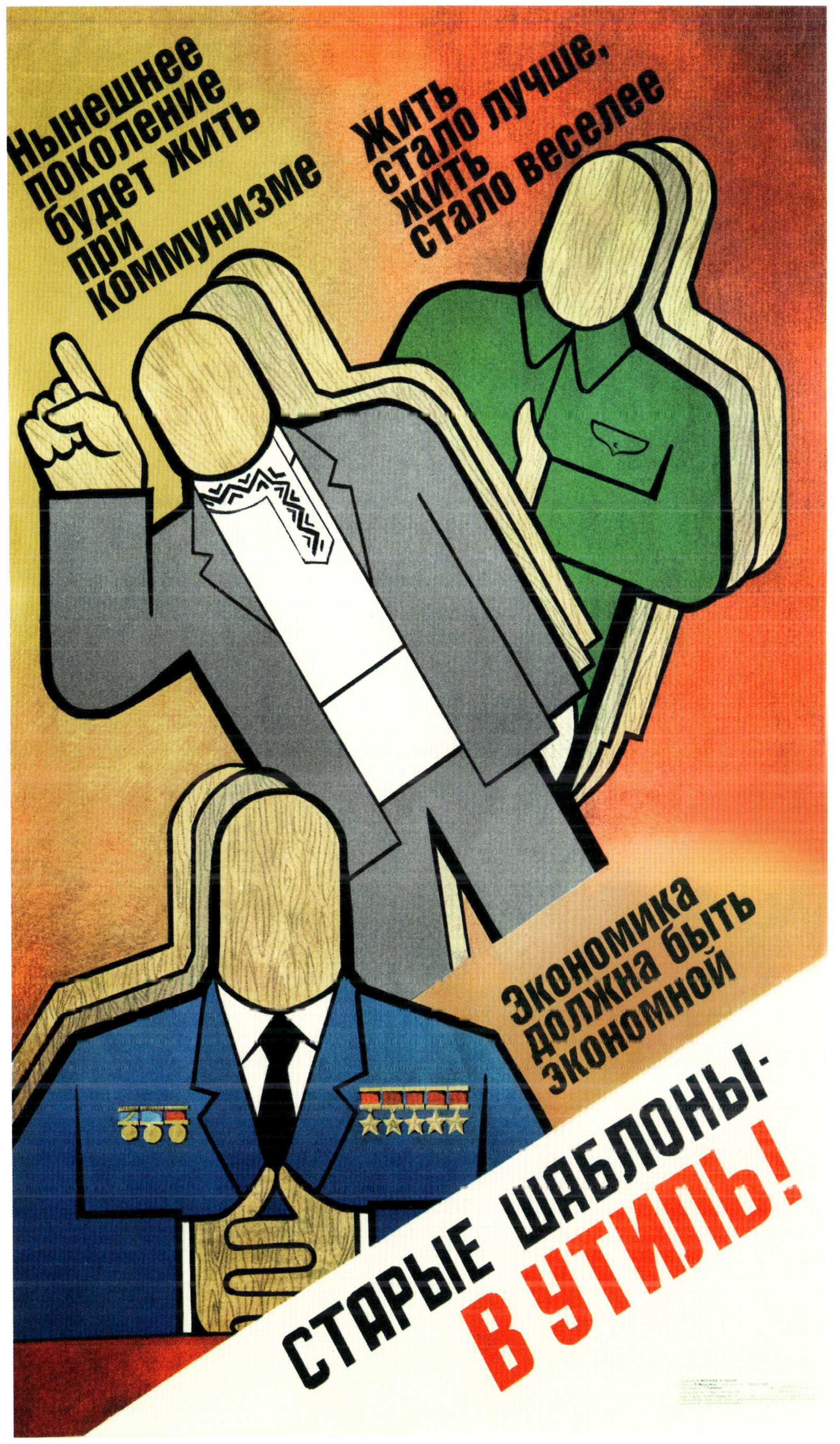
Нынешнее поколение будет жить при коммунизме
Жить стало лучше, жить стало веселее
Экономика должна быть экономной
СТАРЫЕ ШАБЛОНЫ-
В УТИЛЬ!

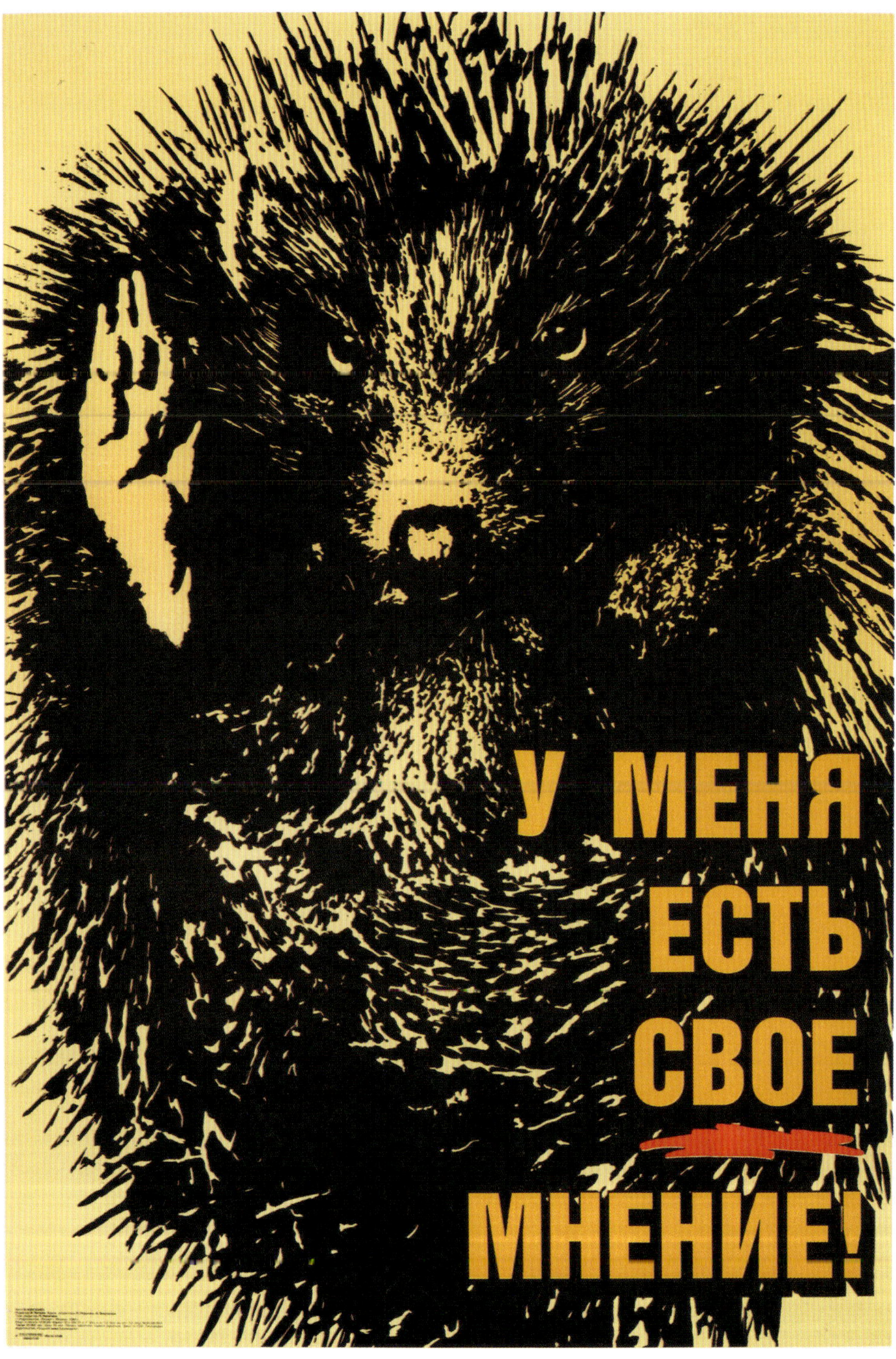

▲ В. Ихтенко (V. Ikhtenko) | 1989

I HAVE MY OWN THOUGHTS ON THIS!
The hedgehog is being difficult and prickly. He is using glasnost dishonestly to stop progress, as his hand gesture indicates.

Л. Заволока (L. Zavoloka) | 1990 ➤

KNOWLEDGE THAT ISN'T BASED ON EXPERIENCE IS FRUITLESS AND FULL OF ERRORS. In keeping with this maxim, a portrait of Leonardo da Vinci is featured on this poster.

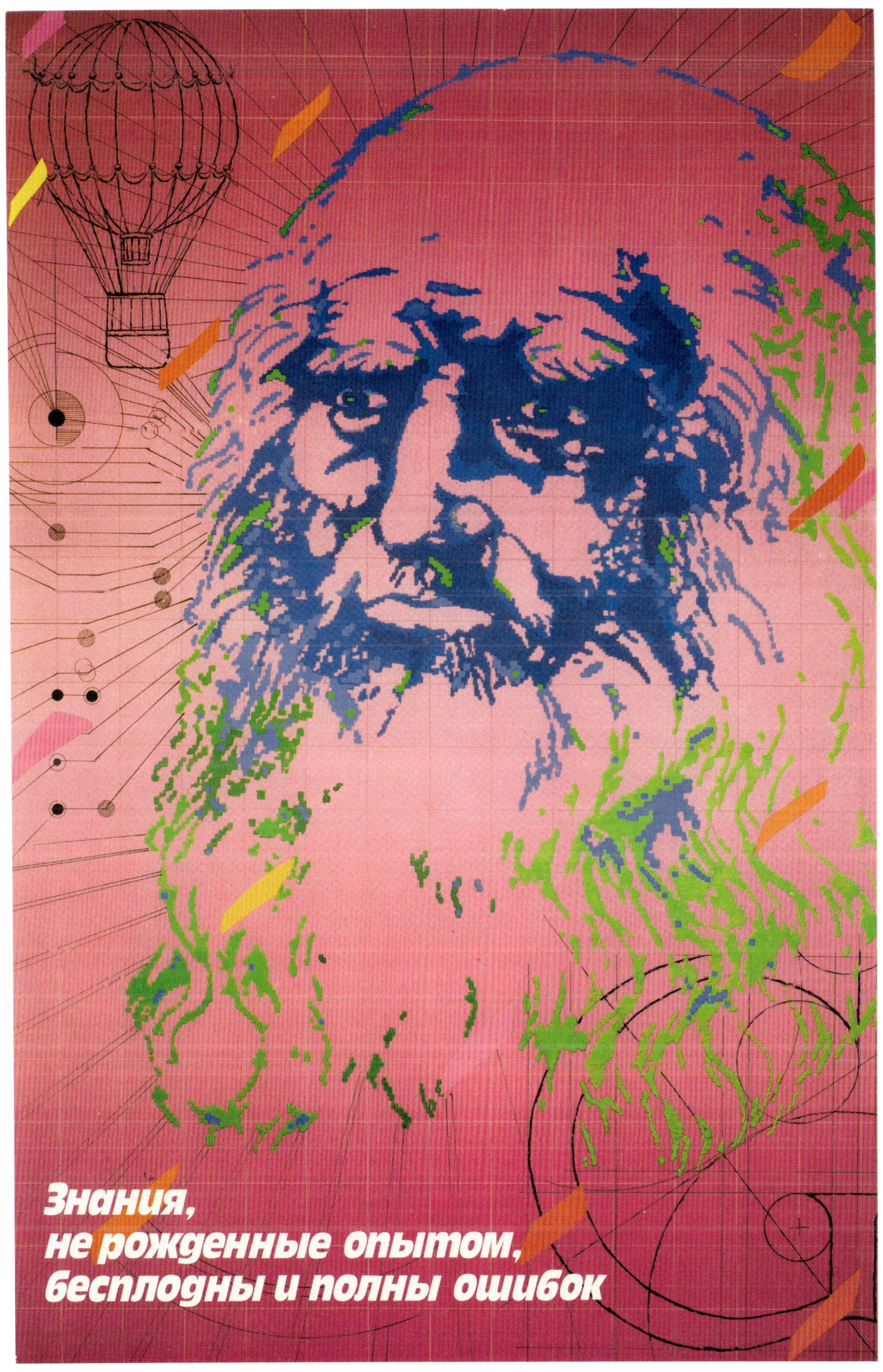
Знания,
не рожденные опытом,
бесплодны и полны ошибок

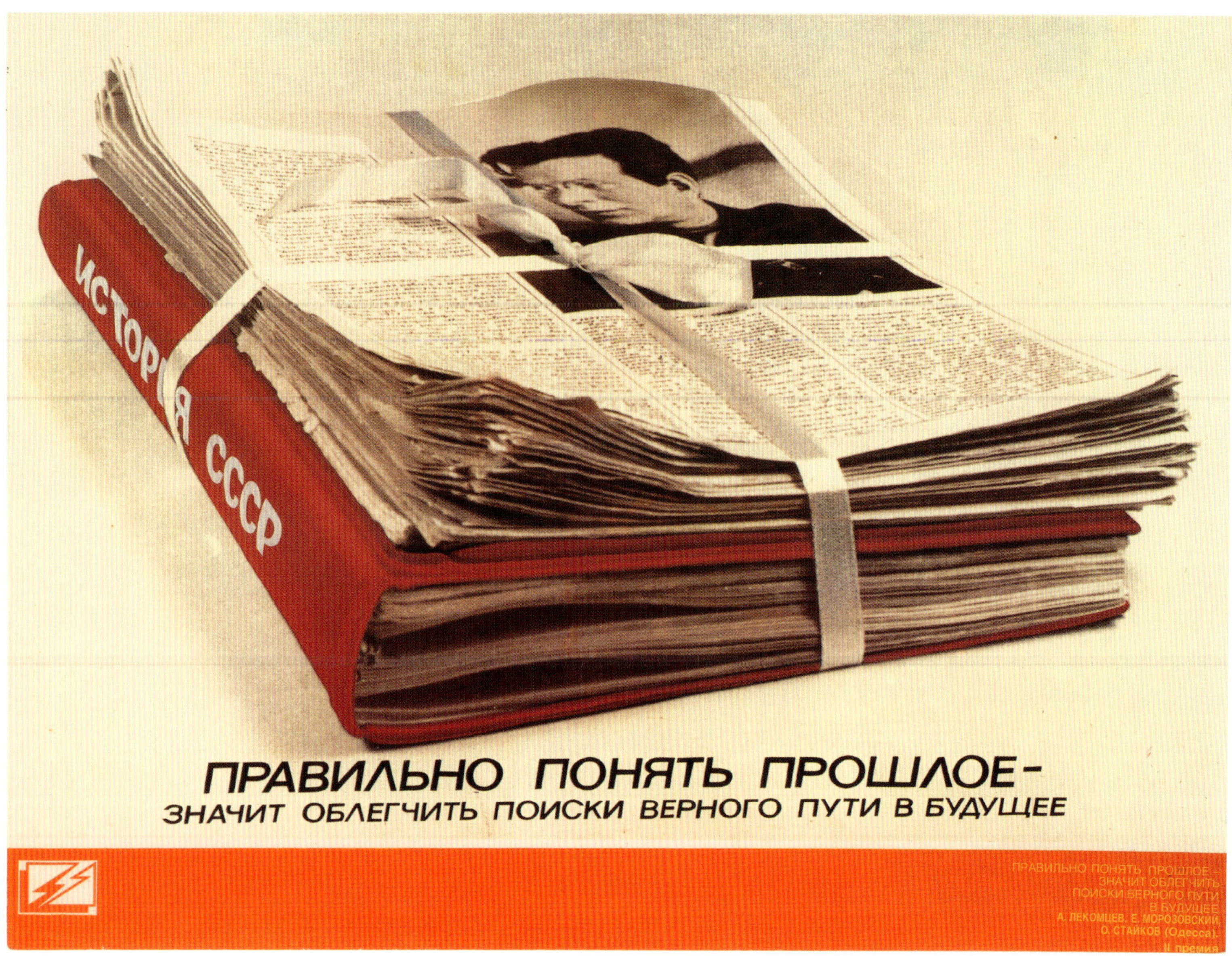

▲ **А. Лекомцев (A. Lekomtsev), Е. Морозовский (E. Morozovsky) | ca. 1988**

A red volume of HISTORY OF THE USSR is tied to a bundle of pages that have been ripped out to distort its version of history. A CORRECT UNDERSTANDING OF HISTORY WILL MAKE IT EASIER TO FIND A TRUE PATH TO THE FUTURE.

И. Горяинов (I. Goryainov) | n.d. ➤

DON'T "SQUEAK"
"Squeaking" is slang for lying, but also the sound that the toy cow makes through its little hole. Text on cow: WE'LL MAKE MORE MILK!

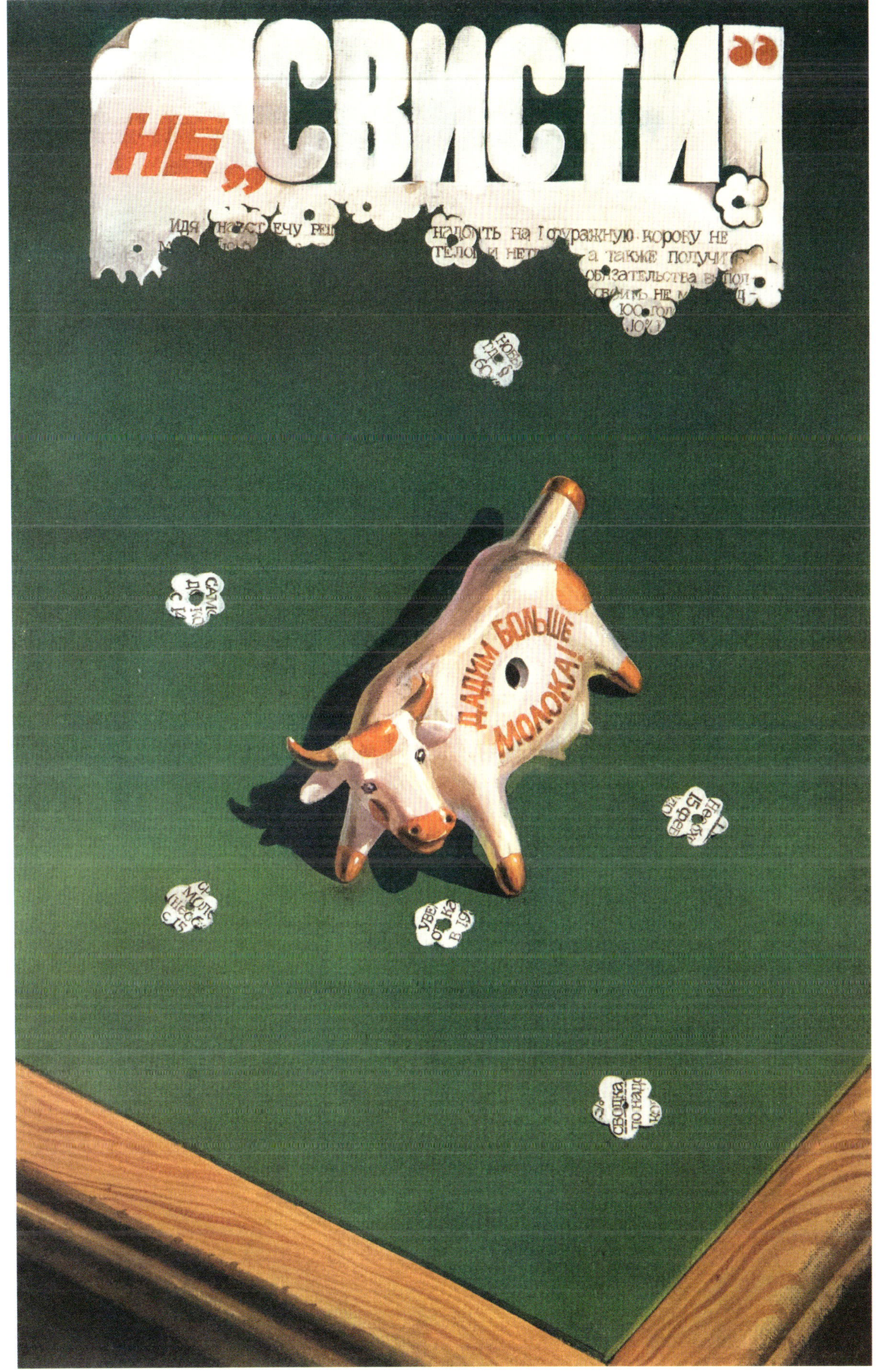
НЕ „СВИСТИ"
ДАДИМ БОЛЬШЕ МОЛОКА!

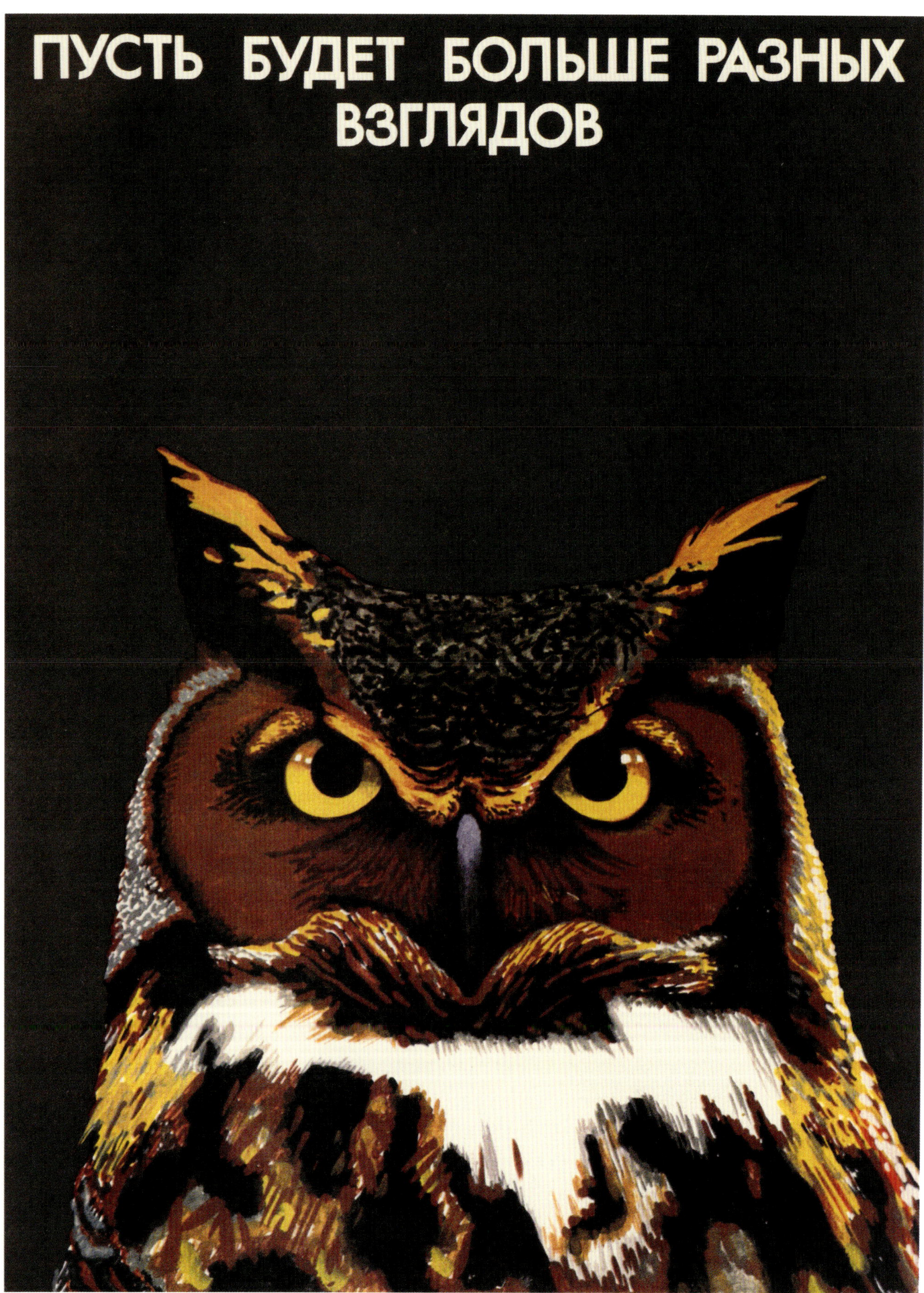
ПУСТЬ БУДЕТ БОЛЬШЕ РАЗНЫХ
ВЗГЛЯДОВ

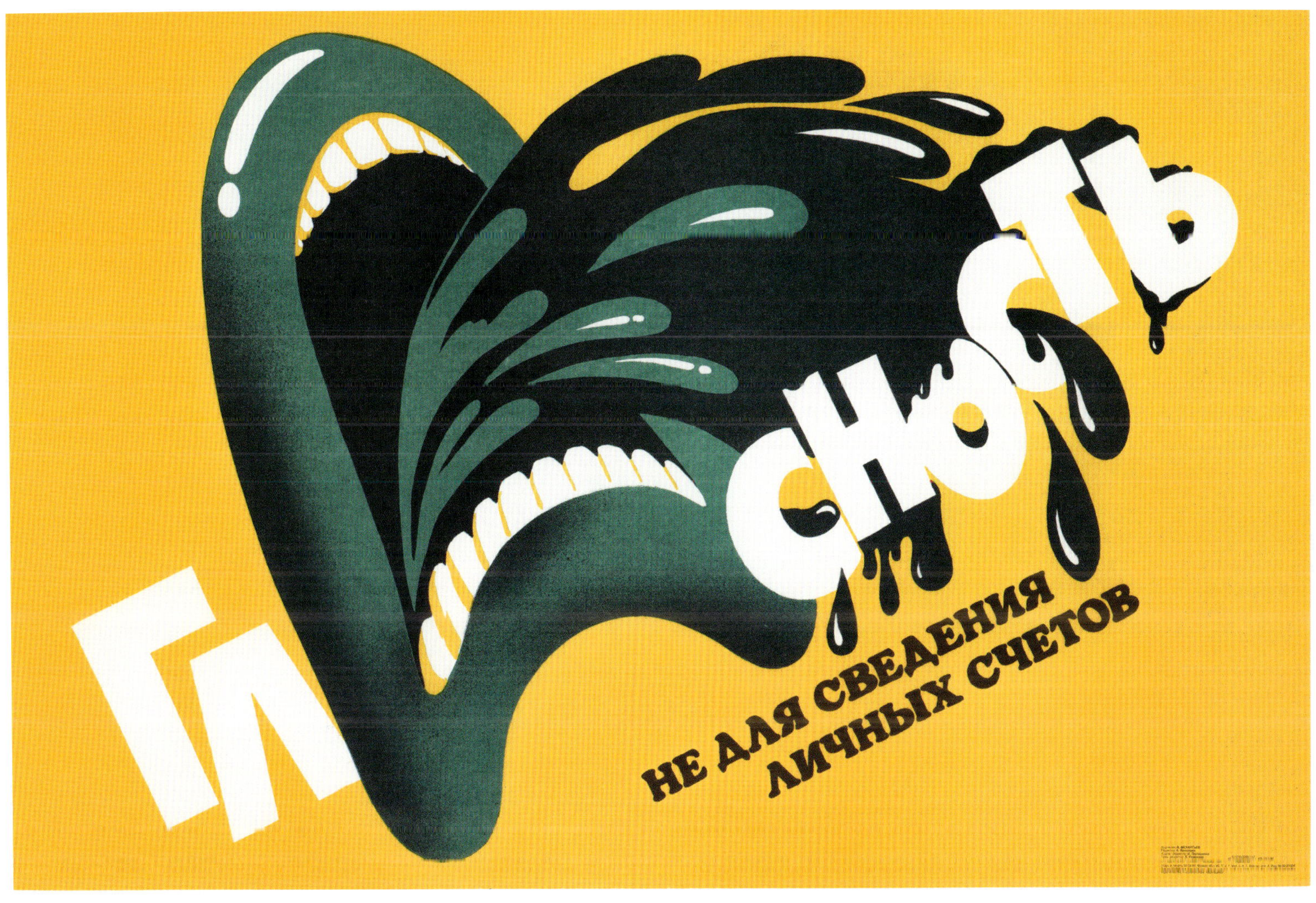

▲ В. Механтьев (V. Mekhantyev) | 1989

GLASNOST IS NOT FOR SETTLING PERSONAL ACCOUNTS!
The "a" in "glasnost" is a vomiting mouth.

◀ С. Каракашев (S. Karakashev) | 1990

LET THERE BE MORE DIVERSE PERSPECTIVES

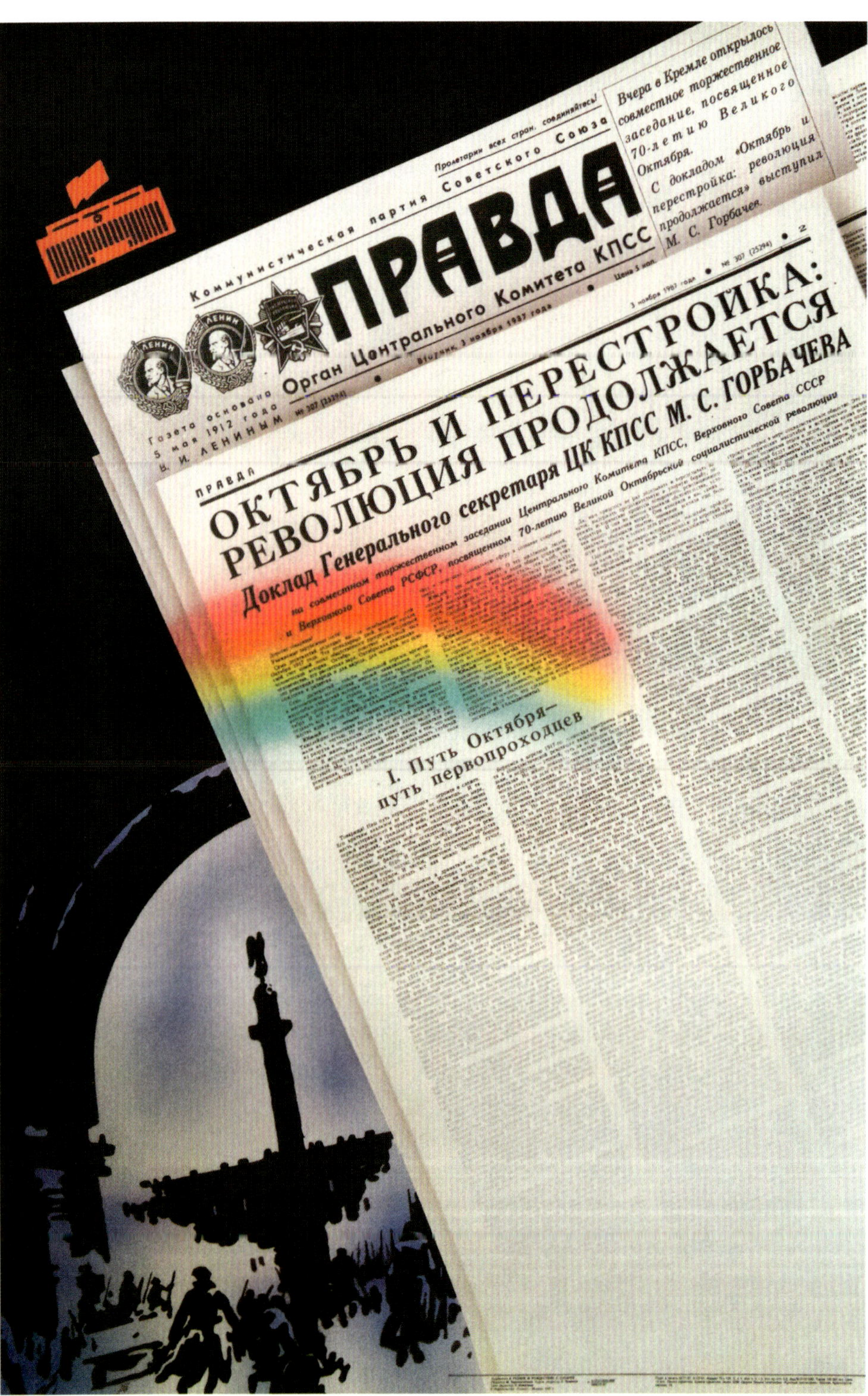

◂ А. Резаев (A. Rezaev), М. Рождествин (M. Rozhdestin), С. Сухарев (S. Sukharev) | 1987

PRAVDA
OCTOBER AND PERESTROIKA: THE REVOLUTION CONTINUES [Headline] REPORT OF THE GENERAL SECRETARY OF THE CENTRAL COMMITTEE OF THE COMMUNIST PARTY OF THE SOVIET UNION (CC OF THE CPSU) M. S. GORBACHEV
I. THE PATH OF OCTOBER IS THE PATH OF PIONEERS

The front page of *Pravda*, the central organ of the CPSU, with a small red silhouette of the Kremlin on top. A fragmented scene from the 1917 October Revolution appears in an underexposed image in the background. The curve of the arch turns into a rainbow connecting the revolutionary past and the present day, emphasizing the link between the Revolution and perestroika as part of the same positive, progressive process.

Н. Пахомов (N. Pakhomov), В. Вострых (V. Vostrych) | 1989 ▸

Text along top: SOCIALIST DUTIES
THE TIME TO ACT IS TODAY. AND THE CONTRIBUTION OF EVERY COMMUNITY, OF EVERY HARDWORKING PERSON, IS MEASURED BY THEIR ACTUAL WORK AND ITS ACTUAL RESULTS
FROM THE MATERIALS OF THE JULY 1988 PLENUM OF THE CENTRAL COMMITTEE OF THE USSR.

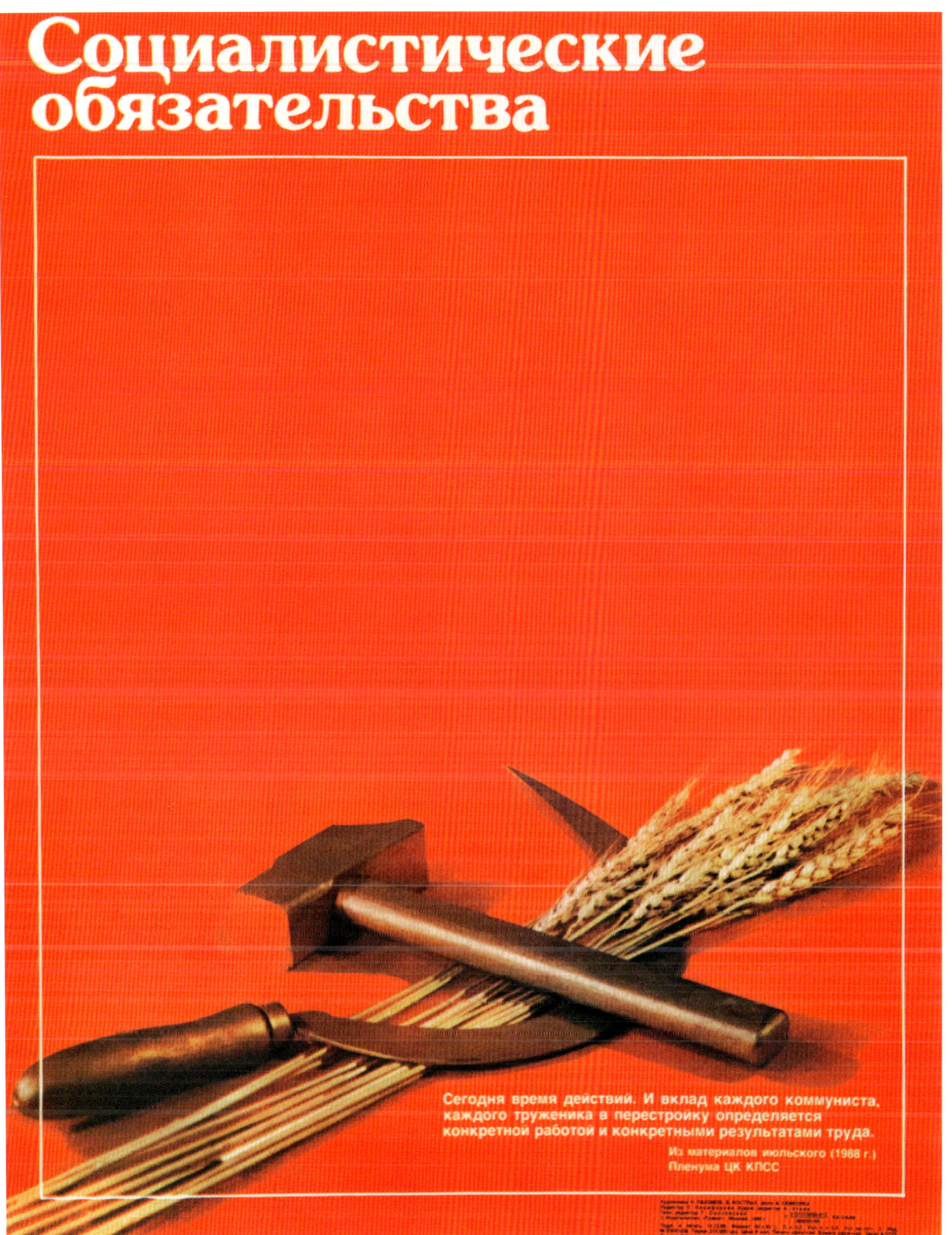
Социалистические обязательства
Сегодня время действий. И вклад каждого коммуниста,
каждого труженика в перестройку определяется
конкретной работой и конкретными результатами труда.
Из материалов июльского (1988 г.)
Пленума ЦК КПСС

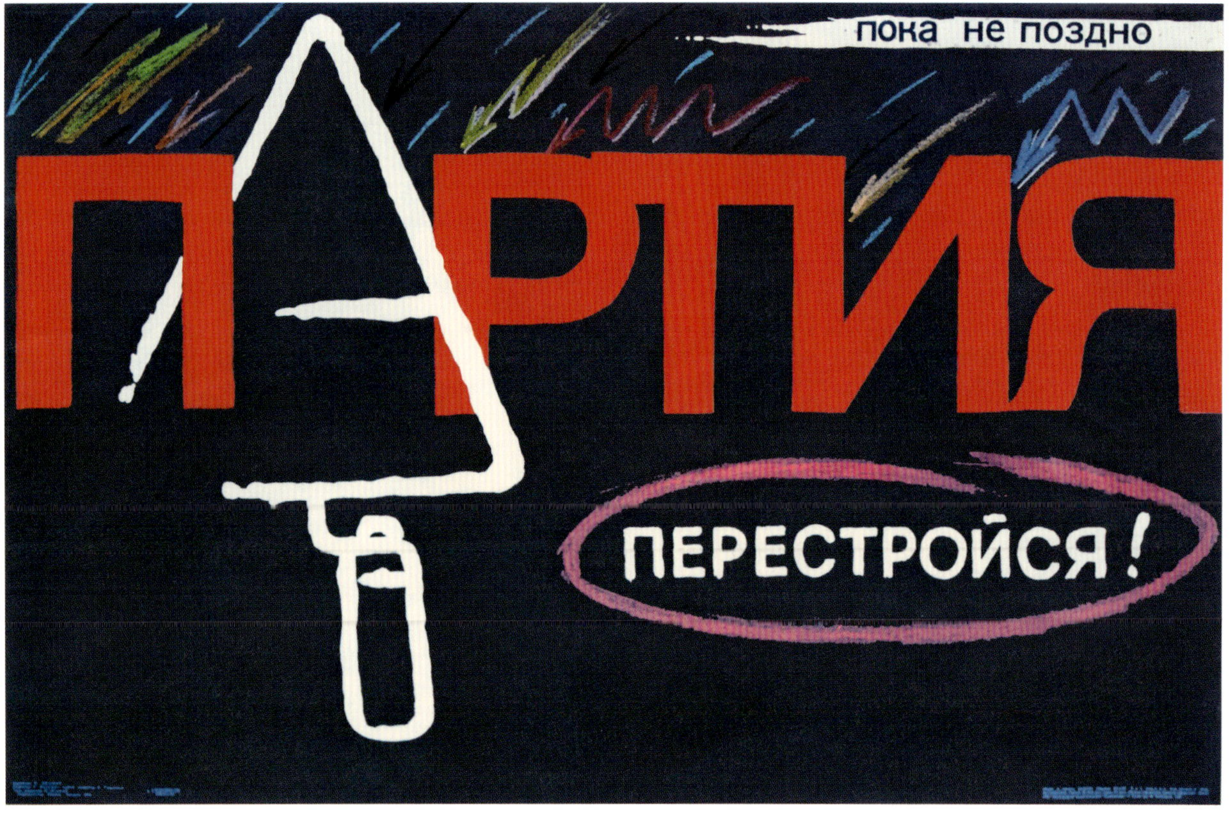

▲ Ю. Леонов (Y. Leonov) | 1990

BEFORE IT'S TOO LATE
PARTY: RESTRUCTURE YOURSELF!

Л. Бельский (L. Belsky), В. Потапов (V. Potapov) | 1989 ➤

OUR COMMON GOALS ARE THE TRUE FOUNDATION FOR A STRONG UNION OF NATIONS
ACCELERATION
PERESTROIKA
GLASNOST
DEMOCRACY

These words are arranged so that one letter in each row stacks vertically to form USSR underneath the hammer and sickle.

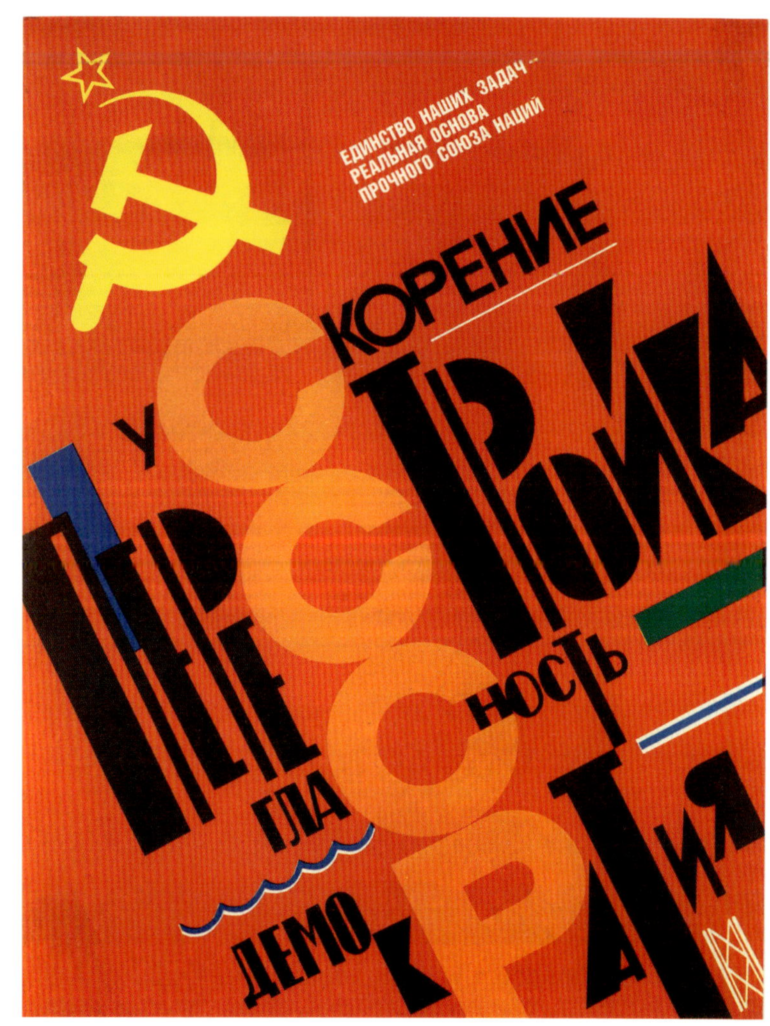

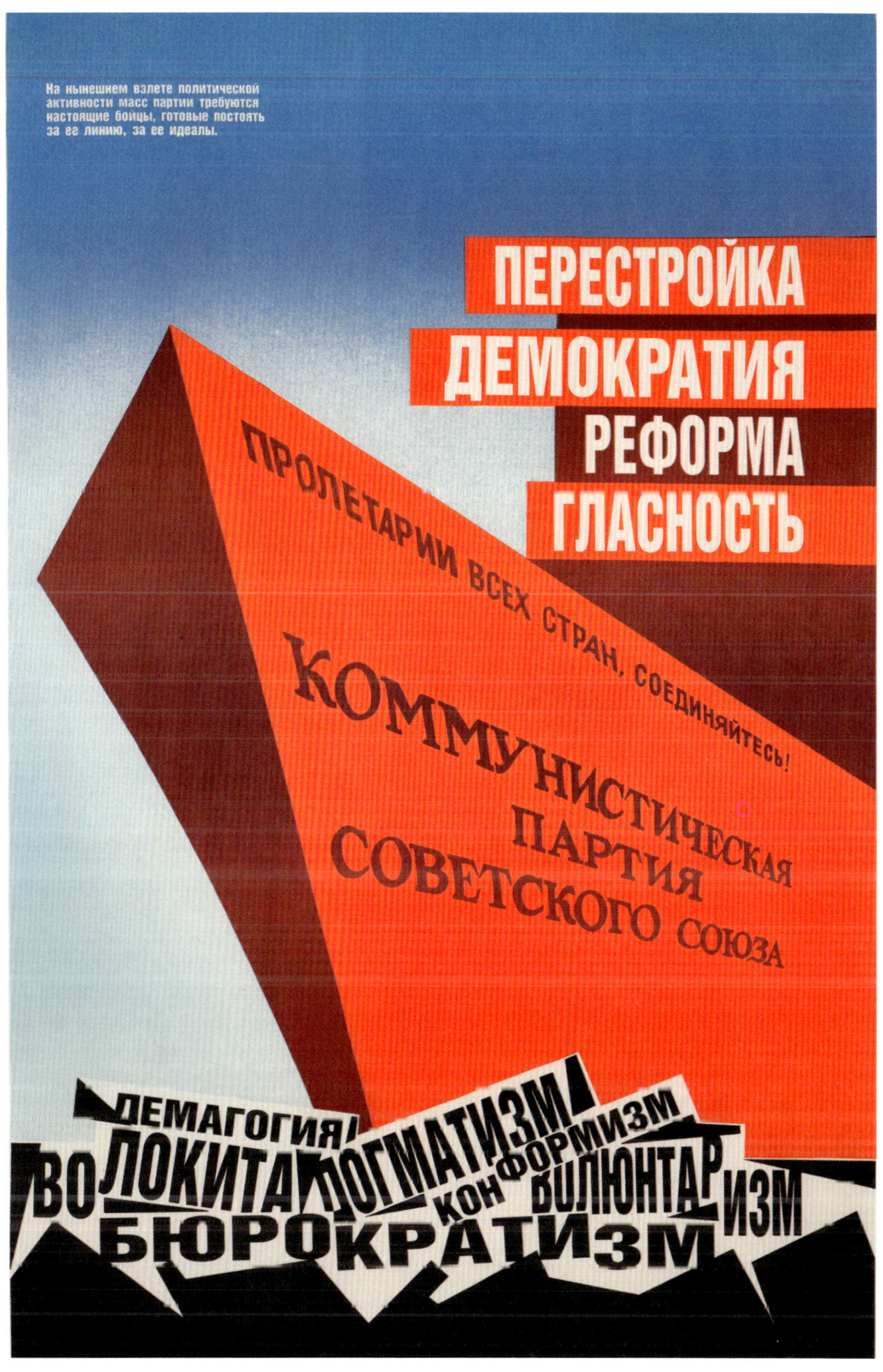

М. Комаров (M. Komarov) | 1989

Caption in white, upper left: THE CURRENT SURGE OF POLITICAL ACTIVITY AMONG THE PARTY MASSES REQUIRES TRUE WARRIORS TO FIGHT FOR THE PARTY LINE AND FOR ITS IDEALS. Text on the icebreaker's bridge: PERESTROIKA / DEMOCRACY / REFORM / GLASNOST. Text on side of ship: PROLETARIANS OF THE WORLD UNITE! Text on ice the ship is breaking through: DEMAGOGUERY / RED TAPE / BUREAUCRATISM / DOGMATISM / CONFORMISM / ABUSE OF POWER.

WORKERS

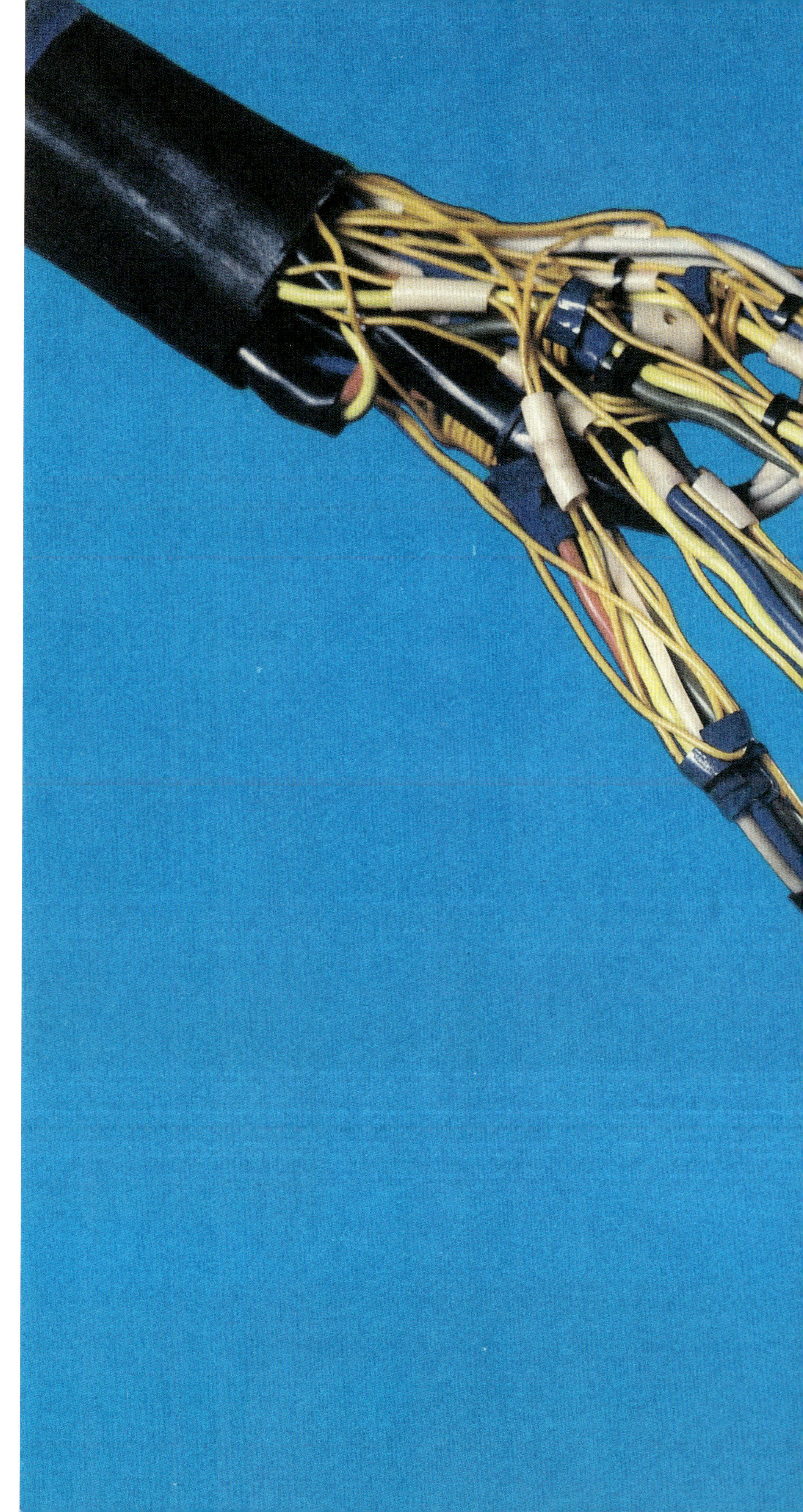

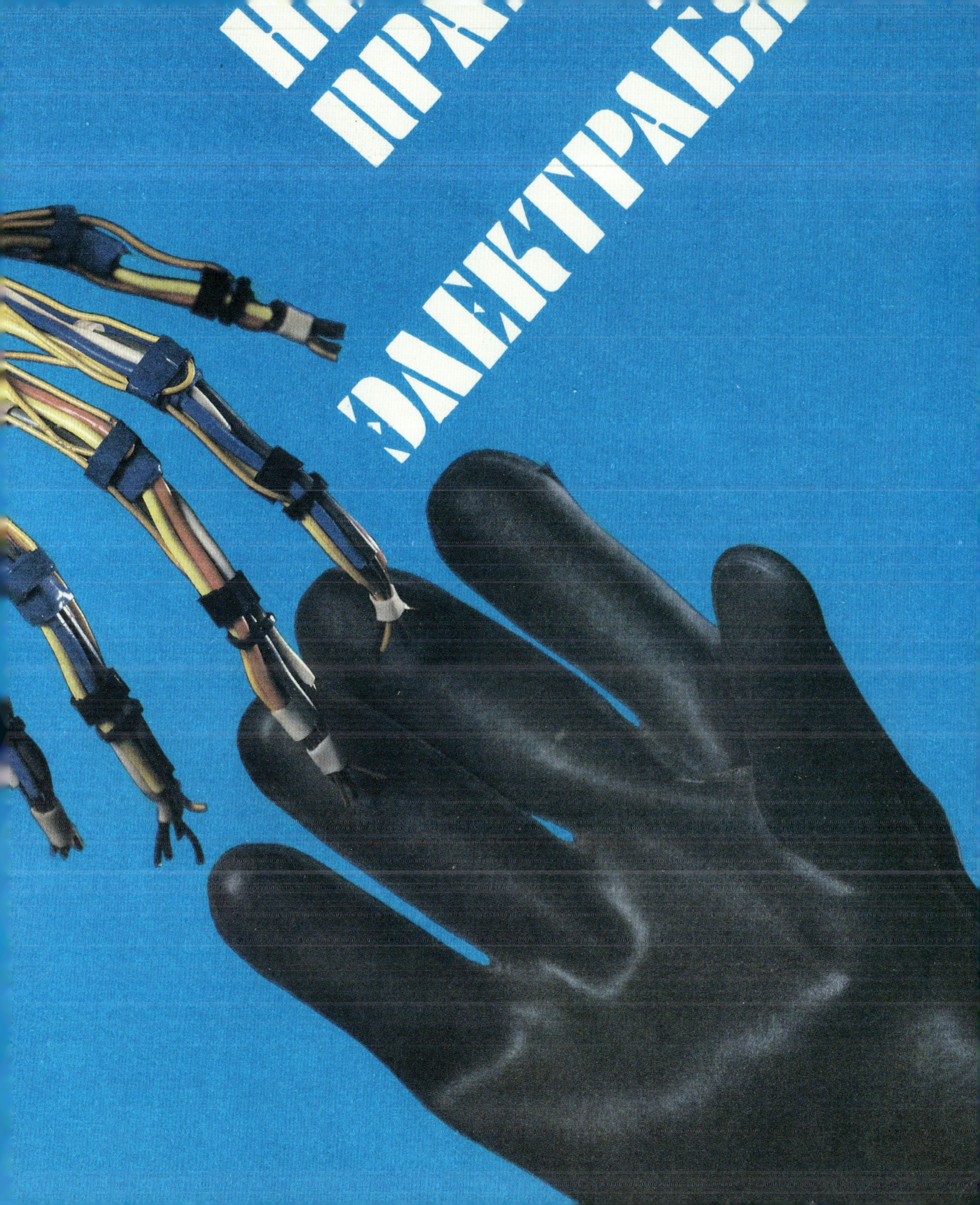

▲ В. Черемных (V. Cheremnykh) | 1989

Text at top: THIS KIND OF PACE IS ON OUR HEADS! Text on worker's helmet: EXCESSIVELY DELAYED CONSTRUCTION

М. Абрамов (M. Abramov), А. Андреев (A. Andreev) | 1985 ➤

PROGRESS REPORT
PLAN EXCEEDED
PLAN: INCOMPLETE
This poster lampoons the tendency of Soviet enterprises to exaggerate the degree to which they have successfully fulfilled annual objectives and quotas for the sake of maintaining appearances dictated by Party propaganda.

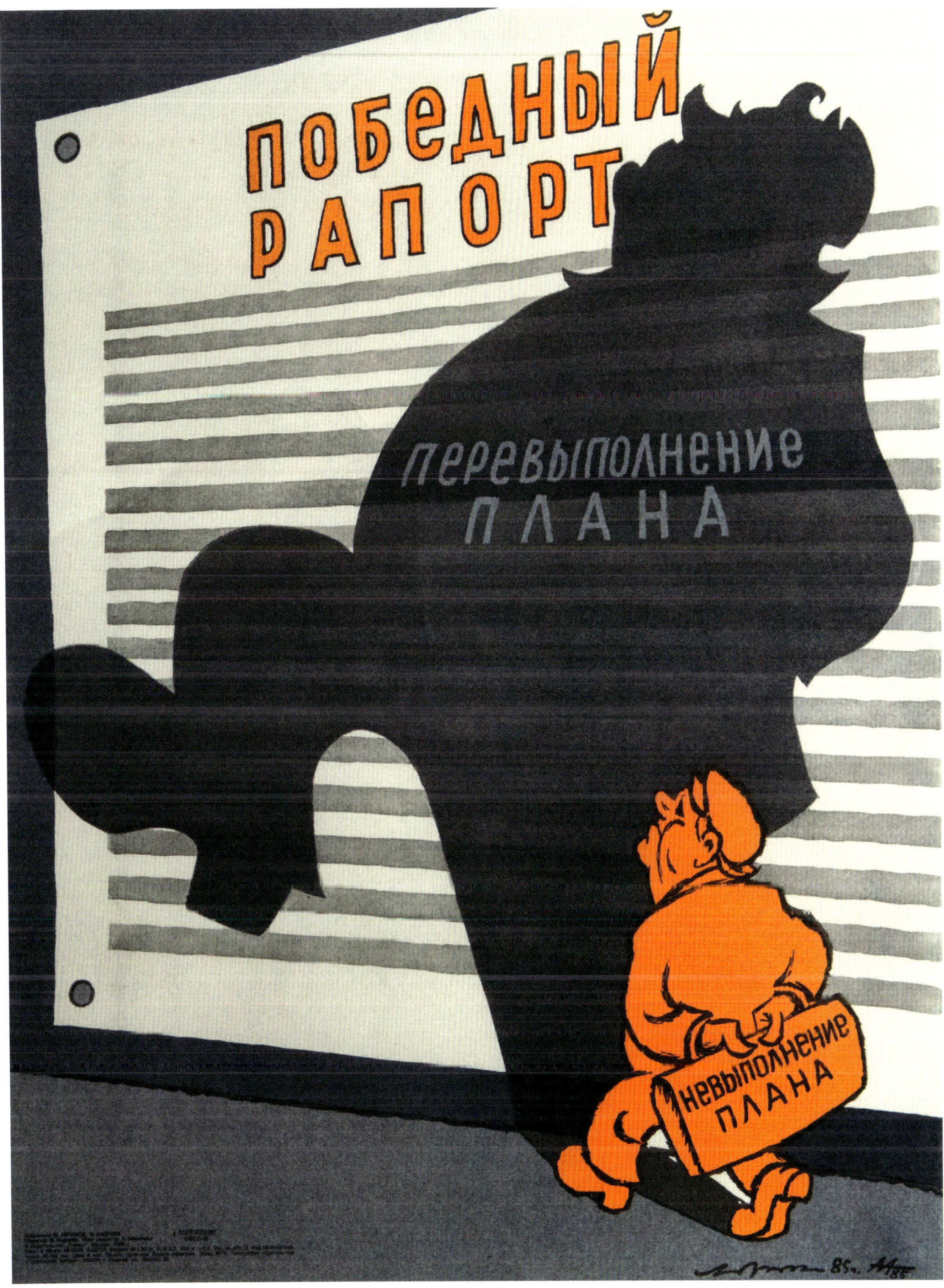
ПОБЕДНЫЙ
РАПОРТ
ПЕРЕВЫПОЛНЕНИЕ
ПЛАНА
НЕВЫПОЛНЕНИЕ
ПЛАНА

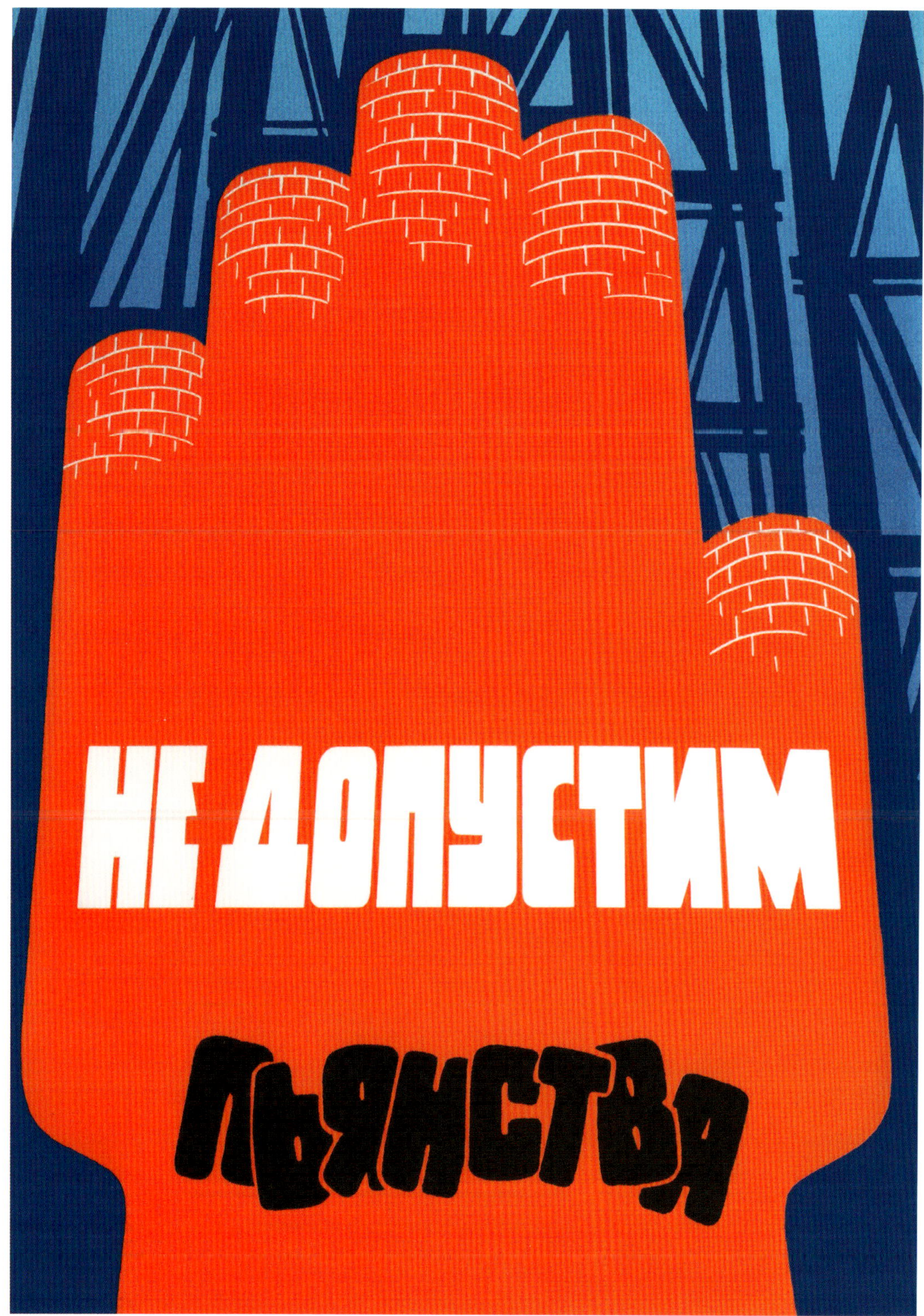

▲ В. Арсеенков (V. Arseenkov) | 1986

NO DRUNKENNESS ALLOWED

The fingers of a hand shaped in the form of factory chimneys are overlaid on industrial scaffolding. The typography of the word "Drunkenness" mimics the staggering gait of an inebriated worker, and the hand's position that of a police officer stopping traffic.

А. Щетилина (A. Shetilina) | 1988 ➤

IS THIS THE WAY WE SHOULD WORK TODAY!?

The image insinuates that it takes nine workers to place a single brick.

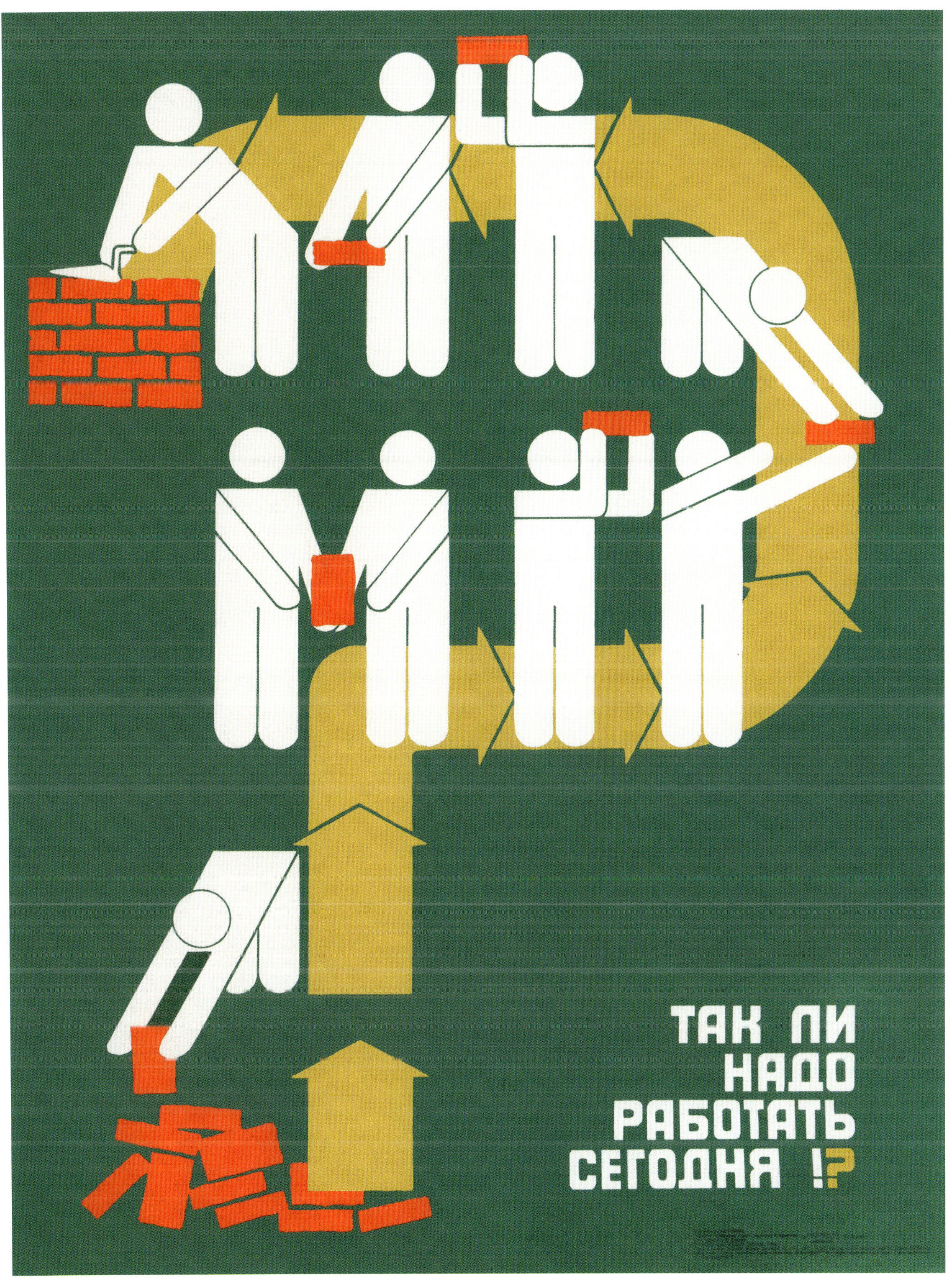
ТАК ЛИ
НАДО
РАБОТАТЬ
СЕГОДНЯ !?

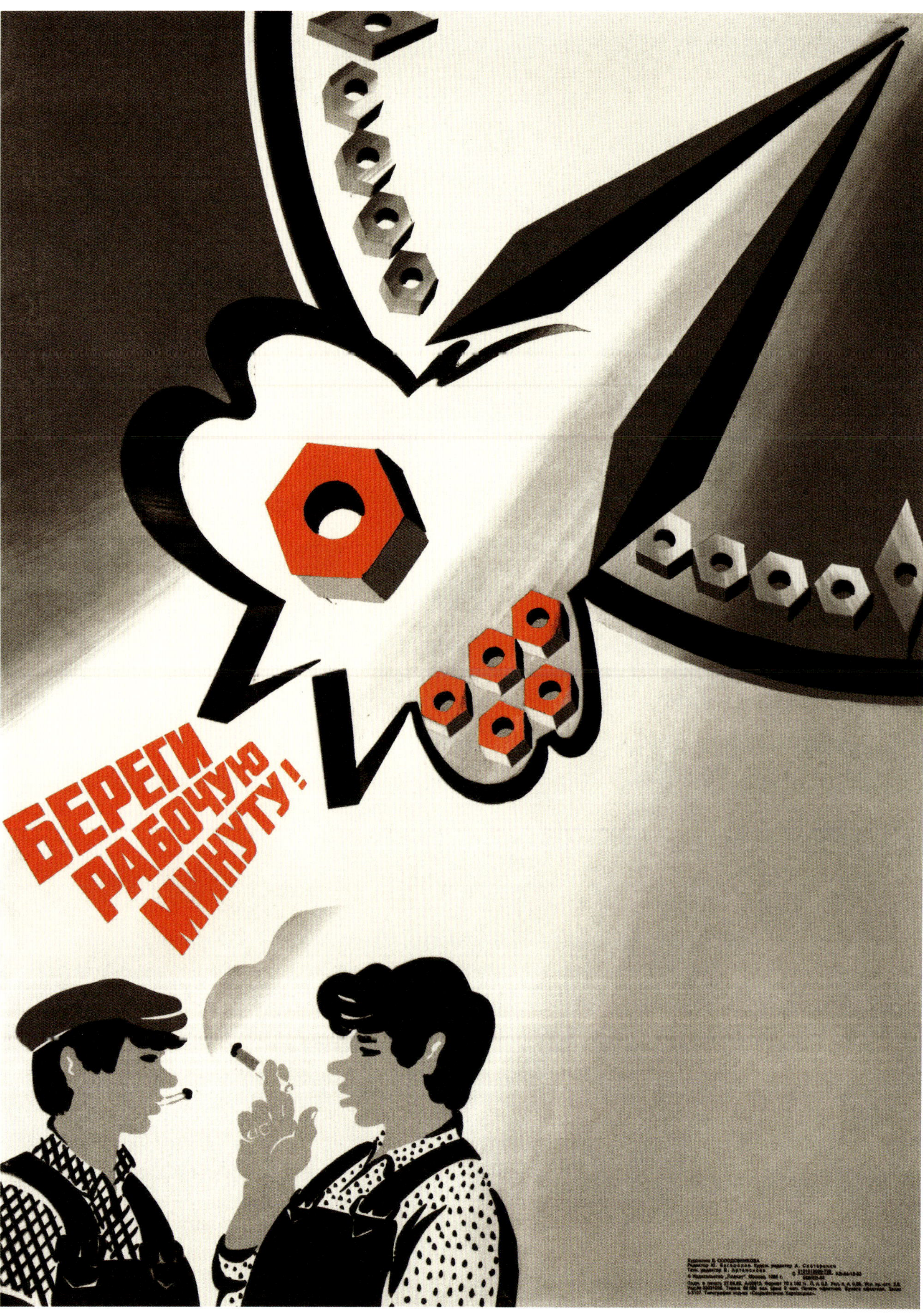
БЕРЕГИ
РАБОЧУЮ
МИНУТУ!

◂ Е. Солодовникова (E. Solodovnikova) | 1986

EVERY MINUTE AT WORK COUNTS!

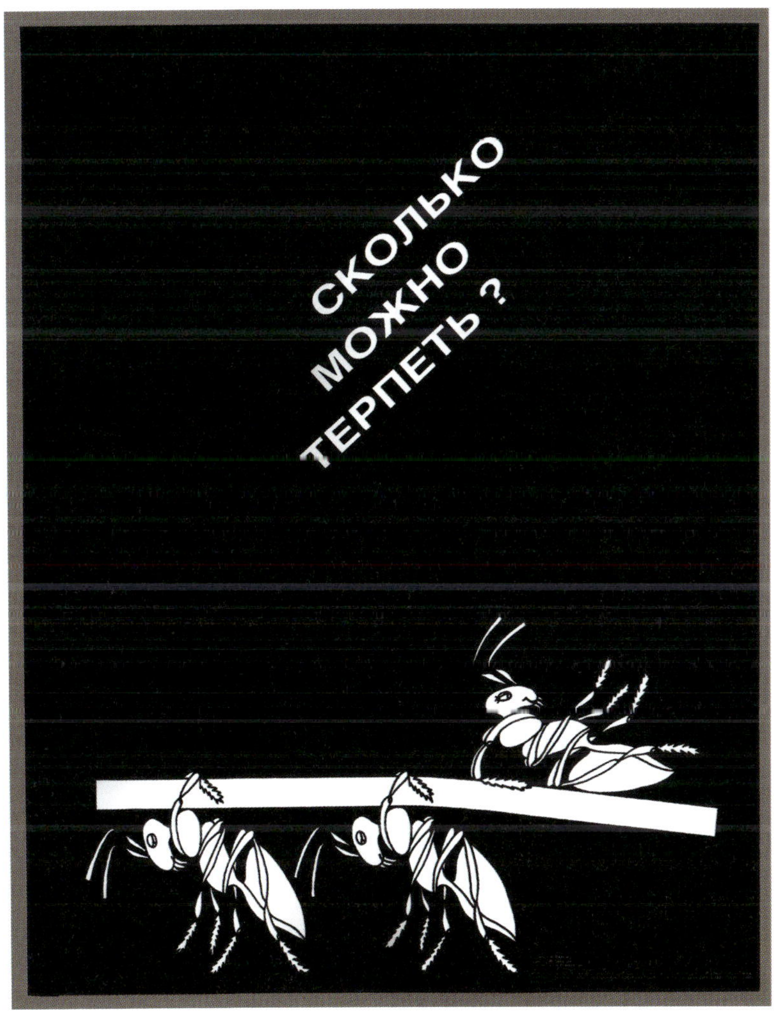

▴ Е. Задко (E. Zadko) | 1987

THE PILFERER IS THE ENEMY OF OUR SOCIETY

◂ И. Варнас (I. Varnas) | 1987

HOW LONG CAN WE TAKE THIS?

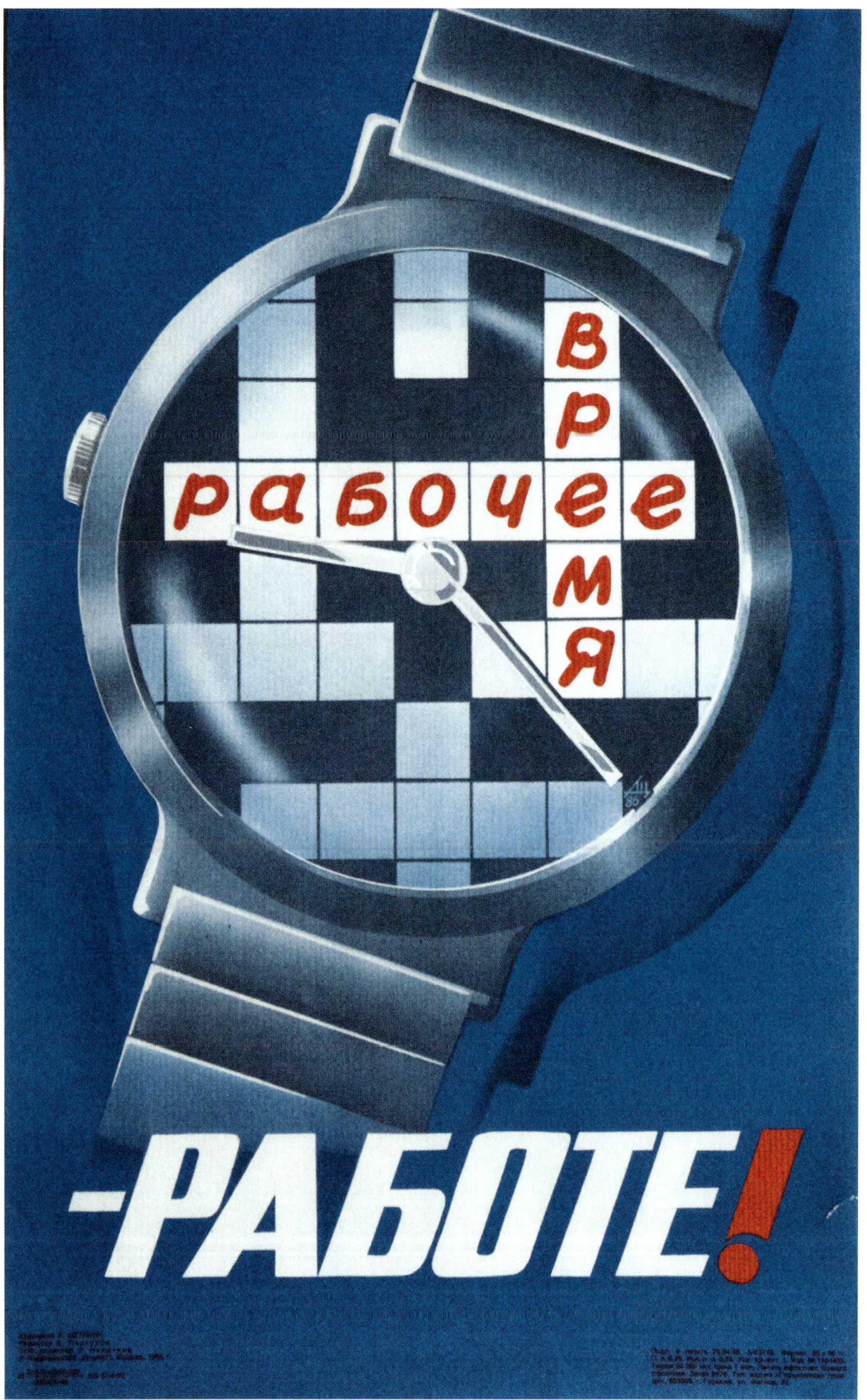

▲ А. Щетинин (A. Shetinin) | 1986

WORK TIME IS FOR WORKING!
The watch face is a crossword puzzle, an activity of leisure, with the words "work" and "time," conveying that working hours are meant exclusively for work.

О. И. Ляшкевич (O. I. Lyashkevich) | 1987 ➤

FOLLOW ELECTRICAL SAFETY RULES!

WORKERS

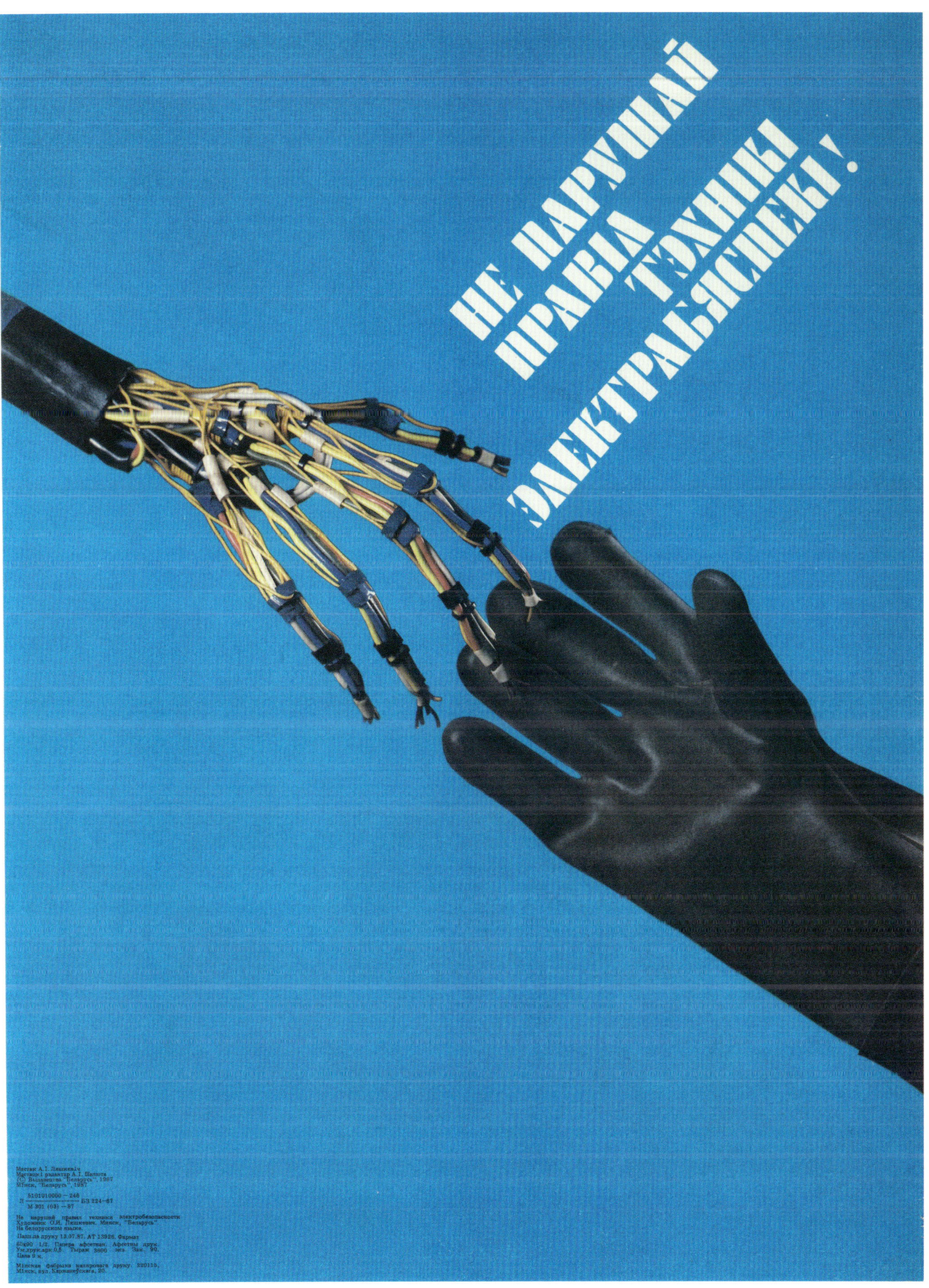
НЕ ПАРУШАЙ
ПРАВІЛ ТЭХНІКІ
ЭЛЕКТРАБЯСПЕКІ!
Не нарушай правил техники электробезопасности
Художник О.И. Ляшкевич. Минск, "Беларусь".
На белорусском языке.

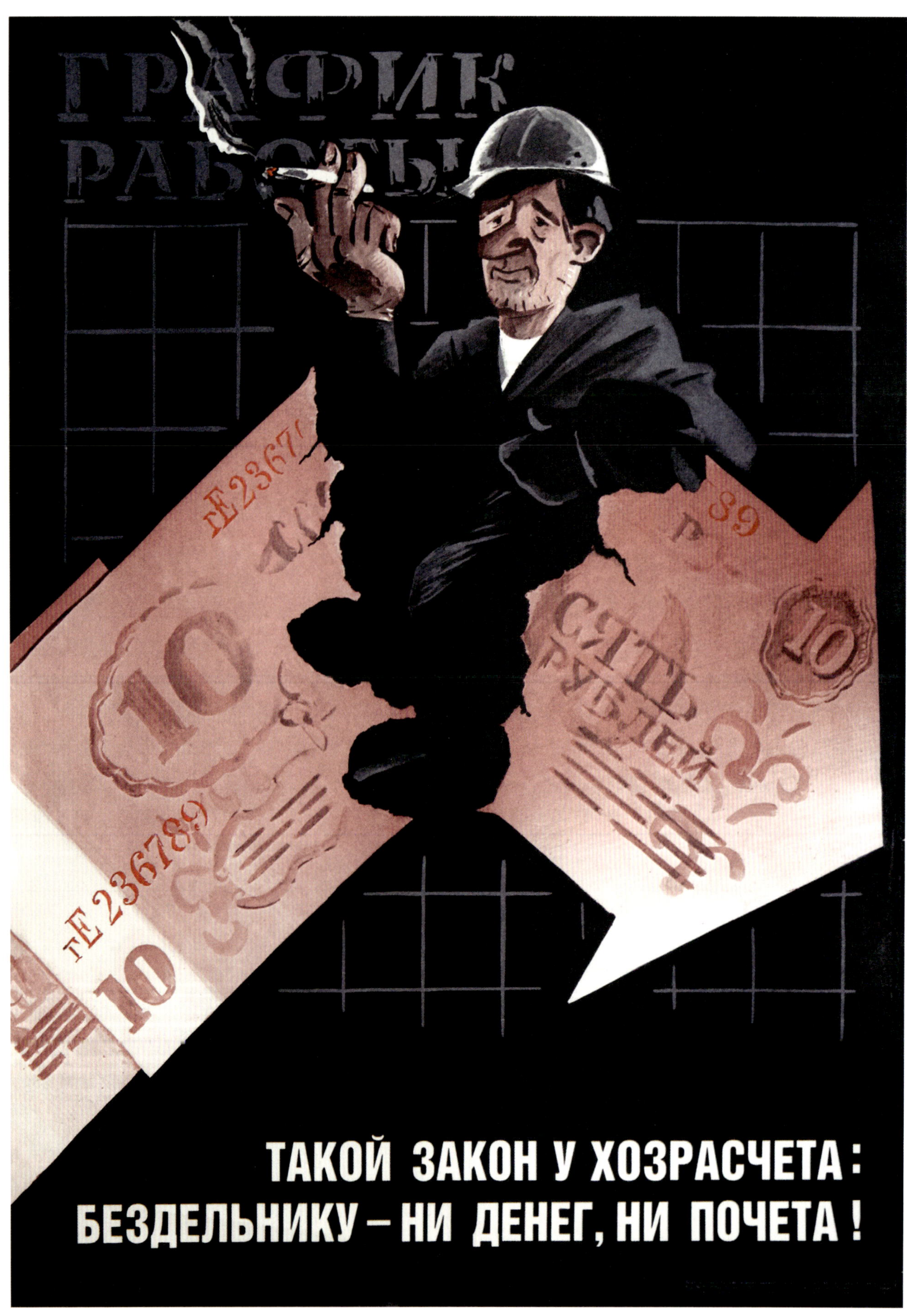
ГРАФИК
ТАКОЙ ЗАКОН У ХОЗРАСЧЕТА:
БЕЗДЕЛЬНИКУ – НИ ДЕНЕГ, НИ ПОЧЕТА!

◂ В. Черемных (V. Cheremnykh) | 1988

Text above worker in background: SCHEDULE
Text at bottom: THE LAW FOR SELF-SUSTAINING PROFITS: NO MONEY, NO RESPECT FOR SLACKERS!
A worker smoking on a red ruble bill causes the graph that is supposed to reflect growth to demonstrate decline instead.

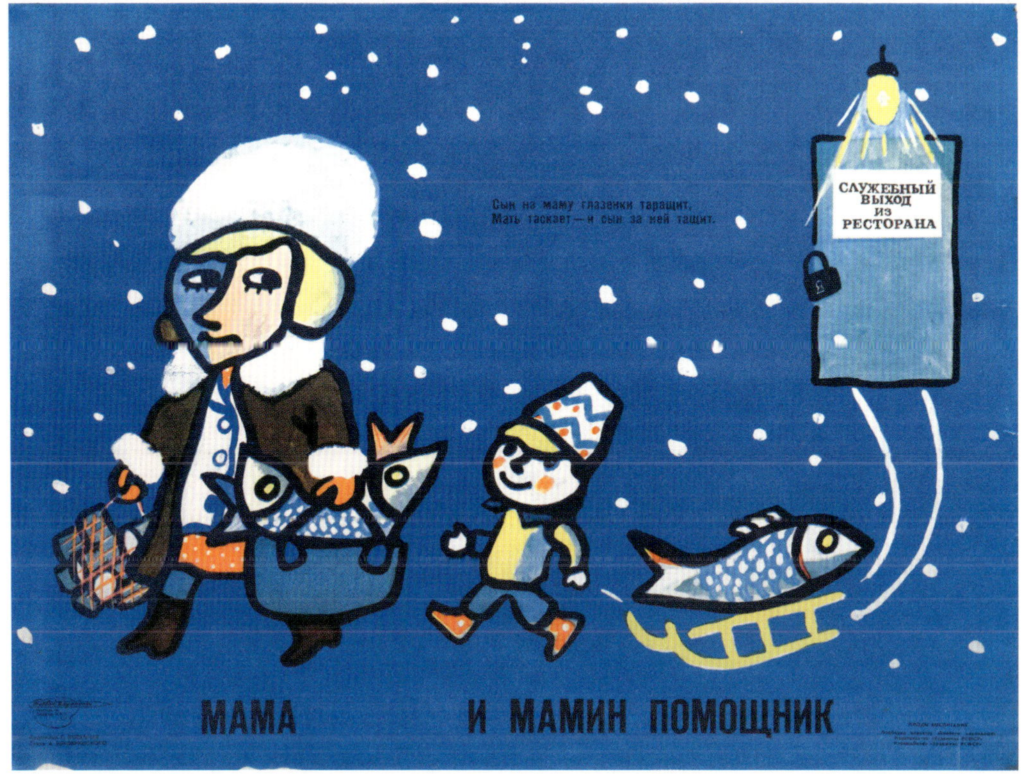

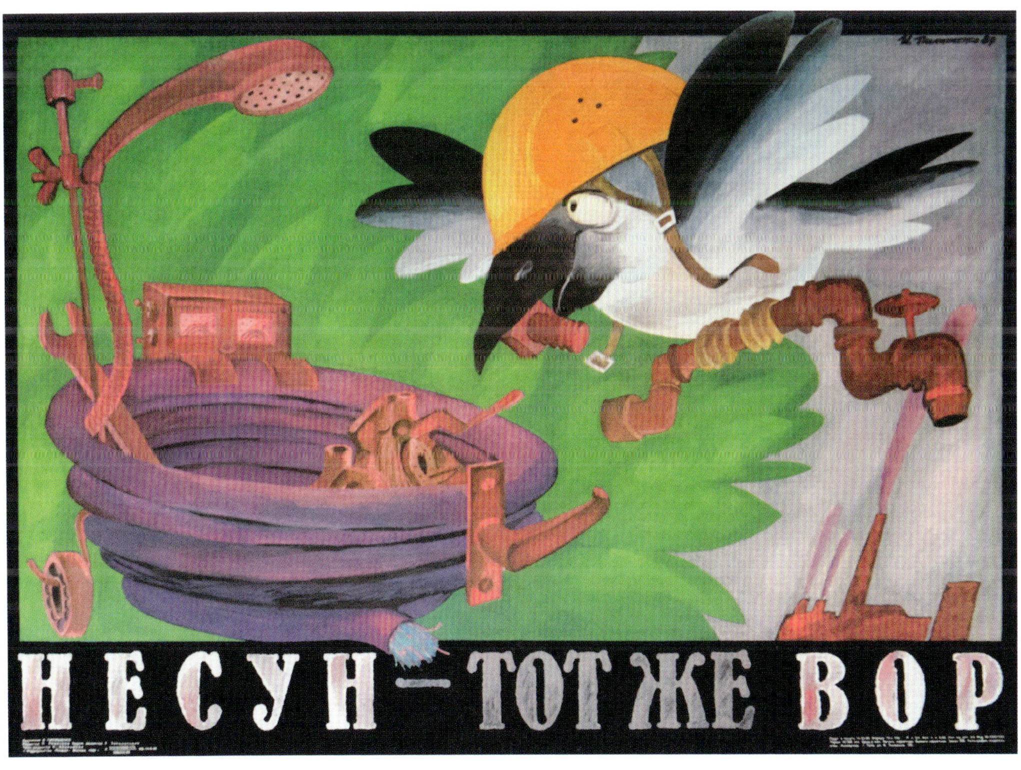

▴ Г. Ковенчук (G. Covenchuk) | n.d.

MAMA AND MOMMY'S HELPER
A mother and son walk out of a door whose sign reads RESTAURANT/EMPLOYEES ONLY carrying bags and pulling a sled with foods taken from the restaurant. THE SON LOOKS TO HIS MOTHER: SHE FILCHES, AND HE FOLLOWS ALONG.

◂ И. Пилишенко (I. Pilishenko) | 1989

A PILFERER IS NO DIFFERENT FROM A THIEF

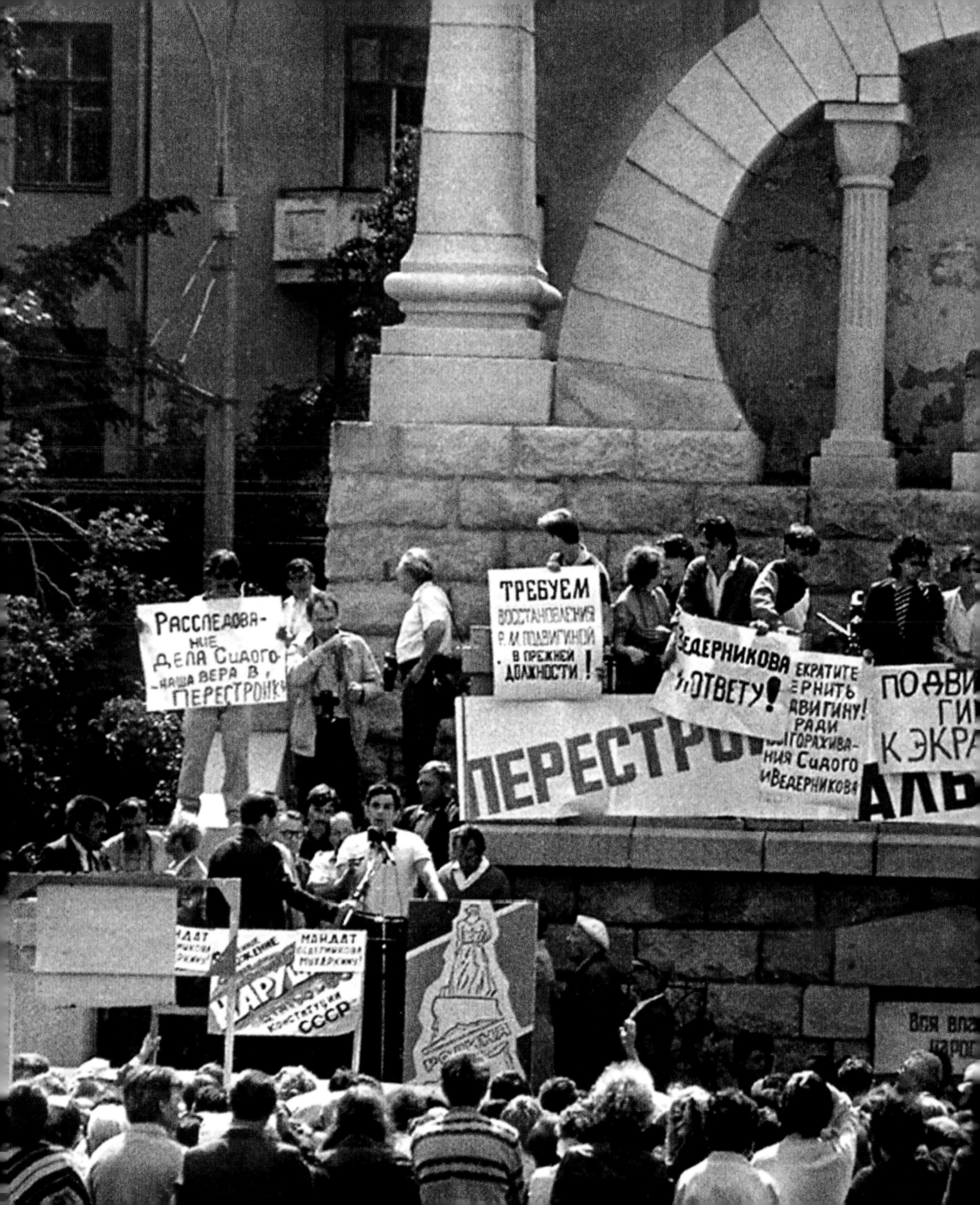
Расследова-
ние
дела Сидого-
ПЕРЕСТРОЙК
ТРЕБУЕМ
восстановления
Р. М. Подвигиной
в прежней
должности!
ЕДЕРНИКОВА
ОТВЕТУ!
ЕКРАТИТЕ
ЕРНИТЬ
АВИГИНУ!
РАДИ
ГОРАЖИВА-
НИЯ Сидого
и Ведерникова
ПЕРЕСТР
ПОДВИ
ГИ
К ЭКРА
АЛЬ
МАНДАТ
КОНСТИТУЦИИ
СССР

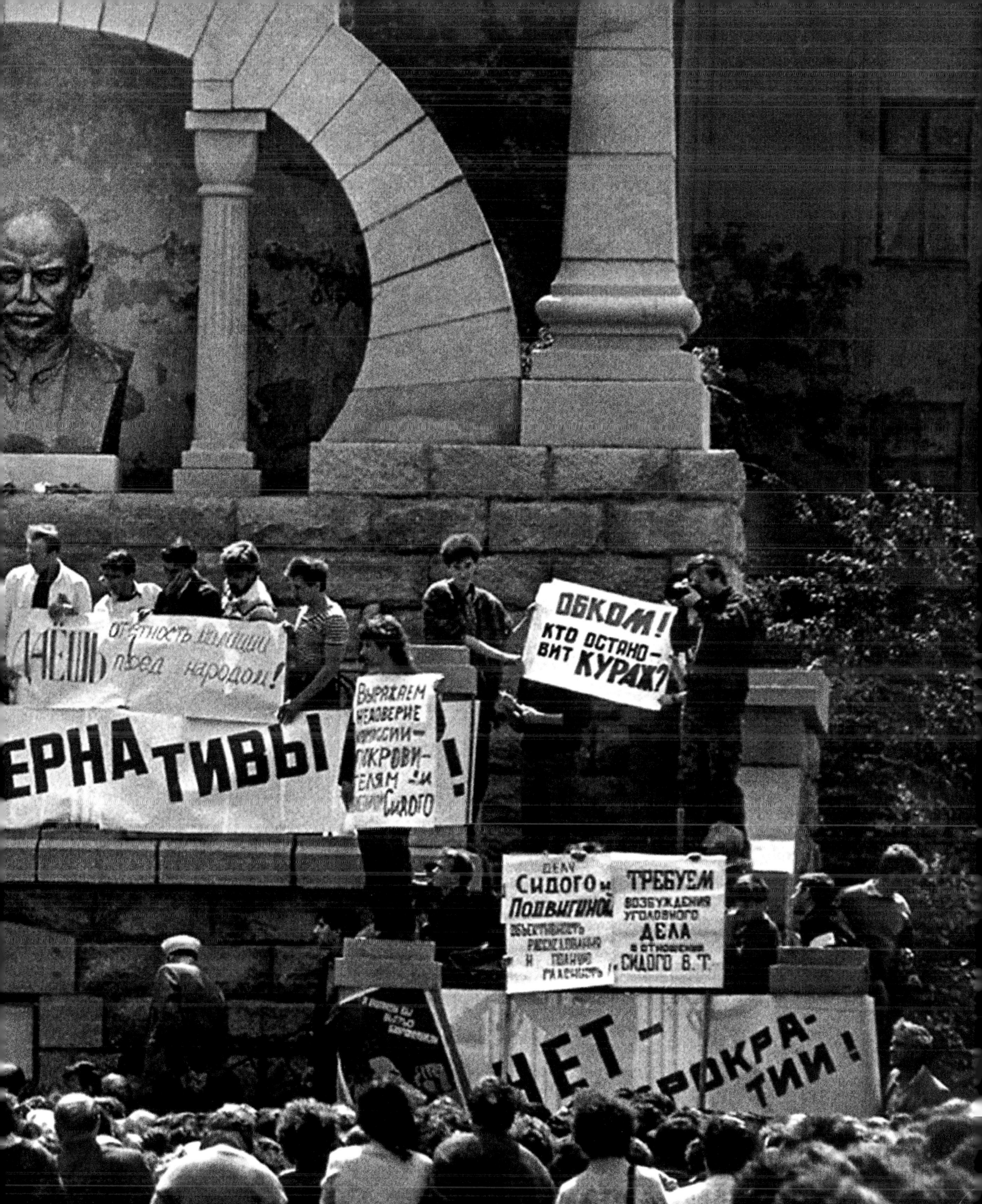
отчетность коллегии перед народом!
ЕРНА ТИВЫ !
Выражаем недоверие
ОБКОМ! КТО ОСТАНО-ВИТ КУРАЖ?
Сидого и Подвигиной
ТРЕБУЕМ возбуждения уголовного ДЕЛА в отношении СИДОГО В.Т.
НЕТ -
ТИИ !

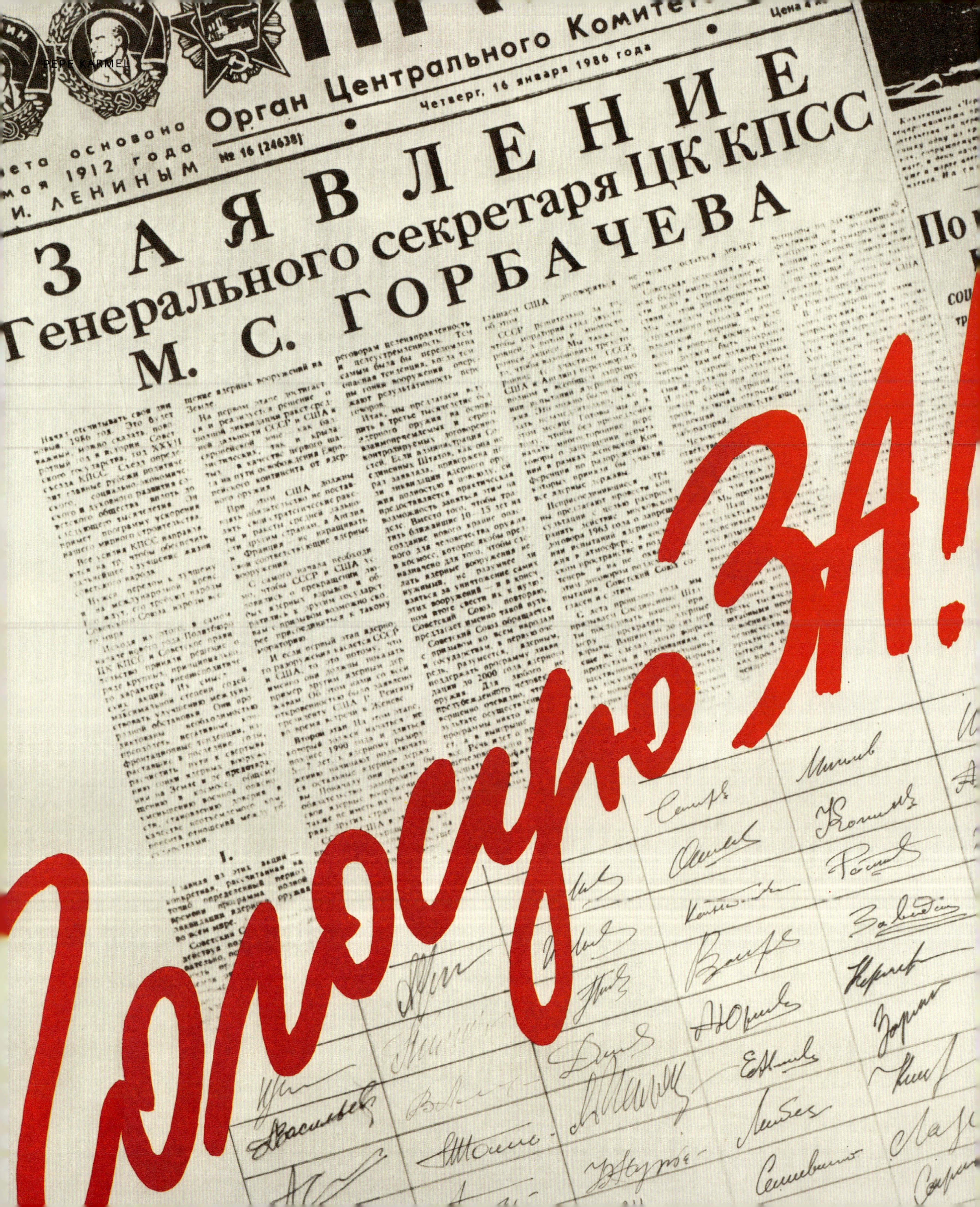
PEPE KARMEL
Орган Центрального Комитет
ета основана
мая 1912 года
И. ЛЕНИНЫМ
№ 16 (24638)
Четверг, 16 января 1986 года
ЗАЯВЛЕНИЕ
Генерального секретаря ЦК КПСС
М. С. ГОРБАЧЕВА
Голосую ЗА!

SOVIET POSTERS FROM THE GLASNOST ERA: THE LANGUAGE OF FORM

PEPE KARMEL

Russian posters of the glasnost era, like Communist art in general, displayed a notable ambivalence toward modernism. In the early years of the Soviet Union, the Ministry of Enlightenment actively supported artistic experimentation, and Russian art movements like Suprematism and Constructivism, briefly, became the cutting edge of the European avant-garde. In the later 1920s, however, Soviet policy shifted, and avant-garde art was condemned as bourgeois and decadent. The task of inspiring and instructing the new men and women of the Communist era required more conventional figuration.

In practice, the officially approved painting and sculpture of the 1930s admitted an impressive variety of styles. The artists privileged to portray Lenin and Stalin stuck close to the example of Parisian Salon painting; other artists, depicting workers, factories, and collective farms, borrowed from French Impressionism, Italian Metaphysical Painting, German New Objectivity, and Art Deco Cubism. Additional figurative styles became acceptable in the cultural thaw that followed Joseph Stalin's death in 1953.[1]

While some poster artists of the 1980s worked in a specifically Russian style of cartoon-like illustration, others took advantage of cultural liberalization to draw on models from Western art and illustration. The ways they utilized these models reflected attitudes widespread in contemporary society. As Alexei Yurchak argues in *Everything was Forever, Until It Was No More: The Last Soviet Generation*, Russian popular culture of the 1980s was marked by a pervasive irony about Communist ideology and by a compensatory fascination with the glamor and vitality of an "Imaginary West." The irony is apparent in jokes that enjoyed a wide circulation:

> What is the difference between capitalism and socialism?
> In capitalism man exploits man, but in socialism it's the other way around.
>
> What does the phrase "capitalism is at the edge of an abyss" mean?
> It means that capitalism is standing at the edge looking down, trying to see what we are doing there.
>
> What would happen if they started building communism in the Sahara Desert?
> There would soon be shortages of sand.[2]

Fascination with the "Imaginary West," a glamorous world glimpsed in magazines and movies, found expression through enthusiasm for jazz and rock and roll, a desire for blue jeans and other garments smuggled into Russia, and an emulation of Western hairdos and posture. Official magazines mocked young Russians who mindlessly mimicked the style of American teenagers while ignoring their own heritage, but the Party tacitly accepted such behavior as a harmless outlet for frustration. Yurchak notes that the Leningrad Rock Club, founded in 1981, was run by the Komsomol (Communist Youth League) and quietly supervised by the KGB. At the same time, Komsomol members who loudly proclaimed their devotion to socialism while secretly embracing Western culture were denounced as corrupt and duplicitous.[3]

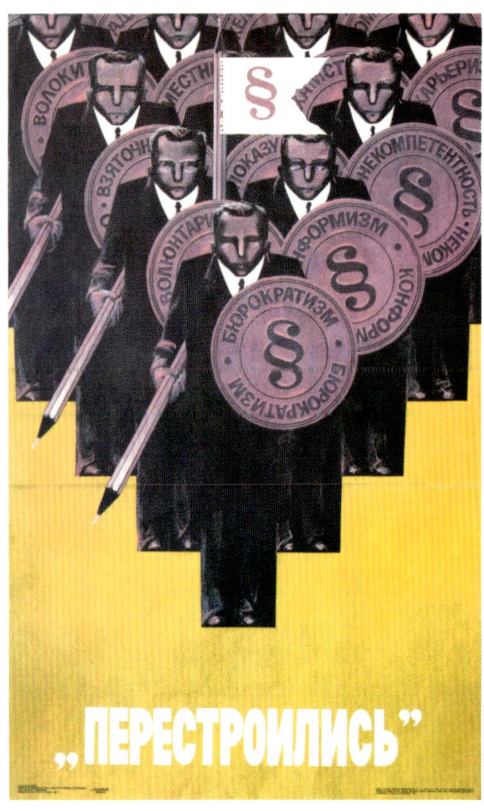

Fig. 1 N. Usov. "Now restructured," 1988. Lithograph, 34 × 21 ½ in. (86.4 × 54.6 cm). Martha H. and J. Speed Carroll Collection.

As discussed by Andy Willimott in his essay for this catalogue, similar ambiguities and contradictions were imbedded in Mikhail Gorbachev's call for glasnost ("openness") and perestroika ("restructuring"). Glasnost acknowledged the need for more open discussion of the problems of the USSR—with the goal of correcting them. It was not a call for Western-style free speech. Perestroika meant a restructuring of the Communist system, not its abandonment in favor of capitalism or Western-style democracy.

Similarly, many of the posters in the Martha H. and J. Speed Carroll Collection call for reform within the existing social and political structure. One poster that resembles the cartoons reproduced in *Everything Was Forever*, "Three 'Heroes'" (n.d., p. 142), criticizes the black market, showing three hirsute men standing behind tables laden with cigarettes, lemons, and bottles of Pepsi-Cola, while construction cranes stand idle in the distance. The implication is that the black market is the result of individual greed and laziness, rather than of the failure of the command economy to produce adequate consumer goods.

Other posters attack bureaucracy as an impediment to change. One example, from 1988, shows bureaucrats defending themselves with swords (pens) and shields (fig. 1). The image is labeled "Now restructured," but the bureaucrats are assembled in a defensive phalanx. Each shield is inscribed with the word "Bureaucracy" on top, while the inscriptions below list the reasons for resistance to change: "conformism / bribery / delay / local nepotism / incompetence / incompetent stubbornness / careerism . . . ." Resistance to perestroika is ascribed to the character flaws of individual bureaucrats, not to the inherent inertia of a command economy.

Working within this minefield of ideological contradictions, creative poster artists drew on a wide range of styles and imagery, sometimes tacitly invoking the repressed history of the Russian avant-garde, sometimes borrowing from Western advertising and Pop art. In some cases, their visual citations reinforced the explicit message of the poster; in others, they suggested a more radical vision of "openness" and "restructuring" than was permitted in official discourse. Often, it is not possible to determine whether the additional meanings suggested by the borrowed imagery were in fact intended by the artists: a haze of ambiguity surrounds their designs.

The inscriptions on V. Arseenkov's 1988 poster (fig. 2) communicate a seemingly straightforward message, reading "Increase the vigor of party organizations . . . Welcome [to speak at the podium] . . . Make Your Speech Precise, Objective, and on Topic." The written message conforms perfectly to Gorbachev's goal of encouraging more open discussion within the Communist Party in order to reform the Soviet state—not to dissolve it. A white podium with four microphones is profiled against a blue and rose sky, inviting the imagined viewers of the poster to step up and speak their minds: vigorously, precisely, and objectively. An upraised hand, fingers extended in parallel, palm facing the viewer, occupies the shallow space between the red lettering in the foreground and the white face of the podium. Seen in isolation, the hand seems simply to be raised in affirmation: a vote in favor of glasnost. For a historically informed viewer, however, it unmistakably echoes the large, raised hand in Gustav Klutsis's 1930 poster "Worker Men and Women: Everyone Vote in the Soviet Elections" (fig. 3).

This is an image with a complex history. Born in Latvia, Klutsis began his artistic career just after the Russian Revolution, making abstract constructions of wooden slats and steel wires. By 1930, Constructivist sculpture was no longer acceptable in Russia, but a degree of abstraction was still tolerated in poster design, and Klutsis survived by making photomontages supporting the Party's propaganda campaigns. The large, raised hand in his poster rises at a dramatic diagonal from a pyramid of smaller raised hands that are interspersed with the faces of men and women workers. The artist first used this design in 1930 for a poster, "Fulfilled Plan, Great Work," celebrating the first two years of Stalin's Five-Year Plan for industrialization. In principle, the raised hands were those of workers enthusiastically endorsing Stalin's policy; in practice, Klutsis used a photograph of his own hand, printing it at larger and smaller sizes to create the image of a crowd of hands.[4] In 1931, Klutsis repurposed the composition by replacing the lettering with a new legend: "Men and Women Workers: Everyone for the Re-Election of the New Soviets." The revised poster thus became a celebration of Communist democracy.

In contrast to bourgeois democracy, where the right to vote is vested, indifferently, in all adult citizens, political power under Communism belonged, in theory, to the working class. Each factory and collective farm was run by a "soviet"—a council, chosen from its own members. The members of these workplace soviets chose representatives to speak on their behalf in a regional soviet, which in turn sent representatives

Fig. 2 V. Arseenkov. "Increase the vigor of party organizations," 1988. Color lithograph, 34 ¼ × 21 ½ in. (87 × 54.5 cm). Martha H. and J. Speed Carroll Collection.

Fig. 3 Gustav Klutsis. "Worker Men and Women: Everyone Vote in the Soviet Elections," 1930. Color offset lithograph on woven paper, 47 × 33 in. (119.7 × 84.7 cm). Collection of the Art Institute of Chicago; Ada Turnbull Hertle Fund.

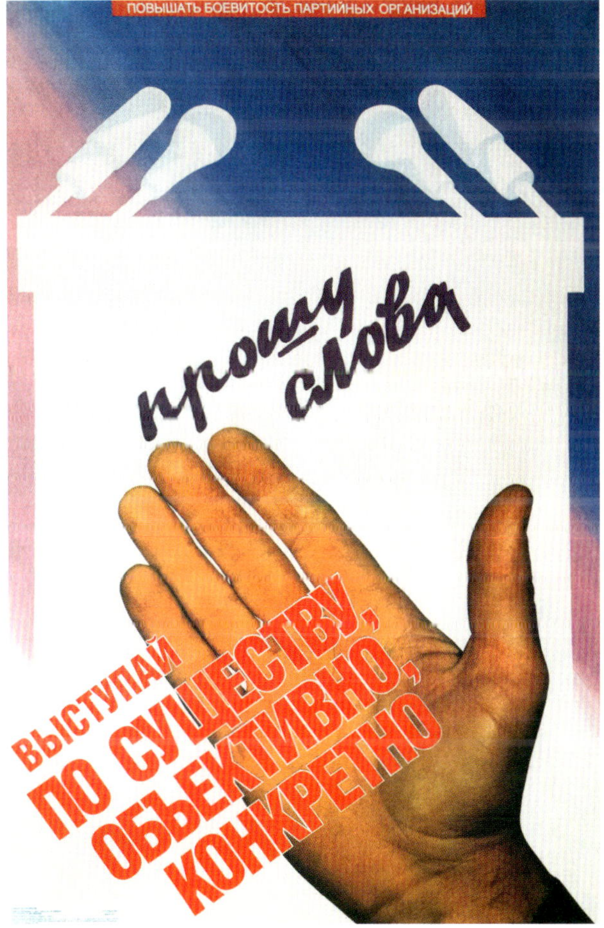

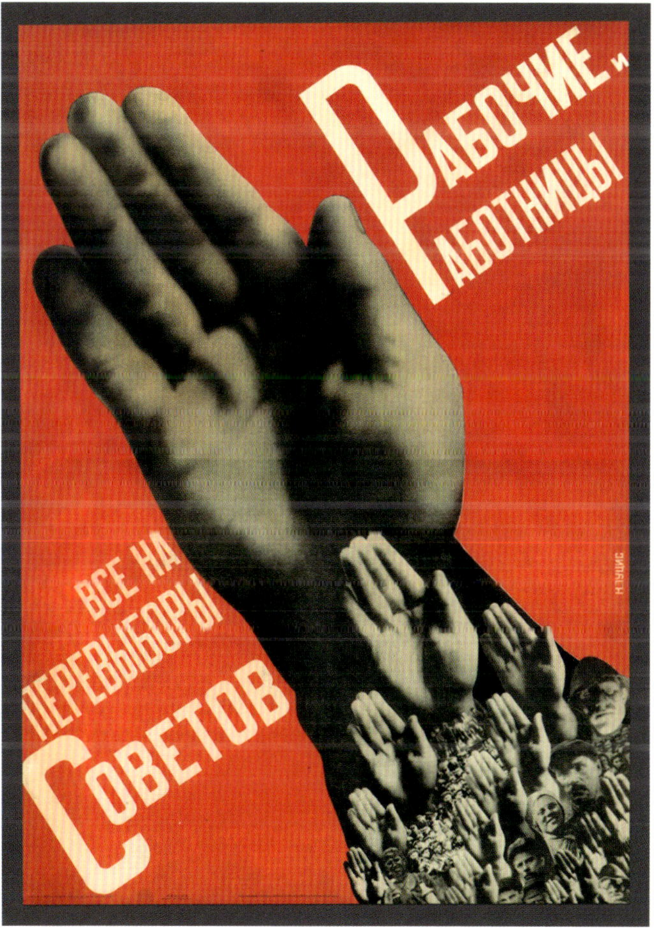

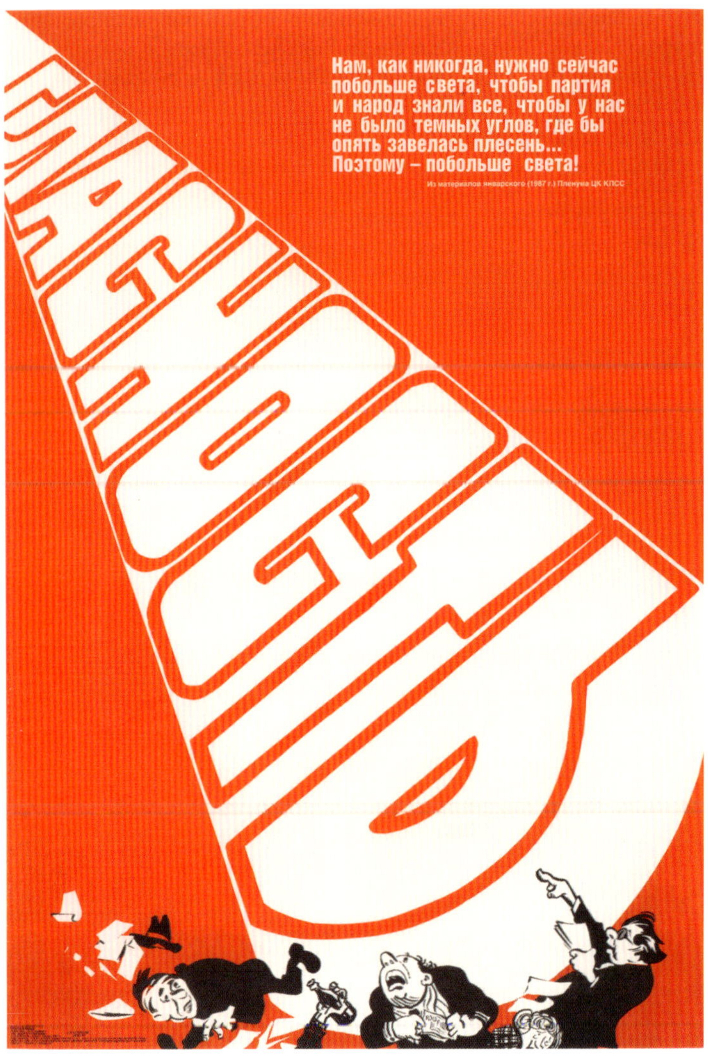

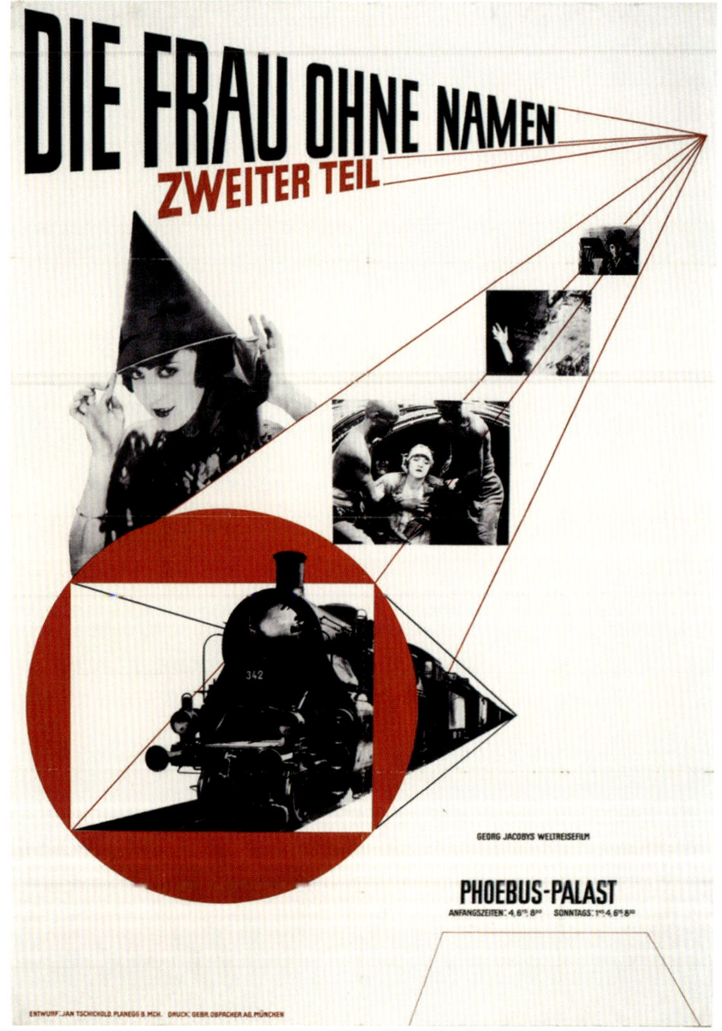

Fig. 4 B. Reshetnikov. "Glasnost," 1987. Lithograph,
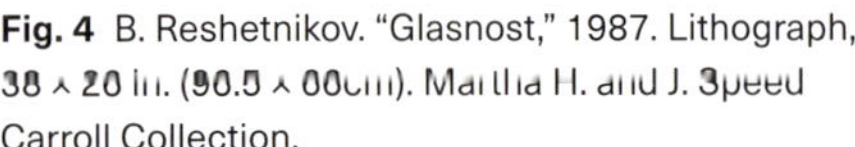
38 × 26 in. (96.5 × 66cm). Martha H. and J. Speed
Carroll Collection.

Fig. 5 Jan Tschichold. Poster for the film: *Die Frau ohne Namen, zweiter Teil (The Woman Without a Name, Part II)*; commissioned by the Phoebus-Palast cinema, Munich, 1927. Photolithograph, 48 ¾ × 34 in. (123.8 × 86.4 cm). Peter Stone Poster Fund; Collection of the Museum of Modern Art, New York.

to the national legislative body in Moscow. Hence the official title of the regime: the Union of Soviet Socialist Republics. Legislative elections, organized according to this process, occurred every few years from 1924 through 1989. In the revised version of Klutsis's poster, the raised hands represent the will of the worker-voters, exercising their democratic rights in the legislative election of 1931.

Needless to say, this was a charade masking the dictatorial power of the Communist Party leadership in Moscow, and, by 1931, of Stalin in particular. Klutsis's 1930 poster evokes the charade rather than the reality of democracy. Despite his faithful service to the Soviet regime, Klutsis was executed in 1938 when Stalin gave orders to suppress a putative Latvian conspiracy against his rule. It seems likely that, even in 1930, the artist was aware of the falsity of his depicted celebration of Soviet democracy.

But what was V. Arseenkov's intention when he paraphrased Klutsis's composition in 1988? Was he using the raised hand to provide an image of participation in Gorbachev's quest to "increase the vigor of party organizations"? Or was the citation intended to suggest that the glasnost campaign was a hollow gesture like the elections of 1931? Perhaps the ambiguity is intentional—the design satisfies both proponents and skeptics.

B. Reshetnikov's 1987 poster "Glasnost" (fig. 4) dramatizes the theme of the Russian bureaucracy's resistance to change. Here, a beam of light inscribed "glasnost" in huge three-dimensional letters exposes a panicked group of corrupt bureaucrats. The text printed at upper right reads: "Now, more than ever before, we need more light, so that the party and the people may see everything clearly, so we no longer have any dark corners where mold can grow . . . and so: let there be more light!" The statement is credited to the January 1987 session of the Communist Party of the Soviet Union (CPSU).

The source of the descending beam of light in this poster is not identified, but it presumably comes from a giant spotlight like those used to celebrate theatrical openings or (during World War II) to reveal attacking planes. That said, the red, black, and white palette corresponds to the color schemes of neither Hollywood posters nor old photographs. It derives, rather, from the Suprematist paintings of Kazimir Malevich and his circle, and from Bauhaus-era designs such as Jan Tschichold's 1927 poster for the film *Die Frau ohne Namen, zweiter Teil* (*The Woman Without a Name, Part II*). Starring Elga Brink as an adventurous American journalist touring the world, the movie was an early example of the kind of "road" picture that was made famous by Bob Hope and Bing Crosby in the 1940s. The poster for Part I of the movie offers a painted image of a blond woman seated at the wheel of a car. In contrast, Tschichold's poster for Part II (fig. 5) is an abstract photomontage with film stills and lettering placed in and around geometric cones that plunge from the foreground into the distance, using abstract forms to convey the idea of rapid, dizzying travel.[5]

In Reshetnikov's 1987 poster, the placement of the beam of light—descending dramatically from the upper left corner—recalls the plunging cone at the center of Tschichold's composition. Obviously, Reshetnikov is not comparing the struggle against bureaucracy to a light-hearted road trip. Rather, he is invoking the utopian associations of Tschichold's style, and its roots in the early Russian avant-garde. Perhaps, the poster implies, glasnost and perestroika will restore the heady optimism of those first years after the Revolution.

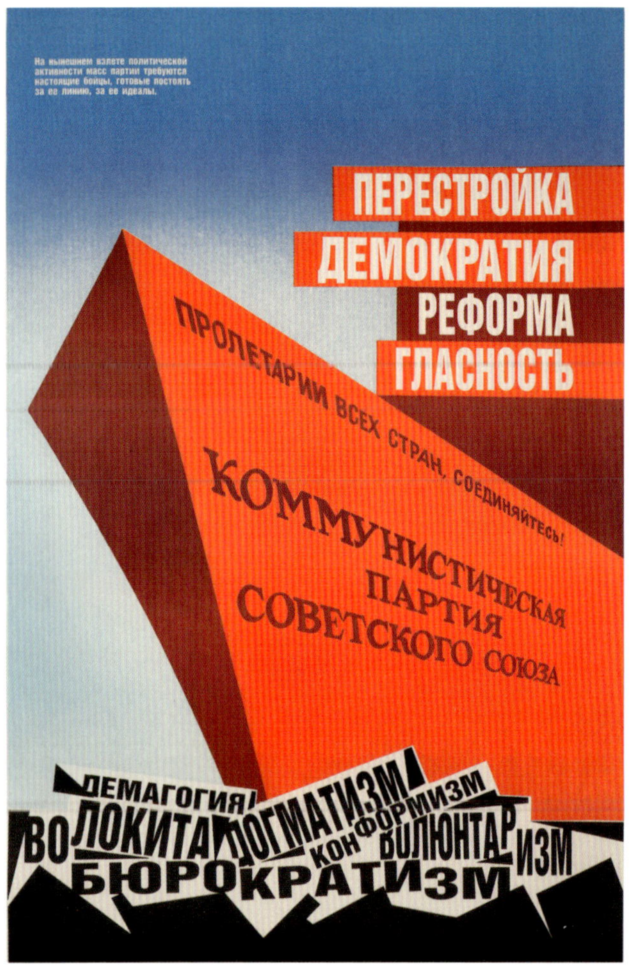

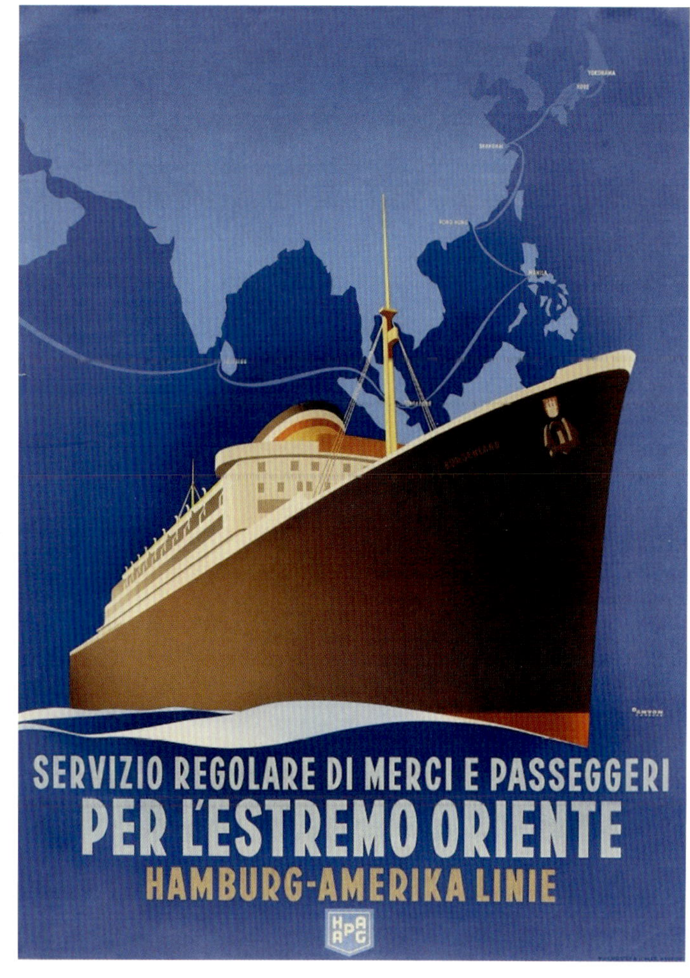

Fig. 6 M. Komarov. "Perestroika, Democracy, Reform, Glasnost," 1989. Lithograph, 38 ¼ × 25 ½ in. (97.2 × 64.8 cm). Martha H. and J. Speed Carroll Collection.

Fig. 7 Ottomar C. J. Anton. "Regular Freight and Passengers Service to the Far East," ca.1935. Lithograph, 25 × 39 ½ in. (63.5 × 100.5 cm).

M. Komarov's "Perestroika, Democracy, Reform, Glasnost," from 1989 (fig. 6), conveys the same message as Reshetnikov's 1987 poster. The poster depicts a ship named *Communist Party of the Soviet Union*, with smaller letters proclaiming, "Proletarians of the world unite!" Its hull is appropriately red. The title of the poster is inscribed across the ship's superstructure. Evidently, the ship is an icebreaker, as it is smashing its way through a clump of floes labeled "Demagoguery/Red Tape/Bureaucratism/Dogmatism/Abuse of Power." The low point of view makes the ship's prow rise above the viewer; its hull is simplified into two geometric planes, each a single color; and it is silhouetted against a featureless blue sky. These formal qualities evoke ocean liner advertisements of the 1920s like Ottomar Anton's poster for the Hamburg-Amerika Line (fig. 7), where the simplified, Art Deco figuration assures the viewer that the vessel is immense, luxurious, powerful, and safe. Clearly, a voyage aboard it will remain a pleasure cruise, even if the destination is the unfamiliar "Far East." Similarly, Komarov's visual equation of the Soviet icebreaker with a capitalist ocean liner promises that the process of glasnost and perestroika will proceed smoothly, without unpleasant incident.

In the years just after 1917, the revolutionary government had encouraged a liberated attitude toward sex, tolerating experiments in "free love," but under Stalin the USSR settled into a repressive puritanism. In the 1980s, the new sexual freedom encouraged by increased contact with the "Imaginary West" ran headlong into the threat of the AIDS epidemic. Poster designers addressing this topic had to be hip enough to hold the attention of young people while simultaneously delivering the unwelcome message that casual sex and promiscuity were in fact dangerous.

O. Dulatova's 1989 poster "Love? Forever?" (fig. 8) offers a visual and verbal response to this challenge. It shows the faces of an attractive young couple, with fashionably spiky hairstyles, staring lovestruck at each other—except red blindfolds cover their eyes. The clear message is that, however close you feel to someone, you may not know very much about them, and it would be prudent to postpone sexual intimacy until you know more. The text at the top poses age-old questions: Is this love? Will it last? But the second question has acquired a new significance in the age of AIDS. If your potential partner is not looking for "eternal" love, then they may have had sex with multiple other partners—increasing the risk of infection. The message of the poster is clear enough to be effective, and indirect enough not to be off-putting.

The purely visual rhetoric deployed by the artist is subtler. The profiles of the young woman and man are almost mirror images, differentiated primarily by the woman's lipstick and earring. Together, they evoke the classic "goblet illusion" popularized by Gestalt psychologists. Focusing on the white profiles, you see two faces. Focusing on the black space between them, you see a goblet with a ringed stem and a wide base. The image hidden in the negative space binds together the faces at either side, emphasizing the importance of a lasting bond.

Furthermore, the couple's spiky hairstyles mark them as young and fashionable. In the West, spiky hair was an element of the punk look of the 1980s. By combining this look with the stark, black-and-white profiles, Dulatova may also have intended to recall Milton Glaser's iconic 1960s poster of Bob Dylan (fig. 9), in which the singer's face is a blank profile but his hair stands up in strands of many colors, charged with vital energy. The immediate implication, in the 1989 poster, is that the most creative people (those with spiked hair) are also the most thoughtful in their choice of romantic partners. But the further implication of citing Glaser's Pop art imagery is to convert love into a kind of consumerism. As a consumer, you want to make the best choice. And the best choice here is caution.

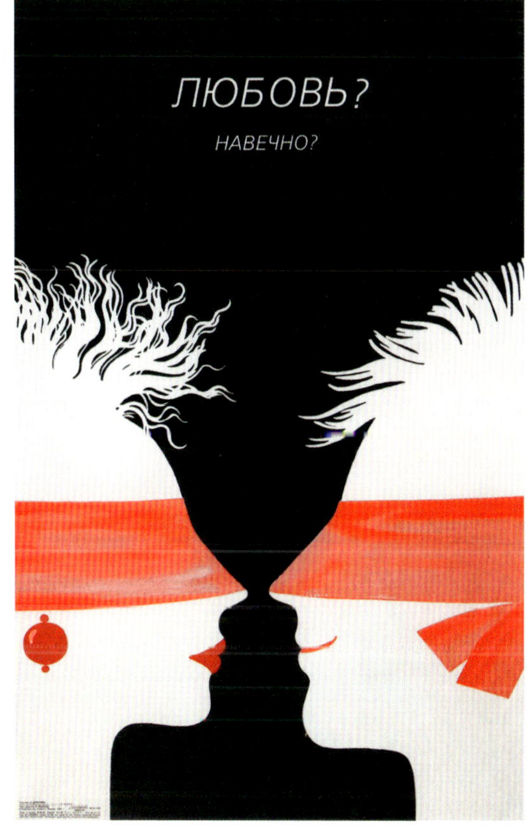

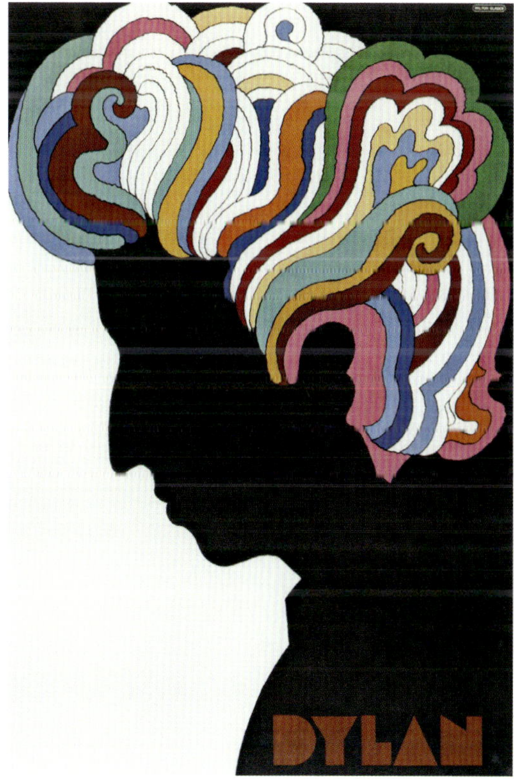

Fig. 8 O. Dulatova. "Love? Forever?," 1989. Lithograph, 34 × 21 ½ in. (86.4 × 54.6 cm). Martha H. and J. Speed Carroll Collection.

Fig. 9 Milton Glaser. *Dylan*, 1966. Offset lithograph, 33 × 22 in. (83.8 × 55.8 cm). Collection of the Museum of Modern Art, New York.

While American Pop art typically celebrated and critiqued consumerism and celebrity, Andy Warhol, the leading Pop artist, was equally obsessed with death. His early silkscreen portraits of Marilyn Monroe and Natalie Wood depicted recently deceased actresses, and his "Death and Disaster" series from the 1960s reproduced newspaper images of car crashes and electric chairs. In 1968, Warhol himself almost died after being shot.[6] In the early 1980s, he created a series of "Gun" silkscreen prints, apparently provoked by the late 1970s surge in handgun deaths. In this example (fig. 10), he used a silkscreened photograph to overlap two images of the same handgun—one black, one red. The violent, funereal associations of the image are underscored by the deliberately uneven printing, which makes the gun itself seem to fade out of existence.

The 1990 poster by R. N. Nayden and A. P. Novozhilov (fig. 11) mimics the grainy, silkscreened look of Warhol's work, but with the added inscription of "1937," referring to one of the grimmest moments in Soviet history: Stalin's Great Purge of 1937–38, which led to the execution of hundreds of thousands of military officers, intellectuals, peasants, national minorities, and Communist Party officials on trumped-up charges of betraying the Revolution. Stalin died of natural causes in 1953. His successor, Nikita Khrushchev, denounced Stalin's horrific abuse of power in a secret speech to a 1956 Congress of Communist leaders; Khrushchev's speech, which soon leaked to a broader public, led to a partial reform of the Soviet system, and could be regarded as an early example of glasnost.

Nayden and Novozhilov, the artists responsible for the poster, came from Belarus, a formerly separate nation that was incorporated into the Soviet Union in 1922 and regained its independence in 1990. Primarily an agricultural country, Belarus suffered badly under Stalin's forced collectivization in the 1930s; evidence of mass killings during the Great Purge was uncovered in 1988. The poster, in sum, recalls the history of Stalinist violence in Belarus to justify the country's quest for independence. The quivering red tongue, painted over the original steel trigger, has been interpreted as a reference to the cowardly officials of the 1930s who denounced their colleagues to save themselves. It might also be read as a symbol of Stalin's insatiable appetite for inflicting suffering and death.

Finally, it is important to consider a visual language that was *not* often used by Soviet poster designers of the 1980s: the distinctive style of the Parisian posters supporting the demonstrations of May 1968, when students joined forces with workers to protest the policies of Charles de Gaulle's government. Posters such as "May '68: Beginning of a Long Struggle" (fig. 12) were produced by the Atelier Populaire (People's Workshop), run by students and faculty members in the lithography studio of the École des Beaux Arts. The demonstrators revived the joyful anarchism of the late nineteenth century, coining slogans such as "It is forbidden to forbid" and "Be realistic, demand the impossible." Rejecting all forms of authority, the students decided to create their own "people's university," while the workers remained on strike despite the pleas of union leaders (including the leaders of the French Communist Party) that they return to work. The poster announcing the "Beginning of a Long Struggle" depicts an iconic red factory with a huge red flag attached to its chimney; building and flag together form a large red square. The date "Mai 68" is written in white across the factory, while "Debut d'une lutte prolongee" is spelled out in red block letters below it.

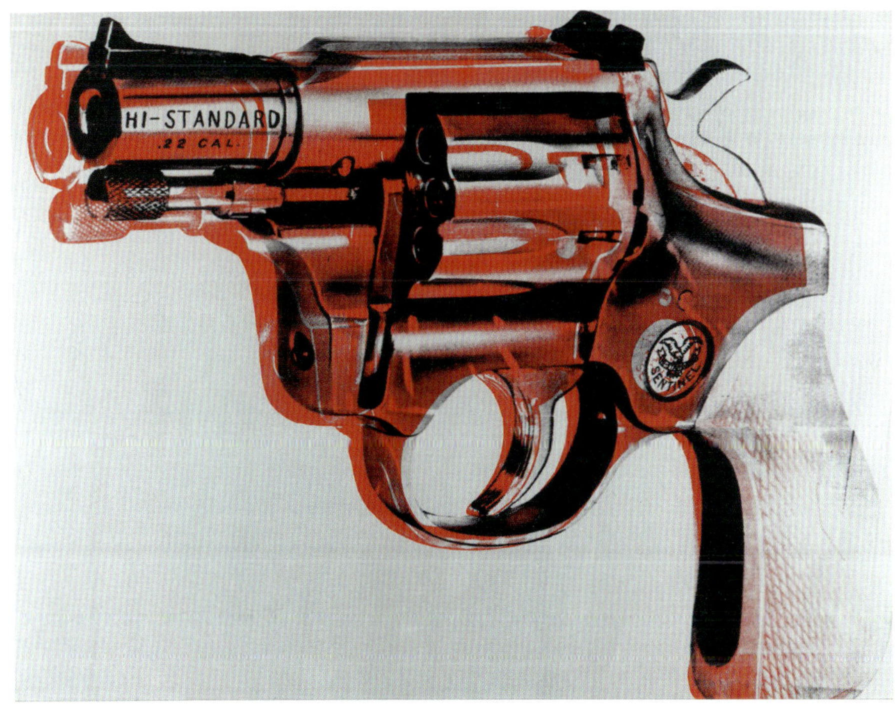

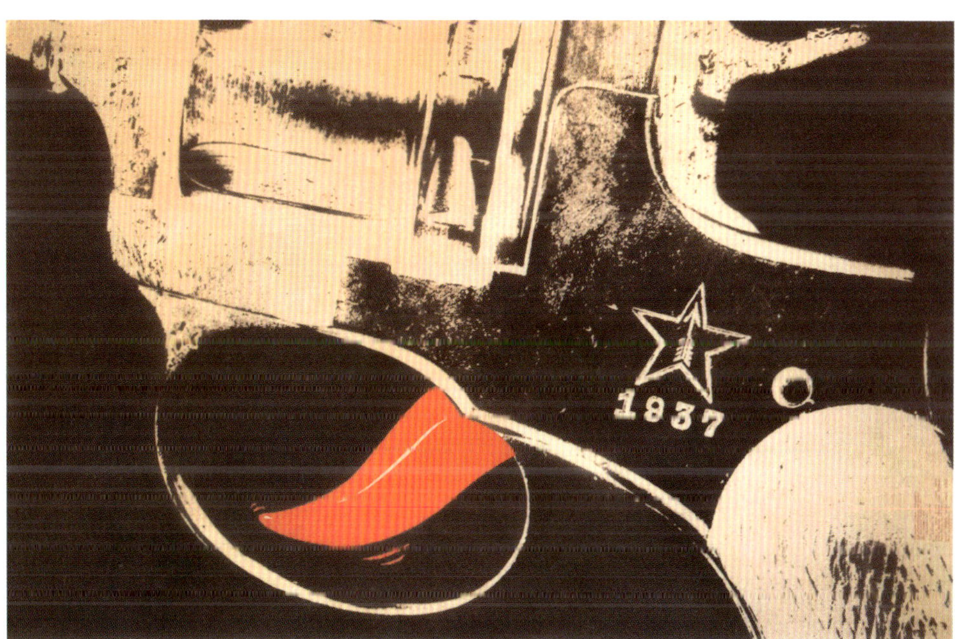

Fig. 10 Andy Warhol. *Guns*, 1981–1982. Acrylic paint and silkscreen ink on canvas, 70 × 90 in. (177.8 × 228.6 cm). Collection of the San Francisco Museum of Modern Art.

Fig. 11 R. N. Nayden and A. P. Novozhilov. "1937," 1990. Lithograph, 24 ¼ × 38 ¼ in. (61.6 × 97.2 cm). Martha H. and J. Speed Carroll Collection.

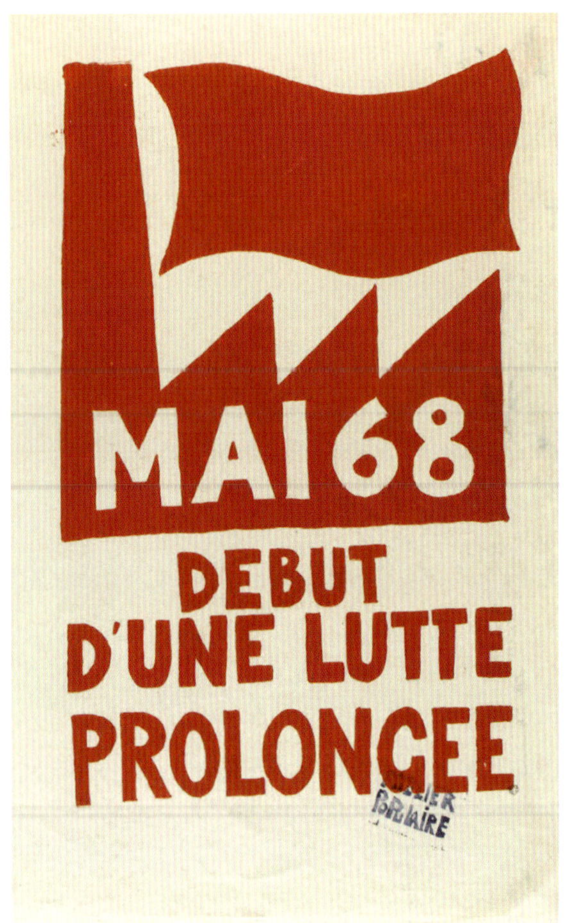

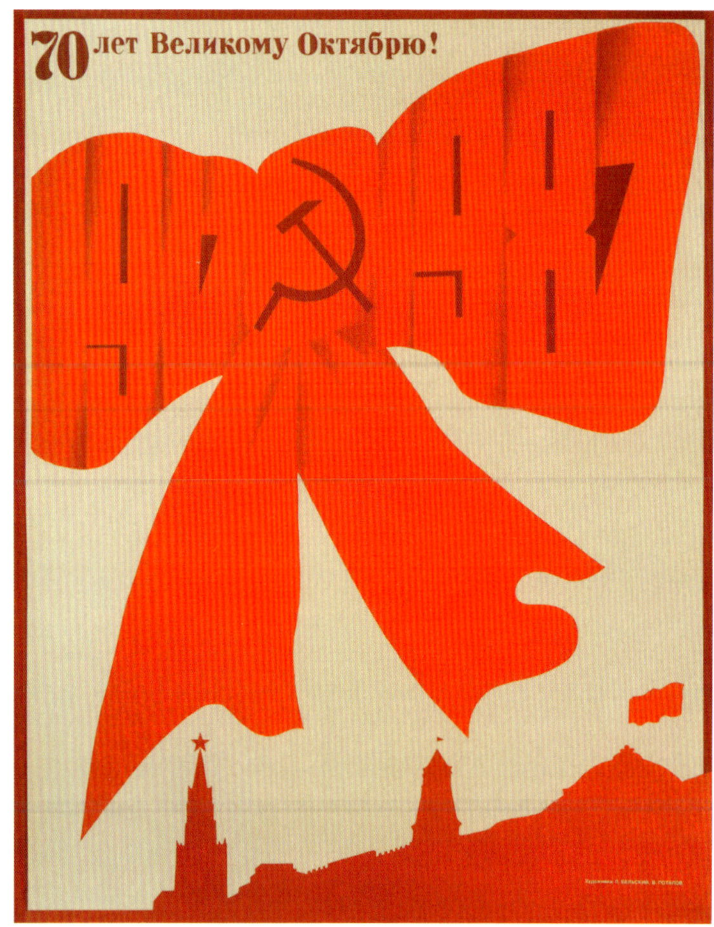

Fig. 12 L'Atelier Populaire. "Debut d'une lutte prolongee," (The beginning of a prolonged struggle), 1968.

Fig. 13 L. Belsky and V. Potapov. "70 years of the Great October!" 1989. Lithograph, 21 ½ × 17 in. (54.6 × 43.2 cm). Martha H. and J. Speed Carroll Collection.

The students' and workers' hopes for a revolution from the bottom up came to a climax on May 30, when 500,000 people marched through the streets of Paris demanding De Gaulle's resignation. It seemed briefly as if the government might collapse. However, a countermarch in support of De Gaulle attracted 800,000 people, and national elections held in June returned De Gaulle and his party to office with an overwhelming majority. The "prolonged struggle" announced on the poster lasted about a month. But the anarchist rejection of authority and the belief in personal liberation as a form of political liberation remained a utopian ideal for the European left for decades.

The Soviet poster celebrating "70 years of the Great October!" (fig. 13) mimics the visual language of the Atelier Populaire. A large red bow floats over the red silhouette of the Kremlin, like the flag floating over the saw-tooth roof of the factory in the 1968 French poster. The dates, "1917–1987," are imprinted in block letters on the loops of the bow. The phrase "70 years of the Great October!" (i.e., the October Revolution) is written at upper left in a plump serif type that looks back, incongruously, to the elegance of Art Nouveau. On the whole, however, the juxtaposition of red, silhouetted forms evokes the joyous anarchism of May 1968.

This style was rarely employed by Soviet designers because its historical associations were dangerously double-edged. On one hand, the demonstrations of 1968 recalled the similar demonstrations that had propelled the Bolsheviks to power in 1917–18 and were frequently restaged by the new Soviet government in the 1920s. On the other, by 1987, the last thing the current Soviet government wanted was to encourage spontaneous demonstrations challenging the authority of the government, the sort of uprisings that had welled up across the West beginning in May 1968. Glasnost and perestroika were intended to restore flexibility to an ossified bureaucracy—not to destroy it.

The collapse of the Soviet Union in 1991 did not mark the end of the second Russian revolution. It turned out that the era of glasnost was merely the "beginning of a long struggle" over the distribution of power and wealth, a struggle that continues to the present day. During this period, contemporary Russian art has experienced alternating periods of liberalization and repression. Despite the passage of time, the Russian posters of the late 1980s retain their fascination, demonstrating how their makers used stylistic allusion to strike a balance between openness and censorship, between the call to restructure the Soviet world and the demand that everything remain the same.

1. The color-infused realism of portraits like Isaak Brodsky's *Lenin Making a Speech* (1933) and Grigori M. Shegal's *Leader, Teacher, and Friend (Comrade Stalin)* (1937) looks back to the example of Parisian Salon painters like Léon Bonnat. In contrast, Vasily Alexandrovich Zverev's *Portrait of the "Shock Worker" I. I. Guiriat, in the Karl Marx Factory* (1931; reproduced in Vladimir Gusev and Yevguenia Petrova, *Radiante Porvenir*, Málaga: Museo Ruso San Petersburgo, 2018, pl. 30) recalls German *Neue Sachlichkeit* (New Objectivity) painters like Rudolf Schlichter, while Vasily Vasilyevich Rozhdestvensky's *Rolling Mill: Hammer and Sickle* (1930; in *Radiante Porvenir*, pl. 23) resembles Claude Monet's 1877 paintings of the Gare Saint-Lazare. The wooden figures and simplified shading of Aleksandr Deineka's *Collective Farm Team* (1934; *Radiante Porvenir*, pl. 48) betray the influence of contemporary Italian art. The sexy Cubist anatomies of Tamara de Lempicka provide the unmistakable model for Vera Mukhina's iconic sculpture *Worker and Collective Farmer* (1937), the Stalinist equivalent to Vladimir Tatlin's *Monument to the Third International* (1919). After Stalin's death in 1953, new styles ranged from the painterly realism of Konstantin Maksimov's *Sashka the Tractor Driver* (1954; reproduced in Matthew Cullerne Bown, *Socialist Realist Painting*, New Haven, CT: Yale University Press, 1998, pl. 950), recalling Frans Hals and the American Ashcan School, to the dramatic profile of Tair Salakhov's *Portrait of the Composer Kara Karaev* (1960; reproduced in Thomas Krens et al, *Russia!*, New York: Solomon R. Guggenheim Museum, 2006, pl. 231).

2. Alexei Yurchak, *Everything Was Forever, Until It Was No More: The Last Soviet Generation* (Princeton, NJ: Princeton University Press, 2006), 279–280.

3. Yurchak, *Everything was Forever*, 166–175, 192–202, 209–212. For an example of a poster criticizing Russian teenagers' mindless imitation of Western styles, see E. Osipov, "Mama gave it to me," in the Martha H. and J. Speed Carroll Collection.

4 Christina Lodder, *Russian Constructivism* (New Haven, CT: Yale University Press, 1983), 190–191.

5. The circle and cones of Tschichold's 1927 composition (fig. 5) were based, in turn, on earlier paintings like Giacomo Balla's *Mercury Passing in Front of the Sun Seen through a Telescope*, 1914 (mumok, Museum moderner Kunst Stiftung Ludwig, Vienna), and Kurt Schwitters' *Revolving*, 1919 (Museum of Modern Art, New York). In contrast, Tschichold's use of photomontage derives from Aleksandr Rodchenko.

6. In 1968, Warhol was shot by Valerie Solanas, a radical feminist and writer, who subsequently received a diagnosis of paranoid schizophrenia.

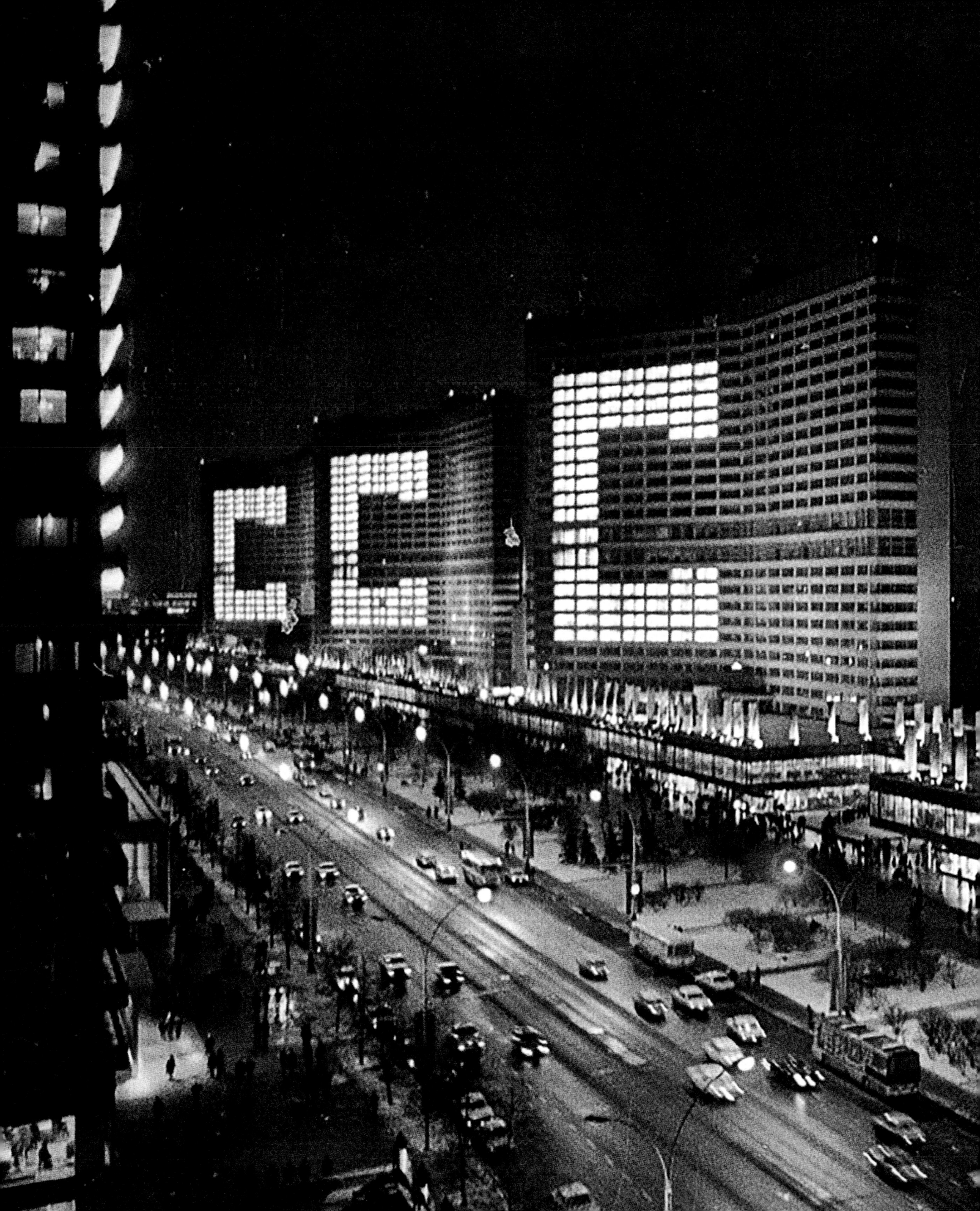

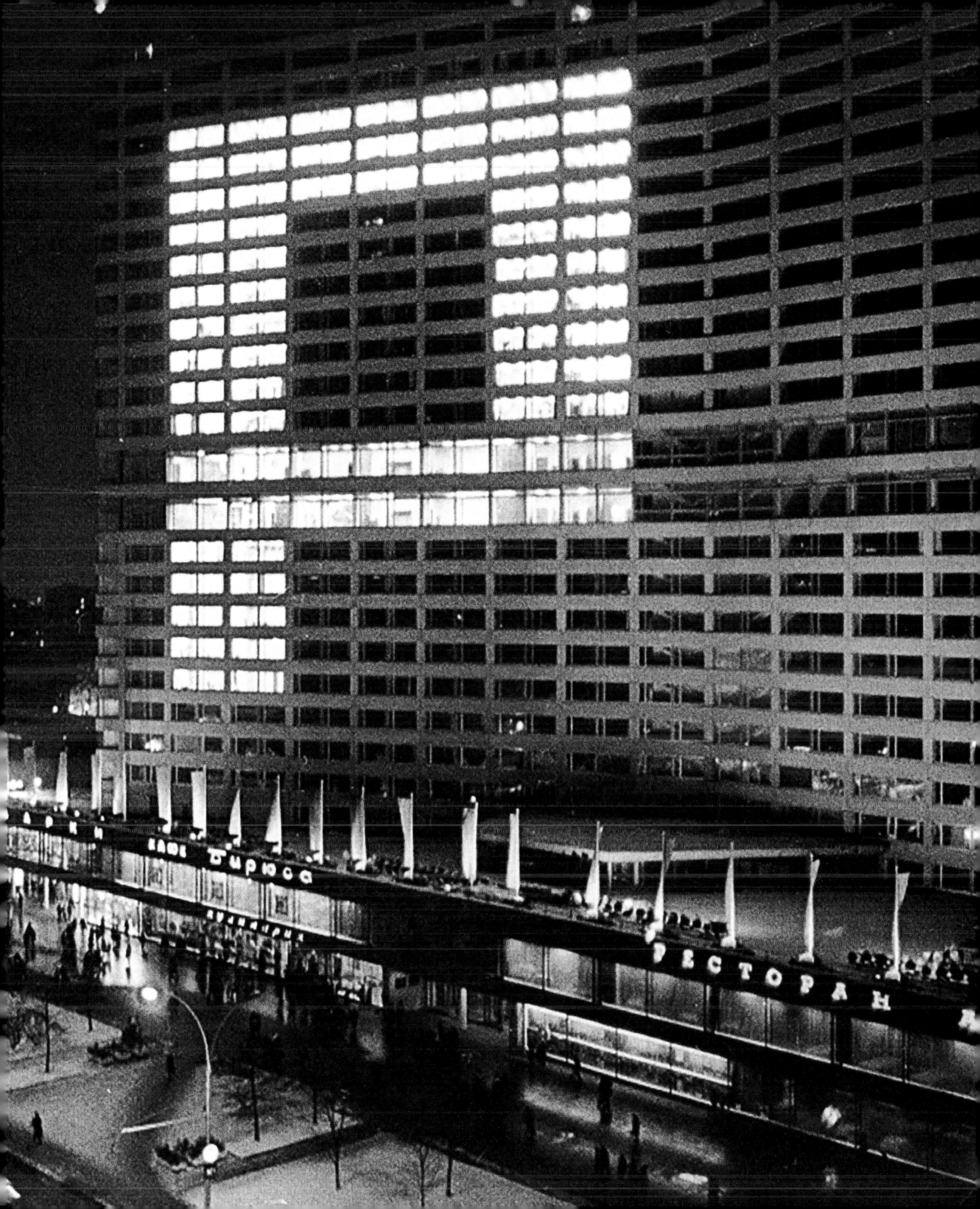
кафе Бирюса
РЕСТОРАН

FUTURE

ENVIRONMENTALISM

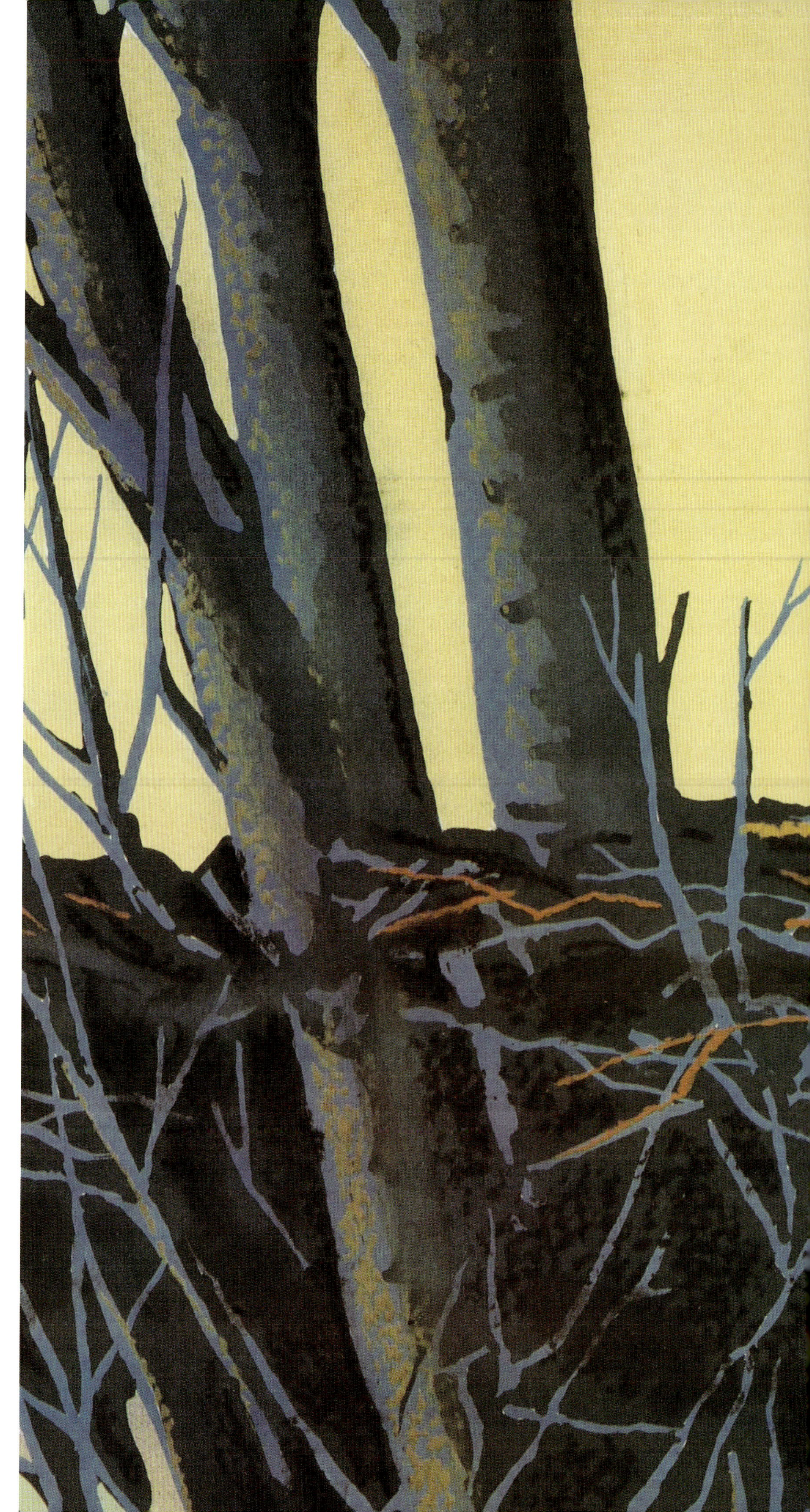

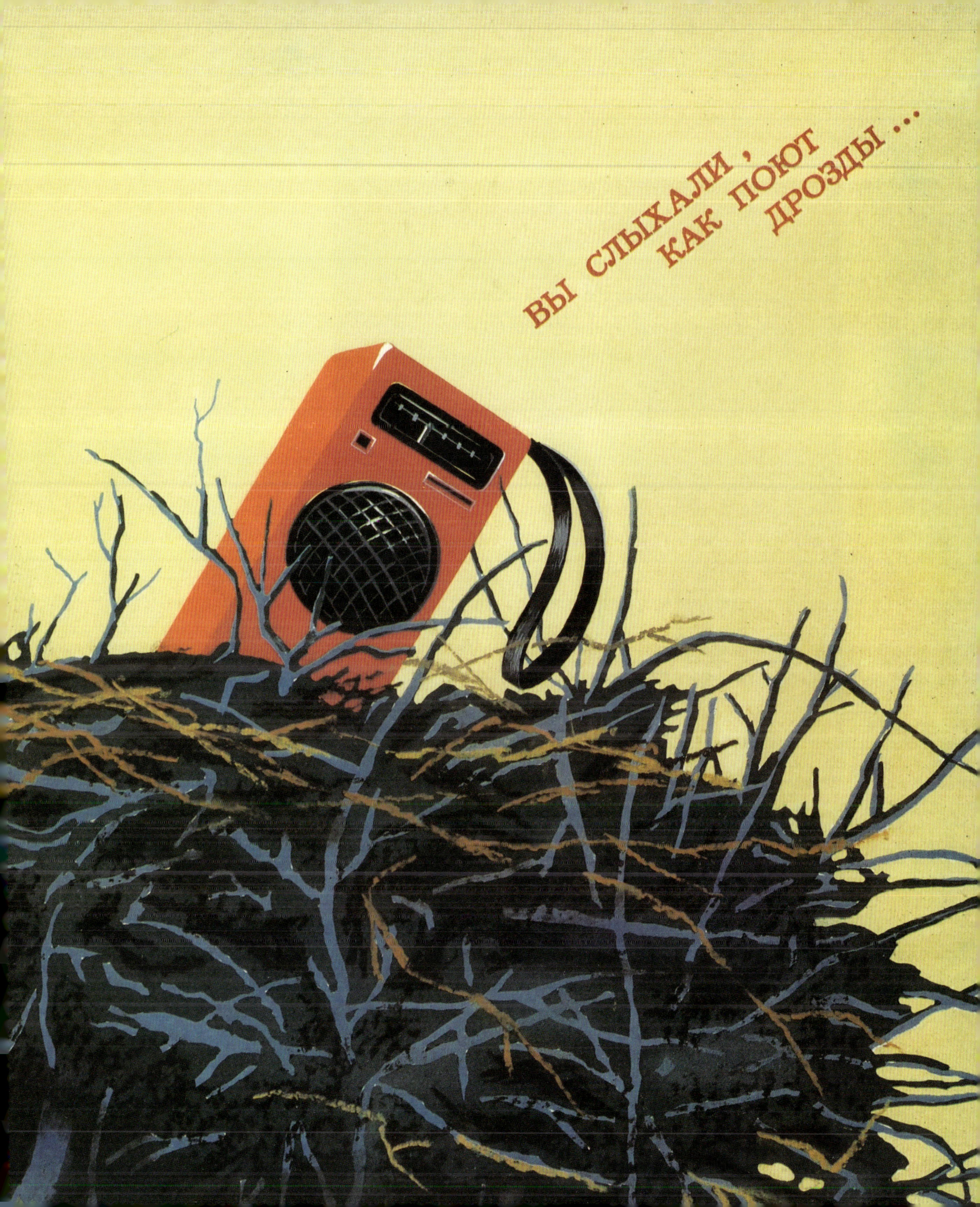
ВЫ СЛЫХАЛИ,
КАК ПОЮТ
ДРОЗДЫ...

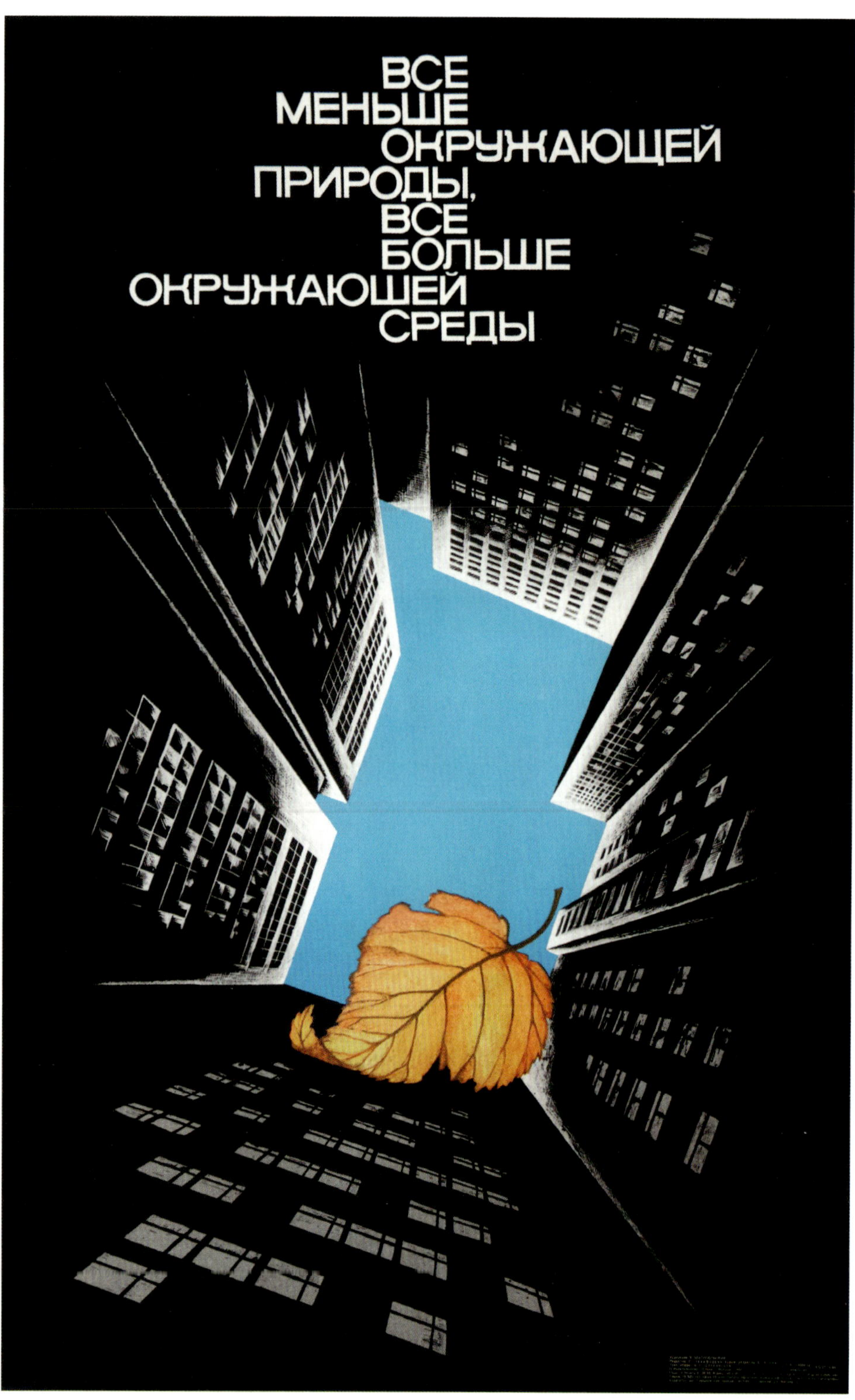

▲ С. Булкин (S. Bulkin), Е. Михеева (E. Mikheeva) | 1989

ALL THE LESS NATURAL ENVIORNMENT,
ALL THE MORE MANMADE SURROUNDINGS

С. Смирнов (S. Smirnov) | 1989 ▶

THE MINISTRY OF LAND AND WATER'S
MISSION ACCOMPLISHED

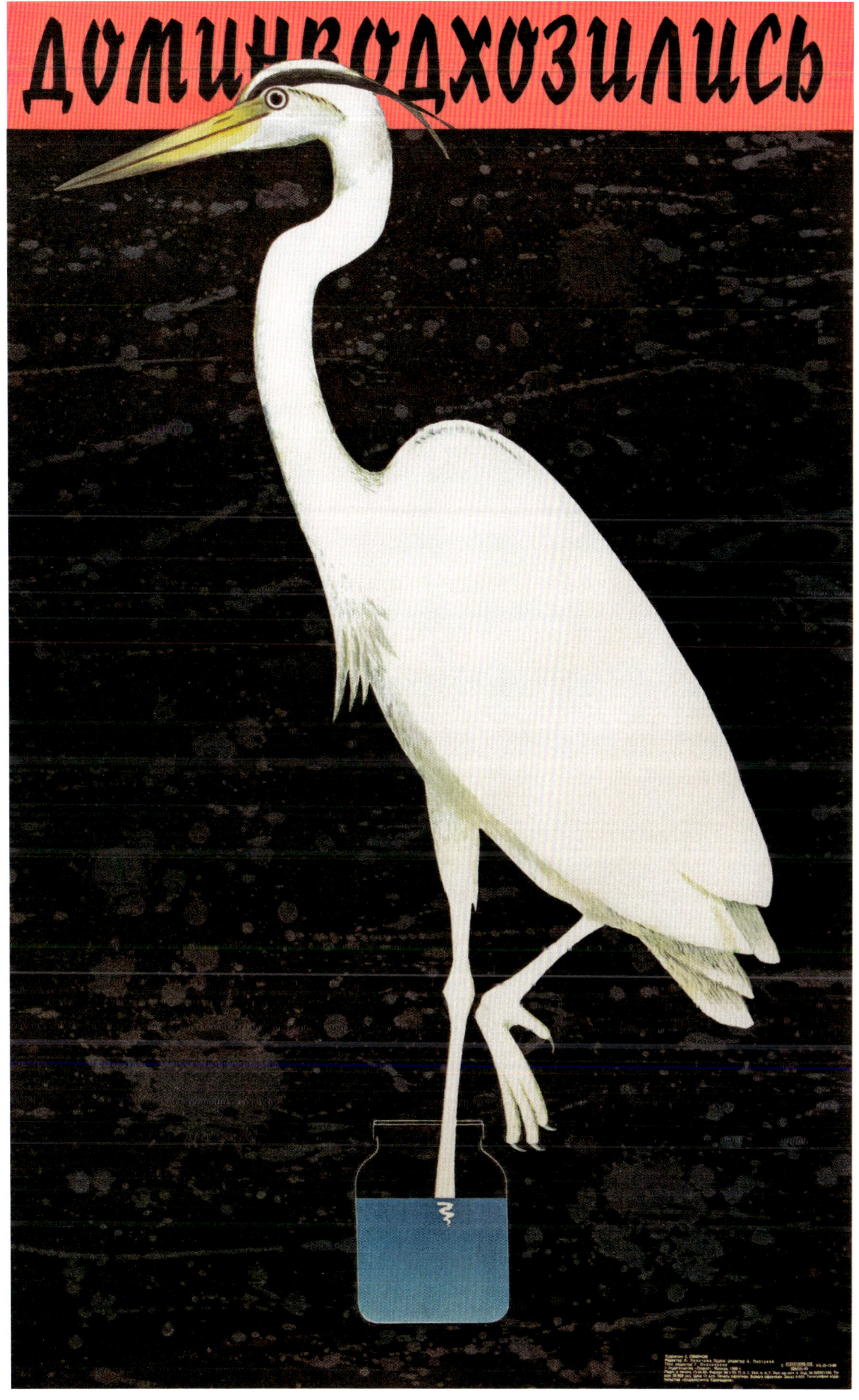
ДОМИНВОДХОЗИЛИСЬ

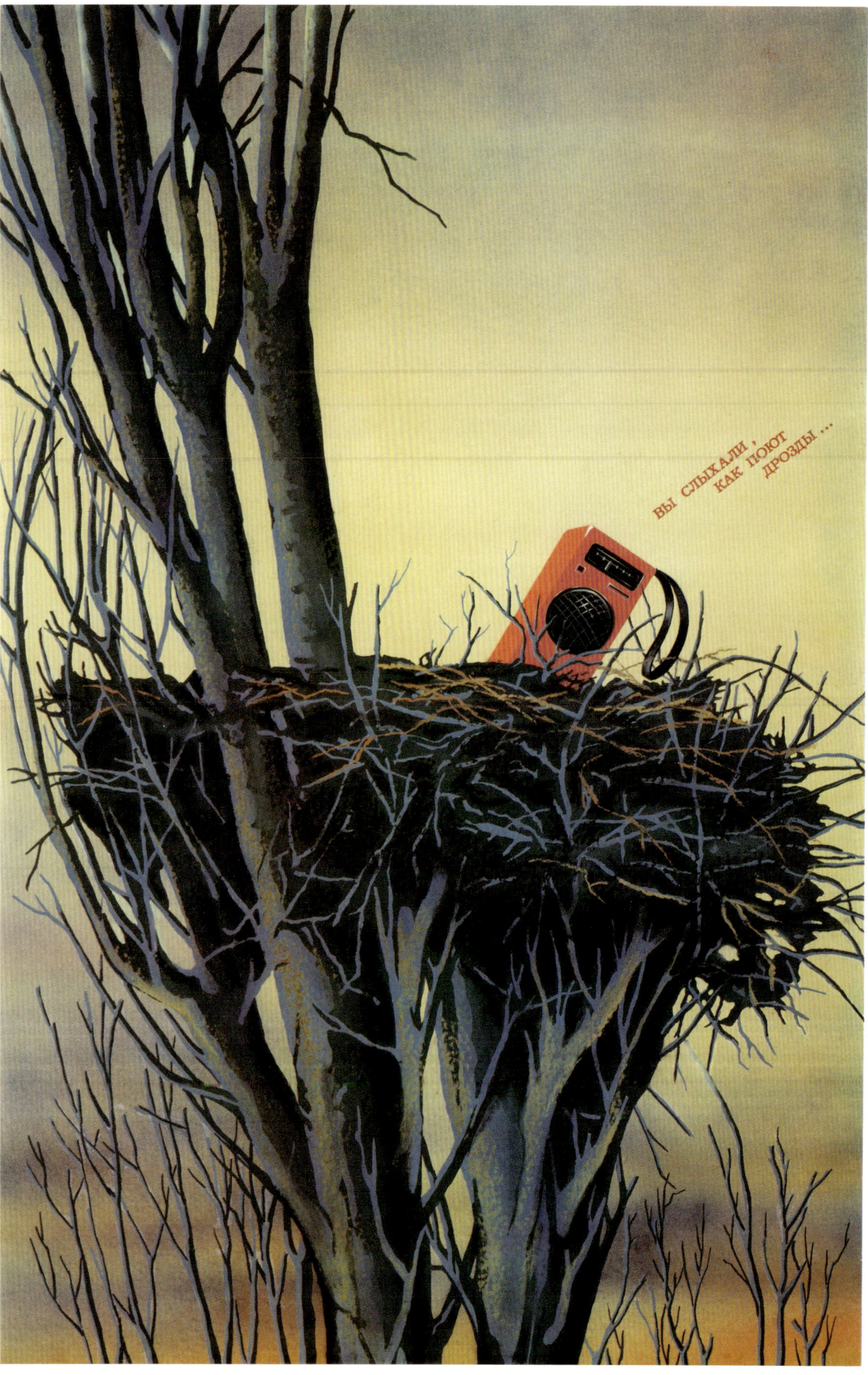
ВЫ СЛЫХАЛИ,
КАК ПОЮТ
ДРОЗДЫ …

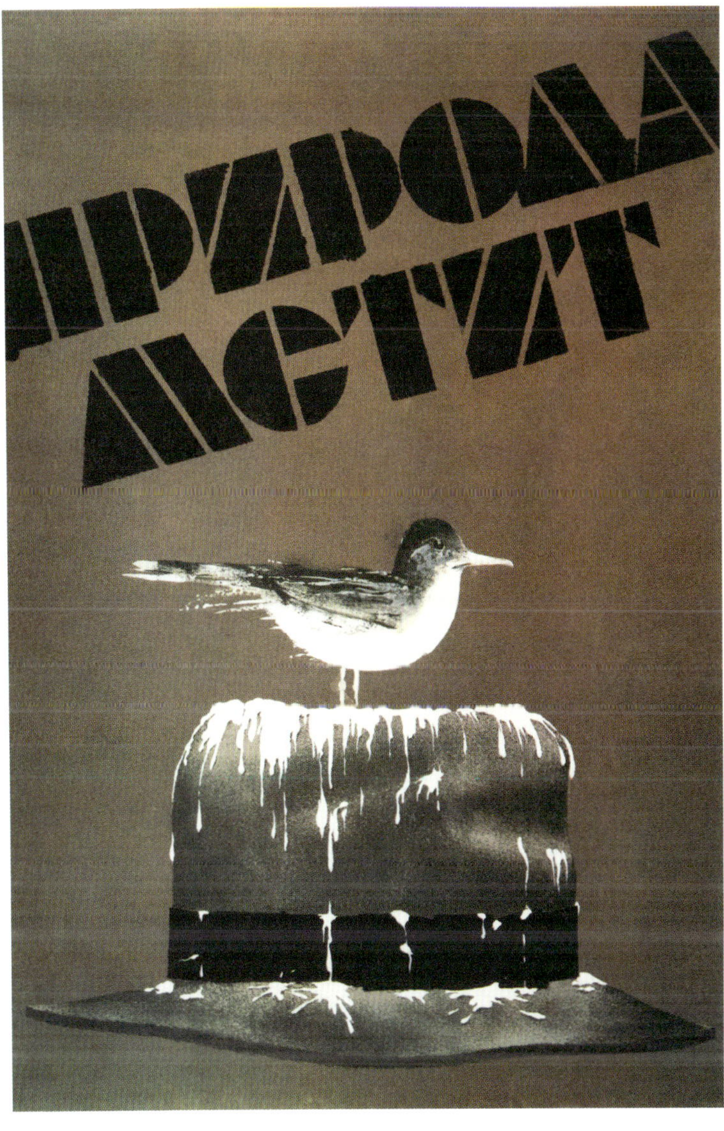

◂ Г. Белозеров (G. Belozerov) | n.d.

NATURE TAKES REVENGE
On the bureaucrats who have, through policies such as large-scale collectivized farming, destroyed much of the natural enviornment.

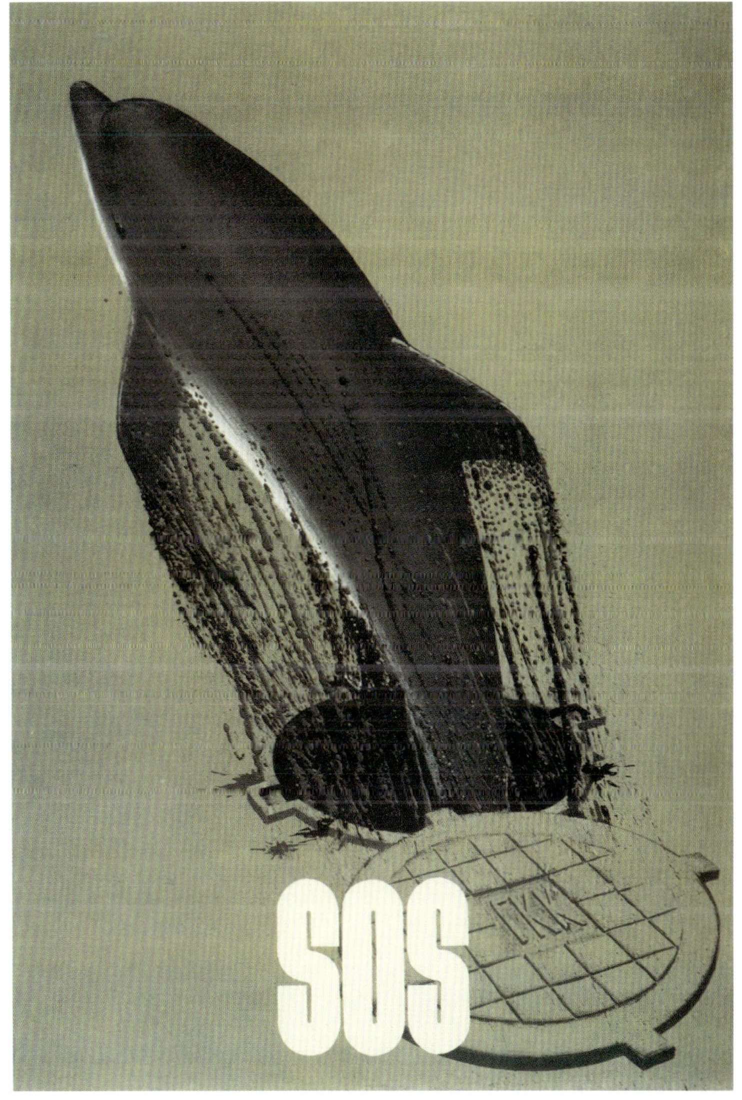

Г. Белозеров (G. Blazered) | n.d. ▸

SOS
A dolphin leaps out of the polluted waters of a sewer.

◂ Н. Литвиненко (N. Litvinenko), В. Тулинов (V. Tulinov) | 1990

HAVE YOU HEARD THE THRUSHES SINGING . . .
A radio emits an old folkloric song in a polluted wasteland.

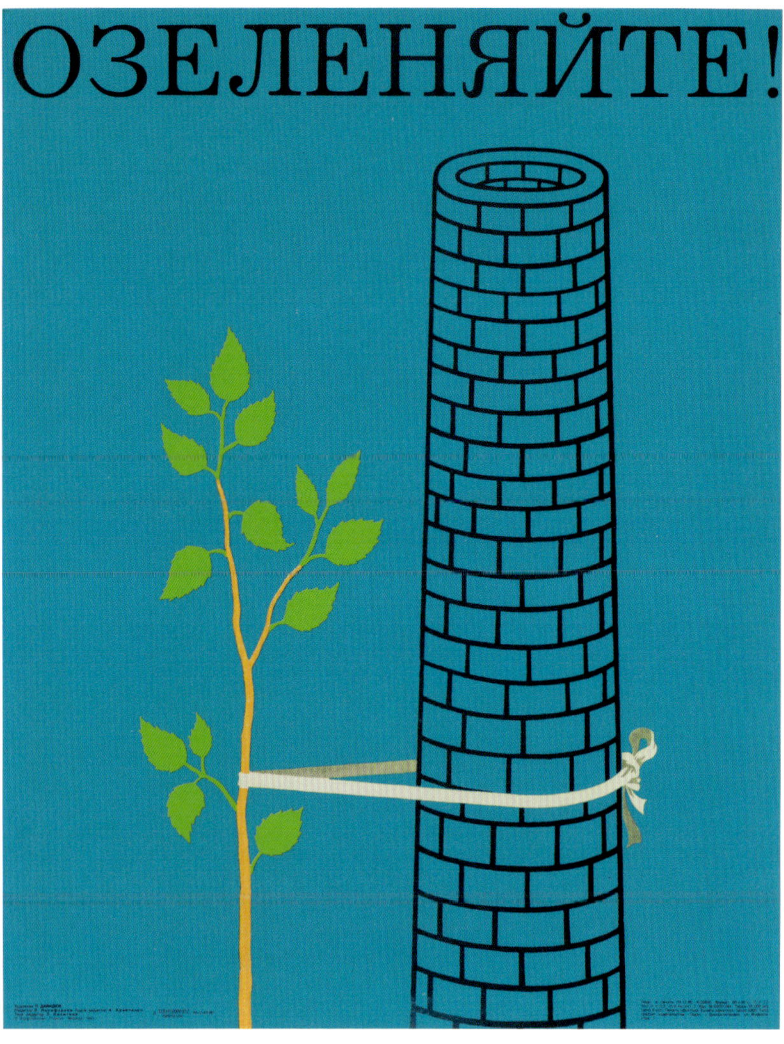

Т. Гардашникова (T. Gardashnikova), Д. Сурский (D. Sursky) | 1988 ➤

A loaf of bread with a paper band, like those used for bundles of money, which reads NATIONAL BANK OF THE USSR and below stamped PRICELESS. Beneath the stamp where there would have usually been an expiration date, it just reads 198, meaning that during the whole decade of the 1980s bread should have been considered priceless, and wrapped up like currency. However, people wasted bread because it was so cheap.

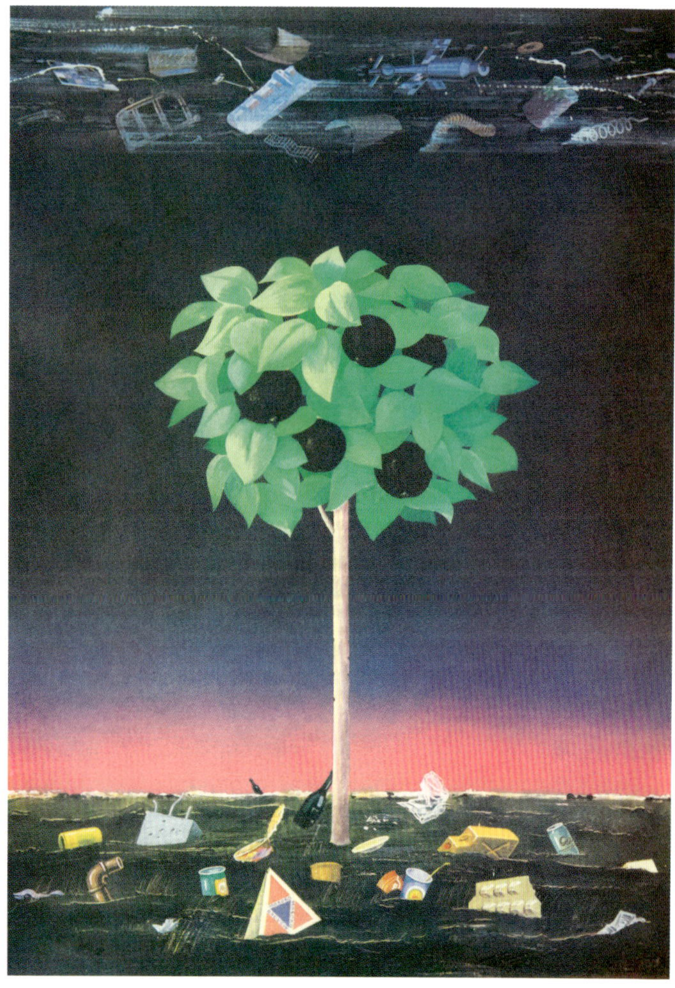

▲ П. Давидюк (P. Davidyuk) | 1986

GREEN IT!
An industrial brick chimney is used as a planting stake for the green sapling—the only source of green—indicating that agriculture should keep pace with industrial growth.

О. Качер (O. Kacher) | n.d. ➤

A solitary tree emerges from refuse; the tree is green but produces only black fruit.

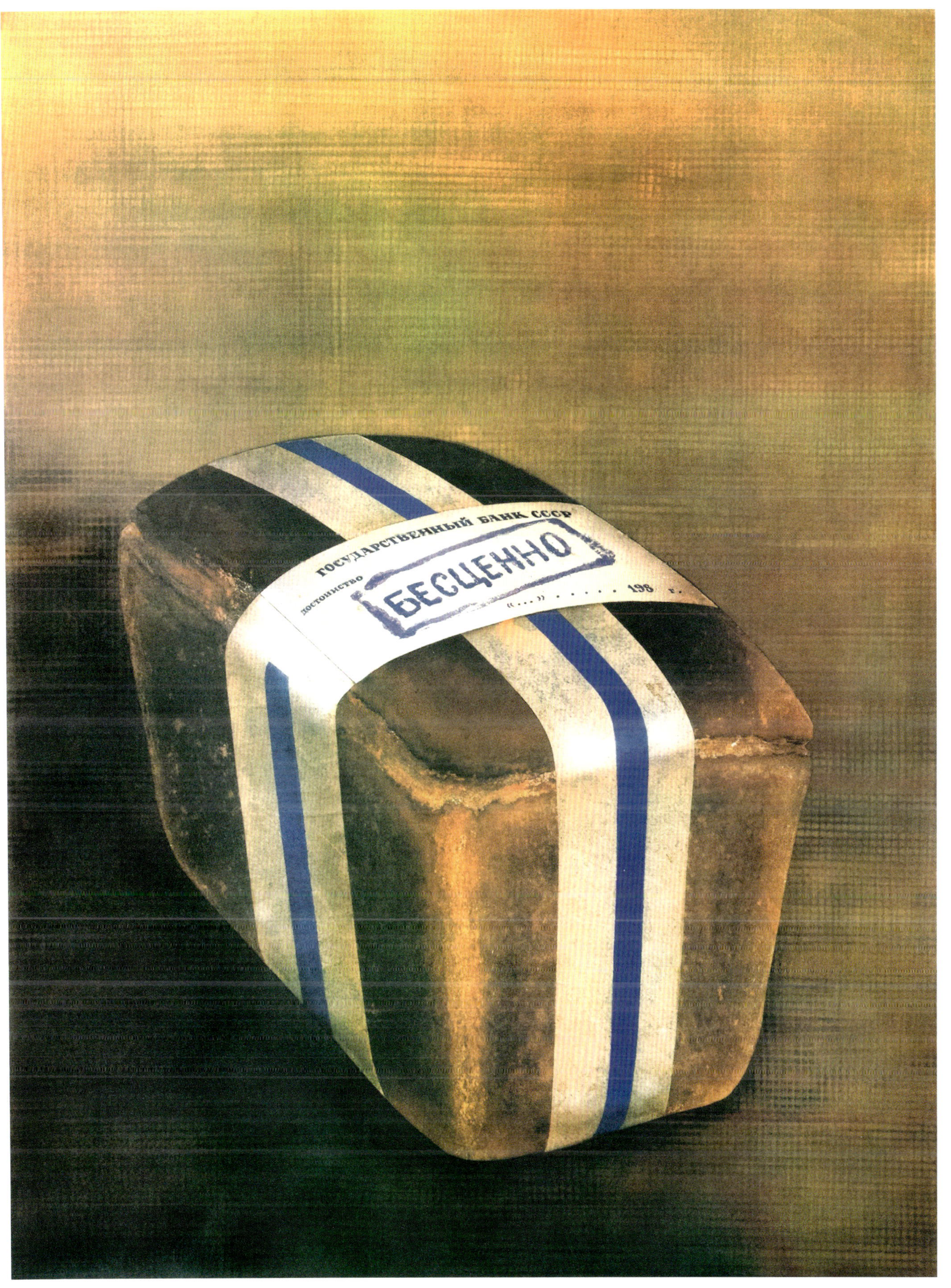
ГОСУДАРСТВЕННЫЙ БАНК СССР
достоинство
БЕСЦЕННО
«...» . . . . . 198 г.

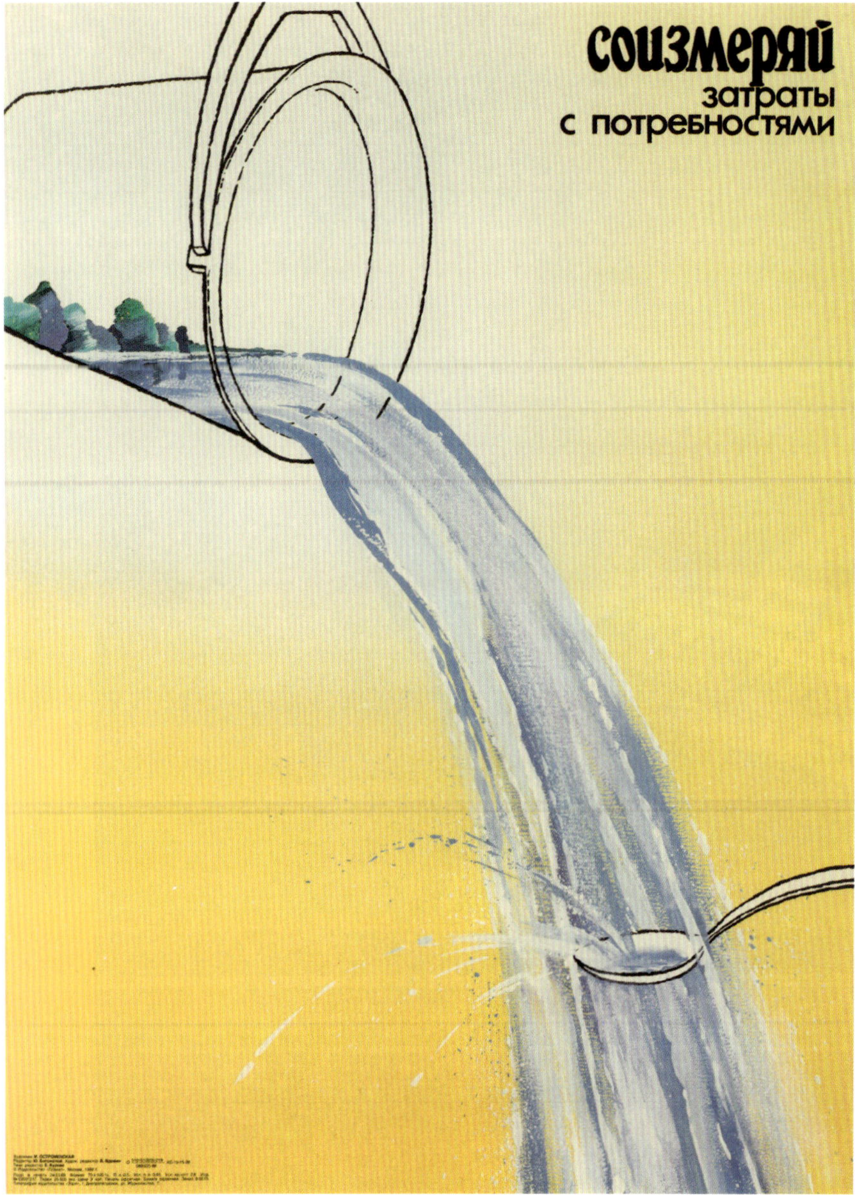

В. Механтьев (V. Mekhantyev) | 1988 ➤

ECONOMIZE!

A giant blue light bulb sits on top of a factory and emits a still larger fan of bright orange light. Beneath the factory, an equally huge single blue drop of water is shown amidst the enormous flow from five wastewater pipes.

▲ И. Остроменская (I. Ostromenskaya) | 1988

WEIGH YOUR CONSUMPTION AGAINST YOUR DEMAND

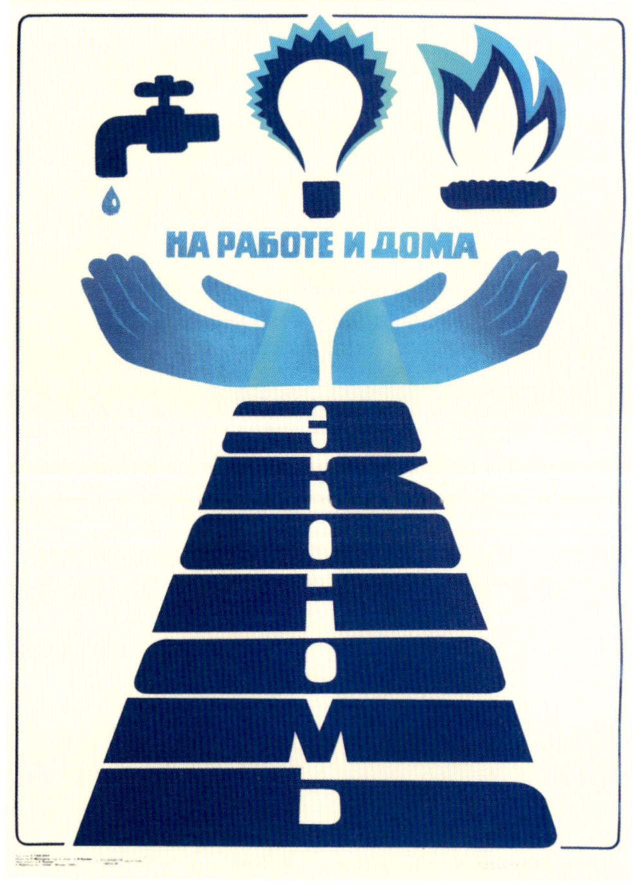

Г. Гаусман (G. Gausman) | 1988 ➤

AT HOME AND WORK: ECONOMIZE

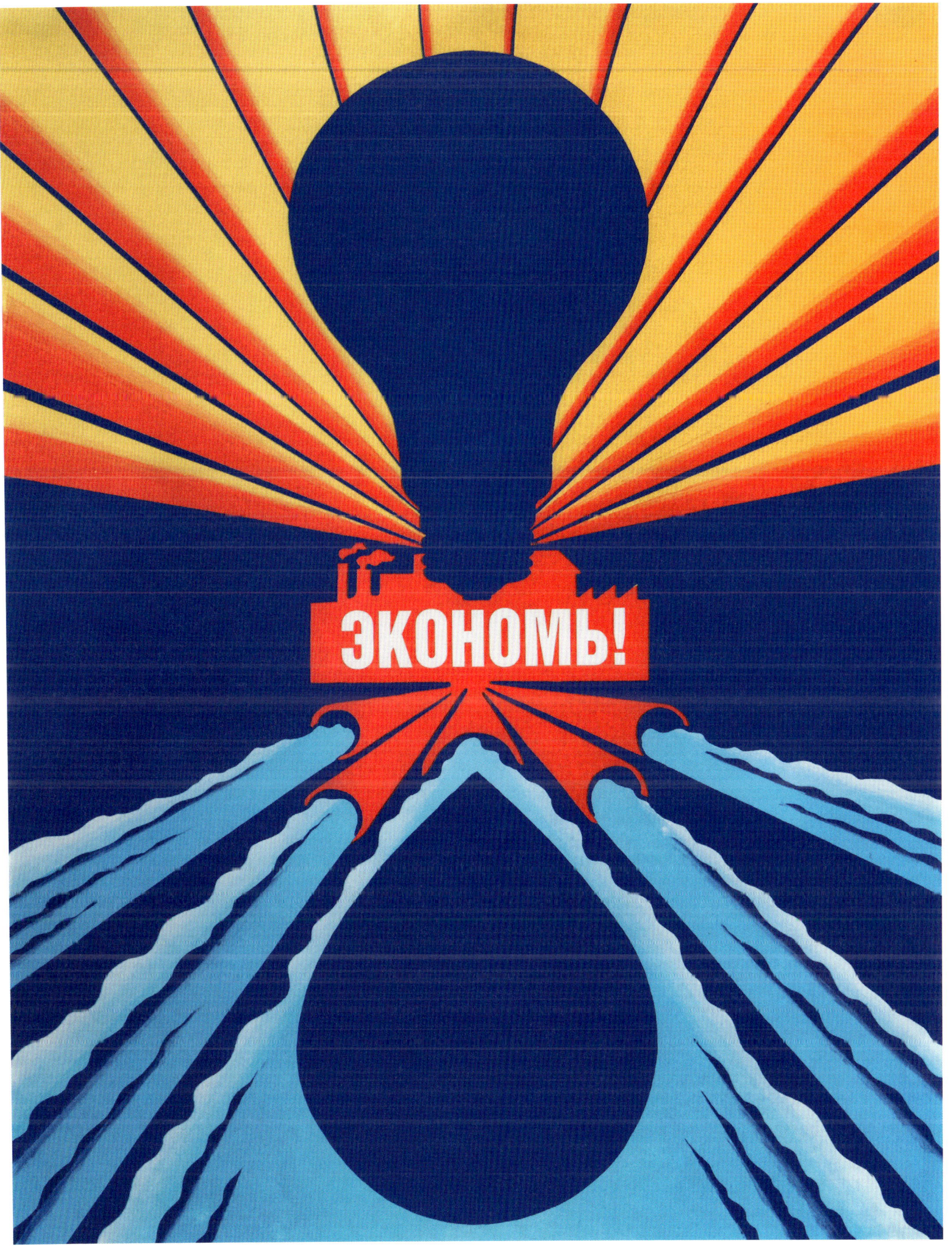
ЭКОНОМЬ!

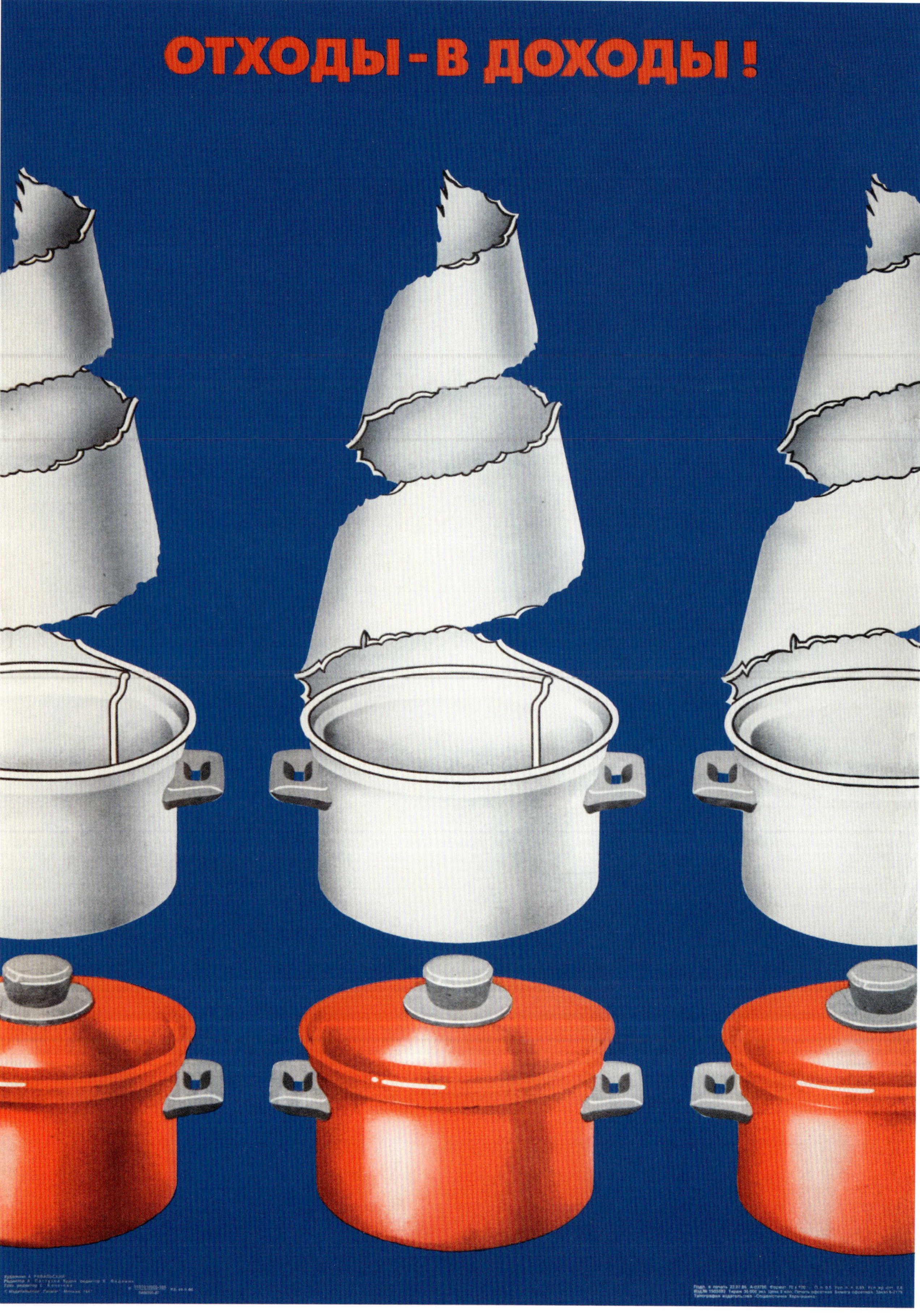
ОТХОДЫ – В ДОХОДЫ !

◂ А. Рафальский (A. Rafalsky) | 1987

FROM WASTE INTO PROFIT!
Giant ribbons of scrap aluminum spiral downward into newly created red cooking pots.

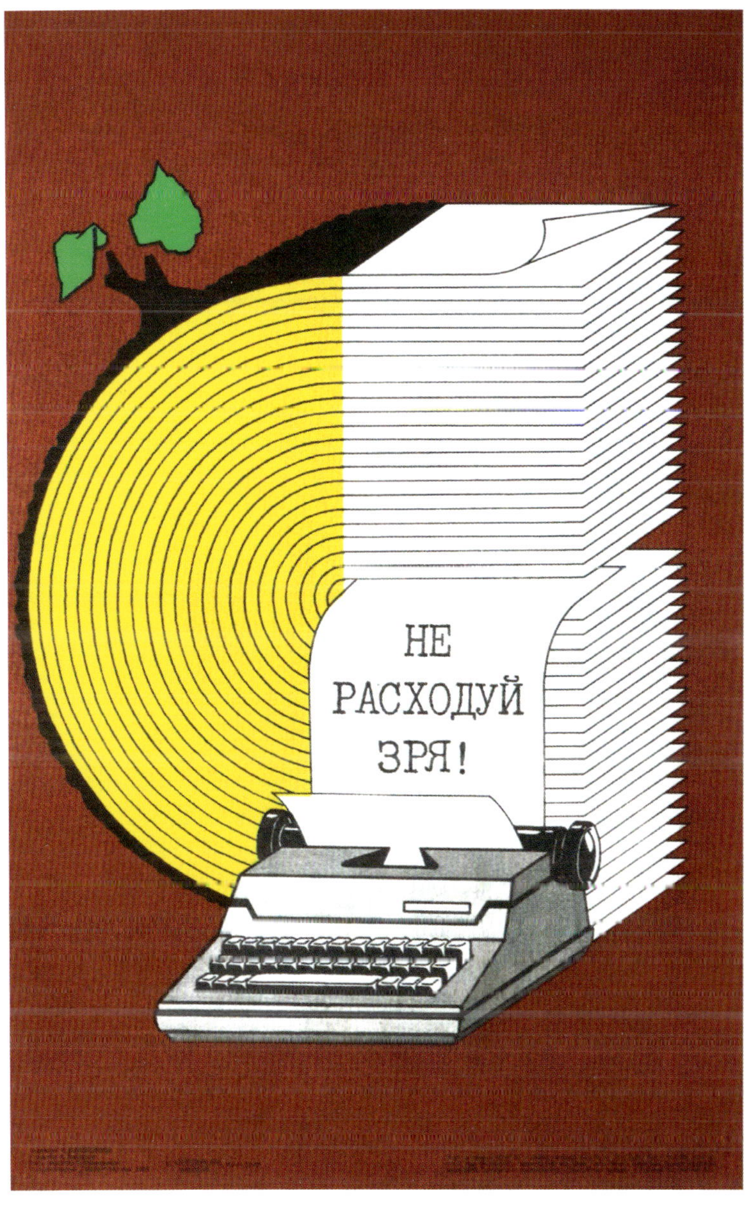

▴ И. Белогорлов (I. Belogorlov) | 1986

DON'T JUST WASTE THINGS!
The rings from a tree log morph into sheets of paper behind a typewriter, as a reminder that every sheet represents a valuable resource.

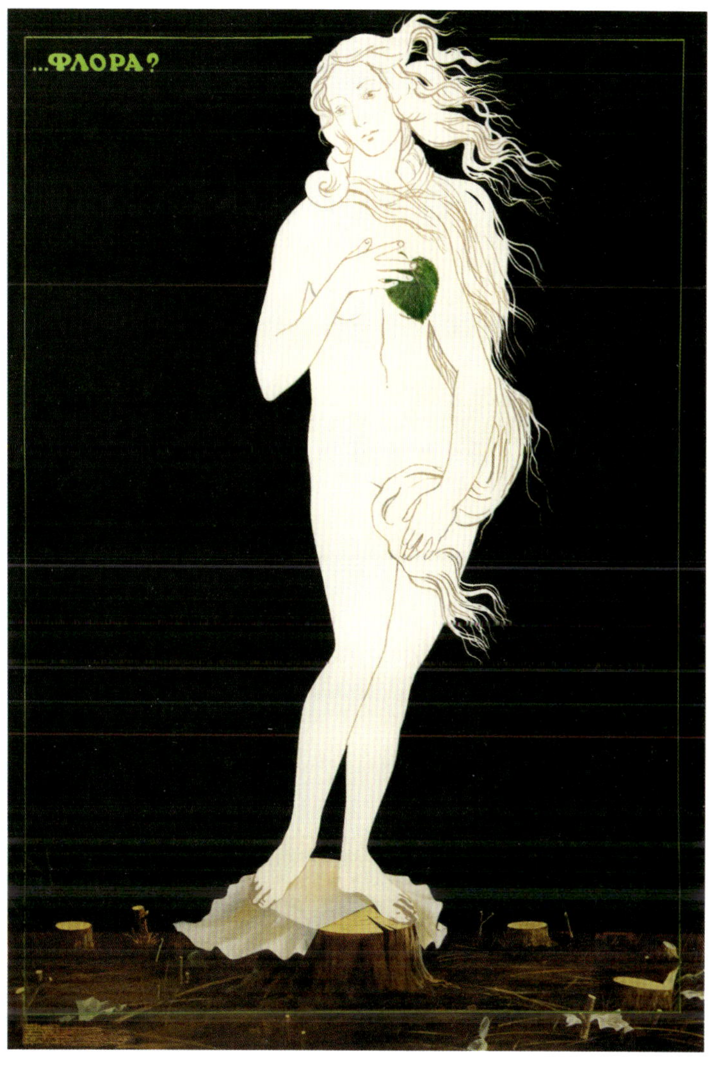

▴ Н. Журавлева (N. Zhuravleva) | n.d.

FLORA?

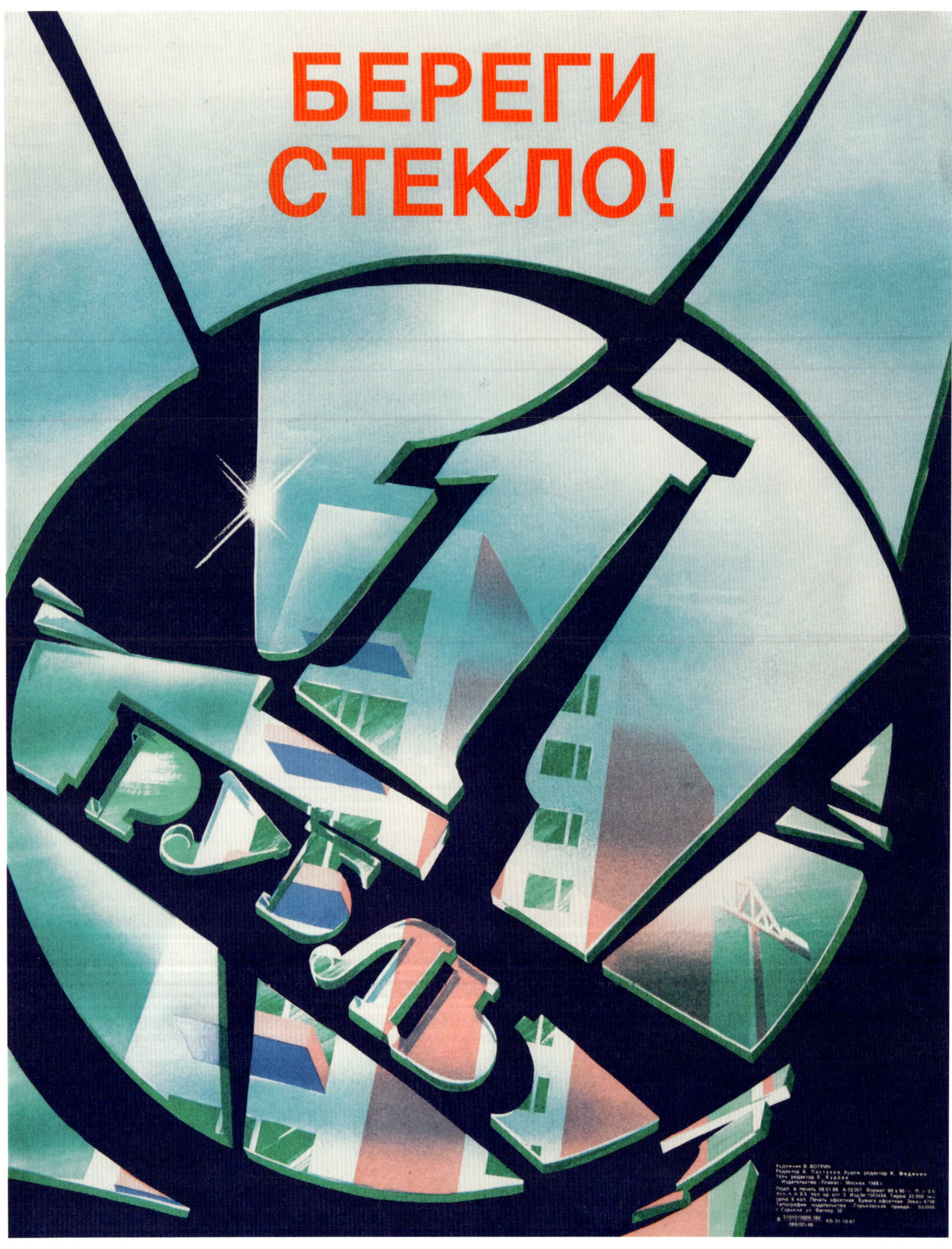
БЕРЕГИ
СТЕКЛО!
1 рубль

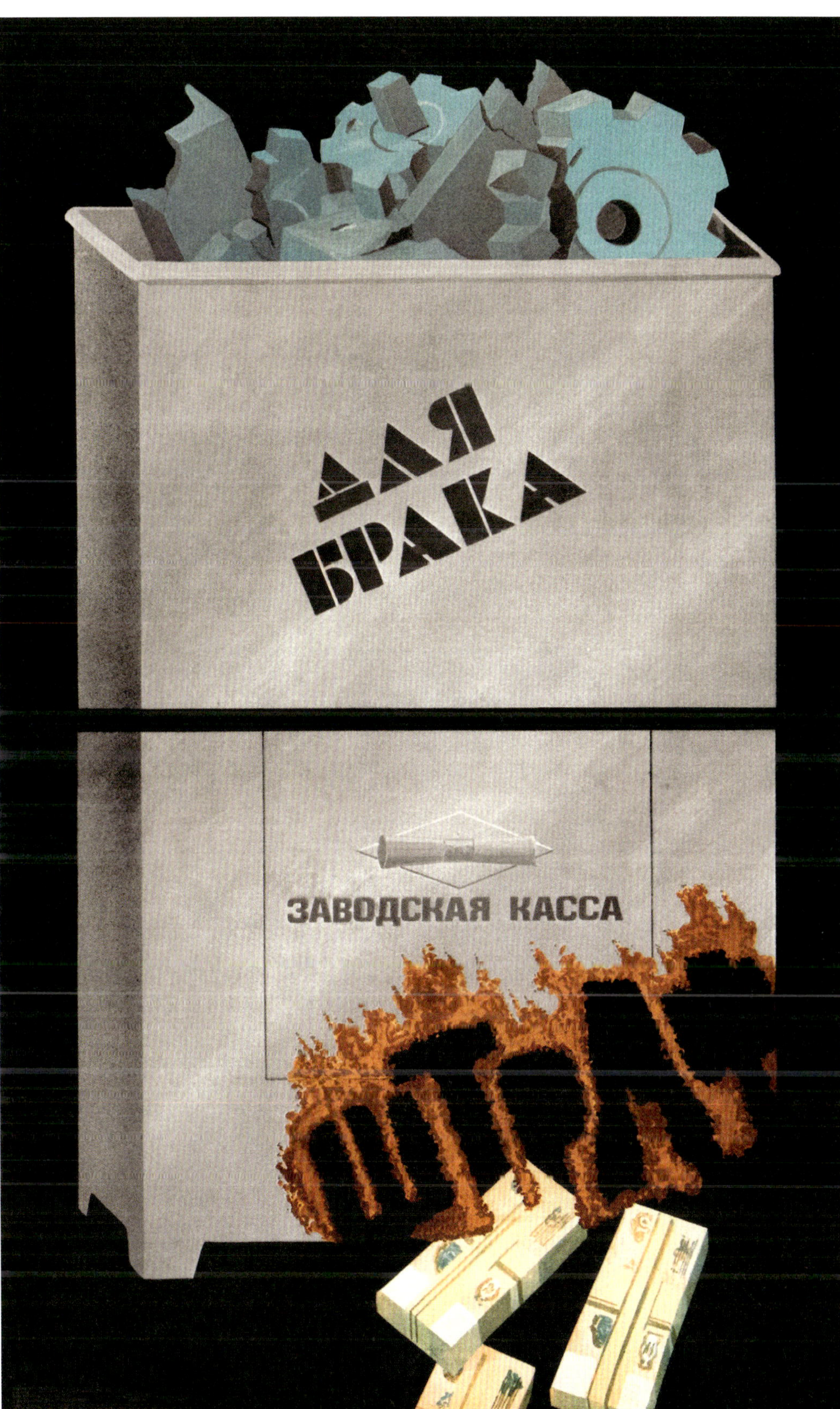

◂ В. Вотрин (V. Votrin) | 1988

BE CAREFUL WITH GLASS!
A piece of shattered glass takes the shape of a broken ruble. In its reflection, there is a building where workers could have used the glass for construction had they not broken it.

С. Смирнов (S. Smirnov) | 1988 ▸

Text on top part of box: FACTORY REJECTS. Text on bottom of box: FACTORY ACCOUNTING DESK. Written in rust at bottom right: PENALTY.
A box in which a factory's defective gears are discarded. Large rust holes from which bundles of rubles drop out from the bottom of the box denote the last profits of the factory accounts. It will cost the enterprise money to produce inferior quality products that will be rejected—for which there will be a penalty.

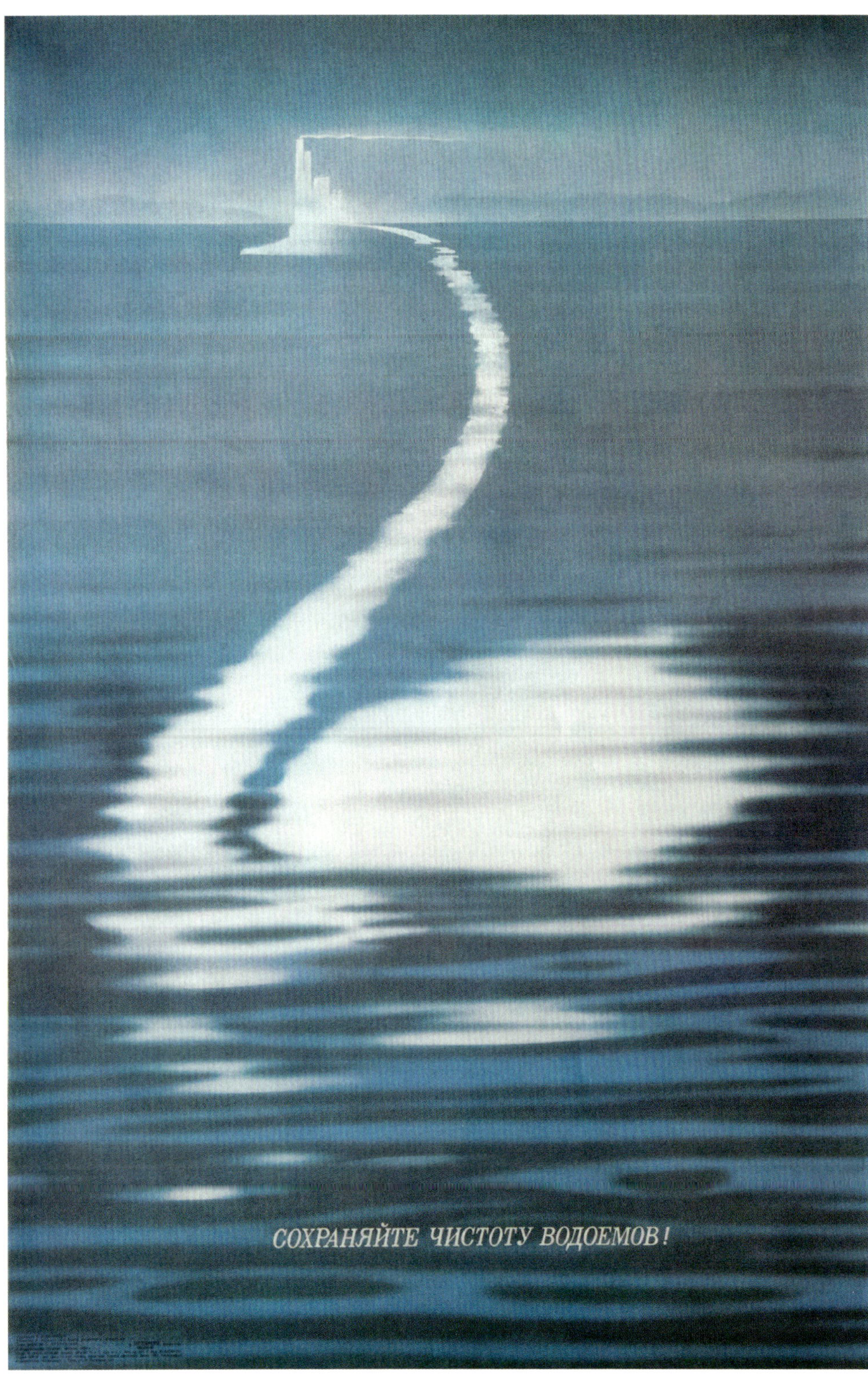

◀ Б. Колесников (B. Kolesnikov) | 1990

KEEP OUR WATERWAYS CLEAN!

В. Лассон (V. Lasson) | 1990 ▶

WELCOME, FEATHERED FRIENDS!

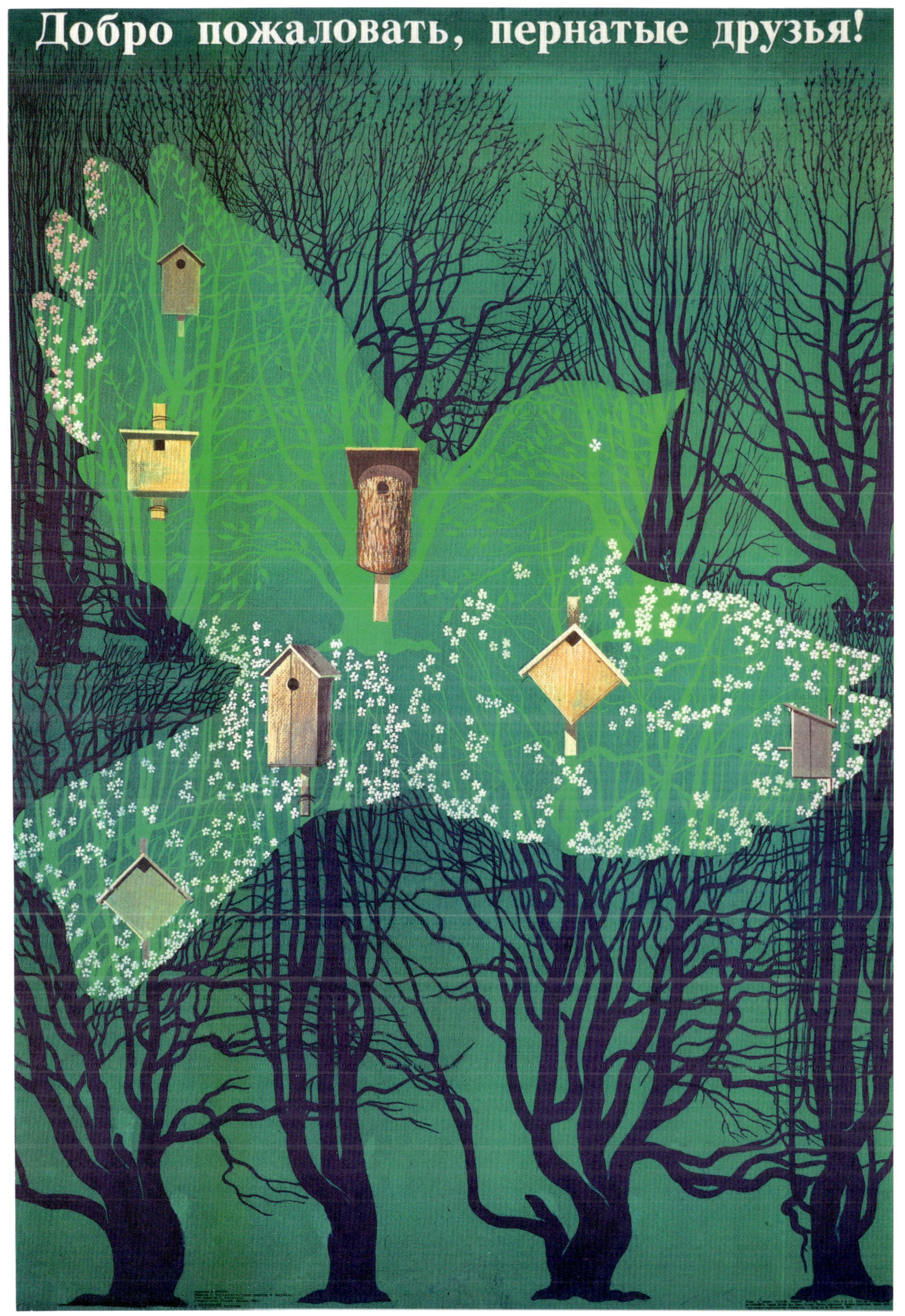
Добро пожаловать, пернатые друзья!

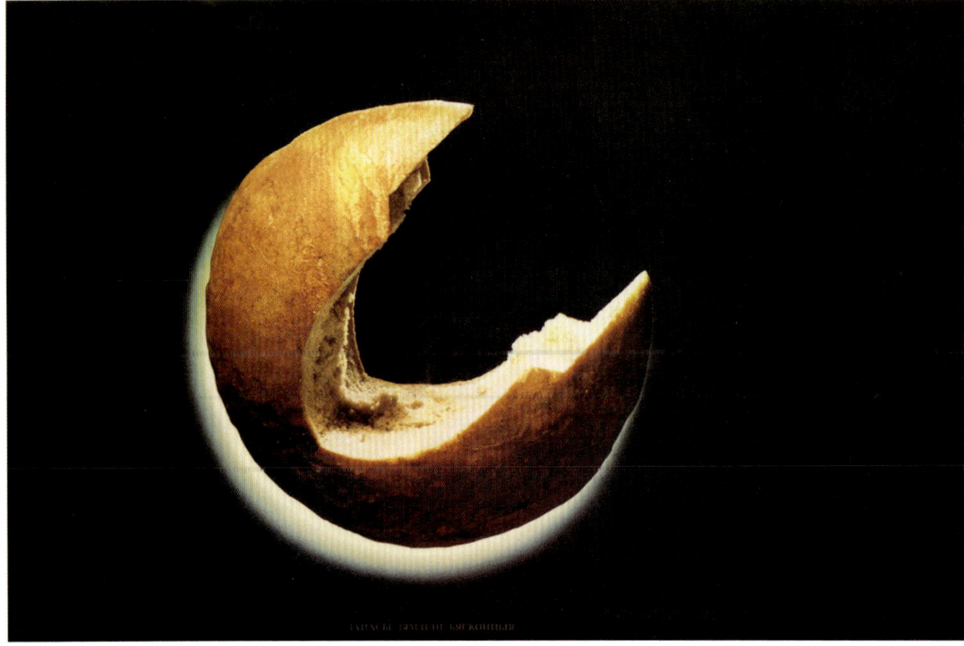

◀ Ю. А. Деев. Минск (Yu. A. Deev. Minsk) | 1989

OUR PLANET'S RESOURCES ARE NOT UNLIMITED
A bread roll is shown with a rocket-shaped bite taken out of it. This depiction indicates that military expenditures are using up resources, and not leaving enough for basic necessities, such as bread.

А. Архипов (A. Arkhipov) | 1990 ▶

MAKE THE RUBLE GREAT AGAIN!
Coffee beans are enfolded in a one ruble note. During this economic period, the ruble note was only worth using as wrapping paper. Coffee beans, on the other hand, were very expensive; at the time this poster was created, they might have cost 60 rubles a kilo.

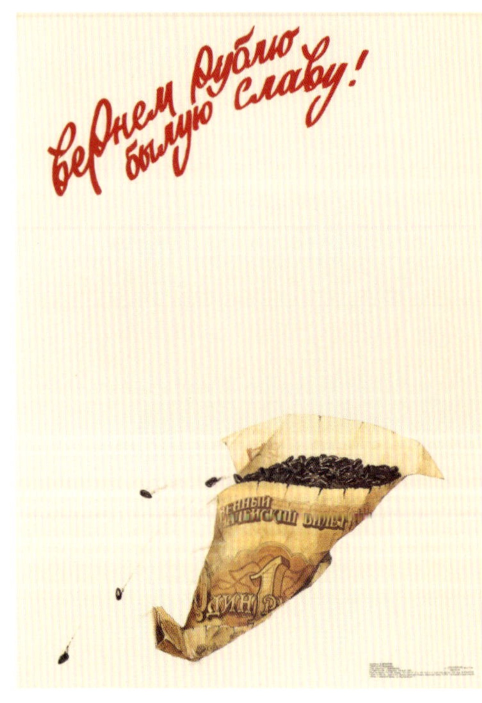

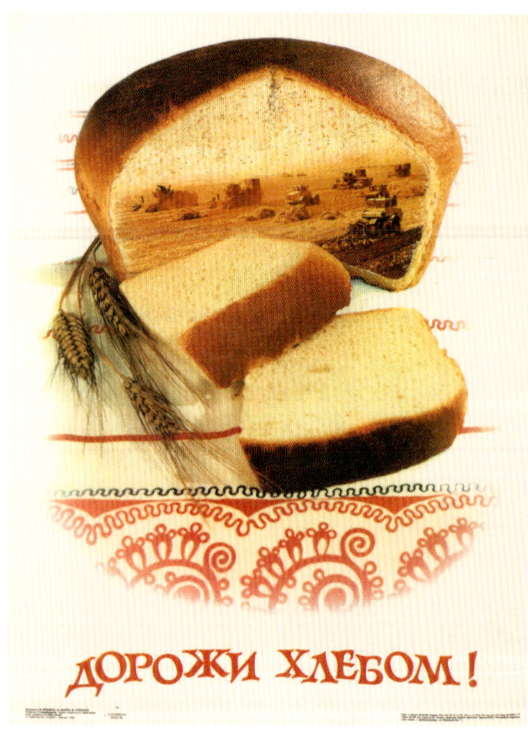

▲ В. Ермаков (V. Yermakov), Ю. Жаров (Y. Zharov), В. Трифонов (V. Trifonov) | 1988

TREASURE BREAD!
A scene of harvesting grain is superimposed onto a sliced loaf of bread on a tablecloth with a traditional, embroidered pattern. Here, the message relayed is not to waste bread as it requires a tremendous amount of work to produce.

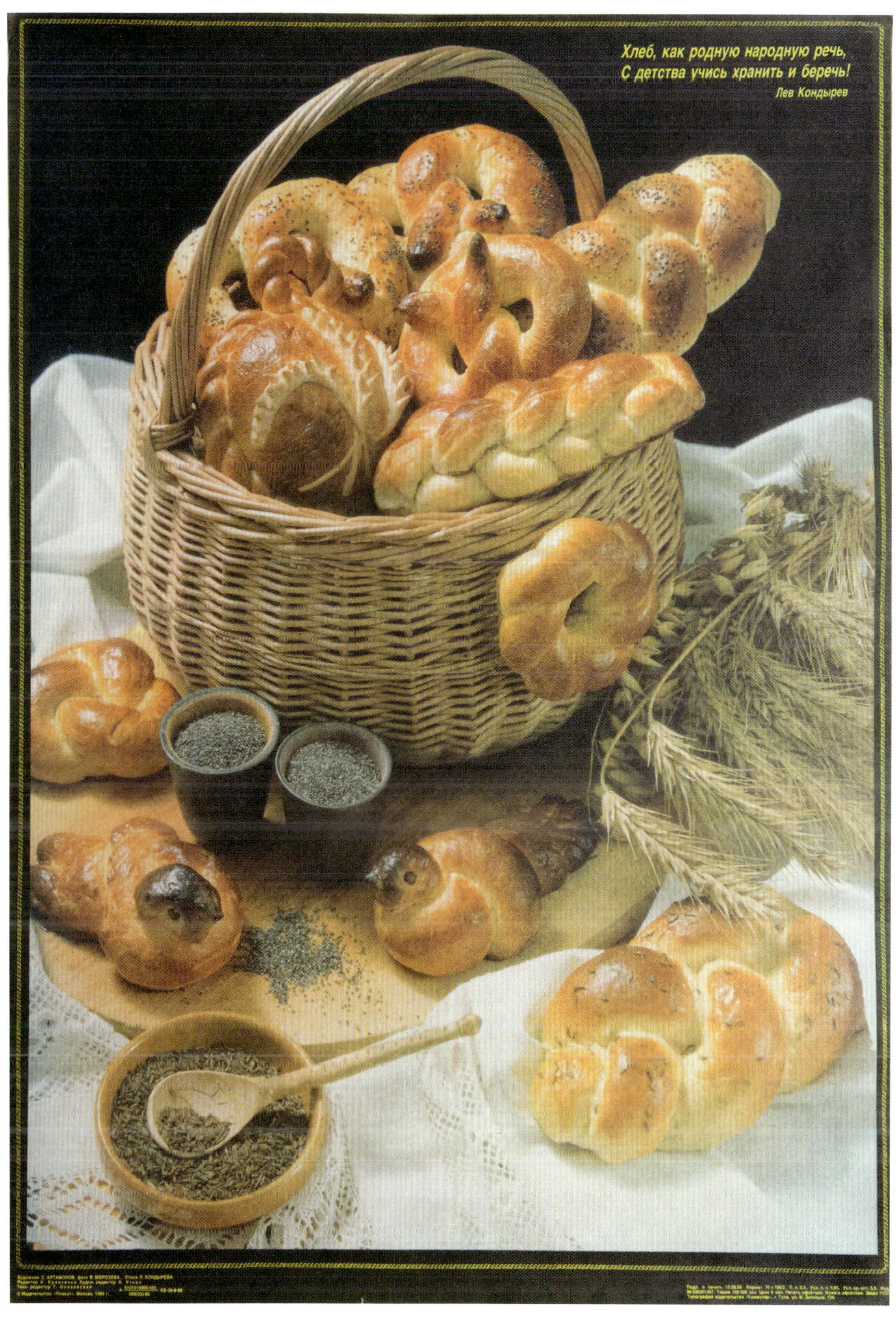

С. Артамонов (S. Artamonov) | 1989

LEARN TO SAVE AND TREASURE BREAD LIKE
IT'S YOUR MOTHER TONGUE!
—LEV KONDYREV

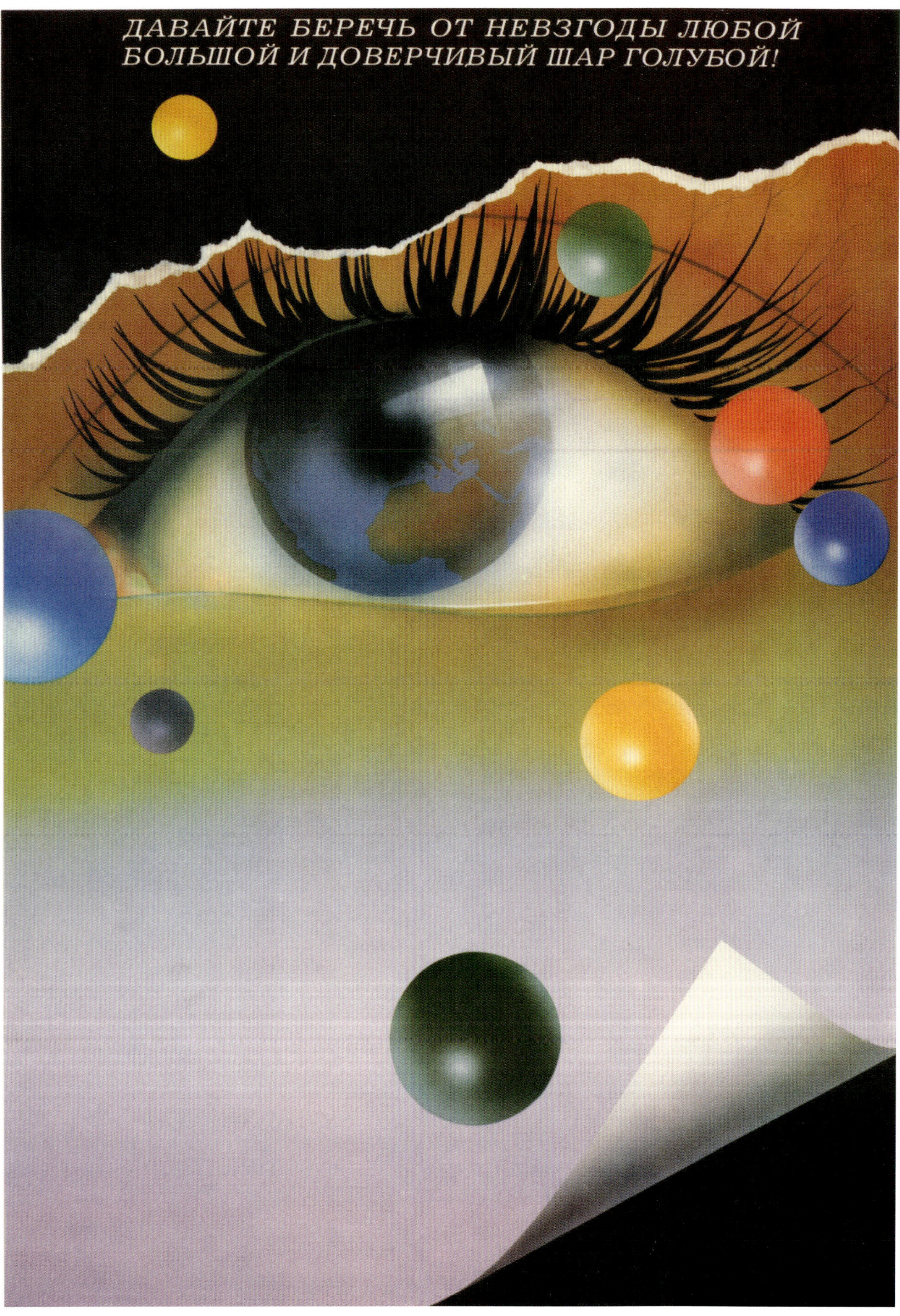

ENVIRONMENTALISM

◂ Здено Браил (Zdeno Bril) | 1989

LET'S PROTECT OUR GLOBE
SO BLUE AND TRUSTING
FROM ANY KIND OF STRIFE
OR SUFFERING!

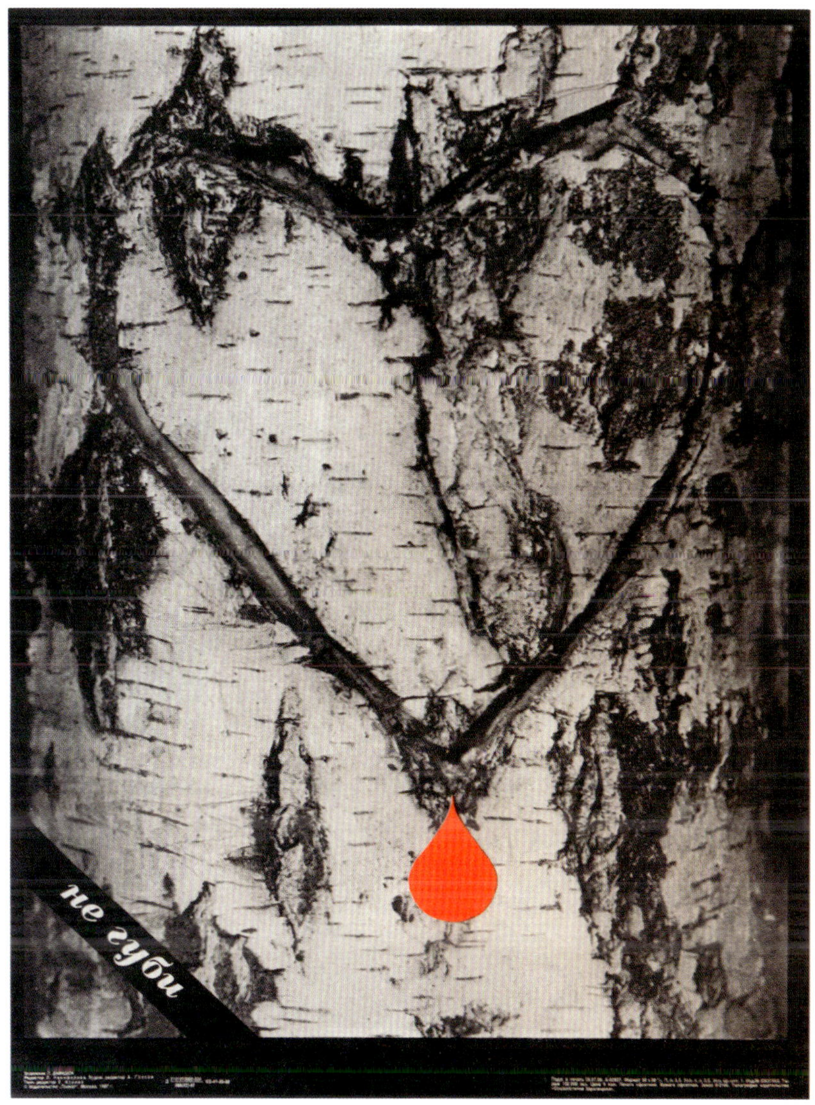

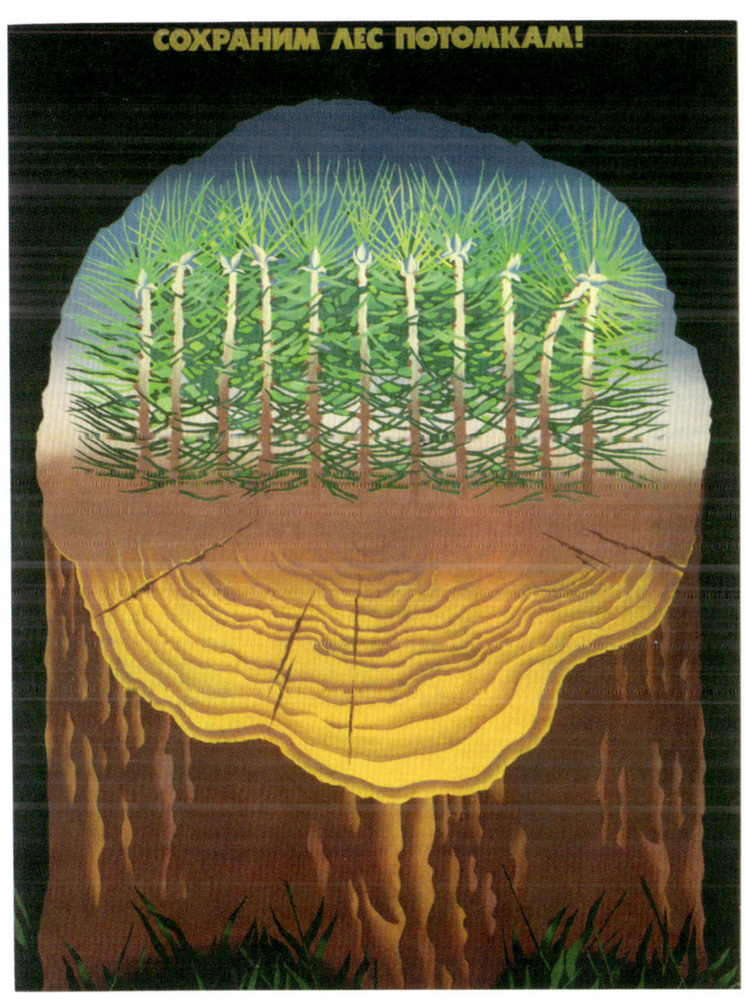

▴ И. Давидюк (I. Davidyuk) | 1987

DO NO HARM

◂ Г. Лопатина (G. Lopatina) | 1987

WE WILL PRESERVE THE FOREST FOR
FUTURE GENERATIONS!

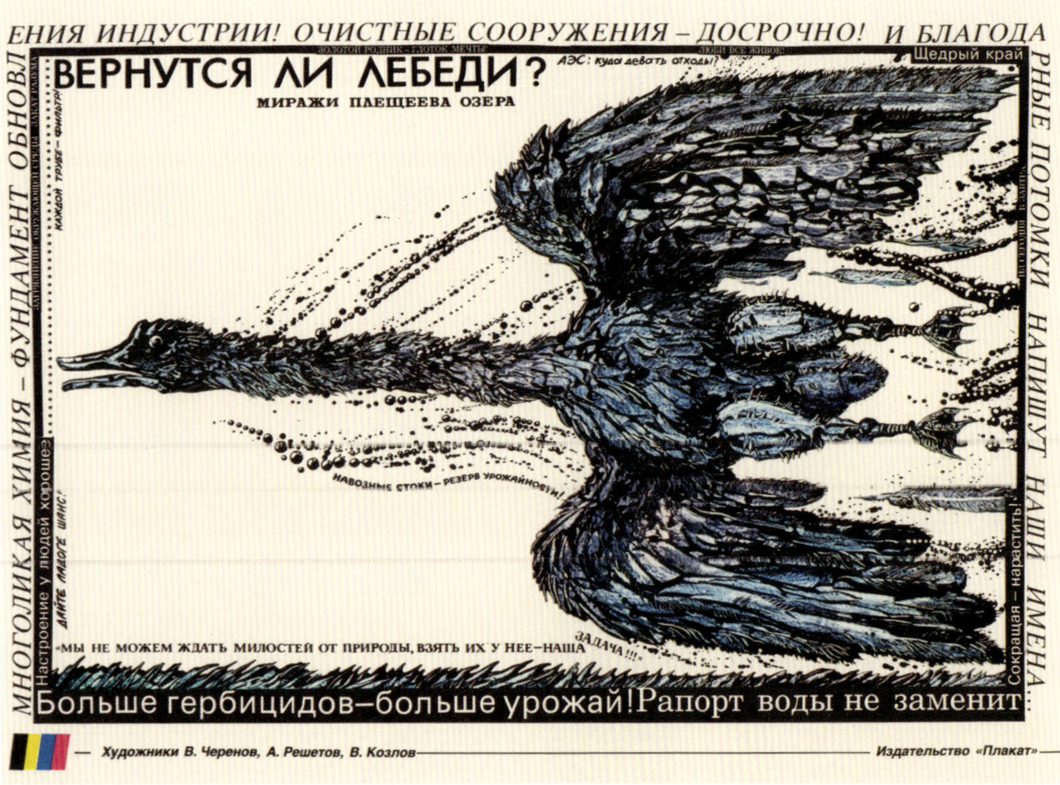

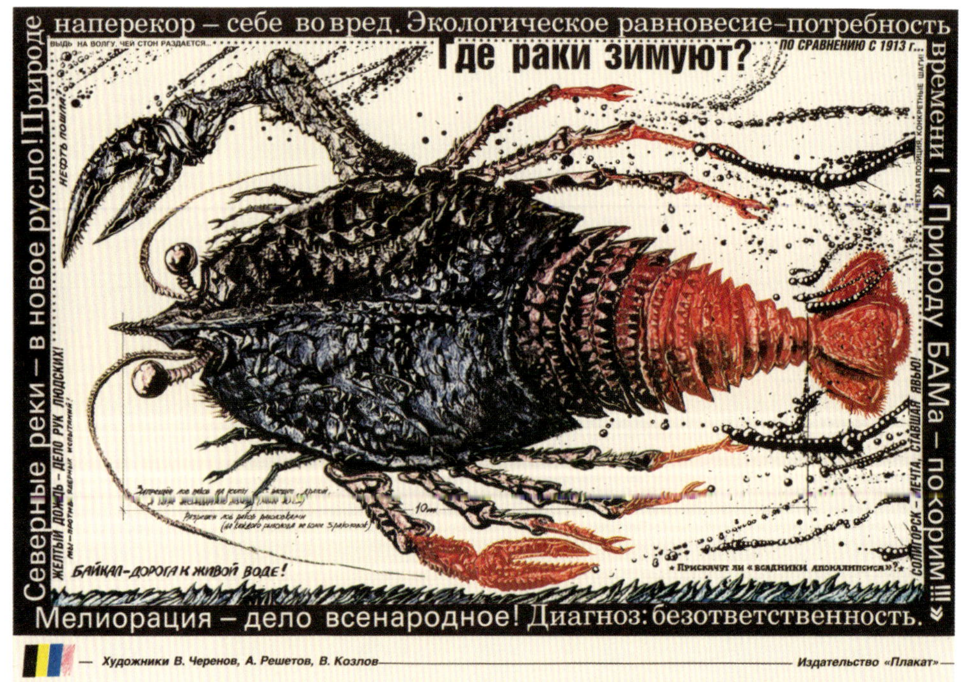

В. Черенов (V. Cherenov), А. Решетов (A. Reshetov), В. Козлов (V. Kozlov) | 1989 ▲

WILL THE SWANS COME BACK? / MIRAGES OF LAKE PLESHCHEYEVO / NUCLEAR POWER PLANTS: WHERE DO WE PUT THE WASTE? / LOVE EVERYTHING THAT LIVES / A GENEROUS LAND / FROM TODAY TO TOMORROW / GROWTH THROUGH REDUCTION! / WE CAN'T EXPECT NATURE TO BESTOW HER GRACES ON US—OUR TASK IS TAKING THEM BY FORCE! / GIVE LADOGA A CHANCE! / THE PEOPLE ARE WELL-DISPOSED / STANDING MANURE IS FERTILITY IN RESERVE! / MORE HERBICIDES —BIGGER HARVESTS! WE NEED WATER, NOT REPORTS ON WATER QUALITY! / A FILTER ON EVERY PIPE! / CONSCIOUS POLLUTION IS THE DEATH OF REASON! / THE GOLDEN SPRING— A GULP OF FANTASY! / CHEMISTRY IS THE FOUNDATION FOR INDUSTRIAL RENEWAL! BUILD WATER TREATMENT PLANTS AHEAD OF SCHEDULE! AND OUR GRATEFUL HEIRS WILL GLORIFY OUR NAMES . . .

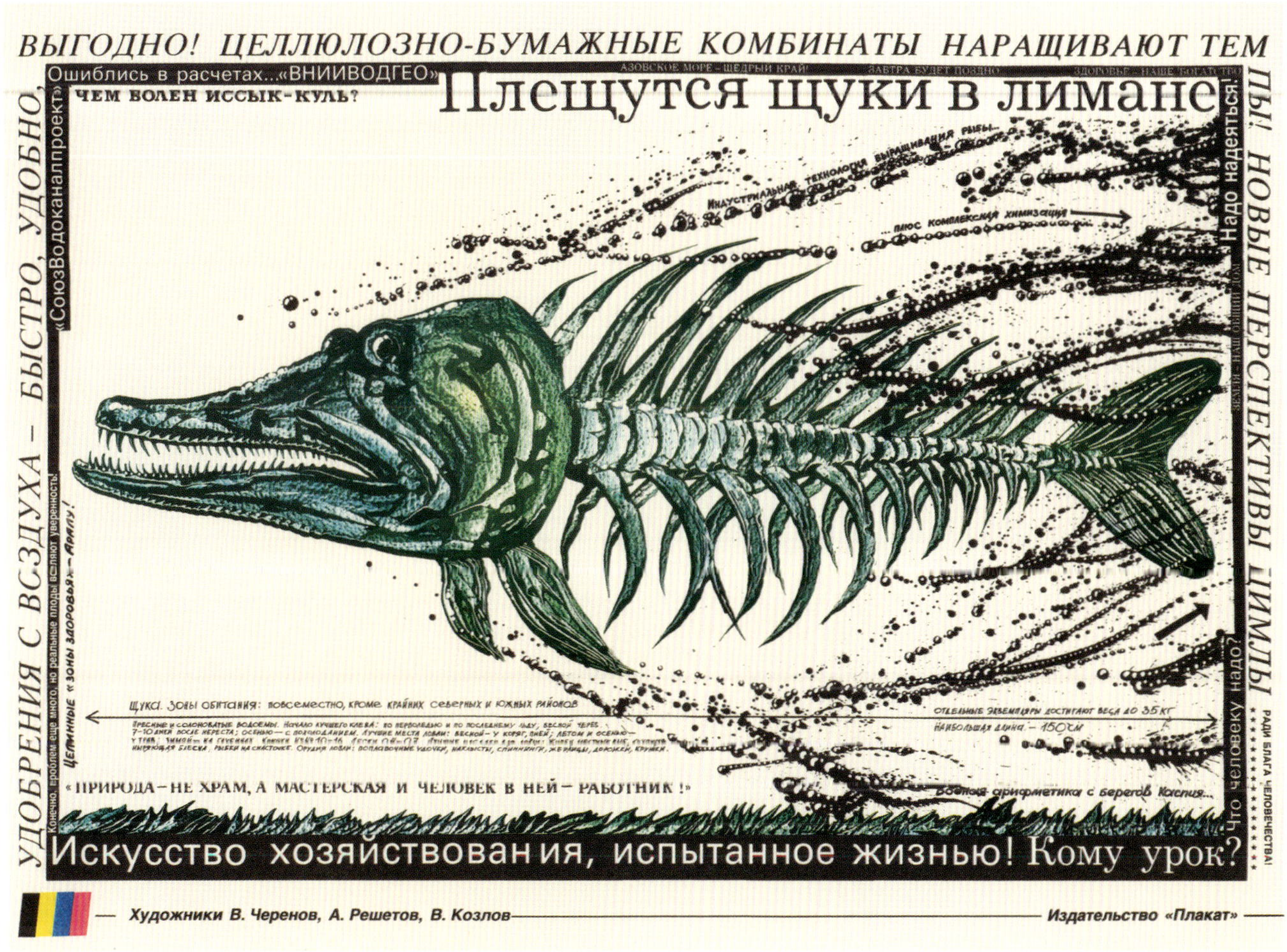

◀ В. Черенов (V. Cherenov), А. Решетов (A. Reshetov), В. Козлов (V. Kozlov) | n.d.

WHERE DO THE LOBSTERS SPEND THE WINTER? Aside from educated tips on how to find and catch lobsters, this question also refers to the folk saying "I will show you where the lobsters spend the winter," meaning "I will do something very bad to you." The implication here is that we should identify the source of this threat to the environment. ACID RAIN IS THE WORK OF HUMAN HANDS! / WE ARE AGAINST NUCLEAR TESTING / LAKE BAIKAL IS THE PATH TO LIVING WATER! / WE'VE STRUCK OIL! / GET THE NORTHERN RIVERS ON TRACK! / GOING AGAINST NATURE IS GOING AGAINST OURSELVES. / ECOLOGICAL BALANCE IS A NECESSITY OF OUR TIME! / WE WILL RETHINK THE BAIKAL-AMUR PROJECT! / SOLIGORSK IS A DREAM COME TRUE! / A CLEAR POSITION, A CONCRETE STEP FORWARD! / COMPARED TO 1913 . . . / DIAGNOSIS: IRRESPONSIBILITY / WILL THE HORSEMEN OF THE APOCALYPSE COME GALLOPING IN?

▲ В. Черенов (V. Cherenov), А. Решетов (A. Reshetov), В. Козлов (V. Kozlov) | n.d.

PIKES ARE SPLASHING IN THE LAGOON / WHAT'S AILING ISSYK KUL? / THE SEA OF AZOV IS A GENEROUS LAND! / TOMORROW WILL BE TOO LATE! / INDUSTRIAL AQUACULTURE AND COMMERCIAL CHEMISTRY . . . [Under the pike is a description of their habitat and how to catch them.] THE EARTH IS OUR COMMON HOME! / HEALTH IS WEALTH / WE HAVE TO HOPE / THE ART OF AGRICULTURE, APPLIED TO LIFE. / WHOSE LESSON IS THIS TO LEARN? WHAT DOES HUMANITY NEED? / NATURE IS NOT A TEMPLE BUT A WORKSHOP, AND MAN—THE WORKER! / OF COURSE, THERE ARE STILL MANY PROBLEMS, BUT OUR TANGIBLE RESULTS INSPIRE CONFIDENCE. / THE UNION OF CANAL PROJECTS / THE ALL-RUSSIAN RESEARCH INSTITUTE FOR RESERVOIRS, SEWAGE, HYDRO-TECHNICAL PROJECTS, AND HYDROGEOLOGICAL ENGINEERING HAS MADE MISTAKES IN ITS CALCULATIONS / AIRBORNE FERTILIZATION IS FAST, CONVENIENT, AND PROFITABLE! / PAPER AND PULP FACTORIES ARE INCREASING THEIR PRODUCTION SPEEDS! NEW HORIZONS FOR THE TSIMLA RIVER!

PEACE

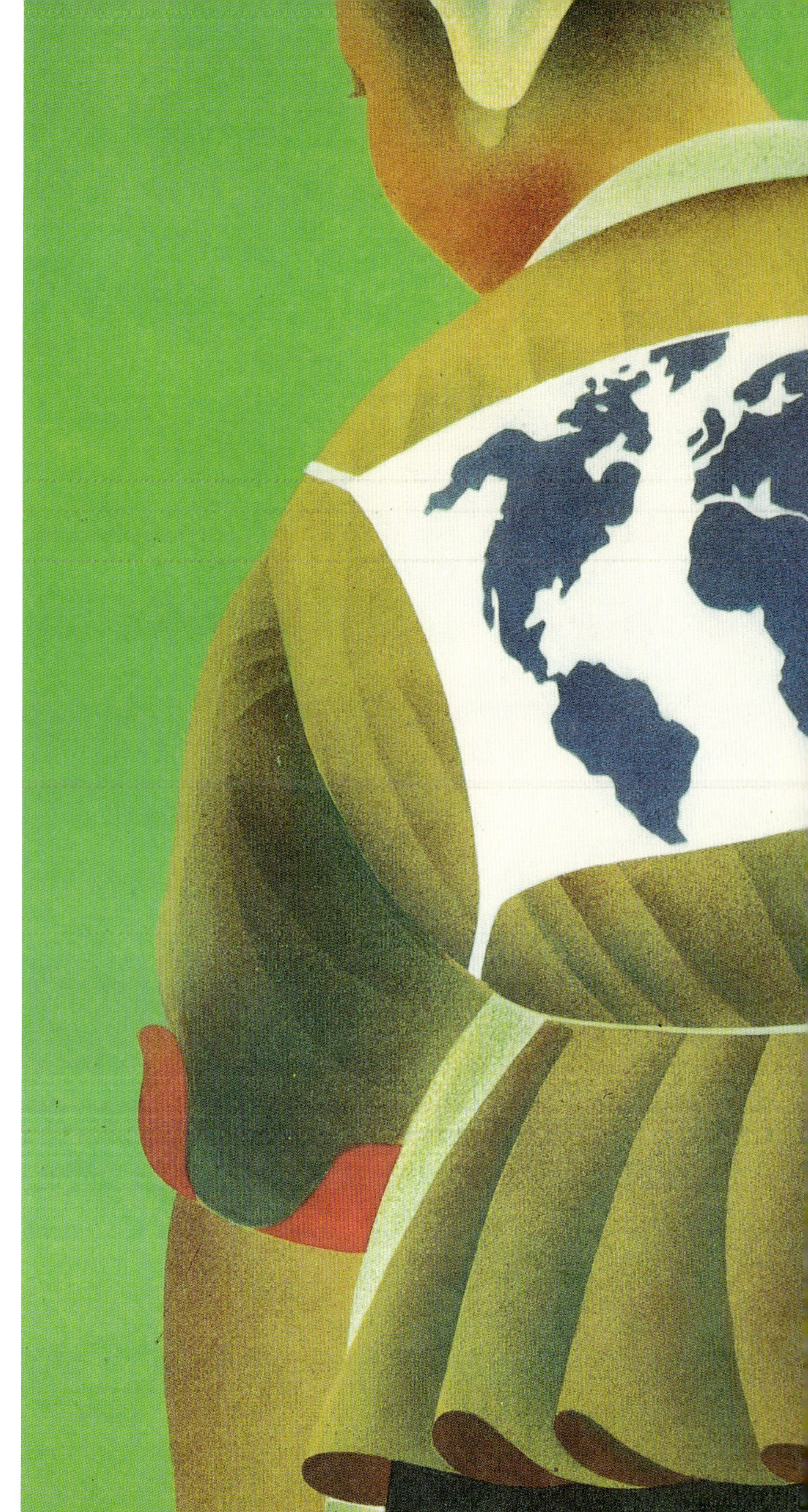

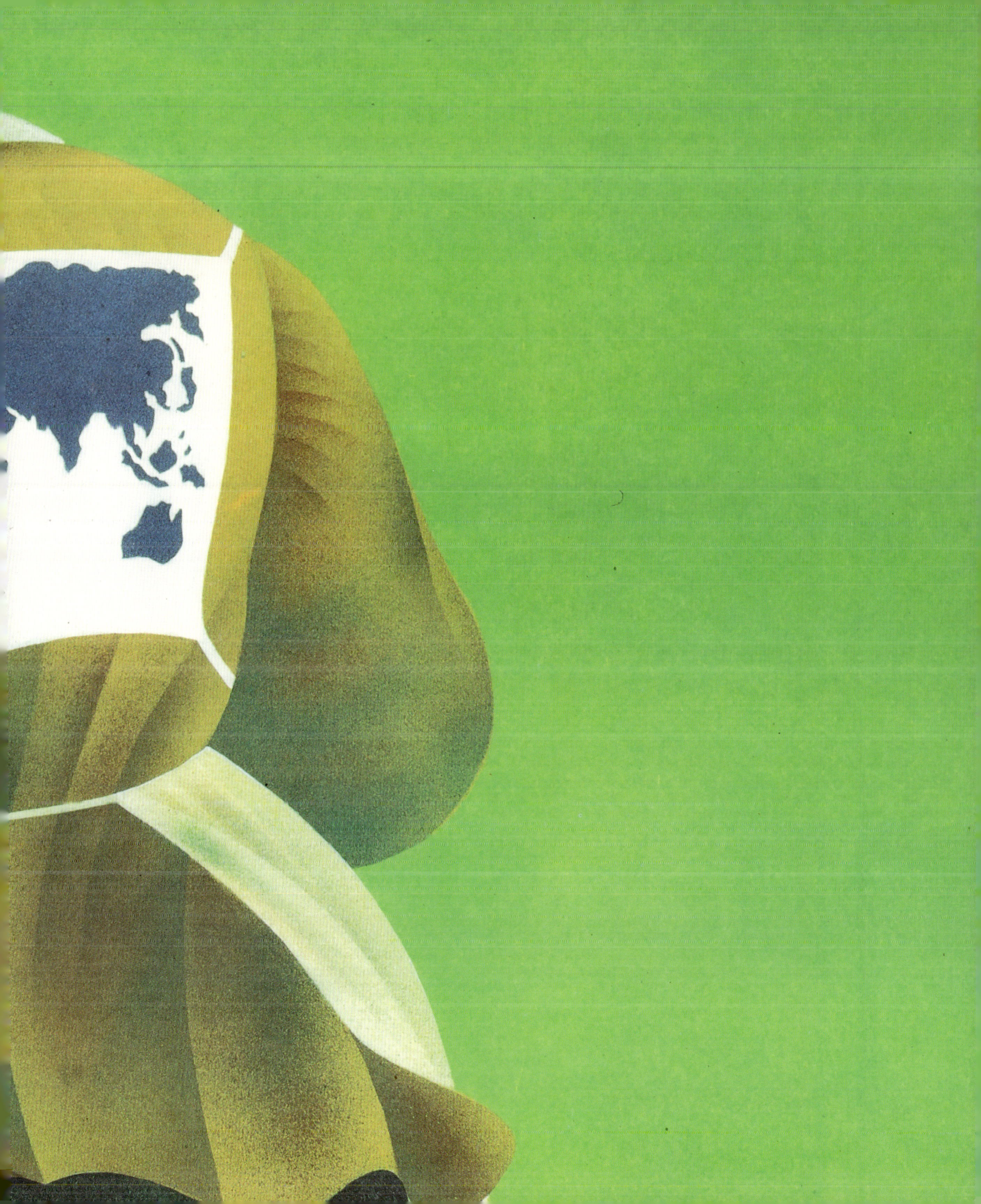

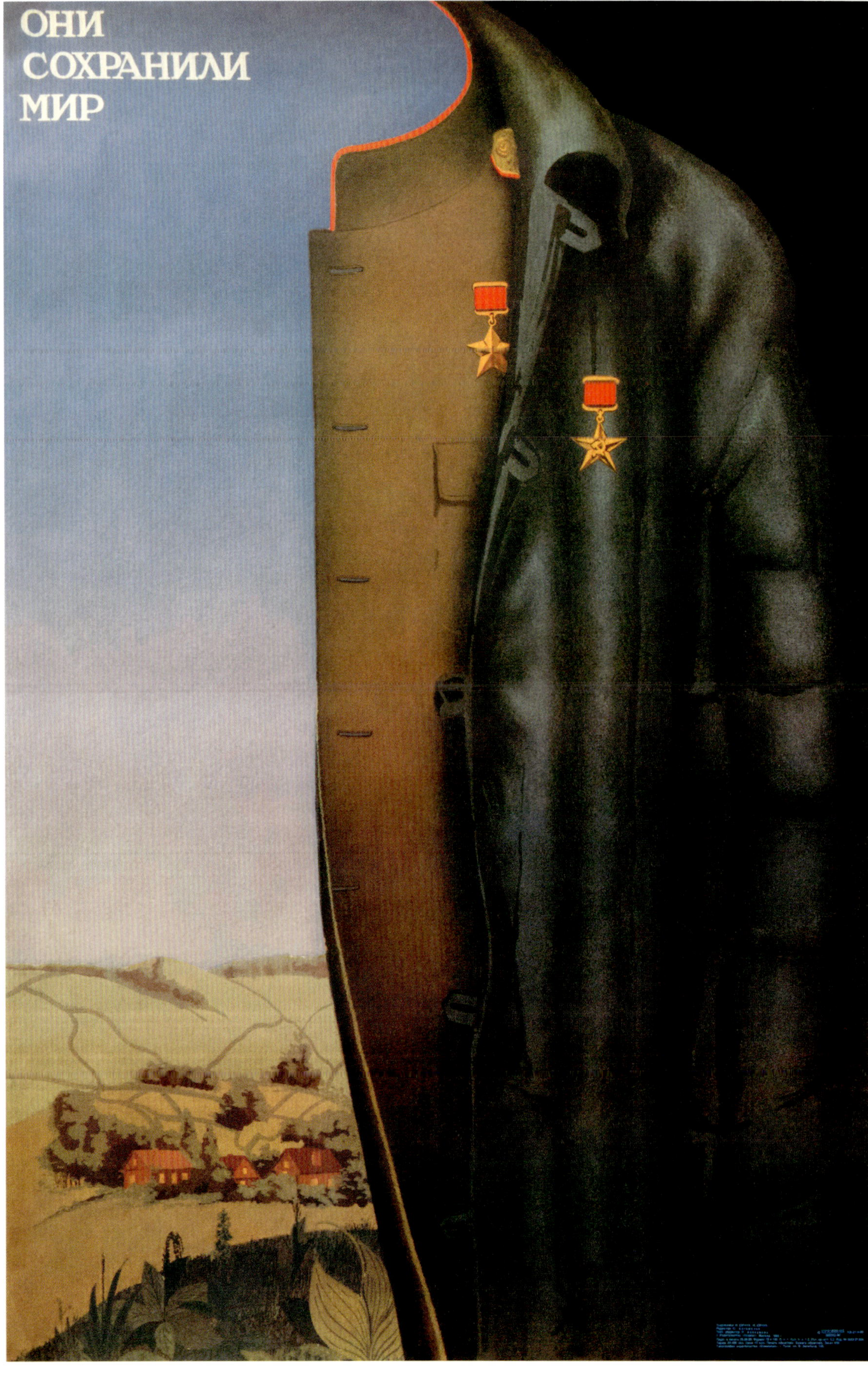
ОНИ
СОХРАНИЛИ
МИР

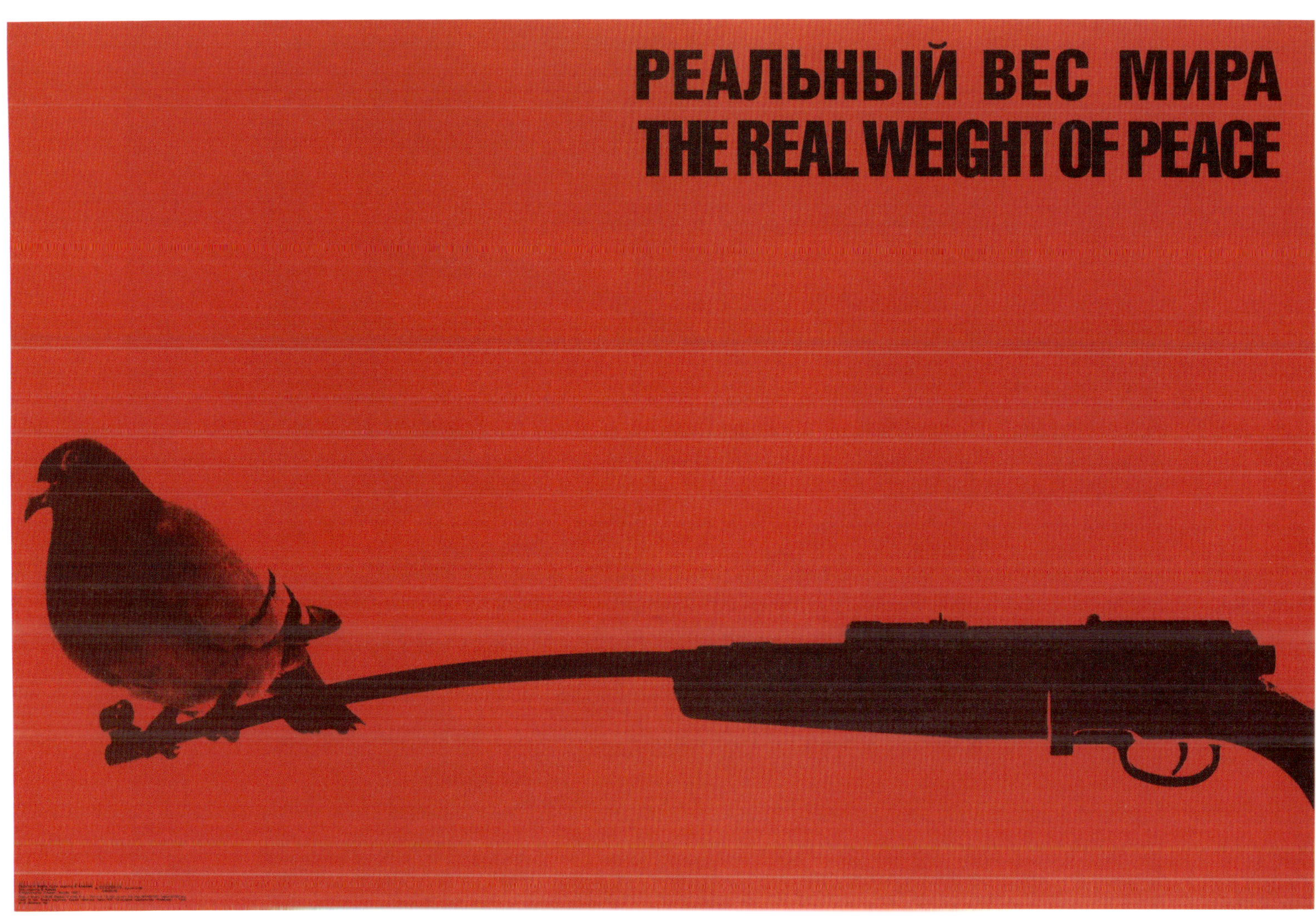

◂ И. Юрчук (I. Yurchuk) | 1990

THEY PRESERVED PEACE
Two men's jackets decorated with medals are depicted against a rural landscape. The interior one is an army jacket, and the exterior one is a peasant jacket, but with a medal of different significance. The army medal is awarded for military heroism; the other for achievements in labor.

Масутэру Аоба (Masuteru Aoba) | 1988 ▴

THE REAL WEIGHT OF PEACE
Text is in both Russian and English.

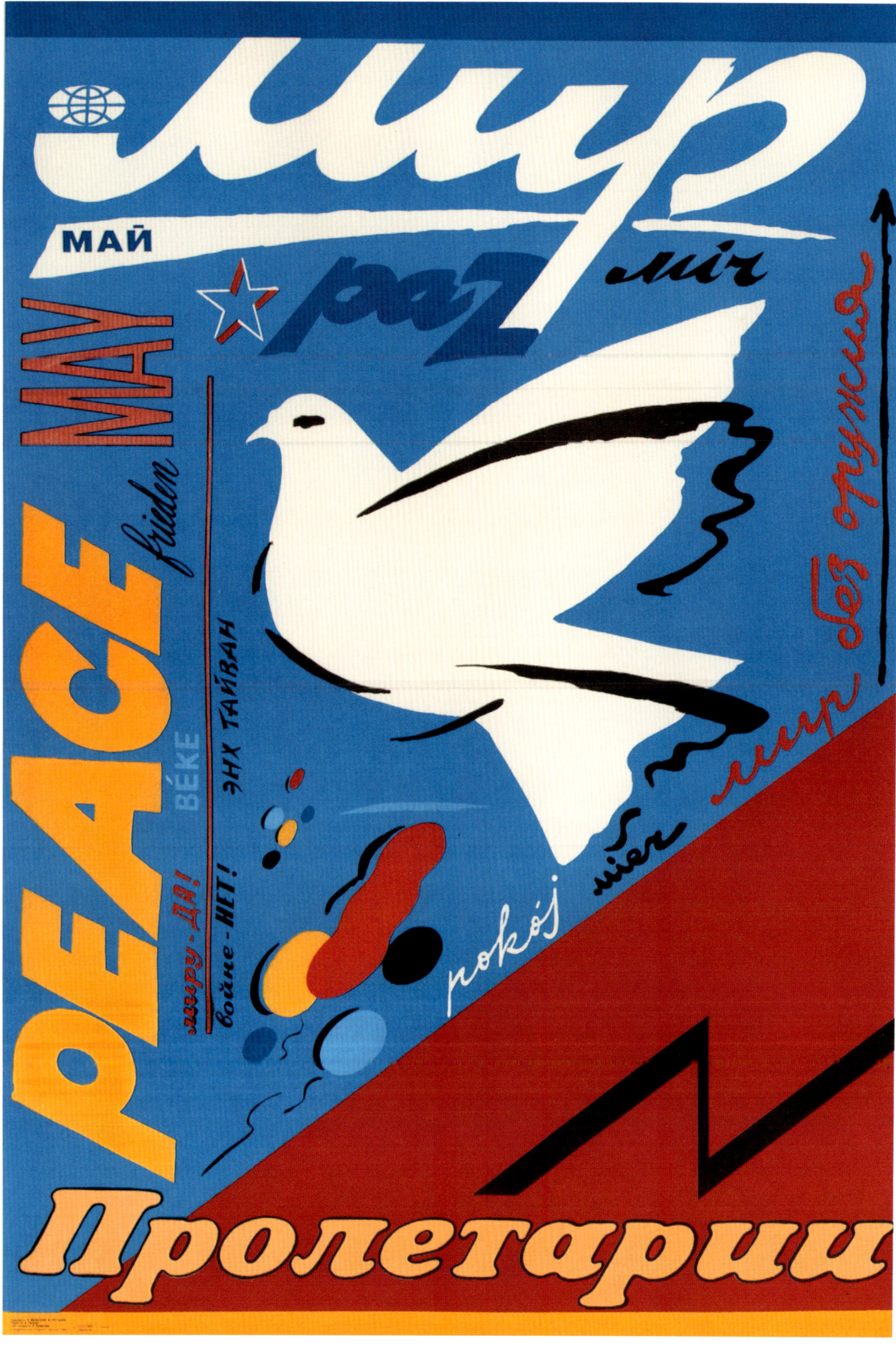
мир
МАЙ
paz
mir
MAY
PEACE
frieden
ВЕКЕ
ЭНХ ТАЙВАН
миру - ДА!
войне - НЕТ!
без оружия
мир
mier
pokój
Пролетарии

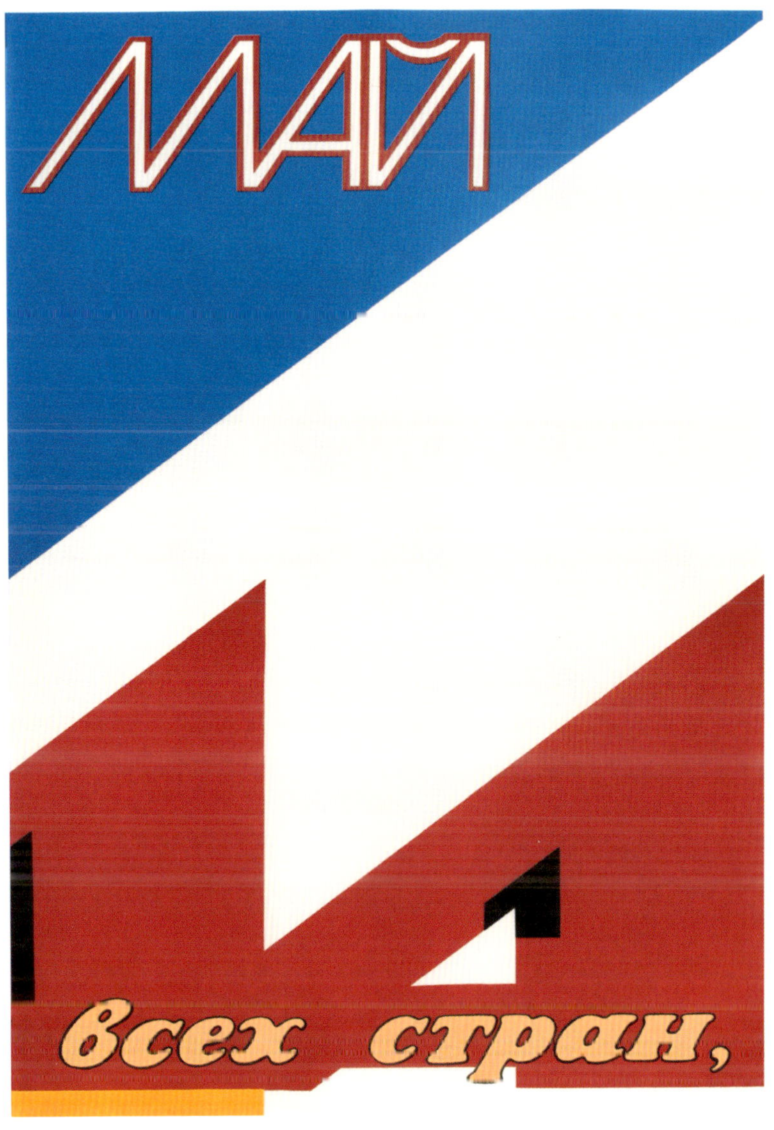

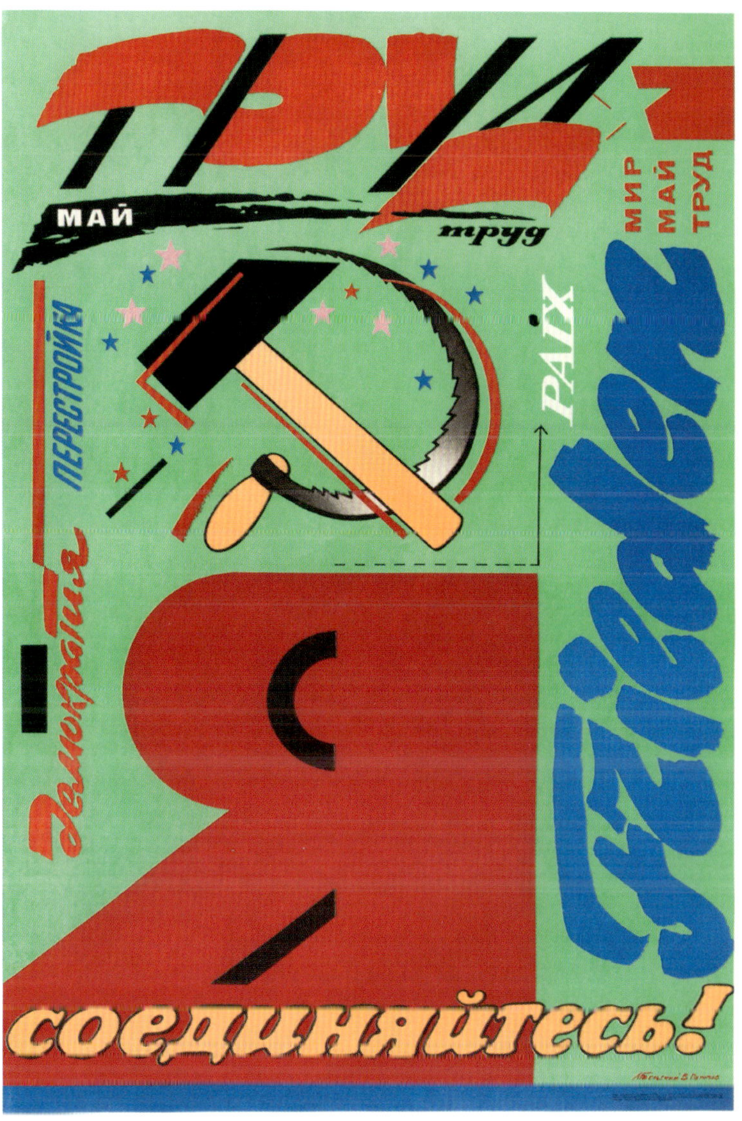

Л. Ебльский (L. Yeblsky), В. Потапов (V. Potapov) | 1989

Three panels of a triptych. Text running sequentially across the bottom of all three panels reads: PROLETARIANS OF THE WORLD, UNITE! Other sequences of texts across the panels read: PEACE / A WORLD WITHOUT ARMS / MAY / LABOR / DEMOCRACY / PERESTROIKA.

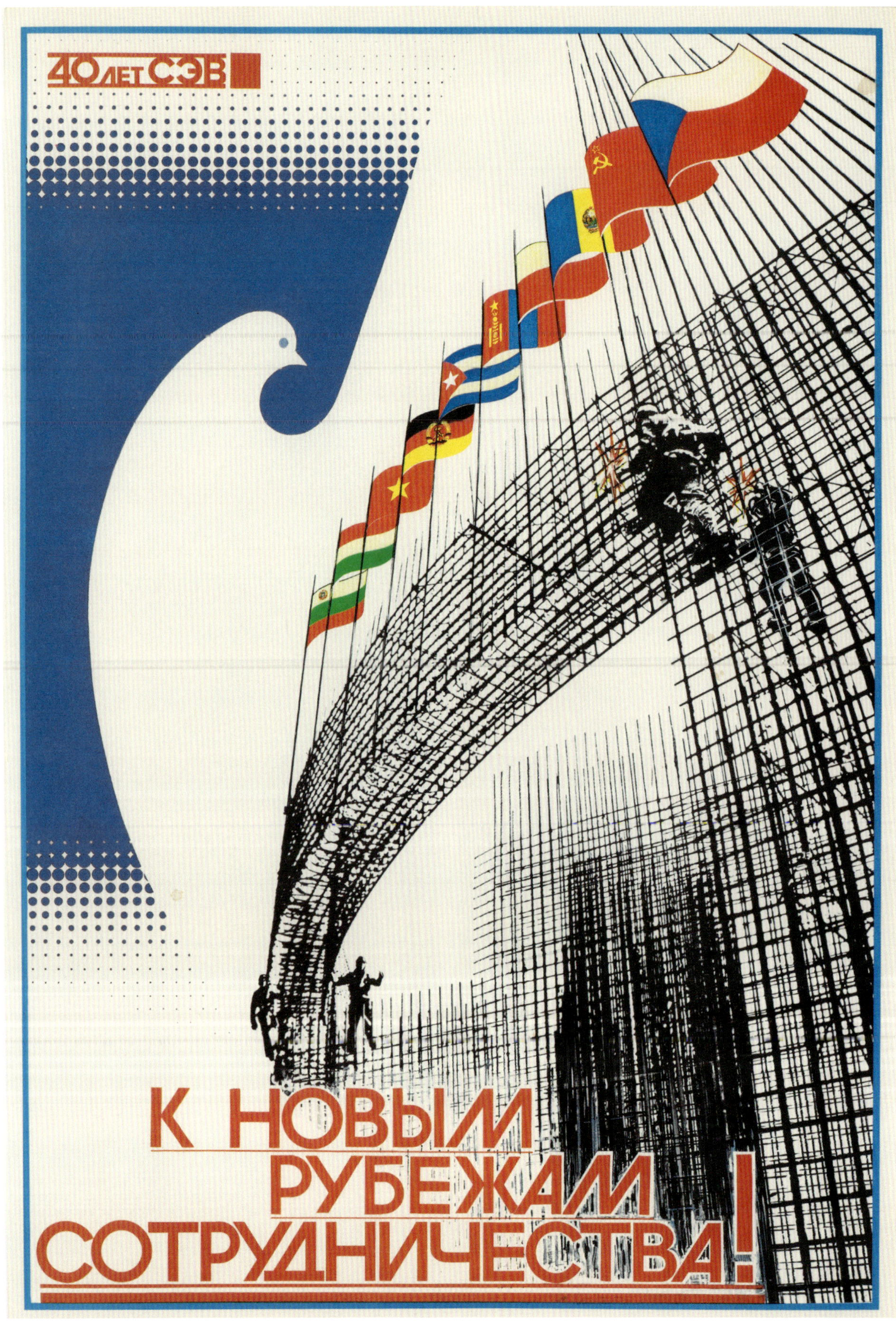
40 лет СЭВ
К НОВЫМ
РУБЕЖАМ
СОТРУДНИЧЕСТВА!

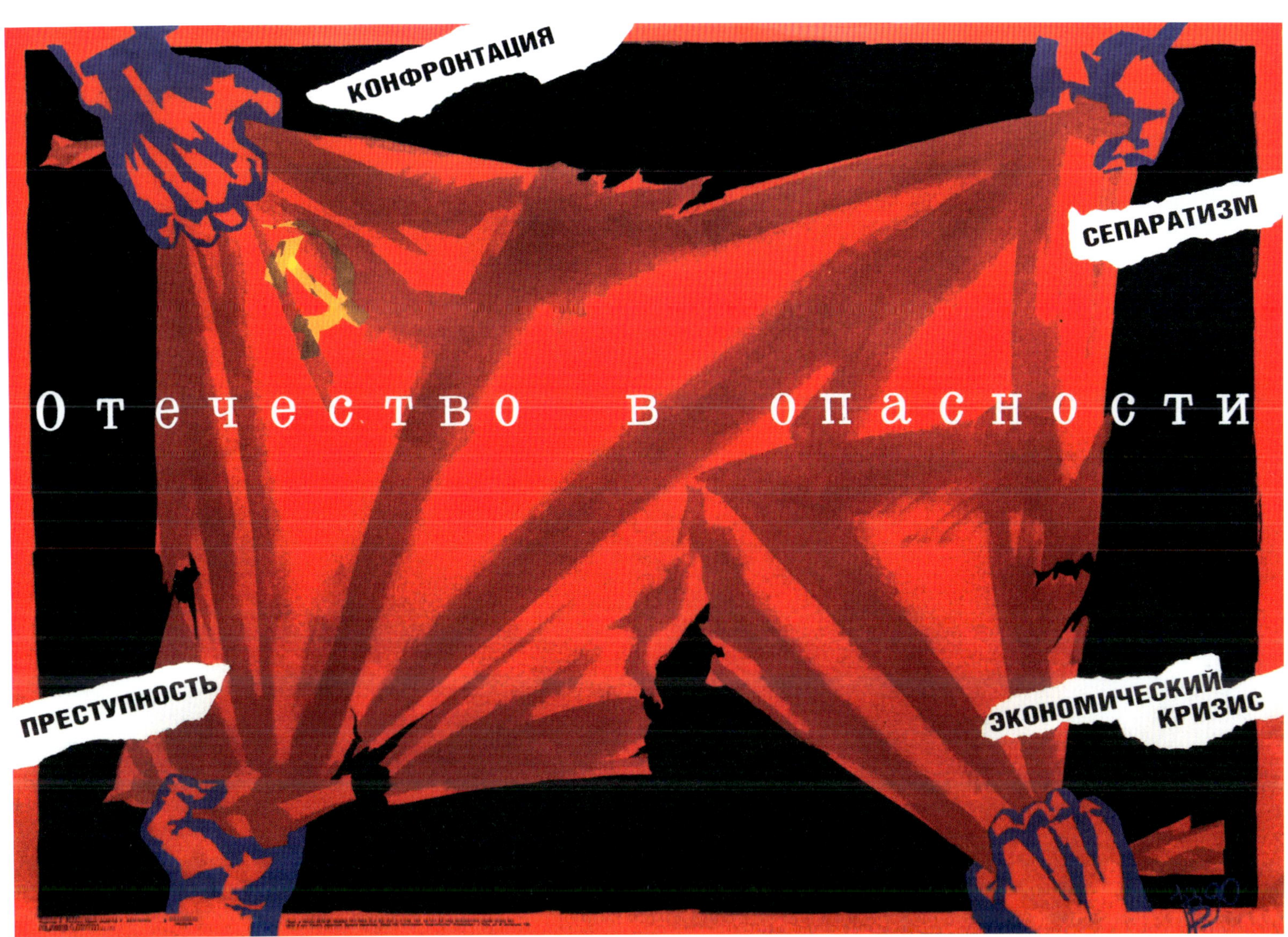

◀ Л. Тарасова (L. Tarasova) | 1988

Text at top: 40 YEARS OF THE COUNCIL FOR MUTUAL ECONOMIC ASSISTANCE
Text at bottom: TO NEW FRONTIERS OF COLLABORATION!
The Council for Mutual Economic Assistance (Comecon) was an international economic organization from 1949 to 1991. Member nations included Albania, Bulgaria, Hungary, Poland, Romania, the USSR, and Czechoslovakia—the Eastern Bloc—along with a handful of other socialist nations whose flags are represented here.

▲ В. Вдовин (V. Vdovin) | 1990

THE HOMELAND IS IN DANGER
Clockwise, left to right: CONFRONTATION / SEPARATISM / ECONOMIC CRISIS / CRIMINALITY. Note that the shape of the USSR flag, as pulled and torn from its four corners, closely approximates the shape of the continental nation.

PEACE

Ю. Николаев (Yu. Nikolaev) | 1989 ➤

THE EARTH IS FOR LIFE ONLY!
A peasant woman is pictured with the map of the world on her back. She is raking up missiles and bombs that have visited death on the land.

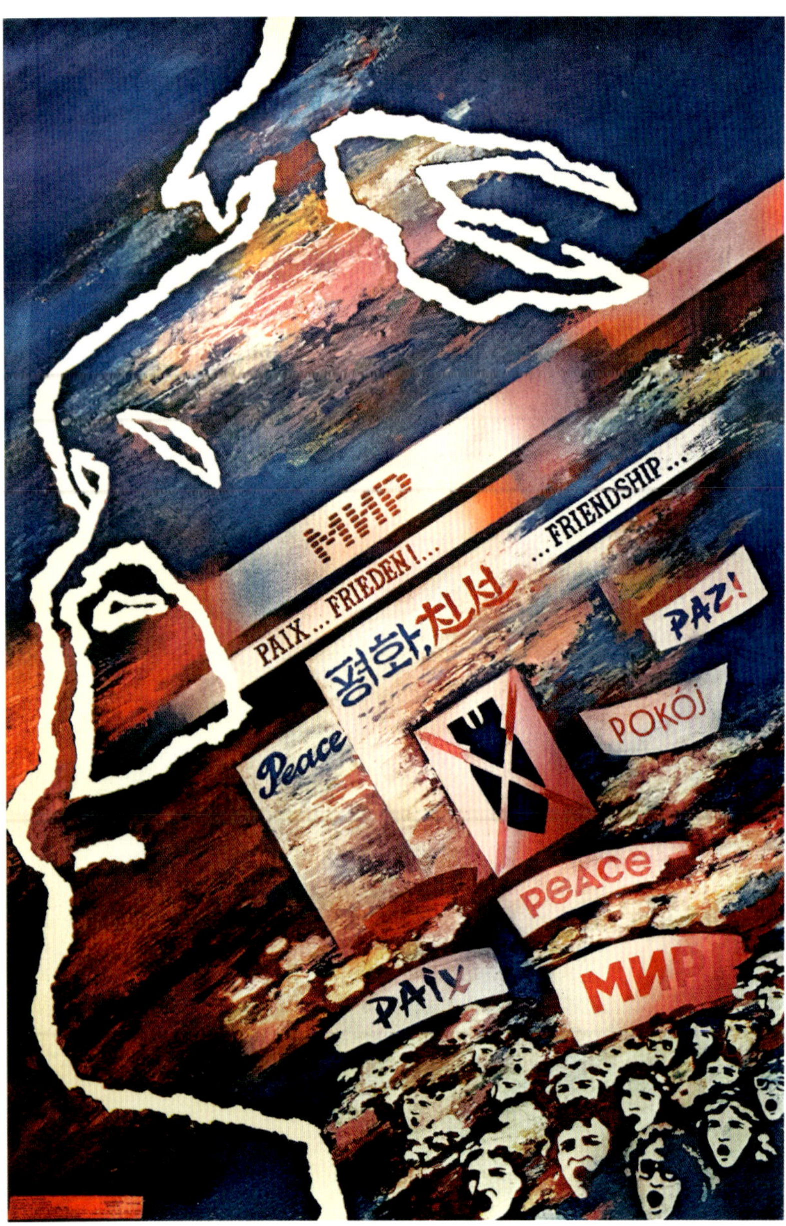

▲ Р. Лопатина (R. Lopatina) | 1989

This image depicts the outline of a face in profile proclaiming PEACE and FRIENDSHIP in many languages.

С. Смирнов (S. Smirnov) | 1988 ➤

WE VOTE FOR PEACE!
Text is in both Russian and English.

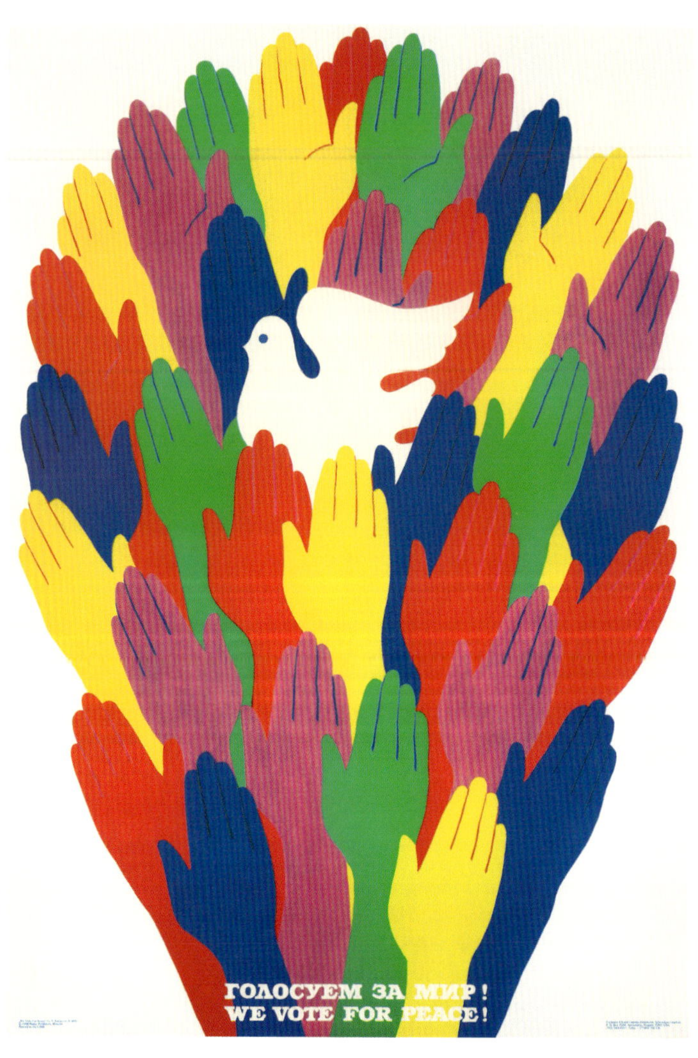

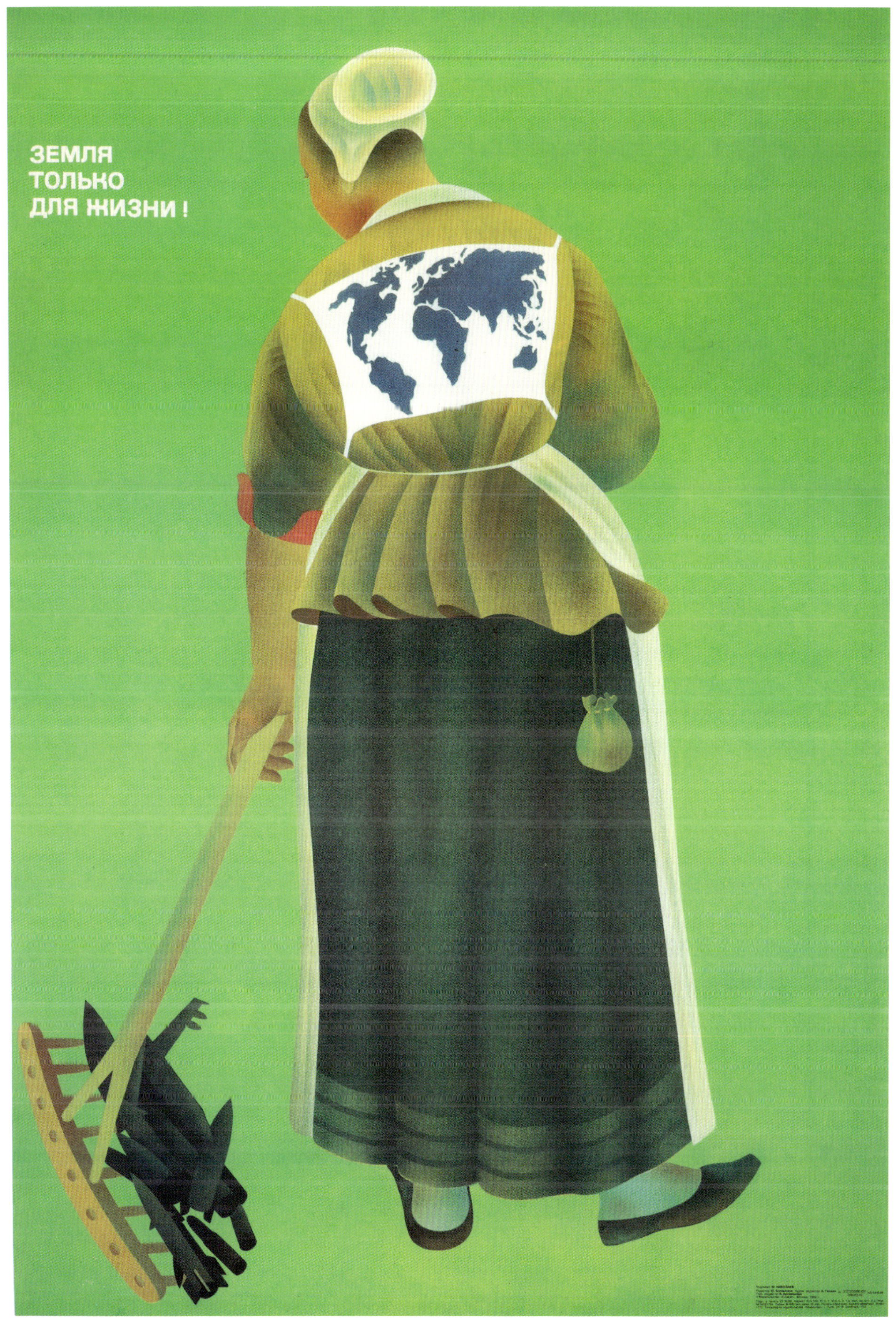
ЗЕМЛЯ
ТОЛЬКО
ДЛЯ ЖИЗНИ !

PEACE

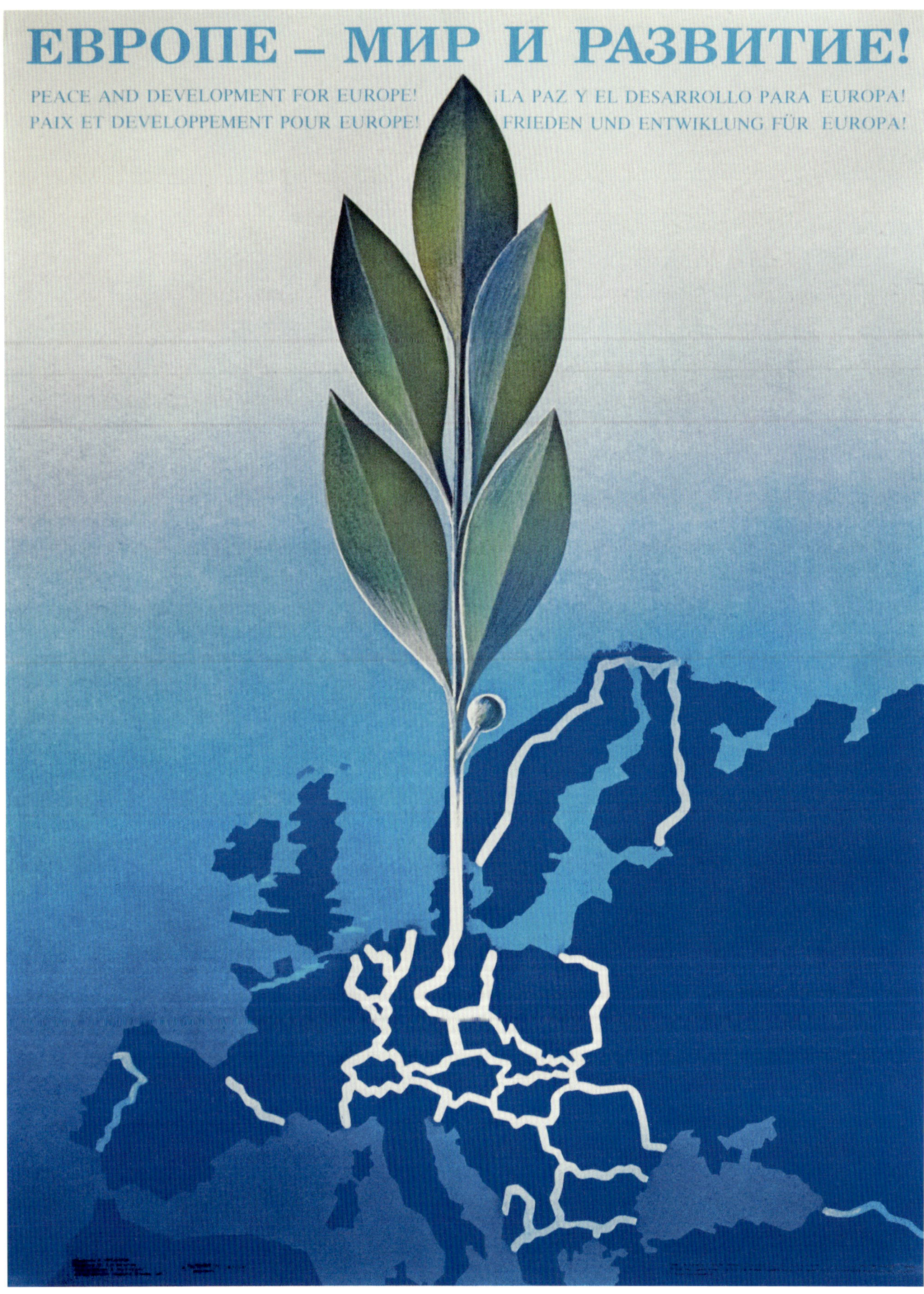
ЕВРОПЕ – МИР И РАЗВИТИЕ!
PEACE AND DEVELOPMENT FOR EUROPE!
PAIX ET DEVELOPPEMENT POUR EUROPE!
¡LA PAZ Y EL DESARROLLO PARA EUROPA!
FRIEDEN UND ENTWIKLUNG FÜR EUROPA!

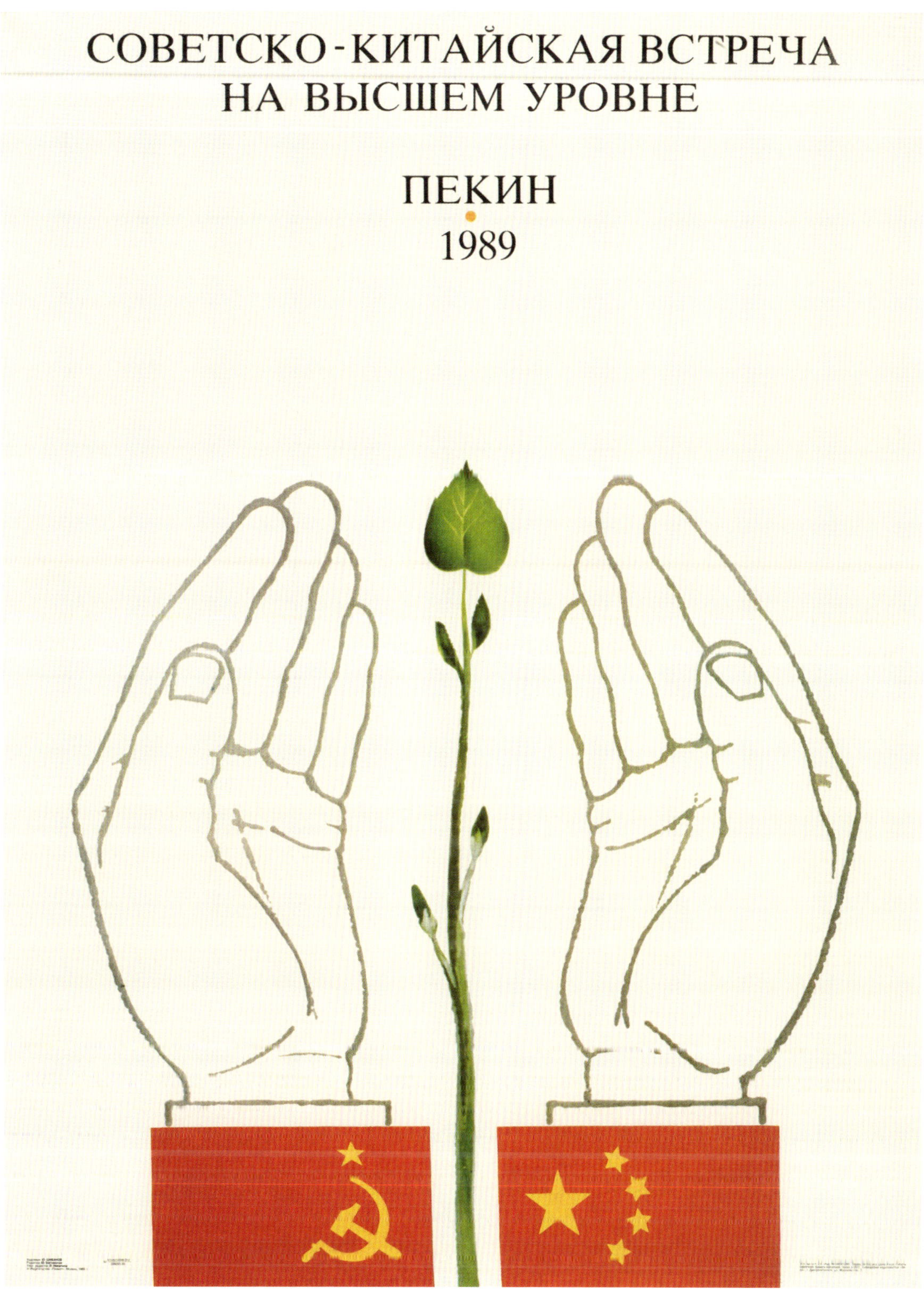

◂ Л. Михайпов (L. Mikhaipov) | 1989

PEACE AND DEVELOPMENT FOR EUROPE!
Beneath the Russian text, the same phrase is repeated in English, French, Spanish, and German.

▴ Ю. Шибанов (Yu. Shibanov) | 1989

SINO-SOVIET SUMMIT
BEIJING
1989

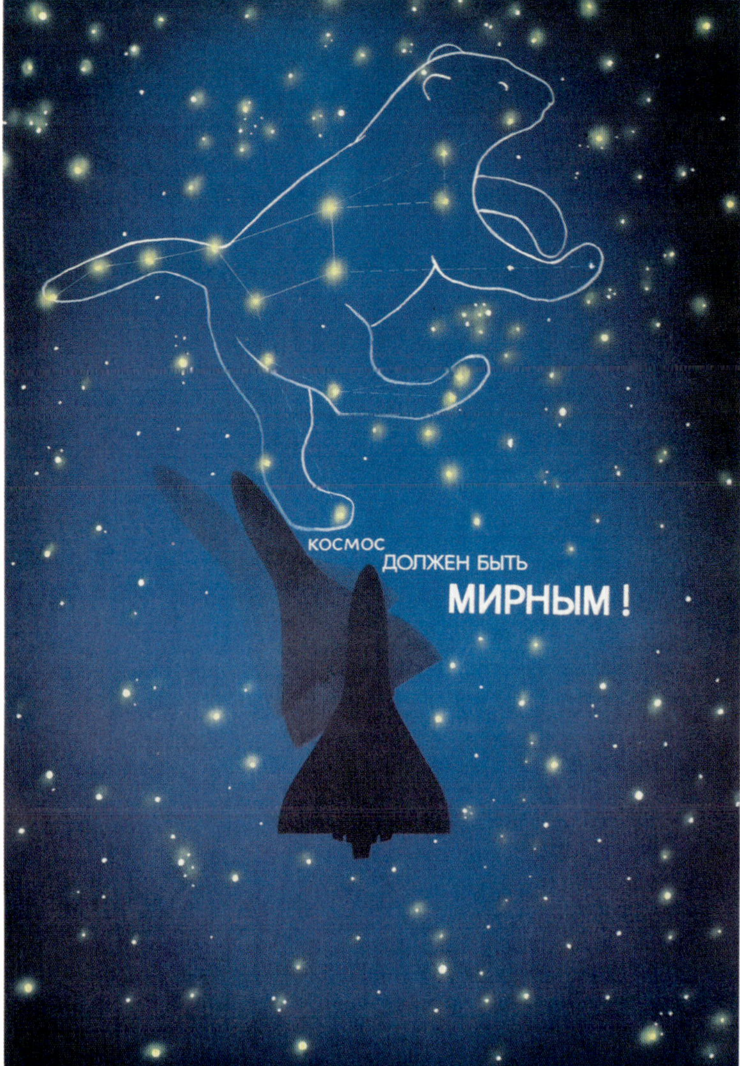

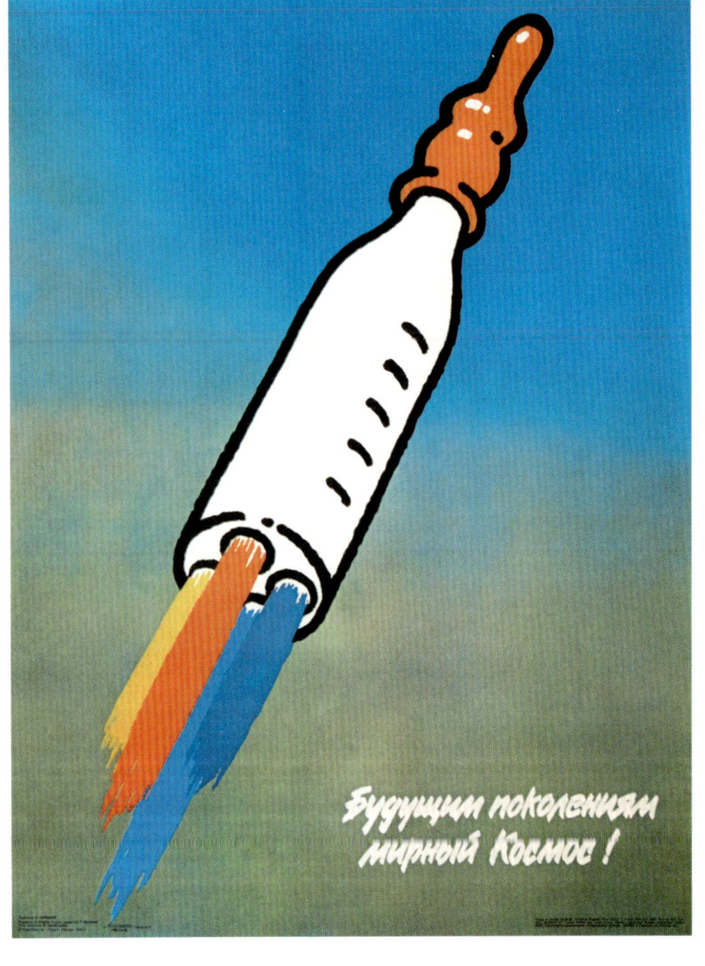

▲ В. Мохначев (V. Mokhnachev) | 1988

THERE MUST BE PEACE IN SPACE!
Initially, a black spacecraft is directed at Ursa Major, at times referred to as the Russian Bear (also known as the Great Bear), then swerves away from the constellation and disappears.

Р. Акманов (R. Akmanov) | 1988 ➤

LESS ROCKETS MORE CONFIDENCE
A rocket with a window shows a plant with leaves composed of the Soviet and US flags. The window opens out to the universe and its infinite promise.

▲ Р. Акманов (R. Akmanov) | 1988

FOR FUTURE GENERATIONS
PEACE IN SPACE!

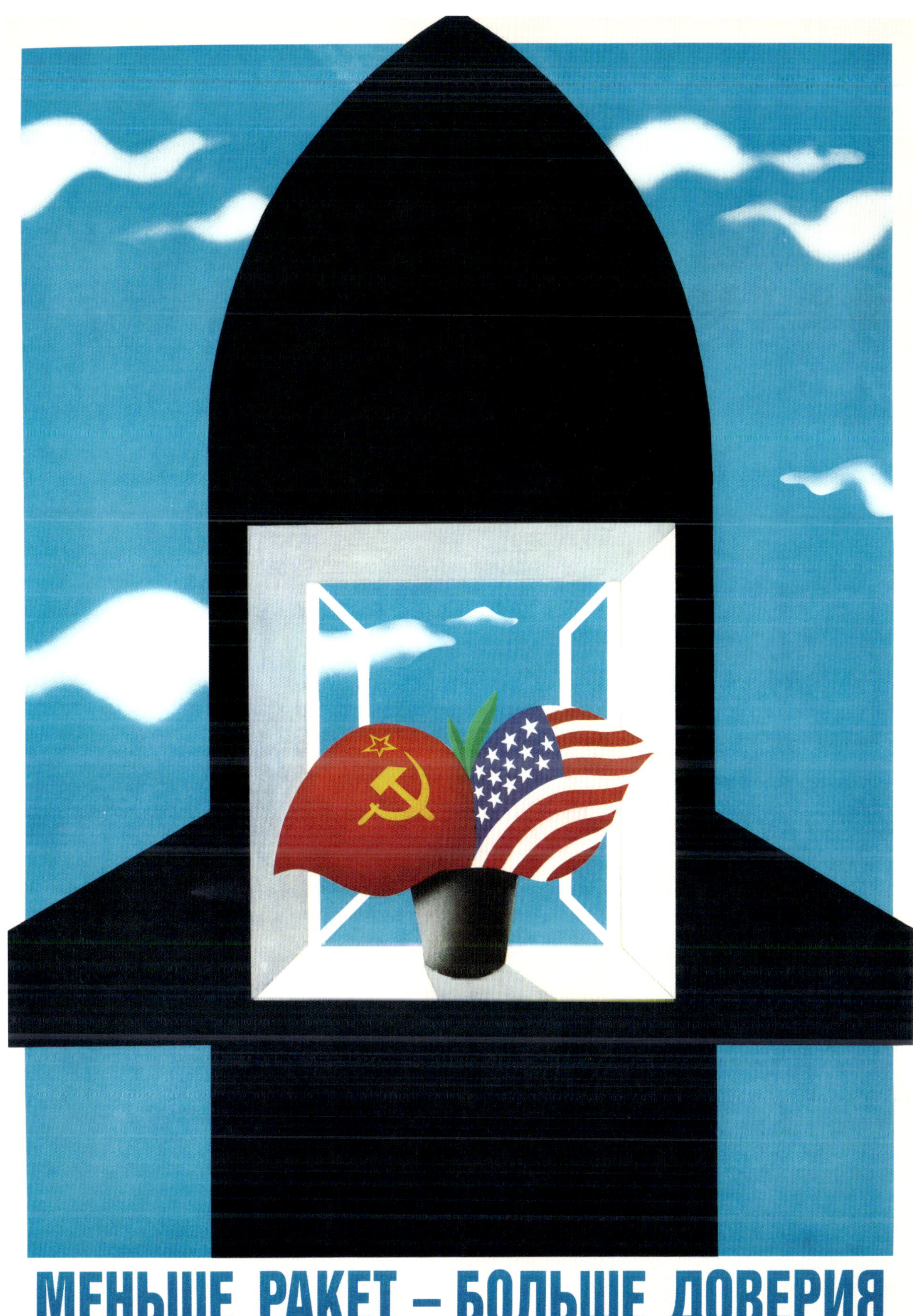
МЕНЬШЕ РАКЕТ – БОЛЬШЕ ДОВЕРИЯ

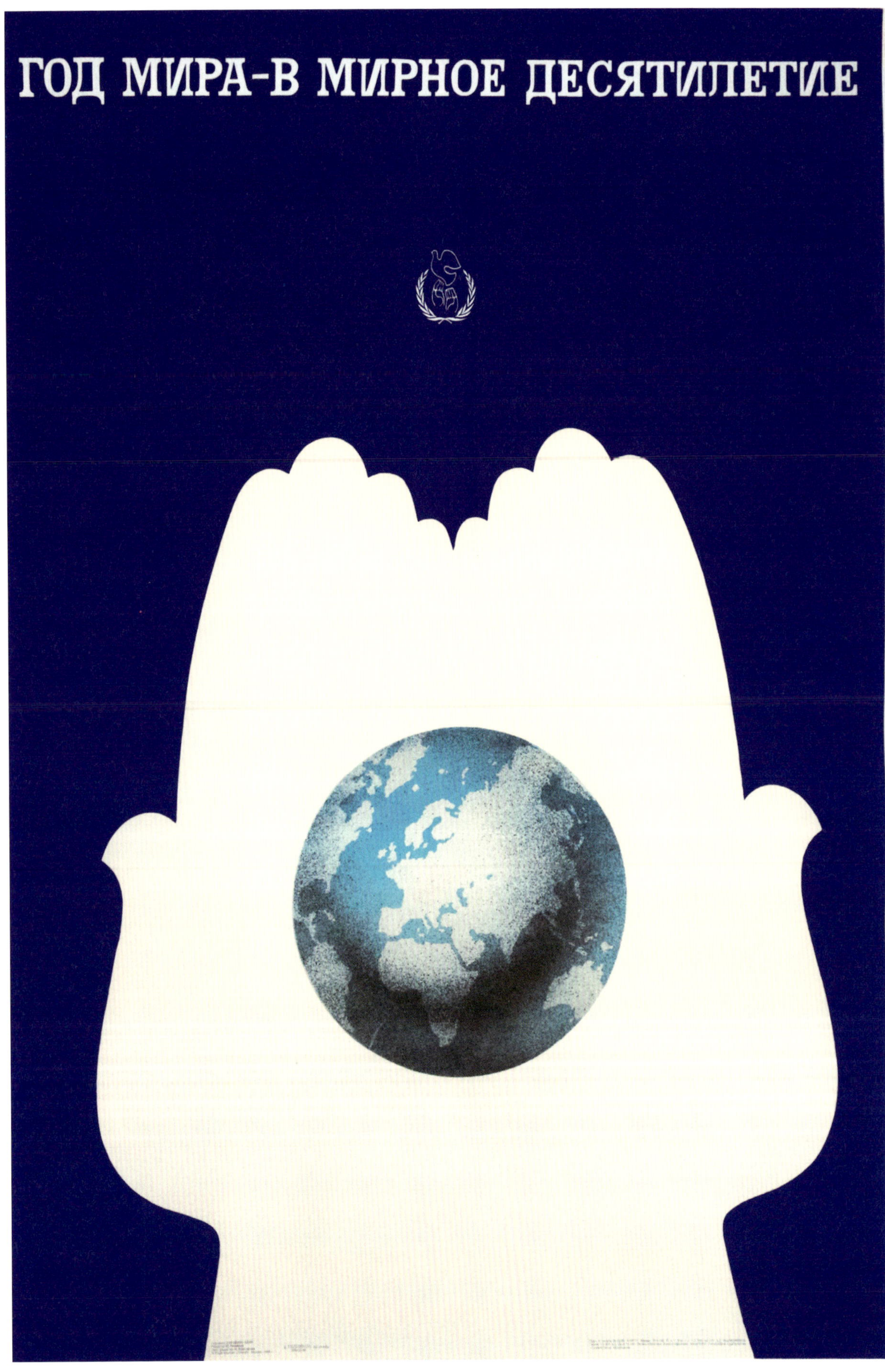

PEACE

◂ Пурэвийн Баяр (Pureviin Bayar) | 1986

LET'S TURN A YEAR OF PEACE INTO A PEACEFUL DECADE

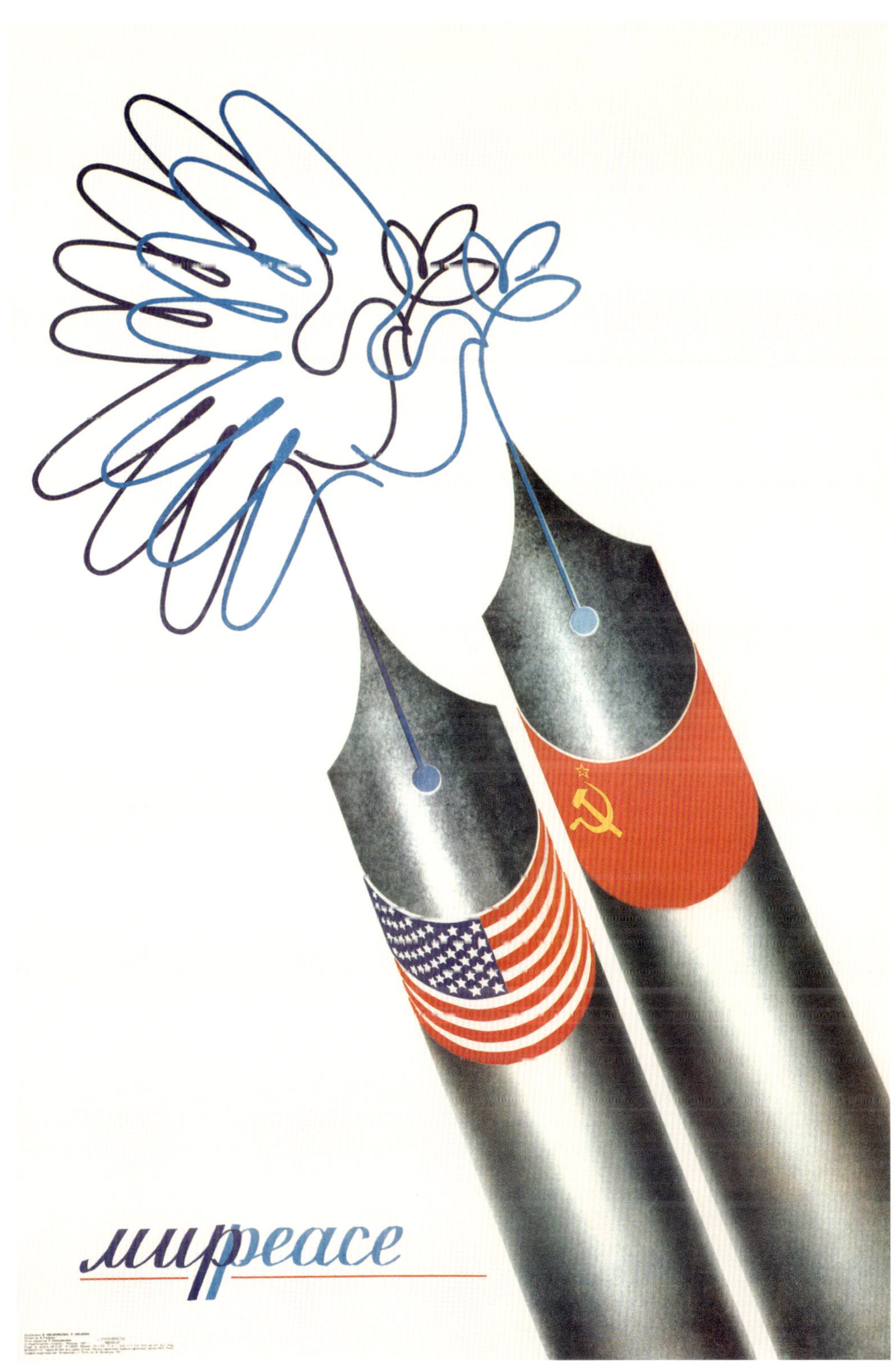

З. Чисарикова (Z. Chysarykova), Л. Чисарик (L. Chisarik) | 1987 ▸

PEACE
Text is both in Russian and English.

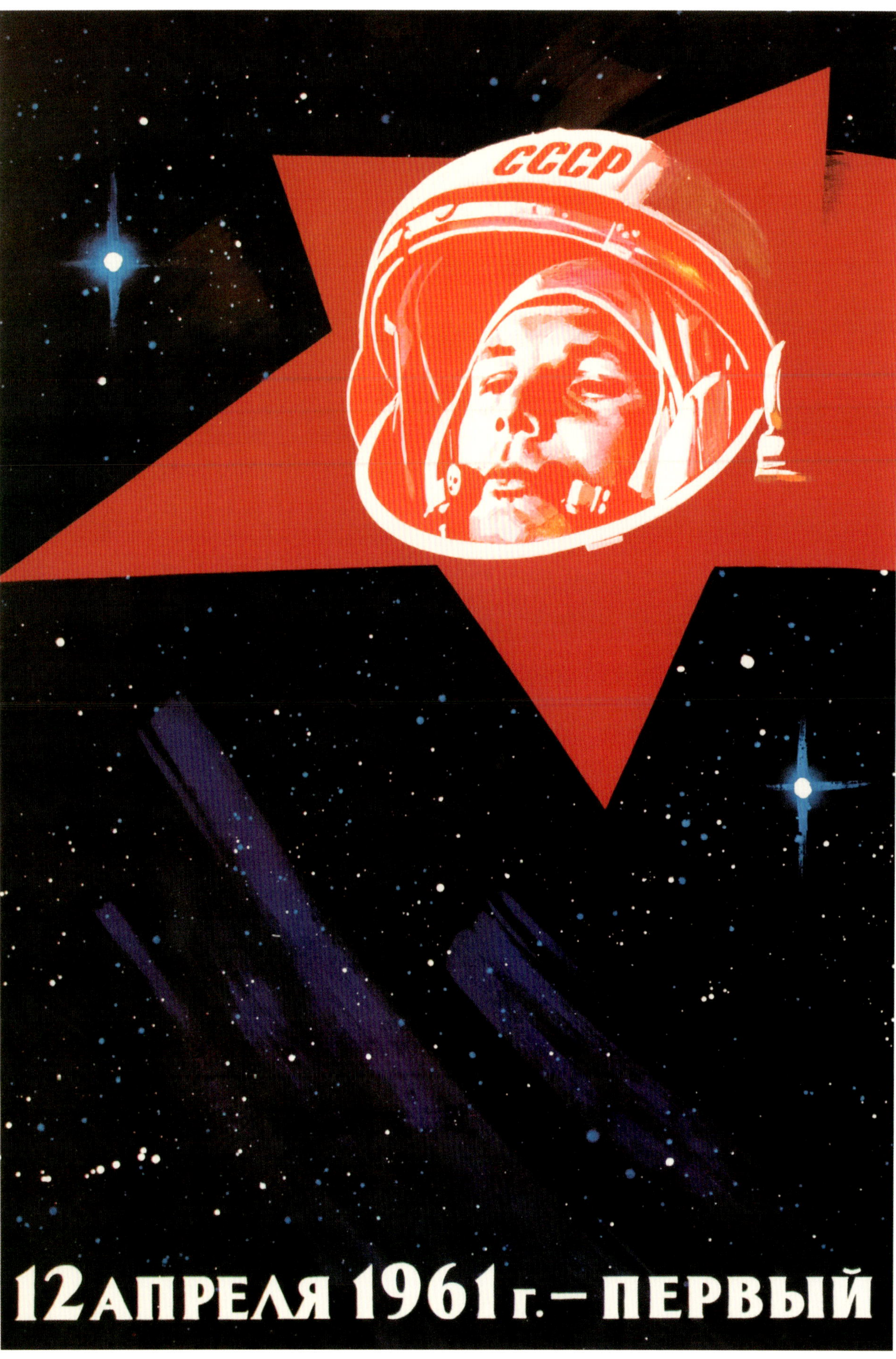
СССР
12 АПРЕЛЯ 1961 г. – ПЕРВЫЙ

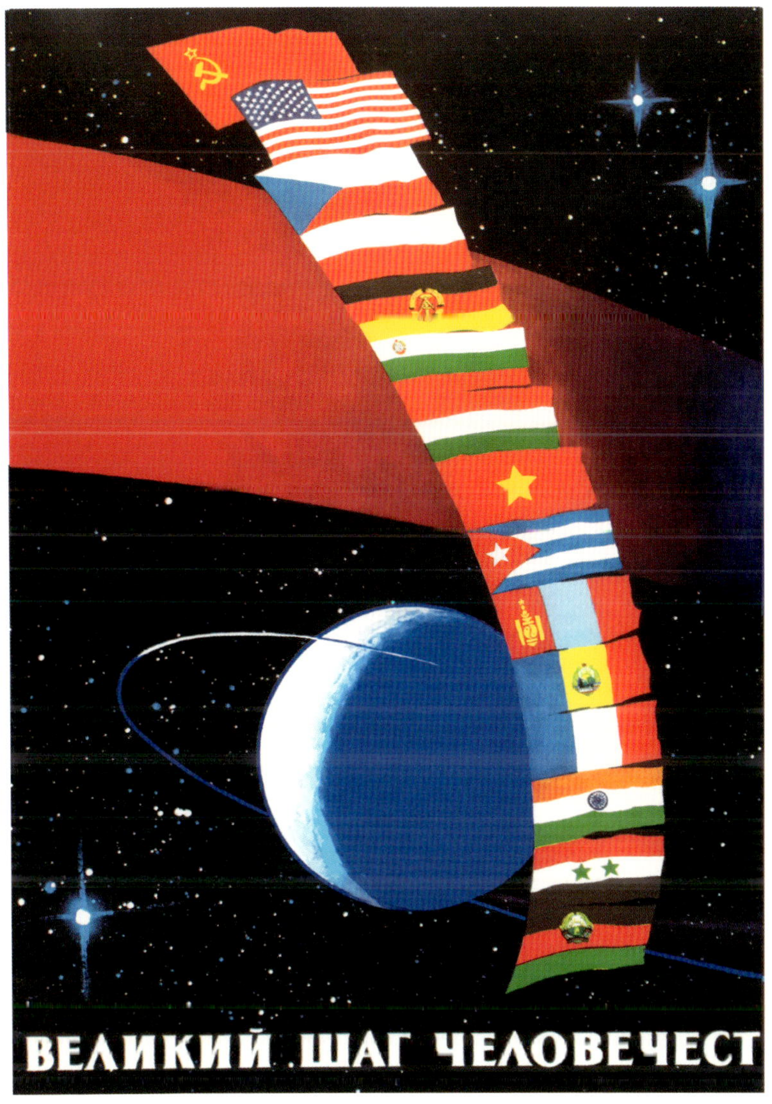

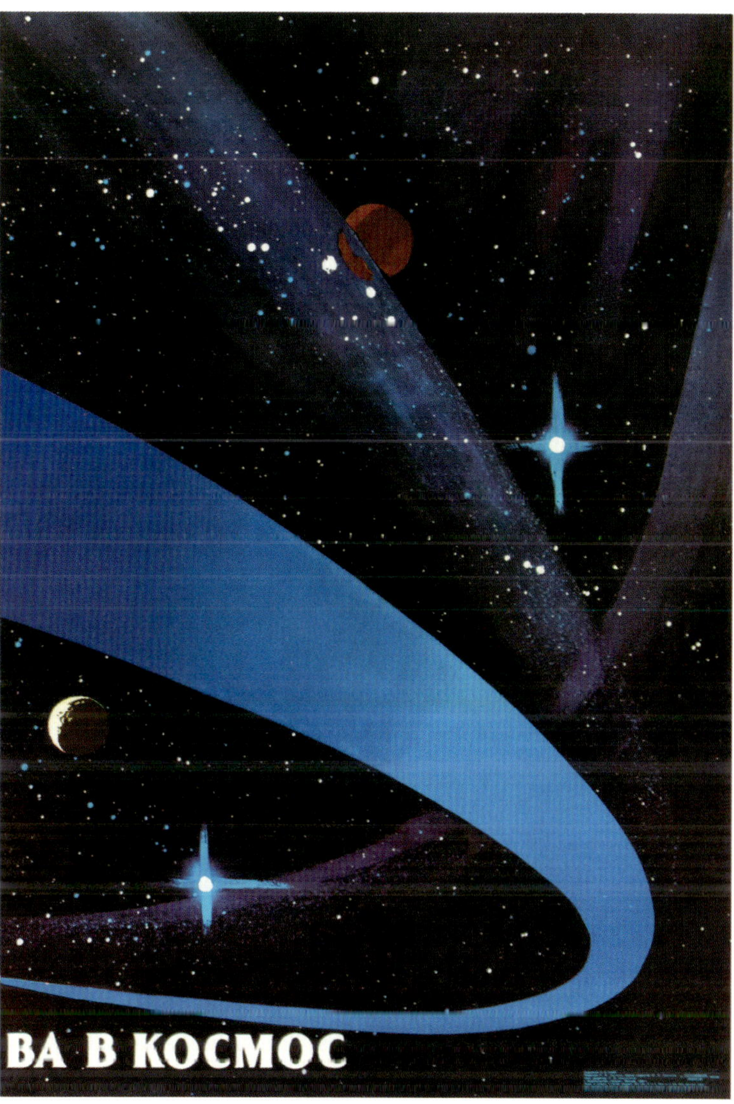

С. Браев (S. Brayev) | 1989

Three panels of a triptych. Text running sequentially across the bottom of all three panels reads: APRIL 12, 1961: THE FIRST GREAT STEP FOR HUMANITY INTO SPACE. The image shows cosmonaut Yuri Gagarin pictured inside a red star in the sky. The date cited is the moment Gagarin became the first human to travel into outer space. In the second panel, a planet is encircled by a band of flags, all of which are of socialist countries except for the US and India.

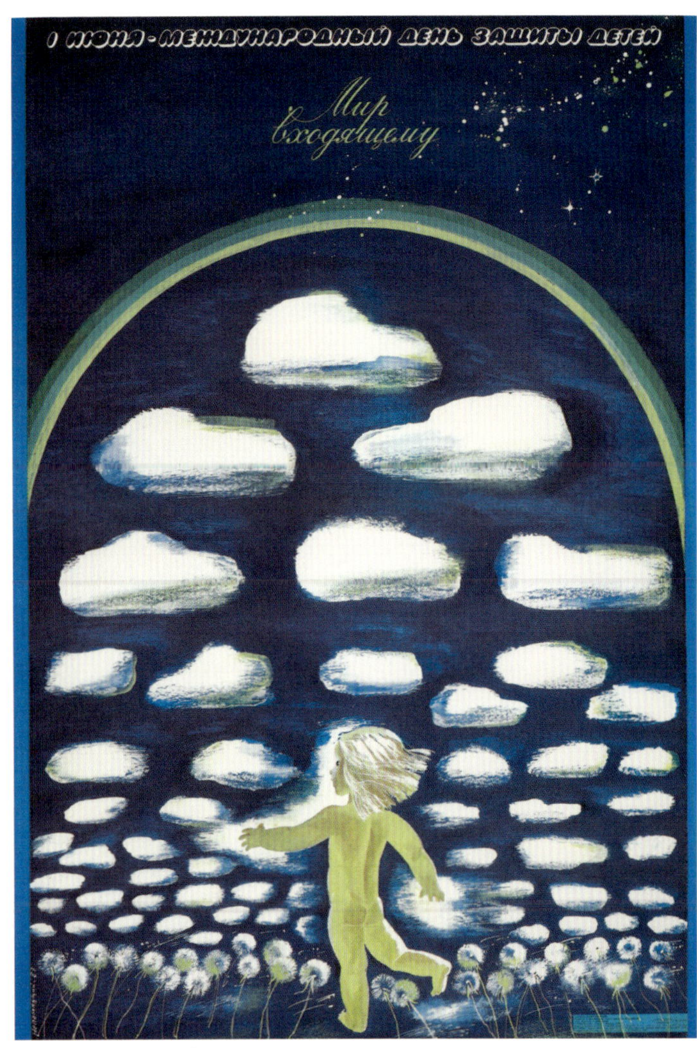

◂ Л. Непомнящий (L. Nepomnyashchiy) | 1987

JUNE 1—INTERNATIONAL CHILD PROTECTION DAY
PEACE TO THE NEW ARRIVALS

В. Шектасов (V. Shektasov) | 1988 ▸

REMEMBER!
EACH DAY OF PEACE HAS COST US 20 MILLION SOVIET LIVES!
The text references the Soviet account that 20 million died under Stalin, and that is considered the cost of each day of freedom following his Reign of Terror.

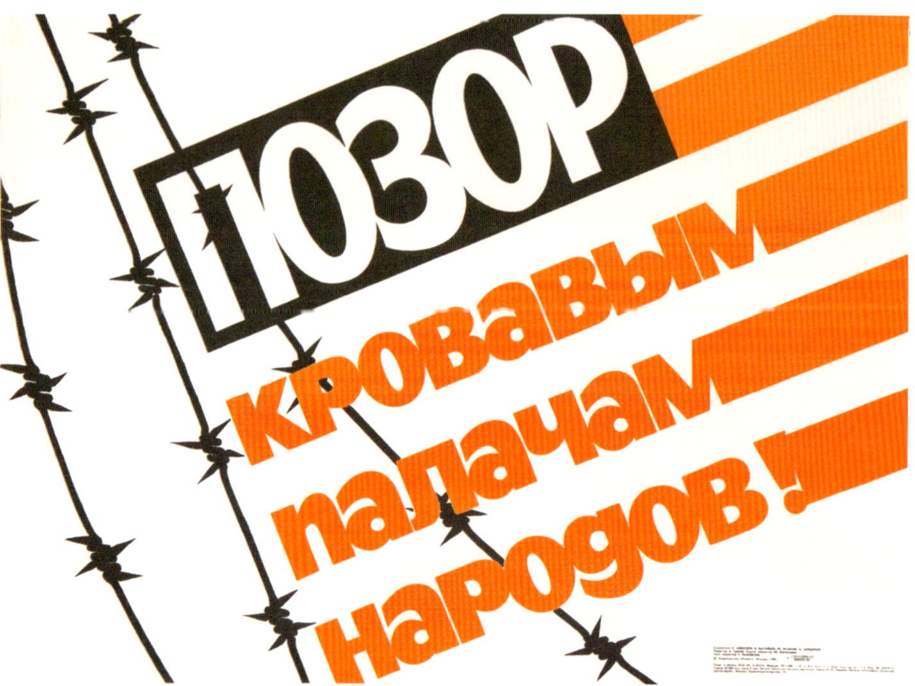

С. Алексеев (S. Alekseev), В. Васильев (V. Vasiliev), Ю. Исаков (Yu. Isakov), А. Моценок (A. Motsenok) | 1984 ▸

SHAME ON THE BLOODY BUTCHERS OF NATIONS!
The barbed wire and stripe motif are meant to be evocative of the American flag.

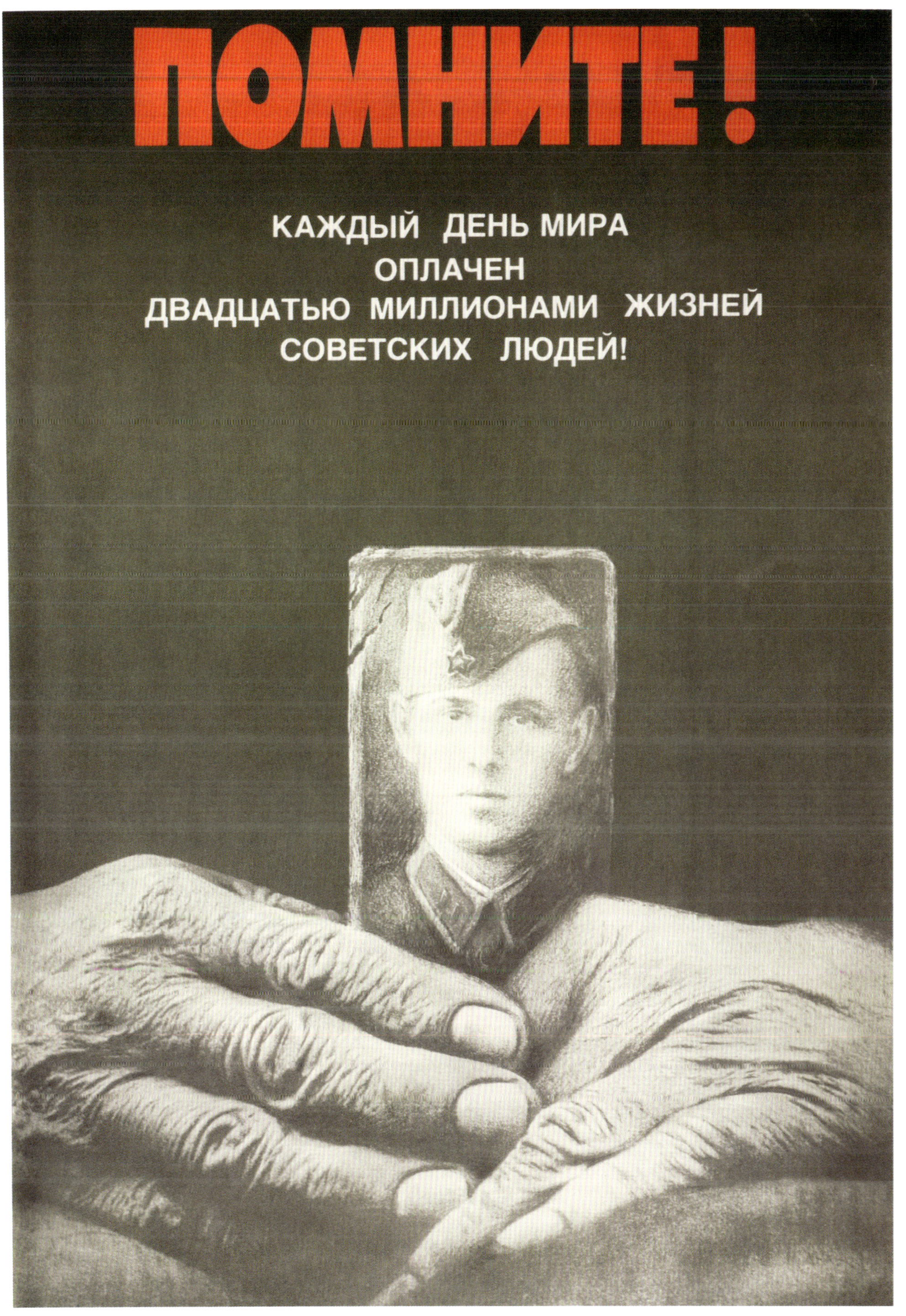
ПОМНИТЕ!
КАЖДЫЙ ДЕНЬ МИРА
ОПЛАЧЕН
ДВАДЦАТЬЮ МИЛЛИОНАМИ ЖИЗНЕЙ
СОВЕТСКИХ ЛЮДЕЙ!

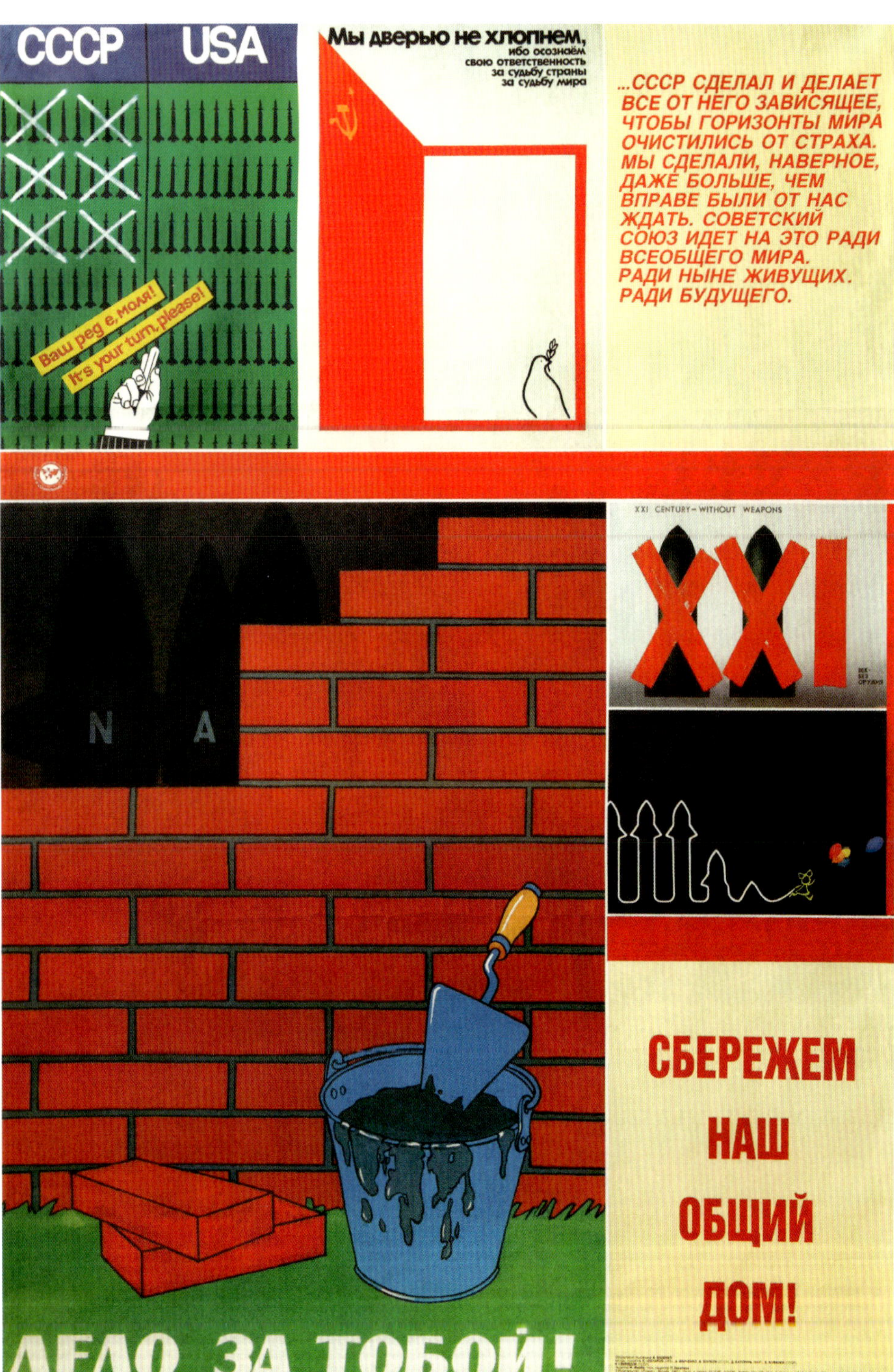

PEACE

◂ А. Бабенко (A. Babenko) | 1987

A collection of seven posters. Clockwise from top left: 1) Shows through crossed out tally marks that the USSR has destroyed a number of atomic weapons; the US, none. NOW IT'S YOUR TURN, PLEASE! 2) A door doubling as the flag of the USSR opens to reveal the dove of peace. WE DON'T SLAM THE DOOR SINCE WE RECOGNIZE OUR RESPONSIBILITY FOR THE FATE OF OUR COUNTRY AND THE WORLD. 3) . . . THE USSR HAS DONE AND IS DOING EVERYTHING POSSIBLE TO RID THE WORLD OF FEAR, AND EVEN MORE THAN WE WERE SUPPOSED TO FOR THE SAKE OF PEACE IN THE FUTURE. 4) XXI TWENTY-FIRST CENTURY WITHOUT WEAPONS. 5) A fuse connected to missiles that peters out to produce colored balloons. 6) PROTECT OUR COMMON HOME! 7) Bricks are being laid to wall out the missiles of NATO. IT'S UP TO YOU!

Б. Ефимов (B. Efimov) | 1985 ➤

The PENTAGON appears on the shark's tail while the word AGRESSION is spelled out by his teeth. The beast swims toward the INDIAN OCEAN. In the background, the island of DIEGO GARCIA displays the flag of a US military base.
THE PREDATOR FROM OVERSEAS IS RARING FOR A BITE
THE INDIAN OCEAN IS WHERE IT'S SET ITS SIGHTS
IT'S HIGH TIME FOR THE FOREIGN "GUESTS" TO TRY TO UNDERSTAND
THAT THE OCEAN IS CALLED INDIAN AND NOT AMERICAN

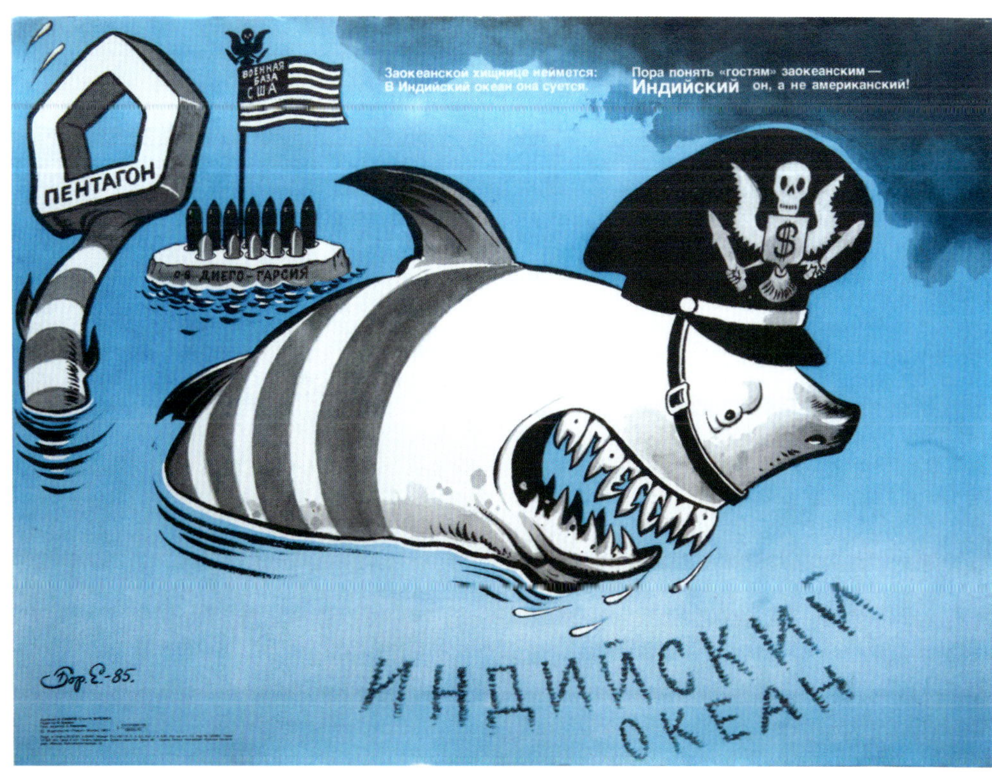

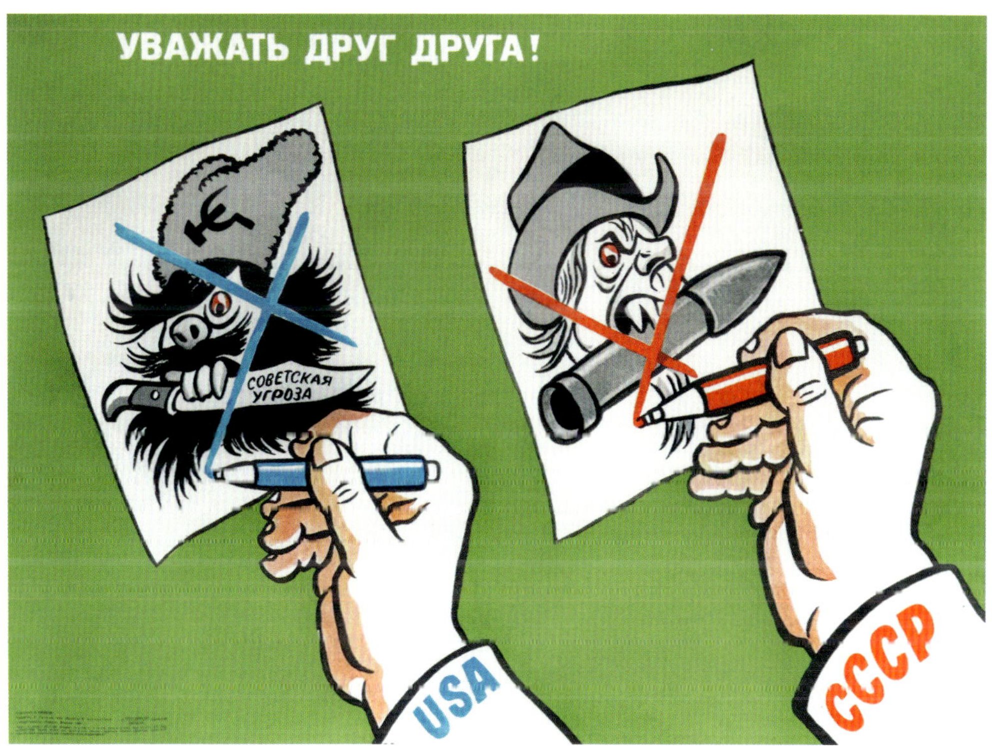

Б. Ефимов (B. Efimov) | 1989 ➤

WE HAVE TO RESPECT EACH OTHER!
On the left, a caricature of a Russian man wears a hat adorned with a hammer and sickle, while wielding a knife in his teeth displaying the message THE SOVIET THREAT. His face is crossed out in blue pen by a hand emerging from a sleeve labeled USA. Meanwhile, a second hand, with a USSR sleeve, uses red pen to cross out a caricature of a cowboy-hat-wearing American who clutches a missile in his teeth.

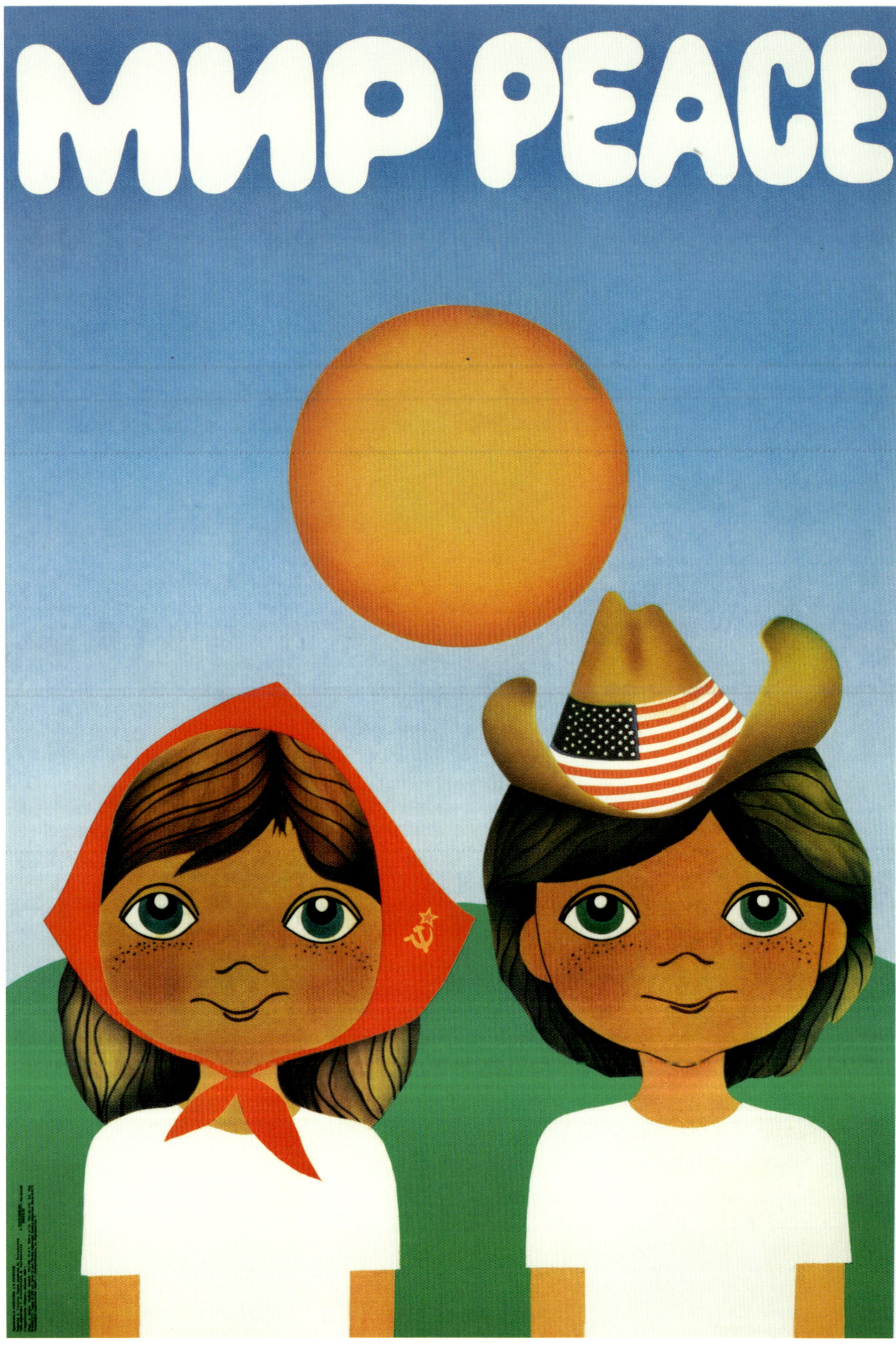
МИР PEACE

◄ Н. Колокова (N. Kolokova), В. Колоков (V. Kolokov) | 1988

PEACE
A young Mother Russia and a young Uncle Sam.

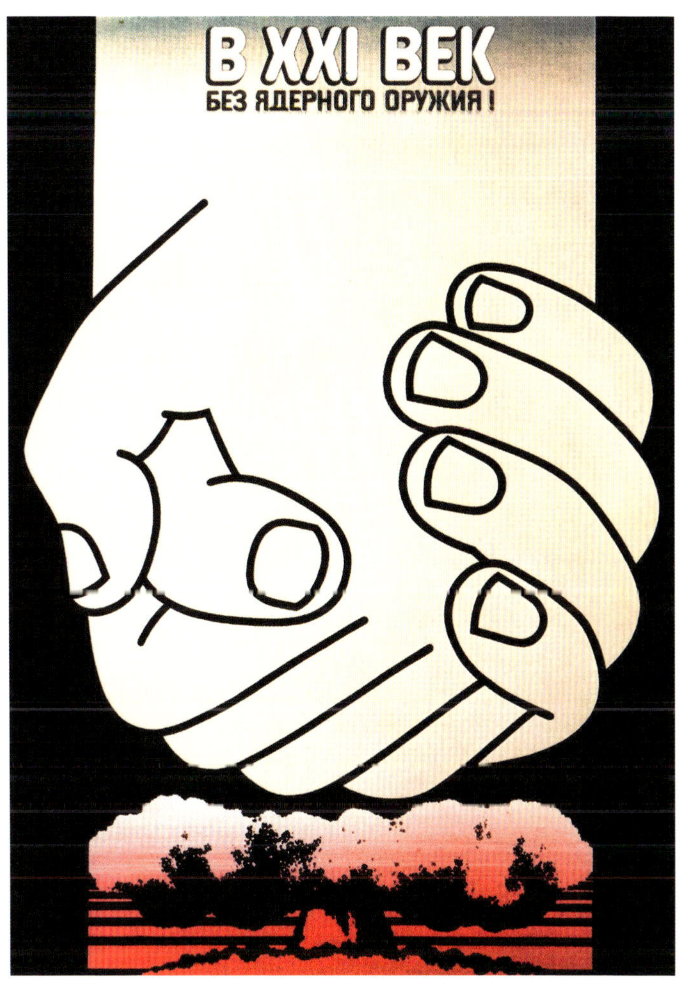

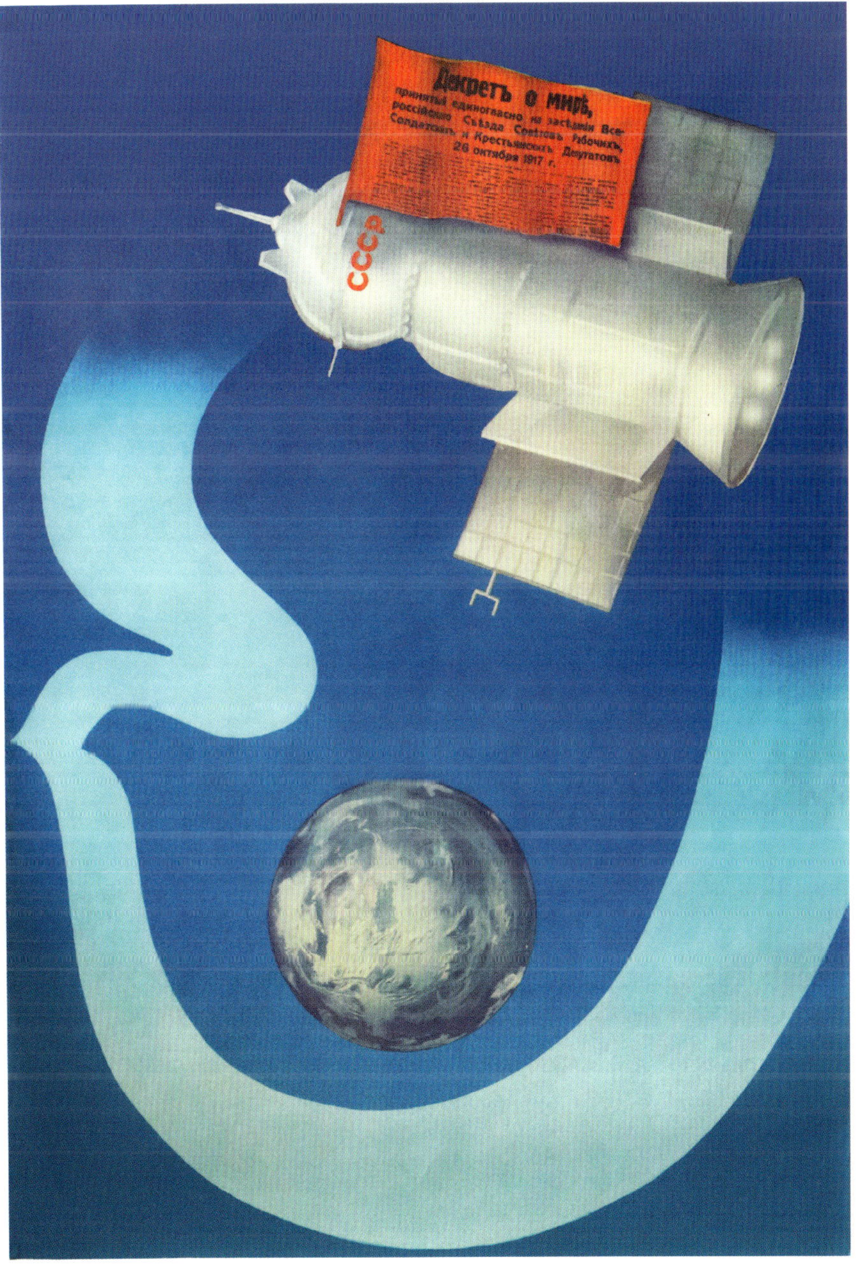

▲ В. Шевченко (V. Shevchenko) | n.d.

INTO THE 21ST CENTURY FREE OF NUCLEAR WEAPONS!
Pictured in this image are clasped hands over a mushroom cloud.

◄ Штефан Штефка (Stefan Stefka) | 1987

A Soviet satellite carries a flag printed with a DECREE ON PEACE. It is a copy of a document from the first Congress of the Communist Party of the Soviet Union, held in 1917. This peace edict, initiated by Lenin, is thus extended into space—into the future—on behalf of the Soviets.

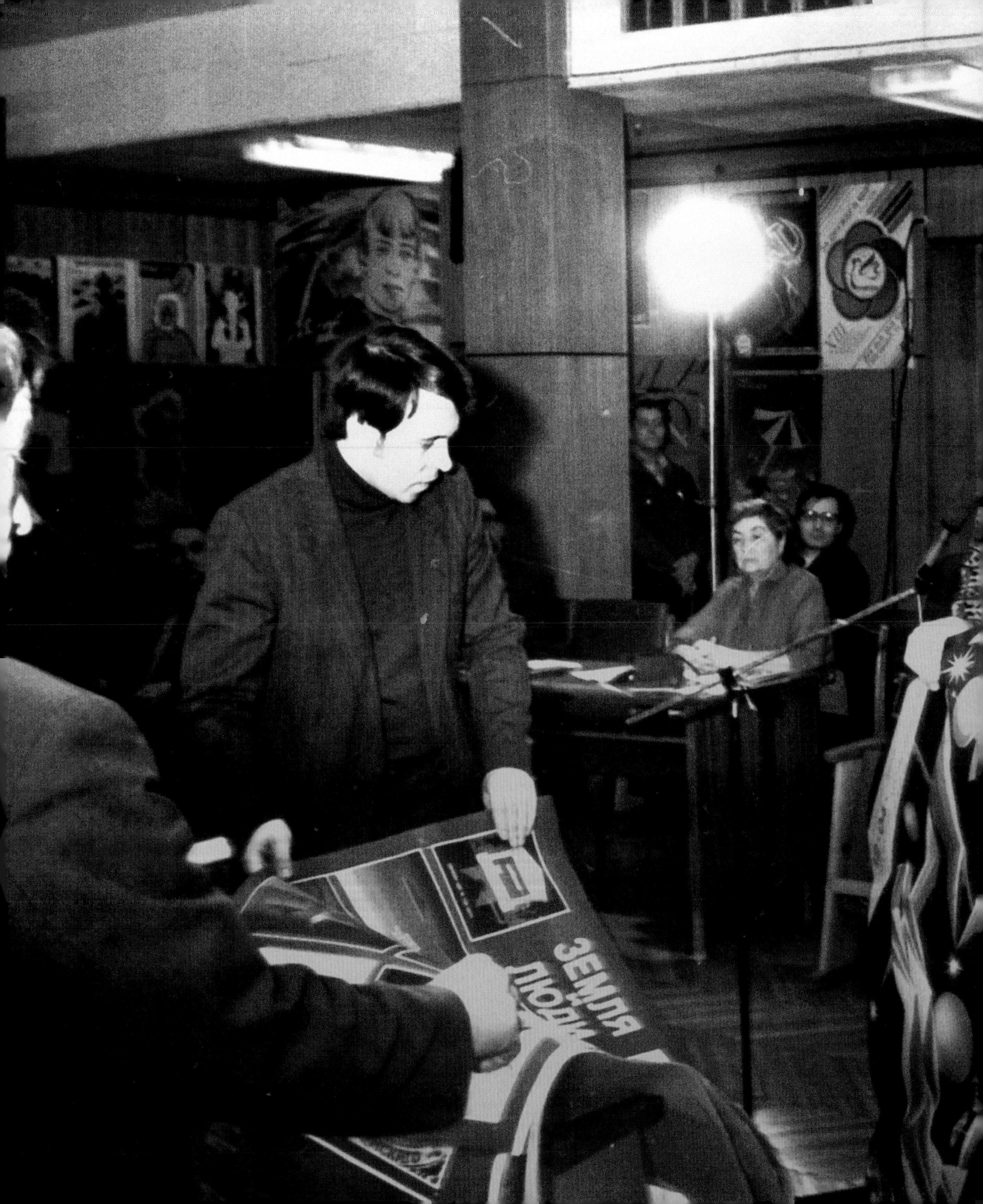
ЗЕМЛЯ

INTERVIEWS

CONDUCTED AND TRANSLATED BY BELA SHAYEVICH

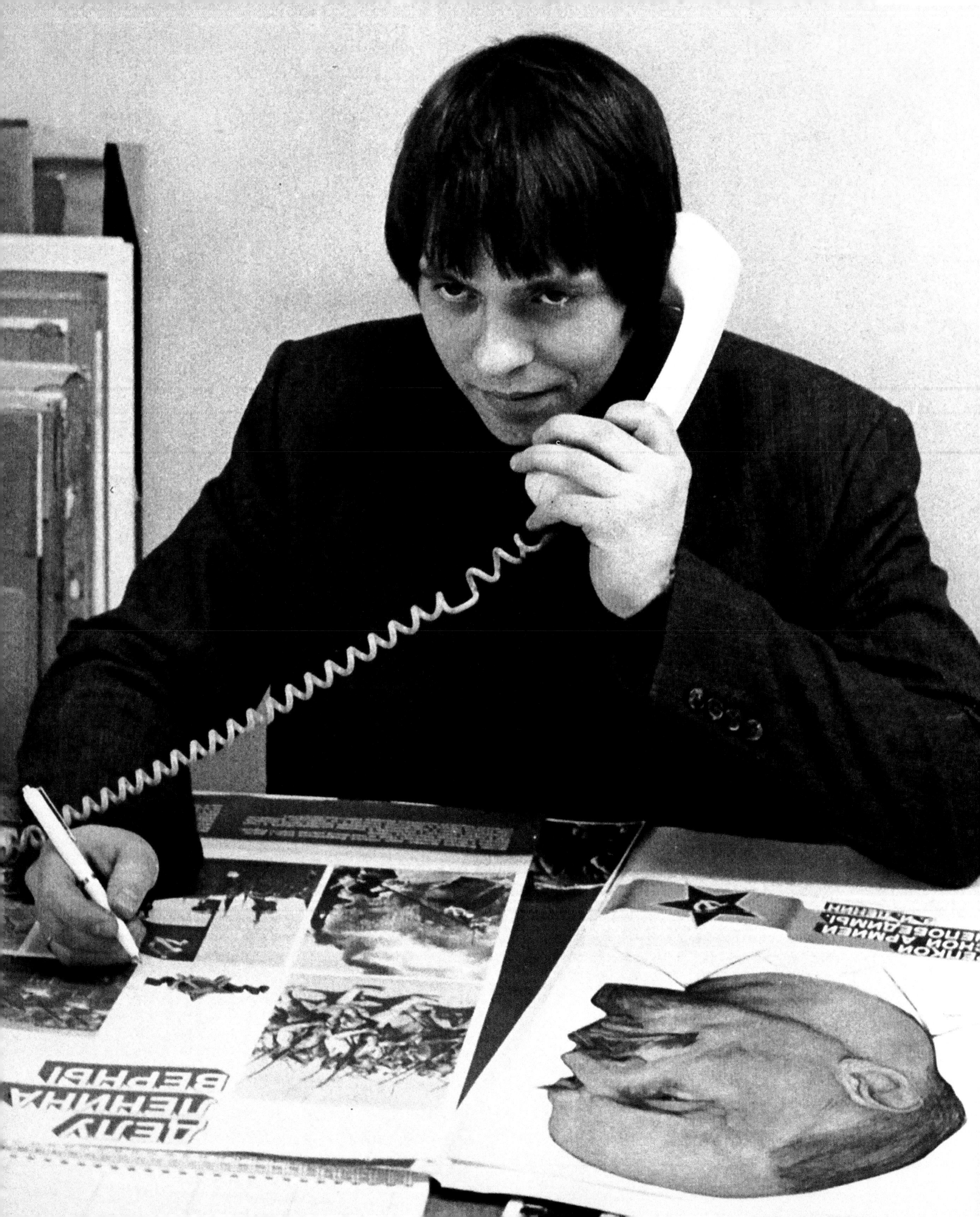
ДЕЛУ ЛЕНИНА ВЕРНЫ!

IGOR PETRYGIN-RODIONOV

How did you start drawing posters? What attracted you to this work? What did you want to accomplish?

I made my first serious poster for an exhibition on the occasion of the 1980 Olympic Games. Before that, I mostly made watercolors—city scenes, portraits. At a certain point, I felt that not many people were working in watercolor, that it was a little too pretty and charming, although the material itself is extremely difficult to work with and does not allow for error. I wanted something harder and sharper.

I never had any specific goals. You make work because you can't help it. It comes of its own accord. That's the secret of art. As the poet wrote, "poems aren't written, they're an event, like the dawn of feeling or a sunset . . . ." However, as an artist becomes more skilled, they start having control over this process. That's why I always remind my students that the difference between an amateur artist and a professional is that the amateur waits to be visited by the Muse while for the professional, she's always on call, ready to show up at a moment's notice. Excuse my frivolity.

Do you remember any posters from your youth that may have inspired or influenced you?

In my early years, I was amazed by the work of masters from the Polish Poster School like Henryk Tomaszewski, Roman Cieślewicz, and Waldemar Świerzy. I was impressed by their power, their creative treatment of traditional topics, the subtle subtext, laconicness, and gorgeous work with image and lettering. I somehow immediately knew that this was for me. It called to my soul. Like Pink Floyd or Vysotsky.

Could you describe the process of creating a poster from beginning to end? Did you pitch your own ideas, slogans, images, or topics?

A poster is a state of mind and spirit. It's a frame you think through. A response to current events. You need to have what I call "the poster mind." If you don't have it, you can't learn or be taught how to make posters. It is impossible to choose this genre the artist needs to be born with it.

An idea for a poster arrives as an image that you try to materialize, always comparing your vision with your work. At a certain moment, your inner voice tells you, "There it is! You did it!" And then you have to stop so you don't ruin it.

Back then and as well as today, most of my work came out of my own ideas, slogans, relationships, and declarations. As a rule, I would develop any topics assigned to me to the point that they were unrecognizable, doing everything in my power to make them as sharp and effective as possible. Oftentimes, I find and found my work breaking all the rules of the commercial genre for the sake of bringing the information to life, as Boris Grebenshchikov sings, "flustering malleable minds."

Как Вы начали рисовать плакаты? Что Вас привлекло к этой работе? Чего Вы ей хотели достичь?

Первый серьезный плакат был сделан к выставке, посвященной Олимпиаде 1980 года. До этого я работал, в основном, в жанре акварели – городской пейзаж, портрет, ню. В какой-то момент почувствовал, что акварельной графики мало, уж больно все красиво и благостно, хотя сам по себе материал сложнейший, не прощающий ошибок. Захотелось чего-то более жесткого и острого.

Цели достичь чего-то конкретного не было никогда. Работу делаешь потому, что не сделать её ты просто не можешь. Она сама собой так складывается. Тайна творчества. Как писал поэт, «стихи не пишутся – случаются, как чувства или же закат...»
Однако с ростом мастерства этот процесс становится управляемым самим художником. Поэтому своим студентам, говоря о том, в чем разница между художником-любителем и профессионалом, напоминаю, что любитель ждет, когда его посетит Муза, а для профессионала она – барышня по вызову, готовая явиться немедленно, уж простите за такую фривольность.

Помните ли Вы плакаты из Вашего детства /юношества которые Вас вдохновили/на Вас повлияли?

В ранние годы меня поразили произведения мастеров польской школы плаката – Г.Томашевского, Р.Чеслевича, В.Свежего. Поразили силой, оригинальной трактовкой традиционных тем, тонким подтекстом, лаконичностью, изумительной работой со шрифтом и образом. Я как-то сразу понял – это мое. Легло на душу. Это как Pink Floyd или Высоцкий.

Могли бы Вы описать с начало до конца процесс создание плаката? Предлагали ли Вы собственные идей, лозунги, образа, или темы? Или все было задано?

Плакат – это состояние ума и души. Ты им мыслишь. Это ответная реакция на происходящее. Надо иметь то, что я называю «плакатными мозгами». Если их нет, плакату научиться или научить невозможно. Этот жанр нельзя выбрать – он должен быть заложен в художнике самой природой

Тема плаката приходит как какой-то образ, который ты пытаешься материализовать, все время сопоставляя увиденное со сделанным. В определенный момент внутренний голос подсказывает «Вот оно! Сложилось!» Значит, надо остановиться чтобы не портить.

Как сегодня, так и в те времена, подавляющая часть моих работ – это собственные идеи, лозунги, отношение и декларации. Как правило, я перерабатывал заданные темы порой до первоначальной неузнаваемости, добиваясь их наиболее острого и эффективного звучания. Часто иду и шел на провокации по всем законам рекламного жанра, чтобы оживить информационное поле и вызвать, как поет Б.Гребенщиков, «смятенье в неокрепших умах».

Did you ever encounter censorship or have your work or ideas rejected on political grounds?

Not in the days of Brezhnev or Gorbachev or Yeltsin or even the early Putin era did I ever encounter censorship. 2019 was the first year when several of my solo exhibitions were forbidden for political reasons.

What changes came with glasnost and perestroika? How were these changes reflected in your work?

Glasnost allowed many people to, in the words of Bulat Okudzhava, "spray out the words that'd long been in the penny bank." The absence of forbidden topics and censorship inspired poster artists who organized independent poster exhibitions that gathered huge audiences and led to the exhibited works being published in thousands of copies by state publishers. Living people, images, and issues took the place of cardboard cutouts of leaders and workers with huge fists. The poster transformed from a propaganda tool into a means for shedding light on the actual pressure points of the people and country as a whole. Posters became a kind of nerve center for processing current events.

You called the perestroika period "one of the best periods in the history of Soviet poster art." Why?

With perestroika, poster art became a space for many young artists to self-actualize, implementing the contemporary artistic and real human language. The perestroika poster breathed in the romantic air of freedom of thought and speech. In those years, there was a high poster culture, which led to the appearance of works that carried on the greatest graphic traditions of the masters of the Bauhaus and Constructivism—Aleksandr Rodchenko, Vladimir Mayakovsky, El Lissitzky, and others. People made posters using a diverse array of styles and mediums, from photography to drawing and painting. People were making interesting decisions with fonts, turning symbols into images.

What was the most difficult/complicated part of your work?

The most difficult part, as always, was dealing with idiot clients and idiot audience members, which is especially hard today under the conditions of the current intellectual, cultural, and moral degradation that has seized Russia over the past 20 years. During perestroika, when frightened communists were running the country, everything was a lot simpler and more cheerful because the intellectual level of the leaders and decision-makers was incomparably higher, and the audiences were educated, well read, and not yet embittered.

Были ли случаи цензуры или отказа на политических основах Ваших работ или идей?

Ни в брежневские, ни в горбачевские, ни в ельцинские, ни во времена раннего Путина не было ни одного случая цензуры. Только начиная с 2019 года последовали запреты на проведение нескольких моих персональных выставок по политическим причинам.

Помните ли Вы какие либо изменение в этой отрасли с приходом гласности и перестройки? Каким образом эти изменения внедрились в Вашу деятельность?

Гласность многим позволила, выражаясь словами Б.Окуджавы, «выплеснуть слова, что давно лежат в копилке» на волю. Отсутствие запретных тем и цензуры вдохновило плакатистов и привело к проведению т. н. «выставок авторского плаката», собирающих огромные зрительские аудитории и многотысячному тиражированию выставочных работ государственными издательствами. Место шаблонно-картонных вождей и рабочих с огромными кулаками заняли живые люди, образы и проблемы. Плакат стал не орудием пропаганды, а средством выявления реальных болевых точек каждого человека и страны в целом. Плакат стал своеобразным нервом современности.

Вы определили период перестройки как «один из лучших периодов в истории советского плаката." Почему?

С Перестройкой в плакатном жанре появилось и самореализовалось много молодых талантливых художников, говорящих на современном графическом и человеческом языке. Перестроечный плакат впитал в себя воздух романтики, свободы мысли и свободы слова. Плакатная культура была в те годы еще на высоком уровне, что способствовало появлению произведений, выполненных в лучших традициях мастеров Баухауса или конструктивизма – А.Родченко, В.Маяковского, Эль Лисицкого и др. Создавались плакаты, выполненные в самой различной технике и стилистике – от фотоплаката, до рисованного или живописного графического листа. Появились интересные шрифтовые решения, где символы превращались в образы.

Что было самое тяжелое/сложное в Вашей работе?

Как всегда и во все времена, самое тяжелое – иметь дело с идиотом-заказчиком и идиотом-зрителем, особенно сейчас, в условиях умственной, культурной и нравственной деградации России, произошедшей за последние 20 лет.
Однако в перестроечные времена, когда страной правили испуганные коммунисты, все было гораздо проще и веселее, потому что интеллектуальный уровень тогдашних правителей и персон, принимающих решения, был несравненно выше, а зритель был образован, начитан и не озлоблен.

What was better about that time?

The best part of that time for me was my almost decade-long career with that All-Soviet monster of publishing, Plakat—the posters they published; participating in many large-scale, All-Soviet, and international shows they organized; and the hope, change, and love that ruled that era.

What do you miss from that era the most as an artist?

Excuse me for repeating myself, but what I miss most is the general atmosphere of reasonableness—people who were free thinkers, unencumbered by a slave mentality; a country that was heading forward into the future, although often going off-course, rather than one that is heading back to the Middle Ages.

I personally have always been and remain free and independent, saying only what I want and need to say, but more and more frequently, this feels like being a voice crying out in the wilderness.

What are you most proud of? What are your favorite posters from this period?

I warmly remember my hooligan series of typographic posters for the First Congress of the National Deputies of the USSR, posters on foreign policies, my collaborative posters that I made with poet Andrei Voznesensky based on his poem "Longjumeau."

I am especially proud of my poster *More of the Party?* from 1993, which I made immediately after the storming of the Russian Parliament, which signaled the end of the era of the Soviet State, perestroika, and glasnost. The Kremlin Cup tennis tournament was happening at the same time and so I drew a silhouette of Yeltsin holding a tennis racket against the backdrop of the burning Supreme Council building and a tennis net that turned into the barbed wire that the building was surrounded by when under siege by the tanks.

Out of the works of my colleagues, I can remember great posters by Georgy Rashkov, Leonid Nepomnyashchiy, Yefim Tsvik, Victor Kundyshev and many others.

Что было лучшее?

Лучшим из того времени я считаю для себя почти десятилетнее сотрудничество со всесоюзным издательским монстром – издательством «Плакат», изданные им плакаты, участие в многочисленных крупномасштабных всесоюзных и международных выставках, само время надежд, перемен и любви.

Что Вам из этого периода больше всего не хватает, как художнику?

Не хватает, простите за повторение, общей атмосферы разума, свободных, не отягощенных рабским менталитетом людей и страны, которая идет, хоть и часто сбиваясь с пути, но вперед и в будущее, а не в Средневековье.

Сам я лично всегда был и есть свободен и независим, говоря только то, что хочу и считаю нужным, но все чаще это смотрится как глас вопиющего в пустыне.

Чем Вы больше всего гордитесь? И/или какой Ваш любимый плакат из этого периода (из Ваших и/или чужих)?

Я с теплотой вспоминаю свою хулиганскую серию шрифтовых плакатов к Первому съезду народных депутатов СССР, плакаты на темы внешней политики, совместную с поэтом А.Вознесенским работу над плакатом по мотивам его поэмы «Лонжюмо».

Особенно дорог плакат «Еще Партию?», сделанный в 1993 году, сразу после расстрела российского Парламента, означавшего конец эпохи Советской власти, Перестройки и Гласности. В это же время в Москве проходил теннисный турнир «Кубок Кремля», поэтому я изобразил силуэт Ельцина с ракеткой в руке на фоне горящего дома Верховного Совета и теннисной сеткой, переходящей в колючую проволоку, которой дом был обнесен во время расстрела из танковых орудий.

Из работ своих коллег могу отметить замечательные плакаты Ю.Леонова, Г.Рашкова, Л.Непомнящего, Е.Цвика, В.Кундышева, да и многих других.

LEONID MIKHAILOVICH NEPOMNYASHCHIY

How did you start drawing posters? What attracted you to this work? What did you want to accomplish?

Because I studied graphic design at the Surikov Art Institute in Moscow, which I graduated from in 1965, I began working on posters as part of my studies. By the middle of the 1960s, when the "severe style" with its "laconism, monumentalism, and expressivity" had reached its peak in Soviet art, the language of poster art was more in tune with the style of that era.

Do you remember any posters from your youth that may have inspired or influenced you?

Of course, I remember the posters from my childhood—from the war and the post-war period, with their positive heroes that looked out at us from every wall: on the street, in the office, at the store, at the building administration office, the guard booth, and the country hut. People confident in what they were doing, their bright, heroic faces. They were our religious icons. I can't say, however, that they influenced my future career. I was more interested in painting. I turned to posters much more consciously and artistically under the influence of the creative atmosphere of the 1960s art scene. The rebirth of our "forgotten people," or, more precisely, the forbidden artists and artists' groups from the 1920s to the beginning of the 1930s—you can see their influence in my poster *May 5th, Printers' Day* (from 1966), reproduced in the 1984 book *Sovetskij politicheskij plakat* (*The Soviet Political Poster*) in which I, a recent art school graduate, quite openly adopted the visual language of expressionism, which I had just recently glimpsed in the work of Aleksandr Deineka.

Visual ideas came to me in different ways; the most important thing was to "see" a color chord or the rhythm of a line.

Could you describe the process of creating a poster from beginning to end? Did you pitch your own ideas, slogans, images, or topics?

As a rule, I received assignments. Most of them were on official topics, not my own ideas. The way things turned out, although I am a pretty apolitical person, I ended up making a lot of political posters. I even got a prize from the Central Committee of the All-Union Leninist Young Communist League for a poster I made for the 50th anniversary of the Komsomol.

Как Вы начали рисовать плакаты? Что Вас привлекло к этой работе? Чего Вы ей хотели достичь?

Поскольку я учился на графика в Суриковском институте /МГХИ им.В.И.Сурикова/, который окончил в 1965 году, то специфика плаката осваивалась уже в самом процессе обучения. Другое дело, что к середине 1960-х годов, когда в советском искусстве своего пика достиг «суровый стиль», с его «лаконизмом, монументализмом и экспрессией», язык плаката, как казалось, мог наиболее соответствовать стилю времени.

Помнито ли Вы плакаты из Вашего детства /юношества которые Вас вдохновили/на Вас повлияли?

Конечно, я помню плакаты моего детства –времен войны и послевоенного времени, с их положительными героями, которые смотрели на нас ото всюду: на улице, в конторе, магазине, в домоуправлении, в сторожевой будке и в избе… Уверенные в своем деле люди, светлые, героические лица были заменой иконных образов. Не могу сказать, что они как то повлияли на мою будущую профессию. Меня больше привлекала живопись. Гораздо более осознанно и творчески я обратился к плакату под влиянием всей атмосферы художественной жизни 60-х годов. Это было возрождение «забытых», а точнее запрещенных художников и объединений 1920-х –начала 30-х годов. Поэтому можно видеть мой плакат «5 мая –день печати» /1966/, воспроизведенный в монографии «Советский политический плакат», вышедшей в 1984 году, где я, недавний выпускник института, довольно откровенно обратился к языку экспрессионизма, так осуждаемого еще совсем недавно в работах А.Дейнеки.

Образы плакатных работ возникали по разному, главным было «увидеть» цветовой аккорд или ритм линий.

Могли бы Вы описать с начало до конца процесс создание плаката? Предлагали ли Вы собственные идей, лозунги, образа, или темы? Или все было задано?

Работу, как правило, «давали». Это были заказы с преимущественно официальными темами, не моими идеями. Так сложилось, что я, довольно аполитичный человек, много проработавший в политическом плакате. И даже получивший премию ЦК ВЛКСМ после выставки к 50 -летию комсомола.

Did you ever encounter censorship or have your work or ideas rejected on political grounds?

I can't remember any specific instances of censorship or my work being rejected. Various committees that also consulted with artists approved our posters. We were supposed to listen to their advice, but how we followed it was up to us. In my younger days, there was something like a professional community among the committees and at the publishing houses that knew how to fight and overcome the obstacles of conservatism.

What changes came with glasnost and perestroika? How were these changes reflected in your work?

Even during perestroika, I had an aversion to the ideological, propagandistic nature of posters and attempted to escape into historical themes, which gave me the opportunity to build more peaceful narratives and distracted me with the beauty of period costumes and artifacts. I got a prize from the Academy of the Arts for my poster *Borodino*, which I consider an important professional achievement.

Because of the increasingly propagandistic nature of poster art, I ended up quitting altogether and turned to illustrating books, which, I think, I was good at, and managed to pursue in both Moscow and Mexico, where I worked for 15 years and even received government prizes.

After returning to Russia, I continued working more on books. And painting.

Были ли случаи цензуры или отказа на политических основах Ваших работ или идей?

Не могу вспомнить точно, случаи цензуры или отказа применительно к моим работам. Ведь и так плакат принимался разными комиссиями, выдававшими свои советы. И мы советы должны были слушать, а уж как им следовать- решал каждый из нас. Но в годы моей юности было что то вроде общности профессионалов в комиссиях или издательствах, которые умели бороться, преодолевать консервативные препоны.

Помните ли Вы какие либо изменение в этой отрасли с приходом гласности и перестройки? Каким образом эти изменения внедрились в Вашу деятельность?

Все же даже в перестроечный период у меня было отвращение к идеологической пропагандистской природе плаката и я пытался «уйти» в историческую тематику, которая давала мне возможности более спокойного рассказа, увлекала живописностью костюмов и миром вещей других эпох. За плакат «Бородино» я получил награду Академии художеств. Его я считаю своей профессиональной творческой удачей.

Из отвращения к усиливавшейся с годами пропагандистской составляющей плакатного жанра я довольно резко перестал работать в плакате и целиком посвятил себя книжной иллюстрации, которая мне, как мне кажется, удавалась и в Москве и в Мексике, где я проработал почти 15 лет и даже получал там правительственные награды.

Вернувшись на родину я также больше работаю в области книги. А также занимаюсь живописью.

YURI BORISOVICH LEONOV

How did you start drawing posters? What attracted you to this work? What did you want to accomplish?

I'm a Leningrader. I've always been interested in posters. In those days, advertising and theater posters were especially memorable. From my childhood, I remember the posters of Nikolay Akimov for the Theater for Satire and Comedy on Nevsky Prospect.

My work in posters began with the film *Moulin Rouge* (1952) about [Henri de] Toulouse-Lautrec, [an artist] who made a huge impression on me. I started seriously pursuing poster art—I was noticed and deemed good. I began participating in poster exhibitions, and my posters were included in international shows and shows at the Manege [Central] Exhibition Hall in Leningrad. In 1977, I was accepted into the poster guild of the USSR Artists' Union, which was led by the wonderful master of poster art Levon Ervandovich Airapetiants, who became a model for me and many other young poster artists who had found themselves a place in the art world.

After I moved to Moscow, I needed to find a job. I went to the Plakat Publishing House and showed my portfolio of posters. They liked them. As a trial assignment, I was tasked with making several posters on economics. They were approved and published, and thus, I was brought on as an art editor.

Could you describe the process of creating a poster from beginning to end? Did you pitch your own ideas, slogans, images, or topics?

Topics for posters were assigned by Editor-in-Chief R. G. Aleyev or his deputies. The publisher's office was always filled with non-staff artists who were also capable poster makers, deftly illustrating any subject assigned to them. They were given various concepts for posters. Usually, an editor would know which artist was best suited for this or that poster. The artists were allowed to use any medium they wanted and choose any images or texts or slogans they cared to. It always came down to the artists' vision. I never imposed harsh guidelines, the artists had total artistic freedom. There were even cases where artists came to us with images and the editors would come up with texts to fit them.

After receiving an assignment, an artist would come back with sketches that were then corrected by the editor if necessary. The poster would be shown to the Artist-in-Chief, the Editor-in-Chief, and then presented to the Arts Council. After it was approved, it would be signed off on by the head of the publishing house before moving on to printing. Posters that failed to pass through the process would be returned to the artists and then submitted to poster competitions and exhibitions. But this was extremely rare.

Как Вы начали рисовать плакаты? Что Вас привлекло к этой работе? Чего Вы ей хотели достичь?

Я ленинградец. Плакат всегда интересовал меня. В то время особенно выделялся рекламный и театральный плакат. Из детства помню плакаты Н. Акимова к спектаклям «Театра сатиры и комедии» на Невском проспекте.

А мое творчество в плакате началось с фильма «Мулен Руж» о Тулузе Лотреке, этот художник произвел на меня огромное впечатление. Я начал серьезно заниматься плакатом, меня заметили, оценили. Я стал участвовать в плакатных выставках, мои плакаты вошли в экспозиции для международных выставок и выставки в ленинградском Манеже. В 1977 году я был принят в секцию плаката Ленинградского союза художников. Дальнейшим развитием в плакатном искусстве явилось для меня обучение в Школе плаката при Союзе художников СССР, которую возглавлял замечательный мастер плаката Л. Айрапетянц, ставший наставником для меня и многих молодых плакатистов, которые нашли свое место в искусстве.

После переезда в Москву встал вопрос об устройстве на работу. Я пришел в издательство «Плакат», показал свои авторские плакаты. Работы понравились. Мне на пробу дали задание создать несколько плакатов на темы по экономике. Их одобрили, они были напечатаны, и я был принят в издательство художественным редактором.

Могли бы Вы описать с начало до конца процесс создание плаката? Предлагали ли Вы собственные идей, лозунги, образа, или темы? Или все было задано?

Темы для плакатов в издательстве давали Главный редактор Р.Г. Алеев или его замы. В редакции были постоянные внештатные художники, которые отлично владели искусством плаката, хорошо раскрывали ту или иную заданную тему. И им давались различные концепции для плаката. Обычно редактор сам представлял себе какой художник способен сделать этот или иной плакат. Автора не ограничивали в выборе техники, изображении образов, текстов или лозунгов. В основном прорисовывалась проблема на видении художника. Я никогда не ставил жесткие условия, давал полную свободу в творчестве. Даже были такие случаи, что художник приносил изображение, а мы в редакции придумывали текст.

Дальше приносились эскизы, поправки вносил редактор (если они были нужны), и плакат показывали Главному художнику, Главному редактору и представляли Художественному совету. После одобрения и подписи директора плакат шел в печать. Плакаты, которые не проходили Худсовет, возвращались автору и попадали на выставки и конкурсы плаката. Но это было весьма редко.

What changes came with glasnost and perestroika? How were these changes reflected in your work?

I was already the head of the First General Political Editorial Board when perestroika began. I was assigned a new task: approving posters with the Ideological Department of the Central Committee of the Communist Party. The head of the publishing house, Anatoly Shumakov, would submit all of the posters there during the editing process. Getting approval had become easier because perestroika had taken effect there, too. In fact, they began to take a special interest in posters, expecting something new from them.

At the office, we were excited about perestroika and glasnost. We got in touch with the Artists' Union and reached out to young artists from Leningrad, Moscow, Kiev, and Penza. At the Chelyuskinskaya House of Artists, a graphic artists' workshop in the suburbs of Moscow, poster artists were offered unusual and daring topics. New, technically-innovative posters with interesting subjects were now published routinely. Many new, talented artists emerged, including Aleksandr Vaganov, Aleksander Chebotarev, Aleksander Lozenko, Vasiliy Chekashov, and many others.

They had to work quickly: some assignments came down from the Central Committee requiring a 24-hour turnaround on difficult and diverse subjects. These were the hardest.

What are you most proud of? What are your favorite posters from this period?

I am proud of having worked with a lot of amazing people, including the legendary poster artist Oleg Savostiuk; that I was on the board of the International Poster Competition at the Central House of Artists, working with Shigeo Fukuda, with whom we judged the final round of the competition. And so much more.

Later on, it became clear that this exciting era of poster art was coming to a sad end. Anatoly Shumakov, who had founded the Plakat Publishing House, a capital-P professional, was forced to retire. Someone was sent in his place who reformed us as the Panorama Publishing House, which focused on books, and quickly vanished.

Today, it's a difficult time for poster art. There are practically no commissions. Posters have been replaced with advertisements created by non-professionals. People believe that anyone can make a poster and it's not worth it to spend the money on an artist. The inner world that unites poster artists has disappeared, as well: we have little sticks, circles, dots, clip art, and fonts—large sheets of paper but no posters! No concepts, ideas, or wit!

My work at Plakat was a very important stage in my professional development. I went on to found my own publishing house, and, for over thirty years, I have been publishing books, brochures, and of course posters. Over the course of such a long creative career, many of these works have gained prominence.

And so I give my thanks to the Central Committee of the Communist Party of the Soviet Union publishing house Plakat for raising an entire generation of poster artists whose works are found in this book.

Помните ли Вы какие либо изменение в этой отрасли с приходом гласности и перестройки? Каким образом эти изменения внедрились в Вашу деятельность?

Когда наступили времена перестройки я был уже Заведующим Первой общеполитической редакцией издательства. На мои плечи легла еще одна инстанция: утверждение плакатов в Идеологическом отделе ЦК. Директор издательства Шумаков А.В. представлял туда все редакционные плакаты. Но уже было легче и проще, потому что и там перестройка внесла свои коррективы: на плакат смотрели с интересом, от него ждали нечто новое.

В редакции восприняли перестройку и гласность с подъемом. Связывались с Союзом художников, молодыми авторами, из Ленинграда, Москвы, Киева, Пензы. В Доме творчества «Челюскинская» плакатистам давались темы необычные, дерзкие. Появились новые интересные по смыслу, технике плакаты, которые потом принимались в печать. Появилось множество талантливых имен в плакате: А. Ваганов, А. Чеботарев, А. Лозенко, В. Чекашов и др.

Работа была и оперативная: заказ от ЦК за 1 день срочно выпустить плакат молнию. Темы сложные, разные. Это было самое трудное.

Чем Вы больше всего гордитесь? И/или какой Ваш любимый плакат из этого периода (из Ваших и/или чужих)?

Я горжусь, что работал с замечательными людьми, легендой плакатного искусства О.М. Савостюком, был в секретариате Международного конкурса плаката в ЦДХ, общался с Шигео Фукудой, с которым вел просмотр последнего тура конкурса. Всего не перечислить.

Далее стало очевидно, что время плаката подходит к печальному концу: отправили на пенсию директора Шумакова А.В., основателя «Плаката», профессионала с большой буквы, прислали другого человека, он сделал издательство «Панорама», которое занялось изданием книг и благополучно исчезло.

Сегодня плакат испытывает сложнейшие времена. Заказов практически нет. Плакат замещается просто рекламой, которой занимаются непрофессионалы, т.к. считается, что плакат может сделать каждый, денег на него тратить жалко. Да и внутренний мир сегодняшних «плакатистов» куда-то исчез: палочки, кружочки, точки, клипы и шрифт - графические листы есть - а плаката нет! Ушла мысль, идея, остроумие!

Издательство «Плакат» стало для меня важнейшей ступенью для дальнейшей профессиональной деятельности. Я основал издательство, занимаюсь уже более 30-ти лет изданием книг, альбомов, буклетов, и конечно плакатов. Многие из них снискали известность за такой долгий творческий период.

Так что «...спасибо издательству ЦК КПСС «Плакат» за воспитание целого поколения плакатистов, работы которых представлены в этом издании.

ACKNOWLEDGMENTS

My initial acknowledgement extends to Mikhail Gorbachev, the eighth and last leader of the Soviet Union, whose sweeping insights, vision, and leadership reformed many of his country's policies, if not its path closer to democracy. Those programs, although short-lived, introduced Soviet citizens to a new, freer way of living that will remain indelible in the annals of history. I admire Gorbachev for his courage to undertake the massive tasks of glasnost and perestroika, and for his accomplishments during their implementation, no matter how short a period it turned out to be. Finally, like a modern day Hephaestus, Gorbachev unleashed the freedom of aesthetic expression and design, without which neither this Collection nor this publication would have come to be.

An undertaking of such vast scope as *Openness and Idealism, Soviet Posters: 1985–1991* would not have been possible without the unwavering support of numerous individuals who have contributed to its long-term development—from its conception in 1987 to its planning and organization, and through to its completion. Bear in mind that neither Martha nor I speak Russian. This means that there are a great number of people who have anonymously, yet invaluably, provided their wisdom, insights, and connections to collectively help lead this project to fruition.

Above all, I wish to express my deep gratitude to the visionary artists whose pioneering graphics fill this volume as they shed new light and introspection on this remarkably rare period in Russian history.

My deepest appreciation also extends to authors Andy Willimott and Pepe Karmel for their discerning and thought-provoking essays that address the historical initiatives of glasnost and perestroika and their sociopolitical consequences through the lens of these posters. I also wish to express my appreciation to Bela Shayevich for the interviews she conducted with three of the artists, whom she tracked down with persistence, and whose posters are featured in this Collection: Yuri Borisovich Leonov, Leonid Mikhailovich Nepomnyashchiy, and Igor Rodionov-Petrigyn. I am also grateful for her fastidious verification of translations throughout this publication.

We cannot forget those who contributed tirelessly to the first iteration of this volume and whose individual efforts have directly affected the outcome of this expanded and comprehensive work. At its inception, Mahir Babayev explained the exquisite subtleties of this Collection, while Thierry Morel perceived its importance and was determined to bring it to the attention of a broader audience, as did Elena Daly and Susan Woodward. Luibov Zakharova deserves a special note of appreciation for her tireless efforts regarding the initial Russian translations, many of which endure in the current version. Nikkita Lary, a friend of very long standing and a resoundingly reliable interpreter of some of the more ambiguous images, also deserves our immense thanks.

I also wish to extend my appreciation to SNAP Editions' brilliant editorial team, led by Sarah S. King and Annikka Olsen, and to the talented graphic designers Tim Laun and Natalie Wedeking. Their dedicated work has produced an intelligent and striking design that amplifies the distinction the Martha H. and J. Speed Carroll Collection has earned from historians and scholars alike. In addition, I wish to thank María José (Coté) Durán Steinman who was critical in the initial layout and photography for this publication's prototype.

I am extremely honored that the noted Skira editore house in Milan, Italy, has agreed to be the publisher of this book, and I wish to extend my gratitude to Edoardo Ghizzoni, International Publications Manager, and to the rest of Skira's editorial and design team as well: Carlotta Santuccio, Emma Cavazzini, Paola Lamanna, Luigi Fiore, Faycal Zaouali, and Doriana Comerlati.

Finally, I am forever indebted to my friends and colleagues Trish Tillman and Ethan Browning for their enduring support, indefatigable work, and aesthetic input in this endeavor, among many others.

—J.S.C., November 2021

J. Speed Carroll is an artist and collector of fine art and ephemera. As a long time partner in the international law firm of Cleary, Gottlieb, Steen & Hamilton, he lived and practiced for substantial periods in both Europe and Asia. During these years, he and his late wife Martha acquired an eclectic and important collection comprising art and ephemera from all five continents, with a focus on Japanese, African, Aboriginal, and pre-Columbian objects, spanning centuries from antiquity to the present day. Their curatorial pursuits also include a unique collection of more than 500 Soviet posters on the themes of Glasnost and Perestroika, from which the examples featured in this volume are drawn. J. Speed Carroll's multi-media artwork is represented by Galerie Mourlot in New York City.

Andy Willimott is an Associate Professor in Modern Russian History at Queen Mary University in London. His previous publications include *Rethinking the Russian Revolution as Historical Divide* (Routledge, 2018) and *Living the Revolution: Urban Communes and Soviet Socialism, 1917–1932* (Oxford University Press, 2017)—recipient of the Alexander Nove Book Prize. He has contributed to the *Journal of Architecture*, *History Today*, *The Architectural Review*, and *Revolutionary Russia*.

Pepe Karmel is an art historian, critic, and Associate Professor in the Department of Art History, New York University. He was previously an art critic for the *New York Times* and *Art in America* and a curator at the Museum of Modern Art, New York. He has curated or co-curated exhibitions of Robert Morris, Jackson Pollock and Pablo Picasso. Karmel's previous publications include *Picasso and the Invention of Cubism* (Yale University Press, 2003); *Jackson Pollock* (Museum of Modern Art, New York, 1998); and *Conceptual Abstraction* (Hunter College Art Gallery, New York, 2012). His most recent book, *Abstract Art: A Global History*, was published by Thames & Hudson, London, in 2020.

Bela Shayevich is a Soviet-American visual artist, writer, and translator. Her book-length translations include Nobel Prize-winner Svetlana Alexievich's *Secondhand Time* (Fitzcarraldo Editions 2016), for which she won the inaugural TA First Translation Prize in 2017, and Yevgeny Zamyatin's *We* (Canongate, 2020). Shayevich also co-translated Soviet underground poet Vsevolod Nekrasov's *I Live I See* (2013), and Igor Kholin's *Kholin 66* (2017), both with Ainsley Morse, for Ugly Duckling Presse. Her translations have appeared in *The New Yorker, Harper's, Little Star*, *St. Petersburg Review*, *Calque*, and *N+1*, among other journals.

First published in Italy in 2022 by Skira editore S.p.A.
Palazzo Casati Stampa
via Torino 61
20123 Milano
Italy
www.skira.net

Printed and bound in Italy. First edition.

ISBN: 978-88-572-4564-5

Distributed in USA, Canada, Central & South America by ARTBOOK | D.A.P., 75 Broad Street, Suite 630, New York, NY 10004, USA.
Distributed elsewhere in the world by Thames and Hudson Ltd., 181A High Holborn, London WC1V 7QX, United Kingdom.

For SNAP Editions, New York
Editor: Sarah S. King
Managing Editor: Annikka Olsen
Associate Editors: Ted Mooney, Nathan Jones, and Nina Wolpow
Design: Tim Laun and Natalie Wedeking

For the Martha H. and J. Speed Carroll Collection
Trish Tillman: Project Director
Ethan Browning: Research and Production Assistant

Original photography: Martha H. Carroll, Trish Tillman, María José (Coté) Durán Steinman
New photography: Jason Mandella

Photo credits:
pp. 4–5: Artiom Romashov © Artiom Romashov
p. 10: © Yuri Inyakin
pp. 12–13: © Fine Art Images/Heritage Images
pp. 40–42. © Roger Tillberg/Alamy Photo
p. 45, fig.2: © Miroslav Zajic/Corbis Historical/Getty Images
p. 45, fig.3: © Gainew Gallery/Alamy Photo
pp. 56–57: © Dennis Brack/Alamy Photo
pp. 180–181: © S. Feofilaktov
p. 189, fig.9: © Milton Glaser Estate
p. 191, fig.10: © The Andy Warhol Foundation for the Visual Arts Inc. by SIAE 2021
pp. 194–195, endpapers © Archive of Valentin Khukhlaev/Архив Валентина Хухлаева
pp. 244–245, 246: © Yuri Leonov
© Mark Aleksandrovich Abramov, Anton Arkhipov, Nikolay Semenovich Babin, Sergej Artamonov, Olga Pavlovna Kacher by SIAE 2022

Captions:
pp. 4–5: The sign reads: "democratization/perestroika/glasnost." November 1988.
p. 10: Mikhail Gorbachev at the First Congress of People's Deputies of the USSR in the Kremlin, Moscow, 1989.
pp. 12–13: Occupation of the city of Kharkiv, in present-day Ukraine, by the Volunteer Army of General Denikin, Russian Civil War, 1918.
pp. 40–41: Conscripts on leave at the Red Square and St Basil's Cathedral, Moscow, 1987.
pp. 56–57: President Ronald Reagan and General Secretary Gorbachev convene in Red Square during a summit in Moscow, May 1988.
pp. 180–181: S. Feofilaktov. *Perestroika*, 1990. Gelatin silver print. The image depicts a rally held in front of the Monument Mausoleum to Lenin situated in the Park Aloye (Scarlet Field), Chelyabinsk, Russia.
pp. 194–195: View of Avenue Kalinina, Moscow. The configuration of lights on the exterior of the buildings form the letters, CCCP—the abbreviation for the full name of the Soviet Union in Russian (Union of Soviet Socialist Republics).
pp. 244–245: Yuri Leonov, Head Editor of the General Political Department, and and Editor-in-Chief of Plakat Publishing V.S. Vorontsov presenting the latest posters in the publishing house conference room, before their exhibition at VDNkh (the All-Soviet Exhibition Center in Moscow), ca. 1984.
p. 246: Yuri Leonov at work, approving and proofreading printed posters, 1984.

Front cover: Р. Акманов (R. Akmanov)
"Less rockets more confidence," 1988

Back cover: Н. Журавлева (N. Zhuravleva)
"SOS!" (detail), 1990